the **penguin** good australian
WINE GUIDE
2007

Ralph Kyte-Powell has more than 30 years' experience in the wine business and hospitality industry. His first wine job was with Seppelt during university vacation. Since then he has worked in marketing and sales for some of Australia's leading wine merchants, managed wine stores, been sommelier at a couple of Melbourne's best restaurants, worked in vineyards and wineries in Australia and France, and lectured on wine at a TAFE college. He's also owned a successful small hotel, and managed a restaurant. He started writing about wine 13 years ago and has a regular column in Melbourne's *Age*. He contributes to other publications including Tourism Victoria's *Wine Regions of Victoria* guide, chairs the imported-wine panel and writes regularly for *Cuisine* in New Zealand, and judges at Australian regional wine shows. A list of Ralph's favourite wines would be encyclopaedic and variable, but would always include champagne, great pinot noir, Rutherglen liqueur muscat and the best Italian reds – and when it all gets too much, he loves a good beer.

Huon Hooke is one of Australia's most experienced and best-qualified wine writers and judges. He is a wine-marketing graduate from Roseworthy Agricultural College and a qualified journalist. His wine-writing career began with the *Australian Financial Review* in 1983 and he's had a weekly column in a Fairfax paper ever since. He has a weekly column in the *Sydney Morning Herald*'s 'Good Living' section, and the *Herald*'s and *The Age*'s *Good Weekend* magazine; he is contributing editor of *Australian Gourmet Traveller WINE* magazine and writes for many other publications. He began judging in wine competitions in 1987 and has judged in most wine shows in Australia, doing about 10 shows a year in Australia and overseas. He is a senior judge and chairman of several shows including (in 2006) the Barossa, Mudgee, Adelaide Hills, Mount Barker, and Boutique Winery Awards. His favourite pastimes, when not up to his nose in wine, are fly fishing, bushwalking, skiing, sailing, music and reading almost anything except wine books.

the **penguin** good australian

WINE GUIDE

2007

Ralph Kyte-Powell and Huon Hooke

Penguin Books

PENGUIN BOOKS

Published by the Penguin Group
Penguin Group (Australia)
250 Camberwell Road, Camberwell, Victoria 3124, Australia
(a division of Pearson Australia Group Pty Ltd)
Penguin Group (USA) Inc.
375 Hudson Street, New York, New York 10014, USA
Penguin Group (Canada)
90 Eglinton Avenue East, Suite 700, Toronto, ON M4P 2Y3, Canada
(a division of Pearson Penguin Canada Inc.)
Penguin Books Ltd
80 Strand, London WC2R 0RL, England
Penguin Ireland
25 St Stephen's Green, Dublin 2, Ireland
(a division of Penguin Books Ltd)
Penguin Books India Pvt Ltd
11 Community Centre, Panchsheel Park, New Delhi – 110 017, India
Penguin Group (NZ)
67 Apollo Drive, Mairangi Bay, Auckland 1310, New Zealand
(a division of Pearson New Zealand Ltd)
Penguin Books (South Africa) (Pty) Ltd
24 Sturdee Avenue, Rosebank, Johannesburg 2196, South Africa

Penguin Books Ltd, Registered Offices: 80 Strand, London WC2R 0RL, England

First published by Penguin Group (Australia), a division of Pearson Australia Group Pty Ltd, 2006

10 9 8 7 6 5 4 3 2 1

Copyright © Penguin Group (Australia) 2006

Cover design by Marina Messiha © Penguin Group (Australia)
Text design © Penguin Group (Australia)
Cover photograph by Photolibrary
Authors photograph by Kevin O'Daly/Aspect Photographics
Typeset in Stone Sans by Post Pre-Press Group, Brisbane, Queensland
Printed and bound in Australia by McPherson's Printing Group, Maryborough, Victoria

ISBN-13: 978 0 14 300523 0.
ISBN-10: 0 14 300523 5.
ISSN 1038–6467.

www.penguin.com.au

Contents

Penguin Wine Awards 2006

It has been a great year for new Australian wines: more wineries, more labels, more brands, and probably more choice than we really need. The ongoing flood of new products makes it increasingly difficult for us to keep up and must be very daunting for many wine drinkers. Thankfully many of the new wines are excellent, so we can't afford to ignore the newcomers.

At the business end of things, there's still a lot of good-value wine at the price levels where most Australians buy their wine – that is, below $20 a bottle. Most of these wines come from the bigger companies and are often made in a rather homogenised style, but our Penguin Wine of the Year is different. From a smaller, fairly new producer, it's a $15 red made from the very fashionable blend of shiraz and viognier. A stylish, Euro-accented, food-friendly type of red. The viognier component is kept nicely in check, adding silky complexity to a core of spicy Victorian shiraz. Simply delicious!

We could easily choose our award winners each year exclusively from the best of the best – the great wines of Australia. But inevitably, that would mean we were filling the pages with super-expensive wines that are beyond most people's budgets, making this guide of limited use to most Australians, and we don't want that!

So our awards are selected with an eye on several criteria: quality, of course, but also price and value for money, quantity and availability (sometimes a problem with a book that's prepared some months before it actually goes on sale). A reasonable quantity has to have been produced. We are a little tired of discovering fabulous wines that ring all our bells, only to find in the fine print that just 100 cases or so were made. People have to be able to buy the stuff. Having said that, the best Australian wines do sell out quickly, even during a wine glut, so be quick if you want to secure any of our award winners. Past experience tells us that some of them will disappear with indecent haste.

THE PENGUIN WINE OF THE YEAR
BEST-VALUE RED WINE

Terra Felix Shiraz Viognier 2005

How do they get so much charmingly flavoursome, beautifully balanced, stylish red wine into a bottle and on the shelf so cheaply? At $15 this is a tremendous bargain. And it's reasonably widely available and therefore not hard to track down. Made by Martin Williams and grown on the Tallarook vineyards near Seymour. (See page 349.)

BEST SPARKLING WINE

Croser 2003

Croser is always good but we fancy the '03 is a little more expansive, more generous and more open-knit in its youth than the usually somewhat austere style of a more typical young Croser. It might not make such old bones, but we're drinking it now! (See page 48.)

BEST WHITE WINE
BEST CHARDONNAY

Toolangi Reserve Chardonnay 2004

This is a majestic chardonnay, which has the Kinzbrunner stamp all over it. (But it's half the price of Giaconda!) By whatever yardstick you choose, this is a great chardonnay which combines finesse and precision balance with mind-bending complexity of flavour. (See page 94.)

BEST RED WINE
BEST SHIRAZ

John Duval Entity Shiraz 2004

The former Penfolds chief winemaker proves he's not just a paper-shuffler! His first straight shiraz is a cracker, showcasing all the best things about Barossa shiraz and avoiding the porty, jammy, over-alcoholic and over-oaked pitfalls others fall into. (See page 318.)

BEST ROSÉ WINE

Spinifex Rosé 2005

This is one of the most European-style Aussie rosés we've ever tasted, and that's a compliment. It has that irresistible complexity, balance, savouriness and drinkability that seems to elude many of its more pristinely clean, but boring, brethren. (See page 204.)

BEST SWEET WINE

Westend Three Bridges Golden Mist Botrytis Semillon 2003

Westend's wines have improved across the board, but the botrytis has always been exceptional and among the Riverina region's best stickies. The '03 is truly a *vino di meditazione*. (See page 380.)

BEST FORTIFIED WINE

Penfolds Grandfather

It's not cheap, but then, this kind of wine is expensive to make. Time is the most costly ingredient and there can be no short cuts. A very great and distinctly Australian fortified wine. (See page 389.)

PICKS OF THE BUNCH

ⓐ BEST RIESLING
Grosset Watervale Riesling 2005

It's aways hard to choose between the two Grosset rieslings – Polish Hill and Watervale – and in 2005 both are great. We came down on the side of the Watervale, which is just that little bit more giving in its youth. (See page 121.)

ⓐ BEST SAUVIGNON BLANC AND BLENDS
Bridgewater Mill Sauvignon Blanc 2005

The last two vintages of this wine have jumped up a gear, and it's now among the best in the country. With all the aromatics you could want, but palate weight and properly ripe flavours as well, the '05 is a winner. (See page 144.)

ⓐ BEST SEMILLON AND BLENDS
Meerea Park Alexander Munro Semillon 2001

For a small maker to release a semi-mature Hunter semillon this calibre is a great service to the wine lover. It is a superb wine, one of the best Alexander Munros we have tasted. (See page 168.)

ⓐ BEST OTHER WHITES AND BLENDS
Ravensworth Marsanne 2005

Bryan Martin, assistant winemaker at Clonakilla, is turning out a superb range of wines from the Canberra district under his own label. The marsanne has an infusion of viognier, producing a distinctive new, aromatic style: rich, spicy and apricot/honey flavoured. (See page 102.)

ⓐ BEST CABERNET SAUVIGNON AND BLENDS
Murdock Cabernet Sauvignon 2001

The few Murdock reds released thus far have been consistently impressive, thanks to the viticultural nous of David Murdock and winemaking skill of Pete Bissell. The '01 is the best yet – and has the bonus of bottle-age. (See page 224.)

🐧 BEST PINOT NOIR
Paringa Estate Pinot Noir 2004

Lindsay McCall's pinots have gone up a few notches, with more subtle oak and greater complexity. The '04 Reserve is even better, but we're giving the award to the '04 Estate because it's cheaper and easier to buy – and also great! (See page 279.)

🐧 BEST OTHER REDS AND BLENDS
Pondalowie MT Tempranillo 2005

For sheer gluggability and hedonistic pleasure we loved this wine. Young it may be; straightforward it may be; unwooded, too; but it's an object lesson in how to produce a delicious fruit-driven young red. (See page 362.)

BEST-VALUE PICKS

🐧 BEST-VALUE SPARKLING WINE
Coldstone Brut Cuvée

From the Vic Alps Winery, this is a new label that should give the big brands something to worry about. (See page 47.)

🐧 BEST-VALUE WHITE WINE
Pewsey Vale Riesling 2005

This has been such a consistently high performer for so long it's almost taken for granted. The price has inched up slightly but it still offers great value for money. We wonder why people drink vegetal, sweet, yucky sauvignon blancs when they can have a quality wine like this for the same money. (See page 132.)

🐧 BEST-VALUE FORTIFIED WINE
Director's Special 10 Year Old Tawny

A lovely soft, fruity port style with some aged character adding complexity. (See page 385.)

BEST NEW PRODUCER

Pondalowie

Pondalowie is based in the Bendigo region and run by the team of Dominic and Krystina Morris, who have both worked in a number of wineries in Australia and Portugal. They planted their own small vineyard at Bridgewater in the mid-90s. Pondalowie has wowed us these past couple of years with a bevy of impressive red wines. Tempranillo, various bottlings of shiraz, reserve shiraz and shiraz viognier, the MT unoaked tempranillo, which is also an award-winner this year, and the Vineyard Blend of shiraz, cabernet and tempranillo all have considerable merit. Their hallmarks are deep, rich colours; fully ripe but not overripe fruit (nor unbalanced alcohol); soft tannins; and generosity of flavour.

The Year in Review

As we write, the news media is full of talk of the 2006 grape glut and record over-supply of Australian wine. When it comes to wine, the mainstream media can't seem to think of anything else. A close second is the ongoing woes of publicly listed wine companies, especially the beleaguered Evans & Tate. The wine industry is really on the nose with the stock-market jocks.

If you take the newspapers as a guide, there is nothing but gloom and doom in the wine business. It is, of course, misleadingly skewed. There is a lot of good stuff happening, and – ever the reactionaries – we've decided to focus on the upside this year. 'Accentuate the positive; eliminate the negative' as Bing Crosby sang.

MORE WINERIES = MORE GREAT WINES

As much as the industry wrings its hands at the 100-plus new producers in Australia alone entering the wine market every year, from our viewpoint there is a lot of good in this. It means that a certain number of exciting, sometimes great, new wines are coming into our viewfinder every year.

For a start, just think of the industry stalwarts who have tantalised us with new wines from their solo ventures in the past year: John Duval Wines from the Barossa, Philip Shaw Wines from Orange, and Stephen Pannell's S.C. Pannell wines from McLaren Vale are just a handful. Pannell was formerly chief red winemaker at Hardys; the other two were senior winemakers for Penfolds and Southcorp, respectively. They have debuted with sensational wines. (As well, Duval is closely associated with Songlines, which launched several outstanding wines in mid-2006, even if the prices are high.) Ex-Houghton winemaker John Griffiths' new Faber Vineyard releases have also impressed. While many newcomers to the wine industry spend several years with the training wheels on, some astonish us by hitting the ground sprinting. Few things excite your jaded authors more than discovering a newcomer whose first offerings thrill our tastebuds. Think Toolangi (Yarra Valley), Savaterre (Beechworth), Spinifex (Barossa), Marius (McLaren Vale), Longview (Adelaide Hills), Chatto (Hunter Valley), Murdock (Coonawarra), Orange Mountain (New South Wales Central Ranges), Word of Mouth (Orange) and Louee (Mudgee) and you'll see what we mean.

Not only do these people bring marvellous wine to the table, they also put pressure on their more established peers, and a bit of friendly competition never hurt anyone. It's never been truer that no one can afford to rest on their laurels in today's dog-eat-dog environment. Whenever we speak to established players in the wine industry, whether they're producers, wholesalers or retailers, they nearly all say they are working harder and trying more innovations just to stay in the race.

CLIMBING THE LEARNING CURVE

The other great news for fine wine lovers is that, as winemakers and grapegrowers in newer cool-climate regions get better at their jobs, the quality of their wines is constantly rising. There's no better example at present than the Mornington Peninsula. A few years ago there were masses of brown-coloured, vegetal, skinny pinot noirs ('rusty water' our late colleague Mark Shield dubbed them) and overworked, over-wooded, over-maloed chardonnays. Not to mention herbaceous green-as-grass cabernets! Today, the cabernet is mostly gone, and its uprooting is unlamented. And the pinots have improved out of recognition. Many of them are truly world class, with good depth of colour and flavour; structure, texture and concentration; length and balance in the mouth; and even some cellaring potential. We're thinking especially of Paringa Estate, Moorooduc Estate, Kooyong, Port Phillip Estate, Stonier, Willow Creek, Yabby Lake and of course Main Ridge Estate, whose pinots were always good but now they're even better. At the same time, winemakers have throttled back on new oak, on malolactic fermentation (so the wines are less likely to smell like a jug of freshly whipped powdered milk); they are more delicate and refined yet more intense, concentrated and persistent in flavour, and more age-worthy.

That's great progress. Other regions have a similar story to tell, especially the Adelaide Hills. Even Coonawarra, which has been in the doldrums for years, no thanks to the over-mechanisation of viticulture over the past 20 years, is showing signs of getting its act together. Vineyards are being converted from minimal pruning back to partial hand-pruning and soil mapping is having a big effect on correct picking times and ripeness levels.

DRINKING TRENDS

What's different about the wine we're drinking? Well, we're drinking more imported wines, more pinot gris and pinot grigio, more sauvignon blanc and semillon-sauvignon blanc blends, more rosé, more affordable pinot noir, more viognier, more oddball exotic varieties such as arneis, barbera, lagrein – even albarino! This year, we've tasted our first Aussie-grown-and-made sagrantino, vermentino and aglianico.

IMPORTS

Woolworths-owned Dan Murphy's, one of the biggest liquor retailers in the country, reports that its sales of imported wine have lifted by 80 per cent in a year. The big movers are cheaper wines such as the cleverly packaged Languedoc red called Arrogant Frog, low-priced beaujolais, and Montes wines from Chile, but well-priced premium-quality wines like Dopff au Moulin (Alsace) and Carpineto (Tuscany, especially its Dogajolo) also contribute. Other retailers and importers are also enjoying a boom in imports, and a rash of new importers rushed into the indent market to take advantage of the high-potential 2005 Bordeaux vintage.

One exciting interpretation of this import boom is that Australians are becoming increasingly adventurous in their wine drinking – less habitual and perhaps less brand-loyal, more risk-taking and open to new experiences. No doubt there are those who've been drinking Aussie wine for many years and have tired of it; no doubt some of the import-drinkers have travelled extensively and discovered foreign wines that they enjoyed while on overseas holidays, then returned home with expanded horizons. They will now pick up a $20 cheap bordeaux where once they might have thought a $20 Australian cabernet merlot was the safer bet. Cheaper Loire sauvignon blancs from regions other than the fashionable sancerre and pouilly-fumé are price-competitive with Marlborough and Australian savvies in the mid-$20s.

LIGHTER WHITES AND REDS

Australian wine drinkers are going for lighter, less-complex wines, 'fridge' wines if you like – such as savvy, semillon sauvignon blanc, rosé and pinot gris/grigio. As noted by the drinks industry analyst for ACNielsen ScanTrack research, Michael Walton, we seem to be 'over' the phase of rich, powerful, oaky and complex, and have decided we all need some light relief.

The authors are all for it. For years we've been questioning winemakers' preoccupation with darkly coloured, strong, complex wines – wines that tend to over-burden the drinker and dominate food to the detriment of eating-and-drinking pleasure. We find ourselves reaching for something light and easygoing to drink (such as pinot noir, a lighter sangiovese, a riesling or semillon) and leaving the heavy artillery in the cellar – and we suspect many others are doing the same.

And yet, as wine writers who receive thousands of samples of wine to taste and review every year, we are increasingly deluged with 'battleship' reds. Shiraz has risen steadily to comprise more than 30 per cent of all the samples we receive, and a disproportionate number of them are big, high-alcohol, gutsy wines. These seem to need cellar time before they can be enjoyed to their fullest. Quite simply, the number of blockbusters is out of balance with what we as critics and you as drinkers could ever want. It's as though every car builder wants to produce a Holden Statesman but no one wants to bother with a Commodore, which ignores the fact that the Commodore is what most buyers want.

Could it be that fame is having an effect? The craving for star status and Parker points is compelling winemakers to produce 'pedestal' wines which they send to the wine shows and critics, while neglecting to shine the spotlight on their 'popular' wines. Everyone wants to be the director of the movie, not the cameraman or editor.

With pinot noir there continues to be an encouraging trend for wineries to release cheaper bottlings priced well below their flagship wines. In specialist pinot noir regions, such as the Mornington Peninsula and Yarra Valley, you're likely to find not only a $60 flag-bearer and a high-$30s mid-ranker, but also a $20 entry-level wine. Frequently, these are pretty good drinks. Fewer of them are green and herbaceous, pale, tart and weedy like they used to be. They include wines such as Pierre Naigeon's Clos Pierre, which gets a rave review in this year's *Guide*, De Bortoli's Windy Peak, the Dromana Estate group's Mornington Estate and Red Hill Estate's Bimaris. This is a good trend: it introduces new drinkers to the delights of pinot noir, with all its easy-drinking and food-friendly advantages, and helps the winery by moving stock and spreading the good news about pinot.

The popularity of sauvignon blanc and semillon-sauvignon blanc blends continues to astonish everyone who is in the business of making or selling wine. The boom seems to be without end. Theories abound, but the most plausible is that the unique phenomenon that is New Zealand 'savvy' has set the whole world aflame, and sauvignon blanc generally as a category has been touched by the heat, causing spontaneous combustion! Even fairly ordinary sauvignon blanc from warm-area Australia is easy to sell, not to mention the popularity of Western Australian semillon-sauvignon blanc blends – which contain very little sauvignon blanc. When a Margaret River wine composed of 90 per cent semillon and 10 per cent sauvignon can have strong demand, why is straight semillon still in the doldrums? When you taste a good semillon beside that kind of blend, the difference is so slight – if indeed there is any difference at all – it suggests that there is a strong element of fashion attached to these names. Are people drinking the wine or the label?

Against this backdrop of rising demand for light-bodied white wines with little or no oak treatment, it's no surprise that pinot gris/grigio is doing well. Pinot grigio is – or will soon turn out to be – easily the bigger category in terms of bottles sold, simply because the Italians have created the market for it over many decades. The market for French-style pinot gris is relatively small. Add in the fact that Italian-style pinot grigio is more of a quaffing wine, with lower alcohol, less richness and less inclination to heaviness, and you have an important difference in drinkability. The canniest marketers of this grape in Australia, including the amazing Brown Brothers, labelled their wines pinot grigio from the outset and have tapped into the bigger market. We suspect that in future, only those making a genuine Alsace style with more weight and alcohol and richer, riper-picked flavours, will label their wine pinot gris; and the market for that will always be smaller. Grigio is more adaptable with food, too, while gris is more selective and needs richer dishes.

And finally, rosé. The number of rosés on the shop shelves continues to swell and although demand is strong, we can't help but wonder if the producers haven't gotten a bit too enthused and over-supplied the market. Rosé has also benefited from the cabernet and merlot over-supply: cheap grapes can be procured even in cooler regions and turned into rosé at very low cost.

We prefer the less-sweet, better balanced styles. While obviously sweet rosés may find a ready market with some drinkers, they are seldom high-quality wines in our experience. The wines which taste soft and smooth and have that all-important quality of quaffability, without obvious sugar, are the wines we enjoy drinking. On the other hand, high-acid rosés – pink wines made like dry whites – are not much fun either because the acidity interferes with their quaffability. It's interesting that De Bortoli's Yarra Valley winemaker Steve Webber and a few others are now making rosés that are softer and lower in acid, as well as drier, even if the colours are not as bright or purple-tinged, because that's the kind of rosé that's good to drink.

THE FOOD CONNECTION

A final observation about all these wine types, which are part of the trend towards drinking lighter wines, is that there is a direct link between what people eat and what they drink. We are eating less rich, elaborate, heavily sauced food, and looking for healthier fodder. We're not visiting 'fine dining' restaurants as much but favouring bistros, fish cafes, sushi bars and other less-formal eateries. Asian foods – Thai, Vietnamese, Japanese and Chinese – are popular, and lighter wines suit these kinds of meals. Your authors frequent Chinese, Japanese and Vietnamese restaurants and in their BYO bags you'll generally find two bottles: a pinot noir and a chilled riesling. It's not that we don't enjoy a hearty Barossa shiraz: there's a time and place for that, too. But the trend to eat and drink lighter is plain to see.

CHEAPER THAN BOTTLED WATER

Never has wine been so inexpensive as today. Newspapers are full of excited stories about wine being cheaper than bottled water. The over-supply has led to remaindering, as the booksellers call it, and the result of that is a loss of profit margin – usually for the producer.

Auctioneers are doing huge business in distressed wine sales. One Sydney auction house was holding an auction every day to get through the quantities flooding into its rooms. In Melbourne, clearance houses have been set up purely to get rid of surplus wine cheaply. Cleanskins are still selling up a storm; although, reading between the lines of what the big operators are saying, the growth in cleanskins has slowed. As a direct result of cleanskins 'cutting their lunch', the big brands are discounting more than ever, as it's the big brands that are most damaged by cleanskin sales. It all means that wine is cheaper than ever, which is good news for you, the buyer.

What is seen less often is discounting of the more expensive, image wines. When these fail to sell sufficiently well, owners tend to dispose of the excess in a more subtle way, such as through hidden discounts to their cellar-door clients, offers to wine-club members, and even as cleanskins or retail/restaurant own-labels. But even those routes are fraught, as word tends to get out: 'Pssst. Did you know this Private Bin R2D2 is actually Joe Bloggs's Old Vine Reserve?' Indeed, Sydney retailer Kemeny's is having massive success selling what it calls Hidden Labels. They are a kind of Kemeny's own-label and the winemaker's name is hidden in the banknote-like filigree detail of the label design. Many of these wines when sold under the producer's label are more than twice the Kemeny's price.

If ever the current spate of discounting and generally cheap wine comes to an end, ordinary wine drinkers won't know what's hit them. Having to pay full price after years of wine-price Nirvana will be a nasty shock. The thing is, though, we can't see it coming to an end any time soon. So enjoy!

Penguin Seals of Approval

The type of closure that seals a wine bottle has been a topic of conversation in the wine world for some years now, and the *Guide* has joined in the debate in past editions. For our part, we've always formed our views based on our experience of wine quality under various closures; telling it like it is without fear or favour.

Many proponents of cork, screw-cap, plastic stopper and their variations argue interminably in favour of this or that closure, often without considering what the wines actually *taste* like under each closure. Then there are those, usually winemakers and commentators, who have the best interests of the wine-drinking public in mind and try to be objective; but there are also vested interests at work, plus quite a few egos to be preened. For our part, this year, we have both taken the opportunity to taste numbers of wines under a variety of closures, in order to better inform our readers. And as with most things that influence wine quality, it's never as clear-cut as you may think.

In our experience, the 'perfect' cork is an excellent way of sealing a wine bottle, both for current consumption and for age, but 'perfect' corks are few and far between. Instead we have corks with a failure rate that makes it a high-risk closure, indeed. A few years ago a friend of ours bought a dozen bottles of an Italian red from Piedmont. Four bottles were spoilt by the classic 'cork taint' of the trichloroanisole (TCA) compound – no less than a third of the wines were rendered undrinkable by the piece of tree bark sealing them. This year a Yarra Valley winery had a similar experience with corks in one of their special reserve chardonnays, and in the end withheld the wine from sale.

And what about age? Corks are especially unreliable seals when it comes to bottle-aged wines. After only five years in bottle, it's unlikely that any two cork-sealed wines from the same bottling will be the same. Varying degrees of oxidation will creep into the wine and some bottles will start to suffer from premature senility. Different bottles of a screw-capped wine, in our experience, age in the same way, even after 10 or 20 years.

Winemakers who hold wines for later release with bottle-age report amazing levels of cork failure. In the Hunter Valley both Tyrrell's and Mount Pleasant regularly release aged examples of their wines and each bottle is individually checked visually before release. With their aged semillons, any bottle containing darker coloured, obviously oxidised, prematurely old or leaking wine is discarded. Both companies report that they cull as much as 30 per cent of each release before sale.

A handful of wine commentators have suggested that wines under screw-cap just don't age as well as those under cork. One even stated that they don't age at all. What absolute twaddle. Our experience across the board is that wines under screw-cap age extremely well and very reliably. In fact in the case of unoaked whites there is no comparison between screw-cap and cork. In a tasting conducted by one of the authors this year of rieslings between three and eight years old under both closures, screw-capped riesling was vastly better in nearly every case than the same wine under cork. The wines evolved a gorgeous interplay of toasty, buttery bottle-aged complexity, concentrated limey-fruit characters, lovely texture and fantastic freshness.

Things aren't quite as clear cut with oak-aged, elaborately handled wines like full-bodied chardonnays and most red wines. In tastings this year we found some screw-capped chardonnays absolutely superb – Cullen and Giaconda immediately spring to mind – but others seem much less evolved at the same stage than their cork-topped brethren. We also found some reds excellent, but others a little 'edgy' under screw-caps, lacking the softness and richness of the very best cork-sealed wines. Do these wines develop better under the best corks? The jury seems to be out still, but it's worth noting that any screw-capped wine is going to be preferable to a corked or an oxidised wine with a cork; and remember that no two older cork-sealed wines are going to be the same.

Screw-caps are the seal of the moment and there can be little doubt that for reliability they beat cork hands down. Are they perfect? Probably close to perfect, providing the wine going into the bottle is as squeaky clean and pure as possible. In the anaerobic environment of a screw-capped bottle, any sulphidey/reductive characters due to the natural process of fermentation, or any excessive dosage of sulphur dioxide (the winery antiseptic) may translate into a notable 'pong' that can mar the pure fruit characters of the wine. The same traits can be found under cork, and such pongy screw-capped wines are still miles more drinkable than wines with even slight TCA cork taint. In Europe sulphide/sulphury qualities are common in many of the greatest wines in youth, and translate into fascinating complexity with age. Should we be worried about this trait in some screw-capped wines? We think not. As winemakers become more experienced and attuned to handling wines destined for screw-cap they will need far less sulphur dioxide and more copper fining – and the problem should disappear. It already is.

Some attempts have been made to overcome the problems inherent in cork seals, and the cork industry PR machine trumpets loudly about technical improvements they are making in cork production, but we've seen little improvement yet. Two other developments to arrive in recent times are interesting. One involves coating the ends of the cork in a membrane that prevents the cork contacting the wine. The other, known as Sabate Diam, is made from granulated cork that is treated with supercritical carbon dioxide to remove any nasties. It works well, although one author has recently had TCA-tainted wine under a Diam cork, highlighting cork's unfortunate ability to pick up taints.

Other wine bottle seals have remained very much in the background. Plastic stoppers, once championed as a real alternative to natural cork, are now only used in cheaper wines designed for early consumption. They look to have a very limited future. Crown seals, the well-known beer bottle top, were found by one large Australian wine company to be the best seal of all, but public acceptance of its use on table wines might be a problem. Commonly used in champagne and high-quality sparkling wine production, then removed after disgorgement and replaced with a fault-prone cork, they are starting to appear on top-notch Australian sparklers – a move we applaud.

Another closure only just off the drawing board is known as Vinlok, a German-developed glass-stopper closure that's very stylish and promises screw-cap-like reliability. Henschke winery is trialling it and early results are good. Watch this space.

Vintage Round-up 2002–2006

A feature of most quality table wines is a vintage date. Few other consumables list the year of production on the label, and then it's usually only as a sort of 'use-by date' that guarantees freshness. With wine, the date means a lot more than that. It gives an indication of age and relative maturity, and it also informs the consumer about what to expect in the bottle. Knowing the vintage and whether it was a good one or otherwise in a particular wine region gives you a chance to avoid the lean, mean and green wines from chilly years, to shy away from the soupy products of roasting-hot vintages, and to grab the great years. If you keep a cellar, however modest, the vintage year allows you to judge the ageing potential of a wine and helps you decide when to open your old treasures.

In Europe, where many outstanding vineyards are found in climatically marginal places, the vintage year was most important. Dramatic changes in weather could occur from year to year, determining whether a wine was a great classic, or glorified dishwater. In Australia table-wine production shrank in the first half of the twentieth century, and those that survived were the safest, most reliable vineyards, and were usually the ones with the least vintage variation. Though vintages could still vary, even in the most stable places, the vintage year in Australia was less vital as a gauge of the wine in the bottle.

The Australian wine boom that began in the 1960s changed all this. As newer, cooler vineyard sites were developed in the search for more finesse in our table wines, and old, abandoned sites were replanted, vintage became progressively more important. In response, each year the *Guide* brings you an independent, five-year, region-by-region vintage overview. This year we look at the vintages 2002–2006, those most likely to be found on the shelves of your local wine shop, or on a restaurant wine list.

2006 VINTAGE

Evaluating the new vintage for the *Guide* each year is a difficult task, especially as the definitive wines from most regions aren't yet available, with many not even in bottle. So we listen, observe, ask questions, and taste what we can to make a preliminary assessment, keeping in mind that some of what we hear about each new vintage is meant to 'talk it up', with commercial issues in mind. This year we had the added advantage of 2006 generally being an early vintage, so there was time to taste more of the unoaked styles before release. We'll have more definite opinions about the 2006 wines when we prepare next year's edition.

NEW SOUTH WALES

Hunter Valley: an extremely hot vintage has provided excellent reds and very good whites.

Riverina: a very good vintage.

Orange/Hilltops: an excellent vintage, especially for reds.

Mudgee: a very good vintage.

Cowra: a very good year.

Canberra: a very good vintage.

VICTORIA

Rutherglen: an excellent year.

Murray Valley: an excellent vintage.

Pyrenees/Grampians: an excellent year.

Bendigo/Heathcote: concentrated, excellent wines.

Yarra Valley: an excellent vintage, especially for red wines.

Mornington Peninsula: a very good year.

Geelong: a very good year.

SOUTH AUSTRALIA

Barossa/Eden Valley: a very good vintage.

McLaren Vale: an excellent vintage.

Clare Valley: another excellent year.

Adelaide Hills: a very good vintage.

Coonawarra/Limestone Coast: a warm, low-yielding year providing some excellent wines.

Riverland: a very good year.

WESTERN AUSTRALIA

Margaret River: a cooler year producing some very fine wines.

Great Southern/Pemberton: a good year.

2005 VINTAGE

NEW SOUTH WALES

Hunter Valley: a very good year generally, for both whites and reds.

Riverina: an excellent vintage.

Orange/Hilltops: a high-quality vintage.

Mudgee: a good middle-of-the-road vintage.

Cowra: some good wines.

Canberra: an excellent vintage of well-concentrated wines.

VICTORIA

Rutherglen: an excellent year.

Murray Valley: an excellent year.

Pyrenees/Grampians: an excellent year. Reds are for long-keeping.

Bendigo/Heathcote: a superb vintage.

Yarra Valley: an excellent year.

Mornington Peninsula: a very good vintage.

Geelong: an excellent vintage.

SOUTH AUSTRALIA

Barossa/Eden Valley: an early vintage of good yields that should produce some excellent wines across the board. The best cabernets are outstanding, as are the Eden Valley rieslings.

McLaren Vale: an excellent year.

Clare Valley: an excellent vintage for both whites and reds.

Adelaide Hills: a first-class vintage.

Coonawarra/Limestone Coast: an excellent year.

Riverland: a very good year.

WESTERN AUSTRALIA

Margaret River: an excellent vintage.

Great Southern/Pemberton: a variable year, but some excellent wines.

TASMANIA

An outstanding vintage.

2004 VINTAGE

NEW SOUTH WALES

Hunter Valley: another of those Hunter vintages where rain intervened with similar results to 2002. Great whites; select reds with care.

Riverina: generally good despite very, very hot conditions.

Orange/Hilltops: a mixed vintage with the Orange area faring best. Generally good wines from the best producers.

Mudgee: generally a good vintage.

Cowra: a warm vintage and generally good wines.

Canberra: a very good vintage with excellent pinot noir and chardonnay. Other wines are less consistent, but the best growers succeeded admirably.

VICTORIA

Rutherglen: a very good vintage.

Murray Valley: heatwave conditions presented some difficulties but quality was generally very good.

Pyrenees/Grampians: an excellent all-round vintage with some age-worthy reds that are generally less formidable than the '03s.

Bendigo/Heathcote: very good wines across the board, with reds standing out. A few reds are overripe and lack freshness.

Yarra Valley: an excellent year, especially for chardonnay and cabernet sauvignon.

Mornington Peninsula: possibly the best vintage for some years.

Geelong: an excellent vintage.

SOUTH AUSTRALIA

Barossa/Eden Valley: one of the worst droughts in history indicated a mixed Barossa vintage, but reds are often superb. Eden Valley produced consistently excellent whites and reds.

McLaren Vale: an excellent vintage.

Clare Valley: this was a mixed vintage with some very hot weather. The best makers' wines look very promising. Some great cabernets.

Adelaide Hills: an excellent year, especially for reds from the best makers.

Coonawarra/Limestone Coast: a very good vintage for the best estates.

Riverland: a hot vintage something like 2001. Good quality though, especially for the new darling of the region, petit verdot.

WESTERN AUSTRALIA

Margarer River: excellent vintage with some outstanding reds. A better year than 2003.

Great Southern/Pemberton: a very good year.

TASMANIA

Patchy weather meant a very mixed vintage. As usual, the name of the maker may be more important than the region. Tread warily and you could be pleasantly surprised.

2003 VINTAGE

NEW SOUTH WALES

Hunter Valley: a small, early vintage that produced very good wines across the board.

Riverina: a very good vintage

Orange/Hilltops: a good vintage.

Mudgee: the rain returned mid-vintage to upset things a bit. Whites were good, reds less impressive.

Cowra: as in other parts of central and southern New South Wales, good whites, so-so reds.

Canberra: good whites, variable reds.

VICTORIA
Rutherglen: drought and nearby bushfires impacted many northern Victorian regions. Reds were very concentrated, quality was mostly fair to good.

Murray Valley: small yields of middling quality.

Pyrenees/Grampians: a low-yielding drought year that produced some massive reds for long-keeping, as well as a few more elegant wines.

Bendigo/Heathcote: similar results to Pyrenees/Grampians.

Yarra Valley: an excellent vintage for both whites and reds.

Mornington Peninsula: a warm, dry vintage that produced some outstanding chardonnays and pinot noirs.

Geelong: an excellent vintage.

SOUTH AUSTRALIA
Barossa/Eden Valley: drought was followed by rain, which wasn't ideal for reds; whites were another matter with great, age-worthy rieslings.

McLaren Vale: a very good smallish vintage, but select carefully.

Clare Valley: as in most southern Australian regions, drought meant very small yields. Good reds and whites, although the rieslings don't have quite the richness of the '02s.

Adelaide Hills: a very good year.

Coonawarra/Limestone Coast: very good wines from a smaller than usual vintage.

Riverland: a good year.

WESTERN AUSTRALIA
Margaret River: a very good year.

Great Southern/Pemberton: a mixed bag but many respectable wines, and some very good.

TASMANIA
A vintage of two parts due to rain mid-vintage: early-picked whites and pinot noir did well, other wines less so.

2002 VINTAGE

NEW SOUTH WALES

Hunter Valley: rain split this vintage in two: early-picked varieties like semillon and most other whites were good, later-picked varieties like shiraz problematic.

Riverina: cool, dry conditions gave Riverina wineries their best vintage in memory. The best wines really show class.

Orange/Hilltops: cool conditions made very good whites. Reds were variable.

Mudgee: an outstanding year, made even more welcome by the series of lousy vintages 1999–2001 that had preceded it. Outstanding reds that combine power with finesse.

Cowra: cool, dry conditions made very good wines.

Canberra: a problematic year due to cool temperatures.

VICTORIA

Rutherglen: mild conditions provided a chance for more elegant editions of Rutherglen's red table wines, although not all took the opportunity presented. Warm, dry autumn conditions proved ideal for fortified wines.

Murray Valley: an excellent year.

Pyrenees/Grampians: a tiny harvest and cool conditions. Better whites than reds.

Bendigo/Heathcote: another Victorian region to produce a much smaller than usual crop. Reds are good.

Yarra Valley: a tiny crop with pinot noir and chardonnay performing best.

Mornington Peninsula: variable quality but some excellent pinot noir.

Geelong: a difficult year but the most skilled winemakers produced very good wines.

SOUTH AUSTRALIA

Barossa/Eden Valley: a cooler vintage that produced much more elegant wines than usual. The best reds are great and Eden Valley rieslings are classical, if a little less concentrated than the '03s.

McLaren Vale: some excellent reds that drink beautifully in youth, but they should age well. Cool summer weather and a mild autumn gave them unusual elegance.

Clare Valley: generally excellent reds and outstanding rieslings.

Adelaide Hills: early-ripening varieties like most whites and pinot noir fared well, other reds less impressive.

Coonawarra/Limestone Coast: cool conditions favoured whites. Reds generally less convincing.

Riverland: an outstanding year in all hot hinterland regions. Great-value reds.

WESTERN AUSTRALIA

Margaret River: refined reds of less concentration than 2001 but still good. Whites were excellent.

Great Southern/Pemberton: early-ripening whites and pinot noir were the pick of the crop. Other reds a mixed bag.

TASMANIA

An Indian summer made for a good vintage.

The Top-quality Wines (🍷🍷🍷🍷🍷)

Among the 1000-odd wines reviewed in this book, there are some that made a special impression. These wines represent, to us, the acme of quality, character and style. Not surprisingly, some are quite pricey, but many are not, and in fact some of them are terrific bargains.

This list includes only our five-glass rated wines, so you can see at a glance which wines really rang our bells. Each one is accompanied by its price and value-for-money star-rating. All the five-glass wines are included, right down to the lowest value-for-money rating – because if you want the very best and can afford it, you'll still want to know that we loved it, despite its price tag!

If there seem to be rather a lot of red wines, especially shirazes, that's because there are a disproportionate number of shirazes on sale. It's simply a reflection of the market. The industry harvests significantly more tonnes of red grapes these days than white (around 55 to 60 per cent, depending on vintage conditions) and more red wine than white is produced. In turn, there is more shiraz wine being made than anything else.

Finally, a word of warning: the best of anything is usually in short supply, so grab 'em while you can!

Wine	Price	Value
SPARKLING WINES		
Hardys Sir James Pinot Noir Chardonnay 2002	$27.00	★★★★★
Jansz Premium NV Rosé	$26.70	★★★★
Brown Brothers Patricia Pinot Noir Chardonnay Brut 2000	$30.80	★★★★
Kamberra Pinot Noir Chardonnay Pinot Meunier 2000	$32.00	★★★★
Croser 2003	$34.00	★★★⁺
Chandon Tasmanian Cuvée 2002	$37.00	★★★⁺

Chandon Vintage Brut Rosé 1999	$37.00	★★★﹣
Hardys Arras Chardonnay Pinot Noir 2000	$53.00	★★★

WHITE WINES

Chardonnay

Wellington Chardonnay 2003	$32.00	★★★★★
Toolangi Reserve Chardonnay 2004	$65.00	★★★★★
Caledonia Australis Estate Chardonnay 2002	$25.00	★★★★﹣
Hungerford Hill Tumbarumba Chardonnay 2004	$25.00	★★★★﹣
Zarephath Chardonnay 2005	$25.00	★★★★﹣
Shaw and Smith M3 Vineyard Chardonnay 2004	$38.00	★★★★﹣
Toolangi Estate Chardonnay 2004	$40.00	★★★★﹣
De Bortoli Yarra Valley Chardonnay 2004	$29.75	★★★★
Gembrook Hill Chardonnay 2004	$30.00	★★★★
Thompson Estate Chardonnay 2004	$35.00	★★★★
Main Ridge Estate Chardonnay 2004	$48.00	★★★★
Oakridge 864 Chardonnay 2004	$50.00	★★★★
Hardys Eileen Hardy Chardonnay 2004	$53.00	★★★★
Voyager Estate Chardonnay 2004	$40.00	★★★﹣
Yabby Lake Chardonnay 2004	$42.00	★★★﹣
Giaconda Nantua Les Deux 2005	$47.00	★★★﹣
Brookland Valley Reserve Chardonnay 2003	$65.00	★★★﹣
Savaterre Chardonnay 2004	$65.00	★★★﹣
Pierro Chardonnay 2004	$65.00	★★★
Giaconda Chardonnay 2004	$115.00	★★★
Penfolds Yattarna 2003	$130.00	★★﹣

Marsanne, roussanne and blends

Tahbilk 1927 Vines Marsanne 1998	$33.00	★★★★

Riesling

The Wine Society Tasmanian Riesling 2005	$15.99	★★★★★
Leo Buring Clare Valley Riesling 2005	$18.50	★★★★★
The Wilson Vineyard DJW Riesling 2005	$19.00	★★★★★
Tim Gramp Riesling 2005	$19.50	★★★★★
Gilberts Mount Barker Riesling 2004	$20.00	★★★★★
Howard Park Riesling 2005	$25.00	★★★★⟩
Knappstein Ackland Vineyard Watervale Riesling 2005	$26.00	★★★★⟩
Seppelt Drumborg Riesling 2005	$30.00	★★★★⟩
Grosset Watervale Riesling 2005	$33.00	★★★★⟩
Leo Buring DW117 Leonay Riesling 2005	$35.00	★★★★⟩
Pikes The Merle Reserve Riesling 2005	$35.75	★★★★⟩
Heggies Riesling 2005	$21.00	★★★★
Frankland Estate Isolation Ridge Riesling 2005	$24.00	★★★★
Petaluma Riesling 2005	$28.00	★★★★
Grosset Polish Hill Riesling 2005	$38.00	★★★★
Penfolds Reserve Bin Eden Valley Riesling 2005	$26.00	★★★⟩
Leasingham Classic Clare Riesling 2002	$33.00	★★★⟩

Sauvignon blanc and blends

Bridgewater Mill Sauvignon Blanc 2005	$18.00	★★★★⟩
Cape Mentelle Wallcliffe Sauvignon Blanc Semillon 2003	$35.00	★★★⟩

Semillon and blends

Huntington Estate Semillon Bin W1 2005	$14.50	★★★★★
Tyrrell's Reserve HVD Semillon 1999	$35.00	★★★★★

Tyrrell's Vat 1 Semillon 1999	$45.00	★★★★⅃
Meerea Park Alexander Munro Semillon 2001	$35.00	★★★★
McWilliams Mount Pleasant Lovedale Semillon 2000	$49.00	★★★★
Tyrrell's Vat 1 Semillon 1994	$72.00	★★★★

Viognier

Meeting Place Viognier 2004	$16.00	★★★★★
Yalumba Eden Valley Viognier 2004	$22.00	★★★★★
Yalumba The Virgilius Viognier 2004	$50.00	★★★★
By Farr Viognier 2004	$55.00	★★★★

ROSÉ WINES

Spinifex Rosé 2005	$23.00	★★★★

RED WINES

Cabernet sauvignon and blends

Poet's Corner Henry Lawson Cabernet Sauvignon 2002	$21.00	★★★★★
Huntington Estate Special Reserve Cabernet Sauvignon Bin FB20 2002	$31.50	★★★★
Faber Vineyard Margaret River Cabernet Sauvignon 2002	$35.00	★★★★
Penfolds Bin 389 Cabernet Shiraz 2003	$40.00	★★★★
Pizzini Il Barone 2001	$40.00	★★★★
Pizzini Il Barone 2002	$40.00	★★★★
Oakridge 864 Cabernet Merlot 2003	$50.00	★★★★
Saltram Winemaker Selection Cabernet Sauvignon 2002	$65.00	★★★⅃
Wynns Coonawarra Estate John Riddoch Cabernet Sauvignon 2003	$75.00	★★★

Durif

All Saints Family Cellar Reserve Durif 2003	$49.00	★★★⸱

Grenache and blends

S.C. Pannell Grenache 2004	$45.00	★★★★

Merlot and blends

Murdock Merlot 2004	$26.00	★★★★

Pinot noir

By Farr Sangreal 2004	$61.50	★★★★⸱
De Bortoli Reserve Release Yarra Valley Pinot Noir 2003	$43.70	★★★★
By Farr Pinot Noir 2004	$57.95	★★★★
Wellington The Hoodster's Blend Pinot Noir 2002	$50.00	★★★⸱
Grosset Pinot Noir 2004	$59.50	★★★⸱
Savaterre Pinot Noir 2004	$65.00	★★★⸱
Paringa Estate Reserve Pinot Noir 2004	$90.00	★★★
Pipers Brook The Lyre Pinot Noir 2003	$95.00	★★★

Sangiovese and blends

Coriole Sangiovese 2004	$20.00	★★★★★

Shiraz and blends

Yering Station Shiraz Viognier 2004	$23.50	★★★★★
Ravensworth Shiraz Viognier 2005	$25.00	★★★★⸱
Peter Lehmann The Futures Shiraz 2003	$29.00	★★★★⸱
John Duval Entity Shiraz 2004	$36.00	★★★★⸱
S.C. Pannell McLaren Vale Shiraz 2004	$45.00	★★★★⸱
S.C. Pannell Shiraz Grenache 2004	$45.00	★★★★⸱
Mount Langi Ghiran Langi Shiraz 2003	$55.00	★★★★⸱

Westend Three Bridges Reserve Limited Release
Shiraz 2003 $25.00 ★★★★

Seppelt Chalambar Shiraz 2004 $30.00 ★★★★

Journeys End Ascent Shiraz 2004 $35.00 ★★★★

Shaw and Smith Shiraz 2004 $38.00 ★★★★

Bress Heathcote Shiraz 2004 $40.00 ★★★★

Euroa Creeks Reserve Shiraz 2002 $42.00 ★★★★

De Bortoli Reserve Release Syrah 2004 $45.00 ★★★★

Heathcote Estate Shiraz 2004 $45.00 ★★★★

Grampians Estate Streeton Reserve Shiraz 2003 $55.00 ★★★★

Henschke Tappa Pass Shiraz 2002 $55.00 ★★★★

Journeys End Arrival Shiraz 2003 $45.00 ★★★★┤

Journeys End Arrival Shiraz 2004 $45.00 ★★★★┤

d'Arenberg Dead Arm 2003 $60.00 ★★★★┤

Pyrenees Ridge Reserve Shiraz 2004 $45.00 ★★★

Abercorn A Reserve Growers' Revenge 2002 $49.95 ★★★

Brokenwood Rayner Vineyard Shiraz 2003 $69.00 ★★★

Henschke Mount Edelstone 2003 $86.00 ★★★

Giaconda Warner Vineyard Shiraz 2004 $87.00 ★★★

Paringa Estate Reserve Shiraz 2004 $90.00 ★★★

Penfolds RWT Shiraz 2003 $130.00 ★★★

Elderton Command Shiraz 2002 $95.00 ★★┤

Barossa Old Vine Company Shiraz 2003 $100.00 ★★┤

Jim Barry The Armagh 2002 $185.00 ★★┤

Penfolds Grange 2001 $450–500 ★★

Henschke Hill of Grace 2001 $500.00 ★★

Other reds and blends

Wood Park Zinfandel 2005 $35.00 ★★★★┤

Centennial Vineyards Limited Release Reserve
      Rondinella Corvina 2004 $30.00   ★★★★

Cape Mentelle Zinfandel 2004 $51.00   ★★★

SWEET WINES

De Bortoli Noble One 2003	$29.00	★★★★★
Westend Three Bridges Golden Mist Botrytis Semillon 2003	$23.50	★★★★⁺
Margan Botrytis Semillon 2005	$30.00	★★★★
McWilliams Limited Release Botrytis Semillon 2004	$30.00	★★★★
Mount Horrocks Cordon Cut Riesling 2005	$32.00	★★★★
Charles Melton Sotto di Ferro 2001	$55.00	★★★★
Turkey Flat The Last Straw Marsanne 2003	$40.00	★★★

FORTIFIED WINES

Noon VP 2004	$18.00 (500 ml)	★★★★★
Seppelt Barossa Valley Amontillado DP116	$21.50	★★★★★
Seppelt Barossa Valley Oloroso DP38	$21.50	★★★★★
Pfeiffer Christopher's VP 2004	$22.50	★★★★★
Baileys Wine Maker Selection Old Tokay	$33.00 (375 ml)	★★★★★
Morris Premium Amontillado	$43.00 (500 ml)	★★★⁺
Morris Premium Liqueur Tokay	$57.00 (500 ml)	★★★⁺
Penfolds Grandfather	$92.00	★★★⁺
Penfolds Great Grandfather	$326.50	★★★

Best-value Wines under $15

Each year there are more and more high-ticket wines flooding onto the market, but still the question we're most often asked when the *Guide* comes out each year is: 'What's the best value?' or 'Which are the best wines under $15?' So, to make it easier for you to find the best-value wines, we list them using $15 as the cut-off point. The wines are sequenced in descending order of value-for-money, using our star ratings (from five down to four), and in ascending order of price, so that you can easily spot the best buys. To save space, we've left out the quality ratings (out of five glasses) but you can easily check these by turning to the review pages.

The prices quoted here are full retail prices, but don't forget that many of these wines can often be found discounted. You will very likely find them substantially cheaper if you shop around, especially if you buy by the dozen. Retailers commonly charge around 10 per cent less for a case purchase, as an incentive to buy more. That discount is usually for both unbroken and mixed dozens. Theoretically, you should be able to buy 11 bottles of Queen Adelaide for Auntie Helen and one bottle of deluxe champagne for yourself, at the case price! So take advantage!

Wine	Price	Value
SPARKLING WINES		
Coldstone Brut Cuvée	$13.00	★★★★⟩
Deakin Estate Brut	$10.75	★★★★
McWilliams Hanwood Estate Pinot Noir Chardonnay	$12.00	★★★★
McWilliams Hanwood Estate Sparkling Shiraz	$12.00	★★★★

WHITE WINES

Chardonnay

Clarence Hill Chardonnay 2004	$15.00	★★★★★
Wolf Blass Eaglehawk Chardonnay 2005	$10.00	★★★★⁺
Bidgeebong Triangle Chardonnay 2005	$14.00	★★★★⁺
Angove's Butterfly Ridge Colombard Chardonnay 2005	$7.00	★★★★
Talinga Park Chardonnay 2004	$9.95	★★★★
Four Emus Chardonnay 2005	$9.99	★★★★
Lindemans Bin 65 Chardonnay 2005	$10.50	★★★★
Bullers Beverford Chardonnay 2005	$13.00	★★★★
Fishers Circle Chardonnay 2005	$13.50	★★★★
Trentham Estate Chardonnay 2005	$14.95	★★★★
Bellarmine Chardonnay 2005	$15.00	★★★★
Pennys Hill Red Dot Chardonnay Viognier 2005	$15.00	★★★★
Printhie Chardonnay 2005	$15.00	★★★★

Marsanne, roussanne and blends

Tahbilk Marsanne 2005	$14.90	★★★★⁺

Pinot gris and pinot grigio

Cheviot Bridge CB Pinot Grigio 2004	$14.00	★★★★

Riesling

Bellarmine Dry Riesling 2005	$15.00	★★★★★
Bellarmine Riesling 2005	$15.00	★★★★★
Richmond Grove Footbridge Riesling 2005	$15.00	★★★★★
De Bortoli Sacred Hill Riesling 2005	$7.00	★★★★⁺
Chrismont Riesling 2005	$14.00	★★★★⁺
Barwite Riesling 2004	$14.60	★★★★⁺
Schild Estate Riesling 2005	$15.00	★★★★⁺

Sauvignon blanc and blends

Trentham Estate Sauvignon Blanc 2005	$12.90	★★★★ｺ
Bellarmine Sauvignon Blanc 2004	$15.00	★★★★ｺ
Cookoothama Sauvignon Blanc Semillon 2005	$15.00	★★★★ｺ
Dalfarras Sauvignon Blanc 2005	$15.00	★★★★ｺ
Angove's Long Row Sauvignon Blanc 2005	$10.00	★★★★
Deen De Bortoli Vat 2 Sauvignon Blanc 2006	$10.00	★★★★
Hungerford Hill Fishcage Sauvignon Blanc Semillon 2005	$14.00	★★★★
Cofield Sauvignon Blanc Semillon 2005	$15.00	★★★★
Rolling Sauvignon Blanc Semillon 2005	$15.00	★★★★

Semillon and blends

Murchison Semillon 2005	$13.00	★★★★★
Huntington Estate Semillon Bin W1 2005	$14.50	★★★★★
Peter Lehmann Adelaide Hills Semillon Sauvignon Blanc 2005	$15.00	★★★★★
Bidgeebong Triangle Semillon Sauvignon Blanc 2005	$14.00	★★★★ｺ
Wolf Blass Eaglehawk Semillon Chardonnay 2005	$10.00	★★★★
Schild Estate Unwooded Semillon 2005	$15.00	★★★★

Verdelho

Faber Vineyard Verdelho 2005	$12.00	★★★★
Kingston Estate Verdelho 2005	$13.00	★★★★
Vercoe's Vineyard Verdelho 2005	$14.00	★★★★
Wyndham Estate Bin 111 Verdelho 2005	$14.00	★★★★

Other whites and blends

Moondah Brook Classic Dry White 2005	$14.00	★★★★
Schild Estate Frontignac 2005	$14.00	★★★★
Primo Estate La Biondina 2005	$15.00	★★★★

ROSÉ WINES

Chateau Mildura Riverboat Rosé 2005	$10.00	★★★★★
De Bortoli Sacred Hill Rosé 2004	$6.99	★★★★⟩
Gordon Parker 'gp' Rosé 2005	$15.00	★★★★⟩
Peter Lehmann Barossa Rosé 2005	$15.00	★★★★⟩

RED WINES

Cabernet sauvignon and blends

Yalumba Y Series Cabernet Sauvignon 2004	$13.65	★★★★★
De Bortoli Sacred Hill Cabernet Merlot 2005	$6.99	★★★★⟩
Woop Woop Cabernet Sauvignon 2005	$14.00	★★★★⟩
Deen De Bortoli Vat 9 Cabernet Sauvignon 2004	$10.00	★★★★
Hardys Nottage Hill Cabernet Sauvignon 2004	$10.60	★★★★
Tatachilla Partners Cabernet Shiraz 2004	$12.95	★★★★
Richmond Grove Weathervane Cabernet Merlot 2004	$15.00	★★★★

Durif

Deen De Bortoli Vat 1 Durif 2004	$10.85	★★★★⟩

Merlot and blends

McWilliams Hanwood Merlot 2004	$12.00	★★★★⟩
Kingston Estate Merlot 2004	$13.00	★★★★
Psyche Smuggler Merlot 2005	$13.00	★★★★
Anderson Merlot 2004	$14.50	★★★★

Pinot noir

Trentham Estate Pinot Noir 2004	$12.50	★★★★
Bellarmine Pinot Noir 2004	$15.00	★★★★
Bellarmine Pinot Noir 2005	$15.00	★★★★

Sangiovese and blends

Piccola Sangiovese Shiraz 2004	$15.00	★★★★
Simon Gilbert Sangiovese Barbera 2004	$15.00	★★★★

Shiraz and blends

Four Emus Shiraz 2004	$9.99	★★★★★
Yalumba Y Series Shiraz Viognier 2003	$13.75	★★★★★
De Bortoli Sacred Hill Shiraz Cabernet 2005	$6.99	★★★★½
Peter Lehmann Barossa Shiraz Grenache 2005	$13.00	★★★★½
Richmond Grove Black Cat Shiraz 2004	$14.00	★★★★½
Lindemans Bin 50 Shiraz 2005	$10.50	★★★★
Hardys Nottage Hill Shiraz 2004	$10.60	★★★★
Deakin Estate Shiraz 2004	$10.75	★★★★
Chateau Mildura Psyche Smuggler Shiraz 2005	$12.50	★★★★
De Bortoli Windy Peak Shiraz Viognier 2003	$13.00	★★★★
Cheviot Bridge Heathcote Shiraz 2004	$13.50	★★★★
Rolling Shiraz 2004	$15.00	★★★★
Terra Felix Shiraz Viognier 2005	$15.00	★★★★

Other reds and blends

Deen De Bortoli Vat 4 Petit Verdot 2004	$10.85	★★★★½
Zilzie Petit Verdot 2004	$15.00	★★★★½

SWEET WINES

Deen De Bortoli Vat 5 Botrytis Semillon 2004	$10.80	★★★★★
Trentham Estate La Famiglia Moscato 2005	$10.00	★★★★

FORTIFIED WINES

Grant Burge Aged Tawny	$13.25	★★★★★
Brown Brothers Reserve Muscat	$14.75	★★★★★
Lillypilly VP Fortified Shiraz 1995	$13.50	★★★★½
Director's Special 10 Year Old Tawny	$12.60	★★★★
Penfolds Club Reserve Tawny	$13.60	★★★★

The Penguin Rating System

This year, for the first time in the 17-year history of *The Penguin Good Australian Wine Guide*, we have included a numerical scoring system. Each wine we review now has a score out of 100. This is in recognition of the fact that over the past few years, the use of this form of rating wine has become increasingly widespread throughout the world. It is an extra service to the reader, as it gives a more precise assessment of how much we liked the wine, in addition to the familiar, at-a-glance glass-rating symbol.

The authors have held out against the global trend towards rating wines out of 100 because we consider that it risks over-simplifying a complex product. There is a well-known tendency among some drinkers in some countries to slavishly follow 100-point ratings, without paying adequate regard to the style and flavour of the individual wine. Retailers, wholesalers, producers and drinkers quote critics' scores without reference to descriptions, and, in our view, this can be dangerous and potentially misleading. We know of collectors who have filled their cellars with expensive 95-point raters only to find they don't enjoy drinking any of them! This is folly in the extreme. The *Guide* has always been, and continues to be, all about reviewing wines with words. Our written descriptions remain detailed because we think it's more important to read the description than just refer to the numbers. But the numbers are an extra guide. Using the 100-point scale gives us more possibilities: it allows us to go up to 97 or even 98 for an especially exciting, great wine.

The authors assess quality using a modified version of the Australasian wine show scoring system. Show judges score out of a possible 20 points – three for colour, seven for nose, and 10 for palate. Any wine scoring less than 10/20 has an obvious fault, so our five-glass range (with half-glass increments) indicates only the top 50 per cent of gradings. When equated to the show system, three glasses is roughly equivalent to a bronze medal;

four approximates silver to high silver; four-and-a-half to five is gold, and five equals a high gold medal or trophy-standard wine. Both authors judge in wine competitions regularly, so are well qualified to use this system.

Everything else is the same: we assess quality and value-for-money separately; we give an estimate of cellaring potential and optimum drinking age; we note the grape varieties used, the source of the grapes, whether they were organically grown; the wine's alcohol content – increasingly important in this age of ever-higher alcohol levels – and where applicable we let you know whether decanting is recommended. We list previous outstanding vintages where we think they're relevant.

Value is arrived at primarily by balancing absolute quality against price. But we do take some account of those intangible attributes that make a wine more desirable, such as rarity, great reputation, glamour, outstanding cellar-ability, and so on. We take such things into account because they are part of the value equation for most consumers.

If a wine scores more for quality than for value, it does not mean the wine is overpriced. As explained below, any wine scoring three stars for value is fairly priced. Hence, a wine scoring five glasses and five stars is extraordinary value for money. Very few wines manage this feat. And, of course, good and bad value for money can be found at $50 just as it can at $5.

If there are more stars than glasses, you are looking at unusually good value. We urge readers not to become star-struck: a three-glass three-star wine is still a good drink.

Where we had any doubt about the soundness of a wine, a second bottle was always sampled.

Quality   Rating

Quality	Rating	
♟♟♟♟♟	95–100	The acme of style: a fabulous, faultless wine that Australia should be proud of.
♟♟♟♟♟	92–94	A marvellous wine that is so close to the top it almost doesn't matter.
♟♟♟♟	90–92	An exciting wine that has plenty of style and dash. You should be proud to serve this.
♟♟♟♟	88–90	Solid quality with a modicum of style; good drinking.
♟♟♟	86–88	Decent, drinkable wine good for everyday quaffing. You can happily serve this to family and friends.
♟♟♟	84–86	Sound, respectable wines, but the earth won't move.
♟♟	82–84	Just okay but, in quality terms, starting to look a little wobbly.

(Lower scores are not usually included.)

Value

★★★★★	You should feel guilty for paying so little: this is great value for money.
★★★★⟩	Don't tell too many people because the wine will start selling and the maker will put the price up.
★★★★	If you complain about paying this much for a wine, you've got a death adder in your pocket.
★★★⟩	Still excellent wine, but the maker is also making money.
★★★	Fair is fair, this is a win–win exchange for buyer and maker.
★★⟩	They are starting to see you coming, but it's not a total rip-off.
★★	This wine will appeal to label drinkers and those who want to impress their bank manager.
★⟩	You know what they say about fools and their money . . .
★	Makes the used-car industry look saintly.

Grapes

Grape varieties are listed in order of dominance; percentages are cited when available.

Region

Where the source of the grapes is known, the region is stated. If there is more than one region, they are listed in order of dominance. Many large commercial blends have so many source regions that they are not stated.

Cellar

Any wine can of course be drunk immediately, but for maximum pleasure we recommend an optimum drinking time, assuming correct cellaring conditions. We have been deliberately conservative, believing it's better to drink a wine when it's a little too young than to risk waiting until it's too old.

An upright bottle ▮ indicates that the wine is ready for drinking now. It may also be possible to cellar it for the period shown. Where the bottle is lying on its side ➤ the wine is not ready for drinking now and should be cellared for the period shown.

▮   Drink now: there will be no improvement achieved by cellaring.

▮ 3   Drink now or during the next three years.

➤ 3–7   Cellar for three years at least before drinking; can be cellared for up to seven years.

➤ 10+   Cellar for 10 years or more; it will be at its best in 10 years.

Alcohol by Volume

Australian labelling laws require that alcohol content be shown on all wine labels. It's expressed as a percentage of alcohol by volume, e.g. 12.0% A/V means that 12 per cent of the wine is pure alcohol.

Recommended Retail Price

Prices were arrived at either by calculating from the trade wholesale using a standard full bottle-shop mark-up, or by using a maker-nominated recommended retail price. In essence, however, there is no such thing as RRP because retailers use different margins. The prices in this book are indicative of those in Sydney and Melbourne, but they will still vary from shop to shop and city to city. They should only be used as a guide. Cellar-door prices have been quoted when the wines are not available in the retail trade.

ⓢ Special

The wine is likely to be 'on special', so it will be possible to pay less than the recommended retail price. Shop around.

⊘ Organic

The wine has passed the tests required to label it as 'organically grown and made'.

▮ Decant

The wine will be improved by decanting.

⬚ Screw-cap

This wine is available with a screw-cap seal. Some of these wines are also available with a cork finish, but at least part of the production has a screw-cap. We recommend them, as a guarantee against cork-taint and random oxidation.

Sparkling Wines

The best Aussie sparklers are being made increasingly from cold-climate grapes grown in Tasmania and high-altitude and/or southerly parts of Victoria. These wines often stand comparison with good non-vintage Champagne, albeit with a decidedly Aussie character. Our cheapie bubblies are remarkable value, especially if you can ensure you're buying a fresh bottle. This is hard to guarantee, as there's no vintage or other indication of age on the label, and these wines get stale quickly. All you can do is try to buy from a shop with a high turnover of that kind of wine. The fizz market is dominated by big company brands, such as Seppelt, Seaview, Yellowglen, Domaine Chandon and Hardys.

Beresford Chardonnay Pinot Noir NV

The Beresford winery at McLaren Vale often attracts our attention for its good-value range of table wines. This sparkling wine shares the same credentials.

CURRENT RELEASE *non-vintage* A very light blush of pink introduces this approachable sparkler. The nose has appetising strawberry aromas with some stone fruits as well, and it's surprisingly delicate. The palate has fine creamy texture with enough underlying structure to keep it interesting, and it finishes dry with a slight firmness and a long fruity aftertaste. Serve it as an aperitif.

Quality	♛♛♛♛
Value	★★★
Rating	91
Grapes	chardonnay; pinot noir
Region	Langhorne Creek, SA
Cellar	🍾 1
Alc./Vol.	12.0%
RRP	$18.00

Bird in Hand Joy

This individual style of sparkling wine comes in a distinctive, skittle-shaped bottle. We like the name – Joy. All too often in the wine biz, people get too serious and analytical and forget that the main purpose of wine is to bring pleasure.

CURRENT RELEASE *non-vintage* The colour is full onion-skin, reflecting the exclusive use of black pinot noir grapes. It is starting to turn bronze with age, and will continue to change as it ages. The wine is big and mouth-filling, generously flavoured and sweetly rich in fruit, but at the same time enlivened by fresh acidity. It's not a wine of subtlety, but big and joyfully hedonistic! Try it with caviar-based canapés.

Quality	♛♛♛♛
Value	★★⁂
Rating	92
Grapes	pinot noir
Region	Adelaide Hills, SA
Cellar	🍾 3
Alc./Vol.	13.0%
RRP	$70.00 ⑤

Bloodwood Chirac

Quality	♥♥♥♥♥
Value	★★★⁣
Rating	93
Grapes	pinot noir; chardonnay
Region	Orange, NSW
Cellar	🍶 3+
Alc./Vol.	11.5%
RRP	$30.00 (cellar door)

The name, of course, is winemaker Stephen Doyle's tongue-in-cheek homage to Jacques Chirac, and was conceived during the French president's last nuclear-testing spree in the Pacific. This vintage spent 48 months on its yeast lees – which is a long time for an Aussie bubbly! CURRENT RELEASE 2001   Orange has great potential for this style, especially in the cooler seasons, and this makes it two great successes on the trot for Stephen Doyle. The wine is still restrained and subtly complex after four years on yeast, with gentle autolysis characters and creamy, cashew-nutty aromas, and just a hint of the oak barrel. The palate is very fine, intense, full of flavour but subtle and discreet, with a clean dry finish. Tops with salmon gravlax on crackers. *Previous outstanding vintage: 2000*

Brown Brothers Patricia Pinot Noir Chardonnay Brut

Quality	♥♥♥♥♥
Value	★★★★
Rating	95
Grapes	pinot noir; chardonnay
Region	north-east Vic.
Cellar	🍶 2
Alc./Vol.	12.0%
RRP	$30.80

Brown Brothers' pinot noir-chardonnay sparkling wine is now named after the Brown family matriarch who passed away in 2004 – it's a fitting tribute to her. CURRENT RELEASE 2000   Another very complex, elegant edition of this premium sparkler. The nose seems to have a little more nutty aged character than past wines, enhancing its vanilla-cream, apple and meringue-like aromas with a hint of the aldehydic complexity you see in some well-known champagnes. In the mouth it has superfine texture, with good depth of baked apple, citrus and nutty flavours that track through a long finish of integrated tangy acidity. Well put together, it has a more-ish quality that has you refilling your glass. Try it as an aperitif with fragrant rice paper rolls.

Brown Brothers Pinot Noir Chardonnay Pinot Meunier NV Brut

Quality	♥♥♥♥⁣
Value	★★★★⁣
Rating	93
Grapes	pinot noir; chardonnay; pinot meunier
Region	north-east Vic.
Cellar	🍶 2
Alc./Vol.	12.5%
RRP	$20.20

Brown Brothers' excellent line of sparkling wines has evolved as a result of their pioneering work with chardonnay and pinot noir in the highlands of Victoria's north-east. This NV version is great value. CURRENT RELEASE *non-vintage*   The nose has attractive vanilla-cream, fig and citrus aromas that are pleasantly fruity and clean. It seems to have evolved a bit more complexity than when we last tasted it, and the palate has a fine, creaming mousse and smooth flavour with a very long tangy finish. Enjoy it with yum cha.

Centennial Vineyards Pinot Noir Chardonnay

This producer is located at Bowral, south of Sydney, where the altitude affords a cool, humid environment, which should be very suitable for growing base wines for sparkling. This one is labelled non-vintage, although our information is that it's a 2003 base wine. Maker: Tony Cosgriff.

CURRENT RELEASE *non-vintage* The wine is bright, clean and well-made, with a bright, light-yellow colour and some yeastiness about the bouquet. There are also white flowers and stone fruits; these characters re-appear in the mouth where it has impeccable balance. It's soft, round and fruity, not too dry but with good commercial balance. Try it with rice crackers or pretzels.

Quality	🍷🍷🍷
Value	★★★★
Rating	90
Grapes	pinot noir 70%; chardonnay 30%
Region	Southern Highlands, NSW
Cellar	🍾 3
Alc./Vol.	11.5%
RRP	$25.00

Chandon Blanc de Blancs Chardonnay

This is frequently our favourite of the large range of premium-quality Chandon bubblies, and in the cooler summer of 2002 the wine is as delicate as we've ever seen it. It's a pure chardonnay wine, which can be a bit simple for some tastes, but those who go for delicacy and finesse will take to it.

CURRENT RELEASE 2002 It has a very persistent collar of foamy mousse, and the aromas are very fruit-driven and youthful, recalling pear, white-peach and greener herbal notes. There's a little straw and some green apple, but autolysed yeast character is hard to find. The taste is soft and seamless, with a little sweetness showing, and just seems to fall away slightly at the finish. Good with trout gravlax.

Quality	🍷🍷🍷🍷
Value	★★★
Rating	92
Grapes	chardonnay
Region	various
Cellar	🍾 4+
Alc./Vol.	12.5%
RRP	$38.00

Chandon NV

The Chandon people have sparkling wine enterprises in seven countries, and we used to be able to name them all. Let's see now, there's France, Australia, the US, Spain, Argentina, Brazil, and, damn, what was the seventh one? But what's it matter? Their Australian wines are probably the best after Champagne.

CURRENT RELEASE *non-vintage* The wine has stacks of flavour but avoids being broad or overly full-bodied. It has a light-yellow colour and a creamy chardonnay-like bouquet, is very fruit-driven with little yeast autolysis character, and the same flavours flow through to the palate. The finish is well balanced and reasonably dry, and it would drink well with dips at a party.

Quality	🍷🍷🍷
Value	★★★
Rating	88
Grapes	chardonnay; pinot noir; pinot meunier
Region	Yarra, Goulburn & King valleys, Vic.; Coonawarra, SA & Tasmania
Cellar	🍾 1
Alc./Vol.	12.5%
RRP	$26.00 ⑤

Chandon Super Riche

Quality	▼▼▼▼
Value	★★★
Rating	90
Grapes	pinot noir; chardonnay
Region	various
Cellar	🍷 2+
Alc./Vol.	12.5%
RRP	· $39.95 (cellar door)

Champagne companies have always tried to pretend their demi-sec or sweeter styles can be served with desserts, but it never works for us. The sweetness of the dessert kills the wine every time. Hence this is Tony Jordan's attempt to make a sweeter style of sparkling wine that really does go with sweet desserts. Only 100 dozen made.
CURRENT RELEASE *non-vintage* This is a substantially sweeter, richer wine than the Cuvée Riche, and even tastes as though there could be some botrytis-affected fruit in the mix. It is very complex. The colour is deep yellow and it smells most unusual – sweetly rich with meaty, toasty, spicy and cooked-fruit aromas, plus herbal sidenotes. It's very sweet and tastes a little strange as a wine with bubbles, but comes into its own with food. Try it with fruit salad and ice-cream.

Chandon Tasmanian Cuvée

Quality	▼▼▼▼▼
Value	★★★┥
Rating	95
Grapes	chardonnay 65%; pinot noir 35%
Region	Coal Valley, Tas.
Cellar	🍷 3+
Alc./Vol.	12.5%
RRP	$37.00

Chandon's chief source of Tassie grapes is the extensive Tolpuddle Vineyard, in the Coal River valley, north of Hobart. The grapes are hand-picked and shipped to Chandon's Yarra Valley winery as whole fruit.
CURRENT RELEASE 2002 There's a significant serving of smoky, toasty complexity from ageing on yeast lees, yet the wine retains its tightness and refinement in the mouth. The palate is a touch less complex than the bouquet suggests, while the back-palate has a little grip from high acidity and phenolics that add structure without being intrusive. It really grows on you as you sip. A very fine, high-quality sparkling wine, which would go well with Japanese sushi.

Chandon Vintage Brut Rosé

Quality	▼▼▼▼▼
Value	★★★┥
Rating	95
Grapes	pinot noir 51%; chardonnay 47%; pinot meunier 2%
Region	various
Cellar	🍷 2+
Alc./Vol.	12.5%
RRP	$37.00

The age of this wine is a surprise. We're not sure if it's intended or accidental, but all we can say is that we are grateful, because the end result is a sheer joy. Makers: Tony Jordan, James Gosper, John Harris and Matt Steel.
CURRENT RELEASE 1999 The colour is quite developed now: a fullish salmon pink; while the bouquet has matured beautifully into a rich, mellow amalgam of smoky and strawberry pinot-led characters. In the mouth it's marvellously smooth and mellow, a big wine with lots of pinot noir body and richness, a full finish and very long aftertaste. It really resonates. A 'pinot noir with bubbles' and very impressive. A delight to drink with quail canapés.

Chandon Vintage Brut ZD

The Chandon people were so encouraged by the success of their original ZD (the pure chardonnay wine with the crown seal) that they decided to do a ZD version of their flagship wine, the Chandon Vintage Brut.
CURRENT RELEASE 2002   This is a very fine wine from the cool year; restrained and harmonious, with that all-important combination of delicacy and flavour intensity that is hard to capture in this 'sunburnt' country. Subtle straw/dry-grass, dried-herb aromas; a good collar of mousse and attractive tightness and fineness of texture in the mouth. It's dry yet smooth, and perhaps just lacks a little charm and Champagne-like complexity. Good drinking with crab canapés.

Quality	♟♟♟♟
Value	★★★
Rating	90
Grapes	pinot noir; chardonnay
Region	various
Cellar	🍶 2+
Alc./Vol.	12.5%
RRP	$37.00 ⑤

Chandon Yarra Valley Brut

Although Chandon's philosophy, like Champagne's, is one of blending – across vineyards, regions and states – it's always fun to see what can be achieved just using grapes grown on your own doorstep, which is what this small-production cuvée is all about.
CURRENT RELEASE 2002   A very good wine, full of straw-like, macaroon, toasty and coconut aromas, and showing some bottle-age development – which seems more forward than the other Chandon '02s. The palate is soft, light and very pleasing but ultimately lacks the persistence of the top wines. It's a very good, more mature style of some finesse. It would suit mushroom puffs.

Quality	♟♟♟♟
Value	★★★
Rating	91
Grapes	pinot noir; chardonnay
Region	Yarra Valley, Vic.
Cellar	🍶 2
Alc./Vol.	12.5%
RRP	$37.00

Chandon ZD

ZD stands for Zero Dosage, which means no sweetening was added at the time of disgorgement (just before release). In Champagne these are also called Brut Absolu, Brut Zero or Non-Dosé wines. The traditional cork's been replaced by a crown seal, in an effort to avoid cork taint and ensure consistency between bottles.
CURRENT RELEASE 2002   This is one of our favourite Aussie sparklers of the moment: a superbly refined, restrained and very sippable bubbly with understated complexity. The aromas are reminiscent of egg custard, straw and melony fruit; the palate is light and delicate yet intense and penetrating, finishing very dry, but taut and seamlessly balanced. Best with food: try a smoked trout pâté.

Quality	♟♟♟♟♟
Value	★★★⧸
Rating	93
Grapes	chardonnay 100%
Region	various
Cellar	🍶 3+
Alc./Vol.	12.5%
RRP	$37.00 ⑤

Charles Melton Sparkling Red

Quality	♜♜♜♜
Value	★★★
Rating	91
Grapes	shiraz
Region	Barossa Valley, SA
Cellar	🍷 10+
Alc./Vol.	14.0%
RRP	$60.00

Graeme 'Charlie' Melton was one of the forerunners of the new wave of bigger, more robust and fruit-driven Barossa sparkling reds, formerly known as sparkling burgundies. They are pretty good upon release, but give them some time in the cellar and you'll be rewarded several times over. CURRENT RELEASE *non-vintage* This is a serious 'spurgle' (sparkling burgundy), which will repay cellaring – Melton suggests you put it away for fully 10 years. The aromas are all about plummy/blackberry shiraz fruit of good ripeness and sweetness. There are some blackberry-jam nuances, and the palate is big and generous. It's a gutsy wine and carries a fair deal of tannin on the finish, which will help it age. Pork spare ribs and plum sauce would be ideal.

Clover Hill

Quality	♜♜♜♜♝
Value	★★★
Rating	94
Grapes	chardonnay; pinot noir; pinot meunier
Region	northern Tas.
Cellar	🍷 4
Alc./Vol.	12.5%
RRP	$41.50

This vineyard and winery are part of the Taltarni company, based in the Pyrenees region of central Victoria but one of the top players in the Tassie fizz game.
CURRENT RELEASE 2001 This is a serious Champagne-style bubbly with a lot of complex characters from extended ageing on yeast lees: oatmeal, macaroon and brioche aromas. It has a long, dry palate with softness and balance despite finishing very dry, and plenty of bodyweight. It would suit quick-seared Tassie abalone. *Previous outstanding vintages: 1994, '96, '99, 2000*

Cofield Sparkling Shiraz T XIV

Quality	♜♜♜♜
Value	★★★
Rating	90
Grapes	shiraz
Region	Rutherglen, Vic.
Cellar	🍷 8+
Alc./Vol.	13.7%
RRP	$30.00

The cuvée number is a code that even Dan Brown couldn't crack. (It means this is the fourteenth tirage.) What he would be able to crack is the seal: it has a sensible crown seal instead of a cork. It's an excellent seal, stays that way for many years in the cellar, and doesn't oxidise or expose your wine to cork-derived taints. Bring it on!
CURRENT RELEASE *non-vintage* This is very much at the drier extreme of sparkling red style; in other words, winemaker Damien Cofield has added relatively little sweetening in the expedition liqueur. Some lovers of the style may find it a little too dry. We like it a lot, but the lack of sugar does expose the tannins on the finish. It has a dense, dark red–purple colour and a bouquet of plum jam, blackberry and oak. It's a big-flavoured style that would go well with food, such as barbecued beef spare ribs.

Coldstone Brut Cuvée

This comes from the Vic Alps Winery, in north-east Victoria's Ovens Valley. The winemaker there is Michael Cope-Williams, formerly of the eponymous sparkling wine facility at Romsey, in the Macedon Ranges, so he knows a thing or two about sparkling wine.
CURRENT RELEASE *non-vintage* **This is a remarkably good fizz for a teensy outlay. It is spotlessly clean and fresh, with a big collar of foam sitting on top and a palish-yellow hue; it smells fresh and lively, with simple fruit aromas but attractively harmonious and with a little creaminess from yeast. The palate is soft and bright, nicely balanced and lively – with no sharp edges, yet it finishes clean and dry. It could give some of the big-company brands a fright, quality wise. Sip with crackers or chips.**

Quality	♟♟♟♙
Value	★★★★⁀
Rating	88
Grapes	pinot noir
Region	north-east Vic.
Cellar	♦ 2
Alc./Vol.	12.0%
RRP	$13.00

PENGUIN BEST-VALUE
SPARKLING WINE

Coldstream Hills Chardonnay Pinot Noir

We first reviewed this vintage a couple of years ago, and it's still current. Does that reflect the slow market? Or is it just a bit obscure for this brand to be somewhat unexpectedly offering a sparkling wine? Winemaker: Andrew Fleming and team.
CURRENT RELEASE 1999 The colour is light to medium yellow and the wine is all-round quite developed, with a complex toasted-bread bouquet and biscuity side-lights. It's very rich and full in the mouth, with developed flavours of complexity and softness in appealing balance and – despite its age – quite Champagne-like finesse. A very satisfying drink, to serve with quail canapés.

Quality	♟♟♟♟♙
Value	★★★⁀
Rating	93
Grapes	chardonnay;
	pinot noir
Region	Yarra Valley, Vic.
Cellar	♦ 1
Alc./Vol.	12.5%
RRP	$27.50 ⑤

Cope–Williams Romsey Brut

This is a non-vintage wine but it has a cuvée number on the bottle: 96/405, which seems to indicate there is at least some 1996 material in the blend. That's quite old! The Cope-Williams winery is a significant contract-winemaking facility these days, run by winemaker David Cowburn.
CURRENT RELEASE *non-vintage* Quite an aged wine, deep-ish yellow in colour with brassy reflections, and it shows quite developed characters with some sherry-like aldehydes. Oatmeal, toasted-bread and biscuity aromas, too. The wine is full of flavour and character with a dry finishing palate. It would go well with caviar on little toasts.

Quality	♟♟♟♟
Value	★★★
Rating	90
Grapes	pinot noir;
	chardonnay
Region	Macedon Ranges, Vic.
Cellar	♦ 2
Alc./Vol.	12.0%
RRP	$39.75

Croser

Quality	🍷🍷🍷🍷🍷
Value	★★★)
Rating	95
Grapes	pinot noir 80%; chardonnay 20%
Region	Adelaide Hills, SA
Cellar	🍾 5
Alc./Vol.	13.0%
RRP	$34.00

PENGUIN BEST SPARKLING WINE

The man Croser officially left the employ of Lion Nathan, Petaluma's present owner, in late 2005 but the name lingers on as the brand of Petaluma's high-profile, and highly refined, sparkling wine.
CURRENT RELEASE 2003   This seems a slightly fuller, richer style than some of the previous Crosers, which have occasionally bordered on austere and overly refined. The macaroon, toast, herbal and honey aromas really shine, together with some bready/autolysis character. Lively acid keeps it all vibrant without being sharp, and the finish is very long and dry. Great with roasted pistachio nuts.

Deakin Estate Brut

Quality	🍷🍷🍷
Value	★★★★
Rating	86
Grapes	chardonnay; pinot noir
Region	Murray Valley, Vic.
Cellar	🍾 1
Alc./Vol.	13.0%
RRP	$10.75 ⓢ

Inexpensive sparkling wine is a big seller. It's fashionable to sneer at these wines in some circles, but approach the Great Western/Carrington/Minchinbury wines with an open mind and you might be surprised at their quality. Deakin Estate is another label that fits the bill.
CURRENT RELEASE *non-vintage*   This is a pale, simple drop of fizz with a clean, uncomplicated nose that suggests apples and stone fruits. It's clean-tasting, fresh and tangy, and represents good value, especially when it's discounted well below $10. Serve it at a noisy party.

Fox Creek Vixen

Quality	🍷🍷🍷🍷
Value	★★★
Rating	92
Grapes	shiraz; cabernet sauvignon; cabernet franc
Region	McLaren Vale, SA
Cellar	▬2–5
Alc./Vol.	14.0%
RRP	$22.00

McLaren Vale's shiraz grapes lend themselves well to sparkling red production. They have the great depth of flavour and naturally smooth, friendly tannin structure that suits the style perfectly.
CURRENT RELEASE *non-vintage*   Purple foam, deep ruby colour – sparkling shiraz! It shows ripe plum, bitter chocolate and floral aromas that are still a tad un-evolved, but a little bit of time in bottle will help it come together. The rawness of youth also shows on the palate, which has some underlying tannic firmness, but the fruit flavour is good and not unduly propped up by sweetness. Try it with spare ribs.

Frogmore Creek Cuvée Evermore

Frogmore Creek is an ambitious Tasmanian venture, jointly owned by Tasmanian and US interests. It's been certified organic, and winemaking is in the competent hands of Andrew Hood.
CURRENT RELEASE 2003   A pale copper-tinged sparkler smelling of juicy apples and strawberry scents with biscuity touches. Some high-toned hints of aldehyde add complexity, but they might intimidate the purists. The palate has fine texture and rich flavour, and the fragrant biscuity finish is carried by fine acidity. A pleasant level of dosage gives a whisper of sweetness in the middle that's perfectly balanced by finely integrated acidity.

Quality	♟♟♟♟♙
Value	★★★★
Rating	92
Grapes	chardonnay; pinot noir
Region	Coal River, Tas.
Cellar	🍾 2
Alc./Vol.	12.5%
RRP	$35.00 Ⓥ

Hanging Rock Macedon Late Disgorged

This is Hanging Rock's answer to prestige champagnes like Bollinger RD and Krug Grande Cuvée. Like the Krug it's an oak-aged non-vintage blend given long lees ageing.
CURRENT RELEASE *Cuvée Six*   This has more depth of golden colour than the standard Hanging Rock fizz, and the bouquet has more subtlety. It opens with restrained, well-integrated toast, honey and apple aromas, and the palate has long nutty, yeasty, vinous flavours. It's all very complex, dry and savoury, yet oxidative and curiously lacking in the lively thrill of the French prototypes that inspired it. An Australian oddity that would go with chicken liver pâté and warm toast.

Quality	♟♟♟♟
Value	★★
Rating	91
Grapes	pinot noir; chardonnay
Region	Macedon Ranges, Vic.
Cellar	🍾 1
Alc./Vol.	12.0%
RRP	$110.00

Hanging Rock Macedon NV Brut

Most Australian sparkling wines with quality aspirations are prized for their squeaky-clean freshness and subtlety, but Hanging Rock is all about complexity and strength.
CURRENT RELEASE *Cuvée XI*   After over four years on its yeast lees, this has a shiny yellow–gold colour and a very fine bubble. The nose is complex with plenty of nutty, caramelly and burnt-bread notes around a centre of stewed-apple-like fruit. The palate is full-bodied, dry and powerfully structured with the oxidative traits hinted at on the nose coming to the fore. It finishes long with an apple-brandy, slightly aldehydic aftertaste. We think it lacks freshness and vitality, but it will suit those who like a big in-your-face glass of bubbles and we've assessed it accordingly. Serve it with brioches filled with veal kidneys.

Quality	♟♟♟♟♙
Value	★★★
Rating	92
Grapes	pinot noir; chardonnay
Region	Macedon Ranges, Vic.
Cellar	🍾 2
Alc./Vol.	12.5%
RRP	$45.00

Hanging Rock Macedon Rosé NV Brut

Quality	♙♙♙♙
Value	✷✷✷
Rating	91
Grapes	pinot noir
Region	Macedon, Vic.
Cellar	▮ 2
Alc./Vol.	12.5%
RRP	$27.00

A new addition to the Hanging Rock range, this pink bubbly has much less lees-ageing than its sparkling Macedon siblings – only 12 months – providing a fresher, more vivacious aperitif style.

CURRENT RELEASE *non-vintage*   An attractive and subtle pink blush introduces this new Hanging Rock sparkling wine, and the nose has a fresh red-berry pinot noir aroma of finesse and delicacy. In the mouth it's clean and fresh with a tangy redcurrant flavour, smooth texture and a tangy finish. Serve it as an aperitif.

Hardys Arras Chardonnay Pinot Noir

Quality	♙♙♙♙♙
Value	✷✷✷
Rating	96
Grapes	chardonnay; pinot noir
Region	Tasmania
Cellar	▮ 4
Alc./Vol.	13.0%
RRP	$53.00 Ⓢ

Arras is Hardys' tilt at the premium sparkling wine market. Made by sparkling guru Ed Carr from cool-climate Tassie chardonnay and pinot, it's made according to the traditional method and priced in the same league as good NV French champagne.

CURRENT RELEASE 2000   We thought this a better Arras than the '99, with everything you would expect from this pedigreed label. The nose shows citrus, apple-custard and toasted-brioche aromas of elegant intensity. In the mouth it has great length and superfine texture, with a subtle interplay between nutty, yeasty bottle-ferment characters and fine fruit flavour. A classy aperitif to sip with topnotch hors d'oeuvres.

Hardys Sir James Pinot Noir Chardonnay

Quality	♙♙♙♙♙
Value	✷✷✷✷✷
Rating	95
Grapes	pinot noir; chardonnay
Region	mainly Tasmania & Macedon Ranges, Vic.
Cellar	▮ 2
Alc./Vol.	13.0%
RRP	$27.00 Ⓢ

This has impressed us greatly over a number of years and we think it offers the best value among the very good Hardys sparkling family, especially as it's rarely sold for full retail price. A smart new package accompanies the 2002 vintage.

CURRENT RELEASE 2002   The nose is rich and quite concentrated with biscuity and smoky aromas coupled to light citrus and strawberry-like fruit. In the mouth it has lovely feel, creamy, long-flavoured and sustained in intensity with a clean dry finish. It combines delicacy and power in the best manner. Try it with little chicken and mushroom pies.

Hardys Sir James Sparkling Pinot Noir Shiraz

This Hardys sparkling red falls outside the mainstream by blending pinot noir with shiraz. It's not quite as robust as the traditional style.

CURRENT RELEASE *non-vintage*   There are aromas of red berries and darker fruits here along with some licorice and earthy notes. It tastes smooth and only slightly sweet with ripe flavour and lively acidity. It's less velvety than the classical style with a slightly angular feel in the mouth. We prefer the Sir James straight shiraz sparkler, although there's nothing really wrong with this one, and it is cheaper. Serve it with BBQ spare ribs.

Quality	♟♟♟♪
Value	★★★
Rating	88
Grapes	pinot noir; shiraz
Region	not stated
Cellar	🍾 2
Alc./Vol.	14.0%
RRP	$16.90

Hardys Sir James Sparkling Shiraz

Hardys is now a part of the massive US-based Constellation Brands empire, but the operation maintains a traditional Aussie feel, and what could be more Australian than sparkling shiraz?

CURRENT RELEASE *non-vintage*   The delicious, ripe, complex nose of this red fizz sums up the style in fine form with sweet-berry, spice, earth and new-leather aromas. The palate flows seamlessly with excellent integration of gentle sweetness and soft ripe tannins underneath. It signs off long and aromatic with good acidity keeping it on track. Enjoy it with roast pork and a fruity stuffing.

Quality	♟♟♟♟♪
Value	★★★♪
Rating	93
Grapes	shiraz
Region	mainly McLaren Vale, SA
Cellar	🍾 3
Alc./Vol.	14.0%
RRP	$26.00

Houghton Pemberton Chardonnay Pinot Noir

In only a few years, this sparkler from Western Australia's 'deep south' has established its own distinctive style. The 2000 vintage is still current at time of writing, perhaps it doesn't sell as well as some of its sparkling stablemates in the Hardys camp, but the bonus is that it seems to have benefited from a little cork age.

CURRENT RELEASE 2000   This has a smooth smoky, nutty bouquet with attractive hints of peach and meringue. In the mouth it's zesty in flavour yet quite soft on the mid-palate, finishing with real finesse. A well-made aperitif style to serve with little steamed shiu mai.

Quality	♟♟♟♟♪
Value	★★★
Rating	93
Grapes	chardonnay; pinot noir
Region	Pemberton, WA
Cellar	🍾 1
Alc./Vol.	13.5%
RRP	$29.50

Jansz Premium NV Rosé

Quality	♥♥♥♥♥
Value	★★★★
Rating	95
Grapes	chardonnay; pinot noir
Region	Piper's River, Tas.
Cellar	🍶 2
Alc./Vol.	12.5%
RRP	$26.70

Originally established in 1986 as a joint venture between the Heemskerk winery and French champagne house Louis Roederer, Jansz is now affiliated with Hill Smith Family Vineyards of Angaston in South Australia.

CURRENT RELEASE *non-vintage* A delicious glass of Tassie fizz awaits those who open this smartly labelled bottle. It's coppery pink in colour with a lively bubble, and the nose shows a strawberries and cream sort of aroma that reflects the use of high-quality cool-grown pinot noir. There's also some richness from bottle fermentation and lees ageing which imparts a light Vegemitey touch. It tastes smooth with good depth, signing off with a clean, fresh aftertaste. Try it with sugar-cured salmon.

Kamberra Pinot Noir Chardonnay Pinot Meunier

Quality	♥♥♥♥♥
Value	★★★★
Rating	95
Grapes	pinot noir; chardonnay; pinot meunier
Region	Canberra region, ACT/NSW
Cellar	🍶
Alc./Vol.	12.0%
RRP	$32.00

Kamberra is the Hardys group's winery in Canberra, which is located in Lyneham. While the wines are made on-site by Alex McKay, no doubt the master of bubbles, Ed Carr, gets into the act when the wine is to be blended and tiraged (bottled for its second fermentation).

CURRENT RELEASE 2000 This is a very impressive bubbly: very mellow, mature and layered; light yellow in colour with a slight coppery tint and toasty, smoky, Vegemite-like developed complexities in the bouquet. The palate is full-bodied, dry and tangy with lots of pinot character, finishing long and clean with lovely texture, strength and persistence. Great with little gougères made with aged gruyère cheese.

McWilliams Hanwood Estate Pinot Noir Chardonnay

Quality	♥♥♥◗
Value	★★★★
Rating	88
Grapes	pinot noir; chardonnay
Region	Riverina, NSW
Cellar	🍶 1
Alc./Vol.	11.5%
RRP	$12.00 Ⓢ

Macs do a remarkable job with this Hanwood range. The wines of various types often punch well above their weight, none better than the two Hanwood sparkling wines reviewed here. Chief winemaker: Jim Brayne.

CURRENT RELEASE *non-vintage* The colour is very pale, suggesting a young base wine. The nose is restrained and has smoky and lanolin touches. It's clean and youthful, but without significant age or yeast autolysis. The taste is very clean and attractive in a young, straightforward, fruit-driven style. It's subtle and understated, as a good bubbly should be. It finishes clean and dry and has plenty of appeal. Serve with party nibbles such as dips and chips.

McWilliams Hanwood Estate Sparkling Shiraz

Great Australian sparkling red is partly about aged complexity, but when they're cleverly done, even the young, fruity ones can have a lot of appeal – especially when the price is as low as Hanwood's.
CURRENT RELEASE *non-vintage* The colour is excellent: a full glowing purple–red. The nose is inviting, with plum, aniseed/licorice and dark-berry aromas – clean and fresh, if a touch young. It's lighter-bodied than you might expect from the colour and nose, but is clean and attractively fruity with well-balanced sweetness. It calls for Chinese pork and plum sauce.

Quality 🍷🍷🍷½
Value ★★★★
Rating **88**
Grapes shiraz
Region Riverina, NSW
Cellar 2
Alc./Vol. 13.5%
RRP $12.00 ($)

Miceli Michael Méthode Champenoise

The Miceli operation is a family affair, with the wines being named after members of the family. Owner is Dr Anthony Miceli, a medico, who took the trouble to gain a degree in wine science from Charles Sturt University. His wines are as distinctive as they are impressive. This won the trophy for the best sparkling wine at Cowra in 2004.
CURRENT RELEASE 2001 We reviewed this last year but it's still available, and we like it a lot. It's still a head-turner, loaded with toasty, smoky, yeast-derived complexities as well as tart appley, straw-like fruit. The acidity is a touch challenging but only if you have it without something to eat. Long, rich, mature and very alive in the mouth, it's a thoroughly enjoyable glass of bubbly. Try it with cheese puffs.

Quality 🍷🍷🍷🍷½
Value ★★★★
Rating **92**
Grapes chardonnay; pinot noir; pinot gris
Region Mornington Peninsula, Vic.
Cellar 3+
Alc./Vol. 12.0%
RRP $32.00

Moorilla Vintage Brut

Moorilla Estate is the 'elder statesman' of Tasmanian wineries, having been first planted by Claudio Alcorso in the 1960s. Winemaker in 2001 was Michael Glover.
CURRENT RELEASE 2001 This is a delicate, shy, youthful glass of fizz with good pale colour, fresh macaroon-like aromas from pinot noir and a touch of yeast complexity. A clean dry palate that has lively acidity makes it a nice, palate-stimulating aperitif style. It's not all that complex or deep, but certainly enlivens the palate before a meal. Serve with oysters.

Quality 🍷🍷🍷🍷
Value ★★★
Rating **90**
Grapes pinot noir; chardonnay
Region Tasmania
Cellar 5
Alc./Vol. 12.5%
RRP $29.50 (cellar door)

Mount Pleasant Sparkling Pinot Noir

Quality	🍷🍷🍷
Value	★★★
Rating	89
Grapes	pinot noir
Region	Hunter Valley, NSW
Cellar	🍾 3+
Alc./Vol.	13.0%
RRP	$21.50 Ⓢ

What better use is there for Hunter pinot than a sparkling red? We can't think of one! Certainly, it's not often a very good table wine in the Hunter. Maker: Phil Ryan.

CURRENT RELEASE 2002   This is a very distinctive style of sparkling red. It's more Hunter in style than anything else, and all the more interesting for it. The colour is a light, developed brick-red; the bouquet is meaty, earthy, leathery and very complex in a classic Hunter sort of way. It's lighter in weight and less boldly fruity than most, but has lovely mellow, aged regional flavour. It's a touch feral perhaps, but in our books it's a great drink. The sweetness is well balanced and it would work with washed-rind cheeses.

Peel Estate Baroque Shiraz Cremant

Quality	🍷🍷🍷
Value	★★★
Rating	88
Grapes	shiraz
Region	Baldivis, WA
Cellar	🍾
Alc./Vol.	13.5%
RRP	$55.00

This sparkling red is given four years in barrel, then four years in bottle before release. No wonder it has such unusual character. 'Cremant' indicates a slightly lower level of effervescence to other sparkling wines.

CURRENT RELEASE 1998   A mature deep-red colour shows age here, and so does the nose. It smells of old leather, licorice, spice and cigar boxes; complex and well out of the sparkling red mainstream. The palate is dry and developed with vanilla and mature berry flavours of good depth and persistence, but the lack of sweetness seems to leave a hole in the middle. It's rather like a very old dry red with bubbles, and its grainy dry tannins add to the oddball feeling. Don't chill it too much and try it with Chinese BBQ pork.

Pondalowie Special Release 'The Black Dog' Sparkling Shiraz

Quality	🍷🍷🍷🍷
Value	★★★⁺
Rating	94
Grapes	shiraz
Region	Bendigo, Vic.
Cellar	🍾 8
Alc./Vol.	14.0%
RRP	$36.00

The sparse black brush strokes that grace the label of Pondalowie's wines actually represent a dog. And there *is* a dog at Pondalowie, Jack the kelpie. Fortunately he is a bit better fed than the emaciated mutt in the logo.

CURRENT RELEASE 2002   This sparkler has the typical Pondalowie look: deep-purplish and youthful. Nose and palate combine regional mint, herb and eucalypt with dense, earthy-blackberry fruit at the core. The smooth palate has good harmony between ripe and savoury flavours, sweetness doesn't take over, and it finishes long with fine-grained dry tannins. Sealed with a crown seal to eliminate the possibility of cork tainting the wine. A classy sparkling red to enjoy with tea-smoked duck.

Preece NV Sparkling

Mitchelton's Preece range of wines covers nearly all bases from sparkling through to whites and reds. Value is always pretty good.

CURRENT RELEASE *non-vintage*   Apple-brandy, meringue and vaguely spicy aromas make this an unusually aromatic sparkling wine, and a hint of nutty aldehyde adds complexity. In the mouth it strikes a good balance between fruit and vinous elements, and it finishes dry and long. Try it with brunch.

Quality	♟♟♟♟
Value	★★★⌐
Rating	90
Grapes	not stated
Region	not stated
Cellar	▮ 1
Alc./Vol.	12.0%
RRP	$15.75 ⑤

Schild Estate Sparkling Shiraz

When these Barossa sparkling shirazes are made without too much sweetness, they truly resemble good Barossa shiraz table wines, and they develop aged complexities in a similar pattern. So, while some are simple, sweet party wines, others are serious wines – and this is such an example.

CURRENT RELEASE 2004   The colour is promisingly deep and the aromas are attractively plummy and aniseed-like, with a chaffy overtone. The taste is all about ripe shiraz fruit, with just the right amount of sweetness, and a smooth, delicious finish that carries well. It would go with prunes wrapped in crispy bacon.

Quality	♟♟♟♟♟
Value	★★★★
Rating	92
Grapes	shiraz
Region	Barossa Valley, SA
Cellar	▮ 5+
Alc./Vol.	13.5%
RRP	$26.00

Seppelt Salinger Chardonnay Pinot Noir

Seppelt was the first Australian winery to release a major commercial run of sparkling wine with a crown seal instead of a cork. That was the 1994 show sparkling shiraz. It was a big success, so Seppelt has extended the innovation to Salinger, its top 'white' bubbly. Crown seals have been used on méthode champenoise wines for many years at the 'tirage' stage, so why not on the finished product?

CURRENT RELEASE 2002   This is the most impressed we've been with Salinger for some years. The 2002 seems to have more generosity and overt character than the Salingers of old, which were often a touch austere. This is light to mid yellow with a handsome bouquet of toasty, smoky cracked-yeast complexities. Meringue and macaroon are to the fore. On the tongue, it has lovely balance and mouth-feel; soft, rich, full, yet with delicacy, and a finish that goes on and on. Smoked salmon wrapped around grissini would work well.

Quality	♟♟♟♟♟
Value	★★★★
Rating	94
Grapes	chardonnay; pinot noir
Region	various, southern Australia
Cellar	▮ 4
Alc./Vol.	12.5%
RRP	$30.00 ⑤

St Leonards Wahgunyah Sparkling Shiraz

Quality	♟♟♟
Value	★★★
Rating	87
Grapes	shiraz
Region	Rutherglen, Vic.
Cellar	➞2–6+
Alc./Vol.	14.1%
RRP	$27.50

St Leonards and its sister winery, All Saints, are both situated on the Murray River at Wahgunyah, just downstream from Albury, near Rutherglen. They were both bought by the late Peter Brown, whose family continues to run them. Maker: Dan Crane.

CURRENT RELEASE *non-vintage* This is a gutsy, fairly aggressive style with plenty of everything. The colour is medium-deep red and some oak is apparent on the nose, which also carries toasted-nut, blackstrap-licorice and ironstone qualities. The taste is a bit 'arms and legs', with some acidity showing out plus some tannin astringency and obvious sweetness. There is also plenty of flavour and, if given some more time, it is likely to all come together. Then serve with stir-fried beef and hoisin sauce.

Stonier Pinot Noir Chardonnay

Quality	♟♟♟♟
Value	★★★
Rating	90
Grapes	pinot noir; chardonnay
Region	Mornington Peninsula, Vic.
Cellar	▮ 2+
Alc./Vol.	12.5%
RRP	$28.00

Stonier chief winemaker Geraldine McFaul has only been in the top job about five years but is already making her mark. She was nominated as one of the eight finalists in the *Australian Gourmet Traveller WINE* magazine Winemaker of the Year Award in 2006.

CURRENT RELEASE 2002 This is ageing gracefully and is still as fresh as when we first reviewed it last year. It has an aroma of candied fruits, macaroon, and smoky pinot noir characters that remind us of chocolate-dipped strawberries. The palate is lively with a fine line of crisp, tart acid leading to a very clean, lip-smacking finish. It would go well with crab.

Taltarni Brut Taché

Quality	♟♟♟♟♟
Value	★★★★⟩
Rating	93
Grapes	chardonnay; pinot noir; pinot meunier
Region	various, Tas. & Vic.
Cellar	▮ 2
Alc./Vol.	13.0%
RRP	$23.00

In recent years Taltarni has been heading in some new directions, and wine quality across the board has been on the improve. The increasing use of Tasmanian material in the sparkling wines has given them a real fillip. By the way, Taché means 'stained' – a reference to this wine's pink colour.

CURRENT RELEASE 2004 This has a delightful pale-salmon colour, and the nose has red-berry, herb and subtle smoky, yeasty aromas. It has pleasant intensity of aroma and flavour without losing its finesse, and fine mouth-feel. The finish is clean and fragrant; a good match for pan-fried trout.

Tigress NV Pinot Noir Chardonnay

Although it's the Bay of Fires 'junior' sparkling wine, it's not really pitched as a secondary line, nor is it priced as such. And Tigress shares the same fine qualities as others in the Hardys folio of fizz.

CURRENT RELEASE *non-vintage*   This is attractive and interesting on the nose, offering zesty citrus and apple aromas with finely integrated bottle-ferment touches. It has good creamy mouth-feel and complex slightly mushroomy flavour, and it finishes dry and zippy, with a lemon meringue-like touch to the aftertaste. Serve it as an aperitif.

Quality	￼￼￼￼￼
Value	★★★↓
Rating	93
Grapes	pinot noir
Region	Piper's River, Tas.
Cellar	￼ 2
Alc./Vol.	12.5%
RRP	$25.80

Tigress Sparkling Rosé

A new sparkling wine from Hardys Tassie outpost, packed in a silver and white label with mauve–pink highlights that will please some and put others off. Like all good modern Oz sparklers it's made from pinot noir and chardonnay.

CURRENT RELEASE *non-vintage*   The colour is just right by us for pink fizz, a pale-salmon blush rather than a confectionery tone. It smells right too with smoky, strawberry and light mushroomy aromas of subtle complexity. In the mouth there's good depth and richness of flavour, with a long dry finish and savoury aftertaste. Try it with sushi.

Quality	￼￼￼￼￼
Value	★★★↓
Rating	93
Grapes	pinot noir; chardonnay
Region	Piper's River, Tas.
Cellar	￼ 2
Alc./Vol.	13.0%
RRP	$25.80

Turkey Flat Sparkling Shiraz

Turkey Flat's vineyard holdings in the Barossa include some of the oldest shiraz vines in Australia. Each year some of the best shiraz barrels are reserved for making this sparkler, which spends 10 months on lees before disgorgement and liqueuring with old Australian vintage port. Sealed with a crown seal to eliminate the possibility of cork tainting the wine.

CURRENT RELEASE *non-vintage*   A dense sparkling shiraz with a deep-purplish colour. It smells luxuriously ripe and luscious with intense aromas of blackberries, spices, Barossa earth and vanilla ice-cream (really). It's smoothly mouth-filling with an essency, deep, long flavour – like old-vine Barossa shiraz – and it has the right balance of drying ripe tannins and measured sweetness. Serve it with roast turkey.

Quality	￼￼￼￼￼
Value	★★★↓
Rating	94
Grapes	shiraz
Region	Barossa Valley, SA
Cellar	￼ 4
Alc./Vol.	12.5%
RRP	$45.00

Yarra Burn Pinot Noir Chardonnay Pinot Meunier

Quality	♟♟♟♟
Value	★★★
Rating	91
Grapes	pinot noir; chardonnay; pinot meunier
Region	mainly Yarra Valley, Vic.
Cellar	🍾 2
Alc./Vol.	12.5%
RRP	$25.00 Ⓢ

Yarra Burn is part of the Hardys group, which is part of Constellation. The base wines come from the Yarra Valley vineyards and are turned into sparkling wine in McLaren Vale by the Hardys group's fizz-meister, Ed Carr.
CURRENT RELEASE 2001   The colour is light yellow with a faint coppery tinge from the black pinot noir grapes, while the bouquet is again pinot-like, with a candied aroma like chocolate-dipped strawberries and a trace of vanilla. It has a fine, creamy mousse of bubbles adding attractive texture, and very good persistence. It would go well with salmon mousse.

Yarrabank Crème de Cuvée

Quality	♟♟♟♟
Value	★★★
Rating	90
Grapes	chardonnay; pinot noir
Region	Yarra Valley & other cool areas, Vic.
Cellar	🍾 2
Alc./Vol.	12.0%
RRP	$36.00

This is a new style for Yarrabank, a sort of answering shot to Chandon's Cuvée Riche, perhaps. This is not so much a 'riche' style as a 'demi-sec' – for those who are into splitting hairs. Makers: Tom Carson and team.
CURRENT RELEASE *non-vintage*   The attractive colour has a pale-pink tinge and some age development, while the bouquet is smoky, strawberry, meringue-like and savoury. Quite complex and very inviting; fairly sweet in the mouth, with a soft, rounded, easygoing personality. It finishes remarkably cleanly for a sweeter style of wine and has good length. We'd serve it with cake or sweet biscuits rather than rich desserts.

Yarrabank Cuvée

Quality	♟♟♟♟♟
Value	★★★⌐
Rating	92
Grapes	chardonnay 53%; pinot noir 47%
Region	Yarra Valley & Mornington Peninsula, Vic.
Cellar	🍾 5+
Alc./Vol.	12.5%
RRP	$35.00

Yarrabank is a joint venture between Yarra Valley winery Yering Station – where the wine is made – and Champagne house Veuve A. Devaux. It is a very Aussie style and in no way an attempt to copy champagne. Its fruit-driven style is enhanced by the prevention of the malolactic fermentation.
CURRENT RELEASE 2001   A very clean, fruit-driven sparkler with subtle creamy yeast overtones, and a decidedly Australian style to it. The chardonnay seems to dominate, with small flowers and peach/stone-fruit aromas, while the palate is again very fresh and clean with abundant fruit and good delicacy, finishing with soft and not particularly high acidity. It would drink well with almond bread.
Previous outstanding vintages: 1995, '99, 2000

Yellowglen Vintage Perle

It amazes us how the bigger companies keep pumping out new brands. Last year it was Bella, this year Perle. The most surprising thing is that they're often pretty good wines – and therefore, hard to ignore! Winemaker is Charles 'Chilly' Hargrave.

CURRENT RELEASE 2001   This is drier and slightly tarter than the regular Yellowglen Vintage Brut, aimed at a more serious drinker we suspect, and that tallies with the higher price. It's also older, with the result being some appealing toasty, macaroon and shortbread-like developed complexities. The palate is smooth and well balanced, finishing with harmony and a clean, dry cut-off. It's quite subtle for its age, and has retained youth and freshness. It would suit salmon roe and crème fraiche on blinis.

Quality	♀♀♀♀
Value	★★★
Rating	89
Grapes	pinot noir; chardonnay; pinot meunier
Region	various, incl. 75% Adelaide Hills, SA
Cellar	🍾 2
Alc./Vol.	12.0%
RRP	$24.00 Ⓢ

Yellowglen Vintage Pinot Noir Chardonnay

A couple of years ago Yellowglen suddenly switched its bread-and-butter range from non-vintage to single-vintage labelling. We suspect it was a reaction to market feedback showing drinkers wanted a year on the label. The quality and style of the wine was unchanged. These days, marketing is critical.

CURRENT RELEASE 2004   This is still a decent, reliable wine with a little more character than the usual mid- to lower-priced fizz. No doubt that's why it's so successful. The nose is smoky, bready and lightly toasty, with some iced-pastry character, but is essentially discreet. The palate is fairly straightforward but again has just enough depth and interest from yeast-derived complexities to hold it above the ruck. We suggest drinking it with smoked salmon and chive sour cream on dry biscuits.

Quality	♀♀♀♀
Value	★★★
Rating	88
Grapes	pinot noir; chardonnay
Region	not stated
Cellar	🍾 2
Alc./Vol.	11.5%
RRP	$18.00 Ⓢ

White Wines
Chardonnay

Chardonnay is the world's favourite white varietal. Despite various knockers, the ABC (anything but chardonnay) reactionaries and the anti-oak brigade, its rise continues. In 1982 our winemakers harvested just over 4000 tonnes of chardonnay grapes; in 2005, 416000 tonnes! Twenty-two per cent of the national crush is now chardonnay, and most of our top-selling white wines are chardonnays. A number of unwooded chardonnays, a less-expensive style Australians have taken to their hearts, are reviewed in the *Guide*. Chardonnay to our minds should be balanced, without excessive oak, residual sweetness or alcohol. We value finesse, flavour persistence and complexity, the last being one of chardonnay's key assets.

Ainsworth & Snelson Chardonnay

Quality	♟ ♟ ♟ ♟
Value	★★★
Rating	92
Grapes	chardonnay
Region	Yarra Valley, Vic.
Cellar	▮ 2
Alc./Vol.	13.5%
RRP	$27.00

Ainsworth & Snelson buy fruit from various places to produce wines that make a clear regional statement. Their chardonnay comes from the Yarra Valley.
CURRENT RELEASE 2004   The nose has fig and citrus fruit of elegance and subtle intensity with a honeyed touch and balanced spicy-oak input. In the mouth it shows good texture and length with medium body and flavours that don't overwhelm with sweet fruit or wood. A gently oaked chardonnay that finishes a tad light on, but it has everything in the right proportions. Serve it beside pan-fried trout with almonds.

All Saints Family Cellar Reserve Chardonnay

Quality	♟ ♟ ♟ ♟
Value	★★★
Rating	88
Grapes	chardonnay
Region	Rutherglen, Vic.
Cellar	▮ 2
Alc./Vol.	13.8%
RRP	$26.50

The silvery-labelled Family Cellar Reserve series is the top of the totem for the All Saints portfolio. These wines contain the cream of the fruit from the substantial 60-hectare Wahgunyah vineyard. Maker: Dan Crane.
CURRENT RELEASE 2004   This shows more reserve than we normally expect in a Rutherglen chardonnay: it's still light-yellow coloured and has a restrained aroma that suggests vanilla, malt and marzipan, suggesting a substantial oak input. The palate entry is sweet, at least partly from the oak, and there is plenty of flavour, again with a degree of refinement. It would suit king prawns marinated in garlic and barbecued.

Amberley Chardonnay

Amberley Estate has had a chequered career. It was started in 1986 by Dutchman Albert Haak and sold to multinational wine company Vincor, who bought Goundrey about the same time, in 2004. It's a substantial operation, with 300 hectares of vines.

CURRENT RELEASE 2004   This has a fair way to go before it's in the same league as the best-known Margaret River chardonnays. It's just too plain and light. The fruit has a herbal, parsley-like style and there is little in the way of complexity. The light fruit is okay but basic, allowing some alcohol heat to appear at the finish. This has a little more weight and character than the Chimney Brush. Try it with a caesar salad with chicken.

Quality	♉ ♉ ♉
Value	★★★
Rating	86
Grapes	chardonnay
Region	Margaret River, WA
Cellar	▮ 3
Alc./Vol.	13.5%
RRP	$22.00 ⊠

Amberley Chimney Brush Chardonnay

This is the cheapest of Amberley's chardonnays, presumably made from bought-in grapes – but also sourced from the Margaret River region. Maker: Paul Dunnewyk.

CURRENT RELEASE 2005   It's like an unwooded chardonnay without declaring as much up-front. It's light coloured, fresh, clean and simple to smell and taste; light, lean and lively on the tongue. There's a trace of sweetness but assertive acid soon cleans up, and dries the finish. It would go with melon and prosciutto.

Quality	♉ ♉ ♉
Value	★★★⤙
Rating	86
Grapes	chardonnay
Region	Margaret River, WA
Cellar	▮ 2
Alc./Vol.	13.0%
RRP	$17.00 ⊠

Angove's Butterfly Ridge Colombard Chardonnay

Colombard is a very handy blending partner for chardonnay. They go together like a hand in a glove. It's surprising we don't see more of it, really. In these days of company takeovers and commercial pressures, Angove's remains a family-owned company.

CURRENT RELEASE 2005   A simple cashew-nut and peach aroma, together with a trace of reduction, is quite adequate at this incredibly low price. It's well-made and offers plenty of fruit, with good balance and mercifully it lacks the obvious residual sugar that props up so many cheap whites these days. We'd serve it with macaroni cheese.

Quality	♉ ♉ ♉
Value	★★★★
Rating	86
Grapes	colombard; chardonnay
Region	Murray Valley, SA
Cellar	▮ 1
Alc./Vol.	13.0%
RRP	$7.00 ⑤ ⊠

Annie's Lane Chardonnay

Quality	♀♀¡
Value	★★¡
Rating	84
Grapes	chardonnay
Region	Clare Valley, SA
Cellar	⬧ 2
Alc./Vol.	13.5%
RRP	$18.00 Ⓢ ⅋

This producer used to try to sell good wine under Quelltaler and several other labels, but they never caught on. Then some bright spark dreamt up Annie's Lane, and whoosh! Off it went. Annie's Lane actually exists, near the vineyard.
CURRENT RELEASE 2005   The colour suggests this is developing fairly quickly, while the bouquet offers peach and herbal aromas with a touch of tropical fruits. Oak is somewhat unintegrated, and the palate is a bit heavy and obvious. There are some green elements in the wine. Clare is not a great source of chardonnay. Serve it with stuffed red peppers.

Artamus Chardonnay

Quality	♀♀♀♀
Value	★★★★
Rating	90
Grapes	chardonnay
Region	Margaret River, WA
Cellar	⬧ 3+
Alc./Vol.	13.0%
RRP	$21.66 ⅋

Artamus is the wine of well-known foodie Ian Parmenter (remember the ABC's *Consuming Passions*?). It's made by contract winemaker Michael Gadd in Margaret River. The wine is sold direct, for $260 a dozen, freight-free anywhere in Australia. www.artamus.com.au
CURRENT RELEASE 2003   The colour is very restrained for its age, and the aromas are of honeysuckle, marzipan and almond, almost as though there were a trace of Italian-style oxidation. But the wine tastes excellent: delicate, lean-ish, subtle and refined in texture, with low-key oak. It's a good food style; you could try it with herb-braised calamari.

Balgownie Yarra Valley Chardonnay

Quality	♀♀♀♀¡
Value	★★★¡
Rating	93
Grapes	chardonnay
Region	Yarra Valley, Vic.
Cellar	⬧ 2
Alc./Vol.	13.5%
RRP	$21.50 ⅋

Balgownie expanded from its pioneering Bendigo headquarters in 2004 to open a Yarra Valley cellar door and cafe complex, incorporating a museum of local wine history. It's well worth a visit.
CURRENT RELEASE 2004   A complex nose shows some skilful winemaking here with mealy, cashew-like seasonings to ripe melony fruit. Oak is carefully applied, and the palate has a creamy texture with good persistence and a soft finish. An attractively understated chardonnay that's a good match for pan-fried fish.

Ballabourneen The Stuart Chardonnay

Ballabourneen is a tiny vineyard in the lower Hunter Valley; the wines are contract-made by Alasdair Sutherland and Andrew Thomas – two very competent winemakers.
CURRENT RELEASE 2004   This is a typical Hunter-style chardonnay, in that the colour has darkened fairly early and it has a big, rich, developed bouquet of roasted hazelnut with almost a hint of rubber. After such a broad, opulent nose the tight, lean, high-acid palate comes as a bit of a surprise. It does have depth and persistence, but is rather pinched and almost tough, possibly because of acid adjustment. It has its charms, and is best with food – try smoked chicken salad.

Quality	♥ ♥ ♥ ♥
Value	★ ★ ★ ┤
Rating	89
Grapes	chardonnay
Region	Hunter Valley, NSW
Cellar	▌ 2+
Alc./Vol.	13.5%
RRP	$25.00 ⓢ

Barwick Estates WA Chardonnay

Barwick Estates is probably a new name to most readers. In fact, it's quite a large player in Western Australia, with nearly 200 hectares of vineyards in three locations – Margaret River, Blackwood Valley and Pemberton.
CURRENT RELEASE 2005   This is a shy, delicate, retiring youngster, with a very light-yellow colour and traces of peach and nectarine in the aroma. It's fruity, soft and round on the palate, and tastes as though it could easily be unwooded. There's a trace of harshness towards the back-palate, which may simply be due to sulphur and will go away in time. Drink it with grilled octopus.

Quality	♥ ♥ ♥
Value	★ ★ ★
Rating	86
Grapes	chardonnay
Region	various, WA
Cellar	▌ 2
Alc./Vol.	13.5%
RRP	$17.50 ⓢ

Bay of Fires Chardonnay

Bay of Fires winemaker Fran Austin is only in her early 30s but she's already making a name for herself with these superfine Tasmanian whites. Her chardonnay is all about subtlety and complexity rather than power.
CURRENT RELEASE 2005   An elegant chardonnay with restrained nectarine and citrus-fruit aromas to start, seasoned with a whisper of classy toasty oak. The creamy palate is more lush and rich than the nose would indicate initially, and it has a long, fine finish. It's a chardonnay that gets better with each sip, and it may repay cellaring short term. Serve it with pan-fried flounder.

Quality	♥ ♥ ♥ ♥ ♥
Value	★ ★ ★
Rating	93
Grapes	chardonnay
Region	northern Tas.
Cellar	▌ 3
Alc./Vol.	13.5%
RRP	$29.00 ⓢ

Bellarmine Chardonnay

Quality	♀♀♀↓
Value	★★★★
Rating	88
Grapes	chardonnay
Region	Pemberton, WA
Cellar	▮ 5
Alc./Vol.	13.6%
RRP	$15.00 ⬚ (cellar door)

All the Bellarmine wines are $15 ex-winery, which has to make Bellarmine one of the most under-priced brands around. The labelling is, like the wines, subtly charming; each variety has a different stone rubbing on its label – of Bellarmine pottery, no less. Maker: Mike Bewsher.
CURRENT RELEASE 2005   The colour is incredibly pale and there's a hint of reduction on the nose – a touch of sulphide, that's been captured by the screw-cap. The wine is all-round light and delicate, which is great if you prize subtlety in your chardonnay. Oak influence is virtually nil. It's a very clean, pure, but slightly simple wine that would not dominate any food. Because of those attributes, it's a superb food wine. Try it with oven-roasted scampi.

Bidgeebong Triangle Chardonnay

Quality	♀♀♀♀
Value	★★★★↓
Rating	91
Grapes	chardonnay
Region	Tumbarumba & Gundagai, NSW
Cellar	▮ 2
Alc./Vol.	13.5%
RRP	$14.00 ⬚

We've been very impressed by the progress of Bidgeebong over the few short years the enterprise has been operating. Quality in the bottle is a good starting point for any new label (and one that isn't understood by some new producers) and Bidgeebong has had it since day one. Pricing is very reasonable, especially for this Triangle range.
CURRENT RELEASE 2005   A fruity young chardonnay with a fresh citrus-like aroma and some notes of nectarine and earth. A whisper of oak provides a very light seasoning, and the palate is fresh and smooth with a long zesty finish. An uncomplicated style that will be a crowd-pleaser, especially at less than $15. Goes well with fried prawns.

Bidgeebong Tumbarumba Chardonnay

Quality	♀♀♀♀↓
Value	★★★★
Rating	92
Grapes	chardonnay
Region	Tumbarumba, NSW
Cellar	▮ 4
Alc./Vol.	13.5%
RRP	$22.00 ⬚

Tumbarumba is a very cool spot and as a result its chardonnay is miles away from the sunny Australian norm. We like these wines for their 'cut' and elegance, and with food they work better than the big, blousy types.
CURRENT RELEASE 2005   Subtle chardonnay with attractive aromas of citrus fruits, melon and subdued nutty oak. It's an understated type that grows on you, evolving subtle complexity in the glass while retaining tight structure. The flavour is ultra-fine and it lasts long and elegant on the palate. There's great balance and just enough oak to give it a little more backbone. Try it with smoked trout terrine.

Boat O'Craigo Black Spur Chardonnay

This Yarra Valley chardonnay is grown near Healesville, a picturesque town on the edge of the main vineyard region. Boat O'Craigo was the Scottish home of the present vineyard owner's great-great-grandfather.
CURRENT RELEASE 2004   The aroma of this chardonnay shows real complexity derived from a mixture of stainless steel and French-oak fermentation, coupled to notable lees influence. Subdued peach and citrus-fruit aromas fill the gaps on the nose, and the palate has a creamy feel to it. The oak component is slightly assertive at the moment, and fruit weight is a little light, perhaps a legacy of young vines, but the wine has style and refinement. A label to watch. Serve this with grilled prawns.

Quality	▼▼▼▼
Value	★★★┤
Rating	90
Grapes	chardonnay
Region	Yarra Valley, Vic.
Cellar	▮ 2
Alc./Vol.	13.5%
RRP	$19.00 ⬙

Brookland Valley Chardonnay

This standard wine is a less elaborate version than the Reserve, but it still has a real touch of class (and a more modest price tag).
CURRENT RELEASE 2003   A well-made chardonnay of less emphatic personality than Brookland Valley's Reserve, this opens with nectarine and citrus aromas, a light hint of cashew and very subtle, well-integrated toasty French oak. It smells savoury and appealing, and it tastes intense and satisfying with a long, smooth mid-palate. Some slight phenolic firmness adds structure at the end but it softens with food. Serve this with cheese and spinach tortellini.

Quality	▼▼▼▼▮
Value	★★★
Rating	93
Grapes	chardonnay
Region	Margaret River, WA
Cellar	▮ 2
Alc./Vol.	14.0%
RRP	$34.75

Brookland Valley Reserve Chardonnay

The first Brookland Valley Chardonnay with a Reserve label was the 2002. It was a super-complex wine that fully justified its Reserve title.
CURRENT RELEASE 2003   There's a lot going on here, in fact we reckon it's even more 'worked' than its predecessor. The winemaking team has thrown everything at it – wild yeast, barrel fermentation, malolactic treatment, extended lees contact, elaborate oak regimes – and it shows. The nose has honey, nutty, yeasty, burnt-match and crème brûlée aromas, along with some peachy fruit. The palate is rich with creamy texture and a long tangy finish, yet all this comes at a relatively low alcohol level of 13 per cent, which shows that a wine doesn't need to be high octane to be impressive. Enjoy it with a creamy seafood pie.

Quality	▼▼▼▼▼
Value	★★★┤
Rating	96
Grapes	chardonnay
Region	Margaret River, WA
Cellar	▮ 2+
Alc./Vol.	13.0%
RRP	$65.00

Bullers Beverford Chardonnay

Quality	♟ ♟ ♟ ♟
Value	★ ★ ★ ★
Rating	88
Grapes	chardonnay
Region	Murray Valley, Vic.
Cellar	▮ 1
Alc./Vol.	14.5%
RRP	$13.00 ⬚ ⑤

Like a number of other Victorian wineries, Bullers of Rutherglen established another vineyard in the Murray Valley to augment their lower-yielding home vineyards, and provide a range of wines for the budget market. CURRENT RELEASE 2005   This is a straightforward commercial chardonnay that will push the right buttons for those who enjoy an inexpensive glass of flavoury white at the end of the day. The nose and palate have ripe-melon and fig-like fruit character, with a light seasoning of vanillin oak. The palate is smooth and satisfying with good length. Good value. Try it with sweet and sour fish.

Caledonia Australis Estate Chardonnay

Quality	♟ ♟ ♟ ♟ ♟
Value	★ ★ ★ ★ ♦
Rating	95
Grapes	chardonnay
Region	South Gippsland, Vic.
Cellar	▮ 3+
Alc./Vol.	13.9%
RRP	$25.00 ⬚

The name sounds like a Scots–Aussie connection. The low-profile owners have 18 hectares of vines in the Leongatha area of South Gippsland, all planted to pinot noir and chardonnay. Master Winemakers, which is Martin Williams's contract winemaking outfit, does a good job on the wines. CURRENT RELEASE 2002   Delayed release has always been part of the Caledonia approach, and happily their style of chardonnay takes bottle-age very well. This one has a very exotic, French kind of personality, with mealy, nutty, malt and honeysuckle (possibly from fermentation on solids and malolactic) aromas of great complexity and charm. The palate has a lot of depth: it's very fine, elegant, understated yet intense. This is quite different to most Aussie chards, and the price is a bonus. Enjoy it with sautéed prawns. *Previous outstanding vintage: 2001*

Callanans Road Chardonnay

Quality	♟ ♟ ♟ ♟
Value	★ ★ ★ ♦
Rating	92
Grapes	chardonnay
Region	Mornington Peninsula, Vic.
Cellar	▮ 2
Alc./Vol.	13.0%
RRP	$20.00 ⬚

Callanans Road is the second label of Tuck's Ridge on the Mornington Peninsula. A good pinot noir was the first wine under the name, and then a chardonnay arrived. They are both lighter editions of the estate's flavoursome flagships. CURRENT RELEASE 2004   Compared to the Tuck's Ridge mainliner, this is lighter in tone, but it does share some of the same qualities. The nose has honeyed melon, citrus and fig aromas with a lightly buttery note adding savoury appeal. Oak is smoothly administered and the palate is lightly creamy with a fine silky finish. Serve it with tempura.

Cannibal Creek Chardonnay

Cannibal Creek is a quiet little corner of Gippsland viticulture making wines of subtle complexity. Chardonnay is a speciality. Maker: Pat Hardiker.
CURRENT RELEASE 2003 A complex type of chardonnay that balances winemaking craft with good chardonnay fruit very well. It has melon, peach and cashew aromas touched by creamy lees influence and a hint of burnt match. Smooth in the mouth, it retains intensity and real richness of flavour without sacrificing freshness and zip. Try it with bug tails, or lobster if you're cashed up.

Quality	♟ ♟ ♟ ♟ ♟
Value	★ ★ ★ ★ ✦
Rating	94
Grapes	chardonnay
Region	Gippsland, Vic.
Cellar	▬ 2
Alc./Vol.	14.0%
RRP	$24.00

Centennial Vineyards Reserve Chardonnay

This ambitious vineyard, winery and restaurant/cellar door complex was built by John Large, who has quite a background in the wine trade. He was one of the founders of Liquorland and, later, the wine club Cellarmasters.
CURRENT RELEASE 2004 This is a very smart chardonnay, even the colour is eye-catching: a bright, light-yellow hue with green glints. It's clean and fresh with aromas of stone fruits and citrus, fruit to the fore and deftly handled oak in the background. There's a suspicion of sweetness on palate, but it has good fruit, style and balance. It would suit buttery grilled scallops on the half-shell.

Quality	♟ ♟ ♟ ♟
Value	★ ★ ★ ✦
Rating	90
Grapes	chardonnay
Region	Orange, NSW
Cellar	▬ 3+
Alc./Vol.	14.0%
RRP	$27.00 ⬱
	(cellar door)

Centennial Vineyards Woodside Single Vineyard Chardonnay

Woodside is the brand for the chardonnay grown in Centennial's own vineyard at Bowral. It's a cool and fairly wet climate, so if some botrytis creeps into the wine some years, it's not unexpected.
CURRENT RELEASE 2004 Botrytis character adds to and modifies the chardonnay varietal personality of this wine. It adds an almost sauternes-like honey/apricot or pineapple aspect, while the palate is sweet-tasting, soft and round – a nice drink but not classic chardonnay in structure. You could team it up with chicken cooked with apricots.

Quality	♟ ♟ ♟
Value	★ ★ ★
Rating	86
Grapes	chardonnay
Region	Southern Highlands, NSW
Cellar	▬ 2
Alc./Vol.	14.0%
RRP	$23.00 ⬱
	(cellar door)

Chapel Hill Unwooded Chardonnay

Quality	🍷🍷
Value	★★★
Rating	85
Grapes	chardonnay
Region	various, SA
Cellar	🍷 2
Alc./Vol.	13.0%
RRP	$14.00 ⑤ 🍷

Industry veteran Pam Dunsford retired from winemaking at the end of 2005. Present winemaker at Chapel Hill is Michael Fragos.

CURRENT RELEASE 2005 Young, simple, fruity and gluggable, this is typical of its genre – except that it's not full of sugar, which we think is a plus. The aromas are herbal and vegetal, with a sweeter note of honeydew melon. It's pale, clean and straight down the line, if a trifle firm from crisp acidity and a clean dry finish. It suits vegetable terrine.

Clairault Estate Chardonnay

Quality	🍷🍷🍷
Value	★★★⅃
Rating	92
Grapes	chardonnay
Region	Margaret River, WA
Cellar	🍷 3+
Alc./Vol.	14.0%
RRP	$30.00

Clair-ault or Clair-oh? The locals pronounce it as the former. Like several other wineries in the same region (think Cape Mentelle, Cape Grace, Leeuwin Estate, Eagle Bay, Hamelin Bay), this one is named after a feature of the local coastline: Cape Clairault.

CURRENT RELEASE 2003 There's a lot happening here: the wine has some burgundy-like funkiness as well as hazelnutty, toasty-barrel aromas. Bottle-age and oak are combining to make a complex bouquet. It's rich, generously flavoured and rounded, with a touch of phenolics well within balance, and plenty of weight. It deserves buttery grilled Western Australian marron.

Clarence Hill Chardonnay

Quality	🍷🍷🍷
Value	★★★★★
Rating	91
Grapes	chardonnay
Region	McLaren Vale, SA
Cellar	🍷 2
Alc./Vol.	14.0%
RRP	$15.00 🍷

This is a new label to us. It's owned by the Curtis family who have more than 100 hectares of vines. It came to light when it won a silver medal at France's Chardonnay du Monde competition in 2005. Maker: Brian Light.

CURRENT RELEASE 2004 What's this? A smart chardonnay from McLaren Vale? That's worth sitting up and taking notice of. It is a very good wine: restrained and seems to be ageing gracefully; the flavours and aromas are of lemon, fig, cashew nut and toasted bread. The structure is soft, rich and slightly broad, with clean acidity and some phenolics. It might not have the finesse of a cool-area wine, but it's a wine of substantial flavour and character. There's a lot to like about it. The price is a bonus. Serve with roast chicken and crispy roast potatoes.

Cobaw Ridge Chardonnay

Alan and Nelly Cooper's Cobaw Ridge is situated in a lovely glade in a forest, and although it's only around an hour's drive from Melbourne, it seems a long way from the big smoke. Wine quality can be first rate.
CURRENT RELEASE 2004   True complexity drives this chardonnay, rather than simple fruit character, yet it stops just short of being worked too hard with winery technique. The nose has grapefruit, white-peach, cream-toffee and subtle nutty-barrel influence. It's smooth and complex on the palate with rich flavours of great length and interest. The finish is dry and tangy. Try it with fettucine all'alfredo.

Quality	♟♟♟♟♦
Value	★★★
Rating	94
Grapes	chardonnay
Region	Macedon Ranges, Vic.
Cellar	▮ 4
Alc./Vol.	13.0%
RRP	$32.00

Coldstream Hills Chardonnay

Coldstream Hills' star seems to have continued to burn brightly despite the oscillations of the parent company Southcorp, which is now part of Foster's. It's still doing well in wine shows and making wines that please the critics, the punters, and pretty well everyone. Maker: Andrew Fleming.
CURRENT RELEASE 2004   A pristine chardonnay in the style that is now typical of Coldstream: fruit-driven, ultra-clean and sensitively oaked, without malolactic. Sweet peach and nectarine aromas greet the nose, and it has terrific vitality on nose and palate, managing to be fruit-driven but also to possess many layers of subtle secondary characters that add complexity. It would go well with prawn and saffron risotto.

Quality	♟♟♟♟♦
Value	★★★★
Rating	93
Grapes	chardonnay
Region	Yarra Valley, Vic.
Cellar	▮ 3+
Alc./Vol.	13.5%
RRP	$26.00 ⑤ 🥂

Craiglee Chardonnay

Made without the fattening influence of malolactic treatment, Craiglee's chardonnay has often surprised us with its age-worthiness. It's a wine that honestly reflects a site and a vintage year without too much winemaking artefact.
CURRENT RELEASE 2005   This is fairly straightforward in style, without quite the complexity of the best southern Victorian chardonnays. The nose is rich in melon and grapefruit aromas with a measure of spicy oak. In the mouth it's quite unctuous in texture with good persistence and a dry finish. It's not subtle but it has plenty of flavour. Pair it with roast chicken drumsticks.

Quality	♟♟♟♟
Value	★★★♦
Rating	91
Grapes	chardonnay
Region	Sunbury, Vic.
Cellar	▮ 4
Alc./Vol.	14.5%
RRP	$28.00

Cumulus Climbing Chardonnay

Quality 🍷🍷🍷
Value ✱✱✱
Rating **86**
Grapes chardonnay
Region Orange, NSW
Cellar 2
Alc./Vol. 13.5%
RRP $20.00 (S)

Cumulus is the re-born Reynolds Wine Company, with its large winery north of Orange and vineyards half an hour's drive in either direction! The new regime brought Aussie Phil Dowell back from his gig at Inniskillin on Canada's Niagara Peninsula to make the wine.

CURRENT RELEASE 2005 A good drinking chardonnay, soft and smooth and round for broad consumer appeal. It smells of toasty oak and butterscotch, suggesting some malolactic fermentation. It has richness and length on palate, and is soft and round with seemingly low acid for ready drinkability. Serve it with buttery grilled scallops.

d'Arenberg The Lucky Lizard Chardonnay

Quality 🍷🍷🍷🍷
Value ✱✱✱
Rating **91**
Grapes chardonnay
Region Adelaide Hills, SA
Cellar 2
Alc./Vol. 13.5%
RRP $25.00

The Lucky Lizards at d'Arenberg are bearded dragons that sun themselves in the vineyard at vintage time, sometimes to be gathered up in loads of grapes destined for the winery. The grapes and lizards pass through the gentle old crusher at the winery together, but luckily the reptiles emerge only shaken from the experience.

CURRENT RELEASE 2005 This young chardonnay shows lots of winery artefact in its make-up. It has burnt-match, nutty, yeasty and beery aromas and flavours surrounding nectarine-like fruit. Is it overworked? Maybe, and those beery overtones are a mite strange, but those who like to slurp rich mouthfuls of big-flavoured chardonnay should enjoy it. Try it with thyme-flavoured roasted chicken.

De Bortoli Gulf Station Chardonnay

Quality 🍷🍷🍷🍷½
Value ✱✱✱✱½
Rating **92**
Grapes chardonnay
Region Yarra Valley, Vic.
Cellar 2+
Alc./Vol. 13.0%
RRP $18.85 (S)

De Bortoli's Yarra Valley winemaker Steve Webber employs both tank and barrel fermentation in this well-priced chardonnay. The result is a wine that retains freshness while showing some attractively subtle complexities of aroma, flavour and texture. It's often on discount, too.

CURRENT RELEASE 2004 This is a very well-made wine at the price, dare we say it, easily equal to some more vaunted 'boutique' Yarra Valley chards . . . and it will give you change out of $20! It opens with restrained melon and grapefruit aromas, a creamy touch, and a well-modulated input of spicy/smoky oak. The smooth palate has fine texture, good length and a tangy dry finish. It's an elegant style of the 'less is more' type. Ideally suited to barbecued prawns with lemon, butter and a twist of pepper.

De Bortoli Yarra Valley Chardonnay

De Bortoli's Yarra Valley Chardonnay has been steadily improving over the years and now it really is one of the region's most consistent for quality and value.
CURRENT RELEASE 2004   Perhaps the most complex De Bortoli Yarra Valley Chardonnay yet, this shows lots of leesy complexity with cashew, yeast and butterscotchy notes interwoven with subtle fig and citrus fruit. The palate is smooth and long with real finesse. Oak treatment shows real restraint. Try it with baked fish.

Quality	♀♀♀♀♀
Value	★★★★
Rating	96
Grapes	chardonnay
Region	Yarra Valley, Vic.
Cellar	▮3
Alc./Vol.	13.0%
RRP	$29.75 ⬧ ⑤

Eldridge Estate Chardonnay

David and Wendy Lloyd bought this vineyard in 1995. It was established 10 years earlier, on Arthurs Seat Road, Red Hill, which must be one of the coolest vineyard sites on the peninsula.
CURRENT RELEASE 2003   A complex and very stylish chardonnay, showing some feral characters on the nose including chookyard or struck match, roast hazelnut and some balsamic wild yeast complexity. The palate is marvellously fine and dry, restrained for its age and developing gracefully, tightly focused, properly dry and very long. The flavours are nicely integrated. Food: barbecued chicken.

Quality	♀♀♀♀▵
Value	★★★↴
Rating	92
Grapes	chardonnay
Region	Mornington Peninsula, Vic.
Cellar	▮5+
Alc./Vol.	13.9%
RRP	$35.00 ⬧ (cellar door)

CURRENT RELEASE 2004   It's definitely a cool-climate style, very Mornington! The malolactic character is evident, in the buttery and 'milk bottle' confectionery aromas. There are nougat scents and there's a lot more than primary fruit occupying centre stage. The palate is shy, delicate, restrained, but also soft and round and deliciously slippery on the tongue. Texture is a highlight. Don't expect a powerhouse: this is subtle. Try it with steamed prawns and beurre blanc.

Quality	♀♀♀♀
Value	★★★↴
Rating	90
Grapes	chardonnay
Region	Mornington Peninsula, Vic.
Cellar	▮4
Alc./Vol.	14.0%
RRP	$35.00 ⬧ (cellar door)

Elgee Park Baillieu Myer Family Reserve Chardonnay

Quality	♟♟♟♟
Value	★★★﹜
Rating	91
Grapes	chardonnay
Region	Mornington Peninsula, Vic.
Cellar	▮ 3+
Alc./Vol.	14.0%
RRP	$31.50 ⬧

Baillieu Myer is a member of the family that started the famous department store chain; they are also among the greatest philanthropists in Australia. Their vineyard dates back to 1972, making it the first of the current generation of Mornington wine properties.

CURRENT RELEASE 2004 Typical of the region, this shows a lot of 'powdered milk' malolactic character, as well as straw-like and buttery aromas. The rich palate has a suggestion of residual sweetness, and is round and smooth and easy to like, with good persistence. It would drink well young with scallops in a bisquey-type of seafood sauce.

Ellender Estate Chardonnay

Quality	♟♟♟♟
Value	★★★
Rating	91
Grapes	chardonnay
Region	Macedon Ranges, Vic.
Cellar	▮ 3
Alc./Vol.	13.2%
RRP	$25.00 ⬧

This little pocket of Macedon Ranges viticulture nestles in the hills behind the pretty hamlet of Glenlyon. This part of Victoria is very picturesque and the interesting spa towns aren't far away.

CURRENT RELEASE 2005 A cool-climate chardonnay with some herbal notes on the nose and tight citrus-accented fruit. The use of old oak for fermentation has resulted in very subtle wood influence, and the flavours echo the nose with herby, lemony flavours, good intensity and a dry minerally finish. It's light years away from the big, fat chardonnay style. Serve it with pan-fried fish.

Epis Chardonnay

Quality	♟♟♟♟♟
Value	★★★
Rating	93
Grapes	chardonnay
Region	Macedon Ranges, Vic.
Cellar	▮ 3
Alc./Vol.	12.9%
RRP	$35.00

Alec Epis was introduced to wine as a young footballer playing for Boulder in Western Australia. His coach served the lads a flagon of sherry as a tonic at half-time! These days Alec's taste in wine is much finer, as evidenced by the elegant wines he produces at his meticulously kept Woodend vineyard. Maker: Stuart Anderson.

CURRENT RELEASE 2004 The nose of this stylish chardonnay has Frenchy notes of minerals and earth, as well as stone-fruit and citrus aromas. It's both subtle and complex and the palate follows suit, understated and refined. A lick of carefully applied oak is integrating nicely and the dry appley-fruit mid-palate is fresh and tasty. It finishes with aromatic persistence. Try it with crab pancakes.

Evans & Tate Chardonnay

The grape glut has hit the bottom line of many wine companies, none more so perhaps than Western Australia-based Evans & Tate. Former managing director and son of the founders, Frank Tate, was removed from the board and from day-to-day running of the company late in 2005. CURRENT RELEASE 2005   Perhaps ironically, the wine quality at E & T has never been better. This is a delicious bottle of chardonnay for your 20 bucks (quite a bit less when discounted). The nectarine and passionfruit aromas are clean and bright, and the cooperage has been applied sparingly. The palate is lean and tight, with lovely flavour and balance, and a firm finish that lingers on and on. A good food wine: enjoy it with baked snapper.

Quality	♀♀♀♀
Value	★★★★
Rating	90
Grapes	chardonnay
Region	Margaret River, WA
Cellar	🍷 3+
Alc./Vol.	14.5%
RRP	$20.00 Ⓢ 🥂

Ferngrove Symbols Chardonnay

Ferngrove is a substantial vineyard in the remote Frankland River region in the far south of Western Australia. Ferngrove's Symbols white wines are designed for uncomplicated drinking young – and they succeed well at it. CURRENT RELEASE 2005   A simple varietal chardonnay with no perceptible oak. It has melon-scented aromas and a direct, fruity palate. The combination of simple, fresh, ripe flavours and tangy succulence makes it a wine to glug down without any fuss. Try it with a seafood salad.

Quality	♀♀♀♀
Value	★★★♪
Rating	88
Grapes	chardonnay
Region	Frankland River, WA
Cellar	🍷 1
Alc./Vol.	14.0%
RRP	$15.00 🥂

Fire Gully Chardonnay

The Fire Gully vineyard at Margaret River is owned by Mike Peterkin of Pierro. The style of the estate's chardonnay is quite different to Pierro, less powerful, less sumptuous, but still excellent. CURRENT RELEASE 2004   A major part of this wine was fermented in stainless steel, while a smaller portion spent some time in French oak. The result is a good balance of complexity and freshness. Melony fruit, honey and hair-gel aromas have a slightly nutty dimension adding subtle complexity. The palate is ripe and succulent with middling body, an ever-so-slight toasty touch, and a long, zesty finish. Pair it with scallops meunière.

Quality	♀♀♀♀♪
Value	★★★
Rating	92
Grapes	chardonnay
Region	Margaret River, WA
Cellar	🍷 3
Alc./Vol.	13.5%
RRP	$27.00 🥂

Fishers Circle Chardonnay

Quality	♟♟♟♟
Value	★★★★
Rating	90
Grapes	chardonnay
Region	not stated, WA
Cellar	🍾 1
Alc./Vol.	13.5%
RRP	$13.50 ⊜

Fishers Circle is a Western Australian label from the Foster's empire. These days the company's outposts stretch to every corner of Australia's vineyard country.

CURRENT RELEASE 2005   If you're looking for a straightforward chardonnay that won't break the bank don't ignore this Western Australian offering. It has a pleasant, clean aroma of citrus, herbs and melon with oak as a light seasoning rather than a definite component. It tastes smooth and succulent, and flavours are fairly simple as these things go, but herby-fresh and satisfying. A lightish chardonnay that goes well with pan-fried fish fillets.

Forester Estate Chardonnay

Quality	♟♟♟♟
Value	★★★
Rating	90
Grapes	chardonnay
Region	Margaret River, WA
Cellar	🍾 3
Alc./Vol.	14.0%
RRP	$25.00

The northern reaches of the Margaret River region haven't quite established themselves for uniformly high-quality wine in the same way as other districts, like Wilyabrup, but the better makers are worth looking out for. Chardonnay is one of the most successful varieties.

CURRENT RELEASE 2004   Melon, citrus fruits and rock candy aromas are dressed in a light veneer of nutty oak. The palate is fresh and clean-tasting, with good texture and subtle flavours. A minerally dryness underpins the fruit in fine style and there's attractive length at the end. Drink it with chicken galantine.

Four Emus Chardonnay

Quality	♟♟♟♟
Value	★★★★
Rating	88
Grapes	chardonnay
Region	not stated
Cellar	🍾 1
Alc./Vol.	12.5%
RRP	$9.99 Ⓢ ⊜

The cutesy, dinky-di Aussie animal labels just keep coming, which is maybe a good thing since at the very least they've saved us from all those Dusty/Creek/River/Ridge/Swagman's Bum type labels. The Four Emus in question are Eddie, Elsie, Ella and Ernie, the rock stars of the outback.

CURRENT RELEASE 2005   This is made in the style we've come to expect from wines under labels adorned with Aussie wildlife. That usually means it's a little bit sweet, and this certainly is. That aside, it *is* a passable commercial chardonnay at a sharp price. Melon and stone fruit, a whisper of oak, soft, juicy and undemanding. No worries. Try it with prawns off the barbie.

Gembrook Hill Chardonnay

Gembrook Hill is situated in the Dandenong Ranges not far from the terminus of the historic Puffing Billy railway. It's cool-climate viticulture in a beautiful part of Australia.

CURRENT RELEASE 2004 A finely constructed, slightly French-accented chardonnay. It has grapefruity aromas that are subtle and clean, with an appetising zest. Hint of minerals and nutty oak add dimension; the palate has complex flavour, smooth texture and a lingering lime-pastille-like aftertaste. A tangy chardonnay to sip with fresh crab.

Quality	🍷🍷🍷🍷🍷
Value	★★★★
Rating	**95**
Grapes	chardonnay
Region	Yarra Valley, Vic.
Cellar	🍾 3
Alc./Vol.	14.0%
RRP	$30.00

Giaconda Chardonnay

One of the authors was lucky enough to buy a case of '96 Giaconda Chardonnay a little before these outstanding wines achieved their rare-as-hen's-teeth cult status. A bottle opened recently was absolutely superb, and very like great French white burgundy. Is this Australia's greatest chardonnay? We think it might be. By the way, none of this wine was released from the bushfire-influenced 2003 vintage.

CURRENT RELEASE 2004 The '04 Giaconda Chardonnay is still in its infancy and full of potential. The nose is ultra-complex, yet oh-so-subtle, with poised nutty, oatmealy and creamy-toffee aromas surrounding refined pear and citrus fruit. It shows a tad more new oak at this stage than the '02, but it's beautifully balanced and will integrate totally with age. The superfine palate is silky and long with a deliciously subtle aftertaste. Try it with grilled king prawns.

Previous outstanding vintages: 1988, '90, '92, '93, '94, '95, '96, '97, '98 '99, 2000, '01, '02

Quality	🍷🍷🍷🍷🍷
Value	★★★
Rating	**97**
Grapes	chardonnay
Region	Beechworth, Vic.
Cellar	▬ 2–8
Alc./Vol.	13.8%
RRP	$115.00 🌀

Giaconda Nantua Les Deux

Nantua Les Deux is labelled as chardonnay, but it does in fact contain a little roussanne that seems to enhance the wine's aromatics. Like all the Giacondas, it's made with an obsessive commitment to quality.

CURRENT RELEASE 2005 This shows typically 'Frenchy' Giaconda chardonnay aromas that offer so much more than the variations on the fruit-oak equation that mark lesser wines. It has a subtle, complex, savoury bouquet that combines nutty touches with earthy, burnt-match, butterscotch, cedar and even lightly floral aromas. The palate is superfine with a deliciously long, dry finish and lingering presence. Try it with buttery grilled salmon steaks.

Quality	🍷🍷🍷🍷🍷
Value	★★★½
Rating	**96**
Grapes	chardonnay; roussanne
Region	Beechworth, Vic.
Cellar	🍾 4+
Alc./Vol.	13.5%
RRP	$47.00 🌀

Giant Steps Chardonnay

Quality	♀♀♀♀
Value	★★★↓
Rating	90
Grapes	chardonnay
Region	Yarra Valley, Vic.
Cellar	▮4+
Alc./Vol.	13.9%
RRP	$25.00 ⊜

Devil's Lair founder Phil Sexton's latest venture is in the Yarra Valley, where he has vineyards and a newly built winery (named Innocent Bystander, after one of his several labels) in Healesville. Winemakers are Sexton himself and Steve Flamsteed.

CURRENT RELEASE 2004   The nose is led by buttery/butterscotch characters, together with fig and melon, and oak nicely tucked into the background. It's soft, gentle and rich in the mouth; seemingly low in acidity with good concentration and length. An attractive, easygoing chardonnay for drinking fairly young – perhaps with oven-baked marron.

Glenguin River Terrace Chardonnay

Quality	♀♀♀
Value	★★↓
Rating	86
Grapes	chardonnay
Region	Hunter Valley, NSW
Cellar	▮1
Alc./Vol.	14.0%
RRP	$23.00 ⊜

The name Glenguin has a lot of significance for the proprietor, Robin Tedder. His grandfather was Lord Tedder, the Baron of Glenguin, which means Robin Tedder is also a Lord and you might wonder what he's doing in Australia growing grapes in the Hunter when he could be in London, sitting in the House.

CURRENT RELEASE 2004   Typical of a Hunter Valley chardonnay, this is very forward-developed and already has a deep-golden colour and a toasty, resiny, Friar's Balsam-like bouquet. It's a bit dried-out and lacks middle-palate fruit and freshness. This is especially puzzling as our sample was under screw-cap, and screw-capped wines usually hold their freshness better than those under cork. Drink it soon, with chicken satays.

Grosset Piccadilly Chardonnay

Quality	♀♀♀♀♀
Value	★★★
Rating	92
Grapes	chardonnay
Region	Adelaide Hills, SA
Cellar	▮3+
Alc./Vol.	13.5%
RRP	$50.00 ⊜

Fastidious is a word that aptly describes Jeffrey Grosset. His wines seldom disappoint, and if they do, it's not for want of effort. You know that what's in the bottle is the best this oenological superman could do in that particular year.

CURRENT RELEASE 2004   This beautifully made wine is all about finesse. Classy aromas of lemon and grapefruit are overlaid with nougat, macaroon and oatmeal notes. It's multi-layered and fresh with a tight, lingering, properly dry, beautifully balanced palate. Nothing is out of place. It goes with Chinese prawn dumplings.

Previous outstanding vintages: 1999, 2000, '01, '02, '03

Hardys Eileen Hardy Chardonnay

Eileen Hardy Chardonnay has evolved over the years into one of Australia's finest. Trendy wine lovers might favour the 'boutique' wines of pocket-handkerchief-sized small producers, but this is better than most of them.
CURRENT RELEASE 2004   Another excellent Eileen that shows some Frenchy burnt-match aromas in its make-up, adding savoury interest to intense grapefruity chardonnay fruit. It has great complexity without any one element taking over – high-class oak, ripe fruit, creamy winemaking artefact – all in harmony. The palate is long and fine in texture with plenty of acidity on a lingering aftertaste. It should age better than most Australian chardonnays. It would be great with salmon.

Quality	🍷🍷🍷🍷🍷
Value	★★★★
Rating	96
Grapes	chardonnay
Region	Tasmania; Yarra Valley, Vic.; Tumbarumba, NSW
Cellar	🍾 4
Alc./Vol.	13.5%
RRP	$53.00 🏅

Hardys Oomoo Unwooded Chardonnay

Once upon a time most whites in Australia were unwooded, but oak made its presence felt as chardonnay became ascendant. Today there's something of a backlash against overt oak character, even in chardonnay.
CURRENT RELEASE 2005   A pale, juicy-smelling chardonnay with attractive aromas of melon, nectarine and citrus. The palate is rather plain, but it is unwooded chardonnay after all. The finish is light but persistent with a lemony tang to it. Try it with fried scallops.

Quality	🍷🍷🍷🍷
Value	★★★↓
Rating	88
Grapes	chardonnay
Region	McLaren Vale, SA
Cellar	🍾 1
Alc./Vol.	13.5%
RRP	$17.00 Ⓢ

Houghton Pemberton Chardonnay

Houghton's Pemberton Chardonnay only arrived on the scene a couple of years ago, but the quality of this wine has already elevated it into the ranks of Western Australia's best.
CURRENT RELEASE 2004   A wine with lots of character and complexity. The nose has grapefruit, melon, a whisper of pineapple, and refined nutty, malty, buttery notes. In the mouth it's smooth and long with stone-fruit and citrus-like flavours, and a thread of spicy oak coming in halfway. It finishes chalky and dry. Serve it with a rich seafood pasta dish.

Quality	🍷🍷🍷🍷🍷
Value	★★★
Rating	92
Grapes	chardonnay
Region	Pemberton, WA
Cellar	🍾 3
Alc./Vol.	13.5%
RRP	$37.90

Howard Park Chardonnay

Quality	♥♥♥♥
Value	★★★
Rating	91
Grapes	chardonnay
Region	Great Southern, WA
Cellar	▮ 3+
Alc./Vol.	13.5%
RRP	$36.00 ⬧

Howard Park is a very state-of-the-art sort of place. At the Margaret River vineyard the feng shui consultants have had a say in things, and the architecture is very modern. The wines more than keep pace with the contemporary image. Maker: Michael Kerrigan.

CURRENT RELEASE 2004 This is a typically refined Margaret River wine, but the '04 shows more notable smoky French oak in its make-up than most. Whether it's overdone is a matter of personal taste. White-peach and grapefruity varietal character stands up to the oak, and some butter/creamy notes add complexity. The palate is fine and long, again with definite barrel input, and while it lacks a little richness at this stage compared to some preceding vintages, it should become more complete with bottle-age. Keep it for a year or so, then try it with sugar-cured salmon.

Hungerford Hill Tumbarumba Chardonnay

Quality	♥♥♥♥♥
Value	★★★★⧫
Rating	95
Grapes	chardonnay
Region	Tumbarumba, NSW
Cellar	▮ 4
Alc./Vol.	13.5%
RRP	$25.00 ⬧

Tumbarumba is true cool-climate vineyard country in the foothills of the Australian Alps in southern New South Wales. Hungerford Hill chardonnay is a regional benchmark.

CURRENT RELEASE 2004 The nose has a grapefuity tang that's fine and elegant, and there's a touch of honeydew melon adding some ripe depth. Subtle mealy and nutty elements from winemaking input and barrel influence add quiet complexity. In the mouth it's smooth and intensely flavoured with real delicacy and great aromatic length. Serve it alongside scallops with beurre blanc.

Jones Road Chardonnay

Quality	♥♥♥♥
Value	★★★
Rating	90
Grapes	chardonnay
Region	Mornington Peninsula, Vic.
Cellar	▮ 2
Alc./Vol.	14.0%
RRP	$24.50 ⬧

Somewhat confusingly this wine is labelled Somerbury Estate on capsule and label, but the Jones Road title also features prominently, so that's what we've called it.

CURRENT RELEASE 2004 There's interesting complexity on the nose here, with nutty and wild, earthy threads woven through a good measure of spicy oak. The oak tends to dominate, but clean, cool-climate, white-peachy fruit hides underneath. The palate is light and dry with reasonable persistence and a dry woody finish. A well-made Mornington Peninsula chardonnay, with the proviso that you have to like oak to enjoy it fully. Drink it with soft cheeses.

Katherine Hills Chardonnay

This brand is a merchant label, marketed by New South Wales wholesaler The Fine Wine Specialist. The wine was made by Langhorne Creek stalwart Rob Dundon. CURRENT RELEASE 2004 It's a very straightforward, basic, fruit-driven chardonnay, and possibly hasn't seen oak at all – although it's not labelled unwooded. The aroma reminds of fresh herbs, especially parsley. The palate is soft, round, low-acid and fairly broad, but at least eschews obvious residual sugar. A respectable quaff, with fish and chips.

Quality	♀♀♀
Value	★★★
Rating	84
Grapes	chardonnay
Region	various, SA
Cellar	▌1
Alc./Vol.	13.5%
RRP	$12.40 ⮑

Kingston Estate Chardonnay

Kingston's Bill Moularadellis is one of the most active people in the wine industry. A dynamo, he has driven the family winery forward with a multitude of products and substantial sales, despite the occasional setback. CURRENT RELEASE 2005 Typical of a Riverland white wine, the medium-yellow colour is already showing a lot of development. The nose is mulchy and a touch vegetal, as well as being a bit developed and not so fresh any more. There are parsley and sundry herbal flavours, and the palate is light, with a touch of sweetness. It would go with whitebait fritters.

Quality	♀♀♀
Value	★★★
Rating	83
Grapes	chardonnay
Region	Riverland, SA
Cellar	▌1
Alc./Vol.	13.5%
RRP	$13.00 ⓢ

Kirrihill Estates Chardonnay

Clare-based Kirrihill is one of the better performing new major wineries of recent years. Firstly under the inaugural winemaker Richard Rowe and now under David Mavor, the wines have been hard to fault, as well as offering good value. CURRENT RELEASE 2004 This is a real crowd-pleaser. It's a soft, rich, round wine which offers plenty of hazelnut, honey and toasty complexities, with a lot of barrel-ferment oak and a degree of class. Nicely balanced on the palate, it seems to be quite dry as well as soft, thanks to a modest level of acidity. Serious chardonnay here. It goes well with chicken risotto.

Quality	♀♀♀♀
Value	★★★★★
Rating	91
Grapes	chardonnay
Region	Adelaide Hills, SA
Cellar	▌3+
Alc./Vol.	12.5%
RRP	$19.00 ⓢ ⮑

Kooyong Clonale Chardonnay

Quality	♟♟♟♟
Value	★★★★
Rating	91
Grapes	chardonnay
Region	Mornington Peninsula, Vic.
Cellar	▮ 4+
Alc./Vol.	13.5%
RRP	$25.00

Kooyong is a very interesting outfit. They make several single-block chardonnays and pinot noirs from their own vineyard, as well as an entry-level bottling of each: the chardonnay is labelled Clonale; the pinot is Massale. This suggests the chardonnay is a single-clone wine, while Massale is the opposite – a blend of clones. Maker Sandro Mosele uses Diam technical corks on all his wines.
CURRENT RELEASE 2005   This is typical of the delicate, non-malolactic, dare we say chablis style favoured by the winemaker. It's very restrained and probably needs a few months to bloom in the bottle. It does have great finesse and balance – fruit dominant and with a piercing intensity and linearity that enables it to go superbly with food. Serve it with any white-fleshed fish, pan-fried in butter.
Previous outstanding vintage: 2004

Lakes Folly Chardonnay

Quality	♟♟♟♟♟
Value	★★★✦
Rating	94
Grapes	chardonnay
Region	Hunter Valley, NSW
Cellar	▮ 5+
Alc./Vol.	13.5%
RRP	$50.00 (cellar door)

Forty-three years down the track, and 'Australia's first boutique winery' is still selling out its chardonnay in three or four weeks! Winemaker Rodney Kempe thinks the '04 is one of the best ever.
CURRENT RELEASE 2004   We'd agree that it's a superb chardonnay. Bottle number 5692 was lovely: lots of nutty, toasty and fruit-compote aromas with traces of fig and apricot. Not overly oaky or in-your-face as a lot of Hunter chardonnays are; it's just beautifully balanced. Rich yet elegant, dry and clean to close, and subtly complex, this is a very fine chardonnay that lives up to its name as one of the two best in the Hunter. It goes extra well with food: try a hard cheese like parmesan.

Leeuwin Estate Prelude Vineyards Chardonnay

Quality	♟♟♟♟
Value	★★★
Rating	91
Grapes	chardonnay
Region	Margaret River, WA
Cellar	▮ 2
Alc./Vol.	14.5%
RRP	$32.00 🍷

Despite being the 'understudy' to the famous Art Series, Leeuwin's Prelude Vineyards Chardonnay is always a rather special wine in its own right.
CURRENT RELEASE 2004   It's definitely a step down from the Art Series in concentration and complexity, but its creamy melon and stone fruit is still intense enough, and it has good texture. Slightly edgy oak is a bit less pronounced than in the '03. Go retro and make a groovy fondue for this wine.

Lillypilly Chardonnay

Riverina chardonnay has a place in the wine diet of many Australians. They find its sunny fruit and smooth texture hits the spot – as a cold drink at social occasions, or at the casual dining table. This example sums up the style admirably.
CURRENT RELEASE 2005   Good varietal keys introduce this straightforward chardonnay. Melon and syrupy stone fruits, and perhaps a hint of pineapple, are found on the fruit-dominant nose. The palate is smooth and easy with a dry finish and a hint of phenolic firmness at the end. Sip it chilled with Balinese-style fried chicken.

Quality	♀♀♀♀
Value	★★★↓
Rating	89
Grapes	chardonnay
Region	Riverina, NSW
Cellar	▯ 1
Alc./Vol.	14.5%
RRP	$14.95 ⊜

Lindemans Bin 65 Chardonnay

One of Australia's export success stories, Bin 65 has spawned a heap of imitators and established sunshiney Aussie chardonnay in some key markets.
CURRENT RELEASE 2005   This has a bright greenish lemon–yellow colour that's very attractive. The aroma is rather obvious, but it is well-made and fault-free. Melony fruit is seasoned with slightly raw oak, and the smooth palate has ripe melon and vanilla flavours, and a whisper of sweetness. It's a direct, commercial chardonnay of good quality with a very handy price tag. Try it with Asian-flavoured fried prawns.

Quality	♀♀♀♀
Value	★★★★
Rating	88
Grapes	chardonnay
Region	not stated
Cellar	▯ 1
Alc./Vol.	13.5%
RRP	$10.50 Ⓢ ⊜

Main Ridge Estate Chardonnay

The White family established this tiny, ultra-cool-climate vineyard in the highest part of the Mornington Peninsula in the mid-1970s. They've always produced some of the area's finest wines, but gradually improving the viticulture continues to pay dividends. The wines are 100 per cent single-estate, wild ferment and malolactic, and aged in new and one-year-old Sirugue oak. Maker: Nat White.
CURRENT RELEASE 2004   This is a crackerjack chardonnay, which shows malolactic character but because of the richness of fruit it holds its balance, with superb white-peach and fig fruit flavours of intensity as well as refinement. There are many other nuances, including smoke and toast. The palate shows great harmony and immaculate balance. Enjoy this with sautéed yabby tails.

Quality	♀♀♀♀♀
Value	★★★★
Rating	96
Grapes	chardonnay
Region	Mornington Peninsula, Vic.
Cellar	▯ 5
Alc./Vol.	14.0%
RRP	$48.00 ⊜ (cellar door)

Moorooduc Estate The Moorooduc Wild Yeast Chardonnay

Quality	🍷🍷🍷🍷🍷
Value	★★★
Rating	94
Grapes	chardonnay
Region	Mornington Peninsula, Vic.
Cellar	🍷 5
Alc./Vol.	14.0%
RRP	$60.00

If ever a chardonnay earned the epithet 'red drinker's white', this does. It's a whopper! We get the impression winemaker Rick McIntyre threw everything at it in an effort to make the most complex wine possible. He succeeds!
CURRENT RELEASE 2003   This is an explosively rich, powerful, in-your-face style. Subtle it ain't. The colour is already deep yellow; the bouquet displays honey and butter, toast, fig and grilled nuts. It's very smooth, rich, gentle and almost unctuous in the mouth, and could cope with the richest poultry or crayfish dish you can cook up. But, like some buttery sauces, it can become just a bit too rich with repeated tasting. A little goes a long way.

Moorooduc Estate Wild Yeast Chardonnay

Quality	🍷🍷🍷🍷🍷
Value	★★★★
Rating	93
Grapes	chardonnay
Region	Mornington Peninsula, Vic.
Cellar	🍷 5
Alc./Vol.	13.5%
RRP	$30.00

Is wild yeast just a marketing gimmick, or does it add something extra? The jury is still out, but there is a strong view that when winemakers stop adding tinned yeast and let fermentation happen naturally, it's actually the same yeast they've been adding for years that's stepping in from the atmosphere to do the job.
CURRENT RELEASE 2003   True to form, this is one of the Peninsula's most powerful, full-bodied chardonnay styles. The medium-deep yellow colour and rich bouquet of grilled bread, toasted nuts and stone fruits show some development, while the taste offers loads of flavour and character. It's fleshy and has some phenolics, but everything's in harmony and still manages to retain elegance and poise. A great success. Serve it with barbecued chicken.

Murrindindi Chardonnay

Quality	🍷🍷🍷🍷🍷
Value	★★★★
Rating	93
Grapes	chardonnay
Region	Yea Valley, Vic.
Cellar	🍷 4
Alc./Vol.	13.5%
RRP	$28.00 🍷

Murrindindi Chardonnay is made in a way that puts it a bit out of the mainstream. It doesn't have any acid-softening, enriching malolactic treatment, and only a small proportion sees any oak. The result is very distinctive.
CURRENT RELEASE 2005   This is about as far away from fruit-bomb Australian chardonnay as you can get. Its inspiration is French chablis: the nose has strong minerality, touches of honey, wax, grapefruit and lime. The intense palate is long, austere and fine in texture, with thrilling acidity giving it a very savoury tang. It won't be to everybody's taste, but fans of the style will be impressed. Try it with shellfish.

Oakridge 864 Chardonnay

Oakridge released a range of super-dooper wines early in 2006, which gave winemaker Dave Bicknell a chance to really stretch out. The wines are sensational – a pity about the rather unimaginative name.

CURRENT RELEASE 2004   Dave Bicknell sure knows how to make chardonnay. His regular wine is superb; this is perhaps even better. It's at least more adventurous, with some of the chookyard, struck-match sulphide-related complexities so beloved of white burgundies. It's tight and restrained in the mouth yet very intense, with great delicacy, line and length. Vibrant, young and vital, its freshness is preserved by the screw-cap. It looks to have a bright future. Serve with lobster.

Quality	🍷🍷🍷🍷🍷
Value	★★★★
Rating	96
Grapes	chardonnay
Region	Yarra Valley, Vic.
Cellar	🍾 4+
Alc./Vol.	13.5%
RRP	$50.00 🗢
	(cellar door)

Otway Estate Chardonnay

Established in 1983, Otway Estate is in a very cool site, one hour south-west of Geelong near Colac. It's a short hop from the Great Ocean Road, one of the world's most superb coastal drives. Winemaker is Ian Deacon.

CURRENT RELEASE 2004   This is a lovely wine indeed, and something of a discovery. It has a light-medium yellow hue and smells of butter, peach/stone-fruit and butterscotch: very complex. The taste is soft and full flavoured with layers of complexity and real finesse. It seems odd to remark on this, but it tastes low in alcohol for an Aussie chardonnay! (And it is. That's a plus in our book.) The finish tapers off slightly, but it's a small point. A delicious wine to serve with sautéed prawns.

Quality	🍷🍷🍷🍷🍷
Value	★★★★✦
Rating	92
Grapes	chardonnay
Region	Otway Ranges, Vic.
Cellar	🍾 4+
Alc./Vol.	13.0%
RRP	$20.00 🗢
	(cellar door)

Paringa Estate PE Peninsula Chardonnay

This understudy to Paringa's 'serious' chardonnay is a totally different critter. The Estate Chardonnay is usually ultra-malolactic, unctuously buttery and over-the-top; we prefer this second-fiddle drop.

CURRENT RELEASE 2005   A generously styled chardonnay, yet one with some finesse. It shows peachy fruit on the nose with nutty oak folded in without any edges. The palate is smooth and plush with ripe-fruit flavour; tangy acidity keeps it clean and bracing at the end. A well-balanced, flavoursome young chardonnay that doesn't show its 15 per cent strength unduly. Serve it with a seafood stew.

Quality	🍷🍷🍷🍷🍷
Value	★★★★
Rating	92
Grapes	chardonnay
Region	Mornington Peninsula, Vic.
Cellar	🍾 2
Alc./Vol.	15.0%
RRP	$18.00 🗢

Peel Estate Chardonnay

Quality	🍷🍷🍷🍷
Value	★★★
Rating	90
Grapes	chardonnay
Region	Baldivis, WA
Cellar	🍾 1
Alc./Vol.	13.5%
RRP	$20.00

One of Peel Estate's specialities is oak-influenced white wine. In the early days chenin blanc and chardonnay thus treated were sometimes a wee bit too oaky, but now there's a bit more moderation.

CURRENT RELEASE 2003   A complex chardonnay with nutty-barrel influence woven through melon fruit. In the mouth the oak shows through a bit more, adding charry/smoky and nutty flavours to a core of fruit. It finishes very dry with a toasty aftertaste. Try it with chargrilled chicken.

Penfolds Bin 311 Tumbarumba Chardonnay

Quality	🍷🍷🍷🍷🍷
Value	★★★
Rating	92
Grapes	chardonnay
Region	Tumbarumba, NSW
Cellar	➡1–5
Alc./Vol.	13.0%
RRP	$35.00 🥂

Penfolds Bin 311 is intended as a single-district chardonnay to highlight regionality and the characteristics of a particular vintage year. This first release comes from Tumbarumba in the cool Alpine foothills of New South Wales.

CURRENT RELEASE 2005   A surprisingly pale young chardonnay that's about as far from the sweetish 'bottled sunshine' type of Oz chard as any. It has a complex nose and while the label states that it has minimal oak influence, there's plenty of evidence of very skilled lees and barrel work adding dimension to a grapefruity cool-grown chardonnay. Nutty cashew-like touches and a minerally underpinning mark the elegant palate. Some may find it a tad hollow in the middle, but it's saved by a long, clean, delicate finish. Serve it with crab.

Penfolds Koonunga Hill Chardonnay

Quality	🍷🍷🍷🍷
Value	★★★★
Rating	90
Grapes	chardonnay
Region	various, South Eastern Australia
Cellar	🍾 2
Alc./Vol.	13.5%
RRP	$15.60 🥂 ⑤

The Koonunga Hill name is mostly associated with red wines, as befits a producer with the red wine pedigree of Penfolds, but the whites can be surprisingly good. Unlike the reds, which can age amazingly well, the whites are for early consumption.

CURRENT RELEASE 2004   This has fresh melon and citrus aromas, the attractive nose of a good-value middle-of-the-road chardonnay. Oak treatment is thankfully subtle and there's a modicum of complexity, unusual in moderately priced chardonnays. It has good texture and weight, finishing clean and lively. One of the best Koonunga Hill chardonnays yet. Try it with spiced chicken kebabs.

Penfolds Thomas Hyland Chardonnay

This competitively priced range of Penfolds wines is named after Thomas Hyland who in 1861 married Georgina Penfold, only daughter of the company's founder Christopher Rawson Penfold.
CURRENT RELEASE 2005 A subtle chardonnay with attractive aromas of melon and understated oak. Its easy-textured palate has good intensity of flavour with a lip-smacking balance of fruit, oak and acidity. Good value, especially when it's discounted. Drink it with ricotta-filled tortellini with a cheesy topping.

Quality	♀♀♀♀
Value	★★★⁴
Rating	90
Grapes	chardonnay
Region	various, SA
Cellar	▮ 2
Alc./Vol.	13.5%
RRP	$19.00 ⬧ ⑤

Penfolds Yattarna

Since the much-ballyhooed (and just slightly disappointing) first vintage of Yattarna in 1995, the wine has been gradually refined to the point where it ranks as one of Australia's most elegant chardonnays. These days the coolest vineyards available to Penfolds are the source.
CURRENT RELEASE 2003 Like the 2002, this Yattarna is relatively pale in colour, and the nose has similar quiet complexity at first, but it grows in stature on acquaintance. Spicy oak is merged with stone-fruit, citrus, mealy and nutty aromas, and the palate has a creamy feel, fine flavour, and an ultra-long finish. A very fine, modern Australian chardonnay. Serve it with grilled scampi.
Previous outstanding vintages: 1996, '98, 2000, '01

Quality	♀♀♀♀♀
Value	★★⁴
Rating	95
Grapes	chardonnay
Region	various SA, NSW & Vic.
Cellar	▮ 4
Alc./Vol.	13.5%
RRP	$130.00

Pennys Hill Red Dot Chardonnay Viognier

We've been seeing a number of chardonnay-viognier blends lately. While chardonnay can temper viognier's way-out-there persona a little, viognier's pungency usually shines through.
CURRENT RELEASE 2005 The nose has emphatic spice and floral aromas from the viognier, but chardonnay's stone-fruit and citrus notes bring it back from the outer limits. It has a smooth and luxurious palate with attractive balance and mellow acidity. Try it with spiced pork chops.

Quality	♀♀♀♀
Value	★★★★
Rating	90
Grapes	chardonnay; viognier
Region	McLaren Vale, SA
Cellar	▮ 1
Alc./Vol.	14.0%
RRP	$15.00

Pepper Tree Grand Reserve Orange Chardonnay

Quality	♥♥♥♥♥
Value	★★★
Rating	92
Grapes	chardonnay
Region	Orange, NSW
Cellar	▮ 4
Alc./Vol.	13.9%
RRP	$35.00 ⬚

From a Hunter Valley base, Pepper Tree has spread its wings to other regions of New South Wales and further afield to South Australia. Orange is one of New South Wales' cooler regions, and chardonnay does well there.
CURRENT RELEASE 2005 Chardonnays of restrained style like this make a welcome change from the voluptuous type. It has a subtle nose of citrus, minerals and melon with some cashew-like richness and a herbal touch. Oak is skilfully handled and well integrated. In the mouth it's rich in flavour with excellent texture and length across the palate.

Pierro Chardonnay

Quality	♥♥♥♥♥
Value	★★★
Rating	96
Grapes	chardonnay
Region	Margaret River, WA
Cellar	▮ 3
Alc./Vol.	13.5%
RRP	$65.00 ⬚

Mike Peterkin's Pierro chardonnays are among Margaret River's most powerful expressions of chardonnay, and although the '04 is a shade less alcoholic than most of its predecessors, it retains tons of character.
CURRENT RELEASE 2004 The nose has citrus and syrupy fig aromas of luscious intensity, along with plenty of buttery richness, and vanillin and nutty complexity. In the mouth it treads a complex path between voluptuous richness and power on the one hand, and true finesse on the other. A tour-de-force in Margaret River chardonnay. Delicious with lobster.

Plantagenet Omrah Chardonnay

Quality	♥♥♥♥
Value	★★★⫯
Rating	91
Grapes	chardonnay
Region	Mount Barker, WA
Cellar	▮ 2
Alc./Vol.	13.0%
RRP	$17.50 ⬚

Omrah is the second label of Plantagenet, the pioneering winery in the Mount Barker region of southern Western Australia. Their unoaked chardonnay is designed for no-fuss drinking in its youth.
CURRENT RELEASE 2005 Omrah is the essence of what commercial unoaked Australian chardonnay is all about (or should be). It has fruity melon and citrus aromas and a clean grapefruity palate that's light and charming. An uncomplicated little thing to sip chilled under a tree when the temperature climbs. Try it with cold chicken.

Port Phillip Estate Chardonnay

Port Phillip Estate (and Kooyong) winemaker Sandro Mosele has become one of the Mornington Peninsula's most proficient chardonnay makers. One of the best places to taste this wine is at Port Phillip's rustic cellar door at Red Hill.
CURRENT RELEASE 2004   This cool-climate chardonnay aims at a very complex style. While white-peachy fruit is at the core of things, it also shows quite a bit of solids influence in its nutty, peaty and matchsticky nuances. Oak is folded in seamlessly as a subtle seasoning. In the mouth it's very creamy in texture with a long-lasting complex, tangy flavour. A full-flavoured chardonnay to drink with roasted salmon.

Quality	🍷🍷🍷🍷
Value	★★★
Rating	93
Grapes	chardonnay
Region	Mornington Peninsula, Vic.
Cellar	3
Alc./Vol.	14.0%
RRP	$30.00

Prancing Horse Chardonnay

Many horses graze on the Mornington Peninsula's green pastures, so this is an appropriate name. Winemaking is in the hands of the highly skilled Sergio Carlei.
CURRENT RELEASE 2004   A relatively pale young chardonnay with a deliciously subtle nose of fine fig-like chardonnay fruit, hints of mealy, nutty complexity, and attractive suggestions of barley sugar and wild honey. In the mouth it has lovely succulent fruit and buttery-rich flavours with a balanced dressing of subtle oak. It finishes long and fine with a vaguely coconutty thread through the aftertaste. Enjoy it with chargrilled salmon.

Quality	🍷🍷🍷🍷🍷
Value	★★★
Rating	92
Grapes	chardonnay
Region	Mornington Peninsula, Vic.
Cellar	3
Alc./Vol.	13.5%
RRP	$40.00

Printhie Chardonnay

Printhie celebrated its tenth anniversary in 2006. It sources its chardonnay grapes from some of Orange's highest vineyards – at 1000 metres above sea level. Proprietor Jim Swift's catch-cry is: 'Wines with altitude'. Winemaker is Robert Black.
CURRENT RELEASE 2005   Swift says his chardonnays need time and evolve slowly. He's right: this is a very tight, shy, backward wine with delicately handled oak. It's very fruit-driven, with some parsley/herbal aromas, lean and delicate in the mouth without a lot of complexity at this stage. No doubt it will build character in the bottle, but it's probably always going to be the lighter, plainer style. Very drinkable all the same, especially with grilled white-fleshed fish.

Quality	🍷🍷🍷
Value	★★★★
Rating	89
Grapes	chardonnay
Region	Orange, NSW
Cellar	3+
Alc./Vol.	13.8%
RRP	$15.00

Pyramid Hill Chardonnay

Quality	♟♟♟♟
Value	★★★↓
Rating	90
Grapes	chardonnay
Region	Hunter Valley, NSW
Cellar	▮ 2
Alc./Vol.	13.5%
RRP	$22.00 ⬧

This large vineyard in the Upper Hunter Valley is a good example of high-tech viticulture providing wines that deliver well above their price-point. The region has a longer history with chardonnay than many other Australian districts and it works well there.
CURRENT RELEASE 2005   A satisfying chardonnay made in a middle-of-the-road style that should have wide appeal. The nose has melon and stone-fruit aromas of good concentration, with a balanced dressing of oak and some buttery notes. It tastes smooth and complete with a long finish and softly integrated acidity. Drink it with pan-fried fish.

Roaring 40s Chardonnay

Quality	♟♟♟♟
Value	★★★
Rating	90
Grapes	chardonnay
Region	southern Tas.
Cellar	▮ 2
Alc./Vol.	13.0%
RRP	$20.00 ⬧

Tasmanian winemaker Andrew Hood is responsible for making a large number of wines for other Tasmanian growers on contract. His chardonnays usually fit the classically cool-climate mould, offering finesse and delicacy lacking in warmer-area wines.
CURRENT RELEASE 2004   Bright and shiny with relatively pale colour, Roaring 40s has some reductive pongs and minerally touches that won't be to everybody's taste. It reminds us a little of chablis. Gentle citrus and earthy aromas lead to a silky-textured palate of good length with grapefruity flavour and a long dry finish. Pair it with shellfish.

Rosabrook Chardonnay

Quality	♟♟♟♟♟
Value	★★★★
Rating	92
Grapes	chardonnay
Region	Margaret River, WA
Cellar	▮ 2
Alc./Vol.	14.0%
RRP	$24.00 ⬧

Rosabrook's wines come with impressive packaging that features a woodcut print of roses. It's one of the less well-known Margaret River operations, but quality is always very good. Maker: Bill Crappsley.
CURRENT RELEASE 2004   The nose is still a little disjointed, slightly resiny oak and nectarine-like fruit seem slightly out of whack on first tasting, but by the time you read this it should have come together. It's much better in the mouth with a delicious silky feel, good intensity of subtly integrated fruit and oak, and a long soft finish. A wine of two parts that grows on you as you sip it. Give it a year or so, then serve it with smoked trout pasta.

Saltram Next Chapter Chardonnay

Like many wines today, the labelling states the origin of the grapes as 'Barossa', as distinct from 'Barossa Valley'. That means the Barossa zone, which is a larger geographical area than the region of Barossa Valley, and includes the Eden Valley region. A subtle distinction; perhaps too subtle. CURRENT RELEASE 2005   Oak is first to arrive when you sniff; then coconut and banana aromas which are quite appealing. The palate is very lean and light, almost a trifle stripped. Previous vintages of this wine have over-delivered on the price-point, so we are surprised. It is very young, and possibly will fill out with a bit more time in the bottle. As it is at time of tasting, it's hard to get excited. Chinese dumplings here.

Quality	♥♥♥
Value	★★★
Rating	84
Grapes	chardonnay
Region	Barossa, SA
Cellar	▮ 2+
Alc./Vol.	13.5%
RRP	$16.00 ⑤

Savaterre Chardonnay

The farmer who Keppell Smith, Savaterre's owner, bought his land from said: 'That's my worst paddock. You're welcome to it.' It's another example of how poorer soils make the best vineyard land – if high quality is your goal. CURRENT RELEASE 2004   This is one hell of a chardonnay. It justifies all the purple prose that's being written about Savaterre these days. It's a wine of great complexity and also great elegance. The bouquet is wonderfully nuanced and multi-faceted; the palate is concentrated, powerful, rich. A Pandora's box of flavours all in marvellous harmony. Serve it with your favourite lobster dish.

Quality	♥♥♥♥♥
Value	★★★⟩
Rating	96
Grapes	chardonnay
Region	Beechworth, Vic.
Cellar	▮ 3+
Alc./Vol.	13.5%
RRP	$65.00 (cellar door)

Seppelt Jaluka Chardonnay

This vintage of Jaluka is entirely from the Drumborg Vineyard, which Karl Seppelt first planted back in the 1970s. It is one of the coolest spots in Victoria, on the west coast near Portland. Maker: Arthur O'Connor and team. CURRENT RELEASE 2005   This is a very good wine but it needs time. It's been released too soon. It's tight and undeveloped, with some free sulphur noticeable on the nose. Despite that, it's a fine, restrained, subtly complex wine with nougat and toasty barrel winemaking inputs, delicate restrained fruit and high acid. This gives an impression of hollowness on the palate but really all it needs is more time. The acidity will ensure this has a good future if you cellar it. Drink with scallops and salad.

Quality	♥♥♥♥
Value	★★★
Rating	89
Grapes	chardonnay
Region	Henty, Vic.
Cellar	▬1–5+
Alc./Vol.	13.5%
RRP	$30.00 ⑤ ≋

Shaw and Smith M3 Vineyard Chardonnay

Quality	🍷🍷🍷🍷🍷
Value	★★★★
Rating	96
Grapes	chardonnay
Region	Adelaide Hills, SA
Cellar	🍾 5+
Alc./Vol.	13.0%
RRP	$38.00

M3 refers to the brothers Michael and Matthew Hill Smith, and their cousin Martin Shaw: the partners in this vineyard. Martin Shaw is chief winemaker, assisted by Daryl Catlin. CURRENT RELEASE 2004   M3 chardonnay has been improving steadily year by year, the twin goals of refinement and age-worthiness firmly in its creators' minds. And they've made great strides with this vintage: it is the best yet and indisputably one of the greatest chardonnays in Australia. A very exciting wine, it's laden with pear, white-peach and honeydew melon aromas; fruit to the fore against a backdrop of classy oak and other winemaking induced complexities. The palate has great finesse and fabulous balance. It's all about understated complexity. And it has the tightness to age well. Serve with prawns in beurre blanc.

Sirromet Seven Scenes Chardonnay

Quality	🍷🍷🍷
Value	★★★
Rating	89
Grapes	chardonnay
Region	Queensland
Cellar	🍾 3
Alc./Vol.	13.5%
RRP	$28.00

Sirromet is the brand name for the Mount Cotton winery south of Brisbane, which takes grapes from vineyards in the Granite Belt and South Burnett. Seven Scenes is one of the top labels. Chief winemaker: Adam Chapman. CURRENT RELEASE 2003   A complex wine with burgundy-style winemaking inputs giving a touch of struck-match character. Smart barrel-ferment oak and lees contact add extra layers. There are some herbal/parsley characters in the fruit, which emerge as the wine warms in the glass. The palate is firm, with fruit sweetness but also a slight astringency at the end. Food: stuffed, roast free-range chicken.

Smiths Vineyard Chardonnay

Quality	🍷🍷🍷🍷
Value	★★★★
Rating	92
Grapes	chardonnay
Region	Beechworth, Vic.
Cellar	🍾 5+
Alc./Vol.	13.9%
RRP	$28.00 ⛉
	(cellar door)

Smiths is the oldest vineyard in Beechworth, established by the Smith family in 1978. With 3.5 hectares of chardonnay, cabernet and merlot, at 550 metres altitude, virtually no irrigation, and minimal input viticulture, this is a hidden gem. CURRENT RELEASE 2005   This has taken some time to settle down in the bottle. It still shows dominant toasty, charry oak and butterscotch winemaking inputs, but it's going to reward cellaring. The palate is tight and restrained, delicate and with underlying complexity. It has lively acid and a linear profile. It could just use a tad more fruit, and we suspect it will fill out over the next year or so. A very fine wine. Enjoy it with sautéed scallops.
Previous outstanding vintage: 2004

St Huberts Chardonnay

St Hubert is the patron saint of hunters, hence the stag's head on the St Huberts labels. Hubert De Castella was also the founder of the original St Huberts, which is the more significant explanation.
CURRENT RELEASE 2005   There's a meaty, funky character in this wine which is probably a function of oak and lees contact. It's peachy and there's a certain grape-skin herbal note as well. It's a fairly straightforward wine with a somewhat clumsy, oak-heavy taste. It does have weight and flavour, but not much delicacy. Serve it with Chinese lemon chicken.

Quality	♉ ♉ ♉
Value	★ ★ ꜝ
Rating	86
Grapes	chardonnay
Region	Yarra Valley, Vic.
Cellar	🍾 4
Alc./Vol.	13.5%
RRP	$25.00 ⑤ ⬚

Stonier Chardonnay

Great name for a winery: the stonier the vineyard the better the quality of the wine. That's because stones facilitate rainwater penetration of the soil and drainage, not to mention acting as little heat-banks to release the day's stored warmth during the night. All of which has nothing to do with Stonier's though – it's the founder's name.
CURRENT RELEASE 2004   For a second-string chardonnay this is pretty smart stuff. Lots of stone-fruit aromas and flavours, with subtle embellishments from background complexities – honey, nuts, toffee – while the palate has more intensity and focus than expected. There is a degree of concentration. Very good indeed, and ideal with smoked chicken and salad.

Quality	♉ ♉ ♉ ♉
Value	★ ★ ★ ★
Rating	92
Grapes	chardonnay
Region	Mornington Peninsula, Vic.
Cellar	🍾 3
Alc./Vol.	13.5%
RRP	$25.00 ⑤ ⬚

Swings & Roundabouts Chardonnay

This brand was started by a small group of people including winemaker Mark Lane, who also has the Laneway brand. Quirky labels and names are their speciality – and the wines are usually very good. Kiss Chasey is their cheaper range.
CURRENT RELEASE 2005   A delicate, shy, light-bodied chardonnay, this has subtlety but should not be mistaken for a simple, basic chardonnay. It's clean and fresh, passionfruity and with a minimal contribution from oak. The palate has lovely balance and fluency. It's a very well-made wine, and would suit crab cakes.

Quality	♉ ♉ ♉ ♉
Value	★ ★ ★ ★
Rating	90
Grapes	chardonnay
Region	Margaret River, WA
Cellar	🍾 3
Alc./Vol.	14.0%
RRP	$20.00 ⬚

Talinga Park Chardonnay

Quality	♥ ♥ ♥ ♥
Value	★ ★ ★ ★
Rating	88
Grapes	chardonnay
Region	Riverina, NSW
Cellar	▮ 1
Alc./Vol.	13.5%
RRP	$9.95 ☒

Talinga Park is a low-priced range of wines from Nugan Estate in the Riverina region of New South Wales.
CURRENT RELEASE 2004   Like a lot of cheaper chardonnays, this looks to be driven a bit by oak (chips?), but at the modest price it's better than some. And the fruit character isn't totally lost, offering a modicum of melony fruit to tease us. The oak tends to dry out the finish but it has some length and depth, and no unpleasant traits to speak of. Serve it with a mildish Malaysian chicken curry and you won't be disappointed.

Tatachilla Keystone Chardonnay

Quality	♥ ♥ ♥ ♥
Value	★ ★ ★ ⦂
Rating	88
Grapes	chardonnay
Region	McLaren Vale, SA
Cellar	▮ 1
Alc./Vol.	14.8%
RRP	$17.95 ⑤ ☒

The 'Keystone' brand was first used by the original Tatachilla enterprise over 90 years ago, on the wines first being exported to the UK in 1913. Today it's reserved for a range of sub-$20 wines of good quality.
CURRENT RELEASE 2005   A chardonnay intended for early consumption, this has lively aromas of melon and citrus, dressed in a moderate amount of spicy oak. The palate follows the formula of straightforward refreshment with very quaffable flavour and texture. There's some depth to it, lifting it a bit above the everyday, and it commendably avoids big doses of winemaking artefact to complicate matters. Simple and light, it matches flash chicken sandwiches well.

Trentham Estate Chardonnay

Quality	♥ ♥ ♥ ♥
Value	★ ★ ★ ★
Rating	90
Grapes	chardonnay
Region	Murray Valley, NSW
Cellar	▮ 1
Alc./Vol.	13.5%
RRP	$14.95 ⑤ ☒

Trentham Estate is one of the star new-wave wineries of the Murray Valley. Despite being reasonably priced (and often discounted), this wine always offers a little more complexity and style than most of the region's chardonnays.
CURRENT RELEASE 2005   The colour is an attractive, bright yellow–green and the nose has clean stone-fruit, melon and fig aromas. Spicy oak is folded in without any sharp edges, and the rich palate has tons of flavour, creamy texture and a long, soft finish. A complete chardonnay at a great price. Drink it young with fettucine and a creamy sauce.

Terra Felix Chardonnay

Terra Felix is the second label of the Tallarook winery, but some of their wines released in recent years have been better than many wineries' top drops. This is an example. CURRENT RELEASE 2005 A more subtle chardonnay than many in this price slot, Terra Felix is driven by grapefruit and white-peach aromas, and a whisper of oak provides a seasoning to the rather delicate fruit. The palate follows the cues of the nose, with smooth texture, attractive lightness and a dry finish. A good alternative for those who like a $15 chardonnay with a bit of finesse. Serve it with pan-fried fish.

Quality	♔ ♔ ♔ ♔
Value	★ ★ ★ ⟩
Rating	92
Grapes	chardonnay
Region	Upper Goulburn, Vic.
Cellar	◗ 2
Alc./Vol.	13.6%
RRP	$14.95 ⅀

Thompson Estate Chardonnay

The Wilyabrup district is the quality heart of the Margaret River region, providing wines of real distinction across a range of grape varieties. Chardonnay is a star with top estates like Moss Wood, Cullen, Pierro and Vasse Felix providing excellent wines. Thompson Estate is cast in the same mould as the best.
CURRENT RELEASE 2004 A very stylish chardonnay. This shows plenty of winemaking input on the nose, but that artefact doesn't overwhelm some great fruit. Nutty, earthy and crème brûlée notes add fascinating complexity to central fig-jam-like aromas. The palate tracks the nose with complex flavours, creamy texture, and a very fine, lip-smacking, long finish. Try it with oven-baked fish.

Quality	♔ ♔ ♔ ♔ ♔
Value	★ ★ ★ ★
Rating	95
Grapes	chardonnay
Region	Margaret River, WA
Cellar	◗ 4+
Alc./Vol.	14.0%
RRP	$35.00 ⅀

Tibooburra Chardonnay

Tibooburra is near Seville, which is a bit off the normal Yarra Valley winery trail. It's picturesque, cool-climate vineyard country and a very good place to grow chardonnay.
CURRENT RELEASE 2004 A welcome change from a diet of big fat chardonnays, this has a delicate aroma that has us thinking of white peaches, grapefruit and lightly floral scents. A very light nutty note adds another aspect, reflecting a restrained hand with oak. It has fine mouth-feel and a clean, dry flavour. A pleasant lighter-bodied chardonnay of charm and finesse that suits delicate seafood well.

Quality	♔ ♔ ♔ ♔ ♕
Value	★ ★ ★ ⟩
Rating	92
Grapes	chardonnay
Region	Yarra Valley, Vic.
Cellar	◗ 3
Alc./Vol.	12.5%
RRP	$29.95

Tigress Chardonnay

Quality	🍷🍷🍷🍷½
Value	★★★½
Rating	**92**
Grapes	chardonnay
Region	Piper's River, Tas.
Cellar	2
Alc./Vol.	13.0%
RRP	$25.80

The Tigress range has a modern informal feel, but the wines can be seriously good. Maker: Fran Austin.

CURRENT RELEASE 2003 Skilfully made chardonnay, this has complexity worked into it with such subtlety that you hardly notice it. Honey, peach and grapefruity characters are interwoven with lightly creamy winemaking inputs, restrained oak handling, and fine acidity to create a smooth, fine, long-flavoured texture. Good now but it should continue to develop short term. Serve it with crab.

Toolangi Estate Chardonnay

Quality	🍷🍷🍷🍷🍷
Value	★★★★½
Rating	**95**
Grapes	chardonnay
Region	Yarra Valley, Vic.
Cellar	3
Alc./Vol.	13.0%
RRP	$40.00

This is Toolangi's mid-range chardonnay. Made by Tom Carson at Yering Station, it's a worthy deputy to the spectacular Reserve wine. It weighs in at only 13 per cent alcohol, substantially less than many top-end chardonnays.

CURRENT RELEASE 2004 This is a subtle wine with less impact than the Reserve, but it still has lots of class. The nose is reminiscent of figs and peaches with nutty, buttery and slightly earthy overlays. Slightly resiny oak should tone down with a little while in bottle. The palate has the customary fine, smooth Toolangi feel, and a lingering, soft finish. Try it with salmon.

Toolangi Reserve Chardonnay

Quality	🍷🍷🍷🍷🍷
Value	★★★★★
Rating	**98**
Grapes	chardonnay
Region	Yarra Valley, Vic.
Cellar	5
Alc./Vol.	14.0%
RRP	$65.00

There's a lot of chardonnay produced in the Yarra Valley. Quality ranges from very good to ordinary, but we've felt that the region's wineries haven't taken the next step and produced a benchmark wine of consistency and classic style. We may have now found it in Toolangi Reserve.

CURRENT RELEASE 2004 Careful viticulture and fruit selection, determination and focus from management, and Rick Kinzbrunner's inspired winemaking has made Toolangi Reserve one of Australia's great chardonnays – and it's only taken a handful of vintages. Who knows what the future might bring? The '04 is a super-complex, Meursault-inspired drop with captivating aromas of citrus, honey, oatmeal, patisserie cream and minerals. It's silky smooth in the mouth, perhaps with a bit more depth than the 2003 edition. Texture and flavour are full of interest and beautifully sustained, finishing savoury and lingering. Delicious with pork cutlets and sautéed apples.

PENGUIN BEST WHITE WINE and BEST CHARDONNAY

Tyrrell's Old Winery Chardonnay

Tyrrell's real expertise lies with semillon – the traditional high-quality Hunter Valley white grape – but chardonnay is a speciality, too. Their Vat 47 has a long pedigree as a national benchmark, while Old Winery is much further down the pecking order.
CURRENT RELEASE 2005   A surfeit of oak tends to overwhelm this young chardonnay, giving it a slightly chippy touch, and toasty notes lead the way over peach and grapefruit flavours. It's dry and long, but just a tad too oaky for us. Try it with grilled chicken.

Quality	�w♟ ♟ ♟ ♟
Value	★ ★ ★ ⁺
Rating	89
Grapes	chardonnay
Region	Hunter Valley, NSW
Cellar	▯ 2
Alc./Vol.	13.9%
RRP	$16.40 Ⓢ ⏛

Tyrrell's Vat 47 Chardonnay

Vat 47 started the chardonnay revolution in Australia via some vine cuttings 'borrowed' from a Penfolds Hunter Valley vineyard and propagated at Tyrrell's Pokolbin headquarters.
CURRENT RELEASE 2004   A restrained and refined chardonnay, not as complex or burgundian as some from Victoria and Western Australia, but it is stylish in its own way. It has melon, fig and mineral aromas with balanced subtle oak, and the light-middleweight palate has an easy feel with flavours that are fresh, long and dry. Try it with baked snapper.

Quality	♟ ♟ ♟ ♟ ♟
Value	★ ★ ★
Rating	92
Grapes	chardonnay
Region	Hunter Valley, NSW
Cellar	▯ 3
Alc./Vol.	13.0%
RRP	$48.00 ⏛

Voyager Estate Chardonnay

Cliff Royle is one of the country's most thoughtful winemakers, and he's always striving to improve his wines with each vintage. Chardonnay is a speciality, and the last few wines have honestly reflected varying vintage conditions, while never straying from the best regional style.
CURRENT RELEASE 2004   This is a lovely Margaret River wine that combines superfine nectarine and citrus-like chardonnay fruit with a skilful seasoning of nutty, creamy and leesy influences. The palate has great depth and presence, yet with less alcohol than many other top chardonnays, proving that you don't need high octane for high quality. It improves with each sip and tastes superb alongside white-fleshed fish simply prepared.

Quality	♟ ♟ ♟ ♟ ♟
Value	★ ★ ★ ⁺
Rating	95
Grapes	chardonnay
Region	Margaret River, WA
Cellar	▯ 4
Alc./Vol.	13.2%
RRP	$40.00

Water Wheel Chardonnay

Quality	♥ ♥ ⅑
Value	★ ★ ★
Rating	85
Grapes	chardonnay
Region	Bendigo, Vic.
Cellar	⟜1–4
Alc./Vol.	13.0%
RRP	$16.00 ⑤ 🍷

At $16 a throw, you'd think they'd go easy on the oak. Barrels are expensive. It's possible they've used chips or inner-staves, of course, which are much cheaper. Screw-capped white wines tend to stay fresher for the first few months than cork-sealed bottles. That can mean the initial oaky edge of a young chardonnay hangs around longer. CURRENT RELEASE 2005 Oak dominates the aroma of this young chardonnay – even when served at a temperature higher than most Australians drink white wines. The palate is intense and broad, with a tickle of early sweetness and then some acid/oak firmness drying the finish. This needs more time in bottle, and then it might need food. We'd suggest crumbed lamb's brains.

Watershed Awakening Chardonnay

Quality	♥ ♥ ♥ ♥
Value	★ ★ ★ ⅃
Rating	90
Grapes	chardonnay
Region	Margaret River, WA
Cellar	🍾 4
Alc./Vol.	14.0%
RRP	$29.00 🍷

Watershed is a relatively new Margaret River outfit (yes, we know, most of them are!) whose early results are impressive across the board. Winemaker is Cathy Spratt, who we first met when she was at St Hallett. CURRENT RELEASE 2005 The colour is bright light yellow, indicating its youth. Charry oak from toasted barrels interacts with rich fruit in the bouquet, giving it lots of personality. The palate is tight, dry and fine, with a touch of leanness. It's soft and smooth and well integrated, with a lingering finish. A good wine to serve with Western Australian marron grilled with garlic, butter and white wine.

Wellington Chardonnay

Quality	♥ ♥ ♥ ♥ ♥
Value	★ ★ ★ ★ ★
Rating	96
Grapes	chardonnay
Region	various, Tas.
Cellar	🍾 3+
Alc./Vol.	13.5%
RRP	$32.00 🍷

This won the trophy for best wine of show at the 2005 Tasmanian Wine Show. Only 420 dozen were bottled. Wellington wines are blended from various vineyards throughout Tasmania; often, winemaking services are exchanged for grapes, and the winemakers can then pick and choose what they want to keep for this brand. CURRENT RELEASE 2003 It's easy to see why this was top wine of the show. It's sensational! It has a full-yellow colour, and a thoroughly seductive bouquet full of rich buttered-toast complexities, grapefruit and nectarine fruit aromas and subtle but supportive French oak. It's quite a big wine, enlivened by fine acidity. There's a lot happening here, and it's all in superb balance. Perfect with sautéed scallops.

Wellington The Hoodster's Blend Chardonnay

The Hoodster is Andrew Hood, fly fisherman extraordinaire and highly influential contract winemaker in southern Tassie. He has serious credentials – as an educator (at Charles Sturt University, Wagga) and as a scientist (at the Australian Wine Research Institute, Adelaide). And his Wellington wines are outstanding – and seriously underrated.
CURRENT RELEASE 2002   This 'reserve' style wine was selected and blended to reward cellaring for 10 years, and only 72 dozen were bottled – happily, under screw-cap. It's an unapologetically high-acid, restrained style. There are lemon-juice and straw aromas, while the palate is very tight, dry and a trifle austere. It's firm and seems a touch ungenerous right now, but we'd love to re-taste it in three or four years. Cellar, then drink with roast chicken and mushrooms in a creamy sauce.

Quality	♔ ♔ ♔ ♔ ♔
Value	★ ★ ★ ⧫
Rating	92
Grapes	chardonnay
Region	various, Tas.
Cellar	🍾 6+
Alc./Vol.	13.5%
RRP	$50.00 ℳ

West Cape Howe Chardonnay

This winery was set up as a contract processing centre by the previous owner. Now, former Plantagenet winemaker Gavin Berry is in charge, and he's rolled his own Mount Trio brand into the company for good measure.
CURRENT RELEASE 2004   A fairly forward style of chardonnay, this has a deep yellow, almost golden, colour, and the bouquet reveals a liberal oak input along with bottle-aged development. This results in a toasted-bread, roasted-hazelnut character which is very appealing. It's a big, complex, but slightly clumsy wine – at least it doesn't stint on flavour. Food: southern fried chicken.

Quality	♔ ♔ ♔ ♔
Value	★ ★ ★
Rating	88
Grapes	chardonnay
Region	Great Southern, WA
Cellar	🍾 2
Alc./Vol.	13.5%
RRP	$24.00 Ⓢ ℳ

Willow Creek Chardonnay

Willow Creek is one of the better-quality Mornington Peninsula wineries, and like a number of them it boasts a good restaurant to tempt visitors.
CURRENT RELEASE 2005   A fresh, juicy chardonnay, a fruit-dominant style made without oak. It has stone-fruit and melon aromas that are simple but pleasantly clean. In the mouth it's smooth with succulent fruit-sweet flavour, simple structure and a dry finish. Try it with spicy chicken satays.

Quality	♔ ♔ ♔ ♔
Value	★ ★ ★
Rating	89
Grapes	chardonnay
Region	Mornington Peninsula, Vic.
Cellar	🍾 2
Alc./Vol.	13.5%
RRP	$20.00 ℳ

Wirra Wirra Sexton's Acre Unwooded Chardonnay

Quality	♟♟♙
Value	★★★
Rating	85
Grapes	chardonnay
Region	McLaren Vale, SA
Cellar	▮2
Alc./Vol.	13.0%
RRP	$16.00 ⓢ ≋

Co-founder of Wirra Wirra, Greg Trott, sadly passed away during 2005 after battling cancer. He was one of the great characters of the wine industry, but fortunately his wines will live on. We remember Trottie every time we see the label and toast him every time we drink Wirra.

CURRENT RELEASE 2005   Exactly what we expect of an inexpensive, unoaked chardonnay. It's light, simple, fruity and soft, with aromas of cashew nut, nectarine and a lacing of citrus. There's lively acidity on the palate and somewhat light fruit with a touch of hollowness. At least they haven't pumped it up with sweetness. It drinks well with vegetable dishes.

Wolf Blass Eaglehawk Chardonnay

Quality	♟♟♟
Value	★★★★↘
Rating	87
Grapes	chardonnay
Region	not stated
Cellar	▮1
Alc./Vol.	13.5%
RRP	$10.00 ⓢ

After a period when it all but vanished from the Eaglehawk label, the magic name of Wolf Blass is now being featured boldly. It certainly is one of the most enduring and valuable brand names in the history of Australian wine.

CURRENT RELEASE 2005   Somewhat advanced for an '05, but who cares when it'll be drunk before you can click your fingers. This is a well-flavoured chardonnay with some cleverly handled oak adding extra interest to the straightforward peach/herb fruit. There's a twinge of sweetness early but the palate finishes cleanly with good balance. It's a crowd-pleaser, and remarkable value for money. It would suit seafood cocktail.

Wolf Blass Gold Label Chardonnay

Quality	♟♟♟♙
Value	★★★
Rating	88
Grapes	chardonnay
Region	Adelaide Hills, SA
Cellar	▬1–4
Alc./Vol.	13.5%
RRP	$22.00 ⓢ ≋

Wolf Blass has a great colour-coded labelling system. The hierarchy is clear: Platinum on top, followed by Black, Grey, Gold, Yellow and Red, below which comes Eaglehawk. Maker: Wendy Stuckey and team.

CURRENT RELEASE 2005   There's a slightly chippy/oaky edge to this youngster. It probably needs a bit more time in bottle, especially as the seal is the totally anaerobic Stelvin screw-cap. The palate has good weight and attractive flavour, melon and peach prevailing, although again the oak is a bit obvious just now. Hold onto it a few months, then drink with pan-fried yabby tails.

Yabby Lake Chardonnay

This vineyard has a common ownership with Heathcote Estate, in Heathcote. Winemakers are Tod Dexter (ex-Stonier) and Larry McKenna, the pinot noir guru of Martinborough.

CURRENT RELEASE 2004   This is a stunning chardonnay, albeit definitely in the Mornington style with lots of malolactic character and complexity at a remove from pure, fruit-driven styles. A strong buttery malo character greets the nose but the more you sniff, the more complex it is revealed to be. There's a lot of nutty sur-lie character as well. The taste is full and rich, dry and savoury, soft and mealy. It's powerful and very long in the mouth. Great with hard cheeses.

Quality	♀ ♀ ♀ ♀ ♀
Value	★ ★ ★ ⊰
Rating	95
Grapes	chardonnay
Region	Mornington Peninsula, Vic.
Cellar	▮ 3+
Alc./Vol.	13.5%
RRP	$42.00

Yalumba Wild Ferment Chardonnay

So-called wild or natural fermentations are becoming common, especially with chardonnay – where winemakers seek to invest the wine with as much complexity and textural quality as possible. There is still some argument over whether such ferments are indeed wild, or whether the yeasts in the environment are simply the ones the winemakers have been shaking out of tins and packets for years . . .

CURRENT RELEASE 2005   This is a delicate, restrained chardonnay with quite a deal of finesse. There are subtle barrel characters plus minerally, chalky overtones that make it quite distinctive and even a touch exotic. The palate is clean, dry and penetrating, despite its lightness of body. A really lovely chardonnay that would go with crab and avocado timbale.

Quality	♀ ♀ ♀ ♀
Value	★ ★ ★ ★ ⊰
Rating	90
Grapes	chardonnay
Region	Eden Valley, SA
Cellar	▮ 4
Alc./Vol.	14.0%
RRP	$18.00 Ⓢ ⧠

Yarra Ridge Unwooded Chardonnay

Unwooded chardonnay tends to get allocated the dregs of the grapes, which is unfortunate. There's a place for good-quality unwooded chardonnay, but somehow the industry has conspired to relegate it to the rejects bin.

CURRENT RELEASE 2004   This is not only a very simple wine, it's green and nettley with almost a mouldy fruit overtone. Aromas of green herbs and vegetation predominate. The palate is very light in weight, and has quite an acid tang to it. Mercifully, it's not overtly sweet. Try it with waldorf salad.

Quality	♀ ♀ ⧠
Value	★ ★ ⊰
Rating	84
Grapes	chardonnay
Region	Yarra Valley, Vic.
Cellar	▮ 1
Alc./Vol.	13.0%
RRP	$20.00 Ⓢ ⧠

YarraLoch Chardonnay

Quality	🍷🍷🍷🍷
Value	★★★
Rating	92
Grapes	chardonnay
Region	Yarra Valley, Vic.
Cellar	🍾 4
Alc./Vol.	13.0%
RRP	$30.00 🍷

We've been very impressed with our first look at the YarraLoch wines – although we've admired Serge Carlei's winemaking for quite a few years. They're not easy to track down, but try Ultimo Wine Centre in Sydney or The Prince and Europa in Melbourne.
CURRENT RELEASE 2004   This is a delicious chardonnay, which we liked even more than the Stephanie's Dream (did the screw-cap help make a difference?). It's a less-worked style, with a bright colour and pristine peachy, nutty aromas of great charm and freshness. Oak has been used sensitively. In the mouth, it's rich and seamless with fine acidity and the merest smidgen of sweetness. A refined chardonnay of great line and length. Serve with lobster.

YarraLoch Stephanie's Dream Chardonnay

Quality	🍷🍷🍷🍷
Value	★★★
Rating	90
Grapes	chardonnay
Region	Yarra Valley, Vic.
Cellar	🍾 2
Alc./Vol.	13.0%
RRP	$40.00 (cellar door)

This is a new brand out of the Yarra Valley. The labels need work: the words Stephanie's Dream are almost invisible in dark lettering on a dark background. The wine quality, however, is impressive from the word 'go'. Winemaker is the highly competent Sergio Carlei of Carlei Estate and The Green Vineyards. Diam corks are used.
CURRENT RELEASE 2004   The wine is fairly developed for its age, but flavour and style are very good. There are toasty and slightly matty-oak aromas, tending towards roast hazelnut, while the palate is full and broad with generous, open-knit structure and appealing drinkability. We'd drink it sooner rather than later, as it seems to be ageing quickly. Team it with chicken shaslik.

Zarephath Chardonnay

The Benedictine community of the Christ Circle who produce the Zarephath wines are continuing a Christian association with wine that goes back two thousand years. **CURRENT RELEASE 2004** The 2004 Zarephath Chardonnay shows more oak influence, solids character and smoky qualities than the '05, but the same grapefruit-like fruit character emerges through it. Creamy notes, cashew and toasty-oak flavours are rich and mouth-filling but it's not heavy. The finish is long and complex. Try it with poached chicken.

Quality	♟♟♟♟⸲
Value	★★★⸴
Rating	93
Grapes	chardonnay
Region	Porongurup, WA
Cellar	▮ 4
Alc./Vol.	13.5%
RRP	$25.00 ⌘

CURRENT RELEASE 2005 A very complex young chardonnay that should evolve well in the short term. It has some savoury, earthy and leesy aromas woven through subtle stone-fruit character in lovely harmony, supported by a sensitive seasoning of oak. The grapefruity palate has creamy texture and deep, rich flavour. It's a deliciously round, complete wine of real complexity, finishing with a tang. Good with Western Australian marron.

Quality	♟♟♟♟♟
Value	★★★★⸴
Rating	95
Grapes	chardonnay
Region	Porongurup, WA
Cellar	▬1–4
Alc./Vol.	13.5%
RRP	$25.00 ⌘

Marsanne, roussanne and blends

Rhône-Valley-styled dry white blends are gaining in popularity, albeit in a small way. Marsanne has been grown in Australia for well over 50 years but has for most of that time been limited to small isolated pockets in Victoria's Goulburn and Yarra valleys. The blending of the two varieties is traditional in the northern Rhône vineyards of Hermitage, Crozes-Hermitage and St Joseph, but single varietals are known there as well. The wines are generally broad, low-acid, bone-dry whites that aren't really built for ageing. Marsanne has a floral to honeysuckle aroma which becomes more honeyed with age; roussanne has less definable character but both tend to be rich and fairly textural, with alcohols on the high side.

Giaconda Aeolia

Quality	♟♟♟♟
Value	★★★
Rating	93
Grapes	roussanne
Region	Beechworth, Vic.
Cellar	▮ 4
Alc./Vol.	13.8%
RRP	$79.00 ➽

Rick Kinzbrunner's take on the exotic Rhône white variety roussanne is one of those wines we look forward to with each vintage. It shows Rick's winemaking thumbprint very clearly, but like all his wines it retains real individuality. CURRENT RELEASE 2005   A brilliant lemon–yellow coloured wine with a charming aroma of honey, wildflowers and citrus. The palate has a silky feel with gently honeyed flavour of length and depth. A background of well-integrated oak seasons it harmoniously and it finishes dry and savoury. Try it with a tuna salad.

Ravensworth Marsanne

Quality	♟♟♟♟
Value	★★★★
Rating	94
Grapes	marsanne; viognier
Region	Canberra district, NSW
Cellar	▮ 5
Alc./Vol.	13.5%
RRP	$20.00 ➽

Bryan Martin is an adventurous soul who's planted a few left-field grape varieties in his Canberra-district vineyard, and marsanne is one of them. Inspired by the success of other Rhône varieties in the region, particularly viognier, Martin has shown that marsanne can work well too. **CURRENT RELEASE 2005   This is one of the most aromatically powerful Australian marsannes we've ever had. It surprised us a lot, until we discovered that it had 10 per cent viognier blended in. The viognier certainly shows in the pot-pourri of floral and spicy scents that leap out of the glass, and some more subtle lemon, nutty and leesy notes give it real complexity. A thread of oak doesn't intrude and it has a smooth, long palate that finishes dry and aromatic. Serve it with feta pastries.**

Tahbilk 1927 Vines Marsanne

At Tahbilk they have one of the most significant, and oldest, plantings of marsanne in the world. This wine, made entirely from a 79-year-old block, shows marsanne's legendary ageing ability well.
CURRENT RELEASE 1998   A brilliant flashing gold colour shows age here, and the nose has the richly honeyed, toasty aromas of maturity. There's a distinctive lime marmalade and honey sort of flavour that's very seductive, the palate is smoothly textured, and it has a very long, toasty aftertaste. A delicious example of what marsanne is capable of. Enjoy it with lemon grass and chilli chicken.

Quality	♟ ♟ ♟ ♟ ♟
Value	★ ★ ★ ★
Rating	96
Grapes	marsanne
Region	Nagambie Lakes, Vic.
Cellar	▮ 5
Alc./Vol.	13.0%
RRP	$33.00

Tahbilk Marsanne

One of Australia's true classics, Tahbilk Marsanne has taken a step up recently with the release of the '98 vintage 1927 Vines special, although older vintages have occasionally been available in the past. This standard wine retains its quality and its price makes it a bargain.
CURRENT RELEASE 2005   A bright young marsanne with an attractive, clean aroma of lightly honeyed pear-like fruit with a floral touch. The palate is smooth and tasty with ripe citrus fruit and a hint of almond. It finishes dry and firm and should age well. Serve it with mildly spiced Indian vegetable fritters.

Quality	♟ ♟ ♟ ♟
Value	★ ★ ★ ★ ⟩
Rating	91
Grapes	marsanne
Region	Nagambie Lakes, Vic.
Cellar	▮ 6
Alc./Vol.	13.5%
RRP	$14.90 ⏚

Turkey Flat Butchers Block Marsanne Viognier

Marsanne and viognier blends aren't common in the Barossa, but this example shows that they work well. By the way, the name of this wine comes from the old 1860s butcher's block now in the Turkey Flat cellar-door sales area. It was used by Ernst Schulz, the local butcher who was present winemaker Peter Schulz's great-grandfather.
CURRENT RELEASE 2004   A deliciously aromatic wine with a complex nose that suggests pears, apricots and peaches. There's also some spice and a thread of old oak. The palate is rich, full-bodied and deeply flavoured with a long, aromatic, apricot-scented finish. A big white for substantial food. Try it with apricot-stuffed roast pork.

Quality	♟ ♟ ♟ ♟ ♟
Value	★ ★ ★ ⟩
Rating	93
Grapes	marsanne; viognier
Region	Barossa Valley, SA
Cellar	▮ 2
Alc./Vol.	14.2%
RRP	$23.00 ⏚

Pinot gris and pinot grigio

There are two broad style groups with this grape: the rich, spicy, high-alcohol Alsace pinot gris style and the earlier-harvested, lower-alcohol, more delicate Italian pinot grigio style. The Alsace style is often slightly sweet and balance becomes a debating point. The Italian style is often the more approachable, with better drinkability and food compatibility. We like both, when they're well done! Australia has embraced this grape with gusto and so have our export markets. While many examples tend towards weak and bland, some have real character and individuality. We consider a faint pink colouring acceptable, as long as it's not the result of oxidation but because of the grape's skin colour.

Bay of Fires Pinot Gris

Quality	♟ ♟ ♟ ♟
Value	★ ★ ★
Rating	91
Grapes	pinot gris
Region	northern Tas.
Cellar	🍾 3
Alc./Vol.	14.0%
RRP	$27.00 🥂

Bay of Fires is Hardys' Tasmanian outpost. The wines are improving all the time under the savvy winemaking of Fran Austin. Chardonnay and riesling are usually the stand-out whites, but the pinot gris is also worth seeking.
CURRENT RELEASE 2005   Notes of pear, spices and nutty touches make a savoury melange on the nose, and the palate has a creamy-smooth feel that's well balanced by fresh cool-climate acidity. It avoids the coarseness that blights so many Aussie pinot gris wines, and it finishes clean and dry. Serve it with buttery scallop brochettes.

Blue Metal Pinot Gris Sauvignon Blanc

Quality	♟ ♟ ♟ ♟
Value	★ ★ ★
Rating	88
Grapes	pinot gris 70%; sauvignon blanc 30%
Region	Southern Highlands, NSW
Cellar	🍾 1
Alc./Vol.	13.5%
RRP	$24.00 🥂

The Blue Metal vineyard is at 790 metres altitude, at Berrima, which is one of those highland towns you used to drive through when travelling on the Hume Highway, but the new freeway bypasses.
CURRENT RELEASE 2005   It's an unusual marriage, but if the wine is improved by blending, why not? The colour has the classic pinot gris copper tinge, and the aromas are also typical of PG, reminding us of spices and pot-pourri, while the palate has good depth of flavour and balance. It has better concentration than many of its kind. It would suit Spanish tapas.

Cheviot Bridge CB Pinot Grigio

Cheviot Bridge likes to describe itself as a virtual wine company, because it doesn't have a winery or vineyards. In fact, various executives do own vineyards, and associated companies do own at least two wineries we can think of (Terrace Vale and Kirrihill), but for the company's many products, the out-sourcing concept holds true.
CURRENT RELEASE 2004   The colour is slightly brassy, which is not unusual for PG, and the main aromas are of green apples with some oak sidelights. It's a light-bodied, simple, fresh wine with a lip-smacking tang and a nice clean, dry finish that ensures it will go with food. We suggest fried calamari.

Quality	♟ ♟ ♟
Value	★★★★
Rating	87
Grapes	pinot grigio
Region	Adelaide Hills, SA
Cellar	▮ 1
Alc./Vol.	12.5%
RRP	$14.00 ⑤ ☕

Chrismont La Zona Pinot Grigio

Chrismont is the vineyard of Arnie Pizzini and family, not to be confused with Alfred Pizzini and his family, who own Pizzini wines at Whitfield. Both are in the upper King Valley.
CURRENT RELEASE 2005   This is very much the easy-drinking, Italian kind of PG, not rich and spicy nor heady and opulent, as it can be. The colour is fairly pale, the aromas are delicately spiced and fragrant; the taste grapey and soft, with a tickle of sweetness; not especially complex but it slips down nicely. Even better with antipasti.

Quality	♟ ♟ ♟ ♟
Value	★★★⸣
Rating	88
Grapes	pinot grigio
Region	King Valley, Vic.
Cellar	▮ 2
Alc./Vol.	13.5%
RRP	$22.00 ☕

Clyde Park Pinot Gris

It is interesting to ponder the varietal character of pinot gris. It doesn't usually have a strong personality. We see a common thread of dried flower petals that is reminiscent of pot-pourri. Others describe it as dishwater, and, for the less successful ones, we can see what that means! Happily, this one falls into the former camp.
CURRENT RELEASE 2005   The colour is pale with a slightly brassy tinge and the bouquet is a riot of dried wildflowers and dried herbs. It's light and fruity in the mouth and lifted by jazzy acidity, giving it a citrusy aftertaste. Indeed, the juxtaposition of high acid with a little sweetness gives a very tangy taste. It needs food, and we'd suggest Thai fish cakes with a light dab of chilli sauce.

Quality	♟ ♟ ♟
Value	★★★
Rating	87
Grapes	pinot gris
Region	Geelong, Vic.
Cellar	▮ 1
Alc./Vol.	14.0%
RRP	$22.00 ☕

Coldstone Pinot Grigio

Quality	♟ ♟ ♟
Value	★ ★ ★ ↓
Rating	86
Grapes	pinot grigio
Region	Victoria
Cellar	⬤ 1
Alc./Vol.	13.0%
RRP	$13.00 ⬷

Yep, it's yet another new brand from the Victorian Alps Winery in Victoria's Ovens Valley. They also make Tobacco Road and Gapsted wines.
CURRENT RELEASE 2005   A delicate, shy, restrained pinot grigio at a very attractive price. It's quite aromatic – powder-puff and musk-stick perfumes waft from the tasting glass. In the mouth, it's light, simple and fairly shy, while the mouth-feel is good. It's rounded, soft and well balanced – albeit with modest length. You could serve it with KFC.

Holly's Garden Pinot Gris

Quality	♟ ♟ ♟ ♟
Value	★ ★ ★
Rating	92
Grapes	pinot gris
Region	Upper Goulburn, Vic.
Cellar	⬤ 2
Alc./Vol.	14.5%
RRP	$25.00 ⬷

Neil Prentice has a long history in the Melbourne food and wine scene, with years of experience in restaurants and bars, and a keen enthusiasm for the life of a vigneron. His Whitlands vineyard was planted in the cool Victorian highlands in the 1990s. Holly is his youngest daughter, whose enchanting pictures of flowers adorn the labels.
CURRENT RELEASE 2005   A rich pinot gris with a high-toned nose of spices, minerals, pear-like fruit and whiffs of creamy-lees and earthy wild-ferment influence. The palate is lush with ripe fruit, silky textured and long in flavour with tangy, natural acid keeping it lively. The palate has attractive softness rather than the phenolic harshness that marks so many other Australian pinot gris wines. Serve it with grilled weisswurst, apples and red cabbage.

Innocent Bystander Pinot Gris

Quality	♟ ♟ ♟ ♟
Value	★ ★ ★
Rating	88
Grapes	pinot gris
Region	Yarra & Alpine valleys, Strathbogie Ranges, Vic.
Cellar	⬤ 1+
Alc./Vol.	13.8%
RRP	$20.00 ⑤ ⬷

Why the name? It's a good question. There is no connection with cartoonist Michael Leunig. Owner Phil Sexton says he often feels like an innocent bystander (remember the confused little figure by Leunig?) when he considers the immensity of the big wine companies and the difficulty for small companies competing.
CURRENT RELEASE 2005   The screw-cap has trapped some reductive aromas in the wine, but the palate is where this one really counts. It has very good flavour, with a spicy, honeyed taste of good varietal integrity and balance. It's an appealing wine with real depth and length of palate, which puts it ahead of most PGs. Try it with an antipasto platter.

Logan Weemala Pinot Gris

Weemala is the brand name of Peter Logan's lower-priced range of wines. They often punch above their weight in the value-for-money stakes. Maker: Peter Logan.

CURRENT RELEASE 2005   This is an excellent PG style: bright and fragrant, intense and spicy with some cured meadow-hay and peachy aromas, underlined by a touch of spice. The palate is rich and deep, but not over-the-top. It's technically A1 and very stylish, with good varietal character and a long, clean, dry aftertaste. It would suit stuffed zucchini flowers.

Quality	♀ ♀ ♀ ♀
Value	★ ★ ★ ★ ⁾
Rating	90
Grapes	pinot gris
Region	Orange, NSW
Cellar	🍷 3
Alc./Vol.	14.0%
RRP	$15.50 ⱬ

Maestro Tasmania Pinot Grigio

This is another label of Sydneysider Robin Tedder, whose main act is the Glenguin vineyard in the Hunter Valley. We reckon Tasmania probably has greater potential for this grape variety than most other places in Australia. Just give 'em time.

CURRENT RELEASE 2005   It's a very attractive, delicate style of PG and should appeal to a broad audience. The aromas are straw-like and faintly spicy with traces of honey, while the palate weight is light but not without intensity. We like the subtlety of it, and the refinement of its texture. A pristine grigio that would drink well alongside tapas or antipasto.

Quality	♀ ♀ ♀ ⸴
Value	★ ★ ★
Rating	88
Grapes	pinot grigio
Region	Launceston, Tas.
Cellar	🍷 2+
Alc./Vol.	13.5%
RRP	$25.00 ⱬ

McVitty Grove Black Label Pinot Gris

This producer has a vineyard, olive grove and cellar door/restaurant in a picturesque setting in the Southern Highlands near Mittagong. The wines are contract-made nearby. The back-label notes suggest a little oak may have been used.

CURRENT RELEASE 2005   The colour is slightly pink from the skins, and this spicy dry white shows toasty oak and a slightly beery aroma, probably from yeast-lees contact. There's a lot happening here, but the oak tends to be a little obvious at this stage. There's some richness to the dry, savoury palate but the wine retains lightness and balance. It's a good drink, and would go with fried calamari.

Quality	♀ ♀ ♀ ⸴
Value	★ ★ ★
Rating	89
Grapes	pinot gris
Region	Southern Highlands, NSW
Cellar	🍷 1+
Alc./Vol.	13.1%
RRP	$24.00 ⱬ

McVitty Grove Silver Label Pinot Gris

Quality	♥ ♥ ♥
Value	★ ★ ★
Rating	87
Grapes	pinot gris
Region	Southern Highlands, NSW
Cellar	▮ 1+
Alc./Vol.	13.1%
RRP	$18.00 🍾

The back label says the grapes were hand-picked from a single block of low-cropping vines – presumably on the McVitty Grove vineyard near Mittagong.
CURRENT RELEASE 2005   This is a very similar wine to the black-label bottling, except that it shows a little sweetness and less oak. It has a pale-copper hue and some leesy yeast aromas, a touch of spice, and rich fruit flavours in the mouth, enhanced by a trace of sweetness. It could be served with bruschetta.

Miceli Iolanda Pinot Grigio

Quality	♥ ♥ ♥ ♥ ♥
Value	★ ★ ★ ★
Rating	93
Grapes	pinot grigio
Region	Mornington Peninsula, Vic.
Cellar	▮ 2
Alc./Vol.	13.5%
RRP	$25.00 🍾

Miceli not only make consistently one of the best PGs in Australia, they release it a year older, which certainly does it no harm and may even lend it an extra degree of character. Winemaker in this small, family business is GP, Dr Anthony Miceli.
CURRENT RELEASE 2005   A remarkably fine wine and further proof that the Peninsula is a happy hunting ground for this grape. It has a spicy, Alsace-like bouquet that almost reminds of gewürztraminer in its exotic character and puissance. Dried flowers, honey and figs continue throughout the wine and we suspect some European winemaking practices have been employed. It's rich and round in the mouth, with glycerol that adds opulence and texture. Clean acidity on the finish: lovely balance and length. It would go with washed-rind cheeses.

Mornington Estate Pinot Gris

Quality	♥ ♥ ♥ ♥
Value	★ ★ ★
Rating	88
Grapes	pinot gris
Region	Mornington Peninsula & King Valley, Vic.
Cellar	▮ 1
Alc./Vol.	13.5%
RRP	$20.00 🍾

Mornington Estate is one of the Dromana Estate brands, along with Yarra Valley Hills and Dromana Estate itself. Winemaker is Rollo Crittenden, son of the redoubtable Garry Crittenden.
CURRENT RELEASE 2005   A very typical gris, which smells of pot-pourri and is soft and light on the tongue, with an ameliorating trace of sweetness. It's a good commercial style, sort of halfway between gris and grigio in style, and the finish is clean and dry with a little thickness from phenolics. It would drink nicely with pasta with peas, bacon and cream.

Ninth Island Pinot Grigio

Pinot gris and pinot grigio are one and the same grape variety. The difference lies in the type of wine the winemaker is attempting. Grigio is usually reserved for lighter, drier, more Italian-accented wines, gris is used on richer, fuller and sometimes sweeter efforts, inspired by the wines of Alsace.

CURRENT RELEASE 2005 Good varietal character here, and it's not as assertively coarse as many in the ever-expanding range of pinot gris/grigio wines we taste. The nose has musky aromas of fresh-cut pear and apple, maybe a hint of banana, and the palate shows good depth and body with a bite of phenolic firmness at the end. It's undoubtedly a food wine rather than a casual sipper, and tastes at home alongside scallops and richer seafoods.

Quality	🍷🍷🍷🍷
Value	★★★
Rating	**90**
Grapes	pinot grigio
Region	northern Tas.
Cellar	2
Alc./Vol.	13.5%
RRP	$21.50

Norfolk Rise Pinot Grigio

Is pinot gris/grigio the most overrated white grape variety in Australia? We think it may be, yet the PGs just keep comin'. Fortunately some makers are creating very good wines with it.

CURRENT RELEASE 2005 A fairly pale-coloured pinot grigio with an attractive nose of spicy pear and banana-like fruit that's quite rich. Hints of minerals and nuts add dimension. The palate has attractively rich flavour with good depth and persistence, finishing with a savoury-dry aftertaste. One of the better PGs around, and the pricing is, too. Try it with caramelised onion tart.

Quality	🍷🍷🍷🍷
Value	★★★★
Rating	**90**
Grapes	pinot grigio
Region	Mount Benson, SA
Cellar	2
Alc./Vol.	13.0%
RRP	$16.55

Punt Road Pinot Gris

Almost submerged in the oceans of awful pinot gris/grigio flooding out of Australian wineries there are some real gems, and this is one of them. Made in the Alsace style, it exhibits true varietal personality without any ugly traits. Maker: Kate Goodman.

CURRENT RELEASE 2005 This has an exotic, musky nose that suggests honey, pears and florist shops, while a whisper of oak adds savoury dimension. It tastes deliciously rich, but not heavy-handed, and the texture is lush and mouth-filling. It shows attractive complexity, and leaves the palate with a long, soft, pear-fragrant finish. Serve it with rich cheeses.

Quality	🍷🍷🍷🍷½
Value	★★★★
Rating	**93**
Grapes	pinot gris
Region	Yarra Valley, Vic.
Cellar	2
Alc./Vol.	13.5%
RRP	$19.00

Scorpo Pinot Gris

Quality	♥♥♥♥
Value	★★★⌐
Rating	91
Grapes	pinot gris
Region	Mornington Peninsula, Vic.
Cellar	▮2
Alc./Vol.	14.0%
RRP	$30.00 ⑤

Sandro Mosele of Kooyong winery is an active contract winemaker and also a great believer in Diam technical corks. He makes Scorpo, Marinda Park, Port Phillip Estate and Murray Darling Collection wines, as well as Kooyong, and all are sealed with Diam.

CURRENT RELEASE 2005 The colour is very bright and youthful; the aromas clean, subtle and fruity with some almost gewurz-like spice as well as savoury/grapey aromas. It became spicier the longer it sat in the glass. There is a whisper of oak adding a subtle extra dimension. The texture is lovely: smooth and refined without obvious sweetness or acid sharpness. It would suit antipasto.

Seppelt Coborra Pinot Gris

Quality	♥♥♥
Value	★★⌐
Rating	86
Grapes	pinot gris
Region	Henty, Vic.
Cellar	▬1–3+
Alc./Vol.	13.5%
RRP	$30.00 ⑤ ⟆

Like several of the white wines in the Seppelt portfolio these days, this one declares in fine print that the grapes came from the Drumborg Vineyard. That's down in south-western Victoria near the coastal town of Portland.

CURRENT RELEASE 2005 Drumborg is a very cool vineyard and this is a tight, ungiving wine in its youth. It may have been released too soon, in which case it will benefit from short-term cellaring. The colour is pale; the aromas are cedary, twiggy and musky/lolly-ish. The palate is a little hollow and the finish a trifle short. If you drink it young, give it plenty of air first, and don't over-chill. Serve it with any white-fleshed fish.

Shadowfax Pinot Gris

Quality	♥♥♥
Value	★★★
Rating	86
Grapes	pinot gris
Region	Adelaide Hills, SA
Cellar	▮1
Alc./Vol.	13.5%
RRP	$24.00 ⟆

Shadowfax was a noble steed, ridden by Gandalf in *Lord of the Rings*. What's that got to do with wine? Nothing, except that fantasy is often identified with wine, and there's nothing wrong with that. We can think of a wine named after another mythical horse, Pegasus . . .

CURRENT RELEASE 2005 This is a pretty straightforward, *comme-il-faut* PG, with a touch of sweetness and some herbal, grassy aromas. It has a little phenolic grip and while it's not a wine of finesse, it does have weight and depth of flavour. It would go with an entrée of pan-fried sardines.

Simon Gilbert Pinot Grigio

This fruit came from the New South Wales zone called Central Ranges. That means it could be from any of the Mudgee, Orange or Cowra regions. Winemaker these days is Andrew Ewart, formerly of Mountadam.
CURRENT RELEASE 2005   The colour is typically pale with a tinge of grey, and the straw-like, faintly earthy aromas are typical of the earlier-harvested style of PG. It's light and lean, with fairly assertive acidity, while the fruit flavour is quite restrained. It's at the savoury/dry rather than fruity end of the spectrum. Try it with grilled sardines.

Quality	♚ ♚ ♚
Value	★★★
Rating	86
Grapes	pinot gris
Region	Central Ranges, NSW
Cellar	▮ 2
Alc./Vol.	13.0%
RRP	$15.00 ⬧

T'Gallant Imogen Pinot Gris

T'Gallant's Kathleen Quealy and Kevin McCarthy have been the greatest champions of pinot gris on the Mornington Peninsula, and have encouraged a large number of other vineyards to plant it. We aren't as convinced of the variety's virtues in the region as they are, but we must agree that some good wines have appeared.
CURRENT RELEASE 2005   Pale-straw in colour, this young PG shows attractive pear and banana varietal aromas with a creamy overtone and a sea-breezy tang. It's smooth in the mouth with ripe flavour and good mid-palate balance, but some alcoholic heat tends to dominate the finish. That said, it works very well with richly sauced scallop dishes.

Quality	♚ ♚ ♚ ♚
Value	★★★
Rating	91
Grapes	pinot gris
Region	Mornington Peninsula, Vic.
Cellar	▮ 2
Alc./Vol.	14.5%
RRP	$19.85 ⬧

Riesling

Riesling was once *the* prestige Australian white wine grape, until chardonnay arrived in the 1970s and became a formidable adversary. At the same time riesling suffered an identity crisis – some became sweeter, which confused everybody, and the word 'riesling' was misused more than ever to denote just about any cheap dry-ish white wine. Riesling's popularity fell with the consumer-friendly result that it became just about the best buy around. And unlike most chardonnay, there's no hurry to drink it; riesling ages superbly. Price tags are starting to climb, but we reckon that many Australian rieslings remain seriously undervalued, a great thing for all of us.

All Saints Estate Riesling

Quality	♀ ♀ ♀
Value	★ ★ ★
Rating	84
Grapes	riesling
Region	Rutherglen, Vic.
Cellar	▮ 3
Alc./Vol.	11.8%
RRP	$17.50 ⬧

Some of the Rutherglen wineries are making riesling these days from grapes grown in higher, cooler altitudes because the finesse and varietal purity is better. This one has no information, so we have to assume the fruit was from the Wahgunyah home vineyard.
CURRENT RELEASE 2005   The colour is a proper, light-yellow hue and it has a pronounced tropical-fruit aroma, perhaps due to some skin contact? There are spicy nuances, too. In the mouth, it's very light and somewhat vapid, the finish disturbed by some harsh acid. It's short and lacks fruit concentration, but is a perfectly acceptable light, quaffing, dry white wine with food. We'd recommend crab cakes.

Annie's Lane Riesling

Quality	♀ ♀ ♀
Value	★ ★ ★
Rating	86
Grapes	riesling
Region	Clare Valley, SA
Cellar	▮ 2
Alc./Vol.	12.0%
RRP	$18.00 ⑤ ⬧

The Annie's Lane wines are pretty reliable for value and quality, although the riesling is made in a decidedly up-front style that we would not recommend for cellaring. Maker: Wendy Stuckey and team.
CURRENT RELEASE 2005   The colour is slightly forward in development and it has a peculiar herbal aroma that recalls chopped basil or perhaps tarragon. It's quite full in the mouth – which tallies with the forward colour – but also has fairly tart acidity. We suggest pairing it with Thai fish cakes, but careful with the chilli sauce!

Barwite Riesling

The Barwite vineyard was planted in 1998 in the cool Victorian High Country. Delicate riesling is the aim here, and to that end the fruit is harvested in the cool of night and then fermented with a slow-acting German yeast strain.

CURRENT RELEASE 2004   This delicious Victorian riesling was a real find for us a vintage or two ago. It's a satisfying style, direct and honest in its appeal. The nose has a minerally/steely backbone to lime-cordial-like fruit. It's well concentrated and genuinely varietal with a vaguely herby European accent. In the mouth it's clean, savoury and balanced, with good mouth-feel and fine flavour, ahead of a delicate finish. Enjoy it with a medium-spiced prawn curry.

Quality	♥♥♥♥♥
Value	★★★★⧽
Rating	93
Grapes	riesling
Region	upper Goulburn Valley, Vic.
Cellar	🍾 3
Alc./Vol.	11.5%
RRP	$14.60 ⧽

Bay of Fires Riesling

The number of good rieslings coming from northern Tasmania is increasing all the time. Bay of Fires has been around for a few vintages now, and it's already one of the best.

CURRENT RELEASE 2005   Classical fine-boned Tasmanian riesling aromas here: floral, limey, quite delicate, yet with a quiet underlying strength. The palate has soft fruit mid-palate with a light mineral touch, leading through to zesty acidity on the finish. Serve it with delicate seafoods.

Quality	♥♥♥♥♥
Value	★★★
Rating	93
Grapes	riesling
Region	northern Tas.
Cellar	🍾 5
Alc./Vol.	12.5%
RRP	$27.00 ⧽

Bellarmine Dry Riesling

Bellarmine's Mike Bewsher makes two rieslings each year: a medium-sweet style modelled on Germany's Mosel Valley kabinetts, labelled simply 'riesling', and a dry version, without residual sugar, labelled 'dry riesling'. Ideally, the dry version should be labelled just 'riesling' and the sweeter one should have some sweetness designation to alert potential buyers to what would come as an unexpected taste.

CURRENT RELEASE 2005   Why isn't there more riesling in Pemberton? This is a cracker. Like most Bellarmine wines, the style is delicate, restrained and pristine. The limey/lemony fruit is smooth and pure, refined and beautifully balanced with a dry yet soft finish. A great fish wine, try it with mixed sashimi.

Quality	♥♥♥♥♥
Value	★★★★★
Rating	94
Grapes	riesling
Region	Pemberton, WA
Cellar	🍾 5+
Alc./Vol.	13.1%
RRP	$15.00 ⧽ (cellar door)

Bellarmine Riesling

Quality	♟ ♟ ♟ ♟
Value	★★★★★
Rating	90
Grapes	riesling
Region	Pemberton, WA
Cellar	🍶 4+
Alc./Vol.	12.8%
RRP	$15.00 ⬛
	(cellar door)

This is the sweeter of the two Bellarmine rieslings (see previous review's comments). When we taste a wine as good as this, we wonder why more Australian rieslings are not sweeter, especially the high-acid, cool-climate ones.
CURRENT RELEASE 2005   This is a good attempt at a German-style riesling of around kabinett sweetness level. It has youthfully estery, spicy aromatics and the tingling cool-climate balance of fruit, acid and sugar is nicely done. The finish is very clean and harmonious. It could suit a mild fish curry.

Bloodwood Riesling

Quality	♟ ♟ ♟ ♟
Value	★★★★
Rating	89
Grapes	riesling
Region	Orange, NSW
Cellar	🍶 5+
Alc./Vol.	12.0%
RRP	$18.00 ⬛
	(cellar door)

The Doyles of Bloodwood are famous for their food as well as their wine, and those who've been lucky enough to be entertained at the cellar-door kitchen rave about the experience – Rhonda's cooking as well as Stephen's unique way with words.
CURRENT RELEASE 2005   This is a richer, more powerful riesling with a lot of depth and spicy – even peppery – flavour. It's still a baby and needs time. The palate is very dry and it seems destined to reward cellaring. It would go well with food, especially grilled garfish.

Capel Vale Riesling

Quality	♟ ♟ ♟
Value	★★★
Rating	87
Grapes	riesling
Region	Mount Barker, WA
Cellar	🍶 4+
Alc./Vol.	12.0%
RRP	$18.00 ⬛

Capel Vale is a big grower of grapes these days, with 220 hectares of vines, spread over four regions (Pemberton, Margaret River, Great Southern and its home base, Geographe). Winemaker until this year was Rebecca Catlin.
CURRENT RELEASE 2004   Mineral and smoky aromas greet the nose, partly from a touch of reduction. There is a sappy/stemmy quality to the fruit as well. At two years, it has a nice bright, light-yellow colour and seems to be ageing gracefully, although the finish is a trifle hollow. It's a slightly oddball wine but makes a decent drink. It goes with tuna tataki.

Cascabel Riesling

Cascabel is a small winery in McLaren Vale specialising in Spanish grape varieties and Spanish-style wines. One of the partners, Susanna Fernandez, is Spanish.
CURRENT RELEASE 2005   Nothing Spanish about riesling, though. This is a straightforward Eden Valley style with a shy aroma and soft, dry, slightly broad palate considering its young age. Dry-straw aromas, delicate floral hints, and a fairly full, ripe palate round out the picture. It tastes as though there's more than 12.5 per cent alcohol. Serve with braised calamari.

Quality	♥♥♥♥
Value	★★★
Rating	89
Grapes	riesling
Region	Eden Valley, SA
Cellar	▮ 4
Alc./Vol.	12.5%
RRP	$23.00 ⬢

Centennial Vineyards Woodside Riesling

This impressive property at Bowral was established by a veteran of the liquor industry, John Large, who started planting vines in the late 1990s. He was a founder of both Liquorland and Cellarmasters.
CURRENT RELEASE 2005   This is a very tight, steely, shy riesling that appears to be developing very slowly. There's a bit of free sulphur that needs time to combine; the palate is dry and delicate, light-bodied and nervy. It could use a bit more fruit. As a youngster, it needs food: try it with any white-fleshed fish.

Quality	♥♥♥
Value	★★★
Rating	86
Grapes	riesling
Region	Southern Highlands, NSW
Cellar	⬢ 1–5
Alc./Vol.	11.5%
RRP	$19.00 ⬢ (cellar door)

Chrismont Riesling

Although the King Valley is perhaps best known these days for its terrific Italian varietals, riesling does very well too. Arnie and Jo Pizzini have produced excellent riesling for some years.
CURRENT RELEASE 2005   An aromatic pale riesling with fresh, fruity aromas of pear, lime and blossom. The palate is light and dry with a juicy middle that's very appealing, ahead of a tangy, powdery-dry signature. Good with fresh river fish.

Quality	♥♥♥♥
Value	★★★★⭑
Rating	91
Grapes	riesling
Region	King Valley, Vic.
Cellar	▮ 4
Alc./Vol.	12.5%
RRP	$14.00 ⬢

Clairault Estate Riesling

Quality	♟ ♟ ♟ ♟
Value	★★★★
Rating	90
Grapes	riesling
Region	Margaret River, WA
Cellar	▮ 5+
Alc./Vol.	12.0%
RRP	$21.50 ➘

The former Cape Clairault is one of the older vineyards in the region, having been started by Ian and Ani Lewis in the mid-1970s. The new owners, the Martin family, have expanded the vineyard as well as modified the name.
CURRENT RELEASE 2005   For a Margaret River riesling this is remarkably austere and restrained. It's pale in colour and very shy and reserved on nose and palate, with a tight, minerally aroma. It is a fairly ungiving wine at the moment but is much better with food than without; food releases the flavour and richness in the wine. It also promises to age well. Try it with oysters.

Cockfighter's Ghost Riesling

Quality	♟ ♟ ♟
Value	★★★
Rating	86
Grapes	riesling
Region	Clare Valley, SA
Cellar	▮ 5+
Alc./Vol.	12.7%
RRP	$23.00 ➘

Cockfighter's Ghost is one of the brands of David Clarke's Pooles Rock outfit, which takes grapes from various regions that suit the grape variety in question. Its home base is in the Hunter, where Patrick Auld is winemaker.
CURRENT RELEASE 2005   This is a shy, retiring style of riesling with a fine apple-blossom aroma and hints of green apple and fresh herbs. It's slightly yeasty and there's a trace of phenolics on the palate. It will be a better wine when time in the bottle has filled it out a little. We'd suggest pairing it with cold roast pork and apple sauce.

Cookoothama Riesling

Quality	♟ ♟ ♟ ♟
Value	★★★★
Rating	88
Grapes	riesling
Region	King Valley, Vic.
Cellar	▮ 3
Alc./Vol.	12.5%
RRP	$17.00 Ⓢ ➘

Cookoothama is one of several brands from the Nugan family of Griffith, orange juice barons, who have risen to become one of the largest grapegrowers and winemakers in the country in quick time. Maker: Daren Owers.
CURRENT RELEASE 2005   A flavoursome and slightly broad riesling with a lot going for it. The aromas recall lemon pith and green herbs such as parsley. The palate is soft and has some fullness and roundness to it. The finish is clean and dry and carries quite firm acidity. It's a good wine and well priced. Try it with stuffed zucchini flowers.

Crabtree Watervale Riesling

Robert Crabtree has seldom been outside the first rank of riesling producers in the Clare Valley. This is a single-vineyard Watervale wine and since the advent of the screw-cap the wine presents better than ever.
CURRENT RELEASE 2005 The nose is shy: delicate lime juice and minerals; the palate is intense and crisp, lively and zesty with a clean, dry, lingering finish. There are traces of bread-dough as well as the stony/pebbly minerality that can make riesling such an exciting wine. It would suit snapper quenelles.

Quality	♟♟♟♟
Value	★★★★᠍
Rating	90
Grapes	riesling
Region	Clare Valley, SA
Cellar	▮6+
Alc./Vol.	12.5%
RRP	$19.00 ⧉

De Bortoli Gulf Station Riesling

The De Bortoli Yarra Valley property was originally part of Gulf Station, a large nineteenth-century pastoral property, hence the name.
CURRENT RELEASE 2006 This opens up with a whiff of sulphur, not an uncommon thing in young riesling, but there's generous fruit character underneath that volcanic edge. It's more at the tropical fruit end of the riesling spectrum, but there's a thread of citrus too. The palate is quite full with rich mid-palate flavour and a dry finish. It probably won't be a very-long-liver like some rieslings, but still worth a couple of years' age. Serve it with a seafood stirfry.

Quality	♟♟♟♟
Value	★★★
Rating	90
Grapes	riesling
Region	Yarra Valley, Vic.
Cellar	▮3
Alc./Vol.	13.0%
RRP	$18.00 Ⓢ ⧉

De Bortoli Sacred Hill Riesling

De Bortoli's Sacred Hill reds get a lot of accolades, and the whites share the same formula of generous style and incredibly low price.
CURRENT RELEASE 2005 The green–yellow colour of this budget-priced riesling shows a wee bit of development, at least in our sample, and the nose is a bit broad and developed too – it all adds up to a rather old-fashioned style. That said, it smells varietally correct with punchy citrus, rock-candy, spice and stone-fruit aromas, and the palate has attractive richness, depth and persistence. Unlike most young rieslings we encounter, it's sealed with a cork, and we wonder whether this has anything to do with its slightly advanced state. Whatever; it remains a great-value white to take along to your local Thai BYO.

Quality	♟♟♟᠍
Value	★★★★᠍
Rating	88
Grapes	riesling
Region	not stated
Cellar	▮1
Alc./Vol.	12.0%
RRP	$7.00 Ⓢ

Don't Tell Dad Murrindindi Riesling

Quality	🍷🍷🍷🍷🍷
Value	★★★★
Rating	93
Grapes	riesling
Region	Yea Valley, Vic.
Cellar	🍾 5
Alc./Vol.	12.5%
RRP	$18.00 🍷

Don't Tell Dad is a new label from the Cuthbertson family's Yea Valley vineyards. They didn't tell Alan Cuthbertson, their Dad, that they were planning this reasonably priced range of table wines.
CURRENT RELEASE 2005   A surprisingly full riesling to come from a cool region, this already shows some complexity despite its obvious youth and freshness. The nose is pungently aromatic, smelling of minerals, lime peel, flowers and a hint of Germanic spice. It shows good depth and richness in the mouth and the varietal flavours are ripe yet with an austere, smoky undercurrent. Serve it with barbecued prawns.

Elderton Friends Riesling

Quality	🍷🍷🍷🍷
Value	★★★★⁴
Rating	92
Grapes	riesling
Region	Eden Valley, SA
Cellar	🍾 5+
Alc./Vol.	12.5%
RRP	$18.00 🍷

The Friends brand appears on a cheaper range of Elderton wines that are made from bought-in grapes. This seems to suggest the Ashmead family has a very amicable relationship with its growers. Maker: Richard Langford.
CURRENT RELEASE 2005   This is a delicious riesling and well priced to boot. It's floral, slightly bread-doughy in its youth, with dried-flower aromas and hints of apricot and honey. There's a steely quality about the palate, good concentration and persistence, and almost a hint of botrytis, which is nothing to be concerned about. It would suit fish in a creamy sauce.

Frankland Estate Cooladerra Riesling

Quality	🍷🍷🍷🍷
Value	★★★
Rating	91
Grapes	riesling
Region	Frankland River, WA
Cellar	🍾 5
Alc./Vol.	13.0%
RRP	$24.00 🍷

Frankland Estate has become a leader of the Australian riesling revival in recent years, promoting this outstanding grape variety all over the country, and producing some fascinating wines from their own vineyards in the south of Western Australia.
CURRENT RELEASE 2005   A fine line of lime-like fruit characterises this tangy young riesling. An earthy, minerally thread adds interest and will probably turn into rich, European-style complexity with age. There's also a slightly sulphidey touch to it that will probably build into another complexing element in time. The palate is tightly built with zesty acidity, and the palate has a long floral aftertaste. Drink it with yabbies.

Frankland Estate Isolation Ridge Riesling

Isolation Ridge was the first of Frankland Estate's individual vineyard rieslings. It was one of the pioneering wines from the Frankland River region to show riesling's suitability to the area.

CURRENT RELEASE 2005   Isolation Ridge often has a little more to it than the pristine standard type of Australian riesling. The '05 is a very minerally/slatey type with dry, spicy stone-fruit and citrus aromas that lead through a concentrated, full-bodied palate of tangy flavours that track the nose accurately. The palate has great aromatic length, and a framework of finely tuned, tart acidity gives mouth-watering succulence. It needs bottle-age, then serve it with Thai marinated and grilled chicken.

Quality	♟♟♟♟♟
Value	★★★★
Rating	94
Grapes	riesling
Region	Frankland River, WA
Cellar	▮ 8
Alc./Vol.	13.5%
RRP	$24.00 ⮀

Frankland Estate Poison Hill Riesling

Poison Hill is an unfortunate name for a vineyard but we can assure you that after drinking it we've never felt better. The name comes from a plant that once grew there that was poisonous to passing sheep.

CURRENT RELEASE 2005   The 'prettiest' riesling of the Frankland Estate individual vineyard trio with a floral delicacy to it that's very charming. Nectarine and lime-like fruit are at the core, and a strongly spicy touch reminiscent of cinnamon runs through it. The palate finishes dry and firm with a long spicy end that's quite exotic. Pair it with a gingery Chinese seafood dish.

Quality	♟♟♟♟♟
Value	★★★↘
Rating	92
Grapes	riesling
Region	Frankland River, WA
Cellar	▮ 8
Alc./Vol.	13.0%
RRP	$24.00 ⮀

Garden Gully Riesling

Garden Gully's cellar door is built on the site of Salinger's Hockheim winery at Great Western, which operated from the 1870s until 1945. Riesling has always been a regional speciality.

CURRENT RELEASE 2005   A classical riesling aroma reminiscent of lime, spice, blossom and minerals marks the nose of this young wine; the palate is finely flavoured – savoury and citrus-fragrant – with good intensity and a long dry finish. Try it alongside home-cured gravlax.

Quality	♟♟♟♟♟
Value	★★★★↘
Rating	93
Grapes	riesling
Region	Grampians, Vic.
Cellar	▮ 6+
Alc./Vol.	12.5%
RRP	$19.00 ⮀

Geoff Weaver Lenswood Riesling

Quality	🍷🍷🍷🍷
Value	★★★★
Rating	90
Grapes	riesling
Region	Adelaide Hills, SA
Cellar	🍷 8+
Alc./Vol.	13.5%
RRP	$23.00 🍷

Lenswood is one of the cooler, higher parts of the Adelaide Hills, where other fine rieslings such as Ashton Hills and Henschke Green's Hill come from. It is one of the best but least-touted riesling regions in the country.

CURRENT RELEASE 2005   The customary Weaver vineyard delicacy is there, and this is a subtle wine that may appear at first to be a touch light-on. It has marvellous delicacy and refinement, and will certainly age well and go beautifully with subtle dishes like sushi. The finish is clean and minerally, and the wine has lovely balance and charm. *Previous outstanding vintage: 2004*

Gilberts Mount Barker Riesling

Quality	🍷🍷🍷🍷🍷
Value	★★★★★
Rating	95
Grapes	riesling
Region	Great Southern, WA
Cellar	🍷 7+
Alc./Vol.	11.8%
RRP	$20.00 🍷

Jim and Bev Gilbert have a 10-hectare vineyard just out of Mount Barker, established in 1985. The vineyard has a great track-record with riesling. The wines are contract-made at Plantagenet by Richard Robson.

CURRENT RELEASE 2004   This is a lovely rich, complex, semi-developed riesling that still has a long life ahead of it. The colour is bright light-medium yellow; the nose shows complex development of honey, toast, fruit compote and quince-jelly aromas. The palate is smooth and flowing, rich and yet refined, with a very long carry. There's a lot of flavour but it's superbly balanced: the epitome of finesse. Serve it with egg and bacon pie.

Goundrey Offspring Riesling

Quality	🍷🍷🍷
Value	★★★
Rating	89
Grapes	riesling
Region	Great Southern, WA
Cellar	🍷 3
Alc./Vol.	13.0%
RRP	$21.50 ⑤ 🍷

This brand is an 'offspring' of the main Goundrey brand, if you like, and price-wise it fits in between the Goundrey Reserve and Homestead ranges. Chief winemaker is David Martin.

CURRENT RELEASE 2005   This is a nicely made riesling, a little forward in development for an '05, perhaps, but then it was not a great year in Western Australia and probably never destined for long cellaring. Ripe floral aromas; rich fruity palate that's soft and balanced and has a slightly tart acid finish – but no harshness. It has length and flavour, but without the finesse you'll find in the top label. Try roast spatchcock.

Grosset Polish Hill Riesling

The 2005 harvest marked the 25th vintage for both of Jeffrey Grosset's rieslings. How time flies. The authors feel kind of ancient when they hear that sort of thing, as we were already grown-ups when the '81s came out. Shucks, we can remember when Grosset worked for Lindemans! CURRENT RELEASE 2005 A beautiful, delicate-but-powerful style as we've come to expect from this label. There are still green tinges in the colour, and aromas of bread dough, fresh flowers, minerals and citrus blossoms. It manages to be both soft and crisp on the palate, with plenty of acid but in no way tart or harsh. Delicate, vibrant and lingering, it has a marvellous 'line' of flavour from entry to finish. Great with any pan-fried white-fleshed fish.
Previous outstanding vintages: all of them

Quality	🍷🍷🍷🍷🍷
Value	★★★★
Rating	95
Grapes	riesling
Region	Clare Valley, SA
Cellar	🍾 8+
Alc./Vol.	13.0%
RRP	$38.00

Grosset Watervale Riesling

The 2005 vintage in Clare was regarded as one of the best in recent times, a great one with which to celebrate Grosset's 25th harvest. Whether it's a better year than 2002 or 1998 is debatable: some say yes; others say it's better than '02 but not '98, and so on . . .
CURRENT RELEASE 2005   This is a magical riesling. The haunting fragrance suggests dried flowers, stone-fruit blossoms and minerals; the palate is creamy-textured, flawlessly balanced and precise, with impressive concentration but also supreme delicacy. A delicious array of refined flavours linger on and on. Food: trout risotto.
Previous outstanding vintages: all of them

Quality	🍷🍷🍷🍷🍷
Value	★★★★⁴
Rating	96
Grapes	riesling
Region	Clare Valley, SA
Cellar	🍾 8+
Alc./Vol.	13.0%
RRP	$33.00

PENGUIN BEST RIESLING

Heggies Riesling

Heggies' vineyard is one of the most significant in the Eden Valley region, making very good white wines, with riesling of typical racy regional style a high point.
CURRENT RELEASE 2005 Like all the best Eden Valley rieslings, this wine combines delicacy with strength in elegant fashion, but it has more concentration than most. The nose has aromas of slate, lime, blossom and white peach, and it tastes intense and deep in ripe, fleshy fruit character, with a zesty thread of minerals and acidity running underneath. It would be tops with garfish.

Quality	🍷🍷🍷🍷🍷
Value	★★★★
Rating	96
Grapes	riesling
Region	Eden Valley, SA
Cellar	🍾 6
Alc./Vol.	12.5%
RRP	$21.00

Henschke Julius Riesling

Quality	♈♈♈♈
Value	★★★
Rating	94
Grapes	riesling
Region	Eden Valley, SA
Cellar	▮ 8+
Alc./Vol.	13.0%
RRP	$26.80 ⬪

The famous Henschke enterprise is best known today as a producer of ultra-collectible red wines, but there was a time when Henschke white wines shared the limelight equally. Riesling has always been a speciality and it continues to be a benchmark.
CURRENT RELEASE 2005   A subdued Eden Valley riesling, very closed up and reserved. It smells fine with lime-pulp, herb and floral aromas of great purity that lead to a fine-boned palate of intense, rather austere varietal flavour. It has real underlying depth though, and the palate, while still youthful, has impeccable balance, structure and great length. Henschke Julius is always age-worthy and this is no exception. Try it with sushi.

Henschke Peggy's Hill Riesling

Quality	♈♈♈♈
Value	★★★
Rating	93
Grapes	riesling
Region	Eden Valley, SA
Cellar	▮ 5
Alc./Vol.	12.5%
RRP	$19.20 ⬪

Peggy's Hill is at the top of the range between Eden Valley and Keyneton in the high country above the Barossa Valley. It's topnotch riesling country.
CURRENT RELEASE 2005   This is a slightly broader, more forward wine than Henschke's Julius riesling, with a nose of steely aromas, citrus and nectarine scents, and a hint of Vichy-water-like minerality. The palate has good depth of mouth-filling flavour that's rich and complete, and some mouth-watering acidity keeps it alive and tangy. It may be slightly less refined than its age-worthy Julius sibling, but it has plenty of character right now. Serve it with smoked trout.

Hewitson Riesling

Quality	♈♈♈♈
Value	★★★ᛃ
Rating	93
Grapes	riesling
Region	Eden Valley, SA
Cellar	▮ 4
Alc./Vol.	12.0%
RRP	$22.00 ⬪

Eden Valley is in the hills above the famous Barossa Valley, and in many ways it's the Barossa's alter ego. It's cooler, lonelier, less commercial. Riesling performs much better up there than it does on the Barossa Valley floor, and quality producers like Hewitson are always seeking it out.
CURRENT RELEASE 2005   Hewitson rieslings are usually a little more forward than some of their regional neighbours, but this is a more reserved edition. It smells varietally correct with lime, white-peach, slate and coriander aromas. The palate is rich and deeply flavoured with good mouth-feel and tight structure. It finishes long and tasty. Great with cured salmon.

Howard Park Riesling

Western Australia's Great Southern region has emerged as an outstanding new source of high-quality riesling; different to but as good as the great South Australian regions. Howard Park has been a star for many years.
CURRENT RELEASE 2005   This youngster looks just right in the glass, a pale-greenish colour of gem-like brilliance and clarity. The nose continues the pristine theme with mineral, citrus, tropical fruit and spice scents of great varietal purity. In the mouth it's typically structured and fine, perhaps with a little more youthful appeal than many past Howard Park rieslings. It tastes clean and focused with limey/spicy fruit that's long and tangy. Lemony acidity underpins it with savoury dryness. We'd suggest pan-fried fresh garfish.

Quality	♟ ♟ ♟ ♟ ♟
Value	★ ★ ★ ★ ⁜
Rating	96
Grapes	riesling
Region	Great Southern, WA
Cellar	🍾 10
Alc./Vol.	12.5%
RRP	$25.00 🍷

Jeanneret Riesling

Ben Jeanneret's estate is one of the smallest recognised Clare Valley producers, making a range of good regional wines that are sold at very good prices.
CURRENT RELEASE 2005   Clare Valley riesling of restraint and finesse, Jeanneret's '05 has apple, spice and lime aromas with a whiff of minerals. In the mouth it is succulent with good fruit concentration dovetailed with a zesty, bracing lick of acidity, and it finishes with a long juicy aftertaste. Try it with grilled fish.

Quality	♟ ♟ ♟ ♟
Value	★ ★ ★
Rating	91
Grapes	riesling
Region	Clare Valley, SA
Cellar	🍾 4
Alc./Vol.	11.8%
RRP	$18.00 🍷

Journeys End The Return Riesling

The journey in question was John Macarthur's odyssey in 1815–16, which took him on a tour of Europe in search of wine lore, knowledge and vine cuttings. On his return he was instrumental in getting Australia going as a wine producer. We should all toast his pioneering work.
CURRENT RELEASE 2005   From a fantastic vintage for Clare–Watervale riesling, this pale young wine has a minerally, slightly Germanic thread on the nose. The fruit character is reminiscent of lime and spiced apple. The palate has the richly flavoured, smoothly textured qualities of the '05 Clare vintage, finishing long, dry and meaningful. Serve it with stir-fried prawns and Chinese mustard greens.

Quality	♟ ♟ ♟ ♟ ♟
Value	★ ★ ★ ★
Rating	92
Grapes	riesling
Region	Clare Valley, SA
Cellar	🍾 6+
Alc./Vol.	12.5%
RRP	$22.50 🍷

Kanta Balhannah Vineyard Riesling

Quality	♉ ♉ ♉ ♊
Value	★ ★ ★
Rating	88
Grapes	riesling
Region	Adelaide Hills, SA
Cellar	▮ 3+
Alc./Vol.	13.5%
RRP	$28.00 ⬚

Kanta is Egon Muller's first attempt at an Australian riesling. It has turned a lot of heads. The Mosel Valley legend had his wine made at Shaw & Smith where it was overseen by Stephen Pannell and Daryl Catlin. The methods were a bit radical (for Aussies): skin contact, solids fermentation, wild yeasts, minimal acid addition, no finings.
CURRENT RELEASE 2005   The wine tastes better than its rather clunky label looks. It's a fuller-bodied, slightly phenolic style of riesling with soft texture and mild acidity. There's a sweaty/gooseberry overtone to the aroma, and the palate has density, alcoholic weight and a little thickness. You could try it with zuppa di pesce (fish soup).

Knappstein Ackland Vineyard Watervale Riesling

Quality	♉ ♉ ♉ ♉ ♉
Value	★ ★ ★ ★ ↕
Rating	95
Grapes	riesling
Region	Clare Valley, SA
Cellar	▮ 5+
Alc./Vol.	13.5%
RRP	$26.00 ⬚

This is the first wine we've seen under this label, and what an impression it made. The vineyard was planted by the Ackland brothers in 1969, and is dry-grown. The soil is classic red loam over the calcareous substance loosely referred to locally as limestone, but which is more correctly termed calcite. Maker: Paul Smith.
CURRENT RELEASE 2005   It's a bigger, more powerful style, and very impressive – but perhaps not for those who prefer the lighter, delicate styles of riesling. The nose is a complex mixture of citrusy, floral and minerally aromas; the palate is rich and full, powerful and structured, with a touch of grip that is all in good balance. It's such a rewarding drink now it's hard to imagine it getting better, but we're sure it will. Drink with pan-fried snapper.

Knappstein Hand Picked Riesling

Quality	♉ ♉ ♉ ♉
Value	★ ★ ★ ★
Rating	90
Grapes	riesling
Region	Clare Valley, SA
Cellar	▮ 7+
Alc./Vol.	13.0%
RRP	$20.00 ⬚

'Hand picked' is not commonly seen on wine labels (also see the Wirra Wirra riesling entry). One reason why wineries favour mechanical harvesters these days is the generally dwindling ranks of people prepared to bend their backs in the heat to do the hard yakka of picking grapes by hand.
CURRENT RELEASE 2005   This is a more delicate, restrained style than the Ackland Vineyard wine, and has a pale colour and a fresh, yeasty, citrusy aroma that is clean and lively. The palate is refined, tangy and bracing, with crisp acidity and a nice firm backbone, without hardness. It's a lovely drink now and would cellar well. Serve it with quiche lorraine.

Lalla Gully Riesling

Lalla Gully is a Tasmanian vineyard associated with Victorian-based Taltarni. Situated in the Piper's River area of north-eastern Tassie, it is true cool-climate viticulture, and riesling suits it well. Maker: Leigh Clarnette.

CURRENT RELEASE 2005   A subdued cool-grown scent meets the nose here with aromas of apples, pears, limes and a delicate floral thread. The palate is dry with good depth of spicy fruit flavour resting on a rather phenolic, austere foundation. It needs food to show its best, perhaps some mint and lettuce-wrapped Vietnamese spring rolls.

Quality	♟♟♟♟
Value	★★★
Rating	90
Grapes	riesling
Region	Piper's River, Tas.
Cellar	▮3
Alc./Vol.	13.0%
RRP	$22.00 ⅏

Leasingham Bin 7 Riesling

Leasingham Bin 7 once occupied the upper level of Australian riesling, but today it's a far more democratic drink, consistently offering classic Clare Valley character at an often discounted price.

CURRENT RELEASE 2005   This has a paler colour than the '04 Bin 7 at the same stage, and the aroma reflects this, showing less evolution than its predecessor, but the same promising intensity. The nose suggests blossom, lime and apple, leading to a classically constructed palate of good depth and savoury persistence. It's a very fine example that's delicious right now, but it will doubtlessly develop well in bottle. Enjoy it with steamed yabbies and herb mayonnaise

Quality	♟♟♟♟♟
Value	★★★⫯
Rating	94
Grapes	riesling
Region	Clare Valley, SA
Cellar	▮6+
Alc./Vol.	12.5%
RRP	$21.00 ⑤ ⅏

Leasingham Classic Clare Riesling

Leasingham provides us with a taste of aged Clare Valley riesling on a regular basis via the Classic Clare wines. The style *is* classical too, always showing some elements of bottle-aged complexity, and now under its screw-cap it has lovely freshness as well.

CURRENT RELEASE 2002   This riesling has just crossed the line between youth and maturity, but it still has some years in front of it. It smells minerally and lightly toasty, adding a deliciously savoury touch to rich, lime-cordial-like fruit aromas. The palate is ripe yet dry with great depth and a viscous texture, finishing with a lingering aftertaste and tangy acidity. A rich, complete riesling that would stand up well to grilled salmon cutlets.

Quality	♟♟♟♟♟
Value	★★★⫯
Rating	95
Grapes	riesling
Region	Clare Valley, SA
Cellar	▮5
Alc./Vol.	12.5%
RRP	$33.00 ⅏

Leo Buring Clare Valley Riesling

Quality	♟ ♟ ♟ ♟ ♟
Value	★★★★★
Rating	96
Grapes	riesling
Region	Clare Valley, SA
Cellar	▮ 5+
Alc./Vol.	13.0%
RRP	$18.50 ⓢ ⛾

No story of Australian wine would be complete without mention of the great Leo Buring rieslings, yet public apathy and corporate idiocy almost destroyed the line some years ago. Now they're back as good as ever. Hallelujah! CURRENT RELEASE 2005 Once again, this classically built young riesling punches well above its weight, delivering excellent Clare character for a relatively modest outlay. The nose is minerally and lime-scented with a touch of leafiness. It smells a bit closed up still, but it really hits its straps on the palate with a rich, dry, stone-fruity thing that's mouth-filling and persistent. It finishes dry with fine, balancing acidity. Not the most delicate regional example, but very flavoursome with mussels mariniere.

Leo Buring DW117 Leonay Riesling

Quality	♟ ♟ ♟ ♟ ♟
Value	★★★★⋆
Rating	98
Grapes	riesling
Region	Eden Valley, SA
Cellar	➡ 2–10+
Alc./Vol.	13.0%
RRP	$35.00 ⛾

Few Australian wines have such an illustrious history as the white-labelled Leo Buring Leonay rieslings. The brand managers and marketers did their best to muck the whole thing up in the 1980s, but now they're back, and as good as ever. Winemaker is Matthew Pick. CURRENT RELEASE 2005 This wine sums up one of Australia's best regional wine types as eloquently as any. It's the essence of Eden Valley riesling: pale with greenish tints, fragrant with floral scents and tight limey-fruit aromas, slaty and subtly rich. In the mouth it has depth of taut-structured, minerally varietal flavour that lingers long and fragrant on the palate. It's still fairly subdued in youth; its glories lie in the future when it should mature into a great wine. Perfect with smoked trout pâté.

Leo Buring Eden Valley Riesling

Quality	♟ ♟ ♟ ♟ ♟
Value	★★★★⋆
Rating	92
Grapes	riesling
Region	Eden Valley, SA
Cellar	➡ 1–5+
Alc./Vol.	12.5%
RRP	$18.50 ⓢ ⛾

The best Leo Buring rieslings have usually been sourced from either the Clare–Watervale or Eden Valley regions over the years. Which is best? Watervale probably gets the nod most of the time, but some of the Eden Valley examples have been every bit as good. CURRENT RELEASE 2005 On first sniff this seems a wee bit less impressive than its '05 Clare Valley sibling. But wait, it builds character with air, developing scented apple and citrus aromas of real charm. The palate is clean and dry with good length and a restrained backbone of tingly acidity. It should reveal itself more with time in bottle, building depth and complexity. Serve it with grilled garfish.

Mac Forbes Riesling

Mac Forbes is a young winemaker who gained experience at Mount Mary before setting up his own label. This wine is unusual in the context of Australian riesling for its sweetness: it should probably carry some qualifier, such as the Germans do with 'kabinett', to distinguish it from drier styles.
CURRENT RELEASE 2005   The colour is pale lemon and it smells dusty, herbaceous, slightly green, also vanillin – and possibly had a touch of botrytis on the fruit. The palate is quite sweet and juicy – somewhere around kabinett to spatlese level – but it's nicely balanced and is a lovely drink. Serve with Thai fish cakes and chilli sauce.

Quality	♀♀♀♀
Value	★★★⌐
Rating	89
Grapes	riesling
Region	Strathbogie Ranges, Vic.
Cellar	▮4+
Alc./Vol.	11.0%
RRP	$22.00 ⬚

Meeting Place Riesling

Kamberra is the name of Hardys' winery in the national capital; Canberra is the name of the city. It's supposed to mean 'meeting place' in the language of the traditional owners, the Aboriginals. Maker: Alex McKay.
CURRENT RELEASE 2005   A cool-cimate wine for sure. It has a slatey, almost Germanic nose that incorporates mineral, honey, lime and herbaceous characters, resulting in a very complex aroma. It's delicate and taut in the mouth, with a juicy, soft, low-phenolic palate that's balanced by a trace of sweetness. A very smart wine that is outside the Australian mainstream. Try it with crab and avocado timbales.

Quality	♀♀♀♀
Value	★★★★⌐
Rating	90
Grapes	riesling
Region	Canberra Region, NSW
Cellar	▮7+
Alc./Vol.	12.0%
RRP	$16.00 ⑤ ⬚

Montara Riesling

The McRae Montara vineyard and cellar door enjoys a panoramic view across undulating pastures and stands of trees towards the distant Pyrenees range. Lovely. The vineyard is now over 35 years old.
CURRENT RELEASE 2005   Floral and herbal aromas first meet the nose, and minerally and lime-like characters are also in the equation. The palate is soft and mellow, due in part to a thread of residual sweetness, but a steely touch adds structure and interest. It finishes dry and aromatic. Drink it with Thai ginger chicken.

Quality	♀♀♀♀
Value	★★★⌐
Rating	89
Grapes	riesling
Region	Grampians, Vic.
Cellar	▮3
Alc./Vol.	13.5%
RRP	$18.00 ⬚

Moorilla Estate Riesling

Quality	♛♛♛♛
Value	★★★
Rating	89
Grapes	riesling
Region	Tasmania
Cellar	➡2–8+
Alc./Vol.	12.0%
RRP	$25.00 ⌛
	(cellar door)

Moorilla Estate has a great track-record for producing riesling with superb ageing potential. For example: its 1989 won the trophy for the best museum white wine at the 2006 Tasmanian Wine Show, at which HH was a judge. The '98 and '96 also won gold medals in the museum class. CURRENT RELEASE 2005 The colour is incredibly pale (reflecting the cool climate) and the aromas are of exaggerated passionfruity/tropical characters and slight sweatiness – not really typical of the maker or region. There's a sweet/sour effect in the mouth, as it has high acidity and also some balancing sweetness. It's a tight, subtle, undeveloped wine that hasn't quite come together yet. Cellar it, and then serve with Tasmanian lobster. *Previous outstanding vintages: 1989, '90, '94, '96, '98, 2001, '03*

Mount Horrocks Watervale Riesling

Quality	♛♛♛♛♛
Value	★★★★
Rating	92
Grapes	riesling
Region	Clare Valley, SA
Cellar	➡1–8+
Alc./Vol.	13.0%
RRP	$28.00 ⌛

If you're in Clare, visit the old Auburn railway station, which Mount Horrocks' owner/winemaker Stephanie Toole bought and renovated as her tasting room and cellar-door sales. There is no railway line these days, instead there's a cycle track so you can bike the length of the valley. CURRENT RELEASE 2005 This vintage seems more austere and designed for long-ageing than usual for Mount Horrocks. The colour has pronounced green tints and the aromas are intensely lime-leafy over mixed citrus fruits. In the mouth, it's slightly hard with firm acidity over a bone-dry finish. It needs time; then enjoy it with, say, fried whitebait. *Previous outstanding vintages: 1999, 2001, '02, '03, '04*

Mount Majura Riesling

Quality	♛♛♛♛
Value	★★★★⌐
Rating	90
Grapes	riesling
Region	Canberra, ACT
Cellar	➡1–5+
Alc./Vol.	11.6%
RRP	$16.00 ⌛

This is one of the few vineyards in the Canberra region that actually lies within the boundary of the Australian Capital Territory. The 9-hectare vineyard includes some unusual types, such as tempranillo, graciano and cabernet franc. CURRENT RELEASE 2005 As we might have expected from Canberra, this is a shy, backward, slightly austere riesling that needs more time to come forward than wines from warmer climes. The nose is still estery and subdued; the palate is juicy, tangy and very lively – almost a touch astringent – with some sweetness helping the balance. It needs time and will go well with shellfish.

Mountadam Riesling

Mountadam has been sold by Moet Hennessy, the
French owners of Cape Mentelle and Cloudy Bay. New
owner David Brown is an Adelaide businessman who
also owns vineyards in the south-east of South Australia.
He lured long-time Petaluma winemaker Con Moshos to
Mountadam in time for the '06 vintage.
CURRENT RELEASE 2004   With a little bottle-age on it, this
riesling is toasty, smoky, slightly fig-jammy to sniff, with just
a little stone-fruit primary aroma remaining. The medium-
yellow colour shows it's no longer a youngster, while the
palate has richness and depth, lots of flavour and body,
and some Alsace-like minerality. It's an unusual style but a
good drink – perhaps with traditional Alsace onion tart.

Quality	♥♥♥♥
Value	★★★⁴
Rating	92
Grapes	riesling
Region	Eden Valley, SA
Cellar	▋3
Alc./Vol.	12.5%
RRP	$24.00 ⓢ

Murdock Riesling

David Murdock was once the chief vineyard man for
Southcorp. This small Coonawarra operation is run by
himself and his family, while Pete Bissell makes the wines
at Balnaves.
CURRENT RELEASE 2005   A very restrained, delicate
riesling that really needs time and requires an act of faith
on the part of the buyer. It needs more time to unfold its
charms. The fruit expression is of the minerally kind, with
lemon sherbet aromas, and the taste is light and subtle
with a reasonably dry finish. Hard to assess at present, but
we feel sure it will be worth more points in another year or
two. It would work with sushi.

Quality	♥♥♥⁴
Value	★★★
Rating	88
Grapes	riesling
Region	Coonawarra, SA
Cellar	➊2–7+
Alc./Vol.	12.5%
RRP	$19.00 ⓢ

Neagles Rock Riesling

At Neagles Rock they saw similarities between the cooler
summer and the slow-ripening 2005 crop and the excellent
2002 vintage. From the very good general standard of '05
Clare rieslings, we'd agree.
CURRENT RELEASE 2005   A bright-looking, green-tinged
wine with excellent varietal and regional aromas of steel,
spice and lime. The palate has elegant, fine flavour that's
absolutely spot-on, although it's a little more muted in
youth than many other '05 Clare rieslings. Texture is
good and there's a feeling of richness, despite its restraint.
Our hunch is that it will build nicely in bottle mid-term,
although it's lovely restrained drinking right now. Match
it with delicate seafood dishes.

Quality	♥♥♥♥⁴
Value	★★★★
Rating	93
Grapes	riesling
Region	Clare Valley, SA
Cellar	▋4
Alc./Vol.	12.5%
RRP	$18.00 ⓢ

Nepenthe Hand Picked Riesling

Quality	⏴⏴⏴⏴⏴
Value	★★★⏴
Rating	92
Grapes	riesling
Region	Adelaide Hills, SA
Cellar	🍶 5
Alc./Vol.	13.5%
RRP	$20.00 🍷

In only a few short years, Nepenthe has become a force to be reckoned with in the Adelaide Hills. With over 150 hectares under vine and a strong commitment to quality, it's a name to watch.
CURRENT RELEASE 2005   The '05 vintage looks to have suited riesling in most areas of South Australia. Nepenthe's version looks built for the long haul. In youth it shows an almost Germanic whiff of sulphur on the nose, along with floral and citrus aromas of good intensity. It tastes intense with broad, fleshy fruit character, some spicy notes, attractive richness, depth and length of flavour. Time will build complexity. Serve it with seafood terrine.

Paradigm Hill Riesling

Quality	⏴⏴⏴⏴
Value	★★★
Rating	91
Grapes	riesling
Region	Mornington Peninsula, Vic.
Cellar	🍶 4
Alc./Vol.	12.5%
RRP	$24.00 🍷

The Mornington Peninsula's best wines are its chardonnays and pinot noirs, but riesling can perform well down there as well. Paradigm Hill is one of the newer vineyards, a meticulously kept place with a very swish cellar-door set-up.
CURRENT RELEASE 2005   A pale riesling with a very fresh, delicate fragrance of blossom, apple and lime. The palate is light and dry with great delicacy of flavour and a fine lip-smacking finish. It hasn't the power that you might find in the great South Australian rieslings, but its finesse is its charm. Try it with grilled whiting.

Pauletts Polish Hill River Riesling

Quality	⏴⏴⏴⏴⏴
Value	★★★⏴
Rating	94
Grapes	riesling
Region	Clare Valley, SA
Cellar	➛2–8+
Alc./Vol.	13.0%
RRP	$21.00 🍷

Those in the know when it comes to Clare Valley riesling always speak well of Pauletts wines. They occupy an ideal spot in the lovely Polish Hill River part of the Valley.
CURRENT RELEASE 2005   There's a steely austerity in the best Clare Valley rieslings that immediately attracts your attention. It's there in this fine example, coupled to more delicate floral and lime-juice qualities. A touch of cinnamon-like spice adds interest as well. In the mouth it's ripe and complete with tangy flavours that should develop into delicious complexity over time. The finish is dry and tightly structured. A classically built regional wine of distinction. It would work with ultra-fresh sashimi.

Penfolds Reserve Bin Eden Valley Riesling

This line of great Eden Valley wines originated from Penfolds' desire to make a statement with riesling, in the same way that Yattarna did with chardonnay. The results have been worth the effort.

CURRENT RELEASE 2005 A very subdued edition of this benchmark Eden Valley riesling, the 2005 opens with a quietly complex melange of lightly floral, quince and lime-like fruit aromas, along with some earthy touches and mineral firmness. It tastes 'serious' with its very restrained vinous and steely flavours, yet there's real depth, richness and structure in there. We reckon that it will be a beauty with some bottle age. It goes well with prawn satays.

Quality	♟ ♟ ♟ ♟ ♟
Value	★ ★ ★ ⟩
Rating	96
Grapes	riesling
Region	Eden Valley, SA
Cellar	➡2–8
Alc./Vol.	13.0%
RRP	$26.00 ⊜

Petaluma Riesling

Petaluma's Hanlin Hill vineyard has been a source of outstanding riesling for many years. The recent series of very good Clare Valley vintages has cemented its reputation as one of the region's best.

CURRENT RELEASE 2005 Some great rieslings have appeared from the near-perfect 2005 Clare Valley vintage, and not surprisingly Petaluma's effort is a real stand-out. It's a bright, green-tinged wine with a superfine, aromatic nose of floral, tropical lime and spice on a firm, slaty background. The palate is rich with plump fruit in the middle, cut through with tangy lime-like varietal notes and zippy acidity. A classy riesling with great cellaring potential. Try it with grilled South Australian whiting.

Quality	♟ ♟ ♟ ♟ ♟
Value	★ ★ ★ ★
Rating	98
Grapes	riesling
Region	Clare Valley, SA
Cellar	▮ 8+
Alc./Vol.	13.0%
RRP	$28.00 ⊜

Peter Lehmann Eden Valley Riesling

Riesling is probably Australia's most age-worthy white wine, and the trend towards sealing it with a screw-cap enhances its potential even more. Peter Lehmann's rieslings are always worth many years in the cellar.

CURRENT RELEASE 2005 This is still a work in progress and ideally it needs time to build flavour and personality. Although the nose shows more extract than the '04, it seems more reserved at the same age. It has slightly estery lime, pear and spice aromas that are still fairly closed up, and the palate shows similar understated fruit. The texture is tight and very fine with promising length and bracing acidity hiding fruit richness. Good with scallops and a buttery citrus-accented sauce.

Quality	♟ ♟ ♟ ♟ ♟
Value	★ ★ ★ ★ ★
Rating	94
Grapes	riesling
Region	Eden Valley, SA
Cellar	➡2–8
Alc./Vol.	12.0%
RRP	$15.65 ⑤ ⊜

Pettavel Evening Star Riesling

Quality	🍷🍷🍷🍷
Value	★★★★
Rating	93
Grapes	riesling
Region	Geelong, Vic.
Cellar	🍾 4
Alc./Vol.	13.0%
RRP	$18.00 🗳

The *Evening Star* was the ship that brought David Pettavel to Melbourne on his epic journey from Switzerland in 1856. He settled near Geelong and was instrumental in the expansion of viticulture and winemaking in the region. His original vineyard was across the road from the modern Pettavel complex.

CURRENT RELEASE 2005   An extraordinarily pungent wine, in some ways reminiscent of Austrian riesling. This has lots of mixed-spice/hot-cross-bun, musky, floral and gingery aromas on the nose, and limey fruit underneath. In the mouth it's exotically rich with great depth of spicy flavour, unctuous texture and a very long, aromatic finish. A forceful young riesling, indeed. Try it with cold soy sauce chicken.

Pewsey Vale Riesling

Quality	🍷🍷🍷🍷
Value	★★★★★
Rating	94
Grapes	riesling
Region	Eden Valley, SA
Cellar	🍾 6
Alc./Vol.	12.5%
RRP	$17.00 Ⓢ 🗳

PENGUIN BEST-VALUE
WHITE WINE

Pewsey Vale Riesling seems to have been around for yonks, but back in the 1960s and '70s it was very new wave. It pioneered a revitalised cool-climate vineyard in the hills beyond the Barossa, and was one of the first high-quality Oz wines bottled with a taint-free screw-cap.

CURRENT RELEASE 2005   The '05 vintage has often imparted an extra dimension of richness to South Australian rieslings, and so it is with Pewsey Vale. It opens pale and brilliant in the glass, and the nose is lush with aromas of sweet lime, peach and spice. In the mouth it's rich and deeply flavoured with fleshy mid-palate fruit dovetailed into a sherbet-fresh finish. Perfect with fried South Australian whiting.

Pfeiffer Riesling

Quality	🍷🍷🍷
Value	★★★★
Rating	90
Grapes	riesling
Region	King Valley & Strathbogie Ranges, Vic.
Cellar	🍾 4
Alc./Vol.	12.5%
RRP	$15.90 🗳

Rutherglen's hot vineyards don't exactly make ideal riesling country, which is why Pfeiffers look to cooler vineyards in other parts of Victoria for their riesling fruit.

CURRENT RELEASE 2005   This pale young riesling smells of tropical fruit, lime-juice cordial, mineral and floral scents. While it hasn't quite the 'cut' of the great South Australians in 2005, it has plenty of ripe varietal character on nose and palate, and in the mouth it's intense and lush in texture. It finishes long, dry and spicy. Match it with steamed yabbies and salsa verde.

Pikes Riesling

Brothers Neil and Andrew Pike and their ancestors have quenched people's thirsts for generations with beer, soft drinks, 'tonics', and now wine. True all-rounders.
CURRENT RELEASE 2005   This pale young riesling is pleasantly aromatic with steely lime and floral elements on the nose, leading to a quite delicately flavoured, attractively structured palate. It tastes fine and long, and there's backbone for ageing too. It doesn't have the impact of The Merle, but it's still a pretty good example of the Pikes riesling style. Good with sushi.

Quality	♟♟♟♟♙
Value	★★★♩
Rating	94
Grapes	riesling
Region	Clare Valley, SA
Cellar	▮ 5
Alc./Vol.	12.0%
RRP	$22.60 ⮿

Pikes The Merle Reserve Riesling

Andrew and Neil Pike have made some of the Clare Valley's best rieslings over the years, especially under the Reserve label, although the standard bottling is no slouch either. The Reserve riesling was renamed 'The Merle' in 2004 in honour of the Pike boys' late mother. It's a worthy memorial.
CURRENT RELEASE 2005   Another absolute classic under this esteemed label. It has everything in precise balance: delicate sherbetty-citrus, floral and green-apple scents combine with understated minerally power, and there's that indefinable 'presence' that the greatest South Australian rieslings have. The texture is very fine, yet there's richness and depth and a long fragrant signature. Tight and tangy now, it will also age superbly. Serve it with scallops steamed with ginger and spring onion.

Quality	♟♟♟♟♟
Value	★★★★♩
Rating	98
Grapes	riesling
Region	Clare Valley, SA
Cellar	▬1–8+
Alc./Vol.	11.8%
RRP	$35.75 ⮿

Pirie South Riesling

Tasmanian winemakers have 'pfaffed' around with all sorts of grape varieties over the last 20 years, with varying degrees of success, but those who've worked with riesling have made some great wines. Andrew Pirie's Pirie South label continues the tradition.
CURRENT RELEASE 2005   Delicacy is the thing here, the orange-lime, floral and apple-drop aromas are light and perfumed, and the fine, clean palate has a gentle suggestion of fruit-sweetness mid-palate in zesty balance. Despite clean, fresh acidity, its long finish is relatively soft. A light, fresh riesling of great charm. Team it with fresh shellfish.

Quality	♟♟♟♟♙
Value	★★★♩
Rating	92
Grapes	riesling
Region	Tamar Valley, Tas.
Cellar	▮ 3
Alc./Vol.	12.5%
RRP	$23.15 ⮿

Plantagenet Riesling

Quality	♥♥♥♥♦
Value	★★★★♦
Rating	93
Grapes	riesling
Region	Great Southern, WA
Cellar	▮ 7
Alc./Vol.	13.0%
RRP	$19.00 ⌕

Plantagenet's wines add weight to the claim that the Great Southern of Western Australia is one of Australia's top riesling regions. They age well, too.
CURRENT RELEASE 2005 This has a very delicate, floral fragrance. It's truly elegant on the nose, and some more substantial lemon and lime touches sit in the background. The flavour is intense, yet light and subtle, with a steely background, a fine texture and long finish. A riesling of true finesse that should develop well mid-term. A good match for sushi.

Radford Dale Eden Valley Riesling

Quality	♥♥♥♥
Value	★★★♦
Rating	90
Grapes	riesling
Region	Eden Valley, SA
Cellar	▮ 4
Alc./Vol.	12.0%
RRP	$19.00 ⌕

Radford Dale is the creation of Barossa native Ben Radford and French-raised Alex Dale. Old Eden Valley vines provide the raw material.
CURRENT RELEASE 2005 The pale, green-tinged colour is spot-on for young Eden valley riesling. The aroma is reminiscent of aromatic limes, apple brandy and steel, leading to a dry, classically austere palate that's long and savoury. It has perhaps a shade less fruit intensity than the greatest Eden Valley riesling wines, but it's still a very good example. Try it with seafood tempura.

Richmond Grove Footbridge Riesling

Quality	♥♥♥♥♦
Value	★★★★★
Rating	92
Grapes	riesling
Region	various, SA
Cellar	▮ 4
Alc./Vol.	12.5%
RRP	$15.00 Ⓢ ⌕

Richmond Grove's rieslings are wines of classical proportions, yet they are priced as quaffers. Who could ask for more? Footbridge is the 'entry level' wine, but it's no also-ran.
CURRENT RELEASE 2005 An angular, taut type of young riesling with a spicy nose reminiscent of citrus, nettles and steel. The palate is intense, persistent and clean with good presence and a tight backbone. Another bargain from Richmond Grove, ideal with grilled whiting meunière.

Rolf Binder Highness Riesling

Most of the better rieslings out of the Barossa come from the eastern side, which includes Eden Valley and Springton, but this one's grown on the western slopes, according to the label. Makers: Rolf Binder and his sister, Christa Deans.
CURRENT RELEASE 2005   This one is rocketing along its ageing curve: the colour is deeper than most '05s and there's some toast already appearing in the bouquet. Herbal and spicy notes are there, too. It's delicate and light on the tongue, with a trace of earthiness. We'd recommend it with cold roast pork and apple sauce.

Quality	♟ ♟ ♟
Value	★ ★ ★ ⟩
Rating	86
Grapes	riesling
Region	Barossa & Eden valleys, SA
Cellar	▮ 4
Alc./Vol.	13.0%
RRP	$16.25 ⊜

Schild Estate Riesling

We are often surprised at the cellaring recommendations we read on back labels, especially those that don't have a significant pedigree. If history shows that a wine cellars well, that's reassuring. Schild Estate's riesling doesn't have a history as far as we know, but the blurb says 'Drink for 20 years'.
CURRENT RELEASE 2005   This is a pleasant, middle-of-the-road riesling with floral, dry-straw and dried-flower aromas, developing lime and lemon on the palate. Its mouth-feel is soft and easygoing, with a trace of richness. It doesn't taste totally bone-dry but is nicely balanced. The acidity is seamless. It drinks well now but we're not convinced about the 20 years. Serve with pan-fried snapper.

Quality	♟ ♟ ♟ ♟
Value	★ ★ ★ ★ ⟩
Rating	90
Grapes	riesling
Region	Barossa Valley, SA
Cellar	▮ 6+
Alc./Vol.	12.0%
RRP	$15.00 ⊜

Seppelt Drumborg Riesling

Drumborg, in the recently gazetted Henty region near Portland in south-west Victoria, is one of the coolest vineyard sites on the Australian mainland. It regularly produces one of our most cellar-worthy rieslings – although some may find it a trifle austere in its youth.
CURRENT RELEASE 2005   Pale coloured and shy of nose, this minerally, crisply acid young riesling is all potential. It's a taut, nervy, tightly packed style with jazzy acidity, intense citrus (lemon, grapefruit) flavour and great delicacy. The flavour flows evenly from start to finish and it really needs time – although it's a sensational drink with fish now. Try grilled whiting.

Quality	♟ ♟ ♟ ♟
Value	★ ★ ★ ★ ⟩
Rating	95
Grapes	riesling
Region	Henty, Vic.
Cellar	▮ 10+
Alc./Vol.	13.0%
RRP	$30.00 ⊜

Skillogalee Riesling

Quality	♥ ♥ ♥
Value	★ ★ ★
Rating	86
Grapes	riesling
Region	Clare Valley, SA
Cellar	▮ 3+
Alc./Vol.	13.0%
RRP	$20.70 ⬚

The 2005 vintage was highly touted by the winemakers of Clare – especially for riesling. They get all excited in Clare whenever they have a cooler summer.
CURRENT RELEASE 2005   We weren't quite convinced by this wine: it seems advanced in colour and forward in flavour. The bouquet is toasty and herbal with hints of geranium. It's a fuller, softer, more up-front style than usual for Skillogalee, and we wonder how it will age. Watch it carefully if you're cellaring it. Food: roast chicken with plenty of garlic.

St Hallett Riesling

Quality	♥ ♥ ♥ ♥ ♦
Value	★ ★ ★ ★ ♦
Rating	92
Grapes	riesling
Region	Eden Valley, SA
Cellar	▮ 10+
Alc./Vol.	11.5%
RRP	$19.00 ⬚

This winery is part of the Lion Nathan juggernaut, but the quality seems quite unaffected by the ownership change. Winemakers Matt Gant and Stuart Blackwell continue to turn out some of the region's best reds – and whites.
CURRENT RELEASE 2005   The '05 harvest was a ripper in Eden Valley and this is a delicious example. It has an aroma of dried wildflowers, citrus blossoms and zesty green apples – the tanginess of which continues in the mouth. It is light, lively and fresh, with the acidity to go really well with fish and crustaceans. We'd choose a trout risotto.

St John's Road Peace of Eden Riesling

Quality	♥ ♥ ♥ ♦
Value	★ ★ ★ ♦
Rating	88
Grapes	riesling
Region	Eden Valley, SA
Cellar	▮ 5
Alc./Vol.	11.5%
RRP	$16.55 ⬚

This is a single-vineyard wine made for the owners by specialist white winemaker Christa Deans. St John's Road is in the Marananga locality, but the grapes were grown in Eden Valley.
CURRENT RELEASE 2005   It seems a very restrained, protectively made style of riesling, with a pronounced green tint in the colour and green-herb aromas with grassy and crushed-lime-leaf notes. The palate is delicate and soft, nicely balanced and easygoing. It could build more interest with further time in bottle. Then we'd suggest drinking it with crab cakes.

Stefano Lubiana Riesling

Steve Lubiana is a very capable winemaker – he even makes his own sparkling wines and does all the work at his winery, without out-sourcing. He and his wife Monique have 19 hectares of vineyard on the Derwent River at Granton. CURRENT RELEASE 2005   This is a tight, nervy, cool-climate style that actually tasted much better after it was topped up and put aside for a few weeks. It's a very fine, delicate, restrained but intensely flavoured wine with a lot of slatey/earthy/mineral aromas rather than the fruity or floral tones. The acidity is a feature: there is plenty of acid but we suspect it's all natural as it's so fine and seamless. Try this with grilled fish and chips.

Quality	♥ ♥ ♥ ♥
Value	★ ★ ★ ﹢
Rating	90
Grapes	riesling
Region	Derwent Valley, Tas.
Cellar	➥1–9+
Alc./Vol.	13.0%
RRP	$27.00

Tim Gramp Riesling

Tim Gramp has riesling in his blood. His ancestors at the venerable Orlando winery pioneered many of the techniques that made modern Australian riesling possible. CURRENT RELEASE 2005   The brilliant greenish-straw colour is perfect, and so are the intense lime-juice/zest aromas and flavours. Understated notes of spring blossom add a delicate touch, and minerally notes provide strength. The dry mouth-filling palate has excellent depth and plenty of extract, and the tight phenolics give real structure without bitterness. This should mature into a traditional style rather than the fruitier modern type. An excellent choice with salmon.

Quality	♥ ♥ ♥ ♥ ♥
Value	★ ★ ★ ★ ★
Rating	95
Grapes	riesling
Region	Clare Valley, SA
Cellar	▮ 6+
Alc./Vol.	13.0%
RRP	$19.50

West Cape Howe Riesling

West Cape Howe is an important contract winemaking and bottling business in the south-west and also markets its own wines, made by the experienced Gavin Berry. It has very little vineyard of its own but relies on local growers for its grapes.
CURRENT RELEASE 2005   The colour is glowing medium-yellow with green tints and it smells of lime-zest, lime-juice and flowers. The taste is bouncy and zesty with green-apple fruit and lovely clean lines. The finish is appetising and dry and it cries out for some pan-fried fish, such as ling.

Quality	♥ ♥ ♥
Value	★ ★ ★ ﹢
Rating	91
Grapes	riesling
Region	Great Southern, WA
Cellar	▮ 5+
Alc./Vol.	11.0%
RRP	$19.00 ⑤

The Wilson Vineyard DJW Riesling

Quality	🍷🍷🍷🍷🍷
Value	★★★★★
Rating	97
Grapes	riesling
Region	Clare Valley, SA
Cellar	🍾 6+
Alc./Vol.	13.0%
RRP	$19.00 🥂

When John Wilson set out to find the site for his vineyard in 1973, the locals told him that the place he'd chosen was totally unsuitable for grapes. It was known as Polish Hill River, and now it's one of the most prized locations for quality riesling in the district. So always remember that local knowledge isn't everything.

CURRENT RELEASE 2005   Like all the best Clare Valley riesling makers, the Wilsons made outstanding wines in 2005. DJW shows bright with green flashes in the glass, and the nose has really concentrated varietal personality reminiscent of limes, apples, pears and dissolved minerals. The finely balanced palate is succulent and intensely flavoured, with a long fragrant finish carried by integrated, racy acidity. Serve it with crab salad.

Windowrie The Mill Riesling

Quality	🍷🍷🍷🍷
Value	★★★★
Rating	89
Grapes	riesling
Region	Cowra, NSW
Cellar	🍾 3
Alc./Vol.	13.5%
RRP	$16.00 ⑤ 🥂

The Mill is an old flour mill right in the heart of the Cowra township. Windowrie's owners, the O'Dea family, restored it as a cellar-door sales and function centre. It's a must-see for wine lovers visiting the area.

CURRENT RELEASE 2005   This is a soft, relatively round style of riesling, which is good value for money. There are citrus-blossom aromas with a touch of earthiness; the palate is forward in development and quite rich, with weight and flesh. The flavoursome palate is not completely dry and finishes soft and smooth. It would go with stuffed zucchini flowers.

The Wine Society Tasmanian Riesling

Quality	🍷🍷🍷🍷🍷
Value	★★★★★
Rating	95
Grapes	riesling
Region	southern Tas.
Cellar	🍾 6+
Alc./Vol.	12.5%
RRP	$15.99 ⑤ 🥂

Julian Alcorso, formerly of Moorilla Estate (until his family sold the property), makes superb rieslings at his contract winemaking business near Hobart. The Wine Society is one of his clients. This wine, blended from three vineyards in southern Tasmania, has won several gold medals.

CURRENT RELEASE 2005   This is an eerily Germanic style of riesling, from a cool year in Tassie. The bouquet is honeyed and fragrant, perhaps with a trace of botrytis: certainly very complex. The palate is deep and juicy in fruit without being overtly sweet. It has lovely flavour, structure and dimension. Superb now, and will only improve with time. It goes well with crisp pork belly with ginger caramel sauce and coconut rice.

Wirra Wirra Hand Picked Riesling

Most grapes in Australian vineyards are picked by machines, but some winemakers still reckon hand picking gives better results – at least for some grape varieties. With delicate whites, any phenolic pick-up from juice contacting broken skins can be a minus. Maker: Samantha Connew.
CURRENT RELEASE 2005   A delicate, spicy riesling with an unusual ginger aspect to its scent. The palate is fresh, subtle and restrained, with plenty of power and drive through to a very dry, slightly firm finish. It's good with food now and should age well. Try Chinese dumplings of pork and spring onions.

Quality	♟♟♟♟
Value	★★★★
Rating	90
Grapes	riesling
Region	Adelaide Hills, SA
Cellar	▮6+
Alc./Vol.	12.5%
RRP	$18.00 ⑤ ⅏

Wolf Blass Gold Label Riesling

Gold Label now stands for quite a range of wines in the Blass portfolio, but this was the wine that started it. Gold Label riesling has always been an excellent style: good to drink young, but some vintages have also aged quite well. Still, it's not a style we would think of when buying riesling to cellar long term.
CURRENT RELEASE 2005   The colour is brilliant and the wine is all-round squeaky-clean and bright. There are herbal/parsley and dusty aromas, with a twist of lime; the palate carries lemon/citrus flavours as well. Texture is a highlight: fine, soft, seamless and easy on the tongue, yet it has plenty of vitality. The fruit-acid balance is excellent and it's clean and dry to finish. Serve with pan-fried flathead.

Quality	♟♟♟♟
Value	★★★★
Rating	90
Grapes	riesling
Region	Clare & Eden valleys, SA
Cellar	▮4
Alc./Vol.	12.0%
RRP	$22.00 ⑤ ⅏

Yellow Tail Riesling

Yellow Tail is the biggest success story in Australian wine, if not the world, sweeping to an enormous market share in the US and other countries in just a few years. This riesling is a recent addition to the portfolio. Maker: Alan Kennett and team.
CURRENT RELEASE 2005   This is a pretty good wine for a tenner and very astutely styled for the audience, with a well-measured lick of residual sugar. The aromas are typical riesling, floral and slightly yeasty, while the palate is fruity and doesn't quite dry off at the finish enough for our likes, but many will no doubt disagree. It would be a good partner for mixed Japanese tempura.

Quality	♟♟♟
Value	★★★⸔
Rating	86
Grapes	riesling
Region	various
Cellar	▮2
Alc./Vol.	12.5%
RRP	$10.00 ⑤ ⅏

Zarephath Riesling

Quality	♇ ♇ ♇ ♇
Value	★ ★ ★ ┤
Rating	90
Grapes	riesling
Region	Great Southern, WA
Cellar	▮ 3
Alc./Vol.	13.0%
RRP	$19.85 ⬙

Zarephath vineyard is owned by a Benedictine community known as the Christ Circle, continuing the link between Christian religious communities and the vine, which goes back well over a thousand years.

CURRENT RELEASE 2005   This is a slightly broader type of riesling than the steely, austere style we're used to from the Porongurup region in Western Australia's south. It's a pale wine with floral aromas and touches of stewed apple, citrus and minerals on the nose. The palate is smooth in the middle with rich flavour of good length, ending clean and tangy. Serve it with seafood tempura.

Sauvignon blanc and blends

In recent years Australia has played underdog to New Zealand with sauvignon blanc. But lately we are seeing more Australian sauvignons which, while they might not rival Marlborough's, are nevertheless excellent. This trend has been boosted by the cool 2005 season. The Adelaide Hills and southern areas of Western Australia seem to do best with this difficult grape. Margaret River's 'sem-sav' style, which can be either semillon- or sauvignon-dominant, has become a classic blend, highly popular with local and overseas drinkers. Sauvignon blanc can be wood-aged but is usually not. The good ones have distinctive varietal character that tends more to the tropical-fruit spectrum rather than the herbaceous aroma/flimsy palate style of the past.

Adinfern Sauvignon Blanc

To most of our readers, this will no doubt be another new name. The *Wine Industry Directory* informs us that there are still around 100 new wine producers entering the fray every year. We wonder why they keep coming, as the market is terribly over-crowded.

CURRENT RELEASE 2005 At least the wine is good! It has an appealing nose with some herbal and lemon/citrus elements, and again lots of citrusy flavours in the mouth. It's light-bodied and vaguely salty at the finish. Juicy but dry, it has a fair degree of charm and is not as simplistic as some. It would go with mussel soup.

Quality 🍷🍷🍷
Value ★★★
Rating **87**
Grapes sauvignon blanc
Region Margaret River, WA
Cellar 1
Alc./Vol. 13.4%
RRP $18.00

Alan & Veitch Lobethal Sauvignon Blanc

This is the Adelaide Hills brand of Robert Johnson, who has vineyards in Eden Valley. The Adelaide Hills grapes are bought from growers. Alan and Veitch are the first-names of his parents.

CURRENT RELEASE 2005 An excellent sauvignon blanc, almost New Zealand-like in its intensity of gooseberry-like, slightly sweaty varietal fruit. The palate is light, clean, fruity and tangy, flowing towards a clean, dry, nicely balanced finish that's lively and refreshing. It's a wine we could drink by the bucket-load. Preferably with a second bucket of fresh prawns.

Quality 🍷🍷🍷🍷½
Value ★★★½
Rating **92**
Grapes sauvignon blanc
Region Adelaide Hills, SA
Cellar 2
Alc./Vol. 13.5%
RRP $22.50

Allira Sauvignon Blanc Semillon

Quality	▼▼⁊
Value	★★★⁊
Rating	84
Grapes	sauvignon blanc; semillon
Region	Strathbogie Ranges, Vic.
Cellar	▮ 1
Alc./Vol.	12.5%
RRP	$13.00 ⑤ ≋

The price impressed us most about this wine. It's very inexpensive for an independent boutique wine from the wilds of sub-alpine Victoria. Allira is the 'second' wine of elgo estate, which is in the Strathbogie Ranges.
CURRENT RELEASE 2004   Okay, it's not going to set the world on fire, but it is a very decent drink – especially at the asking price. Herbal, grassy, slightly stalky aromas rise from the glass and the palate is somewhat sweet, grapey, soft and open-knit – which is not unexpected at two years of age. It's a bit floppy and falls away quickly, but would probably go down well, if chilled, with a Subway.

Alta Sauvignon Blanc

Quality	▼▼▼
Value	★★★
Rating	86
Grapes	sauvignon blanc
Region	Adelaide Hills, SA
Cellar	▮ 1
Alc./Vol.	12.6%
RRP	$19.00 ≋

The Adelaide Hills has become a significant force with sauvignon blanc – and there's not a lot of competition in Australia, other than Margaret River. Marlborough is the main opposition. In the 2005 Adelaide Hills Wine Show, the 2005 sauvignon blanc class had 50 starters. This won a bronze.
CURRENT RELEASE 2005   This is a lighter style; delicate, fresh and clean, with garden-salad aromas, some dusty, peppery and crushed-leaf tones, and a crisp light-bodied, tangy palate that just lacks a bit of depth. The finish is clean and dry, for those who like a drier-style savvy. Match it with a caesar salad.

Angove's Long Row Sauvignon Blanc

Quality	▼▼▼
Value	★★★★
Rating	86
Grapes	sauvignon blanc
Region	Riverland, SA
Cellar	▮ 1
Alc./Vol.	11.0%
RRP	$10.00 ⑤ ≋

This is still a family-owned wine company, with the Angove family now entering its fifth generation in the person of Victoria Angove, who is active in the sales and marketing side of the Renmark-based business.
CURRENT RELEASE 2005   A light, simple, basic sauvignon blanc with pleasant lemonade and lemon-peel aromas with the requisite tangy freshness, but quite different to the flavours one finds in cooler-grown savvies. It's simple and crisp, but not especially varietal. Great value for money, however. We'd suggest a risotto with clams and mussels.

Barwick Estates Sauvignon Blanc Semillon

The good folk at Barwick Estates are fighting a battle against the Western Australian Department of Conservation and Land Management over their controlled fuel-reduction burns at Pemberton. The complaint is that they do this in the lead-up to harvest, when the grapes can become tainted by smoke from the fires. So far, the government is winning.
CURRENT RELEASE 2005   No smoke taint here that we could detect. This is a light, straightfoward, very smart commercial style of sav-sem with lots of mulchy, herbal, vegetal aromas and a lick of sweetness. It finishes cleanly and would drink well with mussel soup.

Quality	♀ ♀ ♀
Value	★ ★ ★ ⫟
Rating	86
Grapes	sauvignon blanc; semillon
Region	various, WA
Cellar	▮ 1
Alc./Vol.	12.5%
RRP	$14.00 ⧖

Bellarmine Sauvignon Blanc

Some of the best sauvignon blancs in the West are coming from Pemberton, which is significantly cooler than Margaret River. Houghton is one, Smithbrook another and now Bellarmine. It takes its name from a type of ancient (seventeenth-century) pottery, which is represented artistically on the labels.
CURRENT RELEASE 2004   The colour is still pale at two years, which is a good sign. The aromas recall lettuce and cucmber; very clean, fresh, crisp and attractive, with a hint of gooseberry that comes through on palate. This is a lovely, delicate, subtle white wine that is drinking superbly. We wanted another glass, and another! It would suit Japanese sushi.

Quality	♀ ♀ ♀ ♀
Value	★ ★ ★ ★ ⫟
Rating	90
Grapes	sauvignon blanc
Region	Pemberton, WA
Cellar	▮ 2
Alc./Vol.	12.5%
RRP	$15.00 ⧖ (cellar door)

Bremerton Sauvignon Blanc

Langhorne Creek isn't the first region that springs to mind when you say sauvignon blanc, but Bremerton winemaker Rebecca Willson does an excellent job with it.
CURRENT RELEASE 2005   Pale in colour, this has a minerally nose of citrus, guava and herbs. The palate is very succulent with good balance between fruit and zesty acidity, and some minerally notes add savouriness. A tad less sweet-fruited than many sauvignons in this price range, it makes a good match with goat's cheese and ripe tomato bruschette.

Quality	♀ ♀ ♀ ♀
Value	★ ★ ★ ★ ⫟
Rating	91
Grapes	sauvignon blanc
Region	Langhorne Creek, SA
Cellar	▮ 1
Alc./Vol.	12.0%
RRP	$17.50 ⧖

Bridgewater Mill Sauvignon Blanc

Quality	♥♥♥♥♥
Value	★★★★↓
Rating	95
Grapes	sauvignon blanc
Region	Adelaide Hills, SA
Cellar	▮ 1
Alc./Vol.	13.0%
RRP	$18.00 ⬜

PENGUIN BEST SAUVIGNON
BLANC AND BLENDS

The label says that Bridgewater Mill Adelaide Hills sauvignon blanc is 'equivalent to the best from anywhere on the globe'. We're not entering into a discussion on the topic, but it is a very consistent performer.
CURRENT RELEASE 2005   In the glass this has a very pale silvery sheen to it, with a hint of a green tinge. The nose is archetypically varietal, smelling of passionfruit and other tropical fruits, crushed green leaves, and a definite hint of cassis. In the mouth it's tangy and alive with juicy tropical flavours that lead to a zippy, dry finish. Great alongside mussels with Thai green herbs.

Brookland Valley Sauvignon Blanc

Quality	♥♥♥♥
Value	★★↓
Rating	91
Grapes	sauvignon blanc
Region	Margaret River, WA
Cellar	▮ 1
Alc./Vol.	13.5%
RRP	$28.50 ⬜

Sauvginon blanc isn't Margaret River's main claim to fame, but it does very well in this beautiful Western Australian region.
CURRENT RELEASE 2005   Typically very pale, this has a thrilling varietal aroma that's reminiscent of passionfruit, with savoury green-herb overtones and a slightly reductive minerality. The palate tracks the nose precisely with tangy, almost tart, varietal flavour that finishes tingly and bracing with just a wee bit of hardness. It goes well with mussels with South-East Asian herbs.

Cape Mentelle Wallcliffe Sauvignon Blanc Semillon

Quality	♥♥♥♥♥
Value	★★★↓
Rating	96
Grapes	sauvignon blanc 70%; semillon 30%
Region	Margaret River, WA
Cellar	▮ 2
Alc./Vol.	13.5%
RRP	$35.00 ⬜

In keeping with current trends, Cape Mentelle has produced a kind of reserve bottling of the blend that has been one of its mainstays for many years. Named after the area where the original vineyard is located, Wallcliffe Road, this wine is made with barrel fermentation and other complexing techniques.
CURRENT RELEASE 2003   We reviewed this last year but the '03 is still current as we write this year's edition. The colour is bright, light yellow and it smells smoky, cedary and gooseberry-ish, with lots of oak as well as varietal signatures showing through. It's a tremendously intense, concentrated, powerful wine with many layers of flavour. The palate is more varietal than the nose at this stage. The finish is clean and dry and lingers superbly. Serve with shellfish cooked with fennel.
Previous outstanding vintage: 2002

Centennial Vineyards Bong Bong White

What a wonderfully Australian-sounding name for a wine! It ranks with Long Flat and Sandy Hollow Dry White (the last no longer in use, regrettably) as a dinky-di brand name. We don't know what 'bong' means in Aboriginal, but when it's repeated it means 'lots of bongs'!
CURRENT RELEASE 2005   This is pretty handy stuff for a generic white wine. Pale coloured, it smells of snow pea and green twig, rather like a Western Australian sem-sav. The palate is fuller than the herbal nose leads you to expect, while it's linear and tapers to the finish, which has some acid hardness. A good drink with food: try it with stuffed capsicums.

Quality	🍷 🍷 🍷
Value	★ ★ ★
Rating	86
Grapes	sauvignon blanc; chardonnay
Region	Southern Highlands, NSW
Cellar	🍾 1
Alc./Vol.	13.0%
RRP	$17.00 🗸 (cellar door)

Centennial Vineyards Woodside Sauvignon Blanc

Woodside – not to be confused with the town in the Adelaide Hills – is the name given to this maker's estate-grown wines. The vineyard is at Bowral. They also buy a lot of grapes from other regions.
CURRENT RELEASE 2005   It's a pale-coloured, shy, nervy, slightly green kind of sauvignon blanc, which smells of cut radish and dusty boiled potato. The mouth is smooth and dry with good intensity and balance, albeit somewhat simple. It's a good drink and has varietal character. It would suit salmon and dill quiche.

Quality	🍷 🍷 🍷 🍷
Value	★ ★ ★
Rating	88
Grapes	sauvignon blanc
Region	Southern Highlands, NSW
Cellar	🍾 2
Alc./Vol.	12.9%
RRP	$20.00 🗸 (cellar door)

Cofield Sauvignon Blanc Semillon

Founders Max and Karen Cofield have been joined by their sons Damien and Andrew who are breathing new fire into the business. The family has eight hectares of vines and make their own wines on-site.
CURRENT RELEASE 2005   This is a very smart effort for Rutherglen, an area not noted for this kind of delicate, aromatic dry white wine. It's clean, crisp and tangy with capsicum aromas and plenty of vitality. The acidity is fairly assertive so it would be best with food. We suggest asparagus quiche.

Quality	🍷 🍷 🍷 🍷
Value	★ ★ ★ ★
Rating	88
Grapes	sauvignon blanc; semillon
Region	Rutherglen, Vic.
Cellar	🍾 1
Alc./Vol.	13.0%
RRP	$15.00 🗸 (cellar door)

Cookoothama Sauvignon Blanc Semillon

Quality	♀♀♀♀
Value	★★★★♪
Rating	90
Grapes	sauvignon blanc; semillon
Region	King Valley, Vic.
Cellar	▌1
Alc./Vol.	13.0%
RRP	$15.00 ⓢ ≋

It brings a smile to our faces whenever we find a big-company wine like this that over-delivers so handsomely on value for money. Owners: the Nugan family of Griffith; winemaker: Daren Owers.
CURRENT RELEASE 2005 Great value for money – this could show a lot of boring big-company products a clean pair of heels. It's vibrant and fruity with an attractive lacing of tidy oak and some herbal, cedary, snapped-twig and cashew-nutty aromas. There's a trace of toast from the beginnings of bottle-age. The palate is intense, fine, long and well-balanced. It drinks well with asparagus grilled with butter and grated parmesan.

Dalfarras Sauvignon Blanc

Quality	♀♀♀♀
Value	★★★★♪
Rating	90
Grapes	sauvignon blanc
Region	not stated
Cellar	▌1
Alc./Vol.	12.5%
RRP	$15.00 ≋

Dalfarras is another range associated with the Purbricks' venerable Tahbilk. It takes its name from winemaker Alister Purbrick's wife Rosa Dalfarra, whose art adorns the label with abstract images inspired by the Tahbilk wetlands.
CURRENT RELEASE 2005 Bright, succulent varietal aromas are an aromatic introduction to this juicy young sauvignon. Suggestions of passionfruit, lime and light grassy scents are pleasantly fresh, and the palate has plump, slightly fruit-sweet tropical flavours kept zippy by a lively tang of acidity. Try it with quick-fried calamari and fresh green herbs.

Deen De Bortoli Vat 2 Sauvignon Blanc

Quality	♀♀♀♀
Value	★★★★♪
Rating	90
Grapes	sauvignon blanc
Region	Riverina, NSW
Cellar	▌1
Alc./Vol.	13.0%
RRP	$10.00 ⓢ ≋

The late Deen De Bortoli presided over one of the Riverina's most successful wineries. Value for money has always been a constant theme, exemplified by this range of wines bearing his name.
CURRENT RELEASE 2006 Bright, juicy varietal cues introduce this young sauvignon with aromas of passionfruit, lime and lightly herbaceous touches. The palate has tingly tropical-fruit flavours made very zesty by fresh acidity. Serve it with warmed goat's cheese and fresh green-leaf salad with a tangy vinaigrette.

Galli Estate Rockbank Vineyard Sauvignon Blanc Semillon

Our Italian is pretty sketchy, but as far as we know 'galli' is the plural of 'gallo', which means chicken. The winery is at Rockbank, which is just outside Melbourne – past the airport.
CURRENT RELEASE 2005   It's a light, simple, rather basic but pleasant sauvignon with a pale hue, shy pepperminty-new-wine aromas and a light, straightforward taste. It has the customary sauvignon tanginess on the palate, and a clean, balanced finish for easy drinking – perhaps with a vegetable terrine.

Quality	♀ ♀ ♀
Value	★★★
Rating	86
Grapes	sauvignon blanc; semillon
Region	Sunbury, Vic.
Cellar	▮ 1
Alc./Vol.	13.0%
RRP	$18.00 ⑤ ⬷

Geoff Weaver Ferus Sauvignon

All around the world, but especially in New Zealand, winemakers are attempting to make another style of sauvignon blanc as an alternative to what Weaver calls the 'outrageously pungent' varietal, simple-fruit style. They do this with natural ferments, solidsy juice, barrel fermentation, lees contact, oak ageing and other techniques, hopefully making a more complex wine.
CURRENT RELEASE 2004   Wow! This is feral alright. The first thing you notice is it's murky, as a result of no fining or filtration. The nose is bizarre: feral, volatile, oak-accented and very eccentric, it also smells like mulched geranium stalks. The oak has a resiny aroma. It's more a feral white wine than a varietal, and more 'out-there' than any sauvignon blanc we've ever tasted! Impossible to score highly by any conventional standards of quality: if you like it, drink it! Try it with stuffed capsicums.

Quality	♀ ♀ ♀
Value	★★➤
Rating	84
Grapes	sauvignon blanc
Region	Adelaide Hills, SA
Cellar	▮ 2+
Alc./Vol.	13.0%
RRP	$40.00 ⬷

Geoff Weaver Lenswood Sauvignon Blanc

Geoff Weaver was for many years a senior winemaker for Hardys, finishing up as chief white winemaker, before leaving to devote himself to his own vineyard. He is also a hobby painter, and his rendition of the vineyard is on the back label.
CURRENT RELEASE 2005   Continuing the top track-record of this wine, the '05 is really excellent, showing lovely ripe-fruit aromas and concentrated, very long palate flavour. Gooseberry, herb and citrus aromas are highly appealing, while the expected tangy/zesty palate qualities we like in sauvignon blanc are there in abundance. Great with steamed coral trout with ginger and spring onions.

Quality	♀ ♀ ♀ ♀
Value	★★★➤
Rating	92
Grapes	sauvignon blanc
Region	Adelaide Hills, SA
Cellar	▮ 2
Alc./Vol.	13.5%
RRP	$23.00 ⬷

Goundrey Offspring Sauvignon Blanc

Quality	♀♀♀♀
Value	★★★
Rating	88
Grapes	sauvignon blanc
Region	Great Southern & Margaret River, WA
Cellar	▮ 1
Alc./Vol.	13.0%
RRP	$21.50 Ⓢ ☕

Goundrey has had a colourful history. Started by local shearing contractor Mike Goundrey and his wife Alison in 1978, it was bought by American businessman Jack Bendat who built it up into a showpiece winery, with massive wine sales second only to Houghton in Western Australia. It's now owned by Canadian-based Vincor.

CURRENT RELEASE 2005 This is a decent wine and right in style for the passionfruity/tropical and herbal flavours that so many people love in sauvignon blanc. It is rather light and perhaps lacks a little concentration, but it has good varietal character, freshness and life. It would suit baked stuffed capsicums.

Gum Bear Sauvignon Blanc

Quality	♀♀♀
Value	★★★
Rating	87
Grapes	sauvignon blanc
Region	Coonawarra, SA
Cellar	▮ 1
Alc./Vol.	12.5%
RRP	$18.00 Ⓢ ☕

A critter wine from conservative Coonawarra! Now that's a turn-up for the books. It's probably the brainchild of some febrile advertising nob from the big smoke. Gum Bear indeed! Eucalyptus koala would be more correct, but it doesn't sound the same.

CURRENT RELEASE 2005 This is a quite acceptable wine, by gum. It has an intense, appealing aroma of tropical fruits with a slight sulphide overlay, and the taste is slightly sweet-and-sour, but is tinged with capsicum flavour and finishes with good balance. It's very commercial with that touch of sweetness, but it's likely to find a keen audience. Drink with Greek stuffed vine leaves.

Hahndorf Hill Sauvignon Blanc

Quality	♀♀♀♀
Value	★★★⬩
Rating	88
Grapes	sauvignon blanc
Region	Adelaide Hills, SA
Cellar	▮ 2
Alc./Vol.	13.0%
RRP	$18.50 ☕

This won a gold medal at a competition in Singapore, which confirms that the highly aromatic, often slightly green/herbaceous, styles of savvy often rise to the top in blind judgings. The winery is run by Larry Jacobs, a former South African who established Mulderbosch in the Cape region of Stellenbosch, before migrating here and buying Hahndorf Hill as a going concern in 2002.

CURRENT RELEASE 2005 The colour is pale and the style of this savvy is lean and light, tangy and herbal, with snapped-twig and snow-pea aromas. It's just a bit mono for our tastes and falls away towards the finish. Still, a good drink in the hi-fi style and it will have many friends. Pair it with roasted red capsicum salad.

Hay Shed Hill Sauvignon Blanc Semillon

Hay Shed Hill's recent history has been beset by changes of ownership and direction, but wine quality is good these days. The vineyard is in one of Margaret River's prime spots.
CURRENT RELEASE 2005   Zippy aromas of fruits like guava and pawpaw meet the nose, and a leafy edge adds an appetising touch. It's lively in the mouth with grassy flavours and a penetrating brisk finish. An aromatic, refreshing wine to sip with shellfish salad.

Quality	♟♟♟♟
Value	★★★┤
Rating	91
Grapes	sauvignon blanc; semillon
Region	Margaret River, WA
Cellar	🍷 2
Alc./Vol.	12.4%
RRP	$20.00 🥂

Henschke Coralinga Sauvignon Blanc

Coralinga was an old estate destroyed by bushfire in the early twentieth century. It was close to the present Henschke vineyard at Lenswood in the Adelaide Hills.
CURRENT RELEASE 2005   The pale, slightly greenish appearance is typical of young Adelaide Hills sauvignon blanc, and the nose shows varietal character that's less penetrating and edgy than many. It has aromas of guava, pawpaw and green leaves, and the palate is in a more vinous vein with a smooth middle and a long, tangy finish. Serve it with goujons of fish with tomato mayonnaise.

Quality	♟♟♟♟♟
Value	★★★┤
Rating	93
Grapes	sauvignon blanc
Region	Adelaide Hills, SA
Cellar	🍷 2
Alc./Vol.	13.5%
RRP	$21.90 🥂

Hesperos Sauvignon Blanc

Hesperos is the going-it-alone brand of former Chateau Xanadu head winemaker Jurg Muggli. Hesperos has its own vineyards, winery and cellar-door sales in Margaret River.
CURRENT RELEASE 2005   This is an exemplary sauvignon blanc: pale coloured with aromas of tangy garden salad and herbs, cut-radish and grass. It's very tangy and crisply tart on the palate, fresh and vigorous with a properly dry, clean acid finish. It has some weight, and its flavour will grow on you as you sip. It suits stuffed zucchini flowers.

Quality	♟♟♟♟
Value	★★★★
Rating	90
Grapes	sauvignon blanc
Region	Margaret River, WA
Cellar	🍷 2
Alc./Vol.	13.0%
RRP	$18.20 🥂

Hewitson Lulu Sauvignon Blanc

Quality	♥♥♥
Value	★★★
Rating	88
Grapes	sauvignon blanc
Region	Adelaide Hills, SA
Cellar	▮ 1
Alc./Vol.	12.5%
RRP	$22.00 ⬗

A new wine from Dean Hewitson, and no wonder: the market for sauvignon blanc has gone ape over the past two or three years. Hewitson is a former Petaluma winemaker who does his thing these days in a former dairy coolstore in suburban Adelaide.

CURRENT RELEASE 2005   There was still a fair bit of sulphur dioxide hanging over the bouquet of our sample, but it has some varietal pungency, with cut-radish and cedar overtones. It's a very light-bodied, delicate style with a lean, soft palate. It's a nice quaffer that could use a bit more intensity. Take it along to a vegetarian restaurant.

Hill Smith Estate Sauvignon Blanc

Quality	♥♥♥♥
Value	★★★⁴
Rating	91
Grapes	sauvignon blanc
Region	Eden Valley, SA
Cellar	▮ 1
Alc./Vol.	12.5%
RRP	$18.95 ⬗

The Hill Smith family's estate in the Eden Valley has specialised in good sauvignon blanc for many years. We think that the latest examples have shown less exuberant fruit than past vintages, but more subtlety and vinosity. Maker: Louisa Rose.

CURRENT RELEASE 2005   A fresh varietal nose of citrus, herbaceous and minerally scents that has some more interesting floral/pot-pourri aromas woven in. In the mouth it's dry and savoury with good texture and length, finishing dry and tangy. It's a more subtle, complex wine than the usual up-front style of Adelaide Hills or Eden Valley sauvignon. Match it with lemon grass prawns.

Houghton Pemberton Sauvignon Blanc

Quality	♥♥♥♥
Value	★★⁴
Rating	92
Grapes	sauvignon blanc
Region	Pemberton, WA
Cellar	▮ 1
Alc./Vol.	13.5%
RRP	$26.00 ⬗

Pemberton is a rather secluded neck of the woods with beautiful countryside and some very picturesque vineyards. Although it's a good four-hour-plus drive from Perth at sensible speeds, it's a worthwhile pilgrimage to make as Houghton's wines are among the region's best.

CURRENT RELEASE 2005   A pale, slightly green-tinged young wine with a nose that sauvignon blanc-haters will . . . hate. It has piercing herbaceous scents, with vegetal, mineral and talc-like touches. The palate has more depth than we expected from the nose, but it's still a penetrating type of wine without much in the way of flesh. That said, it's very true to type, and it should work well with the right food. Serve it with goat's cheese and you should see the point.

Howard Park Sauvignon Blanc

Howard Park's main claims to fame are its excellent cabernet and riesling. Sauvignon blanc didn't feature among the estate's earlier wines, but these days most wineries have a go at just about everything. Maker: Michael Kerrigan.

CURRENT RELEASE 2005   This smells juicy and gorgeous, a surge of passionfruit and assorted tropical fruits lead the way, with an unusual touch of spice in the recipe and nicely subdued herbaceousness. The appetising fruity palate signs off clean and zippy. Try it with goat's cheese and asparagus.

Quality	♥♥♥♥
Value	★★★
Rating	91
Grapes	sauvignon blanc
Region	various, WA
Cellar	1
Alc./Vol.	12.5%
RRP	$25.00

Hungerford Hill Fishcage Sauvignon Blanc Semillon

The significance of the fishcage eludes us, but we've become used to the eccentricities of Hungerford Hill's labelling over the years. Wine quality is good.

CURRENT RELEASE 2005   This has an appealing aroma that merges the lemony cues of semillon with a dab of tropical sauvignon character. The semillon rules even though it's the junior partner in the blend. It's more savoury than many such blends and the palate is dry and tangy. A good dry white for fried whitebait.

Quality	♥♥♥♥
Value	★★★★
Rating	90
Grapes	sauvignon blanc; semillon
Region	not stated
Cellar	1
Alc./Vol.	12.0%
RRP	$14.00

Jamiesons Run Sauvignon Blanc

Although based in Coonawarra, the Jamiesons Run people increasingly use the regional title 'Limestone Coast' on their wines and source fruit from neighbouring areas, suggesting that there may not be enough Coonawarra fruit to satisfy their needs.

CURRENT RELEASE 2005   Steely aromas with a fair whiff of sulphur meet the nose here, but with some exposure to the air it cleans up to reveal simple herby fruit. The palate is soft in the middle with juicy fruit and a dry finish. It suits roasted goat's cheese and onion tartlets.

Quality	♥♥♥
Value	★★★
Rating	86
Grapes	sauvignon blanc
Region	Limestone Coast, SA
Cellar	2
Alc./Vol.	12.0%
RRP	$16.00

Lillydale Estate Sauvignon Blanc

Quality	♉ ♉ ♉ ♉
Value	★★★
Rating	88
Grapes	sauvignon blanc
Region	Yarra Valley, Vic.
Cellar	🍶 1
Alc./Vol.	12.5%
RRP	$19.85 Ⓢ ᵇ

Lillydale Estate is McWilliams' foothold in the lovely Yarra Valley. It's a little off the main Yarra Valley tourist trails, but it's worth a visit for the Great Aussie Indoor Barbecue where you cook your own meat and fish in the smart restaurant.
CURRENT RELEASE 2005   A slightly peppery, edgy sauvignon blanc with zesty herb, snow pea and lime aromas of good intensity. The palate is tight and tangy with light tropical fruit flavour and a dry herbal finish. A good match for shellfish.

Millbrook Sauvignon Blanc

Quality	♉ ♉ ♉
Value	★★★
Rating	86
Grapes	sauvignon blanc
Region	Geographe, WA
Cellar	🍶 1
Alc./Vol.	13.5%
RRP	$20.00 ᵇ

Millbrook's winery and 7-hectare home vineyard are located at Jarrahdale in the Perth Hills, south-east of Perth city. The grapes for this wine, however, were grown in the Geographe region, which is between Perth and Margaret River. Maker: Tony Davis.
CURRENT RELEASE 2005   This is quite a big, robust style of sauvignon, with weight and warmth but without the delicate, crisp structure of cooler-area wines. It has a lolly-shop, confectionery aroma with ripe tropical perfumes, and plenty of palate intensity but not much zing or finesse. It would suit a prawn cocktail with thousand-island dressing.

Moorilla Sauvignon Blanc

Quality	♉ ♉ ♉
Value	★★⁺
Rating	85
Grapes	sauvignon blanc
Region	Tasmania
Cellar	🍶 1
Alc./Vol.	14.0%
RRP	$24.00 ᵇ

We are puzzled by the Moorilla wines of recent times. The quality fluctuates wildly from wine to wine, from bog-ordinary to excellent. Winemaker is Alan Ferry, since Michael Glover moved to Bannockburn during 2005.
CURRENT RELEASE 2005   The aromas are unusually floral, reminding us more of riesling than sauvignon. There could be a touch of botrytis or other rot here: it doesn't smell or taste like pure sauvignon blanc fruit. The palate is slightly sweet and lacks fruit intensity and varietal 'cut'. It's an okay drink but not what we expect from a Tasmanian sauvignon. Goat's cheese is in order.

Mornington Estate Sauvignon Blanc

'Rockin, rollin, ridin, out along the bay; all bound for Morningtown, many miles away . . .' So sang the immortal Seekers. They could easily have been singing about the Mornington Peninsula and Port Phillip Bay. We can pretend they were; it makes it seem a bit more glamorous somehow.

CURRENT RELEASE 2005   A very creditable effort at one of the most popular wine styles in the country. Pale coloured, it's crisp and tangy, tasting of green capsicums and lemon/citrus. The palate is very light and fresh, crisp and clean, with a trace of well-measured sweetness helping soften and make it gentler. You could serve it with grilled garfish and parsley butter.

Quality	♟ ♟ ♟
Value	★★★
Rating	87
Grapes	sauvignon blanc
Region	Mornington Peninsula, Vic.
Cellar	1
Alc./Vol.	13.5%
RRP	$18.00

Nepenthe Sauvignon Blanc

The Adelaide Hills is held to be Australia's best sauvignon blanc region (especially by the Adelaide Hills vignerons) and quality is certainly a step up from many other Aussie districts.

CURRENT RELEASE 2005   This pale wine offers piercing varietal aromas that are herbaceous and tangy, and touches of guava and gooseberry give it a fruity dimension. In the mouth it's a zippy drop with herb and grassy flavours of lively intensity and good persistence. Try it with fresh goat's cheese on toasted olive bread.

Quality	♟ ♟ ♟ ♟
Value	★★★
Rating	90
Grapes	sauvignon blanc
Region	Adelaide Hills, SA
Cellar	1
Alc./Vol.	13.0%
RRP	$20.00

Ninth Island Sauvignon Blanc

Ninth Island wines were created as a second tier to the more prestigious Pipers Brook wines. Quality has varied over the years, usually to do with the vagaries of the marginal weather in some Tasmanian vintages, but when they're good they command attention.

CURRENT RELEASE 2005   A mouth-watering example of Tassie sauvignon blanc, this has a delicately aromatic bouquet reminiscent of asparagus, limes and melon. In the mouth it's a lively drop with excellent varietal flavours in the brisk, cool-climate vein. The finish is appetising and clean, making it a good partner for the freshest of shellfish.

Quality	♟ ♟ ♟ ♟
Value	★★★
Rating	91
Grapes	sauvignon blanc
Region	northern Tas.
Cellar	1
Alc./Vol.	13.7%
RRP	$21.50

Norfolk Rise Sauvignon Blanc

Quality	🍷🍷🍷🍷
Value	★★★★
Rating	92
Grapes	sauvignon blanc
Region	Mount Benson, SA
Cellar	🍾 1
Alc./Vol.	13.0%
RRP	$16.55

There's been quite a rash of new labels from the evolving Mount Benson region on South Australia's Limestone Coast, but few are as promising as Norfolk Rise. It reflects the quality-oriented approach of its owners, Kreglinger, who also have Pipers Brook in Tasmania.

CURRENT RELEASE 2005   Very bright, fresh varietal aromas kick off this pale wine and show excellent varietal character. Passionfruit and grassy scents have real zest, and it tastes lively with a juicy, fruit-sweet mid-palate, a tart backbone and a long, clean finish. Serve it with goat's cheese pastries on a bed of rocket.

Pauletts Sauvignon Blanc

Quality	🍷🍷🍷
Value	★★★
Rating	89
Grapes	sauvignon blanc
Region	Clare Valley, SA
Cellar	🍾 2
Alc./Vol.	13.0%
RRP	$18.50

The Pauletts vineyard is in the Polish Hill River part of the Clare Valley, a prized district that consistently produces some of the region's best wines.

CURRENT RELEASE 2005   A minerally sauvignon blanc with a little more vinous interest than most. It has an aroma of slate, lime, herbs and guava, with a juicy mid-palate, succulent fruit/acid balance, and a dry steely finish. Pair it with pork and coriander dumplings.

Penmara Sauvignon Blanc

Quality	🍷🍷🍷🍷
Value	★★★★
Rating	90
Grapes	sauvignon blanc
Region	Orange, NSW
Cellar	🍾 1
Alc./Vol.	13.5%
RRP	$16.00

This is a mysterious wine company, which seems to be without a central focal point but produces inexpensive wines from five vineyards in several New South Wales regions. The name has something to do with five families being involved, a kind of vinous pentagon. Winemaker: John Hordern.

CURRENT RELEASE 2005   The nose is varietal alright, with cut-radish, capsicum herbaceous notes and a dusty pungency. The taste is soft and smooth, almost with a touch of richness, perhaps with a kiss of oak, but it maintains its essential delicacy and tang, finishing clean and dry. It's very well balanced. Try it with fresh goat's cheese.

Pikes Sauvignon Blanc Semillon

The sauvignon-semillon blend is an odd one, the wines can be green-grassy sauvignon blanc or up-front and tropical. Other examples, like Pikes, show notably more subtle semillon influence on both nose and palate, despite having sauvignon as the major component.

CURRENT RELEASE 2005   Lemon, floral and slightly lanolin-like aromas couple with a dab of tropical fruit in nice harmony here, and it tastes smoothly satisfying with good depth of citrus, nectarine and herby/fruit flavour. It signs off long and clean with an appealing, mouth-watering aftertaste. Good with chilled prawns.

Quality	♥♥♥♥
Value	★★★✦
Rating	91
Grapes	sauvignon blanc; semillon
Region	Clare Valley, SA
Cellar	🍶 1
Alc./Vol.	13.0%
RRP	$19.20 🥂

Rolling Sauvignon Blanc Semillon

Rolling is the lower-priced range of Cumulus Wines, near Orange, made from grapes grown in some of the cooler regions of New South Wales. Winemakers: Phil Shaw and Phil Dowell.

CURRENT RELEASE 2005   A pale young wine with appetising citrus scents in charge, but with a slightly richer, fruit-salady dimension in support. It tastes intense and fresh with good mouth-feel and a long dry finish. A straightforward, clean-tasting dry white. It works well with steamed pipis.

Quality	♥♥♥♥
Value	★★★★
Rating	90
Grapes	sauvignon blanc; semillon
Region	Central Ranges, NSW
Cellar	🍶 2
Alc./Vol.	13.0%
RRP	$15.00 Ⓢ 🥂

Rosily Sauvignon Blanc

Rosily is a fairly low-key operation, relative to Margaret River's big names, and wine pricing is a bit less adventurous than some, but quality is always very good.

CURRENT RELEASE 2005   There's room for various different slants on sauvignon blanc, and these days there are some pretty wines across a broad spectrum of styles. This example is in the riper mould, rather than the ultra-herbaceous camp. It has clean herb and citrus aromas that lead to a palate of some tropical-fruit richness. There's good depth of fruit, balanced by a dry austerity on the finish. A good match for roasted tomato and basil bruschette.

Quality	♥♥♥♥
Value	★★★✦
Rating	91
Grapes	sauvignon blanc
Region	Margaret River, WA
Cellar	🍶 1
Alc./Vol.	13.7%
RRP	$20.00 🥂

Rymill Sauvignon Blanc

Quality	🍷🍷🍷⟩
Value	★★★⟩
Rating	88
Grapes	sauvignon blanc
Region	Coonawarra, SA
Cellar	🍷 1
Alc./Vol.	12.0%
RRP	$15.70 🏷

There's quite a bit of white wine made from Coonawarra fruit, and some of it is good, but in most eyes it's real red wine territory. Rymill make one of the region's better-known sauvignon blancs.

CURRENT RELEASE 2005   A pale young sauvignon with a nose of minerals, tropical fruits and grassy notes. In the mouth it's a juicy, medium-intensity example with reasonable depth of fruit and fairly piercing acidity. Try it with Vietnamese mint-wrapped spring rolls.

Seppelt Victoria Sauvignon Blanc

Quality	🍷🍷⟩
Value	★★★
Rating	84
Grapes	sauvignon blanc
Region	various, Vic.
Cellar	🍷 1
Alc./Vol.	13.5%
RRP	$17.00 Ⓢ 🏷

The Victoria label stands for cheapest wines produced at the Great Western winery, usually from grapes sourced from vineyards across Victoria, wherever the winemakers can find appropriate fruit. Chief winemaker is Arthur O'Connor.

CURRENT RELEASE 2005   Sweet gooseberry aromas with herbal undercurrents confirm the varietal character of sauvignon blanc. It's simple, light and commercial, with a lick of sweetness on the palate. Beneath that, the fruit flavour is a touch insipid. It's not nearly as exciting as the shiraz under the same label, but still fair value. Serve with sautéed scallops.

Shadowfax Sauvignon Blanc

Quality	🍷🍷🍷🍷⟩
Value	★★★★★
Rating	92
Grapes	sauvignon blanc
Region	Adelaide Hills, SA
Cellar	🍷 2
Alc./Vol.	13.0%
RRP	$20.00 🏷

Winemaker Matt Harrop and the gang from Shadowfax are based in southern Victoria, but they take the attitude that if they want to make sauvignon blanc, they get grapes from the best source, which is the Adelaide Hills. They apply that reasoning to other wines, too. We think it's pretty sound thinking.

CURRENT RELEASE 2005   This is one of the more powerful, intensely flavoured savvies we found from the Hills in '05. It is an impressive wine to behold, with intense aromas of crushed lime leaves, herbs and underlying tropical fruits. There may be a subtle element of oaked wine in the blend, adding richness and length. The finish is clean, dry and very long. There's an extra dimension that sets it apart. It would work well with sautéed Balmain bug tails.

Shelmerdine Sauvignon Blanc

This outfit is run by Stephen Shelmerdine, a former chief of the Winemakers Federation of Australia and son of Ross Shelmerdine, founder of Mitchelton. Maker: Kate Goodman.
CURRENT RELEASE 2005 The nose is lifted and slightly edgy, but delivers a lot of lime-leaf and capsicum aromas that have an echo of New Zealand about them. There's some apparent sweetness, and it has a bit more fruit weight than many of its competitors. There's a touch of thickness at the finish, from phenolics. Serve well chilled, with niçoise salad.

Quality	♟ ♟ ♟
Value	★★★
Rating	86
Grapes	sauvignon blanc
Region	Yarra Valley, Vic.
Cellar	🍷 1
Alc./Vol.	13.5%
RRP	$22.00 Ⓢ

Smithbrook Sauvignon Blanc

Smithbrook was established by a syndicate of Western Australians in the late 1980s, bought by Petaluma as a going concern and then absorbed into Lion Nathan along with the rest of the Petaluma group. With 60 hectares, it's one of the big players in Pemberton. Winemaker is Michael Symons.
CURRENT RELEASE 2005 Smithbrook when on song can be one of the best sauvignon blancs in Australia. The 2005 season brought difficulties in the West, however, and this one is a bit too asparagusy/composty on the nose and astringent in the mouth for us. It's lean and dry but lacks palate appeal. Drink it with mussels.

Quality	♟ ♟ ♟
Value	★★★
Rating	86
Grapes	sauvignon blanc
Region	Pemberton, WA
Cellar	🍷 1
Alc./Vol.	14.0%
RRP	$19.00

Smithbrook The Yilgarn Blanc

We're not sure the brand name is catchy enough to make it an instant household word. The idea is to create an identity that transcends the limitations of varietal labelling. That way, they can juggle the proportion of grape varieties from year to year, and also avoid the preconceived expectation of drinkers regarding the way the wine tastes.
CURRENT RELEASE 2005 This is much more than a regulation sav-sem: it's a complex, 'worked' dry white with lots of vanilla, nutty and toasty characters imparted largely by oak barrels, but also other techniques. It has piercing acidity and a touch of austerity, all of which suggests it is intended as a wine for ageing. It certainly has intensity, length and presence. We suggest you cellar it for a year or so, then serve with rich food such as coq au vin made with white wine.

Quality	♟ ♟ ♟ ♟ ♟
Value	★★★★
Rating	92
Grapes	sauvignon blanc 86%; semillon 14%
Region	Pemberton, WA
Cellar	1–5+
Alc./Vol.	14.0%
RRP	$28.00

St Huberts Sauvignon Blanc

Quality	♥ ♥ ♥
Value	★ ★ ★
Rating	86
Grapes	sauvignon blanc
Region	Yarra Valley, Vic.
Cellar	🍷 1
Alc./Vol.	11.5%
RRP	$24.00 ⑤ 🍷

This is the kind of sauvignon blanc that creates enemies for the grape. It has that sweaty, cat-pee pungency that turns some people off. (Is there a correlation between dog lovers and sauvignon blanc haters, we wonder?)
CURRENT RELEASE 2005   The book of Great Yarra Valley Sauvignon Blancs is a very quick read. This one is at least acceptable, as long as you don't mind the aforementioned pungency. If you search, you might find some passionfruit and pawpaw tropical notes, while the palate is lean and lacks strength, falling away towards the finish. Quaff it with a pineapple-topped pizza.

Stoney Vineyard Sauvignon Blanc

Quality	♥ ♥ ♥
Value	★ ★ ⁴
Rating	86
Grapes	sauvignon blanc
Region	Coal River, Tas.
Cellar	🍷 2+
Alc./Vol.	13.5%
RRP	$30.00 (cellar door)

Peter and Ruth Althaus came to Tasmania from Switzerland in the 1980s to take over a tiny established vineyard called Stoney. They greatly expanded the plantings and built an impressive winery into the side of a hill, and set about making some equally eye-opening wines. The flagship wines are labelled Domaine A.
CURRENT RELEASE 2005   It's an unusual style of sauvignon blanc: as always, Peter Althaus follows his own path. The wine has a peppery, herbaceous aroma and flavour with some smoky and compost-like overtones. It's lean and tangy with lively acidity and not a lot of fruit or richness. The finish is dry and lip-smacking. It would go well with fish served with capsicum purée.

Tamar Ridge Sauvignon Blanc

Quality	♥ ♥ ♥ ♥ ⁵
Value	★ ★ ★ ★
Rating	94
Grapes	sauvignon blanc
Region	Tamar Valley, Tas.
Cellar	🍷 1
Alc./Vol.	14.0%
RRP	$20.70 🍷

People get all excited about New Zealand sauvignon blanc these days. Back in Australia, the Adelaide Hills region has carved a niche for itself with this assertive grape, but for our money a handful of top Tasmanian sauvignons merit comparison with the best of the New World. Tamar Ridge is one of them.
CURRENT RELEASE 2005   This bright young wine has lots to recommend it. The aroma is deliciously ripe and juicy with scents of guava, pawpaw and a lightly herbal edge. There's also a touch of slatey minerality. On the palate it has lush fruit, made succulent by a thrilling counterpoint of acidity. Textural interest in the mouth is good, perhaps suggesting a little lees influence. Serve it with scallop and asparagus stirfry.

Trentham Estate Sauvignon Blanc

Sauvignon blanc is riding a wave of popularity in Australia and it's good to know that you don't have to pay a fortune to get true varietal personality.
CURRENT RELEASE 2005   The nose is clean and full of varietal authenticity. It combines a touch of citrus with more juicy tropical fruit aromas, and there are hints of green leaves and asparagus. In the mouth it's ripe and clean with good depth of flavour and it's not boosted by too much residual sugar. There's a bit more 'oomph' to this than we would expect in a sauvignon blanc that's so reasonably priced. It finishes dry and tasty. Try it with fishy canapés.

Quality	♟♟♟♟
Value	★★★★┤
Rating	91
Grapes	sauvignon blanc
Region	Murray Valley, NSW
Cellar	▮ 1
Alc./Vol.	11.5%
RRP	$12.90 Ⓢ 🍷

Voyager Estate Sauvignon Blanc Semillon

Voyager Estate's star is continuing to rise via Cliff Royle's skilled winemaking. We think his chardonnays and shirazes stand comparison with the best, and this take on the ubiquitous Margaret River 'classic white' formula measures up to similar high standards.
CURRENT RELEASE 2005   A shiny, pale wine with a surge of ripe passionfruit on the nose. It also has succulent scents of blackcurrant, lime zest and green leaves. The palate is smooth and agreeable, and a vague suggestion of nutty oak is more about textural interest than flavour. It finishes long and clean-tasting. Delicious with stir-fried calamari.

Quality	♟♟♟♟♟
Value	★★★★
Rating	93
Grapes	sauvignon blanc; semillon
Region	Margaret River, WA
Cellar	▮ 1
Alc./Vol.	13.0%
RRP	$22.00 🍷

Wirra Wirra Sauvignon Blanc

The increasing ranks of sauvignon blanc coming out of the Adelaide Hills seem to get better each year. They do have their ups and downs from seasonal conditions, but the flavours are becoming more agreeable: growers and makers are obviously getting a good handle on style.
Maker: Samantha Connew.
CURRENT RELEASE 2005   Another very good Adelaide Hills '05 savvy. It's pale in colour but has an intense gooseberry aroma that is fresh and vibrant. In the mouth, it is light-bodied but of good intensity; tangy and crisp in mouth-feel, with a firm but not hard finish that lingers well. A wine of vitality and charm to serve with a mixed shellfish platter.

Quality	♟♟♟♟
Value	★★★┤
Rating	90
Grapes	sauvignon blanc
Region	Adelaide Hills, SA
Cellar	▮ 1
Alc./Vol.	13.5%
RRP	$21.50 Ⓢ 🍷

Wirra Wirra Scrubby Rise Sauvignon Blanc Semillon Viognier

Quality	🍷🍷🍷⁅
Value	★★★★⁅
Rating	89
Grapes	sauvignon blanc; semillon; viognier
Region	various, SA
Cellar	🍾1
Alc./Vol.	13.5%
RRP	$15.50 Ⓢ ⧈

The Scrubby Rise is apparently neither scrubby (one would hope there were orderly vines there, not unruly scrub) nor is it on a rise. The late Greg Trott, Wirra's co-founder, would no doubt have found the irony amusing.
CURRENT RELEASE 2005   A curious blend, but it does the job admirably. It's a good fruity, flavoursome quaffing white with a nicely fragrant nose – floral, minerally and vaguely earthy. The palate is full and ripely flavoured, with some tang and zip, thanks to the sauvignon blanc fruit plus lively acidity. The finish is soft and pleasingly dry. It would go with an antipasto platter.

Semillon and blends

The classic Hunter Valley semillon dry white style has enjoyed a high profile over the years. Some of the fame has been deserved, but what's too often overlooked is the good semillon grown in many other parts of Australia. Some excellent wines are emerging from South Australia and Western Australia, and winemakers are honing techniques with semillon to offer another quality white wine alternative. The multiplicity of semillon-sauvignon blanc blends is more of a mixed bag: the best are thrilling, but too many fit a lean-and-mean profile that's far from lovable. As for Hunter semillon, at best it remains a true classic, and the ready availability of aged examples means it's easy to enjoy them at their mature best.

Adinfern Shepherds Rhapsody

This is the basic, entry-level white from Adinfern, whose name sounds more to us like a women's health club or a commercial dried-yeast than a winery. With brands like Musterer's Magic and Shepherd's Dream, who are they kidding? But we wish them well!
CURRENT RELEASE 2005   A simple, soft dry white wine, this smells of the benchmark snow-pea, green-twig characters that typify this kind of wine from the south-west of Western Australia. It's light and lively, soft and straightforward in flavour. The finish is clean and dry. You could serve it with a vegetable terrine.

Quality	♈♈♈
Value	★★★
Rating	86
Grapes	semillon; sauvignon blanc
Region	Margaret River, WA
Cellar	🍾 1
Alc./Vol.	12.9%
RRP	$17.00 🥂

Amberley Semillon Sauvignon Blanc

Amberley was taken over in 2004 by the Canadian-based multi-national company Vincor. Long-term winemaker Eddie Price left soon after. Vincor had also bought Goundrey, and already owns several wineries in the US and Canada. Maker: Paul Dunnewyck.
CURRENT RELEASE 2005   A simple, well-made, very quaffable but ultimately rather basic dry white wine, in typical south-west Western Australian style. The usual herbal, lightly citrusy, vaguely passionfruity flavours are there but the wine lacks a little in depth and interest. A decent commercial quaffer. Have it with stuffed capsicums.

Quality	♈♈♈
Value	★★★
Rating	87
Grapes	semillon; sauvignon blanc
Region	Margaret River, WA
Cellar	🍾 1
Alc./Vol.	13.0%
RRP	$22.00 🥂

Annie's Lane Semillon

Quality	♟ ♟ ♟ ᵻ
Value	★★★ᵻ
Rating	88
Grapes	semillon
Region	Clare Valley, SA
Cellar	⬇ 2
Alc./Vol.	12.5%
RRP	$18.00 Ⓢ ⮕

Annie's Lane is a Foster's brand that is identified with the former Quelltaler winery at Watervale – established way back in 1863. The wines are all Clare Valley wines. The stats tell us the Quelltaler holdings in the valley total 400 hectares. Winemaker: Mark Robertson.

CURRENT RELEASE 2005   There are some traditional straw/hay-like developing semillon aromas, but also some snow-pea, green-stemmy aromas that remind us more of Margaret River. As usual, this wine is a good drink and good value: it has a soft but dry, lemon-flavoured palate of good balance and drinkability. Serve it with chicken Maryland.

Bidgeebong Triangle Semillon Sauvignon Blanc

Quality	♟ ♟ ♟ ♟
Value	★★★★ᵻ
Rating	91
Grapes	semillon; sauvignon blanc
Region	Wagga Wagga, Hilltops & Tumbarumba, NSW
Cellar	⬇ 3
Alc./Vol.	12.0%
RRP	$14.00 ⮕

The 'Triangle' of wine regions involved in the production of this keenly priced range of wines is formed by the regions of Wagga Wagga, Hilltops and Tumbarumba in southern New South Wales.

CURRENT RELEASE 2005   A juicy young wine that shows more semillon character on the nose than sauvignon blanc. It's fresh with aromas of lemon, lanolin, minerals and green herbs. In the mouth it has ripe flavour and good texture with lively citrus flavours of length and vitality. Try it with calamari and green herbs.

Bird in Hand Two in The Bush Semillon Sauvignon Blanc

Quality	♟ ♟ ♟
Value	★★★ᵻ
Rating	86
Grapes	semillon 70%; sauvignon blanc 30%
Region	Adelaide Hills, SA
Cellar	⬇ 1
Alc./Vol.	12.0%
RRP	$16.65 ⮕

If distinctive brand names are their goal, the Nugent family have got the right formula. In fact, their address is Bird in Hand Road, so it probably wasn't their idea. The vineyard is a substantial 26 hectares. Winemaker and viticulturist is Andrew Nugent, assisted by globetrotting consultant-winemaker Kym Milne.

CURRENT RELEASE 2005   This is the cheaper of this winery's two sauvignon-based wines, and is certainly lighter and somewhat greener in flavour than the pure sauvignon blanc. It has a herby, dusty, pyrazine-laden aroma, while the palate is lean and lively with a tangy finish that drops slightly short. The aftertaste is soft and savoury. A good drink with Spanish frittata.

Brokenwood Semillon

Brokenwood Semillon is one of the Hunter's modern benchmarks, a classical style to put away for later. As with most great Hunter Semillons, bottle-age works wonders.
CURRENT RELEASE 2005   Typically pale and restrained in youth, this has a fresh personality that's reminiscent of lime and lemon, dry straw, herbs and minerals. In '05 it has an extra dimension of richness compared to some other vintages, despite being so low in alcohol. The palate is relatively ripe in flavour, leading through to a long, clean, dry finish. It should mature well medium term. Great with delicate fish dishes.

Quality	🍷🍷🍷🍷
Value	★★★★
Rating	94
Grapes	semillon
Region	Hunter Valley, NSW
Cellar	⬤–1–6+
Alc./Vol.	10.5%
RRP	$17.00

Burge Family Winemakers Olive Hill Semillon

Rick Burge is the Barossa's 'other' Burge. His cousin Grant does things very differently. Rick Burge's outfit is small and hands-on, without the grand ambitions of the Grant Burge juggernaut.
CURRENT RELEASE 2005   Typical of Barossa semillon, this has seen the inside of a barrel, and tastes smoky and toasty, while the citrusy, herby semillon varietal fruit is still visible. The palate is rich, soft, rounded and fairly dry, and it drinks well young. It's already quite complex. It would work well with chicken Maryland.
Previous outstanding vintage: 2002

Quality	🍷🍷🍷🍷
Value	★★★★
Rating	90
Grapes	semillon
Region	Barossa Valley, SA
Cellar	🍷 4
Alc./Vol.	13.0%
RRP	$16.00
	(cellar door)

Clairault Semillon Sauvignon Blanc

It's truly remarkable how Margaret River has made its name and fame by blending semillon and sauvignon blanc. If ever there was a case of the whole being greater than the sum of its separate parts, it is SSB.
CURRENT RELEASE 2005   Pale colour introduces a wine of crisp, herbaceous, snapped-twig aromas, with a trace of cedar. This is a plain but agreeable wine with adequate fruit and varietal identity. It's not sugar-reliant like many, and has some strength of structure on palate. You could pair this with trout braised with fennel.

Quality	🍷🍷🍷
Value	★★★
Rating	86
Grapes	semillon; sauvignon blanc
Region	Margaret River, WA
Cellar	🍷 1
Alc./Vol.	13.5%
RRP	$20.00

Cockfighter's Ghost Semillon

Quality	♀♀♀⁌
Value	★★★⁌
Rating	88
Grapes	semillon
Region	Hunter Valley, NSW
Cellar	◊ 3+
Alc./Vol.	12.2%
RRP	$18.00 ⇗

This is one of three brands owned by David Clarke, chairman of Macquarie Bank and a number of other high-profile companies. His other brands are Poole's Rock and Firestick. Clarke bought the former Tulloch winery from Southcorp to give his wines a home base. Maker is ex-Tulloch winemaker, Patrick Auld.
CURRENT RELEASE 2005   A very clean, well-made semillon that seems aimed more at the drink-now market than the hoarders. It's soft and fairly round on the palate, with relatively low acidity. That just means it drinks well young, but lacks the penetrating line and length of a classic. The aromas are of lanolin, lemon and some confectionery esters. Try it with sautéed yabbies.

Crofters Semillon Sauvignon Blanc

Quality	♀♀♀♀
Value	★★★
Rating	91
Grapes	semillon; sauvignon blanc
Region	Margaret River, Pemberton & Mount Barker, WA
Cellar	◊ 1
Alc./Vol.	13.0%
RRP	$23.00 ⇗

Crofters is a range of wines made from Western Australia's more southerly vineyards by benchmark winery Houghton. Semillon-sauvignon is a speciality, and it exemplifies the flavoury style from the West.
CURRENT RELEASE 2005   Quite a voluptuous style of SSB, this has ripe tropical fruit on the nose with some hints of green-pea aroma. The palate has good depth of flavour, and a rounder mouth-feel than many similar blends. It retains typically bracing acidity to keep the palate cleansing. Try it with steamed scallops sprinkled with chopped coriander.

Cuttaway Hill Estate Semillon Sauvignon Blanc

Quality	♀♀♀⁌
Value	★★★⁌
Rating	88
Grapes	semillon; sauvignon blanc
Region	Southern Highlands, NSW
Cellar	◊ 1
Alc./Vol.	11.0%
RRP	$15.00 ⇗ (cellar door)

This vineyard is one of the newer properties in the Southern Highlands, an hour's drive south of Sydney. It's named after the cutting made through a hill to allow for the Hume Highway. Mark Bourne is vineyard manager and Jim Chatto makes the wines at Monarch in the Hunter.
CURRENT RELEASE 2005   This is a good, if not exactly exciting, wine with clean crisp fruit and a modicum of varietal sauvignon blanc character. It's light and fairly plain with lively acidity, herbal and lemony-fruit flavours keeping it all fresh and zippy. The finish is clean, dry and slightly firm, and it would team well with a vegetable-based Lebanese meal.

Cuttlefish Classic White

The Cuttlefish brand comes from the Flying Fish Cove winery, which describes itself as primarily a contract-winemaking and bulk processing facility, located in Margaret River. Classic White is a catch-all name that's used for pretty much anything that doesn't fit into the main varietal wines.
CURRENT RELEASE 2005 It's a fairly plain, nondescript wine but there's nothing wrong with it, and it makes a decent quaffer at a fair price. The aromas are cosmetic, lolly-ish and faintly vanillin; it has a soft, rounded taste with a clean finish and a suspicion of oak. A good quaffing white to drink with fish and chips.

Quality 🍷🍷½
Value ★★★
Rating 85
Grapes semillon; sauvignon blanc; chardonnay
Region Margaret River, WA
Cellar 1
Alc./Vol. 12.5%
RRP $13.25

Edwards Semillon Sauvignon Blanc

The Edwards vineyard was established by the late Brian Edwards, who migrated from England to Australia by flying his Tiger Moth here, and using the trip to raise money for charity. He wrote a book about the experience, which you can buy at the cellar door.
CURRENT RELEASE 2005 A straightforward but pleasing and very typical style of dry white that has become quite the signature of Margaret River. Greenish-stemmy, herbal aromas speak more perhaps of semillon than sauvignon, and it's light-bodied, crisp and lively in the mouth, finishing with crisp tangy acidity that makes the mouth water and prepares the system for food. In other words, it's a good appetite stimulant. Serve it with a seafood salad.

Quality 🍷🍷🍷½
Value ★★★
Rating 88
Grapes semillon; sauvignon blanc
Region Margaret River, WA
Cellar 1
Alc./Vol. 13.0%
RRP $19.00

Glenguin Estate The Old Broke Block Semillon

The Old Broke Block refers to the original plantings of semillon on the white sandy creek-bed soils beside the Wollombi Brook. The original planting was done by Tyrrell's viticulturist Cliff Currie. Robin Tedder bought the property and started the brand in early '90s.
CURRENT RELEASE 2005 There was still a waft of sulphur dioxide obscuring the nose when our sample was tasted; with delicate dry whites, a screw-cap can keep 'free' sulphur from dissipating longer than cork. There are lanolin and mineral aromas too, yet the palate is quite overt and fruity, even juicy, while the finish remains dry. It seems like a riper, more up-front style than we expected from this producer. Try it with baked whole snapper.

Quality 🍷🍷🍷🍷
Value ★★★★
Rating 90
Grapes semillon
Region Hunter Valley, NSW
Cellar 5+
Alc./Vol. 12.0%
RRP $20.00

Hamelin Bay Five Ashes Vineyard Semillon Sauvignon Blanc

Quality	▼▼▼▼
Value	★★★↓
Rating	90
Grapes	semillon 69%;
	sauvignon blanc 31%
Region	Margaret River, WA
Cellar	▮ 2
Alc./Vol.	12.0%
RRP	$20.00 ⊜

Hamelin Bay's Five Ashes vineyard is in the southern part of Margaret River at Karridale. Being a slightly cooler sub-region, it favours white varieties, so two-thirds of their harvest is white grapes. Julian Scott is the winemaker. CURRENT RELEASE 2005   It's a lovely crisp, fresh dry white with typical herbal, citrusy, slightly gooseberry aromas typical of this kind of Western Australian blend. It has delicacy, liveliness and yet also softness on the palate. There's a hint of capsicum and the alcohol level is nice and low – and it's in no way reliant on sweetness. Lovely drinking with prosciutto and melon.

Hamelin Bay Rampant White

Quality	▼▼▼↓
Value	★★★↓
Rating	88
Grapes	semillon; chardonnay;
	sauvignon blanc
Region	Margaret River, WA
Cellar	▮ 2
Alc./Vol.	12.0%
RRP	$17.00 Ⓢ ⊜

This wine won a gold medal and trophy at the Margaret River Wine Show, which must have surprised its connections, the Drake Brockman family. It's the kind of entry-level quaffer that's positioned low in the hierarchy and never expected to do well in shows. CURRENT RELEASE 2005   The aroma presents dusty, peppery pyrazines from slightly underripe grapes while the palate has a lot of acid and is light but piercing in the mouth, with jazzy acidity. The flavours are crisply herbal, snow pea and gooseberry-like. It goes really well with seafood, served cold or hot.

Henschke Louis

Quality	▼▼▼▼
Value	★★★
Rating	92
Grapes	semillon
Region	Eden Valley, SA
Cellar	▮ 2
Alc./Vol.	13.0%
RRP	$27.50 ⊜

Many Henschke wines bear the names of family ancestors, in this case Louis Edmund Henschke, manager of the Hill of Grace vineyard for 40 years. He passed away in 1990. The vines for this Eden Valley semillon are up to 50 years old. CURRENT RELEASE 2005   There's a real juiciness to this semillon, a sort of lemon, melon and apple succulence. It's a ripe, forward style of good depth and drinkability, finishing with some dry, powdery firmness. It comes into its own with food; try it with fried prawns to see what we mean.

Huntington Estate Semillon Bin W1

For the first time, Huntington has used a screw-cap on its semillon, and it just happens to be a stellar vintage. This wine is available ex-winery for $12.50 by the dozen. Given its quality and the track-record of the line, it must be one of the bargains of the year. Maker: Susie Roberts.
CURRENT RELEASE 2005   Semillon is the best white grape in Mudgee, and this puts the case eloquently. It's a beautifully fine, fragrant, intense but smooth, bright wine with an array of lovely aromas: lemon essence, lemon grass, herbal tinges and much more. An extraordinary bargain, and great with pan-fried flathead.

Quality	🍷🍷🍷🍷🍷
Value	★★★★★
Rating	95
Grapes	semillon
Region	Mudgee, NSW
Cellar	🍷 10+
Alc./Vol.	12.0%
RRP	$14.50 ⑤ ⌾

Lenton Brae Semillon Sauvignon Blanc

Lenton Brae is an essential stop for anyone visiting the Margaret River region. The impressive rammed-earth winery is a local landmark, and the stylish wines are usually very impressive. Maker: Edward Tomlinson.
CURRENT RELEASE 2005   This is a shiny young white, with a lively aroma to match its bright appearance. It has a tangy mix of citrus and juicy tropical notes on the nose, and in the mouth it's an intensely flavoured dry wine of good balance. Bracing acidity keeps it clean and penetrating. Try it with salt and pepper calamari.

Quality	🍷🍷🍷🍷
Value	★★★
Rating	90
Grapes	semillon; sauvignon blanc
Region	Margaret River, WA
Cellar	🍷 2
Alc./Vol.	12.5%
RRP	$20.00 ⌾

McWilliams Mount Pleasant Lovedale Semillon

Lovedale is one of the great white wines of Australia: a single-vineyard wine from the block of land beside Cessnock aerodrome, which Maurice O'Shea planted in 1921 after buying it from the Love family.
CURRENT RELEASE 2000   It's six years old but the colour is still medium-full yellow and the bouquet still shows a power of primary fruit: lemon and green-herb aromas, with just a light lacing of toastiness from bottle-age. The palate is soft and round, easygoing, beautifully balanced – without the challenging acidity sometimes found in Hunter semillon. Perhaps the soft acid means it will peak relatively early (by Lovedale standards). Drink with poached white-fleshed fish and a squeeze of lemon.
Previous outstanding vintages: 1984, '86, '96, '98, '99

Quality	🍷🍷🍷🍷🍷
Value	★★★★
Rating	95
Grapes	semillon
Region	Hunter Valley, NSW
Cellar	🍷 5
Alc./Vol.	11.5%
RRP	$49.00 ⑤

Meerea Park Alexander Munro Semillon

Quality	♉♉♉♉♉
Value	★★★★
Rating	95
Grapes	semillon
Region	Hunter Valley, NSW
Cellar	🍷 3+
Alc./Vol.	10.5%
RRP	$35.00

PENGUIN BEST SEMILLON
AND BLENDS

Rhys Eather makes three semillons, at three price levels. The Epoch is released in the year of vintage; the Terra Cotta and Alexander Munro, named after his great-grandfather (also a winemaker), are released with some bottle-age. All are excellent, and made in classic Hunter style.

CURRENT RELEASE 2001 With a medium-deep yellow colour and a complex, aged bouquet of beeswax and honeysuckle, this is a delicious, semi-mature Hunter semillon. It has great depth of flavour and softness, although there's no shortage of acid to help it age and develop. The finish is dry, finely balanced and very long. A superb semillon with several years left in it. Great with any grilled white-fleshed fish – such as bream.
Previous outstanding vintage: 1999

Meerea Park Epoch Semillon

Quality	♉♉♉♉
Value	★★★★
Rating	90
Grapes	semillon
Region	Hunter Valley, NSW
Cellar	🍷 5+
Alc./Vol.	10.5%
RRP	$19.00 🥂

Meerea Park's Eather brothers took over the former Little's winery on Palmers Lane, Pokolbin. They run a busy contract-winemaking business as well as making their own Meerea Park wines.

CURRENT RELEASE 2005 A classic young Hunter sem, with simple lemony-fruit aroma, clean and uncomplicated but bell-like in its clarity. It is remarkably soft and easy to enjoy now, although it will surely live for quite a few years, gathering richness and complexity as it goes. Serve it, while it's young, with any white-fleshed fish.

Merum Semillon

Quality	♉♉♉♉
Value	★★★
Rating	88
Grapes	semillon
Region	Pemberton, WA
Cellar	🍷 4+
Alc./Vol.	13.0%
RRP	$28.00 🥂

Merum is an ancient Latin word, meaning pure, undiluted wine – so says the back label. This excellent brand from Pemberton is owned by Michael Melsom. His wines are made by Jan McIntosh of Margaret River.

CURRENT RELEASE 2005 This shows the obvious effects of oak, which is different from previous Merum dry whites we've enjoyed. The aromas are smoky, toasty and complex; the taste is soft and dry, with some extra richness from the use of barrels. It's nicely flavoursome, even if most of the flavour is from oak at this stage. It could well reveal more fruit as it grows up. We suggest you don't chill it too much, and then serve it with roast chook.

Millbrook Semillon Sauvignon Blanc

This style of white wine has become a huge growth segment throughout Australia. Comments people used to make in the '90s about chardonnay being a generic name for dry white could apply to SSB or SBS today.
CURRENT RELEASE 2005   Another crisp, simple, racy, herbaceous white wine with a trace of reduction on the nose and a fresh, herbal/salady kind of taste. It's clean and youthful with plenty of vitality, leaving the palate with a pleasing impression of balance. Serve it with salads and cold cuts.

Quality	♥♥♥
Value	★★★
Rating	87
Grapes	semillon; sauvignon blanc
Region	Perth Hills, WA
Cellar	🍷 1
Alc./Vol.	13.0%
RRP	$22.00 🍷

Mistletoe Home Vineyard Semillon

Hand picked from Mistletoe's home vineyard on Hermitage Road, and just 300 cases were bottled. It's made as an earlier-drinking style, with 3 grams per litre of sweetness (as opposed to bone-dry for the Reserve). The 2006 vintage was a dry harvest – unusual in the Hunter – giving high-quality, healthy grapes.
CURRENT RELEASE 2006   At time of tasting this had just been bottled and was, as they say in the trade, all arms and legs. It had sweetly floral and cashew-nut aromas, and the palate showed acidity, fruit and sweetness all disjointed, and a slight waft of free sulphur, which dissipated with aeration. We hope and trust people are not drinking this immediately, but that they give it at least a few months to settle down. (Our rating could well be higher in six months or a year.) Then it should drink well with fresh oysters.

Quality	♥♥♥♥
Value	★★★★
Rating	88
Grapes	semillon
Region	Hunter Valley, NSW
Cellar	➡ 2–8+
Alc./Vol.	10.0%
RRP	$17.00 🍷 (cellar door)

Mistletoe Reserve Semillon

This winery was established in 1990 on Hermitage Road, Pokolbin in the lower Hunter Valley. Proprietor Ken Sloan has 6 hectares under vine. Winemaker: Nick Paterson.
CURRENT RELEASE 2005   We wouldn't recommend broaching this for a few years: it's obviously designed as a cellaring wine. When you sniff, you get a great cloud of sulphur dioxide, and when you taste it, the acid is all-pervading. It's far too young. It's also hard to gauge its quality at this time. Suffice it to say it's a classic, low-alcohol, dry, unwooded, high-acid Hunter semillon that should blossom into something pretty smart with age. Then serve it with fish or seafood.
Previous outstanding vintage: 2004

Quality	♥♥♥♥
Value	★★★★
Rating	90
Grapes	semillon
Region	Hunter Valley, NSW
Cellar	➡ 3–10+
Alc./Vol.	10.0%
RRP	$20.00 🍷 (cellar door)

Mitchell Semillon

Quality	♟ ♟ ♟
Value	★ ★ ★
Rating	86
Grapes	semillon
Region	Clare Valley, SA
Cellar	▮ 2
Alc./Vol.	12.5%
RRP	$22.00 ⧈

Semillon does well in Clare; chardonnay does not – to the extent that the Mitchells don't produce a chardonnay at all. But, at least in 2004, their semillon tastes remarkably like a de facto chardonnay! Makers: Andrew Mitchell and Simon Pringle.

CURRENT RELEASE 2004   It's a surprisingly forward style of semillon, with a deep-yellow colour and a rich, oaky but quite complex bouquet. There are peach and fig nuances and it is more reminiscent of chardonnay than semillon. Very full-bodied, it has some toasty feral burgundy-like characters and this is all underlined by emphatic acidity. You could try it with roast free-range chook.

Moss Wood Semillon

Quality	♟ ♟ ♟ ♟
Value	★ ★ ★
Rating	90
Grapes	semillon
Region	Margaret River, WA
Cellar	▮ 3+
Alc./Vol.	14.5%
RRP	$33.00 ⧈

Moss Wood has always set a lot of store in the semillon grape, and together with various other wineries in the region it could mount a strong case for the variety's suitability to the area. We have worried about the elevated alcohol levels in recent years but what we sometimes see as a lack of balance doesn't seem to slow Moss Wood down.

CURRENT RELEASE 2005   The nose is softly herbal and there's a pleasing lack of the hard-edged green, capsicummy aromas that often afflict semillon from Margaret River. It's a lovely wine in the mouth; soft and rounded with fine texture and excellent balance. The 14.5 per cent alcohol doesn't seem to get in the way. Drink it with rich chicken dishes and you'll enjoy it.

Mount Pleasant Elizabeth Semillon

Quality	♟ ♟ ♟ ♟
Value	★ ★ ★ ★
Rating	90
Grapes	semillon
Region	Hunter Valley, NSW
Cellar	▮ 3
Alc./Vol.	11.0%
RRP	$17.00 ⑤

Bottle-age is the mystery ingredient that turns the ugly chrysalis into the beautiful butterfly, to use a rather worn-out metaphor. Certainly, this style needs age, and McWilliams make sure you get to drink the wine in optimum condition by doing the cellaring for you. Makers: Phil Ryan and team.

CURRENT RELEASE 2001   Deep-golden yellow in hue, this mature semillon is very toasty and slightly earthy, with some compost, or fermented herbage notes. The palate is intense and dry, with plenty of vitality, but it's not the most finessed Elizabeth we've tasted. Still, it's won five gold medals to date. It's a good drink with barbecued garlic prawns.
Previous outstanding vintages: 1986, '89, '94, '95, '96, '97, '99

Murchison Semillon

Better known in the past as Longleat, this is one of the prettiest vineyards in the Goulburn Valley, and winemaker Guido Vazzoler and cheesemaker wife Sandra preside over one of the most welcoming cellar doors. Taste the wines, but make sure you try some cheese too.
CURRENT RELEASE 2005 A fresh, juicy young semillon with a fresh nose that's reminiscent of green apples and lemon. The palate is straightforward and very refreshing with flavours that reflect the aroma, and a little hint of honey in the middle. It finishes clean and dry. Serve it with dim sum.

Quality	♟ ♟ ♟ ♟
Value	★ ★ ★ ★ ★
Rating	91
Grapes	semillon; sauvignon blanc
Region	Goulburn Valley, Vic.
Cellar	▮ 2
Alc./Vol.	12.2%
RRP	$13.00 ⬗

Neagles Rock Semillon Sauvignon Blanc

Grown in an old Clare vineyard, this Neagles Rock blend is made with a little barrel fermentation applied to some of the semillon. The result is a wine with a touch more interest than many sem-savs.
CURRENT RELEASE 2005 The nose has many dimensions: lemony semillon, a hint of tropical fruit and a herbal touch from the sauvignon blanc, plus a slight nuttiness from oak. The wood is very subtle and it helps more with texture and 'feel' than flavour. The palate is smooth and vinous, finishing dry and savoury. A good partner for goat's cheese and rocket tarts.

Quality	♟ ♟ ♟ ♟
Value	★ ★ ★ ⭒
Rating	90
Grapes	semillon; sauvignon blanc
Region	Clare Valley, SA
Cellar	▮ 2
Alc./Vol.	13.5%
RRP	$18.00 ⬗

Palandri Semillon Sauvignon Blanc

Palandri's label features an Aboriginal representation of a gecko, a cute little lizard that can defy gravity by climbing up walls and across ceilings. One occasionally sits on the wall and watches one of the authors tasting wine.
CURRENT RELEASE 2005 A fresh, juicy Western Australian white with tropical fruits and hints of apple and blackcurrant on the nose. In the mouth there's clean succulent flavour that's refreshing and zippy. It would go well with chilled prawns.

Quality	♟ ♟ ♟ ♟
Value	★ ★ ★ ⭒
Rating	88
Grapes	semillon; sauvignon blanc
Region	not stated, WA
Cellar	▮ 1
Alc./Vol.	12.5%
RRP	$16.50 ⬗

Penfolds Koonunga Hill Semillon Sauvignon Blanc

Quality	🍷🍷🍷🍷
Value	★★★⯨
Rating	88
Grapes	semillon; sauvignon blanc
Region	not stated
Cellar	🍾 2
Alc./Vol.	12.5%
RRP	$15.60 Ⓢ 🥢

One of the best things about the Penfolds Koonunga Hill range is its reliability. When in doubt you can always grab a bottle and be sure of its quality.

CURRENT RELEASE 2005   A distinctly minerally aroma and a whiff of sulphur introduces this well-made, pale white wine. Lemon/lime and herby scents are there in the mix, and the palate has some depth and presence. And it's dry; unlike many moderately priced young whites, it doesn't rely on too much residual sweetness for its appeal. Try it with shellfish.

Peter Lehmann Adelaide Hills Semillon Sauvignon Blanc

Quality	🍷🍷🍷🍷
Value	★★★★★
Rating	91
Grapes	semillon; sauvignon blanc
Region	Adelaide Hills, SA
Cellar	🍾 2
Alc./Vol.	12.5%
RRP	$15.00 Ⓢ 🥢

Adelaide Hills sauvignon blancs reflect the cool climate in their tangy purity of aroma and flavour, and semillon ripens in similar fashion there. This blend of the two is a well-priced, true reflection of the region.

CURRENT RELEASE 2005   Semillon leads the way here with clean lemon-curd and herb aromas. Some lush tropical notes add another layer, and the clean, appetising palate has good depth and length. Zesty fruit flavours and tingly acidity keep it lively, but it's a step above a simple refresher, offering real interest and great value for money. Serve it with salt and pepper calamari.

Pyramid Hill Semillon

Quality	🍷🍷🍷🍷🍷
Value	★★★★
Rating	93
Grapes	semillon
Region	Hunter Valley, NSW
Cellar	🍾 3
Alc./Vol.	11.0%
RRP	$18.00 🥢

Pyramid Hill is at Denman in the upper reaches of the Hunter Valley. Once this region was regarded as quite separate from the lower Hunter, due to its less humid, more continental climate. Companies like Penfolds put great faith in its potential as a stand-alone region then, but these days the distinctions are blurred.

CURRENT RELEASE 2004   This shows a distinctly minerally note on the nose, along with fragrant lemony aromas. It has a fresh, lively smell, and the palate follows on with similar spring-like lightness and freshness. Its flavour is riper and more forward than most lower Hunters of pedigree at the same stage, and it finishes dry and clean with a soft, fruity aftertaste. A well-made fresh wine to try beside Thai crab cakes.

Quarryman Semillon Sauvignon Blanc

This is a sous-marque of a little-known winery in McLaren Vale called Classic McLaren. The winery was built in a disused quarry – hence the brand name. The business was started only in 1996 and owns 57 hectares of vines in the Vale. Winemaker is Andrew Braithwaite.
CURRENT RELEASE 2005   A light, slightly green (as in underripe grapes), simple dry white that is perfectly good value for money as a basic quaffing wine. The aromas are herbal and vegetal, fruit-driven and uncomplicated, while the taste is light and clean with balanced fruit and acidity, before a fairly short finish. A well-made wine to pair with prosciutto and rockmelon.

Quality	♀ ♀ ♀
Value	★ ★ ★ ◗
Rating	86
Grapes	semillon; sauvignon blanc
Region	McLaren Vale, SA
Cellar	▮ 1
Alc./Vol.	13.0%
RRP	$16.00 ⓢ

Rolf Binder Christa Rolf Semillon

Christa and Rolf are sister and brother, and both Roseworthy-trained winemakers. Christa's surname is Deans – she married another Barossa winemaker, Leon Deans.
CURRENT RELEASE 2004   This is a lovely, tight, vibrant Barossa semillon that's still very fresh. The colour is full yellow and bright; the nose has some developed toasty and lemon-juice/lemon-butter fruit scents. There's also a grass-hay note. It's loaded with flavour but not over-burdened. A superb, semi-developed dry white to drink now, with chicken caesar salad.

Quality	♀ ♀ ♀ ♀
Value	★ ★ ★ ★ ◗
Rating	91
Grapes	semillon
Region	Barossa Valley, SA
Cellar	▮ 3+
Alc./Vol.	13.0%
RRP	$17.90 ⊜

Rosabrook Semillon Sauvignon Blanc

The trend to use a little oak in semillon-sauvignon blanc blends has been growing in Margaret River. Sixteen per cent of this blend was fermented in new French oak. Maker: Bill Crappsley.
CURRENT RELEASE 2005   Nutty oak and a suggestion of leesy complexity add extra interest to citrus, herb and pawpaw-like fruit characters in this young blend. Happily the wood harmonises well, stopping far short of turning ugly, as it can in some similar blends. The clean, fresh palate has attractive richness, and finishes long and aromatic with a pleasantly crisp zip of acidity. Serve it with Vietnamese-style chicken salad.

Quality	♀ ♀ ♀ ♀
Value	★ ★ ★ ★
Rating	92
Grapes	semillon 67%; sauvignon blanc 33%
Region	Margaret River, WA
Cellar	▮ 2
Alc./Vol.	13.0%
RRP	$19.00 ⊜

Rosily Semillon Sauvignon Blanc

Quality 🍷🍷🍷🍷
Value ★★★½
Rating 91
Grapes semillon 65%; sauvignon blanc 35%
Region Margaret River, WA
Cellar 2
Alc./Vol. 13.9%
RRP $21.00

Rosily Vineyard is named after Comte François de Rosily, the French navigator who in 1772 first charted Flinders Bay in Western Australia's south-west.

CURRENT RELEASE 2005 This is a deceptively pale wine that has a nose of some complexity. The usual lemony and herbal varietal hints are there in attractive savoury intensity, and there's a subtle nutty overlay from barrel maturation. It tastes dry and clean with some depth and richness mid-palate. Balance is excellent. A very good, dry, tangy companion to some grilled prawns.

Saltram Next Chapter Semillon Sauvignon Blanc

Quality 🍷🍷½
Value ★★½
Rating 84
Grapes semillon; sauvignon blanc
Region Barossa Valley, SA
Cellar 1
Alc./Vol. 12.0%
RRP $16.00 (S)

New Saltram sub-brands have been sprouting like daisies of late, all with the dullest names imaginable: Eighth Maker, Next Chapter, Maker's Table. Yawn! Often, the wines are as boring as the names.

CURRENT RELEASE 2005 The colour is very advanced for a 2005 wine, but it's obviously made to be drinking at its best when it's sold. The aromas are rather pedestrian: herbal/parsley/stemmy odours. The taste is simple and light, floppy and seemingly low-acid. It lacks intensity and structure, and falls away at the finish. Caesar salad would be in order.

Schild Estate Unwooded Semillon

Quality 🍷🍷🍷🍷
Value ★★★★
Rating 90
Grapes semillon
Region Barossa Valley, SA
Cellar 2+
Alc./Vol. 12.5%
RRP $15.00

'Unwooded' or 'unoaked' are qualifying words normally seen on chardonnay labels, not semillon. However, in the Barossa Valley semillon is quite often oak-matured, so it means more there than it would in, say, the Hunter Valley – semillon's spiritual home in Australia.

CURRENT RELEASE 2005 A very good semillon it is, too. The colour is very light yellow and it smells restrained and shy, which is normal for young semillon. Its aroma reminds of lemon acid drops (confectionery). The palate is fuller than perhaps expected, with some richness and weight reflecting riper fruit and higher alcohol than, say, a traditional Hunter. It has some appealing minerality and really delivers a lot of flavour in the mouth. Try it with Chinese lemon chicken.

Swings & Roundabouts Semillon Sauvignon Blanc

There seems to be no end to the bottlings of this kind of wine emanating from Western Australia in general and Margaret River in particular. There's a pattern to the pricing: the more established and better known the brand, the higher the price. But new brands, such as this one, tend to be cheaper – and better value for money. Maker: Mark Lane. CURRENT RELEASE 2005   It's a simple but appealing wine style and legions of drinkers love it. It's light, straightforward and fruit-driven, smelling of cut cucumber and green herbs, and tasting fruity, simple and soft, with a smidgen of residual sweetness. A good match with zuppa di pesce (fish soup).

Quality	♀ ♀ ♀
Value	★ ★ ★ ◂
Rating	87
Grapes	semillon; sauvignon blanc
Region	Margaret River, WA
Cellar	🍶 1
Alc./Vol.	12.5%
RRP	$16.00 🍷

Tatachilla Growers Semillon Sauvignon Blanc

Tatachilla's Growers is named after the reliable band of growers who supply the grapes for this reliable white wine. Maker: Fanchon Ferrandi. CURRENT RELEASE 2005   Pale and slightly green-tinged, this young wine has an attractive shimmering appearance that gets your mouth watering. It's a middle-of-the-road dry white with light citrus, herb and stone-fruit aromas, and a smooth palate that finishes with a little firmness at the end. It's a simple white to sip chilled with fish and chips.

Quality	♀ ♀ ♀
Value	★ ★ ★ ◂
Rating	87
Grapes	semillon; sauvignon blanc
Region	not stated, SA
Cellar	🍶 1
Alc./Vol.	13.5%
RRP	$12.95 ⑤ 🍷

Torbreck Woodcutter's Semillon

We've said it elsewhere, but although Torbreck produce some formidably priced, formidably built reds, we sometimes prefer the user-friendly wines that occupy the bottom rungs of the Torbreck ladder. This Barossa semillon is one of them. CURRENT RELEASE 2005   This opened with quite a burst of sulphury smells, but it changed with air, a good case for decanting some white wines to expose their true personalities. It evolved into a bright lemon-curd-smelling wine with good intensity and depth, a smooth citrus-flavoured palate, and a long, quite powerful finish. Try it with Chinese lemon chicken.

Quality	♀ ♀ ♀ ♀
Value	★ ★ ★ ◂
Rating	91
Grapes	semillon
Region	Barossa Valley, SA
Cellar	🍶 3
Alc./Vol.	13.0%
RRP	$18.20 🍷 🍾

Tranquil Vale Semillon

Quality 🍷🍷🍷🍷
Value ★★★★
Rating 91
Grapes semillon
Region Hunter Valley, NSW
Cellar ▬3–8
Alc./Vol. 11.0%
RRP \$17.00

Phil Griffiths is another who has made the 'sea change' to take up grapegrowing and winemaking. He gave up a career as a foreign exchange money broker in the UK and various other parts of the world to work the Hunter Valley vineyard he and his wife established in 1996.

CURRENT RELEASE 2006 Very pale, with a vague greenish tinge, this smells totally undeveloped with lemon and lime juice and steely aromas of great purity. In the mouth it shows lemony delicacy with persistent flavour and a tight, long finish. Like most pristine young Hunter semillons, we recommend that you hide it away for some years for it to develop. It would go well with grilled delicately flavoured fish.

Trentham Estate Two Thirds

Quality 🍷🍷🍷
Value ★★★
Rating 86
Grapes semillon; sauvignon blanc
Region Murray Valley, SA
Cellar ▮1
Alc./Vol. 8.5%
RRP \$12.50

Two Thirds refers to the alcoholic content of this wine. At 8.5 per cent by volume it's two-thirds the strength of most white wines.

CURRENT RELEASE 2006 An interesting new type of wine that retains juicy tropical fruit-salad aromas with citrus and herbal touches. It's a deliciously fruity introduction, but in the mouth it really shows its lack of alcohol in a hollow mid-palate. It's smooth, but somehow slightly unsatisfying. That said, it's clean and grapey without any ugly traits, and if you're watching the .05 factor it should do the trick. Try it chilled with some savoury nibbles.

Tyrrell's Lost Block Semillon

Quality 🍷🍷🍷🍷
Value ★★★★½
Rating 92
Grapes semillon
Region Hunter Valley, NSW
Cellar ▮4
Alc./Vol. 11.0%
RRP \$17.00 (\$)

Lost Block is usually a more forward, fruitier type of Hunter semillon compared to Tyrrell's more traditional wines. It originated some years ago when somebody forgot to pick a block of semillon, allowing it to ripen more than usual, hence the 'Lost Block'.

CURRENT RELEASE 2005 A more penetrating lemon-juicy Lost Block than some, this smells fresh and appetising. In the mouth there are clean, persistent lemon/lime flavours of good intensity, finishing zesty with lively acidity. Serve it with Turkish dips and vegetable dishes.

Tyrrell's Reserve Belford Semillon

The Belford vineyard, planted in 1933, is controlled by the fourth generation of the Elliott family, and was the source of some legendary Elliott Hunter semillons 30-plus years ago. Now the vineyard is leased by Tyrrell's and the wine is bottled as an aged Reserve release.

CURRENT RELEASE 1999 Remarkably pale and youthful looking, this rare wine should develop into a real classic. The pristine varietal nose is just starting to develop the savoury richness of maturity, but it still has a way to go. Lightly toasty hints are entering the equation, and the superfine, tight, lemony palate is supported by tingly, almost tart acidity. Try it alongside fish with a lemony sauce.

Quality 🍷🍷🍷🍷½
Value ★★★★★
Rating 94
Grapes semillon
Region Hunter Valley, NSW
Cellar 1–8
Alc./Vol. 9.7%
RRP $28.95

Tyrrell's Reserve HVD Semillon

HVD stands for Hunter Valley Distillery, a name that gives a clue to the past use of this 1908-planted semillon vineyard. Its wines are so distinctive that Tyrrell's bottle them as a single-vineyard release.

CURRENT RELEASE 1999 On opening, this seemed to have less interest than the Vat 1 of the same year, but it evolved in the glass, turning into a memorable example of this unique Australian white wine type. It smells of lemon curd, linseed oil, coriander and toast – very savoury and winning. The palate is rich, smooth and satisfying with a hint of stone fruit among the citrus and lightly toasty flavours. Very more-ish. Perfect with a prawn stirfry.

Quality 🍷🍷🍷🍷🍷
Value ★★★★★
Rating 96
Grapes semillon
Region Hunter Valley, NSW
Cellar 2
Alc./Vol. 10.5%
RRP $45.00

Tyrrell's Vat 1 Semillon

Quality 🍷🍷🍷🍷🍷
Value ★★★★
Rating 95
Grapes semillon
Region Hunter Valley, NSW
Cellar 2
Alc./Vol. 10.8%
RRP $72.00

The authors hold that bottle-age completes the picture with Hunter semillons, and we think Tyrrell's policy of releasing older wines showcases what this classic Oz style is all about beautifully. During the past few months, two different vintages of Vat 1 have arrived, both reasonably priced given their age and quality.

CURRENT RELEASE 1994 A shimmering full-yellow colour looks spot-on for a 12-year-old Hunter sem. The nose is mellow and quietly complex – and only lightly toasty; instead, touches of melon, wood smoke, earth and honey lead the way. The palate is rich and unusually smoky, perhaps reflecting the bushfires during the lead-up to vintage. Serve it with smoked trout salad.

Quality 🍷🍷🍷🍷🍷
Value ★★★★½
Rating 98
Grapes semillon;
Region Hunter Valley, NSW
Cellar 5+
Alc./Vol. 10.3%
RRP $45.00

CURRENT RELEASE 1999 This has a remarkably bright, youthful colour for a seven-year-old, and the nose shows great life. There's a certain earthiness on the nose, along with citrus and green-apple scents, and a whisper of minerality, vaguely reminiscent of chablis, adds savoury dimension. In the mouth it has good mid-palate softness, yet there's solid structure for further ageing. A classic. Delicious with grilled river fish.

Vasse Felix Classic Dry White

Quality 🍷🍷🍷🍷
Value ★★★½
Rating 90
Grapes semillon; sauvignon blanc
Region Margaret River, WA
Cellar 3
Alc./Vol. 12.5%
RRP $19.85

The term 'Classic' is frequently used in Western Australia to denote a very mixed bag of wines. It often has semillon and sauvignon blanc as components, sometimes mixed in with any other white grapes the winery doesn't know what to do with. The Vasse Felix version is always one of the best.

CURRENT RELEASE 2005 Lemony semillon aromas are the first thing you notice here, with sauvignon blanc playing a fruity secondary role. The palate is smooth, ripe and long flavoured with more depth and substance than most 'classics'. It finishes dry and long with a pleasantly brisk tang. Serve it with crispy-fried calamari and lemon wedges.

West Cape Howe Semillon Sauvignon Blanc

The brand was established as part of a contract-winemaking company in the Great Southern by Brenden and Kylie Smith; the company and brand were bought by a syndicate involving former Plantagenet chief winemaker Gavin Berry. All hands are now on deck, building the West Cape Howe brand.

CURRENT RELEASE 2005 An attractive, crowd-pleasing style of sem-sav with green herbal/grassy, crushed-leaf and basil aromas. It has some sweetness and is a trifle short on the finish. A clean, well-made wine that is true to the grape varieties. It would suit Thai-style fish cakes.

Quality 🍷🍷🍷
Value ★★★
Rating 86
Grapes semillon; sauvignon blanc
Region various, WA
Cellar 1
Alc./Vol. 12.0%
RRP $16.00 (S)

Wolf Blass Eaglehawk Semillon Chardonnay

Wolf Blass always had a great love of eagles. His winery office and tasting room used to be a veritable menagerie of the things. Now the new cellar door sales facility at Bilyara has rather a lot of eagles, too. Something to do with Wolf's German origins?

CURRENT RELEASE 2005 You can see the influence of the chardonnay here: it fills out the lean semillon middle palate and adds a certain peachiness to the aroma. There's a touch of vanilla/toast on the afterpalate that may come from a subtle tracery of oak. This is a very good value-for-money dry white. Drink with chicken kebabs.

Quality 🍷🍷🍷
Value ★★★★
Rating 86
Grapes semillon; chardonnay
Region various, SA
Cellar 1
Alc./Vol. 13.0%
RRP $10.00 (S)

Wolf Blass Red Label Classic Dry White

We remember the early days of Wolf Blass Classic Dry White (it always had some crouchen in the blend – an unlamented grape that has sunk without trace). It was a much different wine in the early 1980s, with quite a lashing of oak. The company motto in those days was 'no wood, no good'.

CURRENT RELEASE 2005 It's an acceptable but rather boring, soft, drink-now white wine. The oak has been throttled right back and it has some vaguely vegetal/herbal/compost-like aromas and is plain, clean and balanced, with respectable weight and flavour. It still has some freshness of crisp, herbal fruit. Pair it with salads and cold cuts.

Quality 🍷🍷½
Value ★★★
Rating 85
Grapes semillon; chardonnay
Region not stated
Cellar 1
Alc./Vol. 13.0%
RRP $17.00 (S)

Wolf Blass Red Label Semillon Sauvignon Blanc

Quality	♀ ♀ ♀
Value	★ ★ ★ ⌐
Rating	86
Grapes	semillon; sauvignon blanc
Region	not stated
Cellar	▮ 1
Alc./Vol.	12.5%
RRP	$16.00 Ⓢ

Blass wines are easy for the novice to understand: there's an idiot-simple colour hierarchy, with Eaglehawk at the bottom, then red label, then yellow, then gold, and then the exxy stuff: grey, black and platinum labels, in that order.

CURRENT RELEASE 2005   A typical big-company commercial wine, tasting good from the word go, and offering just a little more than you might expect at the price (which of course is often discounted). Full-yellow colour; lightly toasty nose showing some early maturity but little varietal character; soft and round with good weight and balance. Very easy to drink and enjoy. We'd suggest chicken nuggets.

Yalumba Eden Valley Semillon Sauvignon Blanc

Quality	♀ ♀ ♀ ⌐
Value	★ ★ ★
Rating	88
Grapes	semillon; sauvignon blanc
Region	Eden Valley, SA
Cellar	▮ 1
Alc./Vol.	12.5%
RRP	$18.00 Ⓢ ⧢

Eden Valley is a couple of hundred metres higher than the Barossa Valley floor, so it's no surprise it produces finer white wines. The altitude gives cooler average temperatures, especially at night, which delay the harvest a couple of weeks, giving grapes with different chemical and flavour profiles.

CURRENT RELEASE 2005   A good drink, although the aromatics don't really compare with the likes of New Zealand and the best cool-climate Australian sem-savs. It has some vaguely varietal stemmy/stalky/herbal aromas but comes into its own on the palate, where it has better depth and structure than most of its brethren. It has good length and a firm finish helped along by a well-judged hint of phenolics. Serve it with pan-fried snapper with red capsicum purée.

Verdelho

Verdelho is a chameleon among wine grapes. It can have many expressions depending on where it's grown, how ripe it's picked and how the wine is made. In the Hunter Valley there are some early-picked styles which are delicate and dry, with a certain raciness and excellent food compatibility. They can age well. Others are picked ripe and are richer, more voluptuous and spicy-flavoured, sometimes with some residual sugar. In Western Australia it can be quite herbaceous and in other places, such as Queensland's Granite Belt, tropical-fruity. Verdelho is growing in popularity quite quickly, but off a small base. It is usually inexpensive: a lower- to mid-market wine that's easy to enjoy and doesn't make too many demands on the drinker.

Cassegrain Verdelho

John Cassegrain, principal and winemaker of this outfit at Port Macquarie, has strong links with the Hunter Valley, where he started out as a winemaker (mainly with Tyrrell's). He still brings in some Hunter grapes – of the types that the Hunter does best, such as semillon and verdelho.

CURRENT RELEASE 2005 The wine is dominated by strong confectionery aromas, which could be mainly fermentation esters but probably also include a whisper of oak. It adds coconut and peppermint overtones. The taste is soft and broad, with some sweetness, which is usually a part of the Hunter verdelho style. It's slightly clumsy but certainly has presence and flavour. You could try it with chicken satays.

Quality	🍷🍷🍷
Value	★★★½
Rating	**86**
Grapes	verdelho
Region	Hunter Valley, NSW
Cellar	1
Alc./Vol.	13.5%
RRP	$17.00

Cockfighter's Ghost Verdelho

The story goes that Cockfighter was a racehorse who got bogged in the sandy bed of the Wollombi Brook, and drowned. Not a happy-ending story. The offending creek runs through the vineyards of the Hunter's Broke-Fordwich sub-region.

CURRENT RELEASE 2005 This is a typical Hunter verdelho that will please the many drinkers who buy verdelho. It has a fresh, bread-dough, estery aroma with confectionery overtones and is soft and fruity in the mouth, enhanced by a little residual sugar. The texture is so creamy it's almost fluffy. It would go with an old-fashioned seafood cocktail.

Quality	🍷🍷🍷
Value	★★★
Rating	**86**
Grapes	verdelho
Region	Hunter Valley, NSW
Cellar	1
Alc./Vol.	12.7%
RRP	$18.00 (\$)

Faber Vineyard Verdelho

Quality	♟ ♟ ♟
Value	★★★★
Rating	86
Grapes	verdelho
Region	Swan Valley, WA
Cellar	⬥ 2
Alc./Vol.	13.5%
RRP	$12.00 ⧓
	(cellar door)

John Griffiths named his new venture in the Swan Valley Faber because it's Latin for craft. 'We believe winemaking is a craft, a skill learnt but never perfected.' Admirable sentiments!

CURRENT RELEASE 2005   The colour is light, bright straw; the nose is simple and grapey, hay-like and very clean, with a herbaceous overtone reminiscent of sauvignon blanc. The taste is very grapey and soft, with a smidgen of sweetness. It should be a very popular style. Try it with prawn cocktail.

Kingston Estate Verdelho

Quality	♟ ♟ ♟ ♟
Value	★★★★
Rating	89
Grapes	verdelho
Region	Riverland, SA
Cellar	⬥ 1
Alc./Vol.	13.0%
RRP	$13.00 Ⓢ ⧓

Some of Australia's best everyday drinking wines come from the Murray Valley, aka the Riverland. It is an under-appreciated area, but then it's well known that premium, prestige wines are the ones that make reputations. To that end, Kingston uses grapes from many regions to make its flagship ranges.

CURRENT RELEASE 2005   The green-tinged light-yellow colour first attracts the eye. Then the grassy/herbal, fruity aromas arrive, followed by intense and quite rich tropical-fruit flavours. It's a generous dry white of balance and vitality, to drink with seafood. We suggest yabbies served with a seafood sauce.

Vercoe's Vineyard Verdelho

Quality	♟ ♟ ♟ ♟
Value	★★★★
Rating	88
Grapes	verdelho
Region	Hunter Valley, NSW
Cellar	⬥ 2
Alc./Vol.	14.0%
RRP	$14.00 ⧓

Vercoe's vineyard is in the Belford sub-region of the Hunter, and this wine was made by the hard-working and very talented Jim Chatto, whose contract-winemaking business is based at Monarch in central Pokolbin. Contact: orders@vercoesvineyard.com.au

CURRENT RELEASE 2005   This is a big, pungent, in-your-face verdelho, with generous tropical-fruit aromas and flavours. There are herbal, skinsy side-lights, some alcohol warmth, and sherbetty acidity enlivens the palate. It makes up in flavour what it lacks in subtlety. Serve it with a vegetable terrine.

Wyndham Estate Bin 111 Verdelho

Verdelho has been one of the fastest-growing segments of the white wine market, although the rise of sauvignon blanc might have put a dent in that recently. It's a grape that is traditionally linked with the Hunter Valley and Western Australia's Swan Valley. Chief winemaker is Sam Kurtz.

CURRENT RELEASE 2005   This is a soft, fruity, easy-drinking white, which explains why so many drinkers enjoy verdelho. It's an undemanding wine that slips down easily. This is less sweet than many, which is all the better. The nose is subtly fragrant with touches of mint, coconut and lemon essence. The palate is clean and tangy, with fresh acidity and a clean, dry finish. It manages to balance delicacy and intensity, and would suit fresh crab salad.

Quality	♥ ♥ ♥ ♥
Value	★★★★
Rating	89
Grapes	verdelho
Region	not stated
Cellar	🍾 1
Alc./Vol.	12.0%
RRP	$14.00 ⑤ ⏚

Viognier

The large number of wines in this year's *Guide* shows how fashionable this northern Rhône variety has become across a wide range of Australian vineyard locations from cool Canberra to the torrid Murray. It's being made by all sorts of producers from multinationals to hobby operations, but its potential is a bit of a mystery to us. It can be a rather confronting type of wine, with extraordinary aromatics, elevated alcohol, soft acidity and, all too often, harsh phenolic extraction, which all works against its easy drinkability. In fact, sometimes it's downright ugly. Yet the industry persists with it, and we have to say that some wines are brilliant. Its future will be interesting to watch.

Allies Saone Viognier Chardonnay

Quality	♟♟♟
Value	★★★
Rating	86
Grapes	viognier; chardonnay
Region	Mornington Peninsula, Vic.
Cellar	▮ 2
Alc./Vol.	13.5%
RRP	$23.00 ⊜

The allies here are former chef and waiter David Chapman, and his buddy Barney Flanders, who also has a background in restaurants. Just why they're using the name of a French river (and department) on an Aussie wine is unclear. No doubt the style of their wines has a bit to do with that of the Rhône Valley, where the Saône runs.
CURRENT RELEASE 2005   At this stage it's a fairly neutral, plain wine with faintly herbal vegetal, dusty aromas and a soft, round, alcohol-warm palate that has a subtle suspicion of sweetness. The finish is slightly hot and broad. An estery note suggests it might have had a stuck ferment. All in all, it's a good drink and we think a few months in the bottle will bring out the fruit more. Food: roast corn-fed chook.

By Farr Viognier

Quality	♟♟♟♟♟
Value	★★★★
Rating	96
Grapes	viognier
Region	Geelong, Vic.
Cellar	▮ 4
Alc./Vol.	13.5%
RRP	$55.00

A recent retrospective tasting of all the By Farr viogniers from 1999 to 2004 reinforced our opinion that it's Australia's best. It seems to balance the ethereal perfumed character and the power of the variety better than any other.
CURRENT RELEASE 2004   If you've been disappointed by viognier (we often are), have a go at this one. It's an exquisitely perfumed drop that's more delicate than the bold '03 vintage, but it still encapsulates the spice, apricot and floral qualities of the variety perfectly. The palate is beautifully textured with real richness, great depth and length, leading to a fine finish that's completely at odds with the hot, alcoholic traits or phenolic hardness that mark so many Aussie viogniers. Try it with soft cheeses.

Chateau Mildura Psyche Reserve Viognier

The old Mildara winery on the banks of the Murray at
Mildura has become Chateau Mildura, a name it bore in
its earlier days. The Psyche Reserve wines are the top range
from the reborn winery.
CURRENT RELEASE 2005   A flavoursome viognier that
sums up the variety's emphatic personality well. It has a
concentrated musky nose rich with floral and spicy aromas.
In the mouth it has banana and apricot flavours that are
mouth-filling and rich, without the phenolic hardness that
sometimes spoils viogniers for us. Surprising acidity makes
for a long, clean finish. We'd suggest pongy soft cheeses.

Quality	�
Value	★★★♦
Rating	88
Grapes	viognier
Region	Murray Valley, Vic.
Cellar	▯ 1
Alc./Vol.	14.0%
RRP	$17.00

d'Arenberg The Hermit Crab Viognier Marsanne

Viognier and marsanne both originate in France's Rhône
Valley, where they provide white wines of the typically
hearty type that they love in the south of France. In this
blend the two varieties cohabit without a care.
CURRENT RELEASE 2005   This has a powerfully pungent
nose with the musky aromatics of viognier taking prime
position, but honeyed, peachy qualities temper the
viognier's flamboyance well. The palate begins rich and
smooth with lush mid-palate fruit, and a little dry firmness
enters the equation a bit further down. It finishes dry and
clean. Try it with chicken pie.

Quality	♥♥♥♥
Value	★★★★
Rating	90
Grapes	viognier; marsanne
Region	McLaren Vale, SA
Cellar	▯ 3
Alc./Vol.	13.5%
RRP	$16.95

d'Arenberg The Last Ditch Viognier

d'Arenberg planted McLaren Vale's first viognier vines in
the mid-1990s. Since the Rhône red varieties of grenache,
shiraz and mourvèdre have performed so well there for so
long, it made sense to assume that the white Rhône grapes
would too.
CURRENT RELEASE 2005   A fair measure of barrel-ferment
influence marks the nose of this viognier, providing a
nuttiness that works well with the viognier's personality.
Floral and spice aromas are relatively subdued (for viognier)
but the palate shows plenty of apricotty-varietal flavour
that has an almost syrupy (but not sweet) aspect of
intensity. It finishes dry with a long fragrant aftertaste.
Serve it alongside pork chops with apricots.

Quality	♥♥♥♥
Value	★★★★
Rating	92
Grapes	viognier
Region	McLaren Vale & Adelaide Hills, SA
Cellar	▯ 2
Alc./Vol.	13.5%
RRP	$19.95

Grant Burge Viognier

Quality	♟ ♟ ♟
Value	★ ★ ★
Rating	86
Grapes	viognier
Region	Adelaide Hills & Barossa Valley, SA
Cellar	🍾 1
Alc./Vol.	14.5%
RRP	$20.00 🍷

Last year's version, the 2004, was straight Adelaide Hills; this year it's a blend with Barossa fruit. Perhaps that explains the difference in our reaction: the '05 is just a bit hot and oily. And it happens to have 1 per cent more alcohol, according to the labels.
CURRENT RELEASE 2005   There's some early development showing in the medium-yellow colour and the toasty/dusty, fig and apricot-jam aromas. The wine has ample weight and flavour, but is just a bit too fat and oily, with the alcohol and ripeness blowing it out a little. It needs to be drunk up soon, perhaps with chicken cooked with apricots.

Haselgrove HRS Reserve Viognier

Quality	♟ ♟ ♟ ♟
Value	★ ★ ★
Rating	90
Grapes	viognier
Region	Adelaide Hills, SA
Cellar	🍾 2
Alc./Vol.	13.0%
RRP	$25.00 🍷

HRS stands for Haselgrove Reserve Series, a range of wines the makers say encapsulates the highest standards of quality from a particular region. This single-vineyard Adelaide Hills wine definitely has a touch of class.
CURRENT RELEASE 2005   A fine, elegant viognier, this Adelaide Hills wine adds a subtle touch of oak to the equation, enhancing floral, stone-fruit and limey touches on the nose. The total aroma is refined and classy, but the palate isn't quite as emphatic as we would expect. It has smooth, relatively delicate varietal fruit of moderate intensity, leading to a clean, lean-boned and slightly attenuated, apricot-scented finish. Serve it with soft mild cheeses.

Kangarilla Road Viognier

Quality	♟ ♟ ♟ ♟
Value	★ ★ ★ ↓
Rating	90
Grapes	viognier
Region	McLaren Vale, SA
Cellar	🍾 2
Alc./Vol.	14.0%
RRP	$18.00 🍷

We never cease to be amazed how quickly 'new' grape varieties catch on in this country. Just a few years ago no one had seen Aussie viognier; now everyone's making it – and throwing a bit into their shiraz as well. Makers: Kevin O'Brien and Mike Brown.
CURRENT RELEASE 2005   There's no doubting the grape variety here: it's a big, full wine redolent of apricot, with spicy/exotic nuances, and a rich palate. It's full and round in the mouth with a trace of sweetness. The finish is clean, dry and lingering. A full-on viognier to drink with Chinese honey prawns.

Meerea Park Viognier

Meerea Park is an important winery, not least for its contract-winemaking facilities, which are used by several small vineyards. Brothers Rhys and Garth Eather (try saying that several times after you've had a few) run the show. Their ancestor, Alexander Munro, was one of the Hunter's early winemakers, in the 1850s.

CURRENT RELEASE 2005 Coconut-milk and pineapple scents give a deliciously tropical aroma to this wine. The coconut no doubt comes from a small component of oaked wine. The taste is rich and full, without being overblown as some viogniers are. Peach and nectarine nuances abound in the concentrated flavour, and it finishes with some heat, probably from alcohol. It would suit washed-rind cheeses, like Hunter Valley Gold.

Quality	🍷🍷🍷🍷
Value	★★★½
Rating	**90**
Grapes	viognier
Region	Hunter Valley, NSW
Cellar	3
Alc./Vol.	13.5%
RRP	$21.00

Meeting Place Viognier

The Hardy group has a big winery in Canberra: that is, big compared to the others in the region! It's one of the very few that are actually within the border of the ACT. Winemaker is Alex McKay.

CURRENT RELEASE 2004 This is a lovely viognier, and look at the price! It's bright, fruity, varietal and clean, but also well balanced and avoids the heaviness and excessive alcohol of so many Aussie viogniers. Spicy, apricot and leatherwood honey aromas abound. The palate is rich, smooth and soft, and not overpowering. Clean acidity keeps the finish nice. We'd suggest grilled calamari.

Quality	🍷🍷🍷🍷🍷
Value	★★★★★
Rating	**95**
Grapes	viognier
Region	Canberra region, NSW
Cellar	3
Alc./Vol.	13.5%
RRP	$16.00 ($)

Peerick Viognier

Shiraz performs well in Victoria's Pyrenees region, so it's logical that its Rhône Valley stablemate viognier will be successful there. So goes the reasoning and it seems to work.

CURRENT RELEASE 2005 Peerick pioneered the viognier variety in the Pyrenees and they are doing an excellent job with it. The '05 is a pale young wine with a delicately perfumed floral nose. Some resiny oak adds complexity but it doesn't overwhelm. The palate is creamy in texture with delicious apricot and peach flavours of depth and intensity. It finishes off dry and long with an apricot-fragrant aftertaste. Try it with pickled pork.

Quality	🍷🍷🍷🍷½
Value	★★★½
Rating	**94**
Grapes	viognier
Region	Pyrenees, Vic.
Cellar	2
Alc./Vol.	14.5%
RRP	$25.00

Pepperjack Viognier

Quality	♥♥♥♥♥
Value	★★★↨
Rating	94
Grapes	viognier
Region	Barossa Valley, SA
Cellar	▯ 2
Alc./Vol.	14.5%
RRP	$23.00 ≋

Viognier is one of those French names that anglophones can have a bit of difficulty with. Vignerons aren't daunted by such trifles judging by the number of viogniers we see on the shelves these days. For the record, our French pals say it 'vee-on-yay'. Whatever you do, don't pronounce it 'vinegar'.

CURRENT RELEASE 2005   Very pure varietal scents here. Floral pot-pourri, lavender, stone fruit and subtle oak influence on the nose, and a long finely textured palate with smooth apricot and spice flavour, ending dry, long and fragrant. An excellent varietal wine that works with Thai ginger chicken.

Swings & Roundabouts Viognier

Quality	♥♥♥♥
Value	★★★
Rating	90
Grapes	viognier
Region	Margaret River, WA
Cellar	▯ 2
Alc./Vol.	13.5%
RRP	$20.00 ≋ ▮

The labels on these wines have a fun feel to them. If carefree pleasure and simple *joie de vivre* is the intention, they succeed. Maker: Mark Lane.

CURRENT RELEASE 2005   Here's one for those who don't like the prevalent fat, blousy style of Aussie viognier. It's a much lighter, tighter style; indeed, it's somewhat meagre initially, but opens up with airing. The aromas are minerally and a touch acrid. It's clean and dry to close, and would probably be best left for a while and drunk from late in 2006. Decanting really helps it. Thai fish cakes would suit.

Tollana Viognier

Quality	♥♥♥♥♥
Value	★★★★↨
Rating	92
Grapes	viognier
Region	Adelaide Hills, SA
Cellar	▯ 2
Alc./Vol.	14.0%
RRP	$19.50 ⓢ ≋

Viognier's pungent personality is one of those love-it-or-hate-it propositions for many of us. In Tollana's hands its exuberance is still there, but it's tempered a bit, making a wine of more friendly disposition than the big, over-the-top versions. Viognier haters will remain unimpressed though.

CURRENT RELEASE 2005   Spicy and musky notes are the first thing you notice here, but there are also some notes of apple and citrus to it. The palate has real lushness without the alcoholic heat of some young viogniers, and the ripe apricot and pear flavours have real impact. Serve it well-chilled alongside chilli crab.

Watershed Viognier

This is a young wine company, established as recently as 2002, but it has a sizeable vineyard of 117 hectares, which is big for Margaret River. They have their own winery and crush over 1000 tonnes of grapes. Winemaker is Cathy Spratt, who was formerly with St Hallett.
CURRENT RELEASE 2005   Subtle aromas of pot-pourri and vanillary malted milk – perhaps coming from a portion of barrel-fermented fruit. This is an unusual viognier: sweet/juicy, oily/viscous and sharp on the palate all at once. The acid sticks out a little, making the wine taste disjointed. It's possible a few more months in bottle will help it come together. Food: a creamy chicken dish.

Quality	♀ ♀ ♀
Value	★ ★ ⟩
Rating	86
Grapes	viognier
Region	Margaret River, WA
Cellar	▮ 2
Alc./Vol.	13.5%
RRP	$27.00 ⬥

West Cape Howe Viognier

The grapes for this wine were grown at Bridgetown, which is not in any of the well-known winegrowing regions of Western Australia. Hence, the front label just declares Western Australia. Maker: Gavin Berry.
CURRENT RELEASE 2005   This is an eccentric viognier: the bouquet has some coconut and aldehyde characters – possibly it's a residual fermentation character. There could be a slight oaked component in the wine. The palate is big and generous, perhaps a little too weighty and straying into clumsy territory. The acidity is fairly prominent, leaving the palate a touch hollow. More time in bottle may help – that's months, rather than years. Try it with Indian butter chicken.

Quality	♀ ♀ ♀
Value	★ ★ ★
Rating	86
Grapes	viognier
Region	Bridgetown, WA
Cellar	▮ 2
Alc./Vol.	14.0%
RRP	$19.00 ⬥

Yalumba Eden Valley Viognier

Yalumba is still the leader in viognier in Australia, largely as a result of it having several years' jump on almost everyone else. It usually produces four dry examples each vintage, and sometimes a sweet version too.
CURRENT RELEASE 2004   This is a purer, more fruit-driven style than Virgilius but a lot of people think it's even better. Certainly, it's a clearer expression of varietal character, with subtler oak and winemaking inputs. The spicy, apricot/stone-fruit aromas, coupled with a hint of coconut derived from barrels, come together in a marvellous bouquet, which is faithfully reproduced in the mouth. It's rich yet elegant, concentrated yet refreshing, with terrific length and style, without quite the same awesome might as Virgilius. Serve with rich fish dishes.

Quality	♀ ♀ ♀ ♀
Value	★ ★ ★ ★ ★
Rating	95
Grapes	viognier
Region	Eden Valley, SA
Cellar	▮ 2
Alc./Vol.	14.5%
RRP	$22.00 Ⓢ ⬥

Yalumba The Virgilius Viognier

Quality	🍷🍷🍷🍷🍷
Value	★★★★
Rating	96
Grapes	viognier
Region	Eden Valley, SA
Cellar	🍾 3
Alc./Vol.	14.5%
RRP	$50.00 🍷

This is Yalumba's 'reserve' viognier, not a single-vineyard wine but a barrel selection of the best material. It's an attention-seeking wine – don't expect something subtle or simple! Maker: Louisa Rose.

CURRENT RELEASE 2004   This is a tremendous wine: amazingly complex and flavoursome, very rich and decadent. The flavours include apricot and other stone-fruits, honey and spices – all in generous helpings. The palate really soars: it has concentration and power, but also superb balance. A brickie's labourer in a tutu. Try it with richly sauced roast chicken.

Other whites and blends

Experimentation with 'alternative' white grapes has grown apace in Australia over the past 15 years. This has sprung first from a curiosity on the part of winemakers, which has in turn affected and enthused wine drinkers. Variety is the spice of life, and the saying was never truer than for wine. Who wants a steady diet of chardonnay, sauvignon blanc and riesling? In the white Italian grape varieties alone, we now have people making interesting wine from cortese, arneis, picolit and verduzzo, as well as vermentino grapes. And on the French side we have petit manseng, viognier, the more established colombard, chenin blanc, gewürztraminer and, from Spain, albarino.

Capel Vale CV Chenin Blanc

Chenin blanc is the grape that produces some great wines in the Loire Valley in France, but in Australia it is almost universally pedestrian. This one at least offers some interesting flavours and complexity, and is the best local attempt we've seen for ages. Maker: Rebecca Catlin.
CURRENT RELEASE 2004   As in the best Loire chenins, we suspect there's some botrytis at work here, which adds fig and melon-jam aromas, herbal and honeyed nuances. It also has a reductive overtone that may be compounded by the screw-cap – as is often the case. Interestingly, this adds extra complexity. The taste is rich and full, a trifle broad perhaps, with a little residual sugar. It's better than many Loire chenins we've tasted recently! It could suit smoked trout pâté.

Quality	♟ ♟ ♟ ♙
Value	★★★★
Rating	89
Grapes	chenin blanc
Region	various, WA
Cellar	🍾 1+
Alc./Vol.	12.5%
RRP	$16.00 Ⓢ ⌑

Cassegrain Limited Release Gewürztraminer

John Cassegrain was responsible for reviving grapegrowing and winemaking in the Hastings Valley near Port Macquarie. He's also been a driving force in pioneering viticulture in the New England area of northern New South Wales. Its correct GI (Geographical Indication) is Northern Slopes.
CURRENT RELEASE 2005   The colour is very pale and the nose is shy, although there are some unmistakable gewurz varietal aromas. It's fragrant in a bath-soap perfume kind of way. The palate is also delicate and restrained, low-key and youthful. It may well build more depth and character with a few more months in the bottle. It makes a good drink already, though, and suits quiche.

Quality	♟ ♟ ♟ ♙
Value	★★★⌐
Rating	88
Grapes	gewürztraminer
Region	Northern Slopes, NSW
Cellar	🍾 3⌐
Alc./Vol.	14.5%
RRP	$15.80 ⌑

First Drop Little Rascal Arneis

Quality	♟ ♟ ♟ ♟
Value	★ ★ ★
Rating	89
Grapes	arneis
Region	Adelaide Hills, SA
Cellar	🍷 2
Alc./Vol.	13.5%
RRP	$25.00 🍷

Apparently, arneis means 'little rascal' in its homeland of Piedmont. It's becoming increasingly popular in Australia. First Drop Wines is the after-hours gig of Matt Gant, whose daytime job is as winemaker at St Hallett in the Barossa. These grapes came from the Yacca Paddock vineyard.
CURRENT RELEASE 2005 The colour is very pale, almost water-white, and it has a shy, elusive nose that seems to need time in the bottle to develop a bouquet. The taste is similarly very light, with restrained pear-like flavour. It's clean, soft but dry, finely textured and well balanced, making for a very slurpable, undemanding dry white. We'd suggest prosciutto and melon.

Lillypilly Lexia

Quality	♟ ♟ ♟ ♟
Value	★ ★ ★ ⭐
Rating	89
Grapes	muscat
Region	Riverina, NSW
Cellar	🍷 1
Alc./Vol.	10.0%
RRP	$14.50 🍷

Lexia is strictly speaking a synonym for muscat gordo blanco, the 'fat white muscat' that gives the muscaty flavour to cask whites and some cheaper generic bottled wines. It is the poor relation of frontignac and Muscat of Alexandria, but in the right hands it can make a very good wine.
CURRENT RELEASE 2005 Typical of the maker, this is a spotlessly clean and technically well-made wine that captures the essence of the grape perfectly. It has a spicy, fragrant nose of muscat fruit and is all-round clean and very fresh, with a slight sweetness. It tastes a bit like fresh grape-juice, only less sweet. It's a beautiful wine of its style, but we wonder if labelling it lexia really communicates the right message about how it tastes. You could serve it as an aperitif, or with lightly flavoured dips and pâtés.

Lillypilly Tramillon

Quality	♟ ♟ ♟ ♟
Value	★ ★ ★
Rating	91
Grapes	gewürztraminer;
	semillon
Region	Riverina, NSW
Cellar	🍷 1
Alc./Vol.	12.5%
RRP	$13.50 🍷

Lillypilly's Robert Fiumara is a thoughtful winemaker who explores many different wine styles in his winery with great success. Tramillon is a traminer-semillon blend made into a slightly sweet wine of juicy gluggability.
CURRENT RELEASE 2005 The traminer component definitely leads the way here, imparting exotic lychee and Turkish delight aromas of seductive perfume. It's sweetish in the mouth with spicy traminer flavours of attractive intensity, but the sweetness doesn't quite reach a cloying level. It finishes soft in acidity yet clean and appetising. It might work with sweet and sour Chinese dishes.

Mac Forbes Arneis

Arneis is one of the highest-regarded white grapes of Piedmont, northern Italy, along with cortese and muscat. The most noted is Roero arneis, from the region of Roero, which has its own appellation. It's not a wine of strong personality, and some makers use oak to add extra character. CURRENT RELEASE 2005   The colour is a nice bright, light yellow and it has a definite barrel overtone in its bouquet. The palate is light and dry, clean and fairly plain, with that touch of oak adding length and interest, but also some phenolics. Try it with grilled baby octopus.

Quality	♟ ♟ ♟
Value	★ ★ ★
Rating	87
Grapes	arneis
Region	Yarra Valley, Vic.
Cellar	🍶 2
Alc./Vol.	13.5%
RRP	$18.00 🛒

The Matador Albarino

This one's worth buying just for the packaging. Matt Gant, of First Drop Wines, has done a great job of making this look like a Spanish wine. The model would have been a Galician albarino, such as Rias Baixas. The wine is very good and we reckon albarino has a real future in Australia. CURRENT RELEASE 2005   It tastes nothing like a Galician albarino but it's a very attractive delicate dry white all the same. Bright, light-yellow colour; bright cashew-nutty and melony aromas; and a soft, light-bodied, well-rounded palate with seamless acidity and appealing freshness. There's a subtle hint of oak threading its way through the wine, but not dominating. Try it with tapas.

Quality	♟ ♟ ♟ ♟
Value	★ ★ ★
Rating	90
Grapes	albarino
Region	Barossa Valley, SA
Cellar	🍶 2
Alc./Vol.	13.5%
RRP	$36.00 🛒

Moondah Brook Classic Dry White

Occasionally, trawling through rows and rows of cheap, commercial, big-company products we find something that jumps out and says 'Value!' This is such a wine. It's from the Houghton stable, where the chief winemaker is Rob Bowen. CURRENT RELEASE 2005   For immediate appeal and drinkability, look no further. This is a very gulpable dry white that isn't propped up by sugar or cluttered by wood. It has a bright aroma of herbal, twiggy, snow-pea fruit and is intensely fruity, light and lively in the mouth. It's got a nicely balanced finish that is properly dry and it would probably keep for a year or three. Drink it with seafood and salad.

Quality	♟ ♟ ♟
Value	★ ★ ★ ★
Rating	87
Grapes	not stated
Region	various, WA
Cellar	🍶 2+
Alc./Vol.	13.5%
RRP	$14.00 Ⓢ

Murray Darling Collection Murray Cod Vermentino

Quality	♥♥♥♥
Value	★★★
Rating	88
Grapes	vermentino
Region	Murray Valley, Vic.
Cellar	▮ 2
Alc./Vol.	12.5%
RRP	$24.00

The first release of this wine was called A Murray Cod Called Bruce, in reference to Bruce Chalmers, the grapegrower who is also a part-owner of the brand. They've shortened it this year! The Murray cod, incidentally, is a member of the perch family and one of the great eating fish of Australia. The wine is sealed with a Diam cork.
CURRENT RELEASE 2005   It's a good wine and the winemaker has held back on oak and other inputs, allowing the fruit to shine; however, it's hard to say this is a very distinctive wine. There are savoury dried-herb and mulched-leaf aromas; an echo of cured meadow hay, but it borders on neutral. It is dry but soft, mellow but fresh – and a pleasure to drink, all the same. Grilled seafood would work well.

Olivine Gewürztraminer

Quality	♥♥♥♥
Value	★★★★
Rating	90
Grapes	gewürztraminer
Region	Hunter Valley, NSW
Cellar	▮ 3
Alc./Vol.	12.5%
RRP	$19.00 ⬈

Olivine is the brand name of The Little Wine Company run by Ian and Suzanne Little who are based at Broke in the Hunter Valley. It's not to be confused with Little's in Palmers Lane, Pokolbin, which is no longer connected with the Little family.
CURRENT RELEASE 2005   Not for the first time, this is an excellent traminer from an unlikely source – the Hunter Valley. The aromas are high-toned and spicy, with hints of pepper as well as the more usual lychee and muscat-grape scents. It has very good flavour and styling; the finish is dry and not heavy or phenolic – indeed, it's well balanced and a pleasure to drink with little goat's cheese and fried-onion canapés.

Pewsey Vale Eden Valley Gewürztraminer

Quality	♥♥♥♥♥
Value	★★★⁹
Rating	93
Grapes	gewürztraminer
Region	Eden Valley, SA
Cellar	▮ 2
Alc./Vol.	14.5%
RRP	$27.00 ⬈

Gewürztraminer was among the original plantings when Pewsey Vale was re-established over 40 years ago. It's a variety that works well in the cool highlands.
CURRENT RELEASE 2005   Exotic spice, floral and earthy aromas with a musky touch are typically pungent here. The palate continues the theme with plump texture, rich oriental flavours and a decadent feel. Acidity is soft and it finishes with good length. Try it with pongy cheese.

Pizzini Arneis

Arneis is a white grape from Piedmont in Italy's north. Its obscurity as far as Australians goes hasn't stopped a number of our wineries from playing around with it, sometimes with good results.
CURRENT RELEASE 2005   This has that distinctive canned-pears type of nose that marks arneis for us. There's also a hint of almond icing on the nose. It's delicate, full of interest, and *different*. In the mouth it has the mellow varietal feel and good texture, with a balanced touch of drawing dryness at the end. Delicious with gently flavoured, soft cheese like buffalo mozzarella.

Quality	♟ ♟ ♟ ♟
Value	★ ★ ★
Rating	91
Grapes	arneis
Region	King Valley, Vic.
Cellar	▮ 1
Alc./Vol.	13.8%
RRP	$24.00 ⚥

Pizzini Verduzzo

Italian white wines take a bit of getting used to if you're used to the sunshiny styles of Australia, but there are enough adventurous souls around these days to encourage wineries to make downunder versions. This is one of them.
CURRENT RELEASE 2005   It's a country mile away from modern/traditional Aussie types like riesling and chardonnay, but this verduzzo has its own charm. The nose has delicate floral aromas along with subtle, more savoury/kernelly and hazelnutty threads. In the mouth it shows clean, dry flavour of good persistence. Good with fishy antipasti.

Quality	♟ ♟ ♟ ♟
Value	★ ★ ★
Rating	90
Grapes	verduzzo
Region	King Valley, Vic.
Cellar	▮ 2
Alc./Vol.	14.0%
RRP	$24.00 ⚥

Primo Estate La Biondina

Silk purse from sow's ear. The eminently forgettable colombard grape is endowed with vibrant flair at Primo Estate. Maker: Joe Grilli.
CURRENT RELEASE 2005   You could mistake this for a really zesty sauvignon blanc. The nose is quite herbaceous with blackcurrant and briary aromas, and less of La Biondina's usual passionfruity scent. There's also a slightly sweaty, almost Kiwi sauvignon blanc accent to it. The fruity palate is grapey and crisp with a whisper of sweetness mid-palate adding mouth-watering appeal. We'd suggest a prawn dish fragrant with lemon grass and coriander.

Quality	♟ ♟ ♟ ♩
Value	★ ★ ★ ★
Rating	89
Grapes	colombard
Region	Adelaide Plains, SA
Cellar	▮ 1
Alc./Vol.	12.0%
RRP	$15.00 ⚥

Schild Estate Frontignac

Quality	♀♀♀
Value	★★★★
Rating	88
Grapes	white frontignac
Region	Barossa Valley, SA
Cellar	🍾 1
Alc./Vol.	11.5%
RRP	$14.00 🥂

It's fashionable for leaders of opinion to pooh-pooh this sort of wine, but they are wrong to dismiss it. There is a good market for it, and when it's well made, it can be a delightful casual, summery drink.

CURRENT RELEASE 2005   The colour is typically very pale, while the aromas are fresh and vibrant, very lifted and suggestive of passionfruit and pawpaw. The taste is sweet and grape-juicy, the sweetness being around spatlese level. It does have good fruit flavour and weight beneath the sweetness. Serve it with a plate of fresh fruit, including grapes.

Voyager Estate Chenin Blanc

Quality	♀♀♀♀
Value	★★★
Rating	91
Grapes	chenin blanc
Region	Margaret River, WA
Cellar	🍾 2
Alc./Vol.	13.0%
RRP	$20.00 🥂

If you drive past Voyager Estate's headquarters at Margaret River you'd swear you were in the South African wine country of Paarl and Stellenbosch. The Cape-inspired architecture is very distinctive, and the beautiful garden of roses makes it a must-see place in the region. The parallels don't stop there; chenin blanc is rare in Margaret River, but it's a common grape variety in South Africa.

CURRENT RELEASE 2005   A very respectable chenin, this opens with some sweet tropical-fruit aromas that are ripe but pleasantly subtle. The palate is soft and juicy with clean, fruity flavours that finish dry and clean. An agreeably soft white wine to enjoy with soft cheeses and quince paste.

YarraLoch Arneis

Quality	♀♀♀
Value	★★★
Rating	88
Grapes	arneis
Region	Yarra Valley, Vic.
Cellar	🍾 2+
Alc./Vol.	13.0%
RRP	$25.00 🥂

Arneis looks to be a grape with a future in Australia's cooler parts. We're seeing more and more of them, and they are interesting, if subtle, dry whites with a point of difference. This one's made by Serge Carlei, he of The Green Vineyards.

CURRENT RELEASE 2005   Nice wine, too. It's a delicate, soft dry white that has enough mineral, exotic spice and honey nuances in its bouquet to keep us entertained. It's pretty delicate in the mouth, which means it's very easy to drink, but it doesn't lack intensity. It's tightly wound and has a high level of acid. The notes say it employs 'subtle use of new French oak', but we didn't notice it. That *is* subtle! It would suit a plate of cold antipasti.

Rosé Wines

There's been a revival of interest in this humble wine style in recent years. Scores of wineries which never used to make rosé are having a go. They're making it in just about every region, from a number of different grape varieties, ranging from the logical low-coloured grenache and pinot noir through to shiraz, merlot, cabernet sauvignon and even chambourcin. Occasionally some white grapes are blended in, to further lighten the wine. Australians travelling to places like Spain, Portugal and southern France are enjoying the local habit of drinking rosé, and it stands to reason that rosé should be popular here, with our Mediterranean climate, long dry summers and outdoorsy eating habits.

Amulet Rosato

The Amulet vineyard occupies a beautiful spot in the high country around Beechworth in north-eastern Victoria. It is emerging as one of Australia's most promising table wine districts.

CURRENT RELEASE 2005 A subtle pink colour that's a bit less reddish than most. It smells of red cherries, spicy-sweet biscuits and leather – very sangiovese. In the mouth it shows intense, savoury flavour that isn't reinforced with sweetness, leading to a long dry finish. Good with Italian-style cold meats and salami.

Quality	🍷🍷🍷½
Value	★★★
Rating	**88**
Grapes	sangiovese; shiraz; cabernet sauvignon
Region	Beechworth, Vic.
Cellar	1
Alc./Vol.	13.0%
RRP	$17.00

Angove's Nine Vines Rosé

Nine vines? Nine million might be closer to the mark, in Angove's massive Nanya vineyard near Renmark. Makers: Tony Ingle and team.

CURRENT RELEASE 2005 This is a little more developed than we expected and has a brick-red tinge, while the aromas are very herbaceous, suggestive of cabernet, and the palate is very light and just a touch wishy-washy. The best thing is that it's low in sugar. A lot of its competitors are significantly sweeter. But this kind of balance is much more quaffable and food friendly. It would suit footy franks dunked in tomato sauce.

Quality	🍷🍷🍷
Value	★★★
Rating	**86**
Grapes	grenache; shiraz
Region	Riverland, SA
Cellar	1
Alc./Vol.	12.5%
RRP	$15.00 (\$)

Baldivis Estate Rosé

Quality	🍷🍷🍷
Value	★★★★
Rating	88
Grapes	shiraz
Region	various, WA
Cellar	🍾 1
Alc./Vol.	14.0%
RRP	$14.00 ⬗

Baldivis Estate, on the coastal plain south of Perth, is a subsidiary these days of the ambitious Palandri enterprise based at Margaret River. Prices are reasonable, quality is sometimes good.
CURRENT RELEASE 2005   A subtly coloured pink wine, this smells of red berries and cherries, fruity and fresh. The palate is middling in body and quite intense with sweetish-berry flavour and a clean, dry finish. Serve it chilled at a picnic.

Bird in Hand Pinot Noir Rosé

Quality	🍷🍷🍷
Value	★★★
Rating	87
Grapes	pinot noir
Region	Adelaide Hills, SA
Cellar	🍾 1
Alc./Vol.	12.5%
RRP	$16.60 ⬗

A bird in the hand is worth two in the bush. Not sure how this relates to wine, but as a brand name it is certainly different. The Nugent family are behind this company, and globe-trotting consultant Kym Milne has a hand in the winemaking.
CURRENT RELEASE 2005   A very pretty, likeable rosé with medium-full pink colour, a varietal pinot noir nose showing bubblegum and cherry-like fruit, and a slightly sweet/acidic palate. It's light-bodied and lacks a little softness, with a finish that falls away slightly. There's an attractive peppermint note, too. It would suit steak tartare.

Bloodwood Big Men in Tights

Quality	🍷🍷🍷
Value	★★★
Rating	85
Grapes	malbec
Region	Orange, NSW
Cellar	🍾 1
Alc./Vol.	13.0%
RRP	$15.00 ⬗
	(cellar door)

The name alone gets people in. It's a nice change from bland 'rosé'. And it probably appeals to people who want to think they're drinking something that's subtly different from the popular image of rosé.
CURRENT RELEASE 2005   The colour is at the deeper end of the rosé-style spectrum: medium-full red–purple pink. Our sample was dominated by reductive character: a sulphidic nose and a palate with dulled fruit character. It lacked the usual vibrancy and freshnesss of fruit. Not that it would matter to most rosé drinkers, we guess – it's not a style that is sniffed too much. We'd suggest serving it with baked whole salmon.

Brookland Valley Verse 1 Rosé

Rosés may be on the way back, but we see far too many pink wines that fall short of the quality we'd like. Brookland Valley's is an honest example of good standard without the pretensions of some.

CURRENT RELEASE 2005   A reddish-pink wine with a fruity, sweetish nose that reminds us of flowers, red berries and Turkish delight. In the mouth it's smooth and soft with a juicy hint of sweetness but a non-cloying finish. Try it with summer fare, perhaps ham and salad.

Quality	♟ ♟ ♟ ♟
Value	★ ★ ★
Rating	88
Grapes	merlot; cabernet franc
Region	Margaret River, WA
Cellar	🍷 1
Alc./Vol.	12.5%
RRP	$20.00 ⑤ ⋙

Chateau Mildura Riverboat Rosé

Frankly, we can't imagine a better way to enjoy this pink than while lazing on the deck of a Murray River paddle boat on a balmy summer evening while tucking into a plateful of yabbies.

CURRENT RELEASE 2005   This is a remarkably smart rosé from an unexpected corner. The colour is just right: a medium-light purple–pink, and the intense, fresh aromas are herbal and raspberry-like with some citrus high notes. It tastes as though there's some grenache in it. There is sweetness and it's in good balance with the rest of the wine's components. A more-ish drink, especially with beef carpaccio and shaved parmesan.

Quality	♟ ♟ ♟ ♟
Value	★ ★ ★ ★ ★
Rating	91
Grapes	not stated
Region	Murray Valley, Vic.
Cellar	🍷 1
Alc./Vol.	12.0%
RRP	$10.00 ⋙

Clairault Cape Pink

Cape Pink might sound wussy to steak-chomping big-red drinkers, but at least it's an attempt to be truly Australian and not cosy up to the French. Rosé means pink in French, of course.

CURRENT RELEASE 2005   The signature of cabernet shines through in this non-varietally labelled rosé. The colour is medium-deep pink – on the dark side – and the aromas suggest ripe raspberries or crème de cassis. The palate is quite big, with plenty of sweetness and a lick of tannin together with strong fruit flavour. It's a quality wine with some richness, but not for lovers of light, delicate French-style rosés. Try it with a plate of spaghetti with peas, pancetta and parmesan.

Quality	♟ ♟ ♟
Value	★ ★ ★ ⋆
Rating	87
Grapes	not stated
Region	Margaret River, WA
Cellar	🍷 2
Alc./Vol.	13.5%
RRP	$19.50 ⋙
	(cellar door)

De Bortoli Gulf Station Pinot Noir Rosé

Quality	▆▆▆▆
Value	★★★⁺
Rating	91
Grapes	pinot noir
Region	Yarra Valley, Vic.
Cellar	▮ 1
Alc./Vol.	13.0%
RRP	$18.85 ⑤ ≋

You can make rosé from any red grape, but we think that pinot noir might be the most suitable of all. In the best examples it has a touch of real class.
CURRENT RELEASE 2005   Pale, copper-pink colour gives this the look of some French pink wines, and it smells subtle with an earthy, slightly feral touch that continues the French feel. Some gentle strawberry aromas chime in as well, with a whisper of old oak; the soft, dry palate has a smoothly attractive middle. It's not a squeaky clean, ripe-fruity type – which we think gives it more interest than most. Try it with seared tuna.

De Bortoli Sacred Hill Rosé

Quality	▆▆▆▆
Value	★★★★⁺
Rating	88
Grapes	not stated
Region	not stated
Cellar	▮ 1
Alc./Vol.	12.5%
RRP	$6.99 ⑤ ≋

Inexpensive rosés have always been a minefield populated by winemaking mistakes, stuff nobody knew what to do with, and worse. But don't always shy away from pink wines with a low price tag, they can be a pleasant surprise.
CURRENT RELEASE 2004   The bright confectionery-pink colour is certainly lively, and it's just the ticket for simple refreshment, with a ripe red-berry character that's clean and fruity. The palate is soft and not too heavily boosted by residual sugar as some inexpensive rosés are. It has a light, semi-dry finish. An appealing, undemanding wine for warm weather sipping with light picnic fare.

Devil's Lair Fifth Leg Rosé

Quality	▆▆▆▆
Value	★★★⁺
Rating	92
Grapes	merlot; shiraz; cabernet sauvignon
Region	Margaret River, WA
Cellar	▮ 1
Alc./Vol.	13.5%
RRP	$19.50 ≋

Today it seems everybody makes a rosé. It's all been said before. Yawn. Sadly many of this new generation of pink wines don't exactly send the authors into raptures, but at Devil's Lair they make a good fist of this oft-overrated style. And it really does suit an unpretentious, not-too-groovy Australian lifestyle.
CURRENT RELEASE 2005   This looks promising with a pale-pink colour of bright intensity. The nose has summer-pudding berry smells that are clean and inviting. There's also a bit of light floral/spice character to add interest. In the mouth it continues the fresh theme with berry flavours of good length, and a juicy finish. Outdoorsy summer foods suit this well.

Ellender Estate Rosetta

Rosetta is made from free-run pinot noir juice that's left in contact with its skins for minutes rather than hours, resulting in a pale wine of some delicacy. Cool-grown pinot noir is proving an excellent base for pink wines like this. CURRENT RELEASE 2005 A very pale blush of pink looks light and fresh here, and the floral aroma is delicate too, with hints of raspberries and redcurrants and very gentle spice. The palate is very light, almost ethereal, but it has a spring-like refreshing quality that's quite endearing and a long fragrant finish. Sip it chilled with light picnic fare.

Quality	♍ ♍ ♍ ♌
Value	★ ★ ★
Rating	88
Grapes	pinot noir
Region	Macedon Ranges, Vic.
Cellar	▮ 1
Alc./Vol.	12.0%
RRP	$19.00 ⊗

Gordon Parker 'gp' Rosé

Another new producer from the West, based in the Great Southern. Gordon Parker's wines are available by direct mail only, from: 68 Hill Street, Albany, WA 6330; or admin@gordonparkerwines.com.
CURRENT RELEASE 2005 A very good rosé style, with spot-on medium-light pink–purple colour, and a fresh, strawberry aroma. Vanilla and tutti-frutti tastes come in the mouth and the best thing is that it's low on sweetness. The palate is soft and nicely balanced with a clean dry finish that invites matching with food. We'd suggest an antipasto platter.

Quality	♍ ♍ ♍ ♍
Value	★ ★ ★ ★ ✦
Rating	90
Grapes	shiraz; cabernet sauvignon
Region	Margaret River, WA
Cellar	▮ 2
Alc./Vol.	12.5%
RRP	$15.00 ⊗ (mail order)

Grant Burge Rosé

Barossa rosé is almost a contradiction in terms today – a separate style by itself. Makers like Charles Melton, Turkey Flat and others have invented the rosé that's not a rosé – if you compare it to anything from the Old World (France, Portugal, Spain), that is.
CURRENT RELEASE 2005 Hard to see this as a rosé! It is a rather tannic, harsh wine on the palate which puts it at odds with the soft 'n' slippery style we prefer to quaff in warm weather. It also has a spirity alcohol lift on the nose. The dark colour is appropriate to the style. It needs heartier food than your average rosé: perhaps veal cutlets.

Quality	♍ ♍ ♌
Value	★ ★ ★
Rating	84
Grapes	grenache
Region	Barossa Valley, SA
Cellar	▮ 2
Alc./Vol.	14.0%
RRP	$16.50 Ⓢ ⊗

Mac Forbes Rosé Pinot Noir

Quality	♡ ♡ ♡
Value	★ ★ ★
Rating	86
Grapes	pinot noir
Region	Yarra Valley, Vic.
Cellar	◊ 2
Alc./Vol.	13.5%
RRP	$18.00 ⬚

Gosh, another one! A new producer selling a rosé – where are the buyers for all these new wines? It's no surprise though: when grapes are in over-supply, it's cheap and easy to get wine made, and new brands spring up all over the place. The hard bit is selling it.
CURRENT RELEASE 2005   Clean, fresh, with attractive fruit and not sweet: that's our idea of good rosé. The colour is very hot purple–pink and the nose brings cherry and raspberry confectionery scents. The taste is light and simple, but pleasantly clean and dry. There's a flick of tannin on the finish that firms it up a bit. Try it with a Lebanese-style meal.

Murchison Rosé

Quality	♡ ♡ ♡ ♩
Value	★ ★ ★ ★
Rating	88
Grapes	not stated
Region	Goulburn Valley, Vic.
Cellar	◊ 1
Alc./Vol.	12.5%
RRP	$13.50 ⬚

Guido Vazzoler's ancestors made wine for generations on the Piave River in northern Italy. Rosé is a popular traditional wine type in Italy so it's natural that Guido would make one at his vineyard downunder. Salute.
CURRENT RELEASE 2005   Coloured more in a reddish-pink direction than the lighter colours of most European pink wines, this has red-berry and glace-cherry aromas that are succulent and fruity. In the mouth it's light and clean-tasting with fruity berry flavours and the merest suggestion of sweetness. Take it along to a picnic on a sunny day.

Pepperjack Grenache Rosé

Quality	♡ ♡ ♡ ♡
Value	★ ★ ★
Rating	91
Grapes	grenache
Region	Barossa Valley, SA
Cellar	◊
Alc./Vol.	14.0%
RRP	$23.00 Ⓢ ⬚

Grenache has been the mainstay of pink wine in this country for a long time, as it has in many other parts of the world. Its fruitiness and softness give it broad appeal, especially when the mercury climbs. Maker: Nigel Dolan.
CURRENT RELEASE 2005   This has a bright, ruddy-pink colour of some depth, and there's a slight confectionery thing on the nose that reminds us of kernelly red cherries, raspberries, even a whiff of spring flowers. In the mouth there's a hint of residual sugar to give it substance and softness mid-palate, well-modulated by crisp acidity. A well-made, modern grenache rosé of good quality. Drink it with ham off-the-bone sandwiches.

Peter Lehmann Barossa Rosé

Peter Lehmann's wines offer a cross-section of what the Barossa is all about, and quality is good across the board irrespective of price. Rosé has always been a part of the Barossa scene, and with its sales in Australia increasing by 80 per cent per year we're bound to see a lot more of it. Bravo, if it's all as slurpable as Lehmann's.

CURRENT RELEASE 2005   Party wine! The colour is as bright as a traffic light, a vivid pinkish-ruby, and the nose has a summer-berry aroma that's immediately inviting. In the mouth it's light and fresh with a soft mid-palate that's kept juicy and lip-smacking by zesty acidity. Great with Italian-inspired antipasti.

Quality	♜ ♜ ♜ ⌇
Value	★★★★⌐
Rating	89
Grapes	grenache
Region	Barossa Valley, SA
Cellar	⌂
Alc./Vol.	13.0%
RRP	$15.00 ⑤ ⌇

Shadowfax Rosé

We've long held the view that pinot noir is an excellent grape from which to make rosé. It has the requisite paler colour and less phenolics, a soft sweet-fruit palate, etc. Maker: Matt Harrop.

CURRENT RELEASE 2005   The wine has a little more age development than expected, but – we suspect – that is of little consequence to most drinkers, especially when it tastes so good. The flavours are rich and savoury, with some meaty, gamey complexities which are typical of the pinot noir grape. A lovely wine that finishes with a slight kick of alcohol. It would go well with antipasti.

Quality	♜ ♜ ♜ ⌇
Value	★★★⌐
Rating	89
Grapes	pinot noir
Region	Geelong & Cardinia Ranges, Vic.
Cellar	⌂ 1
Alc./Vol.	13.5%
RRP	$20.00 ⌇

Skillogalee Rosé

Everybody's doing it – making rosé, that is. In Clare, you might expect the rosés to be a bit beefier, and they often are. Winemaker at Skillogalee is Dave Palmer.

CURRENT RELEASE 2005   This is a vibrant, intense rosé style that is almost too confronting. It has a medium-full purplish-pink colour and an exaggerated aroma of raspberry and crushed vine leaves, reflecting the cabernet component strongly. It has some sweetness and acidity in the mouth, which combine to give a rather jarring finish. Try it with fatty tuna sashimi.

Quality	♜ ♜ ♜
Value	★★★
Rating	86
Grapes	cabernet sauvignon 75%; malbec 25%
Region	Clare Valley, SA
Cellar	⌂ 2+
Alc./Vol.	13.5%
RRP	$17.50 ⌇ (cellar door)

Spinifex Rosé

Quality	♥♥♥♥♥
Value	★★★★
Rating	95
Grapes	grenache; cinsault
Region	Barossa Valley, SA
Cellar	▮ 2
Alc./Vol.	14.0%
RRP	$23.00 ⬦

PENGUIN BEST ROSÉ WINE

The proprietors of Spinifex are husband-and-wife team Peter Schell and Magali Gely. They came to Australia from New Zealand in the early '90s and picked up experience in Europe along the way. The stylish, understated packaging and the great character of their small-volume Spinifex wines is most impressive. The rosé was fermented with wild yeasts and matured sur lie.

CURRENT RELEASE 2005   What a superb rosé! We don't often get that excited about rosé, but this is lovely. It has a pale-ish pink colour of good fresh hue and a restrained, cherry/strawberry aroma. The palate is where it all happens, however, with very good intensity and fruit appeal, and a persistent, clean, dry finish that cries out for food. Excellent balance, too. Ideal with smoked salmon canapés.

Taltarni Rosé

Quality	♥♥♥♥
Value	★★★
Rating	91
Grapes	not stated
Region	Pyrenees, Vic.
Cellar	▮ 1
Alc./Vol.	13.0%
RRP	$19.50 ⬦

Taltarni's rosé used to be brightly packaged in a bottle with see-through label and a French feel, but today it's presented more conservatively. The wine inside remains very good. CURRENT RELEASE 2005   Coloured more towards a reddish-pink than the coppery colours you see in some new-wave rosés, this has red-berry and cherry aromas of subtle fruitiness. There's also a very slight reductive touch to it, but it doesn't upset us. The palate is dry with hints of raspberry, and it has good texture and a dry, 'serious' finish. Good rosé to sip with prosciutto, cheese and crusty bread.

The Colonial Estate Enchanteur Rosé

Quality	♥♥♥♥
Value	★★★
Rating	90
Grapes	not stated
Region	Barossa Valley, SA
Cellar	▮ 1
Alc./Vol.	13.0%
RRP	$25.00 ⬦

The Colonial Estate is a lavish new venture that's recently arrived in the Barossa, apparently propelled by a lot of money. It's linked to entrepreneurial winemaker Jonathan Maltus, who makes wine in Bordeaux, notably at Chateau Teyssier in St Emilion. The Barossa winery is in Kalimna Road, Light Pass. CURRENT RELEASE 2005   This is a quite delicious rosé, of the lighter style, resembling a saignée wine. It is light-pink in colour with a developed brick tint, and has a strawberry, dusty aroma. The palate is light and dry, very quaffable, with sappy strawberry flavours and agreeable softness. It's food friendly, and would suit quail canapés.

Tigress Rosé

Tigress is one of many Tasmanian products that feature a thylacine in their labelling. How tragic it is to think that probably the last example of this unique creature died as recently as the 1930s.
CURRENT RELEASE 2005   This has a middling-pink colour of no great intensity; the nose is simple with light-floral hints and simple, smoky red-berry fruit, perhaps from pinot noir. The palate is fresh and light, with simple flavour and a shortish dry finish. A passable rosé to sip with pâté.

Quality	♟ ♟ ♟ ♟
Value	★ ★ ⇁
Rating	88
Grapes	pinot noir
Region	Tasmania
Cellar	🍾 1
Alc./Vol.	12.5%
RRP	$26.00 ⑤ ẞ

Train Trak Pinot Rosé

Twenty-five-odd years ago you could board a little navy blue and yellow railcar at Lilydale to travel through the lovely Yarra Valley as far as Healesville. The trains are long gone, but the remnants of the line run past this vineyard, hence the name.
CURRENT RELEASE 2005   This has a bright colour of some depth, but it's not the fluoro hue of some pink wines. The nose shows exactly why we reckon pinot noir makes such good rosé. It has a fresh strawberryish aroma that's fruity and pure, and it tastes fresh and appetising. It doesn't have the mid-palate sweetness that fills out many pink wines, and it finishes dry. It's all too easy to glug down on a hot day, so do keep in mind the 14 per cent alcohol – it can bite! Serve it with a picnic.

Quality	♟ ♟ ♟ ♟
Value	★ ★ ★ ★
Rating	91
Grapes	pinot noir
Region	Yarra Valley, Vic.
Cellar	🍾 1
Alc./Vol.	14.0%
RRP	$16.00 ẞ

Turkey Flat Rosé

Turkey Flat rosé continues the long tradition of Barossa rosé, with one of Australia's best examples. It's made from a hotchpotch of red grape varieties, but it works well.
CURRENT RELEASE 2005   This has a bright confectionery colour, and the nose is full of ripe red cherries and raspberries. In the mouth it flirts with sweetness, but it remains clean tasting and dry at the finish. The aftertaste is long and fruity with a nicely vinous thread that lifts it above the ordinary, and mouth-watering acidity gives it zip. We'd pair it with nibbles, such as prosciutto wrapped grissini.

Quality	♟ ♟ ♟ ♟
Value	★ ★ ★
Rating	91
Grapes	grenache; shiraz; cabernet sauvignon; dolcetto
Region	Barossa Valley, SA
Cellar	🍾 1
Alc./Vol.	12.5%
RRP	$20.70 ẞ

Wolf Blass Eaglehawk Rosé

Quality	🍷🍷
Value	★★★⁆
Rating	84
Grapes	not stated
Region	not stated
Cellar	🍾1
Alc./Vol.	13.5%
RRP	$10.00 ⑤ 🥢

It's a funny quirk of the wine business that the cheaper you go within a given style of wine, the sweeter the wines become. Evidently the winemakers (or their marketers) believe there's a strong correlation between buyers of cheaper wines and the sweet-tooth syndrome.
CURRENT RELEASE 2005   The colour is an attractive medium red–purple shade of pink, and the nose is high-pitched strawberry/cherry fruit. It's a sweet, rather lolly-ish style of rosé – quite pretty, but there is a lot of residual sugar and some green-fruit flavour lurking beneath it. Try it with pizza.

Red Wines
Cabernet sauvignon and blends

Cabernet runs second to shiraz in the red wine popularity stakes and the gap has widened. Shiraz-mania and the over-planting of cabernet has contributed to its over-supply. That's good news for punters: we can find good-value cabernet in the shops because prices have softened. Whereas top shiraz is grown in many regions, cabernet is more specific and the best sources are Coonawarra and Margaret River, followed by Langhorne Creek, the Yarra Valley, Great Southern and the Pyrenees. We like cabernet to taste like cabernet, with some blackcurrant character; and ripe, with fruit sweetness and elegance. We don't like it herbaceous, as much of it sadly is; and unripe cabernet has green tannins that can be quite bitter.

Ainsworth & Snelson Coonawarra Cabernet Sauvignon

Ainsworth & Snelson's intention of making handcrafted regional classics led them to Coonawarra for their cabernet. CURRENT RELEASE 2003   A well-balanced cabernet that is right in the traditional Coonawarra mould, rather than the blockbuster style favoured by some of the region's makers in the last couple of decades. Lightness and elegance are the themes, with blackcurrant fruit, spice and cedar characters of medium intensity and dry, savoury aspect. It finishes with drying tannins. We'd suggest pairing it with crumbed veal cutlets.

Quality	♟ ♟ ♟ ♟
Value	★ ★ ★
Rating	91
Grapes	cabernet sauvignon
Region	Coonawarra, SA
Cellar	▮ 5
Alc./Vol.	14.0%
RRP	$27.00

Alkoomi Cabernet Sauvignon

Alkoomi celebrated 30 vintages during 2005, and the founding family, headed by Merv and Judy Lange, is still in charge. It's a significantly sized operation, with 110 hectares under vine. Long-time winemaker is Michael Staniford. CURRENT RELEASE 2003   Here's an elegant, fine-boned cabernet in typical Frankland style, with sensitively handled oak that is unobtrusive, and yet the palate has classic cabernet structure. It has some mellow tobacco and meaty aromas as well as cabernet berries, and some complexity from development is starting to come. A wine of finesse and balance, to serve with lamb fillet.

Quality	♟ ♟ ♟ ♟
Value	★ ★ ★ ★
Rating	90
Grapes	cabernet sauvignon
Region	Great Southern, WA
Cellar	▮ 12
Alc./Vol.	13.5%
RRP	$20.00 ▮

All Saints Cabernet Sauvignon

Quality	♀♀♀
Value	★★★⅃
Rating	87
Grapes	cabernet sauvignon
Region	Rutherglen, Vic.
Cellar	➰2–10+
Alc./Vol.	13.8%
RRP	$22.00 🍾

Tragedy struck the Brown family of All Saints in 2005 when Peter Brown was killed in a motorcycle accident. His daughter Eliza Brown is marketing manager, and winemaker is Dan Crane.

CURRENT RELEASE 2004   Sweet blackberry aromas, fully ripe and showing no herbal side at all. It has plenty of weight and flavour, although the balance is upset somewhat by what seems to be over-adjusted acidity. This gives a slight hardness to the palate – which would be less obvious when drunk with food. Try it with cheddar cheese.

Angus The Bull Cabernet Sauvignon

Quality	♀♀♀⅃
Value	★★★⅃
Rating	89
Grapes	cabernet sauvignon
Region	not stated
Cellar	🍷5
Alc./Vol.	13.5%
RRP	$19.00

This is a one-wine label. It was started by Hamish McGowan in 2002 as a hearty red wine to sell to meat eaters in steak restaurants. It's been a tearaway success. The grape source is not disclosed on the package, but is typically from the Barossa and McLaren Vale.

CURRENT RELEASE 2004   It even smells meaty! That is, there's a touch of the roast-meats aroma that comes from ripe, warm-area red wine interacting with toasted oak barrels. There are some cassis and rose-petal aromas, too. The palate is lean-ish and fairly elegant, with acidity showing, which tends to shorten up the finish. This would not be an issue when drunk with steak. It's not as robust as you might expect from the publicity material, but a good drink with rare steak.

Anvers Cabernet Sauvignon

Quality	♀♀♀♀⅃
Value	★★★★
Rating	92
Grapes	cabernet sauvignon
Region	Langhorne Creek, SA
Cellar	🍷6+
Alc./Vol.	14.5%
RRP	$28.00 🍾

The Keoghans of Anvers source grapes from all around South Australia, suiting the grape to the region. Langhorne Creek is one of the most under-sung Australian regions. It has very few actual wineries but lots of vineyards, and part of the problem is that much of its fruit is trucked out to wineries in other places, which don't always acknowledge its provenance.

CURRENT RELEASE 2002   This is a slightly forward wine, showing some age already. It has some brick-red tinges in its colour and smells of smoky charcuterie, leather, earth and rose petals. It's quite an elegant wine, with soft tannins and a smooth, mellow texture for easy-drinking. It's medium-weighted and perhaps a touch oak-pushed, but a very good drink and ready to go. Food: shish kebabs.

Balnaves Cabernet Sauvignon

Balnaves' Coonawarras are hard to find but they are consistently among the region's best. They're often sold with the added bonus of an extra year or so in bottle-age. CURRENT RELEASE 2002 Intense and finely poised, this treads an attractive line between savouriness and ripe, tangy blackcurrant fruit, with some lightly leafy hints and a touch of mint. Oak takes a back seat but it adds a balanced seasoning, and the palate has tight structure with some typical Coonawarra cab austerity. It's a fine understated style that would work well with a Middle-Eastern-inspired lamb dish.

Quality	♥♥♥♥♪
Value	★★★
Rating	93
Grapes	cabernet sauvignon
Region	Coonawarra, SA
Cellar	▮ 6
Alc./Vol.	14.0%
RRP	$35.00

Barossa Valley Estate Ebenezer Cabernet Sauvignon

Barossa Valley Estate's Ebenezer range usually features a cabernet merlot blend, but in 2002 a straight cabernet has appeared for the first time that we can remember. It's from one of the best Barossa cabernet vintages in memory. CURRENT RELEASE 2002 The nose is complex, yet nicely underplayed with black-plum, high-toned oak and lightly leafy aromas. In the mouth it is smooth and well flavoured, with good balance and a tangy, cool-vintage feel. The finish is fine and long. It would go well with lamb chops.

Quality	♥♥♥♥
Value	★★★
Rating	90
Grapes	cabernet sauvignon
Region	Barossa Valley, SA
Cellar	▮ 5
Alc./Vol.	14.0%
RRP	$32.00

Barossa Valley Estate Epiphany Cabernet Merlot

We didn't have an epiphany after tasting this red, nothing unusual happened at all, so don't expect miracles from it. It remains a modest, easy-drinking red of the type that the big makers churn out effortlessly. CURRENT RELEASE 2003 This smells pretty good at the price, ripe and interesting with some herby notes to a core of juicy blueberry and blackcurrant fruit, dressed lightly in subtle oak. In the mouth it shows similar flavours of reasonable intensity and light- to medium-weight. It has zesty acidity and soft tannins making it a fresh, early-drinking style of good character. Serve it with steak and onion pie.

Quality	♥♥♥♪
Value	★★★
Rating	88
Grapes	cabernet sauvignon; merlot
Region	Barossa Valley, SA
Cellar	▮ 3
Alc./Vol.	14.0%
RRP	$15.25 ⑤

Ben Potts Lenny's Block Cabernet Malbec

Quality	♟♟♟♟♟
Value	★★★
Rating	92
Grapes	cabernet sauvignon 80%; malbec 20%
Region	Langhorne Creek, SA
Cellar	▮ 8+
Alc./Vol.	14.5%
RRP	$34.00

Maurice 'Lenny' Potts, grandfather of Ben Potts, started working in the family's Langhorne Creek vineyards in the 1950s and he's still part of the team. This wine honours his contribution.

CURRENT RELEASE 2003 This has blackcurrant-like fruit on the nose with some briary, plum-cakey malbec aromas in the background, and an oak input that's subtly appropriate to the style of the wine. There's some savoury earthiness as well, and the palate has traditional Langhorne Creek generosity of flavour and smooth texture. Ripe tannins are beautifully integrated and it has a long signature. Good with steak and kidney pudding.

Berrys Bridge Cabernet Sauvignon

Quality	♟♟♟♟♟
Value	★★★
Rating	93
Grapes	cabernet sauvignon
Region	Pyrenees, Vic.
Cellar	➥2–12
Alc./Vol.	15.0%
RRP	$32.00

You don't see Berrys Bridge wines everywhere, but make sure to try them when you can. They are good examples of the intense Pyrenees regional-style red wine.

CURRENT RELEASE 2004 A dense young wine with a penetrating nose of black fruits, seasoning spices, meaty notes, mint and aromatic oak. In the mouth it has concentrated cabernet fruit of depth and persistence. Firm tannins back things up well. A solid cabernet that will undoubtedly benefit from long ageing. Roast lamb with rosemary and garlic will suit it well.

Bremerton Tamblyn Cabernet Shiraz Malbec Merlot

Quality	♟♟♟♟
Value	★★★★
Rating	90
Grapes	cabernet sauvignon; shiraz; malbec; merlot
Region	Langhorne Creek, SA
Cellar	▮ 4
Alc./Vol.	14.5%
RRP	$18.00 ⬗

Tamblyn is a family name relating to the ancestors of the Willsons, who own Bremerton. They came to Australia from Cornwall generations ago.

CURRENT RELEASE 2003 A fruit-dominant cabernet blend of direct, ripe appeal, Bremerton is a typically flavoursome Langhorne Creek red. Blackberry-like fruit has some nice syrupy ripeness, there are touches of pepper and spice, and oak is subdued. It's medium-bodied and well balanced with an attractively chewy texture. Partners homemade lamb and vegetable pasties really well.

Canobolas–Smith Alchemy Cabernet Sauvignon

What a great name for a blended red wine! It's all about turning base metals into gold by some form of wizardry. The blend saw about 50 per cent new oak and is available in both cork and screw-cap finishes. Chief wizard: Murray Smith.

CURRENT RELEASE 2002   A briary, smoky, faintly vegetal kind of red that doesn't really reflect any one grape variety, but is an interesting amalgam. It's not oaky but fruit-driven, and has a full-bodied, vibrant, elegant palate of good concentration and grip. The tannins are smooth and ripe and the finish is very long. It will still benefit from ageing, then serve it with hard cheeses such as pecorino.
Previous outstanding vintages: 1996, '97, '98, 2001

Quality	♥♥♥♥♥
Value	★★★
Rating	92
Grapes	cabernet sauvignon 60%; cabernet franc 25%; shiraz 15%
Region	Orange, NSW
Cellar	⬤–1–5
Alc./Vol.	14.5%
RRP	$35.00 (cellar door)

Cape Mentelle Cabernet Sauvignon

Cape Mentelle has been through some changes lately, but under the ownership of Moet Hennessy and with Tony Jordan overseeing the production, it seems to be on a stable footing now. Makers: Simon Burnell and Lara Bray.

CURRENT RELEASE 2002   The 2002, from a cool summer, has that extreme briary Margaret River regional character, which is possibly due to some less-ripe grapes in the mix. It is certainly a powerful, vibrant cab, with sharply defined cabernet flavours in the blackcurrant/cassis/crushed-vine-leaf spectrum. A deep, well-structured wine, it's just held back a little by herbaceous characters that hover on the cusp of ripeness. Serve it with a rich beef casserole.
Previous outstanding vintages: 1991, '94, '98, '99, 2000, '01

Quality	♥♥♥♥♥
Value	★★★
Rating	92
Grapes	cabernet sauvignon
Region	Margaret River, WA
Cellar	⬤–2–12+
Alc./Vol.	14.5%
RRP	$73.00

Capel Vale Cabernet Sauvignon

Young winemaker Rebecca Catlin recently left Capel Vale for Tasmania, where her family have bought the Tamar Valley vineyard and winery, Holm Oak.

CURRENT RELEASE 2002   This is a complex, bordeaux look-alike (read: slightly funky) that also carries a thread of bitterness in the palate. The nose is very captivating: cedary, meat-stocky and slightly animal. The palate has flesh and softness, punctuated by noticeable acidity. A wine straight out of left-field. Try before you buy! Food: gourmet meat-pies.

Quality	♥♥♥♥
Value	★★★
Rating	88
Grapes	cabernet sauvignon
Region	south-west WA
Cellar	5
Alc./Vol.	14.5%
RRP	$23.00

Clairault Estate Cabernet Sauvignon

Quality	♥♥♥♥♥
Value	★★★♦
Rating	93
Grapes	cabernet sauvignon
Region	Margaret River, WA
Cellar	▮ 8+
Alc./Vol.	14.0%
RRP	$36.50 ▮

This winery was established by the Lewis family in 1976 as Cape Clairault. It now has new owners and a fresh lease on life. Winemaker: Will Shields.

CURRENT RELEASE 2002   A very good, and typical, Margaret River cabernet. It has complex aromas of seaweed, tomato ketchup and cassis, which actually tastes a lot better than it sounds! The palate is medium-weight and very fruit-sweet, with attractive cabernet flavour and a firm tannin backbone enlivening it all. Delicious wine and appropriately priced. It would go well with roast leg of lamb.

Clairault Estate Cabernet Sauvignon Merlot

Quality	♥♥♥♥♥
Value	★★★★
Rating	92
Grapes	cabernet sauvignon; merlot
Region	Margaret River, WA
Cellar	▮ 6+
Alc./Vol.	14.0%
RRP	$30.00

Often, wineries market two cabernet-based reds, a straight cabernet sauvignon and a cabernet merlot blend. The blend is usually the cheaper wine, more fruit-driven and designed to drink younger. This is exactly the case with Clairault.

CURRENT RELEASE 2002   Lovely cassis and crushed-leaf typical cabernet aromas greet the nose and the taste is smooth and juicy with plenty of sweet, ripe fruit and high-quality oak lending a complementary rather than dominant embellishment. The palate is fleshy but the acidity is a touch obvious. A good food wine: drink it with veal saltimbocca.

Climbing Cabernet Sauvignon

Quality	♥♥♥♥
Value	★★★★
Rating	88
Grapes	cabernet sauvignon
Region	Orange, NSW
Cellar	▮ 4+
Alc./Vol.	13.5%
RRP	$20.00 ⑤ 🍷

Climbing is the more upmarket brand of the Cumulus winery near Orange in the New South Wales Central Highlands. Former Southcorp chief executive Keith Lambert is CEO and former Southcorp chief winemaker Philip Shaw is in charge of winemaking. Ex-Coldstream Hills winemaker Phil Dowell is the hands-on man.

CURRENT RELEASE 2004   A straightforward red wine with some vanilla and blackberry aromas. It's very bright and slightly raw, lacking complexity at this stage but tastes as though the grapes were properly ripe. The palate is quite fleshy but the tannins are on the firm side, and it could drink better with protein-rich food. We'd recommend T-bone steak.

Crittenden Cabernet

Garry Crittenden is a survivor of the first order. After Dromana Estate, the company he founded, was floated publicly and he had rid himself of all connections, he started again, using the original vineyard beside his house, which now contains 24-year-old vines.
CURRENT RELEASE 2004   Packaged – unusually – in a burgundy bottle, this is a soft, fragrantly cassisy wine, which is ripe and varietal and refreshingly light and tangy in the mouth. It maybe lacks a little in power and persistence, but it's a very pleasant drink. It would suit pan-fried veal escalopes.

Quality	▼▼▼↓
Value	★★★
Rating	88
Grapes	cabernet sauvignon
Region	Mornington Peninsula, Vic.
Cellar	▮ 5+
Alc./Vol.	13.5%
RRP	$30.00 ⬙ (cellar door)

d'Arenberg The Galvo Garage

d'Arenberg's homespun wine names celebrate the rustic and the everyday. Galvo garages and sheds are fixtures of most wineries around Australia – even the new-wave, trendy places.
CURRENT RELEASE 2004   A densely hued wine that needs breathing to lose some of the rawness of youth. Decanted, it reveals briary aromas of black fruits, with some anise, herb and cedary touches. The palate has lush texture and ripe earthy flavours that are slightly old-fashioned in true d'Arenberg fashion. It has length and depth, and it finishes with dry sinewy tannins. Try it with roast beef.

Quality	▼▼▼▼
Value	★★★
Rating	91
Grapes	cabernet sauvignon; merlot; petit verdot; cabernet franc
Region	McLaren Vale, SA
Cellar	⬋1–6
Alc./Vol.	14.5%
RRP	$30.00 ⬙

d'Arenberg The High Trellis Cabernet Sauvignon

The High Trellis vineyard was the first at d'Arenberg to be trained above knee height in the 1890s. Its cabernet sauvignon has been a regional benchmark since the 1960s.
CURRENT RELEASE 2004   d'Arenberg's traditional methods show in this cabernet. Earthy/rustic aromas, and a herby edge trim black-plummy fruit; it has good texture and depth of flavour in a middleweight package. The finish is dry and grainy with good length. Serve it with kidney pastries.

Quality	▼▼▼▼
Value	★★★↓
Rating	90
Grapes	cabernet sauvignon
Region	McLaren Vale, SA
Cellar	▮ 6
Alc./Vol.	14.0%
RRP	$19.95 ⬙

De Bortoli Sacred Hill Cabernet Merlot

Quality	♟ ♟ ♟
Value	★★★★⸲
Rating	86
Grapes	cabernet sauvignon; merlot
Region	Riverina, NSW
Cellar	🍷 2
Alc./Vol.	13.5%
RRP	$6.99 Ⓢ ⮯

Yet another Sacred Hill red to tempt those on a budget, the Cabernet Merlot maintains the standard of the range. It's not the most refined red you can get, but it does its job better than wines selling for many dollars more.
CURRENT RELEASE 2005   This has a typical earthy Riverina nose with aromas of ripe berries and spice, plus a complementary dab of oak. In the mouth it has a touch of fruit-sweetness in the modern manner, and an agreeably soft texture, finishing with very easy tannins. Try it with a pizza.

Deen De Bortoli Vat 9 Cabernet Sauvignon

Quality	♟ ♟ ♟ ⸾
Value	★★★★
Rating	88
Grapes	cabernet sauvignon
Region	Riverina, NSW
Cellar	🍷 3
Alc./Vol.	13.5%
RRP	$10.00 Ⓢ

This great-value range of wines was named after the late Deen De Bortoli, patriarch of the De Bortoli family, who passed away prematurely in 2003.
CURRENT RELEASE 2004   The Deen De Bortoli Vat 9 Cabernet doesn't excite in the same way as the more oddball Vat 1 Durif and Vat 4 Petit Verdot, but it does offer excellent value as a reasonably priced quaffer, especially when it's discounted well below $10. The '04 wine has juicy raspberry and blackcurrant-like fruit of good intensity, with attractive, easy texture and a soft but savoury dry finish. Serve it with lasagna.

Don't Tell Dad Murrindindi Cabernet Sauvignon

Quality	♟ ♟ ♟ ♟ ⸾
Value	★★★★⸲
Rating	92
Grapes	cabernet sauvignon
Region	Yea Valley, Vic.
Cellar	🍷 5
Alc./Vol.	13.5%
RRP	$16.00 ⮯

The dad in question is Alan Cuthbertson, who established the Murrindindi vineyard in Victoria's Yea Valley over 25 years ago. One of the authors helped out with vintage at Murrindindi in the early days and the Cuthbertsons were very gracious, showing great tolerance of his slothful ways and general uselessness in the vineyard.
CURRENT RELEASE 2003   This densely coloured young cabernet has absolutely classic varietal character. The nose reminds us of blackcurrant syrup, cedar and dried herbs with a superbly bordeaux-like combination of ripeness and austerity. The persistent palate is concentrated in flavour, but light in the sense that it doesn't weigh you down, and it finishes with very fine-grained tannins. We'd suggest pairing it with roast lamb.

Edwards Cabernet Sauvignon

Founder Brian Edwards passed away after fighting cancer, but his family very ably continues the tradition. Son Michael makes the wines at Voyager Estate, where he is assistant winemaker; another son Christo manages the 25-hectare vineyard.
CURRENT RELEASE 2003   In typical Edwards style, this is a very intense, elegant cabernet, and a classic Margaret River wine. It has serious depth of blackcurrant/cassis fruit, sensitively backed by quality oak. Some hints of raisined fruit, too. It shows good depth and balance, and should cellar well. Food: rare roast beef.

Quality	♟ ♟ ♟ ♟ ♟
Value	★★★★
Rating	92
Grapes	cabernet sauvignon
Region	Margaret River, WA
Cellar	▯ 10+
Alc./Vol.	14.0%
RRP	$25.80

Elderton Cabernet Sauvignon

The Ashmeads of Elderton now have three cabernets in their list. The Friends is the cheapest, then this one, and the top of the totem is The Ashmead at $83 a bottle – a partner for their Command Shiraz. Winemaker: Richard Langford.
CURRENT RELEASE 2003   This is a typically smooth, early-mellowing Barossa style of cabernet. There are leathery, earthy, smoked-meats aromas reflecting ripe grapes and the liberal use of oak maturation. The taste is beautifully balanced and supple – almost elegant. It's full-bodied, smooth and savoury and would make a fine accompaniment to braised beef.

Quality	♟ ♟ ♟ ♟
Value	★★★★
Rating	91
Grapes	cabernet sauvignon
Region	Barossa Valley, SA
Cellar	▯ 6+
Alc./Vol.	14.5%
RRP	$25.00 ▯

Elderton Ode to Lorraine

For reasons best known to themselves, brothers Cameron and Allister Ashmead suddenly came over all sentimental about their Mum, and decided to dedicate a wine to her. Hence, the 'Ode to Lorraine' – a highly respected wine woman of the Barossa.
CURRENT RELEASE 2002   It's definitely an Elderton red! The trademark oak is there in full cry, and the bouquet is loaded with mocha, chocolate, vanilla, timber and subdued berry aromas. It's a big, solid, amply proportioned red with plenty of mild, smooth tannins, and flavours of oak and ripe fruit intertwined on an opulent palate structure. Not very cabernet-varietal, but very Elderton! It would go with hard cheeses, especially aged cloth-bound cheddar.

Quality	♟ ♟ ♟ ♟
Value	★★★
Rating	90
Grapes	cabernet sauvignon 68%; shiraz 25%; merlot 7%
Region	Barossa Valley, SA
Cellar	▯ 10+
Alc./Vol.	14.5%
RRP	$40.00 ▯

elgo estate cabernet sauvignon

Quality 🍷🍷🍷
Value ★★★
Rating **87**
Grapes cabernet sauvignon
Region Strathbogie Ranges, Vic.
Cellar 1–6+
Alc./Vol. 14.0%
RRP $26.00 ($)

The Strathbogie Ranges is a significant winegrowing region in the highlands of central Victoria. It's long been a grape supplier to wineries in other regions, but its public profile has been held back because of the small number of wineries there. There are just 10 wineries and we'd never heard of half of them.

CURRENT RELEASE 2004 The cool climate is evident here, in the minty, eucalyptus-like aroma and the high level of acidity on the palate. The colour is excellent: a youthful medium-deep purple–red, and there are some nice smooth red-berry aromas, too. It's a bit sharp on the tongue, but it is young, and it needs to be served with food. Try vitello tonnato.

Evans & Tate Cabernet Merlot

Quality 🍷🍷🍷🍷
Value ★★★★
Rating **91**
Grapes cabernet sauvignon; merlot
Region Margaret River, WA
Cellar 1–7+
Alc./Vol. 14.5%
RRP $20.00 ($)

It's amazing how many countries a medium-sized winemaker like E & T can be exporting to. A glance at their list of export destinations shows no less than 32 countries spread across the globe: from Canada to East Timor, from Denmark to Vietnam. Maker: Richard Rowe and team.

CURRENT RELEASE 2003 A slightly lighter style of cab merlot from this region, which is noted for full-bodied reds. It's medium-weight and fine-boned, with raspberry and rhubarb aromas, and a hint of gumleaf mint. The tannins are fine and long, providing backbone without obvious grip. It's a little tight and unevolved and will benefit from more time in the cellar. Serve it with pasta with a rich duck sauce.

Faber Vineyard Margaret River Cabernet Sauvignon

Quality 🍷🍷🍷🍷🍷
Value ★★★★
Rating **95**
Grapes cabernet sauvignon
Region Margaret River, WA
Cellar 10+
Alc./Vol. 14.0%
RRP $35.00

John Griffiths, former head winemaker for Houghton, runs this impressive new operation in the Swan Valley. He says, rather teasingly, that the grapes for this cab were 'grown on one of the [Margaret River] region's pioneer vineyards.'

CURRENT RELEASE 2002 This is a serious cabernet all right. The colour is deep and dark; the bouquet is very bordeaux-like with cedary oak-fruit interplay and lovely sweet-berry cabernet fruit of pinpoint ripeness. It's rich and yet elegant, with fine-grained tannins and superb balance. One to seek out. Delicious with pink roast lamb.

Ferngrove The Stirlings

The Stirlings is Ferngrove's flagship red. It's named after the mountain range that forms a backdrop to the Ferngrove vineyards.
CURRENT RELEASE 2003   Despite the shiraz component there's a hint of bordeaux here. It has savoury scents of violets, herbs, blackcurrant and cedary oak that are intense yet subtle. There's also a slight medicinal hint that won't necessarily be to everyone's taste. The palate has medium body and good intensity, with complex cabernet and oak-derived flavours. There's appealing grainy texture and the tannin structure tracks down the palate with lovely integration. An interesting wine. We'd recommend racks of lamb.

Quality	🍷🍷🍷🍷
Value	★★★
Rating	94
Grapes	cabernet sauvignon 71%; shiraz 29%
Region	Frankland River, WA
Cellar	1–10
Alc./Vol.	14.0%
RRP	$40.00

Forest Hill Cabernet Sauvignon

This vineyard's had a chequered career. It was the first vineyard planted in the Mt Barker area of the Great Southern, by the Pearse family in 1965. It got shoved from pillar to post, was owned by Vasse Felix for a time, and is now independent, with its own winery. Smith & Son distribute the wines, as they do Vasse Felix. As well, Bruce Pearse, son of the founders, is Vasse's viticulturist. There's order in the universe!
CURRENT RELEASE 2004   The colour is excellent, whetting the appetite for a treat. The nose is all coffee, raspberries and spices: attractive fruit and stylish oak handling. It's very elegant in the mouth, with great intensity, length and focus. A classy number, and it will age superbly. Have it with top-quality cheddar.

Quality	🍷🍷🍷🍷
Value	★★★★★
Rating	92
Grapes	cabernet sauvignon
Region	Great Southern, WA
Cellar	12+
Alc./Vol.	14.0%
RRP	$22.00

Forester Estate Cabernet Sauvignon

Forester Estate is at the northern end of the Margaret River region in an area that once had a prosperous timber industry. Giant eucalypts still surround the vineyard. Maker: Kevin McKay.
CURRENT RELEASE 2003   This has that succulent, sweet-and-sour sort of nose that typifies cabernet sauvignon: leafy blackcurrant and minty aromas are touched by toasty/spicy oak. The wood factor is quite restrained, especially given the wine's 20 months in new French oak. In the mouth it's ripe enough, but it retains those appetising savoury characteristics well. The palate is fine-boned and long in flavour, backed by ripe fine tannins. Try it with Vietnamese beef and mint.

Quality	🍷🍷🍷🍷
Value	★★★
Rating	92
Grapes	cabernet sauvignon
Region	Margaret River, WA
Cellar	6
Alc./Vol.	14.0%
RRP	$28.00

Giaconda Cabernet Sauvignon

Quality	♥♥♥♥♥
Value	★★★
Rating	93
Grapes	cabernet sauvignon
Region	Beechworth, Vic.
Cellar	🍾 4
Alc./Vol.	13.5%
RRP	$58.00

Cabernet sauvignon is often overlooked by wine tragics in favour of the more fashionable Giaconda chardonnay and shiraz, but they shouldn't ignore it – when the vintage suits cabernet it's very good indeed.

CURRENT RELEASE 2004   There's a typically herbal-blackcurranty aroma here, along with cedary oak, and some meaty, funky notes give it a slightly rustic edge. The palate is smooth and long with good depth and balance, ahead of a grippy finish. Serve it with lamb and kidney pie.

Grosset Gaia

Quality	♥♥♥♥♥
Value	★★★⁺
Rating	92
Grapes	cabernet sauvignon 75%; cabernet franc 20%; merlot 5%
Region	Clare Valley, SA
Cellar	🍾 7+
Alc./Vol.	14.0%
RRP	$54.00 🍷 (cellar door)

Expect the unexpected from Jeffrey Grosset. Having decided to withhold his '04 Gaia and '05 pinot noir and chardonnay till March 2007 (about a year later than usual), he released to the mailing list a quantity of older Gaia ('01 and '02) and Piccadilly chardonnay ('02 and '03). He'd bought them from a very cool chalk-lined underground cellar in England. No doubt the prices include a component for two lots of sea freight!

CURRENT RELEASE 2001   This took some time to open up with aeration. It showed a lot of stemmy-vegetal aromas, including tomato bush, spiked with raspberry cordial. Later: more cassis and charry oak with black-olive development. In the mouth, it was delicious: elegant sweet fruit of fine texture and impeccable balance. The tannins are soft and fine-grained and it already drinks well, although it's hard to avoid the conclusion that it's still in the early stages of its life. Cork-sealed. Drink with a meat and vegetable casserole.

Hardys Nottage Hill Cabernet Sauvignon

Quality	♥♥♥♥
Value	★★★★
Rating	89
Grapes	cabernet sauvignon
Region	not stated
Cellar	🍾 3
Alc./Vol.	13.5%
RRP	$10.60 Ⓢ

Nottage Hill is named after Tom Nottage, the nephew of founder Thomas Hardy, who joined his uncle in 1866 and managed Hardys' Tintara vineyard and winery for over 60 years.

CURRENT RELEASE 2004   A pleasant, straightforward red as befits its moderate price. It smells clean and inviting with aromas of ripe black fruits and herbs of good intensity. An earthy touch gives it savoury appeal and the palate is medium in concentration and length. Food: BBQ lamb chops.

Hay Shed Hill Cabernet Merlot

Margaret River produces the best cabernet blends in Western Australia. Hay Shed Hill's version doesn't earn the accolades of some of its neighbours, but the vineyard is ideally situated in the region's cabernet heartland.
CURRENT RELEASE 2004   There's unusual pungency on the nose here. It shows concentrated aromas of mint, violets and savoury herbs, dressing up a core of blackcurrant and blackberry fruit. In the mouth it has intense tangy flavour and good texture with firm grainy tannins and a long finish. It needs time for its emphatic characters to integrate, but it should be excellent in a few years. Serve it with a leg of lamb.

Quality	♈♈♈♈♙
Value	★★★★
Rating	92
Grapes	cabernet sauvignon 75%; merlot 20%; cabernet franc 3%; petit verdot 2%
Region	Margaret River, WA
Cellar	➥2–8+
Alc./Vol.	13.9%
RRP	$24.00 🍷

Henschke Cyril Henschke Cabernet Sauvignon Cabernet Franc Merlot

Henschke's top cabernet remembers Cyril Henschke, father of present winemaker Stephen. Cyril was a pioneer of bottling single-estate wines at a time when most Aussie reds were labelled 'Claret' or 'Burgundy'.
CURRENT RELEASE 2002   Cyril Henschke Cabernet seems to have been a little off the pace in recent years but this latest offering is headed in the right direction. It has aromas of raspberries and blackcurrants, with some mocha and olive-like touches. Oak is well handled. There's also an herbaceous thread in there. In the mouth it's a finely textured wine with a hint of herbal character, black-fruit flavour and good length – richness should build in the bottle, as Cyrils do have a good record in the cellar. Try it with veal chops and caramelised onion sauce.

Quality	♈♈♈♈♙
Value	★★♪
Rating	93
Grapes	cabernet sauvignon 75%; cabernet franc 12.5%; merlot 12.5%
Region	Eden Valley, SA
Cellar	▮8
Alc./Vol.	14.5%
RRP	$99.00 🍷

Hungerford Hill Fishcage Cabernet Merlot

The Hungerford Hill name has meant a lot of things over the years as the company went through various permutations, eventually becoming an under-performing Southcorp 'brand'. Now it's in private ownership and it seems to have the direction that was lacking for such a long time.
CURRENT RELEASE 2004   A loose-knit cabernet made in a modern commercial style of ripe, plummy, earthy fruit, straightforward fruit-sweet flavour, middling body and intensity, and some gently grainy dry tannins behind. A no-fuss drop to serve to the Friday-night pizza fraternity.

Quality	♈♈♈♙
Value	★★★♪
Rating	88
Grapes	cabernet sauvignon; merlot
Region	not stated
Cellar	▮2
Alc./Vol.	13.5%
RRP	$14.00 Ⓢ 🍷

Huntington Estate Special Reserve Cabernet Sauvignon Bin FB20

Quality	♥ ♥ ♥ ♥ ♥
Value	★ ★ ★ ★
Rating	95
Grapes	cabernet sauvignon
Region	Mudgee, NSW
Cellar	🍾 15+
Alc./Vol.	13.5%
RRP	$31.50 ⑤ 🍾

Huntington Estate is regarded as the flagship winery of Mudgee, and Bob Roberts, its founder, the godfather. Sadly for the region, he retired at the end of 2005 and the winery has been sold to neighbouring Abercorn. Maker: Susie Roberts.

CURRENT RELEASE 2002 This vintage is more chocolatey in youth than usual for Huntington, as well as rich, fleshy and tannic on the palate. This will all mellow in a year or two, which is the pattern, and we suspect that the '02, being a cooler season with slower-evolving wines, is a little backward. It is a superb wine with a big future. Delicious with stuffed lamb roast.

Jeanneret Cabernets

Quality	♥ ♥ ♥ ♥ ♥
Value	★ ★ ★ ♦
Rating	92
Grapes	cabernet sauvignon; merlot; cabernet franc; malbec
Region	Clare Valley, SA
Cellar	➖ 1–7
Alc./Vol.	14.5%
RRP	$22.00 🍷

Jeanneret's label features a representation of the Fibonacci sequence (or Golden Spiral): the geometric depiction of a precise mathematical sequence that often occurs in nature. Yes, well . . . what more can we say?

CURRENT RELEASE 2003 There's plenty of regional choc-mint aroma to this cabernet, and black fruit is mixed in appetisingly, as well as subtle spicy oak. The palate has attractive intensity and delicious freshness, with tangy flavours and a savoury, grainy texture provided by long, ripe tannins. A great companion to minty lamb cutlets.

Kangarilla Road Cabernet Sauvignon

Quality	♥ ♥ ♥ ♥ ♥
Value	★ ★ ★ ★
Rating	92
Grapes	cabernet sauvignon
Region	McLaren Vale, SA
Cellar	🍾 10+
Alc./Vol.	14.0%
RRP	$18.50 ⑤

For some reason, in our childish imagination, the name Kangarilla conjures up images of an Aussie version of a cross between Godzilla and King Kong, with a massive kangaroo thrashing through the streets of McLaren Vale on a lovesick rampage.

CURRENT RELEASE 2004 This is a fresh young cabernet with a youthful purplish colour and a bright aroma of dark plums, cassis and black cherries. It has a smooth, flowing palate with soft ripe tannins, plenty of sweet fruit and a silky texture. There are some grainy tannins towards the back and the palate is harmonious and nicely integrated. A lovely wine, indeed. It suits hearty winter stews.

Leasingham Bin 56 Cabernet Sauvignon

Bin 56 is usually titled Cabernet Malbec, but the 2002 vintage has such a high proportion of cabernet sauvignon that the label has left the malbec component off.
CURRENT RELEASE 2002   A deeply coloured wine with a nose of mulberries, plums, leather and slightly medicinal minty notes. The palate is rich, dry and firm with a minty, leathery feel and ripe, grainy tannins. It has a slightly overripe/underripe thing that has us a little mystified, but it's not a bad wine, especially with appropriate food. We'd suggest pairing it with a minty lamb dish.

Quality	♙ ♙ ♙ ♙
Value	✶ ✶ ✶
Rating	90
Grapes	cabernet sauvignon; malbec
Region	Clare Valley, SA
Cellar	🍶 5
Alc./Vol.	14.0%
RRP	$24.50 Ⓢ

Leconfield Cabernet Sauvignon

Leconfield was once a name to be reckoned with in Coonawarra, but the wines have been somewhat wayward for many years. The quality direction seems to be returning under ex-Rouge Homme winemaker Paul Gordon.
CURRENT RELEASE 2003   This has a whisper of the mulchy qualities that have marked Leconfield's cabernets for too long, but there's also savoury blackcurrant aroma and flavour of some intensity. It's at the tart, austere end of Coonawarra cabernet, but it's clean and brisk in the mouth, finishing dry and firm. Serve it with Vietnamese mint-wrapped beef.

Quality	♙ ♙ ♙ ♙
Value	✶ ✶ ✶
Rating	90
Grapes	cabernet sauvignon
Region	Coonawarra, SA
Cellar	🍶 5
Alc./Vol.	13.5%
RRP	$32.00 ⬢

CURRENT RELEASE 2004   A densely coloured youngster with a herby nose of blackcurrant fruit that's light and savoury. It has a middleweight palate that's fresh and tangy without much in the way of complex flavour development. But it's clean and well balanced, and slightly reminiscent of some Coonawarra cabs of yore, back in the days when the style wasn't as big and robust as it often is these days. A clean-cut young cabernet to enjoy with lamb cutlets.

Quality	♙ ♙ ♙ ♙ ♙
Value	✶ ✶ ✶ ⁊
Rating	92
Grapes	cabernet sauvignon
Region	Coonawarra, SA
Cellar	🍶 5
Alc./Vol.	13.5%
RRP	$32.00 ⬢

Lenton Brae Cabernet Sauvignon

Quality	♟♟♟♟
Value	★★★
Rating	90
Grapes	cabernet sauvignon 85%; merlot 15%
Region	Margaret River, WA
Cellar	⊸1–6
Alc./Vol.	13.6%
RRP	$34.00

Margaret River has less vintage variation than some of Australia's newer vineyards, but it still exists. In describing the near-perfect 2001 vintage and the cooler 2002 vintage, most makers favour the former year, but we think Lenton Brae's '02 might have the edge over the estate's '01.
CURRENT RELEASE 2002 A fine, austere cabernet nose introduces this well-made cabernet. It has plum and blackcurrant varietal cues and dusty/cedary oak in harmony. There's good mid-palate concentration and length in the mouth. It finishes dry and firm, but with less astringency than the 2001 wine. It needs time in the bottle, then serve it with racks of lamb.

Longview Devils Elbow Cabernet Sauvignon

Quality	♟♟♟♟♟
Value	★★★⟩
Rating	93
Grapes	cabernet sauvignon
Region	Adelaide Hills, SA
Cellar	▮5
Alc./Vol.	14.5%
RRP	$26.00

Longview Vineyard is an exciting new label from Duncan MacGillivray, the man behind Two Dogs alcoholic lemonade. The winery is a lovely place to visit with views over an unspoilt South Australian landscape.
CURRENT RELEASE 2004 A ripe style of Adelaide Hills cabernet that has a complex nose of black fruits, spice, mocha and licorice. It tastes smooth but unevolved, with a fruit-sweet, almost anise-flavoured mid-palate that scores plenty of points for intensity. It finishes with fine, soft tannins in good balance. Italian sausages with lentils suit it well.

M. Chapoutier Cabernet Sauvignon

Quality	♟♟♟♟
Value	★★★
Rating	89
Grapes	cabernet sauvignon
Region	Mount Benson, SA
Cellar	▮4+
Alc./Vol.	13.5%
RRP	$25.00 ▮

Rhône Valley guru Michel Chapoutier established a presence in Australia several years ago, with joint ventures at Mount Langi Ghiran and Jasper Hill as well as Mount Benson. He is an enthusiast for Australian wine and pays regular visits.
CURRENT RELEASE 2001 This is a left-field style of cabernet – possibly because of the French influence, possibly because Mount Benson is a new region and still a bit unsettled about styles. Charry-oak, charcoal, seaweed and black-olive aromas are more about complexity and secondary character than primary fruit. It's medium-bodied, smooth, elegant and harmonious in the mouth, with mild but positive tannins. It's different. Try before you buy. Food: gourmet hamburgers.

Maglieri Cabernet Sauvignon

Steve Maglieri started this winery in 1972 and sold it to Beringer Blass some years ago. He's gone on to create a new winery called Serafino, but we're pleased to report the style and quality of the Maglieri red wines is as good as ever. Winemaker: Charles 'Chilly' Hargrave.

CURRENT RELEASE 2004   This is outstanding value for money: a bright, bouncy young cab with generous flavour; a typical McLaren Vale core of sweet fruit, and balanced tannins. We like the aromas of blackberry and ripe plum, which display good varietal character and no greenness. The acidity firms the tannin on the finish, which ends a touch grippy, but it's well within the bounds of style and would go well with food. We suggest osso buco.

Quality	🍷🍷🍷🍷🍷
Value	★★★★⁣
Rating	92
Grapes	cabernet sauvignon
Region	McLaren Vale, SA
Cellar	🍾 10+
Alc./Vol.	14.0%
RRP	$20.00 Ⓢ

Maxwell Lime Cave Cabernet Sauvignon

Maxwell winery was established in 1979 by Ken Maxwell, father of the present winemaker Mark Maxwell. They also make mead – one of the very few wineries that still do make this old-fashioned honey wine.

CURRENT RELEASE 2003   This is a typically big, dense regional style of red. It has a slightly medicinal, earthy, leathery nose, and a chunky, full-bodied palate with chewy tannins. It's not a 'bright fruit' style but aims to be more than that. It has stacks of flavour and palate length and would benefit from cellaring – or if you can't wait, breathe it. Food: shepherd's pie would suit.

Quality	🍷🍷🍷🍷
Value	★★★⁣
Rating	90
Grapes	cabernet sauvignon
Region	McLaren Vale, SA
Cellar	⬤–1–10+
Alc./Vol.	14.5%
RRP	$33.00 🍾

McWilliams Barwang Cabernet Sauvignon

Barwang is a pioneering vineyard planted by the Robertson family at Young in 1969 and sold to McWilliams 20 years later. The area of land under vines has been increased several times over since then.

CURRENT RELEASE 2001   As usual, this is an excellent value-for-money red. But again, as usual, it's an oak-driven style. The aromas are meaty, earthy, woody, a touch mulberry-like and with an 'animal' aspect. The palate has slight hardness and the acid is noticeable. It's best served with food, such as a hearty beef casserole.

Quality	🍷🍷🍷🍷
Value	★★★★
Rating	90
Grapes	cabernet sauvignon
Region	Hilltops, NSW
Cellar	🍾 6+
Alc./Vol.	13.5%
RRP	$24.00 Ⓢ 🍾

Mitolo Jester Cabernet Sauvignon

Quality	♀♀♀♀₷
Value	★★★★
Rating	92
Grapes	cabernet sauvignon
Region	McLaren Vale, SA
Cellar	▲ 7+
Alc./Vol.	14.5%
RRP	$28.00 ⊠

The nickname of this wine is Baby Serpico, because 20 per cent of the grapes were air-dried for seven weeks before fermentation, as with the more-expensive Serpico cabernet. The drying is not really necessary to achieve correct ripeness in a region like McLaren Vale – it simply softens the tannins and takes away any sharp edges. CURRENT RELEASE 2005 The colour is typically dark and the aromas are subdued, but remind of tomato-bushy cabernet, toasty oak and dark chocolate. It tastes of ripe, sweet fruit, and has a solid tannin backbone. It has good concentration, ample ripe tannins and plushy texture. It's good value, and would suit venison braised with cherries.

Moondah Brook Cabernet Sauvignon

Quality	♀♀♀₷
Value	★★★★↓
Rating	89
Grapes	cabernet sauvignon
Region	various, WA
Cellar	▲ 5+
Alc./Vol.	14.0%
RRP	$16.60 Ⓢ

Moondah Brook is one of the least-talked-about brands among hard-core wine aficionados, but in our experience it offers some of the best-value red wine in the entire wine market, year after year. It's one of the Western Australian brands of the Hardys group. Chief winemaker: Peter Dawson. CURRENT RELEASE 2002 This is a good cabernet with weight and concentration, even if it's a tad oak-reliant. There are smoky, toasty-barrel aromas with some meaty and sweaty overtones, and the berry/leafy fruit is developing some cigar-box accents. The palate is smooth and elegant, if a trifle lean, and the finish has some acidity showing. It goes with grilled lamb chops.

Murdock Cabernet Sauvignon

Quality	♀♀♀♀₷
Value	★★★↓
Rating	93
Grapes	cabernet sauvignon
Region	Coonawarra, SA
Cellar	➡ 1–15+
Alc./Vol.	13.5%
RRP	$48.00 ▮

PENGUIN BEST CABERNET
SAUVIGNON AND BLENDS

The Murdock family has two vineyards, one in Coonawarra, the other in the Barossa. David Murdock was once a viticulturalist with Southcorp, and knows how to achieve quality in the vineyard. Pete Bissell does the rest in the winery. **CURRENT RELEASE 2001 The Murdock cabernet style is very particular: restrained, elegant and tidy, with real tightness of focus and fine texture. It's quite bordeaux-like, with classy cedary oak and nicely ripened fruit well harmonised in the bouquet and flavour; oak fairly evident at this early stage of the wine's life. The finish is long and tannins mouth-puckering. It has the kind of firmness and authority that bode well for a long-cellaring future. It will go well with all hard cheeses.** *Previous outstanding vintages: 1999, 2000*

Murdock The Merger Cabernet Sauvignon Shiraz

The Merger is all about merging the best features of the grape varieties and regions. This is the second release of the wine, and it's a blend of Coonawarra cabernet with Barossa shiraz (remember Penfolds Bin 60A?), which the Murdocks describe as a 'classic Australian claret-style red'. CURRENT RELEASE 2004   The Barossa component seems to have a big influence on the texture of this wine: it's thick and chewy with mouth-coating tannins – very atypical of Coonawarra reds! The aromas are of biscuity oak and subdued berries, and there is plenty of appeal here, although the tannins are a little heavy-handed. It needs more time. Then serve it with aged Heidi gruyère cheese.

Quality	♟ ♟ ♟ ♥
Value	★ ★ ★ ┤
Rating	89
Grapes	cabernet sauvignon 60%; shiraz 40%
Region	Coonawarra & Barossa Valley, SA
Cellar	➡2–10+
Alc./Vol.	13.5%
RRP	$20.00 ➰

Neagles Rock Cabernet Sauvignon

Neagles Rock reds encapsulate the robust style of the Clare Valley very well. Due to some hot weather late in the 2004 growing season the '04 wines are even more macho than usual.
CURRENT RELEASE 2004   Big Clare reds such as this are like a three-course meal in a bottle! It has very concentrated black-fruit, capsicum and mint aromas with definite charry oak in the background. The smooth, complete palate has a ripe core of blackcurrant fruit, balanced by some more savoury elements, well-handled wood and ripe tannins in support. Its 15 per cent alcohol was a bit of a warning sign to us, but actually it doesn't show too much. Try it with braised oxtail stew.

Quality	♟ ♟ ♟ ♟ ♥
Value	★ ★ ★ ★
Rating	92
Grapes	cabernet sauvignon
Region	Clare Valley, SA
Cellar	▮ 10
Alc./Vol.	15.0%
RRP	$22.00

Oakridge 864 Cabernet Merlot

Oakridge released a new range of cellar-door-only, super-premium wines early in 2006. They are named after the winery address on the Maroondah Highway at Coldstream. Maker: David Bicknell. Only 120 dozen made.
CURRENT RELEASE 2003   This is an elegant, typical Yarra Valley style of cabernet, although it is nice and ripe and has none of the greener aromas that can bedevil Yarra Valley cabernet and merlot. This has a lot of blueberry, cassis and toasty influences, suggesting fully ripe grapes and liberal oak contact. Medium- to full-bodied, it has smoothness, balance and easy-drinkability – but we suspect it will richly reward cellaring. Drink with pink roast beef.

Quality	♟ ♟ ♟ ♟ ♟
Value	★ ★ ★ ★
Rating	95
Grapes	cabernet sauvignon; merlot
Region	Yarra Valley, Vic.
Cellar	▮ 10+
Alc./Vol.	13.0%
RRP	$50.00 ▮ ➰ (cellar door)

Oakridge Cabernet Sauvignon Merlot

Quality	♥♥♥♥♥
Value	★★★★★
Rating	92
Grapes	cabernet sauvignon; merlot
Region	Yarra Valley, Vic.
Cellar	🍾 6+
Alc./Vol.	13.5%
RRP	$20.00 ⑤ 🥂

This brand was established by the Zitzlaff family in 1978 in the Seville area. They sold up there, moved to the Gruyere/Coldstream district and started afresh. They 'went public' and the company was bought by go-ahead Western Australians Evans & Tate.
CURRENT RELEASE 2003 There is a seaweed-like aroma in this wine – not unusual in cabernet, especially the more leafy styles. It also shows raspberry and rose-petal. There's a mulchy, slightly gamey influence as well. A less classy, less structured wine than the same maker's 864 bottling. But a very good drink in its own right and agreeably priced. A good companion to pan-fried veal.

O'Leary Walker Cabernet Sauvignon

Quality	♥♥♥♥
Value	★★★★
Rating	90
Grapes	cabernet sauvignon
Region	Clare Valley, SA
Cellar	🍾 10+
Alc./Vol.	14.5%
RRP	$21.50 🍾 🥂

David O'Leary and Nick Walker became friends in 1979 while studying winemaking at Roseworthy Agricultural College near Adelaide. They each had successful careers with big companies before starting O'Leary Walker in 2000, soon afterwards building a new winery at Clare.
CURRENT RELEASE 2004 These guys never dud us. Their wines are always generously flavoured and good value. This cab is no exception. The youthful aromas are of toasty oak, plum and blackberry, with side-lights of earth and roast meats. This leads into a palate that's big and ballsy, with lashings of tannin and oak and stacks of flavour. It's not all that elegant, but over-delivers on character. It would go with T-bone steak.

Oliver's Taranga Corinna's Red Wine

Quality	♥♥♥♥
Value	★★★⫯
Rating	90
Grapes	cabernet sauvignon; shiraz
Region	McLaren Vale, SA
Cellar	➡ 2–10
Alc./Vol.	14.5%
RRP	$28.00 🍾

The label tells us that Corinna is the first member of the Oliver family to make wine, although the family has been growing grapes at Taranga since William Oliver's time in 1841.
CURRENT RELEASE 2003 This is a mellow, fairly developed style of red, with some dusty/earthy and herbal elements in its bouquet, translating to a rich, chewy, densely textured wine on the palate. It's a robust, traditional McLaren Vale style and needs time. Then serve it with hard cheeses, such as cheddar.

Orlando Jacob's Creek Reserve Cabernet Sauvignon

We've said it before, and we'll say it again. There is
astonishing value for money to be had in big-company
wines priced at this level, if you are a discerning buyer.
The main reason many of the more fashionable, much
more expensive but less enjoyable wines are favoured
over the likes of JC Reserve is sheer snobbism.
CURRENT RELEASE 2002   An aromatic style of cabernet;
this has high-notes of peppermint and blackcurrant, plus
a lacing of spices. The colour is bright and young; the
bouquet is fresh, showing fairly strong but not excessive
oak, and the taste is medium- to full-bodied and elegant,
with linearity and persistence. In short, a classic cabernet
profile. It would drink well with roast lamb and mint sauce.
Great value!

Quality	♟♟♟♟
Value	★★★★★
Rating	90
Grapes	cabernet sauvignon
Region	various, SA
Cellar	▮5+
Alc./Vol.	13.5%
RRP	$17.00 ⓢ

Peel Estate Cabernet Sauvignon

Peel Estate's cabernets are released with a bit more age
than most of the competition, a good thing as cabernet
sauvignon really does need a bit of age to mellow.
CURRENT RELEASE 2001   A deeply coloured cabernet
with rich blackberry aromas mixed with some notes of
capsicum, earth and briar. The medium-bodied palate has
savoury berry and dry herb flavours that lead to a grippy
finish. Try it with herbed veal chops.

Quality	♟♟♟♟
Value	★★★
Rating	90
Grapes	cabernet sauvignon
Region	south-west coast, WA
Cellar	▮4
Alc./Vol.	14.5%
RRP	$32.50

Penfolds Bin 389 Cabernet Shiraz

Few Australian wines enjoy the pedigree of Bin 389. First
made under the guidance of Max Schubert in 1960, it
comes from the same stable as Grange, Bin 707 and all
those other famous Penfolds reds – and shares a distinct
family resemblance.
CURRENT RELEASE 2003   A fuller example of Bin 389 than
the preceding vintage, this sums up the style beautifully: a
nucleus of ripe, lush berry character, some touches of sweet
spice, hints of cedar, vanilla and coconut, generous flavour,
great length and balance. A classical Australian style. An
excellent partner for kidney-stuffed roast leg of lamb.
*Previous outstanding vintages: 1961,'64, '66, '71, '76,'86,
'90, '91, '94, '96, '98, 2001, '02*

Quality	♟♟♟♟♟
Value	★★★★
Rating	95
Grapes	cabernet sauvignon; shiraz
Region	McLaren Vale, Barossa Valley, Padthaway, Langhorne Creek & Bordertown, SA
Cellar	▮8
Alc./Vol.	14.5%
RRP	$40.00 ⓢ ▮

Penfolds Bin 407 Cabernet Sauvignon

Quality	♥♥♥♥♥
Value	★★★⸴
Rating	92
Grapes	cabernet sauvignon
Region	Coonawarra, Langhorne Creek, McLaren Vale & Bordertown, SA
Cellar	▮ 7
Alc./Vol.	14.5%
RRP	$35.00 ⓢ ▮

Bin 407 was launched with the 1990 vintage, giving the Penfolds Bin range a straight cabernet to slot in below the famous 707. It shows more elegant, cool-climate characteristics than its illustrious sibling, and is usually great value for money.

CURRENT RELEASE 2003 Penfolds won't be releasing a Bin 707 from the 2003 vintage, so 407 benefits from the premium fruit usually reserved for its big brother. This is a great effort from a vintage that wasn't kind to cabernet, offering intense, leafy, blackcurranty varietal cues on the nose with nicely underplayed oak folded in. The palate is middling in body, harmonious and well concentrated, finishing dry and savoury. Try it with herbed minute steaks. *Previous outstanding vintages: 1990, '91, '94, '96, '98, 2001, '02*

Penley Estate Phoenix Cabernet Sauvignon

Quality	♥♥♥♥
Value	★★★
Rating	90
Grapes	cabernet sauvignon
Region	Coonawarra, SA
Cellar	▮ 6
Alc./Vol.	14.5%
RRP	$23.00

The Tolley branch of Penley winemaker Kym Tolley's family established their first winery, the Phoenix Wine and Distilling Co., in 1888. The main product was TST Hospital Brandy, a far cry from fine table wine.

CURRENT RELEASE 2004 An interesting young cabernet of surprising softness. It opens with plummy, almost merlot-like, fruit aromas, with hints of licorice and raisins. There's a slightly rustic earthy thread to it, and an almost porty thing. The palate has smooth ripe flavour of depth and persistence, finishing with balanced tannins. A good match for roast rack of veal.

Pepperjack Cabernet Sauvignon

Quality	♥♥♥♥♥
Value	★★★★⸴
Rating	93
Grapes	cabernet sauvignon
Region	Barossa Valley, SA
Cellar	▮ 6
Alc./Vol.	14.0%
RRP	$22.00 ⓢ

Few widely distributed Barossa Valley labels offer the consistent quality of Pepperjack. They are designed by winemaker Nigel Dolan to encapsulate what the Barossa is all about, and they do the job well.

CURRENT RELEASE 2004 Generously proportioned reds like this are very Barossa. It's a deeply coloured drop smelling of syrupy blackcurrant fruit with balanced input from subtly spicy oak. It has a clean appetising aroma, and is followed by a smooth, velvety mid-palate that leads to finely balanced savoury, grainy tannins. A ripe, satisfying red at a good price. A good companion to lamb.

Pizzini Il Barone

The Pizzini name is strongly associated with the emergence of Victoria's King Valley as a source of top-quality wines. Italian-origin grape varieties have been a speciality for some years, and in Il Barone they share the spotlight with more conventional cabernet and shiraz.

CURRENT RELEASE 2001   A very interesting and satisfying blend. The colour shows some maturity, developing towards brick-red from ruby. On the nose there's a savoury, rather Italianate amalgam of cedar, licorice, mint, spice and old leather; plum and prune-like fruit fill the gaps. A complex and appealing introduction to a pretty special drop. The palate is richly flavoured, yet very dry, more-ish and long. Tannins are grainy, ripe and firm. Great with furred game.

Quality	🍷🍷🍷🍷🍷
Value	★★★★
Rating	96
Grapes	cabernet sauvignon; shiraz; sangiovese; nebbiolo
Region	King Valley, Vic.
Cellar	🍾 8
Alc./Vol.	14.0%
RRP	$40.00 🍾

CURRENT RELEASE 2002   Despite a few years in barrel and bottle, the '02 Il Barone is still relatively unevolved, but its complex personality promises much for the future. It opens with savoury Italianate aromas that suggest tar, licorice, black fruits, leather and gravelly earth. There's a lovely savoury 'Italian cafe' sort of vibe to it with its profound, elaborate flavours of great intensity, and it finishes with perfectly integrated dry tannins. Try it with wild mushroom risotto perfumed with truffle oil.

Quality	🍷🍷🍷🍷🍷
Value	★★★★
Rating	95
Grapes	cabernet sauvignon; shiraz; sangiovese; nebbiolo
Region	King Valley, Vic.
Cellar	🍾 10
Alc./Vol.	14.0%
RRP	$40.00 🍾

Poet's Corner Henry Lawson Cabernet Sauvignon

Quality	♥♥♥
Value	★★★
Rating	86
Grapes	cabernet sauvignon
Region	Mudgee, NSW
Cellar	🍶 3
Alc./Vol.	14.0%
RRP	$21.00 ⑤ 🍾

The poet Henry Lawson spent part of his upbringing in the Mudgee district, which emboldened the Orlando Wyndham Group to name its Mudgee winery Poet's Corner and brand some of its wines Henry Lawson. It strikes us as odd that poets of the distant past are glorified, yet contemporary poets are paid little attention by society.
CURRENT RELEASE 2001   This, the current release at time of tasting, is an earthy, edgy, mineral wine with a slight lack of freshness and a touch of astringency, although the colour is very good for a five-year-old red. It has an ironstone character and the acidity makes the palate taste a bit lean. It needs food: we'd suggest Wiener schnitzel.

Quality	♥♥♥♥♥
Value	★★★★★
Rating	95
Grapes	cabernet sauvignon
Region	Mudgee, NSW
Cellar	🍶 8+
Alc./Vol.	14.0%
RRP	$21.00 ⑤ 🍾

CURRENT RELEASE 2002   A trophy winner at the 2005 Mudgee Wine Show, this is a youthful, vibrant wine with brilliant purple–red colour and a superb nose of violets, herbs and dark berries. The palate is very intense, tremendously elegant and filled with delicious cabernet flavour. The balance is exemplary. Serve it with hard cheeses, like reggiano.

Punt Road MVN Cabernet Sauvignon

Quality	♥♥♥♥¼
Value	★★★
Rating	93
Grapes	cabernet sauvignon
Region	Yarra Valley, Vic.
Cellar	🍶 8
Alc./Vol.	13.5%
RRP	$48.00

MVN is Punt Road's prestige label, named after the late Michael Vivian Napoleone who restarted the Punt Road vineyard after purchasing it in a run-down condition in 1987.
CURRENT RELEASE 2003   From a very warm vintage, this Yarra Valley cabernet shows strong varietal aromas of ripe, mouth-watering blackcurrant and spiced plum. Charry French oak makes an impression, but the inviting, savoury austerity of ripe cabernet fruit is at the heart of things. It's a middleweight in the mouth, with sustained, clean, juicy flavour of excellent length, supported by fine, soft tannins. Try it with lamb shanks braised in cabernet.

Reynell Basket Pressed Cabernet Sauvignon

The feel of the Reynell brand borrows from the old Chateau Reynella labels that graced some of Australia's best cabernets a generation or two ago. The old Reynella cellar in Reynell Road, Reynella, now part of the Hardys empire, is another reminder of this great Australian wine name.

CURRENT RELEASE 2004 A dense, glass-staining red with a nose of essency black fruit, violets, herbs and spices dressed in a good dose of slightly raw, cedary, clove-like oak. The palate is intense with blackcurrant and toasty-barrel flavour that's savoury and tightly structured. In contrast to a lot of modern South Australian cabernets, it has a relatively moderate level of alcohol that provides nice mid-palate weight while maintaining freshness. Fine ripe tannins provide a dry backbone and tie it together. Great with racks of lamb roasted pink.

Quality	🍷🍷🍷🍷½
Value	★★★
Rating	**93**
Grapes	cabernet sauvignon
Region	McLaren Vale, SA
Cellar	2–10+
Alc./Vol.	13.5%
RRP	$49.50

Richmond Grove Weathervane Cabernet Merlot

The weathervane in question sits atop the spire of Richmond Grove chateau's tower at Tanunda in the Barossa. It features a goshawk guarding a bunch of grapes.

CURRENT RELEASE 2004 This has promising intensity and depth of colour, and the nose is an attractive amalgam of blackcurrant fruit, more savoury/minty/leafy notes, and just a whiff of sweet oak. The middleweight palate has good tangy black-fruit flavour that's nicely poised, and although it falls away a little in the mouth it's still a satisfying drop at the price. It signs off with ripe soft tannins. Try it with little lamb cutlets.

Quality	🍷🍷🍷🍷
Value	★★★★
Rating	**90**
Grapes	cabernet sauvignon; merlot
Region	not stated
Cellar	3
Alc./Vol.	13.5%
RRP	$15.00 ($)

Saltram Mamre Brook Cabernet Sauvignon

The biblical Mamre Brook name at Saltram dates way back to the days of the founder, William Salter. It is still a premium line for cabernet and shiraz although the Eighth Maker and No.1 Shiraz, and Winemaker Selection Cabernet have lately been slotted in above it. Maker: Nigel Dolan.

CURRENT RELEASE 2004 This is a top vintage for this wine. It's very youthful, with deep purple–red colour and an undeveloped nose of plums, dark berries and walnuts, with a hint of prune. The tannins are abundant: grippy but ripe. There is a lot of ultra-ripe fruit character, and the negative is that it's not especially cabernet-like. A very smart drink though, to drink or cellar. It would go well with rare steak and onions.

Quality	🍷🍷🍷🍷
Value	★★★★
Rating	**90**
Grapes	cabernet sauvignon
Region	Barossa Valley, SA
Cellar	15+
Alc./Vol.	14.0%
RRP	$25.50 ($)

Saltram Winemaker Selection Cabernet Sauvignon

Quality	▼▼▼▼▼
Value	★★★⁖
Rating	95
Grapes	cabernet sauvignon
Region	Barossa Valley, SA
Cellar	◆–2–20+
Alc./Vol.	14.5%
RRP	$65.00 ▮

This is a 'Limited Release' wine from Nigel Dolan, produced from a special batch of fruit off a single vineyard at Dorrien. We wonder if it's the same vineyard that used to go into Seppelt's now-deleted Dorrien Cabernet. (Both companies are under the Foster's umbrella now.)
CURRENT RELEASE 2002   This is a whopper of a cabernet: a very dark, concentrated, oaky number that suggests a boiled-down essence, with deeply infused oak giving strong mocha, coffee aromas. It's almost too much of a good thing: very concentrated, thick and chewy, with lots of fleshy texture and tannin galore, but no astringency whatever. It makes an emphatic statement. Cellar it, then serve with hard cheeses, such as reggiano.

Sandhurst Ridge Fringe Cabernet Sauvignon

Quality	▼▼▼▼
Value	★★★
Rating	91
Grapes	cabernet sauvignon
Region	Bendigo, Vic.
Cellar	▮ 4
Alc./Vol.	14.0%
RRP	$29.00 ⧰

Sandhurst Ridge has its own smallish vineyard in resurrected old-vineyard country near Bendigo providing the estate wines. The Fringe range of wines are made from grapes grown by neighbours to Sandhurst Ridge specifications.
CURRENT RELEASE 2004   The nose has savoury mint and eucalypt scents, a regional characteristic that's not too strong in this wine. There are also deep black-fruit, cedar and subtle spice aromas that carry through the palate in fine balance. It has real charm in the mouth, with good intensity but without formidable weight. It finishes with fine, ripe tannins. Serve it with herbed minute steaks.

Sandstone Cabernet Sauvignon Merlot

Quality	▼▼▼⧸
Value	★★★⁖
Rating	89
Grapes	cabernet sauvignon; merlot
Region	Margaret River, WA
Cellar	▮ 4
Alc./Vol.	13.5%
RRP	$33.00 ▮

A marital split between the partners in the Sandstone brand has resulted in Mike Davies departing and Jan McIntosh continuing to make the wines. Sandstone is based on a small estate vineyard in the Wilyabrup sub-region.
CURRENT RELEASE 2002   Some development shows in this wine already: our sample had a brick-red tinge to the colour and was dominated by savoury, secondary characters as opposed to primary fruit. It may have been a less than perfect cork; however, we liked the wine anyway! The bouquet suggests olives, earth, roast meat, dust and leather, quite complex but advanced. It's a good drink but the palate has some drying qualities that are likely to become accentuated by further ageing. We'd suggest osso buco.

Schild Estate Cabernet Sauvignon

Schild Estate is located at the Lyndoch end of the Barossa, where Ed Schild has been a grapegrower for some years and only recently ventured into selling wine. This wine was sealed with a Diam cork (which seems to be less prone to taints).
CURRENT RELEASE 2004   A solid cabernet; full-bodied and chunky, with a smooth, weighty palate and plenty of drinkability. Black-olive and creosote aromas, reflecting liberal oak contact. Chocolate and vanilla too. It's not especially complex but could reward short-term cellaring. Smooth for early drinking appeal. Serve with T-bone steak.

Quality	♥ ♥ ♥ ♥
Value	★ ★ ★ ★
Rating	90
Grapes	cabernet sauvignon
Region	Barossa Valley, SA
Cellar	▮ 5+
Alc./Vol.	14.5%
RRP	$24.00 (cellar door)

Seppelt Moyston Cabernet Merlot

The brand name Moyston is a very old one with a proud history. The first red wine HH ever tasted was a '60s Moyston. Seppelt has for generations grown and made great shirazes at Great Western. Cabernet is very much the poor relation there. That's probably why they're blending Bendigo fruit with the local stuff.
CURRENT RELEASE 2004   The aroma contains a bit more gumleaf/mint than we like in our red wine, but that's not a cardinal sin. What is questionable is the amount of oak – it tastes too much like oak-barrel staves and this leaves a harsh, bitter aftertaste. It could come good with further bottle-age: it's hard to tell. Cellar, then try it with hard cheeses, such as pecorino.

Quality	♥ ♥ ♥
Value	★ ★ ⊣
Rating	86
Grapes	cabernet sauvignon; merlot
Region	Bendigo & Grampians, Vic.
Cellar	➡ 2–8+
Alc./Vol.	14.0%
RRP	$30.00 ⓢ ⧉

Sevenhill Cabernet Sauvignon

Sevenhill was started in 1851 by an Austrian Jesuit priest, Father Kranewitter, in the Sevenhill sub-region, named after the Seven Hills of Rome. There have been few winemakers, as they tend to have long careers, but the last couple have broken away from the tradition of Jesuit winemakers. The latest is Liz Heidenreich.
CURRENT RELEASE 2002   The 2002 season was a cool one and herbal flavours were unusually prevalent in Clare reds. This year, the traditionally minty Sevenhill aroma has a pronounced green, vegetal, almost weedy accent. It is fruit-driven as usual, oak taking a back seat, and the palate seems lean and a trifle astringent. It needs time: cellar, then serve with barbecued kangaroo backstraps.

Quality	♥ ♥ ♥
Value	★ ★ ★
Rating	86
Grapes	cabernet sauvignon
Region	Clare Valley, SA
Cellar	➡ 1–10
Alc./Vol.	13.5%
RRP	$24.50 ▮

Shottesbrooke Cabernet Sauvignon

Quality	♟ ♟ ♟ ⸴
Value	★ ★ ★ ⸴
Rating	88
Grapes	cabernet sauvignon
Region	McLaren Vale, SA
Cellar	▮ 5+
Alc./Vol.	13.5%
RRP	$21.00

While the wine industry has been chasing high-Baumé, high-alcohol and opulent, sweet-fruited, low-acid reds during the last few years, Shottesbrooke's Nick Holmes has stuck doggedly to his guns and continued to make a more elegant, lighter style. Sometimes they look decidedly green beside the modern wines.

CURRENT RELEASE 2003   This is very much in the house style: lean-ish, medium-bodied, with a good but not particularly deep colour, and a smooth, pleasant-drinking palate finishing with bright acidity. There are plenty of inviting oaky, earthy, new-leather and vanilla/chocolate aromas. There's a suggestion of new barrels and the wine has good balance for current drinking. It would suit roast duck breast.

Skuttlebutt Cabernet Merlot Shiraz

Quality	♟ ♟ ♟ ♟ ⸴
Value	★ ★ ★ ★ ★
Rating	93
Grapes	cabernet sauvignon; merlot; shiraz
Region	Margaret River, WA
Cellar	▮ 6+
Alc./Vol.	14.0%
RRP	$16.00 ⸘

Skuttlebutt – a lovely word, isn't it? With lots of old-fashioned charm. Apparently, the word comes from a communal barrel of water around which people used to meet and gossip in olden times, spinning yarns and spreading rumours. Which is its modern meaning: a rumour.

CURRENT RELEASE 2004   The colour isn't all that deep but this is a lovely bright-fruited red, loaded with cassis and mulberry/sweet berry aromas and flavours; a flick of peppermint, too. The flavour is nicely focused on the palate and the balance and structure are excellent. Good length too, and low-key oak. We can't see why this wine is so cheap – there's nothing ordinary about it at all! Perhaps it just reflects the over-supply of Margaret River cabernet and merlot grapes. Serve it with braised lamb shanks.

St Huberts Cabernet Merlot

Quality	♟ ♟ ♟ ♟ ⸴
Value	★ ★ ★ ★
Rating	92
Grapes	cabernet sauvignon; merlot
Region	Yarra Valley, Vic.
Cellar	▮ 8+
Alc./Vol.	13.5%
RRP	$24.00 ⑤

A proud old Yarra Valley name that's now a brand in the giant Foster's Wine Estates' portfolio. It would be tempting to pooh-pooh these wines – St Huberts don't even have their own winery in the Yarra Valley any more – but the quality and style are being maintained well.

CURRENT RELEASE 2004   This is a typically elegant St Huberts red, with moderate alcohol and lively acidity that may put some people off, but to others it just demands a bit of cellaring time. Sweet cassis aromas with fruit leading the way; lots of berry flavours and excellent varietal characteristics. Modest tannins. Perfect with roast lamb.

Stella Bella Cabernet Sauvignon Merlot

All the Stella Bella wines are sourced from the southern half of the Margaret River region – between the towns of Margaret River and Augusta. In this area they own, lease or have long-term contracts with five small vineyards, with which they are 'striving to develop an identifiable Stella Bella style'. Bravo.

CURRENT RELEASE 2003   Another lovely Stella Bella red, with bright fruit aromas supported by subtle but fine-quality oak, and achieving that winning combination of concentration with elegance. The palate is young and tight, but accessible, with lashings of pure blackcurrant/crème de cassis flavours and appealing fleshiness. It will cellar well, and should drink nicely with beef stroganoff.

Quality	♥♥♥♥♥
Value	★★★★
Rating	92
Grapes	cabernet sauvignon; merlot
Region	Margaret River, WA
Cellar	🍷 12+
Alc./Vol.	14.0%
RRP	$25.00 ⊠

Stringy Brae Cabernet Sauvignon

The 2002 summer was exceptionally cool, giving the warmer South Australian regions such as Clare and the Barossa a season more resembling Coonawarra. This often translated to unusually good cabernet.

CURRENT RELEASE 2002   This is a puzzling wine, at once herbal and slightly underripe tasting, and at the same time a bit feral with one foot in the funky camp. But there are many appealing sides to it: it's concentrated and deep, with solid structure, a very youthful colour and some raspberry- and blackberry-fruit notes. There's an echo of bordeaux in the wine, but that may also be a function partly of its off-characters. Definitely a case of 'try before you buy'.

Quality	♥♥♥♥
Value	★★★
Rating	89
Grapes	cabernet sauvignon
Region	Clare Valley, SA
Cellar	🍷 7+
Alc./Vol.	14.5%
RRP	$18.50 🍷 ⊠

Swings & Roundabouts Cabernet Merlot

Mark Lane and Ian Latchford, the principals of this nascent wine company, reckon they've gained considerable experience (and expertise, we daresay) riding the swings and roundabouts of the turbulent wine industry.

CURRENT RELEASE 2004   This wine benefits from some airing, as many screw-capped reds do. It has a toasty-oak and coffee/mocha bouquet, with a hint of funk from a reductive overtone. It's just a touch unresolved on the palate and needs time to mature. At present it's a little too raw and aggressive for our preference. Cellar, then serve with roast venison.

Quality	♥♥♥♥
Value	★★★
Rating	88
Grapes	cabernet sauvignon 60%; merlot 40%
Region	Margaret River, WA
Cellar	⊷1–6+
Alc./Vol.	14.0%
RRP	$20.00 ⊠

Taltarni Three Monks Cabernet Merlot

Quality	♥♥♥♥
Value	★★★
Rating	91
Grapes	cabernet sauvignon; merlot
Region	Pyrenees, Vic.
Cellar	▬ 6
Alc./Vol.	14.0%
RRP	$21.20

The label's three shadowy monks are in fact the three 'cellar monkeys' of Taltarni: winemakers Leigh Clarnette, Loic le Calvez and Louella McPhan. Together they are rebuilding Taltarni's reputation as one of the Pyrenees region's leading labels.
CURRENT RELEASE 2003   Slightly sunburnt aromas of plums, prunes, wood smoke and dry herbs are savoury and intense. In the mouth this wine has strong structure and intense flavours, finishing dry and very firm with tannins that would do the tough Taltarnis of old proud. A flavoursome wine to serve with a steak.

Tatachilla Keystone Cabernet Sangiovese

Quality	♥♥♥♥
Value	★★★★
Rating	90
Grapes	cabernet sauvignon; sangiovese
Region	McLaren Vale, SA
Cellar	▬ 2
Alc./Vol.	14.9%
RRP	$17.95 ⬧

Cabernet sauvignon and sangiovese are the basis of a number of Italian wines these days. They combine savoury Italian tradition with international fashion to create some very good wines. In Australia the idea is gaining ground.
CURRENT RELEASE 2004   A middle-of-the-road style that combines these two quite different grape varieties well. It leads off with blackcurrant, earth, herb and leathery aromas of medium intensity. It tastes succulent and flavoury with a real tang. Tannins are very soft, making it a wine to drink young and fresh. Try it with scaloppine.

Tatachilla Partners Cabernet Shiraz

Quality	♥♥♥♥
Value	★★★★
Rating	88
Grapes	cabernet sauvignon; shiraz
Region	Langhorne Creek, McLaren Vale & other, SA
Cellar	▬ 3
Alc./Vol.	14.5%
RRP	$12.95

The Tatachilla spiel says that these wines 'wear the thumbprint of McLaren Vale', and although a proportion of the grapes are sourced from further afield, they do bear a distinct regional feel.
CURRENT RELEASE 2004   This opens with an earthy, funky 'old Southern Vales' aroma that takes us back to the good (or bad) old days. Plummy fruit is straightforward in flavour, and it has medium body and soft tannins. An old-worldly, meaty type of red, not squeaky-clean like most modern cab-shirazes, but it does have honest regional qualities. Drink it with lamb's fry and bacon.

Thorn–Clarke Shotfire Ridge Quartage

The Thorn-Clarke label was launched about four years ago, but its proprietors' families have a Barossa grape-growing history going back to the 1870s. Not surprisingly the wines have been very good from the word go.
CURRENT RELEASE 2004   The deep-purplish colour looks promising here, and it smells appetisingly of blackberries and blackcurrants, juicy and ripe with spicy touches and a savoury hint of briar. It tastes ripe and intense with medium body, fine texture and soft tannins. It's a well-made middle-of-the-road type, and it's quite dry, not bolstered by sweetness like some modern Barossa reds. Serve it with grilled pink lamb chops.

Quality	♟ ♟ ♟ ♟
Value	★ ★ ★ ✦
Rating	91
Grapes	cabernet sauvignon 43%; shiraz 29%; cabernet franc 13%; merlot 11%; petit verdot 4%
Region	Barossa Valley, SA
Cellar	🍾 4
Alc./Vol.	14.1%
RRP	$23.00

Tim Gramp Clare Valley Watervale Cabernet Sauvignon

The Gramp family made Orlando one of the best-known wine names in Australia, before selling the business in the 1970s. This great winemaking pedigree is continued by Tim Gramp with his excellent range of classic South Australian wine types.
CURRENT RELEASE 2003   A forceful, complex mouthful of cabernet with intense aromas of black fruits, mocha, spice and toasty oak. It tastes concentrated with full body and good depth of sustained flavour. Fine, ripe tannins are in perfect harmony. It's a bargain at the price and it can only get better in the bottle. It would suit aged Heidi gruyère cheese.

Quality	♟ ♟ ♟ ♟ ♟
Value	★ ★ ★ ★ ✦
Rating	93
Grapes	cabernet sauvignon
Region	Clare Valley, SA
Cellar	🍾 8
Alc./Vol.	14.0%
RRP	$19.50 🥂

Tollana TR222 Cabernet Sauvignon

The Tollana label was a victim of the carnage wrought a few years ago on the Southcorp organisation by a new administration. Always a good source of well-priced, hearty, regionally authentic Eden Valley wines; we lamented its passing. In the last year or two, Tollana wines have reappeared under another, more enlightened management team.
CURRENT RELEASE 2004   Tollana has returned with a bright young Eden Valley cabernet that has everything in the right place. It smells ripe and attractive with intense briary black-fruit aromas nicely trimmed in subtly spicy oak. The palate is smooth and easy on the gums with good depth and persistence of flavour, balanced by friendly dry tannins. Good value with roast beef.

Quality	♟ ♟ ♟ ♟
Value	★ ★ ★ ✦
Rating	90
Grapes	cabernet sauvignon
Region	Adelaide Hills, SA
Cellar	🍾 4
Alc./Vol.	13.5%
RRP	$19.50 Ⓢ 🥂

Trentham Estate Cabernet Sauvignon Merlot

Quality	♥♥♥♥
Value	★★★┤
Rating	89
Grapes	cabernet sauvignon; merlot
Region	Murray Valley, NSW
Cellar	▮ 3
Alc./Vol.	13.5%
RRP	$14.00 Ⓢ ⧉

The Trentham wines nearly always punch above their weight. The cellar door on the highway between Swan Hill and Mildura is well worth a visit if you're passing through. CURRENT RELEASE 2004   There's a deliciously ripe nose here that shows excellent cab and merlot traits. There are spicy-blackcurrant and richer plummy notes, and a whisper of vanilla in the background. It has a juicy palate that falls away just a little, but the purity of fruit carries it well, finishing in soft, grainy tannins. Enjoy it with penne and pumpkin and crispy prosciutto.

Turkey Flat Cabernet Sauvignon

Quality	♥♥♥♥♥
Value	★★★
Rating	93
Grapes	cabernet sauvignon
Region	Barossa Valley, SA
Cellar	▮ 6
Alc./Vol.	15.0%
RRP	$40.00

The shiraz from Turkey Flat is perhaps better known than this cabernet sauvignon, but both are very good regional examples. Maker: Peter Schulz. CURRENT RELEASE 2004   Despite its decidedly warm 15 per cent alcohol, this Barossa cabernet stops short of being too fumy, but only just. It opens with stewed-plum and blackcurrant-pastille-like fruit of generous proportions with touches of dark chocolate and sweet oak. In the mouth it has a round, generous feel with attractive concentration and velvety texture. A balanced foundation of tannins keeps it together. Try it with braised lamb.

Tyrrell's Rufus Stone McLaren Vale Cabernet Sauvignon Malbec

Quality	♥♥♥♥
Value	★★★
Rating	91
Grapes	cabernet sauvignon; malbec
Region	McLaren Vale, SA
Cellar	▮ 6
Alc./Vol.	14.5%
RRP	$24.00 ⧉

Where once they solely championed the Hunter Valley (while importing tons of grapes from South Australia and Victoria) these days Tyrrell's produce wines openly sourced from all three states. CURRENT RELEASE 2003   An aroma of warm, sweet oak opens proceedings in this wine, with raspberry-ish malbec and black-fruit cabernet aromas filling the gaps. It tastes succulent and quite complex with smooth texture, plenty of palate interest, and balanced furry tannins. It has adequate length and a nice tang to it. Try it with pot-roasted topside of beef.

Vasse Felix Cabernet Merlot

The Vasse Felix cellar-door and restaurant complex is a must for any visitor to Margaret River. Wine quality from this pioneering Margaret River estate is generally good and the surroundings very picturesque.
CURRENT RELEASE 2003   This shows distinct green pepper and herbal aromas with some tart blackcurrant fruit in the middle. It's not as bad as it sounds, being a tad savoury rather than simply unripe. There's an attractive thread of cedary oak, and the palate is succulent and tangy with dry tannins in support. Ideal with minty lamb cutlets.

Quality	♀♀♀♀
Value	★★★
Rating	90
Grapes	cabernet sauvignon; merlot
Region	Margaret River, WA
Cellar	▮ 4
Alc./Vol.	14.0%
RRP	$21.35

Voyager Estate Cabernet Sauvignon Merlot

Margaret River and cabernet sauvignon enjoy a symbiotic relationship that has made it a classic Australian style in less than 40 years. Quality varies though, so don't automatically assume that Margaret River on a cabernet label is a guarantee. Happily Voyager Estate's reputation is excellent.
CURRENT RELEASE 2002   The '02 Margaret River cabernet vintage wasn't up to the great 2001 standard, having less plush fruit character, and Voyager's cabernet reflects this. It has a slightly leafy, green-peppery nose with some juicy blackcurrant-like fruit at the core. The palate is tightly wound and long, with minty mid-palate fruit of clean flavour. Tannins are dry and grippy. Serve it with minty Thai beef stirfry.

Quality	♀♀♀♀
Value	★★★
Rating	92
Grapes	cabernet sauvignon; merlot
Region	Margaret River, WA
Cellar	➥1–6
Alc./Vol.	14.0%
RRP	$39.50

Voyager Estate Girt by Sea

'Australians all let us rejoice . . . da-da-da-da-de-dum . . . with da-de-da-de-da-de-dum, Our home is girt by sea.' For many Australians, this is how the national anthem goes, but most know that the country is 'girt by sea'. And the Margaret River vineyards are girt by sea, too.
CURRENT RELEASE 2004   This is a savoury cabernet blend with a nose of redcurrant, plum, leafy and clove-like notes. It tastes smooth and clean with medium body and balanced tannins. It's not sweetly fruity like much of the competition, but this sort of dry, structured red works better with food than much of the competition. Try it with minty lamb cutlets.

Quality	♀♀♀♀
Value	★★★⁺
Rating	92
Grapes	cabernet sauvignon 50%; merlot 41%; shiraz 9%
Region	Margaret River, WA
Cellar	▮ 3
Alc./Vol.	14.0%
RRP	$24.00 ⅏

Warburn Estate Barossa Valley Cabernet Sauvignon

Quality	❢ ❢ ❢ ❢
Value	★★★
Rating	88
Grapes	cabernet sauvignon
Region	Barossa Valley, SA
Cellar	➥ 1–6+
Alc./Vol.	14.0%
RRP	$23.00 ⑤ ▮

Warburn Estate is one of the many labels that used to be called Riverina Wines, run by long-time wine industry player Tony Sergi. It's a big operation, with 1100 hectares of its own vineyards. Winemaker: Sam Trimboli.
CURRENT RELEASE 2003   It's the first time we've seen this company playing with interstate fruit. The wine has an excellent deep, young colour and a lovely clean, sweetly ripe aroma of cassis, generously laced with coconutty oak. It's full-bodied and fully ripe, with a slightly aggressive salty, acid/tannin grip to close. It needs time to mellow, and is best with food. Try spicy Italian pork sausages.

Water Wheel Cabernet Sauvignon

Quality	❢ ❢ ❢ ❢
Value	★★★★
Rating	90
Grapes	cabernet sauvignon
Region	Bendigo, Vic.
Cellar	➥ 1–6+
Alc./Vol.	14.0%
RRP	$19.50 ⑤ ⧆

The Cumming family of Water Wheel have 120 hectares of vineyards, and grow some pretty flavoursome cherries and tomatoes commercially as well. Winemaker is Peter Cumming.
CURRENT RELEASE 2004   Good depth of colour and fruit richness are the hallmarks of this excellent, sweetly fruit-driven style. It's not as high-alcohol as some prior releases, and we approve of the change. There are raspberry, cassis aromas with a side-note of crushed leaves. There's no question about fruit ripeness. The profile is more elegant than usual, perhaps, with slightly leaner plum, blackberry and herb flavours. It has plenty of structure and finishes with bite. It would suit hard cheeses such as grana padano.
Previous outstanding vintages: 1996, '97, '98, 2000, '03

Windows Cabernet Merlot

Quality	❢ ❢ ❢
Value	★★★﹢
Rating	86
Grapes	cabernet sauvignon; merlot
Region	Margaret River, WA
Cellar	▮ 5
Alc./Vol.	14.1%
RRP	$16.00 ▮ ⧆

Yet another new brand from Margaret River. Why Windows? Perhaps the owners saw a window of opportunity to enter the wine business because of the plentiful supply of cheap red grapes in this region.
CURRENT RELEASE 2004   There's a definite sulphide pong about this wine, and we wondered – not for the first time – whether the screw-cap could be implicated: a totally inert seal will keep a young wine in a reductive state longer than a cork. Whatever the issues, this wine needs air, so decant it first. You may find it improves on the palate as well as the nose. It's won a gold and silver medal at significant shows, so it's obviously been perceived as having considerable merit earlier in its life.

Wirra Wirra The Angelus Cabernet Sauvignon

The name of this wine refers to the magnificent bell that sits in the belfry, which was recently incorporated into the new Wirra Wirra winery building. The bell came from a demolished Jesuit church, St Ignatius in Norwood, Adelaide.
CURRENT RELEASE 2002   Following a trend in South Australian big reds, this seems to have become thicker and more chewy in recent vintages, more McLaren Vale than Coonawarra in style, for sure. Lots of black-olive and earthy notes, richly constructed and generously oak-infused, with a lot of extract and density. It should age well, and go with barbecued kangaroo fillet.

Quality	🍷🍷🍷🍷🍷
Value	★★★
Rating	93
Grapes	cabernet sauvignon
Region	McLaren Vale; Coonawarra, SA
Cellar	⊂→1–15+
Alc./Vol.	14.5%
RRP	$50.00 🍾

Wolf Blass Eaglehawk Cabernet Sauvignon

The Eaglehawk range comes with a Procork these days. That's an Australian invention: a regular one-piece (or agglomerate) cork with a polymer membrane attached to each end. This is designed to reduce the incidence of tainting and 'random oxidation'.
CURRENT RELEASE 2004   Eaglehawk is a simple, grapey kind of red intended for immediate quaffing without too much deep philosophical discussion. Its aromas recall cherry pip and plum skin, together with some greener herbal notes. It's not very vinous or complex. The finish is merely adequate. Pair it with herbed rissoles and tomato sauce.

Quality	🍷🍷🍷
Value	★★★⁴
Rating	85
Grapes	cabernet sauvignon
Region	not stated
Cellar	🍾 2
Alc./Vol.	13.0%
RRP	$10.00 ⑤

Wolf Blass Gold Label Cabernet Sauvignon

There's something of the spiv about Wolf Blass – bow-ties, racehorses, flash cars and a certain gift of the gab. He sold the business many years ago, but there's no doubting the Wolf Blass brand is one of the most successful in the history of Australian wine.
CURRENT RELEASE 2003   There is plenty to like about this cabernet, although it seems to have been made in a forward, ready-drinking style. The colour has some development and there are woodsy, earthy, savoury characters about the nose, plus mint. Oak is the most prominent characteristic. Give it some air and you'll find a very pleasing drink. Serve with gourmet sausages.

Quality	🍷🍷🍷🍷
Value	★★★⁴
Rating	90
Grapes	cabernet sauvignon
Region	Coonawarra, SA
Cellar	🍾 5
Alc./Vol.	14.0%
RRP	$23.00 ⑤ 🍾 🥩

Wolf Blass Grey Label Cabernet Sauvignon

Quality	♟♟♟♟
Value	★★⟩
Rating	89
Grapes	cabernet sauvignon
Region	Langhorne Creek, SA
Cellar	⬤–3–10+
Alc./Vol.	14.5%
RRP	$40.00 🍾 ⧈

It's one of the conundrums of the modern wine industry (not only in Australia) that red wines are more concentrated, more alcoholic and more tannic than ever and yet they're being released onto the market earlier than ever. It's called cash-flow – the need to turn wine into cash ASAP. It's left up to the buyer to cellar the wine, but how many drinkers actually do that? Maker: Caroline Dunn.
CURRENT RELEASE 2004   Another big, brash, bold red from the Blass bunker: a wine that, in all sincerity, we could not enjoy at the moment. It needs several years in our view. The colour is very deep, the nose is heavy with timbery and minty smells, and in the mouth it's numbingly tannic, chewy and dense. Cellar; then drink with aged cheddar.

Wood Park Cabernet Sauvignon Shiraz

Quality	♟♟♟♟
Value	★★★★
Rating	92
Grapes	cabernet sauvignon; shiraz
Region	King Valley, Vic.
Cellar	🍾 5+
Alc./Vol.	14.0%
RRP	$20.00 ⧈

Wood Park's 2005 reds were on the market at a tender young age. They are lovely fruit bombs now but we wonder about the ageing pattern of such wines that have spent a worryingly short time in barrel. Generally, we find reds need a certain amount of time in oak to evolve and mature, otherwise they won't develop along classic lines.
CURRENT RELEASE 2005   This is a delicious fruit-forward red for drinking young. A stylish cabernet shiraz with excellent varietal cues of both cassis and plum, it may not be terribly complex but is a well-proportioned red with nicely ripe flavours, good intensity and length. Will complexity come with time in bottle? We're not sure. But it's so good young, you might not care. It would go well with a rare fillet steak.

Woodstock Cabernet Sauvignon

Quality	♟♟♟♟
Value	★★★★
Rating	90
Grapes	cabernet sauvignon
Region	McLaren Vale, SA
Cellar	⬤–1–8+
Alc./Vol.	14.0%
RRP	$20.00 ⧈ (cellar door)

Woodstock has produced some lovely McLaren Vale cabernets over the years, especially in the vintages preceded by cooler summers. That seems to be the key in the Vale: hotter years and cabernet don't get on too well.
CURRENT RELEASE 2004   It's a wine of substance! Dark coloured, big and dense, with liberal grainy tannins and slightly chunky softness, it has ripe, warmer-region cabernet fruit of a blackcurrant essence style, with major overtones of peppermint. Delicately handled oak adds a subtle extra dimension. There's a faintly green tinge to the tannins on the back-palate but the overall picture is of power with elegance. It would suit roast lamb with pesto sauce.

Woodstock Five Feet Cabernet Sauvignon Shiraz

Why Five Feet? Woodstock was named after the town in Oxfordshire, England, and in that town the unusual local stocks were said to have five leg-holes, for five feet. Woodstock's flagship wine is named The Stocks. CURRENT RELEASE 2004 This is a big, generous bear of a wine with a lot of peppermint and garden-mint aromatics. It's full-bodied and somewhat gruff to taste, with slightly aggressive tannins that need time to soften. It will also build some complexity if given time. There's plenty of weight, the colour is a promising deep purple–red, and there's no shortage of flavour or potential. It's great value and would go with barbecued butterflied leg of lamb.

Quality	🍷🍷🍷🍷
Value	★★★★
Rating	89
Grapes	cabernet sauvignon; shiraz
Region	McLaren Vale, SA
Cellar	▬1–7+
Alc./Vol.	14.5%
RRP	$17.00 ⬚ (cellar door)

Woop Woop Cabernet Sauvignon

Some retailers we know write about this wine as though it is the ant's pants; one even rated it 94/100 in his newsletter. Well, we would just remind readers that retailers are in the business of selling wine, and newsletters and price-lists are promotional tools . . . Maker: Ben Riggs. CURRENT RELEASE 2005 It is an impressive wine, especially for the price. The colour gets you in immediately: deep purple–red – but then it's a very young wine. The nose is a riot of simple, sweet, ripe plummy fruit, no oak in evidence, and a twist of nutmeg/spice – more like shiraz than cabernet! The palate is likewise bold and fruity, simple but lively, with a hint of green tannin and a fair belt of acid. Lovers of fruit bombs will go for it. It needs hard cheeses.

Quality	🍷🍷🍷
Value	★★★★⑂
Rating	87
Grapes	cabernet sauvignon
Region	South Eastern Australia
Cellar	🍾3+
Alc./Vol.	14.0%
RRP	$14.00 Ⓢ

Wynns Coonawarra Estate Cabernet Sauvignon

Both Wynns cabernets from the 2003 harvest have a special strap-label telling us that this vintage celebrates 50 years of Wynns cabernet sauvignon. Not many wineries can make such a boast. Maker: Sue Hodder and team. CURRENT RELEASE 2003 Another excellent cab from Wynns, albeit in a slightly denser style than usual. Cassis fruit is infused with darker, black-olive aromas suggesting plenty of time in wood, while the palate is full-bodied and almost thick, with an abundance of tannin. It has good depth and weight, and the tannins are nice and ripe. We'd suggest roast wild duck.
Previous outstanding vintages: 1954, '55, '58, '62, '66, '76, '82, '84, '85, '86, '88, '90, '91, '94, '96, '97, '98, '99, 2001, '02

Quality	🍷🍷🍷🍷🍷
Value	★★★★
Rating	92
Grapes	cabernet sauvignon
Region	Coonawarra, SA
Cellar	▬1–20
Alc./Vol.	13.5%
RRP	$30.00 Ⓢ 🍾

Wynns Coonawarra Estate John Riddoch Cabernet Sauvignon

Quality	🍷🍷🍷🍷🍷
Value	★★★
Rating	95
Grapes	cabernet sauvignon
Region	Coonawarra, SA
Cellar	➡3–25
Alc./Vol.	13.5%
RRP	$75.00 🍾

The previous release of this flagship wine was the '99. Its price was almost halved by the previous owner, Southcorp, which was catastrophic for the brand – although most observers agreed it was over-valued at the time. Several years' breathing space has allowed a style change and price rise.
CURRENT RELEASE 2003   We love the new direction of this wine: it's less oaky, less tannic, not overripe, and more elegant than before. Fine red–purple colour; marvellous cabernet aromas of cassis, mulberry and blueberry, and the oak so well balanced you barely notice it. The medium- to full-bodied palate is smooth and fluent, with lovely flavour and balance. It needs time and will richly reward cellaring. Hard cheeses are the best match.
Previous outstanding vintages: 1982, '86, '90, '91, '94, '96, '98, '99

Xanadu Cabernet Sauvignon

Quality	🍷🍷🍷🍷
Value	★★★⁺
Rating	90
Grapes	cabernet sauvignon
Region	Margaret River, WA
Cellar	➡2–6
Alc./Vol.	14.5%
RRP	$25.00 🍷

Xanadu started off as a rather eccentric establishment, but these days it's a more mainstream place with excellent facilities for visitors.
CURRENT RELEASE 2004   Snappy blackcurrant, floral and herby aromas are archetypically varietal, and these days Xanadu's cabernet style is riper and more satisfying than it once was. A thread of cedary French oak sets the fruit off well, and it has good persistence of austere flavour, finishing savoury and grippy. Try it with roast racks of lamb.

Yalumba Y Series Cabernet Sauvignon

Quality	🍷🍷🍷🍷
Value	★★★★★
Rating	90
Grapes	cabernet sauvignon
Region	not stated
Cellar	🍷3+
Alc./Vol.	13.5%
RRP	$13.65 ⑤

The sub-$15 region of the red wine market for the bigger companies has become quite a battleground, with some extraordinary value for money if you taste first, and then shop around. This is a newie from Yalumba, offering similarly marvellous value as its stablemate, the Y Series shiraz viognier.
CURRENT RELEASE 2004   This is a really lovely young cabernet, medium-bodied and very, very drinkable. The colour is vibrant and youthful; the nose offers violets, anise, crushed leaves and berry fruits. Oak is underplayed, so is tannin. It's a drink-now red with a smooth slurpy texture: balanced and understated. There are some less-ripe fruit elements that will worry technical tasters more than most people. Enjoy it with a beef and vegetable stirfry.

Durif

Durif is a selection of the lesser French grape variety peloursin, according to Jancis Robinson's *Guide to Wine Grapes*. It's all but disappeared in France, while America's petite sirah is widely thought to be durif. Whatever, durif is capable of making memorable wines in north-east Victoria, especially Rutherglen, the Australian region most closely identified with it. There, durif makes full-bodied, tannic, high-alcohol reds which are among the biggest red table wines made anywhere. They can be outstanding and quite long-lived. In the Riverina and Riverland some very tasty, inexpensive durifs can be found that are good early drinking, but tend not to age well. The wine is dark coloured with rich blackberry, sometimes jammy or even porty flavours.

All Saints Family Cellar Reserve Durif

This wine is 15 per cent alcohol but it's not porty or overripe, doesn't have dead-fruit character or a spiry finish. Instead, it's a well-made, vibrant, big but balanced red wine. Not all of them are – but then, 15 per cent is probably only mid-range alcohol for a durif! Maker: Dan Crane.
CURRENT RELEASE 2003   This is the best All Saints wine we've seen for many a year. It is most impressive. Black as night and dense as tar – a good sniff might prompt you to think of dusty boots, old-leather armchairs, blackberry jam and blackstrap licorice. It's solid, gutsy, powerful and loaded with delicious ripe fruit, the palate concluding in a wall of tannin that only barbecue-blackened steak or sausages could tame. A red for heroes.

Quality	🍷🍷🍷🍷🍷
Value	★★★⟩
Rating	95
Grapes	durif
Region	Rutherglen, Vic.
Cellar	🍾 12+
Alc./Vol.	15.0%
RRP	$49.00 🍾
	(cellar door)

Campbells The Barkly Durif

Barkly was once the name of the town that is now known as Rutherglen. There's a sign on the edge of town that reads: 'Sydney has a nice harbour, but Rutherglen has a great port.' And a pretty decent durif, too.
CURRENT RELEASE 2002   This one is a bit on the hot side for us; the alcohol overheats the finish leaving a spiry after-burn. With dusty/earthy and discreet plum-jam aromas and a big palate full of bold, aniseed-like flavour, it is a solid but not especially complex red. You could try serving it with hard cheeses, such as Italian grana.

Quality	🍷🍷🍷⟩
Value	★★⟩
Rating	89
Grapes	durif
Region	Rutherglen, Vic.
Cellar	🍾 7+
Alc./Vol.	15.0%
RRP	$41.00 🍾

Deen De Bortoli Vat 1 Durif

Quality	🍷🍷🍷🍷
Value	★★★★⁊
Rating	90
Grapes	durif
Region	Riverina, NSW
Cellar	🍶 3+
Alc./Vol.	13.5%
RRP	$10.85 Ⓢ

This wine originated in Darren De Bortoli's belief that durif had great potential in his warm Riverina vineyards. Previously the grape was exclusively grown in Victoria's Rutherglen district.

CURRENT RELEASE 2004 This is right in the solid durif mould, but it has a bit more breeding than many of the Rutherglen durifs. It has a dense purplish appearance, and it smells of blackcurrant, spice and licorice, with some vanillin touches. The palate has good texture and a tight structure of dry tannins. A very satisfying red with barbecued meats.

Westend Three Bridges Durif

Quality	🍷🍷🍷🍷⁊
Value	★★★★★
Rating	92
Grapes	durif
Region	Riverina, NSW
Cellar	🍶 6+
Alc./Vol.	14.5%
RRP	$23.35 🍾

Durif originated in the Rhône Valley, but is now little grown in France. It is closely identified with Rutherglen; however, the Riverina is doing increasingly interesting things with it. Maker: Bryan Currie.

CURRENT RELEASE 2003 This is a whopper! Its super ripe fruit verges on jammy but retains its vibrancy nicely. It's a big, dense, concentrated wine, more fruit-driven than the Reserve bottling, and possessed of masses of flavour and tannin. This needs protein: hard cheeses like parmesan would work.

Westend Three Bridges Limited Release Durif

Quality	🍷🍷🍷🍷⁊
Value	★★★⁊
Rating	92
Grapes	durif
Region	Riverina, NSW
Cellar	🍶 5+
Alc./Vol.	14.5%
RRP	$25.00 🍾

Westend has risen to the top of the Riverina pack in recent years. Its wines are second to none in the area. The Limited Release wines are hard to find but worth the effort. Best go direct to the cellar door in Griffith (see our Directory of Wineries for contact details).

CURRENT RELEASE 2003 A big, solid red that has been given plenty of oak. The colour is dark and dense; the bouquet offers coffee/mocha, toasty and dusty-oak aromas. It's very dry, savoury and tannic in the mouth and really demands food. Proteins readily soak up those chewy tannins. For all that, the wine finishes admirably smoothly. Drink it with shish kebabs.

Grenache and blends

Not that long ago South Australians were being paid a bounty to pull it out, but after being a wallflower for many years, grenache is now the belle of the ball. Old-vine material is being bought at a premium, and the resulting wine, whether made as a straight varietal or blended with traditional companions like shiraz and mourvèdre, is attracting raves both locally and internationally. Grenache is mainly grown in the older wine regions of South Australia and styles vary from soupy and hot with alcohol, through smooth, generous, delicious middleweights, to spicy Rhône look-alikes. The cool 2002 vintage was especially kind to old-vine, dry-grown grenache. They are disappearing from the shelves fast, so grab some of these beauties while you can.

Charles Melton Nine Popes

Charlie Melton never tires of reminding us all what a rich resource the Barossa Valley has in very old grenache and shiraz vines, which have managed to escape the ravages of phylloxera, the pest that has wreaked its havoc in other important vineyards of the world, necessitating re-planting. CURRENT RELEASE 2003   This vintage has a very dry, savoury-style bouquet with little primary fruit showing, but lots of earthy, dusty herb, mint and jam aromas. The taste is very big, chewy and gutsy, with ample drying tannin. There's a deep buried core of concentrated ripe fruit which the tannin structure holds up like a pillar. The finish is very dry and savoury and it needs food. We recommend medallions of buffalo fillet.
Previous outstanding vintages: 1990, '96, '98, 2002

Quality	♟♟♟♟♟
Value	✶✶✶
Rating	92
Grapes	grenache; shiraz
Region	Barossa Valley, SA
Cellar	➤1–7+
Alc./Vol.	14.5%
RRP	$45.00

d'Arenberg The Custodian Grenache

d'Arenberg kept the faith with poor old grenache when it had been deserted by all but a few, back in the days when all the smart young things in the wine industry were cooing about the charms of weedy cabernet sauvignon. The worm has turned, and now those wizened old-grenache vines are nothing short of national treasures. CURRENT RELEASE 2004   There's a warm familiarity about the bouquet of this red; earthy, raspberryish fruit has sweetly spicy overtones, and it shows little oak influence to confuse things. In the mouth it's ripe and at the same time savoury in time-honoured grenache fashion, with a dry structure of tannins to support it. Try it with Chinese claypot beef.

Quality	♟♟♟♟♟
Value	✶✶✶✶
Rating	93
Grapes	grenache
Region	McLaren Vale, SA
Cellar	4
Alc./Vol.	14.5%
RRP	$19.95

d'Arenberg The Derelict Vineyard Grenache

Quality	▼▼▼▼⟨
Value	★★★⟩
Rating	94
Grapes	grenache
Region	McLaren Vale, SA
Cellar	▮5
Alc./Vol.	14.5%
RRP	$30.00

The Derelict Vineyard Grenache comes from a 30-year-old McLaren Vale vineyard that was neglected and forgotten until it was rejuvenated by d'Arenberg. The vines were a tangle of wild, gnarled, struggling wrecks – 'resembling Medusa's hair' says Chester d'Arenberg – but now these low-yielding vines are the source of top grenache grapes. CURRENT RELEASE 2004   A more subtle, perfumed version of d'Arenberg's grenache. It has very fine red-berry and minerally fruit aromas with subtle ironstone overtones. The palate is excellent with just the right balance of focused regional fruit, smooth texture, length of palate and ripe tannins. Serve it with steak and kidney pies.

Gilligan Shiraz Grenache Mourvèdre

Quality	▼▼▼
Value	★★★
Rating	87
Grapes	shiraz; grenache; mourvèdre
Region	McLaren Vale, SA
Cellar	▮5
Alc./Vol.	14.4%
RRP	$20.00

Leigh Gilligan has been a familiar face in the McLaren Vale wine industry for many years. This is the first wine to bear his name, however. It's sealed with a Diam cork, which is a good move in our view; 450 dozen were produced. CURRENT RELEASE 2004   Strawberry-jam grenache flavours dominate this blend. There's a floral note, too, in its captivating nose, and a trace of animal. It's complex, but there's a touch too much extraction on the palate and a trace of bitterness creeps in. It would go well with game pie.

Grant Burge The Holy Trinity

Quality	▼▼▼▼
Value	★★★
Rating	90
Grapes	grenache; shiraz; mourvèdre
Region	Barossa Valley, SA
Cellar	▮5+
Alc./Vol.	14.0%
RRP	$33.00 ▮

They're a religious lot over there in the Barossa, largely Lutherans, of course (but not the Burges, they're of British stock). But that's not what the name of this wine is referring to. It's the three revered red grapes of the Barossa, from which it's vinified. CURRENT RELEASE 2002   This is so jammy you could almost feel tempted to spread it on your breakfast toast. It's got a wealth of super-ripe aniseed, plum-jam, blackberry and eucalyptus/mint aromas, which translate into a generously flavoured, rich, supple textured palate. It's not really southern Rhône-like at all, but a damn good Aussie red. We'd recommend pot-roasted venison.

Hardys Oomoo Grenache Shiraz Mourvèdre

The success of Hardys' Oomoo Shiraz has now bred a couple of other Oomoo wines. This blend employs these three traditional McLaren Vale red grape varieties to make a wine of old-fashioned style and generosity.
CURRENT RELEASE 2005   A ripe, slightly jammy red that doesn't have the class of Oomoo Shiraz, but it does deliver plenty of character. The nose has earthy plum and berry aromas that say McLaren Vale very clearly. In the mouth it's smooth and ripely flavoured with medium body and ripe, balanced tannins. It's a tad short compared to its shiraz sibling, but it does have generosity. Drink it with lamb tagine.

Quality	♥♥♥♥
Value	★★★⟩
Rating	88
Grapes	grenache; shiraz; mourvèdre
Region	McLaren Vale, SA
Cellar	▮ 3
Alc./Vol.	14.0%
RRP	$17.00 Ⓢ ⪥

Hardys Tintara Grenache

These Tintara wines are packaged in a bottle with a wonderfully retro feel. The wine inside is a very traditional drop, too.
CURRENT RELEASE 2003   Grenache with real complexity. The nose has black-cherry-jam, spice, dark-chocolate and Siena-cake aromas of good concentration and richness. The palate is ripe and round with great depth of flavour and beautifully integrated fine tannins. A very easy-drinking, friendly grenache to sip with chorizo and lentils.

Quality	♥♥♥♥♥
Value	★★★
Rating	94
Grapes	grenache
Region	McLaren Vale, SA
Cellar	▮ 6
Alc./Vol.	14.5%
RRP	$42.50

Henschke Johann's Garden

There are plenty of Johanns in the history of the Barossa Valley and surrounding areas. The Henschkes respect the region's German/Lutheran heritage a great deal, so this traditional regional blend is dedicated to all those Johanns past and present.
CURRENT RELEASE 2004   This has a brighter colour than some grenache-driven Barossa reds, and the nose seems fresher too, but that doesn't mean it's a wimp, quite the contrary. Its spice, dark-berry and earthy aromas aren't exactly delicate, and they lead to a full-bodied, rich and jammy palate with an alcoholic feel that says 'take care'. It finishes soft and generous, and will suit those looking for a big, smooth red to accompany a hearty dish. Try it with oxtail braised in red wine and see what we mean.

Quality	♥♥♥♥
Value	★★★
Rating	91
Grapes	grenache 69%; mourvèdre 19%; shiraz 12%
Region	Barossa Valley, SA
Cellar	▮ 5
Alc./Vol.	15.5%
RRP	$35.50 ⪥

Hewitson Miss Harry Dry Grown and Ancient

Quality	♟ ♟ ♟ ♟
Value	★ ★ ★ ⟩
Rating	91
Grapes	grenache 44%; shiraz 43%; mourvèdre 13%
Region	Barossa Valley, SA
Cellar	🍷 4
Alc./Vol.	14.0%
RRP	$22.00 🍷

Dean Hewitson treats the 50- and 80-year-old vines that create this wine with appropriate respect. Good on him, it was only a couple of decades ago that growers were getting government assistance to pull up similar ancient Barossa vineyards.

CURRENT RELEASE 2004   As you would expect from this blend of varieties, coupled to a hot vintage, this has a wild Rhône-ish feel to it. The nose has red fruit, spice and minerally aromas of good intensity. The palate is velvet-smooth, long and easy with soft ripe tannins and barely a whiff of oak to it. The old-vine fruit does the talking. We'd recommend enjoying it with a lamb pie.

Izway Mates Grenache Shiraz Mataro

Quality	♟ ♟ ♟ ♟
Value	★ ★ ★
Rating	88
Grapes	grenache 60%; shiraz 25%; mataro (mourvèdre) 15%
Region	Barossa Valley, SA
Cellar	🍷 3
Alc./Vol.	14.5%
RRP	$28.00 🍷

The Izway wines have a chummy style, as expressed in their packaging. The back label says: 'Each vintage . . . will be dedicated to people who have inspired, influenced and entertained us – our mates. The 2005 vintage is dedicated to Bendo and Ty, and our many shared outlandish adventures.'

CURRENT RELEASE 2005   The grenache is most apparent in this blend, through its bubblegum confectionery aromas, and a light- to medium-bodied, fruity, sweetish palate. It's a rather raw, straightforward, slightly cooked-fruit style with some alcohol warmth bringing up the finish. It would suit pork spare ribs with plum sauce.

Jeanneret Grenache Shiraz

Quality	♟ ♟ ♟ ♟
Value	★ ★ ★ ⟩
Rating	90
Grapes	grenache; shiraz
Region	Clare Valley, SA
Cellar	🍷 4
Alc./Vol.	15.0%
RRP	$18.00 🍷

Grenache has a long history in the Clare Valley, but it was a bit out of favour until recently. Fashion changes and interest in these generously proportioned, warmly alcoholic wines is growing again.

CURRENT RELEASE 2004   A fresher interpretation of a grenache-dominant red wine than many in South Australia, but this still has plenty of substance. It shows blackberry, raisin, mint and slightly porty aromas that have a hearty warmth. In the mouth it's a ripe, sun-drenched style with good body, density, length and soft, agreeable tannins. Serve it with mature, firm cheeses.

Penfolds Bin 138 Old Vine Grenache Shiraz Mourvèdre

One of the newer Penfolds Bin reds, Bin 138 differs from most of its siblings in being aged only in old oak hogsheads. It's also the first to be bottled under screw-cap.

CURRENT RELEASE 2004 A smooth, fruit-dominant wine that's a bit at odds with the traditional Penfolds red style, which usually shows definite oak influence. It smells of red berries, plums, spice and earth, and it has a delicious, mouth-filling, hearty personality, yet it's not overripe or blown out by alcohol like some other Barossa grenache blends. Good with braised steak and onions.

Previous outstanding vintages: 1994, '96, '98, 2001

Quality	🍷🍷🍷🍷
Value	★★★½
Rating	**91**
Grapes	grenache; shiraz; mourvèdre
Region	Barossa Valley, SA
Cellar	5
Alc./Vol.	14.5%
RRP	$26.00 (Ⓢ)

Quarryman Grenache

Quarryman is a sub-label of Classic McLaren, a fairly new winery whose reds debuted at high prices in the wake of the initial buoyant response from the American market. Things have got much tougher since those heady days, and it was no surprise to see a cheaper label emerging.

CURRENT RELEASE 2003 A very smoky, almost burnt nose, opens up to reveal chocolate and spices and a hint of raisin. The palate is deep and fleshy, with a firmer tannin spine than we're used to seeing in grenache from this region – which is all to the good. Lovely balance and has that intangible 'drink me!' quality. Delicious with steak and kidney pie.

Quality	🍷🍷🍷🍷
Value	★★★★★
Rating	**90**
Grapes	grenache
Region	McLaren Vale, SA
Cellar	3
Alc./Vol.	14.5%
RRP	$16.00

Reynell Basket Pressed Grenache

This grenache has been around for a while, and we suspect that despite the hype about grenache and the 'Rhône' varieties, they don't exactly speed off retail shelves.

CURRENT RELEASE 2002 This is definitely one of the better of the current crop of South Australian grenaches. It has a concentrated nose reminiscent of raspberry with notes of spice, chocolate and crème brûlée. The palate is velvety and juicy with attractive textural interest, leading to soft smooth tannins at the end. Try it with Chinese steamed duck.

Quality	🍷🍷🍷🍷½
Value	★★★½
Rating	**93**
Grapes	grenache
Region	McLaren Vale, SA
Cellar	4
Alc./Vol.	14.0%
RRP	$31.75

S.C. Pannell Grenache

Quality	♟♟♟♟♟
Value	★★★★
Rating	95
Grapes	grenache
Region	McLaren Vale, SA
Cellar	🍾 10+
Alc./Vol.	14.0%
RRP	$45.00 (mail order)

This is scarce as hen's teeth: just 40 dozen were allocated to all of Australia. Steve Pannell reckons he spent $1.80 on each cork, and got the best money could buy. He is a former Hardys chief red winemaker, and a son of the founder of Moss Wood, so he knows something about quality. CURRENT RELEASE 2004 The deep purple–red colour is remarkable for grenache. As is the depth of flavour, concentration, the quality of tannins and overall balance. Aniseed, vanilla, chocolate, blackberries, leather and black olive are among the flavours. It's not often a new label arrives and three out of three score gold medals in HH's blind tastings. But Pannell's three '04 reds did. They are extraordinarily good. Food: roast pork with rosemary.

Schild Estate Grenache Mourvèdre Shiraz

Quality	♟♟♟♟
Value	★★★⟩
Rating	92
Grapes	grenache; mourvèdre; shiraz
Region	Barossa Valley, SA
Cellar	🍾 3
Alc./Vol.	15.0%
RRP	$22.00 🛍

GSM blends, or in the case of this one, GMS blends, are a small but important part of the red-wine scene. They are well suited to Australian conditions, which are not too different climatically from the southern Rhône Valley. CURRENT RELEASE 2005 This one is a bit young to be on sale, but considering it's smooth and full of charm, why not? Some drinkers just adore fresh primary fruit. They're happy to be into red wine within a year of harvest. The aromas are attractively spicy, with black-pepper, floral and jammy nuances from the grenache, a touch of sap and alcoholic warmth. Strangely delicious! It's hard to know how this sort of wine will develop, but we suspect it's best young. Beef spare ribs and plum sauce would suit.

Shingleback Grenache

Quality	♟♟♟♟
Value	★★★⟩
Rating	91
Grapes	grenache
Region	McLaren Vale, SA
Cellar	🍾 4+
Alc./Vol.	14.5%
RRP	$27.00

The Shingleback wines are grown and made by the Davey family, who also have the side-brands White Knot/Red Knot, and The Gate. They've only been in the wine market a few years but have already kicked a swag of goals. Maker: John Davey. CURRENT RELEASE 2004 This is a delightful grenache, made – appropriately – in a soft, lightly oaked, low-tannin style that's immediately captivating. There's a lather of sweet, syrupy grenache fruit to taste, with spice and herb flavours galore, and even a little streak of tannin to give it a backbone. The alcohol is warm and lingering on the finish, which is part of the style. Drink it with lamb kidneys.

Temple Bruer Grenache Shiraz Viognier

Temple Bruer's organic credentials have been certified by the ACO, one of an increasing number of producers using organic methods in vineyard and winery.
CURRENT RELEASE 2004 A very ripe, aromatic drop with a complex nose of spice, pepper, stewed prunes, raspberries and apricot jam. In the mouth it shows distinct viognier influence adding apricot notes to meaty and berry-fruit flavours. Medium- to full-bodied, it's a hearty mouthful of honest red wine, ending with spicy warmth and sinewy tannins. Serve it with hearty sausages.

Quality	♛♛♛♛
Value	★★★⟩
Rating	90
Grapes	grenache; shiraz; viognier
Region	Langhorne Creek, SA
Cellar	🍾 5
Alc./Vol.	14.0%
RRP	$18.50 ⬱ Ⓥ

Torbreck Juveniles

Originally made for Juveniles Wine Bar in Paris, Torbreck Juveniles is made from a blend of grenache, mourvèdre and shiraz, a combination of grapes that's just as traditional in parts of France as it is here.
CURRENT RELEASE 2005 A very ripe, rather soupy nose that's typically Barossa with its sweet red-berry aromas, slightly jammy touches and nuances of earth. The palate is smooth and fruit-sweet with a slight jamminess that's part and parcel of such ripe, old-vine grenache-based reds. It has soft tannins and a long sweetish finish. Try it with soy-braised beef ribs.

Quality	♛♛♛♛
Value	★★★
Rating	92
Grapes	grenache; mataro (mourvèdre); shiraz
Region	Barossa Valley, SA
Cellar	🍾 3
Alc./Vol.	14.6%
RRP	$26.50 ⬱

Torbreck The Steading

Torbreck founder Dave Powell once worked as a woodcutter in Scotland, which explains the Scottish allusions that give many of his wines their names. A 'steading' is a collection of sheds found scattered around a Scottish farm.
CURRENT RELEASE 2003 This is an aromatic grenache blend that smells of spices, earth and berry fruit, with smoky/meaty touches in the background. It's more savoury and complex than some similarly cultish Barossa reds, a Barossa-meets-Rhône style with a viscous, mouth-coating feel, fruit-sweet flavour, and ripe tannins that give just a hint of bitterness to the warm finish. It would go well with Spanish-influenced lamb, chorizo and chickpeas.

Quality	♛♛♛♛⟩
Value	★★★
Rating	92
Grapes	grenache; mourvèdre; shiraz
Region	Barossa Valley, SA
Cellar	⊶1–5
Alc./Vol.	14.5%
RRP	$39.75 🍾

Merlot and blends

Merlot is one of the fastest-growing varietal categories not only in Australia but around the world. This puzzles your authors because they are finding the good ones few and far between. What is it that appeals to wine drinkers about merlot? Perhaps it's the *idea* of merlot, which all the back labels will tell you is supposed to be soft, rounded, low in tannin and easy on the gums. Good merlot *is* like that, with a soft, plum or raspberry-like, sometimes olive-like fruit character. In reality much of it is underripe and green-tasting, often with harsh, astringent tannin or residual sugar 'papering over' its hardness. This section encompasses wines that are majority merlot: most will be between 51 per cent and 100 per cent merlot.

Alan & Veitch Woodside Merlot

Quality	♥♥♥♥
Value	★★★
Rating	89
Grapes	merlot
Region	Adelaide Hills, SA
Cellar	▮ 5+
Alc./Vol.	14.0%
RRP	$28.00 ▮

Woodside is a town in the Adelaide Hills, where lies the vineyard from which Robert Johnson bought the grapes for this wine. It's the Corbally vineyard, which is at 480 metres altitude.

CURRENT RELEASE 2004   There's plenty of green-bean, cool-climate merlot character on the bouquet of this wine, together with some Ribena/blackcurrant cordial and vegetal notes. That seems to indicate some less-than-ripe grapes, but the palate is good: full-bodied, with density, flesh and richness. The texture is a feature: it's slinky, velvety and rather sexy. The only negative is a little bitterness on the back-palate. Drink it with beef and black-olive casserole.

Anderson Merlot

Quality	♥♥♥♥
Value	★★★★
Rating	90
Grapes	merlot
Region	Rutherglen, Vic.
Cellar	▮ 5
Alc./Vol.	14.5%
RRP	$14.50 ▮
	(cellar door)

It's funny how wineries seldom mention bronze medals, but this one does. In fact, the details are printed on the front label, as opposed to the customary sticker. The medal was gained at the Victorian Wines Show in 2005. Winemaker is Howard Anderson.

CURRENT RELEASE 2004   Cassis, mulberry and blueberry aromas pour from the glass. It's a fruit-forward style of merlot, enhanced no doubt by the fact that it didn't undergo a malolactic fermentation. With penetrating flavour and plenty of weight and extract, it's bigger than most merlots. A pleasant touch of oak embellishes it, and the palate has structure and length. It would go with a steak sandwich.

Berrys Bridge Pyrenees Merlot

Berrys Bridge vineyard occupies an out-of-the-way little enclave near St Arnaud in central Victoria. The town of St Arnaud has one of the most picturesque nineteenth-century streetscapes in the state, a great spot to visit on any trip to the vineyards of the Pyrenees.
CURRENT RELEASE 2004   An intense varietal nose suggests plums, spices, mushrooms and undergrowth, with a hint of cedary oak in the background. The palate isn't as big and concentrated as the other Berrys Bridge wines but it has good intensity, with medium body and fine-grained, sinewy tannins in support. Try it with a veal and mushroom pie.

Quality	♟ ♟ ♟ ♟
Value	★★★
Rating	91
Grapes	merlot
Region	Pyrenees, Vic.
Cellar	▮ 4
Alc./Vol.	13.5%
RRP	$42.00

Big Hill Vineyard Merlot

The Bendigo gold rush led to the planting of a number of vineyards to slake the diggers' insatiable thirst, but the dreaded phylloxera bug and efforts to eradicate it led to their demise in late-Victorian times. Today many vineyards have been replanted on the same sites as those pioneering plantings, and Big Hill is one of them.
CURRENT RELEASE 2004   An emphatic young merlot, deeply pigmented, with intense stewed-plum and raspberry-fruit character and a leafy varietal touch. The palate is well-concentrated with mint, plum and spice-like varietal fruit, medium body and firm tannins. Serve it with lamb's fry and bacon.

Quality	♟ ♟ ♟ ♟
Value	★★★◗
Rating	91
Grapes	merlot
Region	Bendigo, Vic.
Cellar	▮ 6+
Alc./Vol.	13.0%
RRP	$20.00

Centennial Vineyards Reserve Merlot

This winery and its vineyard are located in a very difficult viticultural environment: the high-rainfall, high-altitude Southern Highlands, where soils are also rather fertile. Hence there is a lot of out-sourcing going on. Maker: Tony Cosgriff.
CURRENT RELEASE 2004   Eucalyptus, peppermint herbal fruit is the dominant theme here. The wine also has rather sharp acid on the palate. It has a slightly doughnut shape and could use a bit more flesh and fruit sweetness. Good length; firm tannin finish. It needs food, and would team well with pink lamb loin chops.

Quality	♟ ♟ ♟ ◖
Value	★★★
Rating	88
Grapes	merlot
Region	Orange, NSW
Cellar	▮ 5
Alc./Vol.	14.5%
RRP	$28.00 (cellar door)

Chateau Mildura Psyche Smuggler Merlot

Quality	♈♈♈
Value	★★★★
Rating	86
Grapes	merlot
Region	Murray Valley, Vic.
Cellar	🍾 3
Alc./Vol.	14.0%
RRP	$13.00 🥂

This brand emanates from a very old, historic winery called Chateau Mildura. It was built about 1888 by the Chaffey brothers, who pioneered irrigation in the Mildura area, and has been lying idle since Mildara Blass stopped making sherry there in 1997. A local, Lance Milne, bought it in 2002 and installed a boutique winery inside, without altering the original structure. Winemaker: Neville Hudson. CURRENT RELEASE 2005 Another surprising young red from this new label. The colour is good, the nose is tutti-frutti: simple ripe-berry fruit, unencumbered with oak or other complexities. There are cherry-pip and tomato-bush flavours, and it's smooth and flavoursome in the mouth. Hard to quibble about the price here. Take it to a barbecue.

Climbing Merlot

Quality	♈♈♈♈
Value	★★★★
Rating	90
Grapes	merlot
Region	Orange, NSW
Cellar	🍾 5
Alc./Vol.	14.0%
RRP	$18.00 ⑤ 🥂

The Cumulus people have broken out of the envelope in respect to coining new brand names. Rolling and Climbing, forsooth! The Climbing label depicts men in tights climbing trapezes, and reminds us of a famous painting by Leger that lives in the National Gallery, Canberra. CURRENT RELEASE 2004 This topped the merlot class with a silver medal in the '05 Orange Wine Show, and we can see why. It has a smoky aroma of charred oak and bold red fruits. The palate is sweetly berry-fruited with good structure and elegance. A nice drinking red, rather than a great wine. It would suit Wiener schnitzel.

Giant Steps Merlot

Quality	♈♈♈♈
Value	★★★★
Rating	90
Grapes	merlot
Region	Yarra Valley, Vic.
Cellar	🍾 6
Alc./Vol.	14.0%
RRP	$25.00 🥂

The winemaker at Giant Steps, Sexton and Innocent Bystander is Steve Flamsteed, who is not only an accomplished winemaker but also an experienced chef and trained cheesemaker. CURRENT RELEASE 2003 An impressive merlot, this has an excellent colour and lovely ripe-fruit aromas of blackberry, with a sappy/crushed-leaf overtone (suggesting there may be a little cabernet in it) and some attractive black-olive characters. Oak is subtly handled. There's an abundance of tannin but it's soft and smooth. A serious merlot with some potential for cellaring. Drink with a casserole of beef and olives.

Heggies Merlot

In a world where lolly-ish merlot is everywhere, thank heaven for wines like Heggies. It's serious merlot, worthy of the big occasion.
CURRENT RELEASE 2002   If you want to try excellent merlot varietal character, Heggies is a good place to start. This has a mellow bouquet that hints at spicy fruitcake, dark plums and cedar, with a subtle wisp of violets. It smells classy, but there's nice meaty richness to satisfy the true sensualists. In the mouth it has a velvety feel with good integration of ripe fruit and more savoury elements, finishing with fine-grained dry tannins. Works well with herbed roast veal.

Quality	♟ ♟ ♟ ♟ ♟
Value	★★★★
Rating	93
Grapes	merlot
Region	Eden Valley, SA
Cellar	🍾 4+
Alc./Vol.	14.0%
RRP	$25.70

Henschke Abbotts Prayer

Once a merlot-cabernet blend, Abbotts Prayer is now almost a straight merlot, with small inputs from other varieties. Merlot is a grape type that enjoys some popularity in the cool Adelaide Hills.
CURRENT RELEASE 2001   The '01 was still the current vintage at time of publication, which suggests that it's probably not the fastest-moving line in the Henschke portfolio. It's a more successful Abbotts Prayer than some past examples, with attractive aromas of plum, savoury herbs, mulberries and spicy oak, but it still has a slight leafy thread. It tastes smooth and soft, and the flavours track the nose exactly. It signs off with balanced tannins. Good with Swedish meatballs.

Quality	♟ ♟ ♟ ♟
Value	★★⁺
Rating	90
Grapes	merlot
Region	Adelaide Hills, SA
Cellar	🍾 4
Alc./Vol.	14.5%
RRP	$68.20

Hungerford Hill Orange Merlot

Hungerford Hill's portfolio of wines is tilted towards the New South Wales wine regions, often exploring newer, or more obscure, places outside the realms of conventional wine country. Orange is a cool region providing good conditions for growing merlot.
CURRENT RELEASE 2004   A leafy, fresh varietal nose suggests raspberries and dark plums, with a hint of fruitcakey-merlot spice and a thread of savoury oak. The palate has a silky-smooth feel that's very merlot, and it finishes long and soft with very fine-grained, ripe tannins. It's a merlot that grows on you as you sip, and it responds well to decanting. Try it with roast veal.

Quality	♟ ♟ ♟ ♟ ♟
Value	★★★
Rating	92
Grapes	merlot
Region	Orange, NSW
Cellar	🍾 4
Alc./Vol.	14.0%
RRP	$26.50 🍾 ⌇

Kingston Estate Merlot

Quality	🍷🍷🍷½
Value	★★★★
Rating	**88**
Grapes	merlot
Region	Langhorne Creek, Clare Valley & Riverland, SA
Cellar	4+
Alc./Vol.	14.5%
RRP	$13.00 (\$)

What should a merlot taste like? This is a question that puzzles many punters. They vary from green and weedy to big and porty, from firm and drying to sickly sweet, and with every red-wine flavour known to humankind.

CURRENT RELEASE 2004 This is a big bruiser of a red wine for $13. In one sense, it's good value – a lot of wine for your money. In another, it's too much of a good thing: people who buy $13 merlot are probably looking for something softer and easier to drink than this tannic number. Mid-purple–red in colour, the aromas are of raspberry and mint with a distinctly odd gooseberry overtone. The taste is thick and oaky with mouth-coating tannins, plenty of weight and flesh. It needs food, so serve it with barbecued meats.

Margan Merlot

Quality	🍷🍷🍷
Value	★★★
Rating	**86**
Grapes	merlot
Region	Hunter Valley, NSW
Cellar	3+
Alc./Vol.	13.5%
RRP	$20.00

The film *Sideways* did no favours to the public image of merlot. The film's (non-) hero, Miles, takes wine so seriously that he refuses to dine out with people who want to order merlot. His famous outburst struck a chord with a lot of people in the wine business, and we suspect it's been immortalised.

CURRENT RELEASE 2004 This is a light-bodied merlot with a medium-light colour of good red–purple hue and a shy, herbal/minty aroma. The taste is light again, lean and fairly leafy, without a lot of flesh on the bones. It's fruit-driven, low-tannin and non-confronting, which probably means it will have plenty of fans. It could be partnered with veal saltimbocca.

McWilliams Hanwood Merlot

Quality	🍷🍷🍷½
Value	★★★★½
Rating	**88**
Grapes	merlot
Region	mainly Riverina, NSW
Cellar	2
Alc./Vol.	13.5%
RRP	$12.00 (\$)

We notice the Hanwood labels now say 'Hanwood Estate', which is a bit misleading. If all the grapes for these big-selling, budget-priced wines came from McWilliams' own property, it would have to be the biggest vineyard in Creation!

CURRENT RELEASE 2004 This is a remarkably decent drink for the money! Nice deep colour; attractive nose of aniseed and blackberry (with no obvious wood); and a very fruity/plummy, sweet palate that owes a bit to residual sugar but it's cleverly done and it's not so sweet as to offend the purist. This would appeal to a broad audience. Try it with a cheeseburger.

Murdock Merlot

The Murdock family is one of the best boutique-sized producers in Coonawarra – a region that is pretty much dominated by big-company activity. The wines are very capably made at Balnaves by *Gourmet Traveller Wine* magazine Winemaker of the Year 2005, Pete Bissell. CURRENT RELEASE 2004   This screw-capped wine was very closed upon opening, but after some breathing it emerged as a very stylish merlot, indeed. With lively, crisp, raspberry-like flavour and a hint of mint, this is a fruit-driven style that is elegant and finely structured, almost a touch lean where merlot is generally plump, while the finish is well balanced and satisfying. A classy merlot to serve with duck braised with fennel.

Quality	🍷🍷🍷🍷🍷
Value	★★★★
Rating	95
Grapes	merlot
Region	Coonawarra, SA
Cellar	🍾 5+
Alc./Vol.	14.0%
RRP	$26.00 🍾

Plunkett Strathbogie Ranges Merlot

Merlot is a variety that's championed a lot in cooler regions by winemakers looking for an alternative early-ripener to pinot noir. This example is from the cool Strathbogies in central Victoria.
CURRENT RELEASE 2004   This young merlot smells of beef stock, plums and gentle spice. In the mouth it's medium in body and intensity, with smooth texture and attractive varietal flavour. It finishes soft and agreeably persistent. A tasty, straightforward merlot to serve with corned beef.

Quality	🍷🍷🍷🍷
Value	★★★
Rating	91
Grapes	merlot
Region	Strathbogie Ranges, Vic.
Cellar	🍾 3
Alc./Vol.	14.0%
RRP	$21.00 🍾

Primo Estate Merlesco

Merlesco is merlot made into an early-drinking style by Joe and Dina Grilli of Primo Estate. It imitates the type of wine he, and his parents, and their parents, sipped as an everyday beverage.
CURRENT RELEASE 2005   A savoury, uncomplicated nose of earthy-plum fruit is juicy and simple. In the mouth it's supple and fresh with no-fuss flavour and soft tannins. It's a succulent wine to guzzle, not a wine to think about, and it goes well with homemade pizzas with simple toppings.

Quality	🍷🍷🍷🍷
Value	★★★
Rating	88
Grapes	merlot
Region	not stated, SA
Cellar	🍾 1
Alc./Vol.	13.0%
RRP	$18.00 🍾

Rees Miller Estate Cotton's Pinch Merlot

Quality	♥ ♥ ♥ ♥
Value	★ ★ ★
Rating	90
Grapes	merlot
Region	Yea, Vic.
Cellar	🍾 2
Alc./Vol.	14.5%
RRP	$35.00

The modest Rees Miller winery and vineyard is at Yea on the road to the Victorian snowfields. Proprietors Sylke Rees and David Miller reckon the site is ideally suited to merlot. CURRENT RELEASE 2003   This merlot shows attractive ripeness and there's a rustic edge that almost gives it a touch of Europe. It smells wild and gamey with smooth plum fruit, notes of sweet spice and harmonious cedary oak input. The palate has high-toned ripe fruit flavour that shows a hint of volatility that might displease the purists, but it does have plenty of personality. It's probably drinking at its best right now. Serve it with game.

Robert Johnson Vineyards Merlot

Quality	♥ ♥ ♥ ♥
Value	★ ★ ★
Rating	90
Grapes	merlot
Region	Eden Valley, SA
Cellar	▬ 1–6+
Alc./Vol.	14.5%
RRP	$40.00

Merlot can be a confronting beast, whose vegetal characteristics tend to polarise tasters. Even when sugar-ripe and high in alcohol, it often retains green herbaceous characters. You can find overripe and underripe grape flavours in the same wine. This one comes from Robert Johnson's own vineyards in the Eden Valley. CURRENT RELEASE 2004   The colour is an appealing deep red–purple and the nose reflects extensive use of new oak with its toasty-barrel, mocha/chocolate aromas. In the mouth, this is joined by raspberry and red-cherry flavours with a spicy lift. It builds licoricey, slightly porty traces towards the back-palate. There are herbaceous/green-leafy scents that unfold more as the wine sits in the glass. It's a good but confusing wine – a wine of contrasts.

Schild Estate Merlot

Quality	♥ ♥ ♥
Value	★ ★ ★
Rating	86
Grapes	merlot
Region	Barossa Valley, SA
Cellar	🍾 4
Alc./Vol.	14.5%
RRP	$24.00 (cellar door)

We wonder who buys all the varietal merlot that's on sale these days. So much of it is very ordinary. Schild Estate has more runs on the board than most. Its 2003 won a gold medal and trophy for best merlot at the Boutique Winery Awards 2005. This one is sealed with a Diam cork. CURRENT RELEASE 2004   The mint and coconut aromas lead the way to a rather oddball merlot. It has harsh acid and possibly some residual sugar on palate. The tannins are a shade green and astringent. It does have weight and flavour, but just fails to sing. Decent rather than inspiring. Try it with veal in a creamy mushroom sauce.

Shottesbrooke Merlot

The generation switch we see so much now in Australian wineries has happened at Shottesbrooke, with the Holmes family hopping up a generation. Founder Nick Holmes now has a winemaker: his stepson Hamish Maguire.
CURRENT RELEASE 2004   There's a lot happening in this merlot: vegetal seaweedy/jungley, black-olive aromas intermingled with fine-quality oak. It has a fairly high acidity giving it a tangy finish. With the softening effect of food, it's a good drink. Drink it with veal parmigiana.

Quality	♥ ♥ ♥
Value	★ ★ ★
Rating	86
Grapes	merlot
Region	McLaren Vale, SA
Cellar	🍾 4+
Alc./Vol.	14.0%
RRP	$18.00 🥂

Smith & Hooper Limited Edition Merlot

Smith & Hooper is a joint venture between the Hooper family, local landholders in what is now the Wrattonbully wine region, and the Hill Smiths of Yalumba. The wines are made in the Barossa.
CURRENT RELEASE 2002   A savoury style of merlot, beginning to show some development, with an earthy, olivey kind of character. The finish is dusty/oaky and the palate flavours are very much in the savoury spectrum (rather than grapey). It has good flavour and balance in the mouth. An elegant as opposed to opulent style, which should go well with rabbit casserole.

Quality	♥ ♥ ♥ ♥
Value	★ ★ ★
Rating	89
Grapes	merlot
Region	Wrattonbully, SA
Cellar	🍾 4
Alc./Vol.	13.5%
RRP	$37.00

Tateham's Merlot

Tateham's is a micro-boutique operation run by Mike and Isabelle Jeandupeux. All Tateham's wines are sourced from a vineyard in the Polish Hill River sub-region.
CURRENT RELEASE 2004   This is a pleasant, medium- to light-bodied merlot with a shy nose of mint, raspberry and crushed leaf. It tastes as though it could have the odd cabernet berry in it. The palate is interesting: it's lean and wiry with a touch of astringency and not a lot of flesh or richness. It turns cassisy towards the back-palate. A nice food-style red to serve with veal rib roast.

Quality	♥ ♥ ♥
Value	★ ★ ★
Rating	87
Grapes	merlot
Region	Clare Valley, SA
Cellar	🍾 3+
Alc./Vol.	14.3%
RRP	$24.00 🥂
	(cellar door)

Thorn–Clarke Sandpiper Barossa Merlot

Quality	♟ ♟ ♟ ♟
Value	★ ★ ★ ★ ⌐
Rating	90
Grapes	merlot
Region	Barossa Valley, SA
Cellar	▮ 2
Alc./Vol.	14.1%
RRP	$16.00

The quality of the Thorn-Clarke Barossa wines exceeds expectations across a broad range of price points. The Sandpiper wines sit at the bottom of the tree, but still offer plenty.

CURRENT RELEASE 2004   This inexpensive merlot has a surprisingly dense, glass-staining colour, and the wine is well concentrated with smooth, ripe, plum, raspberry and spice aromas. The palate is plump and velvety with persistent flavour and soft fine tannins to give mellow support. Enjoy it with spaghetti and ragu sauce.

Trentham Estate Merlot

Quality	♟ ♟ ♟ ⌐
Value	★ ★ ★ ⌐
Rating	89
Grapes	merlot
Region	Murray Valley, NSW
Cellar	▮ 2
Alc./Vol.	13.5%
RRP	$14.50 ⑤ ⌘

Trentham Estate's formula for reasonable prices and high-quality wines is bringing them plenty of success. Thankfully their merlot doesn't rely on sugary sweetness like some of its competitors.

CURRENT RELEASE 2004   A medium-intensity merlot with attractive berry character, a lick of spicy oak and a suggestion of Vegemite (no, we're not losing our minds.) The palate is clean and uncomplicated with smooth ripe flavour, medium body and soft tannins. A pleasant, crowd-pleasing type of red. Try it with a Chinese beef claypot dish.

Wood Park Myrrhee Merlot

Quality	♟ ♟ ♟ ♟
Value	★ ★ ★ ⌐
Rating	90
Grapes	merlot
Region	King Valley, Vic.
Cellar	▮ 5
Alc./Vol.	13.5%
RRP	$20.00 ⌘

Myrrhee – pronounced 'my-ree' – is in the King Valley near Milawa, where John Stokes's Wood Park vineyard and winery are situated. In our experience, the King produces some of the better values in Australian merlot. The grapes were grown by one Neville Bussell.

CURRENT RELEASE 2004   Typical of the Wood Park style, this is a fruit-driven user-friendly wine: a sweetly plummy, lightly leafy aroma and a soft, rounded palate with gentle tannins for easy drinking. It has some intensity and persistence and is an excellent drink-now red. You could serve it with vitello tonnato.

YarraLoch Stephanie's Dream Merlot

Another new brand, and yet another brand using the word Yarra in its name! Well, there's nothing to say you can't do that, as long as the grapes come from the Yarra Valley. This outfit seems to have the smarts. The wines are good, and they've got Sergio Carlei to make them. He's bottled them with Diam corks, which is no bad thing.

CURRENT RELEASE 2004   This is a pretty handy merlot. It has the requisite olivey, meaty aromas together with slightly funky/sweaty merlot characters and it goes a lot further than just simple bright fruit. The palate is lean and has a touch of elegance. The finish carries some firm, tight tannins. It's a good drink, especially with veal saltimbocca.

Quality	♛ ♛ ♛ ♛
Value	★ ★ ┤
Rating	89
Grapes	merlot
Region	Yarra Valley, Vic.
Cellar	🍾 4+
Alc./Vol.	14.0%
RRP	$40.00 (cellar door)

Pinot noir

The holy grail? Maybe. Pinot noir certainly excites the interest of our more quixotic winemakers, and frustrates them too. We've watched pinot's trials and tribulations in Australia over many years and we're pleased to report that the news gets better all the time. Increasing vine age, levels of experience and improving technique mean that wine quality has been moving ahead, and now pinot noir's mysterious, sensuous delights aren't as rare as they once were. It's still best to follow good advice to find the best wines, and if in doubt exercise caution, but in good years places like Tasmania, southern Victoria, the Adelaide Hills and Western Australia's far south are really coming of age with pinot. One welcome development in recent times has been the democratisation of pinot via a new crop of sub-$20 wines – some are surprisingly good.

Allies Pinot Noir

Quality	♛♛♛♛
Value	★★★★
Rating	90
Grapes	pinot noir
Region	Mornington Peninsula, Vic.
Cellar	ⓘ 3
Alc./Vol.	13.2%
RRP	$23.00 ⬗

The allies are a couple of young men who have been around the Melbourne and Mornington Peninsula food and wine scene for some years. They seem a passionate pair with a desire to make some fine vino of their own. CURRENT RELEASE 2005 The colour is quite pale and the aromatics are sweetly fragrant and bubblegum/raspberry-ish. But the palate has real richness and intensity, with some of the jammy characters – possibly from a hot ferment – that pinot occasionally presents. It's a succulent, sexy wine of depth and persistence. It goes well with hare and beetroot pithivier.

Balgownie Pinot Noir

Quality	♛♛♛♛
Value	★★★★⊣
Rating	91
Grapes	pinot noir
Region	Yarra Valley, Vic.
Cellar	ⓘ 4+
Alc./Vol.	13.5%
RRP	$22.00 ⬗

Balgownie has made a tiny quantity of pinot from its Bendigo vineyard since founder Stuart Anderson's day; now it also sources grapes from the Yarra Valley to make this wine of not-so-limited production. The Yarra Valley is a more suitable region for pinot. Tobias Ansted makes the wine at Balgownie's Bendigo winery. CURRENT RELEASE 2004 This is a savoury style of pinot with noticeable oak and quite a deal of muscle. It has tannin and structure that set it apart from most Aussie pinots. There are strawberry and black-cherry aromas with walnutty oak-derived characters, while the mouth has penetrating cherry flavour and good length. A very good wine and excellent value for money. Serve it with roast squab.

Bellarmine Pinot Noir

This is a relatively little-known new producer in Pemberton, owned by a German, Dr Willi Schumacher. They're doing things the right way. From young vines, winemaker Mike Bewsher has turned out some lovely stuff already, and the prices (everything is $15!) are amazingly low.

CURRENT RELEASE 2004 The colour is paler than the '05 while the bouquet is meaty, gamey, perhaps slightly reductive, with fragrant berry-jam and confectionery aromas. It's a lighter-weighted wine, delicate and almost ethereal, sweetly plummy with some oak flavour, finishing with firm tannin. It's best with food, such as parmesan cheese.

Quality	🍷🍷🍷½
Value	★★★★
Rating	**89**
Grapes	pinot noir
Region	Pemberton, WA
Cellar	3
Alc./Vol.	13.5%
RRP	$15.00 (cellar door)

CURRENT RELEASE 2005 Delicacy is the keynote with all Bellarmine wines and this is a fine, fragrant style of remarkably deep colour and slightly grippy tannin. The aromas are very appealing: sweet ripe cherry – and it seems to have some beaujolais-like carbonic maceration character. A good wine that could be even better in a year or so. Try beef carpaccio here.

Quality	🍷🍷🍷½
Value	★★★★
Rating	**88**
Grapes	pinot noir
Region	Pemberton, WA
Cellar	4
Alc./Vol.	14.5%
RRP	$15.00 (cellar door)

Bloodwood Pinot Noir

Orange has the kind of climate and soils that should suit pinot noir well, but as with all 'new' regions, it takes time to produce great pinot. We can look forward to charting its progress as the vines mature and the growers gain experience with this tricky variety.

CURRENT RELEASE 2004 There's a stalky touch of gumleaf/mint in this pinot, which obscures the varietal fruit somewhat, but it is a very pleasant wine all the same. There are mulberry, sappy and vanilla flavours as well, and the palate has good depth and weight. The structure is still tight, which suggests it will cellar quite well in the short term. It would suit pink roast lamb.

Quality	🍷🍷🍷½
Value	★★★
Rating	**89**
Grapes	pinot noir
Region	Orange, NSW
Cellar	4
Alc./Vol.	13.5%
RRP	$32.00 (cellar door)

Bress Yarra Valley Pinot Noir

Quality	♟ ♟ ♟
Value	★ ★ ★ ★
Rating	91
Grapes	pinot noir
Region	Yarra Valley, Vic.
Cellar	➡ 1–4
Alc./Vol.	13.0%
RRP	$19.00 ⪤

Bress is the name of Adam Marks's vineyard and winery at Harcourt in the Bendigo region. It used to be the Mount Alexander vineyard, and it's not the only source of fruit for the Bress wines. Adam also fashions wines like this pinot from other regions he sees as Australian classics.
CURRENT RELEASE 2005   A very youthful pinot that still seems a bit raw and edgy. There's a stemmy backing to the fruit and some earthy pongs, but the core of pinot fruit is ripe and quite rich. The palate has good length and strength of flavour on the finish. It needs to be forgotten about for a year or two to get its act together, but it should evolve nicely. Try it with paella.

By Farr Pinot Noir

Quality	♟ ♟ ♟ ♟
Value	★ ★ ★ ★
Rating	95
Grapes	pinot noir
Region	Geelong, Vic.
Cellar	▮ 5+
Alc./Vol.	13.5%
RRP	$57.95

Gary Farr makes two pinot noirs from his family vineyard near Geelong. A 'standard' wine and Sangreal. Sangreal is made entirely from his oldest plantings, while this sibling is a blend of new plantings and old-vine material.
CURRENT RELEASE 2004   The difference between this wine and the rarer Sangreal is one of tone rather than style. They both have a family resemblance; this one is less concentrated but still fragrantly seductive. It has ripe, spicy, cherry-like fruit, with musky/foresty notes and minerally undertones. The palate is silky and long with lovely balance and texture. Tannins are a tad more edgy than in the Sangreal, but they integrate well. Excellent with 'coq au pinot noir'.
Previous outstanding vintages: 1999, 2000, '01, '02, '04

By Farr Sangreal

Quality	♟ ♟ ♟ ♟ ♟
Value	★ ★ ★ ★ ┧
Rating	98
Grapes	pinot noir
Region	Geelong, Vic.
Cellar	▮ 5+
Alc./Vol.	13.5%
RRP	$61.50

Gary Farr is one of only a small handful of Australian winemakers to have truly mastered the capricious pinot noir grape. In fact it could be argued that he is *the* master, especially with consistency factored in.
CURRENT RELEASE 2004   A superb Australian pinot, exotically rich and super-complex. It starts off with gamey, spicy, foresty aromas set against a substructure of plummy fruit. The 100 per cent new oak is perfectly integrated, and the velvety, multi-layered palate is sumptuous and lingering. Balance is excellent and the very soft, ripe and ultra-fine tannins are an object lesson in how a pinot should be structured. Serve it with roasted pigeons.

Callanans Road Pinot Noir

This is the second-string pinot noir of Tuck's Ridge. It shows good varietal personality, albeit in a lighter vein.
CURRENT RELEASE 2004   A lightish pinot with attractive strawberry and spiced-cherry aromas leading to a clean-tasting palate. It doesn't show a great deal of concentration, but the pinot flavour is correct, and the light underlying structure dries the finish well. Be adventurous and serve it with cured salmon.

Quality	♀♀♀♀
Value	★★★★
Rating	90
Grapes	pinot noir
Region	Mornington Peninsula, Vic.
Cellar	2
Alc./Vol.	13.0%
RRP	$20.00

Cape Bernier Pinot Noir

This small producer is located at Bream Creek, on the East Coast of Tasmania. The wine will be hard to find; the price we quote is from a Sydney stockist: Annandale Cellars.
CURRENT RELEASE 2004   This is a 'fruit bomb', with lots of things to like. It has a good colour and a complex bouquet of spicy, sappy, black-cherry and mint aromas. It's highly aromatic but just a trifle green, as the palate confirms. It certainly has a lot of flavour and fills the mouth, although the tannins and acidity are somewhat disjointed and there's a little hardness in the tannins. Another year in the bottle might help it harmonise. We suggest pairing it with barbecued seafood.

Quality	♀♀♀♀
Value	★★★
Rating	89
Grapes	pinot noir
Region	East Coast, Tas.
Cellar	4
Alc./Vol.	13.9%
RRP	$28.50

Carlei Estate Pinot Noir

Sergio Carlei is one of the more interesting characters on the wine scene. He is a former chiropractor and biochemist, he believes in biodynamic viticulture, and is a highly intelligent, intuitive and skilful winemaker. All his wines are sealed with Diam corks.
CURRENT RELEASE 2002   This is a pleasant, attractive wine rather than a great pinot. It's showing the beginnings of bottle-age and is maturing gracefully. The bouquet is complex with gamey, minty and herbal aromas while the palate has good intensity and character, albeit with slightly elevated acidity. It does retain freshness and vitality. It would suit roast pork.

Quality	♀♀♀♀
Value	★★★
Rating	90
Grapes	pinot noir
Region	Yarra Valley, Vic.
Cellar	2+
Alc./Vol.	13.5%
RRP	$49.00

Centennial Vineyards Woodside Pinot Noir

Quality	�w♟♟♟
Value	★★★
Rating	88
Grapes	pinot noir
Region	Southern Highlands, NSW
Cellar	▯ 2+
Alc./Vol.	13.1%
RRP	$20.00 (cellar door)

No visit to the Southern Highlands is complete without a visit to this impressive complex, followed by lunch in the restaurant. This unfiltered, single-vineyard wine was grown on their own vineyard at Bowral. Maker: Tony Cosgriff. CURRENT RELEASE 2004 Strawberry, cherry-essence and vanilla aromas have immediate appeal, while the palate is soft and sweetly fruity, with a mouth-filling generosity. It has some carbon dioxide prickle, and is not especially structured – more of a fruit bomb. It drinks well with cold meats and salads.

Clos Pierre Pinot Noir

Quality	♟♟♟♟
Value	★★★★★
Rating	90
Grapes	pinot noir
Region	Yarra Valley, Vic.
Cellar	▯ 2
Alc./Vol.	13.0%
RRP	$15.99

This wine is the result of collaboration between fifth-generation French vigneron Pierre Naigeon, De Bortoli's Yarra Valley winemaker Steve Webber, and the Dan Murphy retail chain. The result is a Yarra Valley pinot noir that offers real, French-accented varietal character on a budget. CURRENT RELEASE 2005 A relatively pale-coloured wine with a succulent nose reminiscent of cherries and plums. It tastes light, and it has an almost beaujolais-like feel and succulent gluggability. The palate has attractive intensity of flavour with silky softness and a clean dry finish, ahead of a fragrant, long aftertaste. Great value. Serve it with grilled spiced quails.

Clyde Park Bannockburn Pinot Noir

Quality	♟♟♟♟
Value	★★★
Rating	90
Grapes	pinot noir
Region	Geelong, Vic.
Cellar	▯ 3
Alc./Vol.	14.0%
RRP	$28.00

The vineyard was established by Gary Farr at Bannockburn township in 1979, but he sold it to Melbourne restaurateur Donlevy Fitzpatrick, and it has ended up in the hands of the Jongebloed family. Mature vines may partly explain the wine quality. Winemaker is Simon Black. CURRENT RELEASE 2004 It's a lighter-bodied, fine-boned pinot of considerable charm. Foresty, chaffy aromas predominate. In the mouth, the complex savoury fruit/oak interactions are quite stylish, and it's a wine of good depth and balance. We'd like to try it with coq au vin.

Coldstream Hills Pinot Noir

This company, which is part of Foster's Wine Estates, has been at the forefront of Australian pinot noir development for many years, and has gradually refined its styles to arguably set the standard for commercial pinot noir. This regular label is made in decent-sized licks and has consistent quality and style. Maker: Andrew Fleming. CURRENT RELEASE 2005 It opens with a sandalwood-like aroma, presumably from oak – perfumed but not very varietal – and airs to reveal a complex pinot nose with some subtle stalk overtones, plus dark cherry and a whiff of oak beneath. It has a lot of flavour and plenty of body considering it's the junior wine in the portfolio. Lovely ripe, sweet fruit and good value. It goes well with oxtail ravioli. *Previous outstanding vintages: 1996, '99, 2000, '01, '03, '04*

Quality	♟♟♟♟♟
Value	★★★★
Rating	92
Grapes	pinot noir
Region	Yarra Valley, Vic.
Cellar	🍷 5+
Alc./Vol.	13.5%
RRP	$26.00 Ⓢ 🥢

Curly Flat Pinot Noir

The 14-hectare Curly Flat vineyard was established at Lancefield in 1992 by Phillip and Jennifer Moraghan. They have never met cartoonist Michael Leunig, the creator of Curly Flat and Mister Curly. That's curious, because Leunig likes wine and has a vineyard of his own. CURRENT RELEASE 2003 This is an altogether more serious pinot than its little bro, the Williams Crossing, and has more depth, structure, concentration and all-round richness. The fruit flavours are riper and more complex black-cherry/ plum, charcuterie, smoke and spice, with some of the extra nuances coming from whole-bunch fermentation and stylish but subtle oak. It's fleshy and refined and the flavours linger long after the wine is gone. It's perfect with roast squab.

Quality	♟♟♟♟♟
Value	★★★
Rating	93
Grapes	pinot noir
Region	Macedon Ranges, Vic.
Cellar	🍷 5+
Alc./Vol.	13.5%
RRP	$44.00 (cellar door)

De Bortoli Reserve Release Yarra Valley Pinot Noir

The fruit for this 'special' from De Bortoli's Yarra Valley winery came from the original vineyard blocks, planted 25 to 35 years ago on the property then known as Yarrinya. The maturity of the vineyards is a good indicator of potential quality. CURRENT RELEASE 2003 This has a fragrant and complex bouquet of lovely delicacy. Aromas of raspberry eau-de-vie, exotic spice, wood smoke and forest undergrowth are very inviting, and it builds in the glass with air. The silky palate is long and fine in texture, with succulent flavour and very soft ripe tannins underneath. A deliciously drinkable pinot of real elegance. Try it with pot-roasted quail.

Quality	♟♟♟♟♟
Value	★★★★
Rating	96
Grapes	pinot noir
Region	Yarra Valley, Vic.
Cellar	🍷 4
Alc./Vol.	13.5%
RRP	$43.70

Diamond Valley Estate Vineyards Pinot Noir

Quality	♥♥♥♥♦
Value	★★★
Rating	93
Grapes	pinot noir
Region	Yarra Valley, Vic.
Cellar	▮ 6
Alc./Vol.	13.0%
RRP	$63.00

Diamond Valley pinot noirs have enjoyed extraordinary success in wine shows. The brand changed hands in 2005, but the Lance family retain the winery facilities and vineyard, and winemaking continues in the same hands. CURRENT RELEASE 2004 Like all the best pinots, this is a wine that reveals itself slowly. The nose has deep plum and dark-cherry fruit of delicious concentration with notes of spice, deli and some undergrowthy scents. It's silky in texture with lovely depth of intense varietal flavour, underpinned by subtle oak and superfine tannins. A good companion to terrine en croûte.

Domaine A Pinot Noir

Quality	♥♥♥♥
Value	★★♦
Rating	90
Grapes	pinot noir
Region	Coal River, Tas.
Cellar	▮ 4+
Alc./Vol.	13.5%
RRP	$65.00 (cellar door)

The back label proudly proclaims that this single-vineyard wine was bottled unfiltered, and that there were 5000 bottles produced. Winemaker and proprietor Peter Althaus is a Swiss migrant who made the jump from the computer industry to wine many years ago.
CURRENT RELEASE 2003 This is quite a substantial pinot but just a touch dry-reddish for us, and lacks some of the pinot charm we look for. The colour is deep for three-year-old pinot – medium-full red–purple – and there is a definite eucalypt-forest aroma. Not just gumleaves, but earth and decomposing humus, which is not unusual in Australian pinot. The taste is big and has some firmness from tannin and acid. It has enough flavour to be balanced, but it needs food. A ballsy, solid kind of pinot, to serve with kangaroo seared on the barbecue.

Domaine Day One Serious Pinot Noir

Quality	♥♥♥♥
Value	★★★
Rating	90
Grapes	pinot noir
Region	Eden Valley, SA
Cellar	▮ 4
Alc./Vol.	13.0%
RRP	$28.00 ⬚

Robin Day was chief winemaker for Orlando in the early 1990s. Now his own Domaine Day has hit the streets with some interesting and adventurous wines that fall well outside the Eden Valley norm, including one very serious pinot noir.
CURRENT RELEASE 2004 A slightly dry-reddish pinot on the nose that has plenty of ripe character but not much subtlety. There are red-berry aromas with a thread of oak through them, and the palate has simple ripe-berry fruit of moderate intensity, supported by light dry tannins. It has good length of flavour but it lacks the complexity of the best. Try it with teriyaki chicken.

Eldridge Estate Pinot Noir

Eldridge Estate's owner David Lloyd is a pinot noir fanatic, to the extent that he grows several different clones of pinot and sometimes bottles them in single-clone batches. These are only available occasionally, in fiddly quantities, but they make fascinating tasting.
CURRENT RELEASE 2003   The colour is excellent for a three-year-old pinot: medium-deep purple–red. It's a chunky pinot, fairly tannic and oaky and perhaps lacking a bit of pinot charm. There are mint, cherry and coconutty oak aromas. It's a bit dry-reddish. It will certainly age, but to what end we are not entirely sure. We'd suggest pairing it with grilled lamb backstraps.

Quality	▾▾▾▾
Value	★★★
Rating	89
Grapes	pinot noir
Region	Mornington Peninsula, Vic.
Cellar	▮ 5
Alc./Vol.	14.0%
RRP	$35.00 ⬜ (cellar door)

Eldridge Estate West Patch Pinot Noir

Eldridge Estate's David Lloyd is intense about his pinot noir, but he also produces one of the best gamays you're likely to find in Australia.
CURRENT RELEASE 2004   A very fine, pure, natural-tasting pinot with a medium-light red–purple colour, fragrant cherry-fruit-driven aroma and a degree of complexity. Use of oak is subtle. It's light-bodied and has good fruit intensity with excellent balance and finishes with a very gentle touch of tannin. An enjoyable easy-drinking pinot. Serve it with roast pigeon breast.

Quality	▾▾▾▾
Value	★★★⯪
Rating	90
Grapes	pinot noir
Region	Mornington Peninsula, Vic.
Cellar	▮ 4+
Alc./Vol.	14.0%
RRP	$30.00 ⬜

Elgee Park Baillieu Myer Family Reserve Pinot Noir

The Myer family's fortunes began when migrant Sidney Myer opened his first department store in Bendigo. It moved to Melbourne where it became one of the icons of Australian retailing. The wine came much later, when 'Bails' Myer planted vines in 1972.
CURRENT RELEASE 2004   This opened up with pronounced coconutty, oak-barrel aromas but after extended aeration it became wonderfully fragrant, with brandied-cherry aromas galore. The palate is smooth and has a neat combination of fruity and savoury characteristics. A lighter-weighted pinot of charm and length. It would suit barbecued kebabs of chicken and vegetables.

Quality	▾▾▾▾
Value	★★★⯪
Rating	90
Grapes	pinot noir
Region	Mornington Peninsula, Vic.
Cellar	▮ 4
Alc./Vol.	14.0%
RRP	$32.50 ⬜

Frogmore Creek Pinot Noir

Quality	�wineglass ♥♥♥
Value	★★★
Rating	88
Grapes	pinot noir
Region	Coal River, Tas.
Cellar	3+
Alc./Vol.	13.5%
RRP	$30.00

The email address (before they changed service providers) used to be morefrogs@bigpond.com. Not only does it reveal the wit of proprietor Tony Scherer, it gives an insight into the 'green' philosophy in practice at Frogmore Creek, which is an organic vineyard.
CURRENT RELEASE 2004 Minty, cherry, vanilla and plum aromas herald a pleasant enough lighter-bodied pinot. It has some appealing flavours and drinkability is good, despite the herbal aspects. The minty/crushed-leaf overtones and the rather firm, perhaps slightly green, tannins seem to go hand in hand. A little more age would be advised, then serve it with veal saltimbocca.

Geoff Weaver Lenswood Pinot Noir

Quality	♥♥
Value	★★★
Rating	84
Grapes	pinot noir
Region	Adelaide Hills, SA
Cellar	2+
Alc./Vol.	13.0%
RRP	$35.00

The Adelaide Hills generally don't impress as one of the great pinot noir regions of Australia. The coolest years and the highest altitudes seem to bring the best results, but, as ever, pinot noir is a chameleon.
CURRENT RELEASE 2003 This is a most unusual wine, smelling of crushed oyster shells and mint, which seems to add up to underripe grapes. There's a hint of superphosphate too, of all things. The mouth-feel is strangely 'cold' and tart, with oak and acid sitting apart and firm tannins closing in at the finish. Perhaps it needs more time. At present it is uninspiring.

Giaconda Pinot Noir

Quality	♥♥♥♥
Value	★★★
Rating	92
Grapes	pinot noir
Region	Beechworth, Vic.
Cellar	2–6
Alc./Vol.	13.5%
RRP	$84.00

Pinot noir has been the most variable of Giaconda's wines over the years, with some outstanding wines interspersed with lesser lights. At its best it's a full-flavoured style of jammy intensity.
CURRENT RELEASE 2004 An earthy, wild thread pervades this pinot, giving some meaty and earthy elements to a nucleus of cherry-like fruit. The palate is intense and slightly gamey with grainy texture and a firm, slightly astringent backbone. It's still immature and we suspect that it will build more complexity and smoothness with time. Good with duck risotto.

Giant Steps Pinot Noir

Winemaker Steve Flamsteed is one of those rare people who straddle the two worlds of wine and food in a big way. A former chef and cheesemaker, he is now a full-time winemaker whose previous gig was with Hardys in the Yarra Valley. One of his tasks at Giant Steps is to open a restaurant at the new winery in Healesville.

CURRENT RELEASE 2004 The structure is certainly there, but we're not sure there's enough fruit intensity to balance it. The aromas are very inviting: cherry liqueur, vanilla and cherry essence, then there's a bit of a dip in the mid-palate, before firm tannins bring up the rear. A good rather than exciting pinot, which would suit roast pork belly.

Quality	🍷🍷🍷
Value	★★★
Rating	**87**
Grapes	pinot noir
Region	Yarra Valley, Vic.
Cellar	3
Alc./Vol.	13.5%
RRP	$25.00

Grosset Pinot Noir

Jeffrey Grosset has a continuing relationship with the 8.5-hectare Barratt vineyard at Summertown in the Piccadilly Valley – a superb place to grow pinot noir and chardonnay. These days there are two vineyards, but he's coy about their identities. An unusual feature is that 40 per cent of the wine was fermented as whole-bunches – including stalks.

CURRENT RELEASE 2004 This is a very impressive pinot. Good depth of colour; lovely bouquet of black cherry, backed up by classy oak. It's nicely concentrated with lots of flesh, fruit-sweetness and extract. The tannins are supple and almost chewy. A pinot of real power and density, the flavour persisting in the mouth for a long time after swallowing. Absolutely yummy! Try it with rabbit casserole.

Quality	🍷🍷🍷🍷🍷
Value	★★★½
Rating	**96**
Grapes	pinot noir
Region	Adelaide Hills, SA
Cellar	5
Alc./Vol.	14.0%
RRP	$59.50

Hillcrest Pinot Noir Premium

Hillcrest's name might not be the best known in the Yarra Valley, but it was one of the earliest plantings, going back to the early 1970s. For most of the vineyard's life it has supplied grapes to other winemakers, but in recent years its own label has appeared. Winemaking is by pinot noir guru Phillip Jones.

CURRENT RELEASE 2004 The aroma of this wine is very complex, and it responds well to decanting, revealing meaty, spicy and thyme-like notes alongside dark-plum and earthy smells. It's savoury rather than fruity, and the palate has foresty flavours that are dry and aromatic. It lacks a little fruit depth mid-palate, and finishes a tad stemmy, but it should be worth watching as it ages. An out-of-the-mainstream style. Try it with roast duck.

Quality	🍷🍷🍷🍷
Value	★★★
Rating	**91**
Grapes	pinot noir
Region	Yarra Valley, Vic.
Cellar	4
Alc./Vol.	12.6%
RRP	$48.00

Hurley Vineyard Lodestone Pinot Noir

Quality	♟♟♟♟
Value	★★★
Rating	90
Grapes	pinot noir
Region	Mornington Peninsula, Vic.
Cellar	▮ 5
Alc./Vol.	14.3%
RRP	$38.00 ▮ (cellar door)

Hurley Vineyard is a labour of love for Kevin Bell and Tricia Byrnes. Winemaking concepts are based on French-artisan traditions.

CURRENT RELEASE 2004   Kevin Bell often mentions burgundy when speaking of his wines, and there's a definite French accent to this one. It has some mystery and a touch of wildness on the nose, and while it's not as squeaky clean and fresh as some, it has character. Smoky, dark plum aromas are coupled to spicy, earthy complexities and subtle cedary oak in powerful fashion; the palate has good body, depth and structure. Sip it with roast pork and prunes.

Kooyong Massale Pinot Noir

Quality	♟♟♟♟
Value	★★★⁴
Rating	92
Grapes	pinot noir
Region	Mornington Peninsula, Vic.
Cellar	▮ 3+
Alc./Vol.	13.5%
RRP	$26.00

The French term *selection massale* means the vineyard was planted using a range of different clones of pinot noir vine, not just one. A single clone would mean *selection clonale* – like the standard Kooyong chardonnay. In pinot, multiple clones are thought to encourage complexity.

CURRENT RELEASE 2005   This is a lovely pinot with an encouragingly deep colour, a high-toned perfume of cherry and strawberry, pure-fruited without whole-bunch funkiness, and just a lick of oak. The palate is balanced and smooth with a harmony of flavours and textures. The tannin is light and soft by Kooyong standards. It's light-bodied but has good intensity and spot-on pinot flavour. We'd suggest veal sweetbreads.

Main Ridge Half Acre Pinot Noir

Quality	♟♟♟♟⁵
Value	★★★
Rating	93
Grapes	pinot noir
Region	Mornington Peninsula, Vic.
Cellar	▮ 5
Alc./Vol.	14.0%
RRP	$52.00 ▨ (cellar door)

Nat and Rosalie White's pioneering Mornington Peninsula vineyard is run with a perfectionist approach, necessary to get the most out of a region that's one of the coolest on the Peninsula.

CURRENT RELEASE 2004   This has a relatively pale colour but that's not a problem with pinot noir, and the nose has the delicacy that we've always associated with the Main Ridge pinots. It's a less substantial wine than the '03, but it has real charm. It smells of nougat, glace cherries and floral hints with some underlying savoury notes. In the mouth it has a silky feel, soft cherry flavour, very soft tannins and a long, almost ethereal aftertaste. Delicious with pot-roasted quail.

Marinda Park Pinot Noir

Marinda Park is a smartly run, newer Mornington Peninsula winery with a cosy restaurant where you can dine well next to the barrels, perhaps listening to some jazz. Wine quality is good, and if you're tired of wine (we never are, of course!) you can sip Marinda Park's own French's Cider. CURRENT RELEASE 2004   A spicy, plummy pinot nose greets you here, and there's a foresty touch to the nose. In the mouth it's clean and ripe with medium body and a fine finish that lingers long on the palate. Serve it with soft cheeses.

Quality	♟ ♟ ♟ ♟
Value	★ ★ ★
Rating	90
Grapes	pinot noir
Region	Mornington Peninsula, Vic.
Cellar	🍾 3
Alc./Vol.	13.5%
RRP	$31.00

McRae Mist Pinot Noir

This relatively unknown Victorian pinot noir has surprised us with its quality and value before. The lacklustre, washed-out mauve label won't do it any favours in the marketplace though.
CURRENT RELEASE 2004   A pleasant, light pinot with attractive plum and spice aromas that lead to a succulent palate. It shows a tad more depth than the nose would indicate, with fleshy cherry-like flavours of good intensity, and a backbone of lightly grainy tannins. A very presentable pinot at a very sharp price. Try it with a charcuterie selection.

Quality	♟ ♟ ♟ ♟
Value	★ ★ ★ ★ �’
Rating	90
Grapes	pinot noir
Region	Mornington Peninsula, Vic.
Cellar	🍾 2
Alc./Vol.	13.2%
RRP	$16.99 ☗

Merricks Creek Close Planted Pinot Noir

The quality and character of Mornington Peninsula pinot noir has soared recently, and the early days of thin, green, 'rusty water' pinots are a distant memory. The wines we've tasted this year have been especially memorable. It's great to see all the work down there at last bearing fruit.
CURRENT RELEASE 2004   This is a step up from the standard Merricks pinot, with hints of stalk and feral complexities, coupled with brandied-cherry and cherry-conserve aromas that have more layers and nuances. There's a lacing of oak among the abundant flavours, finished with a little tannin firmness that lends structure. It would go well with duck confit.

Quality	♟ ♟ ♟ ♟
Value	★ ★ ★
Rating	91
Grapes	pinot noir
Region	Mornington Peninsula, Vic.
Cellar	🍾 4+
Alc./Vol.	13.5%
RRP	$48.00

Merricks Creek Merricks Pinot Noir

Quality	♟♟♟
Value	★★★
Rating	89
Grapes	pinot noir
Region	Mornington Peninsula, Vic.
Cellar	▮ 3+
Alc./Vol.	13.5%
RRP	$38.00

We normally wouldn't review all three pinots from such a small and relatively obscure boutique winery, but the three '04s are such delicious wines that we wanted to let you know that there's a new star in the Mornington firmament. This is its entry-level bottling.

CURRENT RELEASE 2004   A delicious light-bodied, introductory pinot that lacks the stalk and oak complexities of the dearer wines, but emphasises clarity of lush, properly ripened pinot noir fruit, instead. The aromas are of strawberry, cherry and sappy leaf, and there's a touch of acid showing on the finish. It's soft and fruit-sweet and drinks well now, with duck braised with fennel.

Merricks Creek Nick Farr Pinot Noir

Quality	♟♟♟♟
Value	★★★
Rating	93
Grapes	pinot noir
Region	Mornington Peninsula, Vic.
Cellar	▮ 5+
Alc./Vol.	13.5%
RRP	$62.00

This is the dearest and most substantial of this maker's pinots. The wine is named after Nick Farr, son of Gary and Robyn (of By Farr), who despite being a young slip of a chap is the consulting winemaker at Merricks Creek. He seems to have inherited his dad's great touch with pinot.

CURRENT RELEASE 2004   This is a stemmier and more 'out there' wine than the other two Merricks pinots, with a spectrum of aromas and flavours that give it layers of interest, which unfold as it airs and you work your way through a glass or three. It's medium-full red–purple in hue, and there's a hint of gumleaf mint at first, which morphs into foresty complexities. It's a lot more than just simple cherry fruit. The mid-palate is nicely fruit-sweet and it leaves you wanting more. Delicious, and would go with pink roast lamb.

Moorilla Estate Pinot Noir

Quality	♟♟
Value	★★⟩
Rating	84
Grapes	pinot noir
Region	Tasmania
Cellar	▮ 2
Alc./Vol.	13.0%
RRP	$30.00 (cellar door)

We admit to being puzzled by the Moorilla wines; they are all over the place, some are good, some not so good. The confusion is compounded by the fact that most years they make several pinots, and the dearer ones don't always taste the best.

CURRENT RELEASE 2003   There are some earthy, gamey characters in this wine that tend to polarise tasters. The wine is fairly developed, and the palate is unbalanced with tinny acidity and harsh, drying tannins. There's a thinness to the palate flavour that disappoints. Those who revel in funky, 'out there' pinots might go for it.

Moorilla Estate Reserve Pinot Noir

The Reserve package certainly looks the part: the wine comes in a very heavy bottle with a cloth label – which harks back to the days of founder Claudio Alcorso, whose first wines wore cloth labels, too.
CURRENT RELEASE 2003 The low (12 per cent) alcohol may be telling. The wine tastes green, hollow and tartly acidic to us. It is peculiar, because it also has some pungent fruity aromas that remind us of strawberry jam. The palate has a decidedly 'cold' feel to it, with dominant acidity compounding hard, grippy tannins. The best thing about it is the colour, which is excellent.

Quality	♟ ♟
Value	★ ★
Rating	82
Grapes	pinot noir
Region	Tasmania
Cellar	🍶 2
Alc./Vol.	12.0%
RRP	$75.00 🍶

Moorilla GV Block 28 Pinot Noir

Most vineyards are planted in sections, called blocks, with space in between for machinery to move around. Because properties have variable topography and soils, blocks of vineyard emerge as yielding wines of differing characteristics and qualities. To celebrate those differences, winemakers sometimes bottle them separately.
CURRENT RELEASE 2005 This is a fruit-driven strawberry- and cherry-scented pinot that has some greener herbaceous side-lights. It's light-bodied and fairly simple, without obvious oak and the tannins are very mild. It's a little under-powered, but the price is modest. It would drink well with vitello tonnato.

Quality	♟ ♟ ♟
Value	★ ★ ★
Rating	87
Grapes	pinot noir
Region	northern Tas.
Cellar	🍶 3
Alc./Vol.	13.0%
RRP	$24.50 🍷
	(cellar door)

Moss Wood Pinot Noir

Margaret River's strength does not lie in pinot noir, but Moss Wood persist with the grape. Every now and then, they come up with a very good wine. Makers: Keith Mugford and Ian Bell.
CURRENT RELEASE 2003 It really benefited from some breathing time, opening up over several hours into a very pleasing drink. Ripe cherry and plum aromas with a touch of jam; it's a light- to medium-weighted wine but has good flavour coupled with richness and better structure than a lot of Aussie pinots. It could even repay short-term cellaring. It would suit washed-rind cheeses.
Previous outstanding vintages: 1986, '95, '98, '99, 2002

Quality	♟ ♟ ♟ ♟
Value	★ ★ ★
Rating	90
Grapes	pinot noir
Region	Margaret River, WA
Cellar	🍶 5+
Alc./Vol.	13.5%
RRP	$52.50 🍷

Narkoojee Pinot Noir

Quality	☐☐☐☐☐
Value	★★★★☐
Rating	93
Grapes	pinot noir
Region	Gippsland, Vic.
Cellar	☐ 4
Alc./Vol.	13.5%
RRP	$19.00 (cellar door)

Gippsland can produce excellent pinot noir, but standards are annoyingly inconsistent across the region. Narkoojee's pinot has been steadily improving in recent times, and the latest effort is very good.

CURRENT RELEASE 2004   A fragrant pinot noir with a nose of syrupy plum preserves, spice, earth and warm undergrowth elements. A measure of bacony oak enters the equation, but it's not intrusive. In the mouth it's on the lightish side of medium-bodied, but it has generous proportions with fine texture and very long flavour. A classy Gippsland pinot to try with crispy roast pork.

Nepenthe The Good Doctor Pinot Noir

Quality	☐☐☐☐☐
Value	★★★
Rating	93
Grapes	pinot noir
Region	Adelaide Hills, SA
Cellar	☐ 2–6
Alc./Vol.	14.0%
RRP	$44.00 ☐

This doctor in question is Dr Ed Tweddell, the founder of Nepenthe who sadly passed away in 2005. This Limited Release wine commemorates his commitment to producing the best wine possible from his Adelaide Hills vineyards.

CURRENT RELEASE 2003   A complex pinot with plenty of foresty aromas mixed with strawberry and spiced-cherry fruit. The palate has rich flavour and good length, with gamey and earthy touches to ripe fruit, as well as a stemmy touch. That stemmy influence adds a whisper of bitterness to the finish, but it's not too worrying and should soften with a little more time in bottle. Try it with veal chops.

Ninth Island Pinot Noir

Quality	☐☐☐☐
Value	★★★☐
Rating	91
Grapes	pinot noir
Region	Piper's River, Tas.
Cellar	☐ 2
Alc./Vol.	13.5%
RRP	$23.50

Ninth Island Pinot Noir appeals to us a great deal. It fulfils a real need in the Australian wine market. In a way it's rather like French beaujolais, a succulent, lightish, low-tannin quaffer of high quality, designed to be glugged down young.

CURRENT RELEASE 2005   As usual, this is a fantastically drinkable drop. Bright colour heralds juicy raspberry and cherry varietal aromas, and there's a savoury Tassie touch of undergrowth. In the mouth it's slick in texture, light and tangy. A great wine to slurp down with a selection of good charcuterie.

O'Leary Walker Pinot Noir

The grapes for this company's several Adelaide Hills wines come from the O'Leary family vineyard at Oakbank. Makers: Dave O'Leary and Nick Walker.
CURRENT RELEASE 2005   It's a fairly simple, basic pinot but at this price, it's fair value. The colour has good depth and the nose shows some herbal and stewed-fruit notes, while the taste is pleasant enough for its straightforward plummy/vanilla characters, finishing with a little alcohol warmth and tannin grip. It could be served with rabbit casserole.

Quality	♟ ♟ ♟
Value	★ ★ ★
Rating	86
Grapes	pinot noir
Region	Adelaide Hills, SA
Cellar	▯ 2
Alc./Vol.	14.0%
RRP	$21.50 ⧫

Paradigm Hill L'ami Sage Pinot Noir

This pinot noir used to be called Oracle, but after a tussle over the name with another winery, George and Ruth Mihaly of Paradigm Hill decided to change it to L'ami Sage, 'the wise friend'. The name is in recognition of some handy advice proffered by a friend of theirs.
CURRENT RELEASE 2004   A pinot with an intense nose of spices, dark plums and cherries, undergrowth and notable new-oak input. There's good texture in the mouth with ripe, complex varietal flavour of depth, backed up with an unusually firm grip of tannin that seems to come partly from fruit, partly from wood. It's a well-concentrated pinot that might reward bottle-age, allowing that firmness to mellow. Serve it with beef fillet.

Quality	♟ ♟ ♟ ♟
Value	★ ★ ★
Rating	91
Grapes	pinot noir
Region	Mornington Peninsula, Vic.
Cellar	⬷ 2–6
Alc./Vol.	14.0%
RRP	$40.00

Paringa Estate Pinot Noir

Paringa Estate has established itself as one of the Mornington Peninsula's best pinot noir producers over many vintages. With increasing vine age and a series of warm vintages, some of the most recent wines have been outstanding.
CURRENT RELEASE 2004   This is Paringa's mid-range pinot – there's a Reserve above it and a Peninsula pinot below it – and it sums up the estate's style well. The nose has wild-strawberry and cherry aromas of some delicacy, and foresty, slightly sappy notes add complexity. A light layer of spicy oak seasons things well, and the palate has silky texture, gentle complexity and a dry finish. Try it with roast chicken and bacon.

Quality	♟ ♟ ♟ ♟ ♟
Value	★ ★ ★
Rating	93
Grapes	pinot noir
Region	Mornington Peninsula, Vic.
Cellar	▯ 4
Alc./Vol.	14.9%
RRP	$55.00 ⧫

PENGUIN BEST PINOT NOIR

Paringa Estate Reserve Pinot Noir

Quality	♟♟♟♟♟
Value	★★★
Rating	97
Grapes	pinot noir
Region	Mornington Peninsula, Vic.
Cellar	▮ 6
Alc./Vol.	14.9%
RRP	$90.00 🥂

These Special Barrel Selection wines are the top of the Paringa Estate tree, wines of extra richness and complexity. They aren't released every year, only when conditions are just right.

CURRENT RELEASE 2004   An exquisitely rich and complex pinot nose of plum-like fruit with a gamey touch and some foresty notes, even a slightly floral dimension. Spicy oak has been seamlessly absorbed by the wine. In the mouth it has a velvety feel and very long, fine flavour. Dry tannins give structure and it has a lingering, warm aftertaste. It would be perfect with beef fillet.

Pipers Brook The Lyre Pinot Noir

Quality	♟♟♟♟♟
Value	★★★
Rating	95
Grapes	pinot noir
Region	Piper's River, Tas.
Cellar	▮ 4
Alc./Vol.	13.6%
RRP	$95.00

Tasmania has benefited from some consistent vintages in recent years, and the general standard of pinot noir is constantly improving. Pipers Brook is one of the champs, with a broad range of different wines made to exacting standards.

CURRENT RELEASE 2003   Typical Tassie glace-cherry pinot noir aromas meet the nose here, and there are some complex meaty, spicy and chocolatey overtones. The palate is finely textured with satiny fruit flooding the mouth and persisting through a long, gentle finish. Succulent acidity frames it well and keeps it light and tangy in the mouth. Very good. Keep it for roast duck.

Pirie South Pinot Noir

Quality	♟♟♟♟
Value	★★★⁺
Rating	91
Grapes	pinot noir
Region	Tamar Valley, Tas.
Cellar	▮ 3
Alc./Vol.	13.5%
RRP	$23.20

Andrew Pirie's work with pinot noir in Tasmania's north has resulted in some very good wines over the years, especially given the vagaries of the climate in some years. Pirie South wines celebrate cool-climate viticulture in a range designed to enhance light modern cuisine.

CURRENT RELEASE 2005   A very juicy, brightly coloured Cru-beaujolais-style red with an intense nose of raspberries and red cherries uncomplicated by apparent wood or winemaking artefact. The palate is straightforward with light, clean flavours that aren't very complex, but varietally correct and very fresh. It finishes soft and easy. Serve it with veal sausages and onions.

Port Phillip Estate Pinot Noir

Port Phillip Estate's Pinot Noir is packed in one of those heavy burgundy bottles that say 'serious wine'. It's made by Sandro Mosele, a winemaker who is very serious about pinot noir.
CURRENT RELEASE 2004   This has good depth of colour, and the nose shows a good level of ripeness. It has dark-cherry, spice and undergrowthy aromas, and the palate has moderately intense plummy-pinot flavour, with a whisper of firmness behind. It finishes with good length. Delicious with coq au vin.

Quality	🍷🍷🍷🍷
Value	★★★
Rating	93
Grapes	pinot noir
Region	Mornington Peninsula, Vic.
Cellar	4
Alc./Vol.	14.0%
RRP	$38.00

Savaterre Pinot Noir

'Anything starting with "sh" works here,' says Keppell Smith, referring to chardonnay and shiraz in Beechworth. We're not sure where that leaves pinot noir, but when the right season comes along, Savaterre gets that right, too.
CURRENT RELEASE 2004   A remarkably good pinot, considering the relatively young vines (planted 1997) and not-all-that-practised maker. The bouquet is complex: sappy, floral and sweet cherry; the palate is deep, soft and layered, with stacks of flesh and fruit sweetness. A wine of great charm and more-ish drinkability, to serve with duck confit.

Quality	🍷🍷🍷🍷🍷
Value	★★★⭒
Rating	95
Grapes	pinot noir
Region	Beechworth, Vic.
Cellar	4+
Alc./Vol.	14.0%
RRP	$65.00 (cellar door)

Shelmerdine Pinot Noir

The Shelmerdine family, who are related to the Myer family, are Melbourne aristocracy. They are big grapegrowers, as well as emerging wine producers, with large vineyard holdings in the Yarra Valley and Heathcote. This comes from their Lusatia Park vineyard.
CURRENT RELEASE 2004   The colour is medium-pale and it's a fragrant, light-bodied, ethereal style of pinot that is easy to enjoy. There's a tickle of acid that tends to dominate the finish and gives an impression of mid-palate hollowness. A pleasant immediate-quaffing pinot, to team with lightly seared tuna.

Quality	🍷🍷🍷
Value	★★★
Rating	86
Grapes	pinot noir
Region	Yarra Valley, Vic.
Cellar	2
Alc./Vol.	13.4%
RRP	$26.00 $

St Huberts Pinot Noir

Quality	♟ ♟ ♟
Value	★ ★ ★
Rating	87
Grapes	pinot noir
Region	Yarra Valley, Vic.
Cellar	▯ 3+
Alc./Vol.	13.0%
RRP	$26.00 ⑤ ≋

Like Yarra Ridge, this is a brand owned by Foster's, but at least St Huberts has a vineyard associated with it. Whether all the fruit comes from that vineyard these days is a moot point.

CURRENT RELEASE 2004   This is a reasonable pinot but not a stand-out example of what the region is capable of. It has a medium-light colour and a pleasing nose of raspberry with a chaffy/straw-like overlay. The palate is somewhat dominated by acid and tannin and thins out towards the finish. It needs more stuffing. It would drink better with food than without – say, Italian prosciutto and grissini.

St Leonards Pinot Noir

Quality	♟ ♟ ♟
Value	★ ★ ★
Rating	86
Grapes	pinot noir
Region	Rutherglen, Vic.
Cellar	▯ 3+
Alc./Vol.	13.0%
RRP	$21.50 ≋

Pinot noir has a high 'degree of difficulty', but in Rutherglen it's higher again, as pinot seems to make its finest wine in cool-climatic areas. A diving analogy would be a reverse three-and-a-half somersault in pike position from the three-metre springboard.

CURRENT RELEASE 2004   This is a fair drink although not really a definitive varietal pinot. It has a touch of the regional gumleaf aroma and the palate is somewhat strong in tannin for the weight of the fruit. This tends to dry off the palate. Have it with protein and you'll probably find it's still a good drink. Try savoury meatballs.

Stonier Pinot Noir

Quality	♟ ♟ ♟ ♟
Value	★ ★ ★ ⫞
Rating	91
Grapes	pinot noir
Region	Mornington Peninsula, Vic.
Cellar	▯ 4
Alc./Vol.	13.5%
RRP	$26.50 ⑤ ≋

Stonier, while owned by the Lion Nathan grog group these days, is serious about pinot, and makes several examples. Every year it mounts a public tasting celebration called SIPNOT, which includes pinots from all over the world. Winemaker is Geraldine McFaul.

CURRENT RELEASE 2004   This is the kind of pinot that grows on you as you sip it. The colour is fairly light while the bouquet has some subtle sap and cooked-strawberry notes. The taste is mellow and sweetly fruity. It has some weight and volume in the mouth, albeit slightly disjointed at this stage. It has some hidden charms and would go well with veal saltimbocca.

Tarrington Artemisia Pinot Noir

The Tarrington winemakers refer to their Artemisia pinot as their 'bourgogne rouge' rather than an 'entry level' wine. It does share characteristics with some French burgundy. CURRENT RELEASE 2004 A relatively deeply coloured, controversial wine that should interest some pinot-philes. Its complex, lush, powerful and decadently rich smells remind us of dark fruits, mushrooms, undergrowth, earth and spices. Its Achilles heel is a fair measure of volatility that puts it on the edge of acceptability. A pity. If the sharp edge and high-toned flavours don't worry you, the wine does show good texture with long, deep flavours. It lingers long on the palate, finishing with fine, grainy tannins, but that VA is a problem. Try it with confit duck.

Quality	♀ ♀ ♀
Value	★ ★
Rating	86
Grapes	pinot noir
Region	Henty, Vic.
Cellar	▮ 4
Alc./Vol.	13.4%
RRP	$40.00 ▮

Ten Minutes by Tractor Pinot Noir

Ten Minutes by Tractor has changed hands, but the wines still come from the three family vineyards that originally established the label. The three vineyards are all 10 minutes by tractor from each other. This pinot selection used to be labelled Reserve and in '04 it came solely from the Judd vineyard. Maker: Richard McIntyre. CURRENT RELEASE 2004 The better pinot noirs have the sort of complexity and finesse that keeps you returning to your glass. This fits that description and we like it a lot as a result. It shows strawberry and plum fruit with some farmyardy and gamey threads that are decadently rich and naughty. It tastes long and silky with a clean signature of fine tannins. Good with 'coq au pinot noir'.

Quality	♀ ♀ ♀ ♀ ♀
Value	★ ★ ★
Rating	93
Grapes	pinot noir
Region	Mornington Peninsula, Vic.
Cellar	▮ 4
Alc./Vol.	13.5%
RRP	$52.00

T'Gallant Tribute Pinot Noir

T'Gallant is now owned by the Foster's empire via Beringer-Blass, but founders Kevin McCarthy and Kathleen Quealy still play a part. The wonderfully eccentric feel of some of the wines hasn't changed much since the takeover. CURRENT RELEASE 2004 This pinot has a brilliant ruby colour and a sweetly fruity aroma reminiscent of glace cherries, cassata and similar confections. There's a surge of juicy, plummy fruit in the mouth, with a silky texture and subtle length, underpinned by soft tannins. It's not as powerful as some past Tribute pinots, being quite light but pleasantly persistent. Try it with chorizo, boiled eggs and vegetables baked inside bread dough.

Quality	♀ ♀ ♀ ♀ ♀
Value	★ ★ ★ ┥
Rating	93
Grapes	pinot noir
Region	Mornington Peninsula, Vic.
Cellar	▮ 3
Alc./Vol.	13.0%
RRP	$35.00

Tigress Pinot Noir

Quality	♟ ♟ ♟ ♟
Value	★★★⟩
Rating	91
Grapes	pinot noir
Region	Piper's River, Tas.
Cellar	▮ 3
Alc./Vol.	13.5%
RRP	$30.00

The Tasmanian wine industry is promoting the idea that it's one of the best places in Australia for pinot noir. A decade ago we would have disagreed, but in recent years as vineyards and winemakers have matured the claim doesn't sound so silly.
CURRENT RELEASE 2004   An uncomplicated young pinot that may not have the elaborate flavours that make pinot-tragics swoon, but its lightness and freshness are still attractive. It has aromas of strawberry ice-cream, herbs and cherries, and the palate has pleasant red-fruit flavours of moderate length, finishing dry and savoury. Enjoy it with vegetable risotto.

Tokar Estate The Reserve Pinot Noir

Quality	♟ ♟ ♟ ♟ ♟
Value	★★★⟩
Rating	92
Grapes	pinot noir
Region	Yarra Valley, Vic.
Cellar	▮ 4
Alc./Vol.	14.0%
RRP	$40.00 (cellar door)

Tokar Estate is one of the newer players in the Yarra Valley. It has one of the most beautiful views in the valley, looking across pastures, woods and mountains. The wines ain't bad either.
CURRENT RELEASE 2003   A power-packed pinot worthy of the Reserve title, this has a very concentrated nose of dark cherries, black chocolate and tea leaves. The palate follows suit with lush black-cherry jam-like fruit, great persistence and succulence. Soft tannins underpin it perfectly. A big pinot, sure to attract attention. Try it with Peking duck.

Trentham Estate Pinot Noir

Quality	♟ ♟ ♟ ♟
Value	★★★★
Rating	89
Grapes	pinot noir
Region	Murray Valley, NSW
Cellar	▮ 2
Alc./Vol.	13.5%
RRP	$12.50 ⑤ ⧳

From the warm climes of the Murray Valley, this wine defies all the conventional wisdom saying that cheap pinot noir can't be any good. Okay, it's not Chambertin, but it does have surprising varietal honesty.
CURRENT RELEASE 2004   Authentic varietal character starts off with a nose of sweet-red fruits and spice with a hint of sappy undergrowth. It tastes soft and agreeable with lightish-medium body and a pleasantly fruity flavour. Serve it with prosciutto-topped pizza.

Turramurra Estate Pinot Noir

Turramurra has one of the most picturesque cellar doors on the Mornington Peninsula. It's in a more isolated spot than many Peninsula wineries and the peaceful ambience of the place is superb.
CURRENT RELEASE 2003   This has a very complex bouquet of plums, earth, undergrowth and those gamey smells of the soil that mark the most interesting pinots. A thread of spicy oak integrates well, and the lush palate has complex flavour and velvety texture. It's a lush, hedonistic style with a very fine, dry, long finish. Drink it with prune-stuffed loin of pork.

Quality	♟ ♟ ♟ ♟ ♟
Value	★ ★ ★ ↘
Rating	93
Grapes	pinot noir
Region	Mornington Peninsula, Vic.
Cellar	◖ 3
Alc./Vol.	14.0%
RRP	$40.00

Warramate Pinot Noir

Warramate is a new entrant into the pinot noir game. Although one of the oldest vineyards in the Yarra Valley, it has been limited to cabernet, riesling and shiraz for most of its 36 years. Maker: David Church.
CURRENT RELEASE 2004   This is the first Warramate pinot we've tasted and it's very good indeed. A smooth, fleshy wine of good depth and weight, it has appealing sap, earth, straw and forest-floor aromas. Nicely concentrated and quite rich, it would go well with marinated quails thrown on the barbie.

Quality	♟ ♟ ♟ ♟
Value	★ ★ ★ ★
Rating	92
Grapes	pinot noir
Region	Yarra Valley, Vic.
Cellar	◖ 3+
Alc./Vol.	14.5%
RRP	$19.00 ⅋ (cellar door)

Wedgetail Estate Single Vineyard Pinot Noir

French-Canadian-born Guy Lamothe has made a speciality of pinot noir since planting his Yarra Valley vineyard in 1994. In our view, quality has been variable at times, with some ripeness issues in a few vintages, but they are improving.
CURRENT RELEASE 2003   There's a wildness to this pinot that might displease the techno-tasters, but it has a sort of rustic charm that wins you over. The nose has dark cherry, earth and spice with a dab of caramel, and the palate is smoothly structured and long with fine, dry tannins underneath. More subtle than the big-fruit pinot styles, it suits quail well.

Quality	♟ ♟ ♟ ♟
Value	★ ★ ★
Rating	90
Grapes	pinot noir
Region	Yarra Valley, Vic.
Cellar	◖ 3
Alc./Vol.	13.5%
RRP	$40.00

Wellington The Hoodster's Blend Pinot Noir

Quality	♥♥♥♥♥
Value	★★★⧸
Rating	95
Grapes	pinot noir
Region	various, Tas.
Cellar	▮ 5+
Alc./Vol.	13.5%
RRP	$50.00

Andrew Hood – aka The Hoodster – resisted the temptation to bottle reserve wines for many years, until 2002 came along. There's a chardonnay as well. His aim was to select parcels of wine that he believed would age especially well.

CURRENT RELEASE 2002 Tassie pinot can be long-lived, and at four years this is still a baby. It has great depth of colour and inviting aromas of black cherry, peppermint and sweet mulberry, ageing slowly and gracefully. The palate has a tight, compact structure and is lively and powerful. Surprising as it may sound, the wine has yet to hit its peak. Serve with roast duck.

Wignalls Pinot Noir

Quality	♥♥♥
Value	★★★★
Rating	90
Grapes	pinot noir
Region	Great Southern, WA
Cellar	▮ 3
Alc./Vol.	13.5%
RRP	$30.00

In the early 1990s, Wignalls was one of the pacesetters for pinot noir in Australia. Then the train ran off the rails for a few years: the wines were too vegetal and faded very quickly. Something was wrong in the vineyard. Now, with Rob Wignall, son of the founders, at the helm, things seem to be returning to the tracks.

CURRENT RELEASE 2004 This won the trophy for best pinot noir at the 2005 Mount Barker WA Wine Show. It's a well-structured pinot with backbone and length, and nice purity of black-cherry pinot flavour with some sappy and sous-bois overtones. A succulent pinot of real charm. Delicious with pink roast lamb.

Quality	♥♥♥
Value	★★★★
Rating	90
Grapes	pinot noir
Region	Great Southern, WA
Cellar	▮ 5+
Alc./Vol.	14.5%
RRP	$30.00 ⬧

CURRENT RELEASE 2005 Bright light-medium red–purple in colour; the aroma is the feature of the wine: it's very lifted, fragrant, high-toned and inviting. Sappy, black-cherry, strawberry, slightly minty and herbal aromas, with deftly handled oak. The palate is medium-bodied and nicely balanced – again, nothing is out of place. There's a slight tannin astringency at the finish, but it goes well with food. Try roast chicken, gravy and vegetables.

Williams Crossing Pinot Noir

The second label of Curly Flat is – as you might expect – a lighter, fruitier, simpler style than its more expensive big brother. It doesn't state Macedon Ranges on the label, but the grapes are all estate grown. Maker: Phil Moraghan.
CURRENT RELEASE 2004   There are some greener, herbal aromas here possibly from young vines or less well-ripened fruit, while the taste is lighter and plainer than the Curly Flat, but still nice and fruity, with youthful vigour and a trace of firmness. A clean, well-made pinot of a lighter style that nevertheless packs plenty of fruit intensity and charm. It would go well with garlicky barbecued king prawns.

Quality	❛❛❛❜
Value	★★★❹
Rating	89
Grapes	pinot noir
Region	Macedon Ranges, Vic.
Cellar	🍶 3+
Alc./Vol.	13.5%
RRP	$20.00 ⧜
	(cellar door)

Winbirra Vineyards Southern Basalt Pinot Noir

Another new producer from the Mornington Peninsula. This one has two tiny vineyards, at Merricks and Merricks South, and sold its grapes for the first seven years, before enlisting Sandro Mosele to make some wine at Kooyong. Diam corks are used.
CURRENT RELEASE 2004   This is quite a chunky, four-square pinot with a rather tannic palate and slightly reductive nose. The finish is certainly dry, but not disagreeable. It really needs food, so serve it with something pinot-friendly, like roast pork belly.

Quality	❛❛❛
Value	★★★
Rating	86
Grapes	pinot noir
Region	Mornington Peninsula, Vic.
Cellar	🍶 3+
Alc./Vol.	14.0%
RRP	$28.00

Yabby Lake Vineyard Pinot Noir

It's probably a mystery to the uninitiated tourist, but in Australia a yabby (or yabbie) is a small freshwater crustacean, a kind of crayfish. Sautéed yabby tails are a delicacy even the humblest farmer's kids can indulge in. Maker: Tod Dexter.
CURRENT RELEASE 2004   Another very good pinot from this fairly new Mornington outfit, albeit in a fairly oak-influenced style. It has a deep, solid bouquet of mocha and toasty barrel, black cherry and chocolate. It's full, soft and rich in the mouth, with good length and a nice measure of tannin, which firms up the finish and provides backbone. We wonder if a fraction less oak might have been better, but maybe we're splitting hairs. We'd recommend veal sweetbreads.

Quality	❛❛❛❛❜
Value	★★★
Rating	92
Grapes	pinot noir
Region	Mornington Peninsula, Vic.
Cellar	🍶 3+
Alc./Vol.	14.5%
RRP	$60.00

Yarra Ridge Pinot Noir

Quality	¶ ¶ ¶ ¶ ¡
Value	★★★★¡
Rating	92
Grapes	pinot noir
Region	Yarra Valley, Vic.
Cellar	▮ 5
Alc./Vol.	13.0%
RRP	$23.20 Ⓢ ≋

While Yarra Ridge is seldom considered among the very best pinot noir makers in the Yarra Valley, its wines are usually above average and represent especially good value for money. The wines are no longer made at Yarra Ridge; the winery has been sold to Rob Dolan (who was once the resident Yarra Ridge winemaker).

CURRENT RELEASE 2004   This is a pinot of weight and structure, whose aromatics are more in the earthy spectrum than your fragrant strawberries and cherries. Sous-bois and earthy low-notes combine with some hints of black cherry; the palate is firm and a trifle tannic, but it does have uncommonly good depth. It should take some age well. Then serve with roast duck breast.

YarraLoch Pinot Noir

Quality	¶ ¶ ¶
Value	★★¡
Rating	86
Grapes	pinot noir
Region	Yarra Valley, Vic.
Cellar	▮ 2
Alc./Vol.	14.0%
RRP	$30.00

YarraLoch is a new producer, at least to us. And we've been impressed by most of its wines. Having a real pro like Sergio Carlei as contract winemaker doesn't hurt, of course. And the wines are all sealed with Diam corks.

CURRENT RELEASE 2003   Pinot noir is the most difficult of grapes and it's probably no surprise this was the least of the new releases from YarraLoch. It has a chaffy/compost kind of aroma with a bit of animal eccentricity, while the taste is a tad lacking in definition and pinot charm, and the high acidity gives it an almost tinny taste and a drying finish. It needs food: try it with crumbed lamb's brains.

Zarephath Pinot Noir

Quality	¶ ¶ ¶ ¶
Value	★★★¡
Rating	90
Grapes	pinot noir
Region	Porongurup, WA
Cellar	➡1–4
Alc./Vol.	14.0%
RRP	$26.00 ≋

Most of Western Australia doesn't really suit pinot noir that well, but the timeless landscape of the Porongurup ranges in the far south is different. Zarephath's Porongurup pinots are heading in the right direction.

CURRENT RELEASE 2005   This has a bright-ruby colour and a fresh, fruity nose that's deliciously fragrant. It reminds us of red-glace cherries, Asian spices and dry forest undergrowth. The palate has intense cherry-like flavour with reasonably fleshy texture, but it finishes a little hard and slightly stemmy at the moment. It should soften with a year or two, and it will go well with roast quail.

Sangiovese and blends

With so many Aussies claiming Italian ancestry, and Italian culture and cooking so popular, it's surprising that only in the last decade have we begun to take Italian wine really seriously. Perhaps the improving quality of wine from Italy has shown us what's possible with varieties like sangiovese, or maybe it's our thirst for innovation, but plantings are increasing in many corners of the country. Victoria's King Valley leads the way via growers of Italian heritage, and the home-grown sangiovese is starting to achieve typically savoury dry fruitiness and attractive structural interest. The best sangiovese is excellent with a variety of foods, and it's also excellent as blending material, sometimes to give a savoury, appetising edge to cabernet or merlot.

Amulet Sangiovese

Sangiovese is becoming almost mainstream in Australia these days. Its savoury, more-ish personality is ideal with the modern Mediterranean food that's so popular in Australia today.
CURRENT RELEASE 2004   This sangiovese from Beechworth has savoury Italian-wine smells that suggest cherries and spices. It's a more low-key sangiovese than some, with an attractive silky texture, gentle, long flavour and moderate tannins. An easy-going style to accompany a cheesey risotto.

Quality	♟♟♟♟
Value	★★★
Rating	89
Grapes	sangiovese
Region	Beechworth, Vic.
Cellar	▮ 2
Alc./Vol.	14.0%
RRP	$18.00 🍷

Coriole Sangiovese

Coriole's label rightly reminds their fans that they were the first consistent producer of sangiovese in Australia – with first plantings in 1985. The wines have been quite light in the past, but we sense a new style direction in the last few vintages, none better than the 2004. Maker: Grant Harrison.
CURRENT RELEASE 2004   The colour is medium-deep red–purple and the bouquet is fresh, youthful and fruit-driven, smelling almost tutti-frutti with attractive berry-like characters and no herbaceousness. The palate is where it really impresses, though: with real weight and concentration, intense cherry and raspberry flavours, good length and harmony, this is a very smart sangiovese. Serve with Tuscan-style grilled lamb cutlets.
Previous outstanding vintages: 2002, '03

Quality	♟♟♟♟♟
Value	★★★★★
Rating	95
Grapes	sangiovese
Region	McLaren Vale, SA
Cellar	▮ 5+
Alc./Vol.	14.0%
RRP	$20.00 🍷

Piccola Sangiovese Shiraz

Quality	♟ ♟ ♟ ♟
Value	★ ★ ★ ★
Rating	90
Grapes	sangiovese; shiraz
Region	Central Ranges, NSW
Cellar	▮ 2
Alc./Vol.	14.0%
RRP	$15.00 ⬗

A new label from Robin Tedder of Glenguin in the Hunter Valley made from grapes grown elsewhere in New South Wales. Piccola is designed as a food-friendly, savoury style. CURRENT RELEASE 2004 Despite its shiraz component, this has a savoury accent that fits more with an Italian philosophy of wine than with an Australian tradition. It smells complex with cherry, cedar, leather and spice aromas, and it tastes savoury with subdued fruit character, dry flavour and a slightly angular, food-friendly finish. Easy to sip with saltimbocca alla romana.

Ravensworth Sangiovese

Quality	♟ ♟ ♟ ♟
Value	★ ★ ★ ⟩
Rating	90
Grapes	sangiovese
Region	Canberra district, NSW
Cellar	▮ 2
Alc./Vol.	14.0%
RRP	$21.00 ⬗

Sangiovese is an oddity in the Canberra district, and Ravensworth's Bryan Martin reckons the region's climate is marginal for the variety. This hasn't stopped him playing around with it, and the results so far have been good. CURRENT RELEASE 2005 This youngster has the sort of Italian deli smells that encapsulate sangiovese's unusual charm: dark-cherry, prune, spice, and rustic smoky aromas and flavours are ripe, yet typically savoury. The palate is just as much about texture as flavour. Cherry-scented and slightly aniseedy varietal fruit is coupled to a grainy mouth-feel and a grippy aromatic finish. Very interesting. Try it with pasta and tomato-based sauces.

Simon Gilbert Sangiovese Barbera

Quality	♟ ♟ ♟ ♟
Value	★ ★ ★ ★
Rating	90
Grapes	sangiovese; barbera
Region	Central Ranges, NSW
Cellar	▮ 3+
Alc./Vol.	14.0%
RRP	$15.00 Ⓢ

Italians might blanch at the thought of Tuscan and Piedmontese grape varieties in bed together, but if it works – why not? Simon Gilbert is a public wine company based at Mudgee and sourcing grapes from throughout the New South Wales Central Ranges. CURRENT RELEASE 2004 Here's a good pasta wine at an everyday price with some distinctive Italianate character: fragrant raspberry, mulberry, leafy aromas and a touch of dried banana. The palate has good intensity, is medium-bodied and finishes with the kind of grip that's typical of Italian-style reds. Food: spaghetti bolognese.

Tateham's Sangiovese

Tateham's is also the name of the proprietors' cafe/restaurant in the little town of Auburn, at the foot of the Clare Valley. This is a real boutique: they declare their crush at less than 10 tonnes of grapes a year!

CURRENT RELEASE 2004   The colour is not deep, merely medium-red with a purple tint, but the wine has good flavour. It is fruit-driven and somewhat herbal, while the palate is medium- to full-bodied and smooth, with some floral, licorice, earthy and dried-herb accents. A mild tannin grip adds authority to the finish. Try it with game birds, such as squab.

Quality	�w♟♟♟
Value	★★★
Rating	89
Grapes	sangiovese
Region	Clare Valley, SA
Cellar	▯ 4+
Alc./Vol.	14.5%
RRP	$24.00 ⬚
	(cellar door)

Shiraz and blends

Shiraz is Australia's signature grape, our most popular red wine both locally and overseas. In 2005, shiraz grapes made up about one-quarter of the total wine harvest: 454 000 tonnes. The real gob-smacker, though, is comparing that with 20 years ago: 56 500 tonnes! An eight-fold increase in two decades – largely export driven. The great thing about Aussie shiraz is its diversity: we can drink elegant, spicy styles from cooler climates; rich, chocolatey ones from the hotter regions; and many other permutations. There's a new fashion for viognier blends (just four or five per cent can make a big difference) and a trend towards using more French oak and less American. We like many styles of shiraz but, as in everything, balance is the key: wines that are too oaky, tannic or alcoholic or have 'dead fruit' character aren't rated highly.

Abercorn A Reserve Growers' Revenge

Quality	♛♛♛♛♛
Value	★★★
Rating	95
Grapes	shiraz; cabernet sauvignon; merlot
Region	Mudgee, NSW
Cellar	▮ 12+
Alc./Vol.	14.0%
RRP	$49.95 ▮ (cellar door)

This won a gold medal at the 2005 Mudgee Wine Show where HH was officiating. At the very least, it's an answering shot for those arguments about which grape variety suits Mudgee best – cabernet or shiraz. Maker: Tim Stevens. CURRENT RELEASE 2002 The colour is still young for its age and there are lovely smoky, mellowing, semi-developed complexities on nose and palate. There's a seductive combination of primary fruit and secondary barrel and bottle-age components to the flavour. Fleshy, smooth and seamless across the palate, the blend succeeds handsomely and no single grape dominates. Try it with roast venison.

Abercorn A Reserve Shiraz

Quality	♛♛♛♛♛
Value	★★★⁴
Rating	92
Grapes	shiraz
Region	Mudgee, NSW
Cellar	▬ 2–15+
Alc./Vol.	14.0%
RRP	$36.00 ▮ ⊗

In 2005, Tim and Connie Stevens of Abercorn bought their neighbour, Huntington Estate, from the retiring founders, Bob and Wendy Roberts. It was a scaled-down version of the minnow swallowing the whale. It's a good fit, as the styles of the two wineries' reds are distinct and separate. CURRENT RELEASE 2003 A big, rich, succulent style of Mudgee shiraz with chocolate and vanilla aromas, spot-on fruit ripeness and a solid but supple structure of ripe tannins. Smoky barrel-ferment characters add an extra sheen to the bouquet, while dark-plum and earthy regional elements also chime in. It has the structure to age long term and is a great cellaring proposition. Then serve it with hard cheeses.

All Saints Family Cellar Reserve Shiraz

Like the related Brown Brothers operation, All Saints likes to play up the 'family' nature of the business. Presumably, they think wine drinkers are more warmly disposed towards family businesses than to cold, faceless corporations. CURRENT RELEASE 2004   It's not at all what we expected from a flagship Rutherglen red; not a big battleship wine at all. The colour is merely medium-deep and the aromas recall raspberry, mint, cassis and herbs – almost as though there was some cabernet blended in. It's quite fruit-driven and youthfully vibrant, promising to age slowly and long. It's an elegant – if not all that complex – drink, today. Try it with roast lamb and mint sauce.

Quality	♟♟♟
Value	★★★
Rating	89
Grapes	shiraz
Region	Rutherglen, Vic.
Cellar	●–1–10+
Alc./Vol.	14.2%
RRP	$49.00
	(cellar door)

Anvers The Warrior Shiraz

This company started off as Annvers, with two 'n's, and then dropped one. Their literature tells us the name comes from Antwerp, Belgium, as does the mythological Brabo, which is their logo. The proprietors are Wayne and Myriam Keoghan; Myriam hails from Antwerp. CURRENT RELEASE 2003   This is a whopper, as we've come to expect from flagship South Australian shirazes these days. It's not shy in alcohol and the palate is hefty and tannic. There are hints of raisin, roast meat and earth and it's more savoury than fruity, with slightly forward development. It even smells tannic, if that's possible! Not a wine of charm, but brutal muscle. It needs more time, then serve with casseroled beef.

Quality	♟♟♟
Value	★★★
Rating	89
Grapes	shiraz
Region	52% Adelaide Hills & 48% McLaren Vale, SA
Cellar	●–2–10+
Alc./Vol.	14.9%
RRP	$45.00

Baddaginnie Run Shiraz

The Baddaginnie Run vineyard is part of an environmentally conscious enterprise in the Rotherlea Valley in Victoria's Strathbogie Ranges. One hundred thousand trees have been replanted and the vineyard is run along sustainable lines – an admirable venture that deserves success. CURRENT RELEASE 2002   There are cool-climate spice, mint and herbal notes on the nose here, but it's still nicely ripe and complete. Tangy mulberry-like fruit fills it out with hints of mocha and spice in the mix. Balance is good and it finishes long and fresh. We'd recommend roast lamb.

Quality	♟♟♟♟
Value	★★★★
Rating	91
Grapes	shiraz
Region	Strathbogie Ranges, Vic.
Cellar	▮5
Alc./Vol.	14.5%
RRP	$20.00

Baileys 1920s Block Shiraz

Quality	♥♥♥♥♥
Value	★★★⟩
Rating	93
Grapes	shiraz
Region	Glenrowan, Vic.
Cellar	➡2–12
Alc./Vol.	14.5%
RRP	$35.00

Big reds and the Glenrowan region go hand in hand. The reds were pretty rough and ready 40 years ago, but they've been civilised since. They're still no blushing violets, though.
CURRENT RELEASE 2003   A very deep, blackish shiraz with plenty of punch. It has a demiglaze-like concentration of jammy black fruit on the nose, and there's a typical earthy ironstone regionality to it. Oak is in good balance. The powerful palate is rich and deeply flavoured with a firm, dry tannic grip supporting it. A wine to lay down for the long haul, then drink with rare rump steak.

Balgownie Estate Shiraz

Quality	♥♥♥♥♥
Value	★★★
Rating	92
Grapes	shiraz
Region	Bendigo, Vic.
Cellar	➡2–10
Alc./Vol.	14.0%
RRP	$31.00 ⑤

This pioneering vineyard of the reborn Bendigo *vignoble* continues to grow under new ownership. Stuart Anderson's original plot has been extended and it has reinforced its place as the region's premier winery.
CURRENT RELEASE 2004   Balgownie shiraz remains a brawny character, very deep in colour with a potent nose of dark berries, earth, mint and spice. The palate is rich and youthful, showing deep black-fruit flavours and a touch of gaminess. It has full body and is still totally unevolved. Give it time, then enjoy it with a rare steak.

Balnaves Shiraz

Quality	♥♥♥♥
Value	★★★
Rating	91
Grapes	shiraz 95%; cabernet sauvignon 5%
Region	Coonawarra, SA
Cellar	➡2–8
Alc./Vol.	14.5%
RRP	$28.00 ⑤

Pete Bissell goes about the business of winemaking without too much fanfare, but the unfussed approach conceals one of Coonawarra's best winemakers. His skill coupled with the Balnaves' outstanding fruit has made this label one to search for.
CURRENT RELEASE 2004   A dense young shiraz that smells of pepper, dark berries and currants. It's spicy and savoury and there's a mild seasoning of cedary oak. The palate is spicy but subtle, with medium-weight. Unusually for a Balnaves wine it's a rather old-fashioned type of lean-boned dry Coonawarra shiraz. In time it should develop into a wine of understated elegance. Try it with racks of lamb.

Barossa Old Vine Company Shiraz

This label has been created by the Langmeil winery to highlight the fruit from Barossa shiraz vineyards planted over 100 years ago. It's a true benchmark wine.
CURRENT RELEASE 2003 A very powerful essay in Barossa shiraz with a nose of great concentration and harmony. To us it's reminiscent of dark beef stock, dark fruits, bitter chocolate and smoky oak, all seamlessly melded together. The velvety palate has great texture and the intense flavour is vinous and complex, yet very subtle. It finishes with perfectly balanced fine-grained ripe tannins and a long nutty aftertaste. Serve it with roast beef at a grand dinner.

Quality	♟♟♟♟♟
Value	★★⟊
Rating	97
Grapes	shiraz
Region	Barossa Valley, SA
Cellar	🍾 12
Alc./Vol.	15.0%
RRP	$100.00

Battle of Bosworth Shiraz

As we all know only too well, the Battle of Bosworth was fought during the Wars of the Roses in 1485, but the one referred to here was Joch Bosworth's battle to convert his McLaren Vale vineyard to organic viticulture.
CURRENT RELEASE 2003 A solid, potent critter. Concentrated blackberry-like McLaren Vale shiraz of great purity and concentration leads the charge, and touches of bitter chocolate, vanilla and spice add interest. The palate is full-bodied with intense, ripe fruit that finishes long and powerful. A warm and welcoming style for those who like big reds. Try it with a thick T-bone steak.

Quality	♟♟♟♟⟊
Value	★★★★⟊
Rating	92
Grapes	shiraz
Region	McLaren Vale, SA
Cellar	🍾 10
Alc./Vol.	14.5%
RRP	$25.00 ⓥ

CURRENT RELEASE 2004 The aroma of raisined fruit gives an almost muscaty feel to this big, ripe red. There's also some earthy spice and a slightly charry touch. In the mouth it's warm and alcoholic with raisined fruit flavour, and porty and amarone-like touches. It finishes with relatively soft, ripe tannins. It's a style that might score a stratospheric rating in certain American wine commentaries, and it doesn't have any faults, but to our taste it's a bit overdone. We'd suggest soft cheese.

Quality	♟♟♟⟊
Value	★★★
Rating	89
Grapes	shiraz
Region	McLaren Vale, SA
Cellar	🍾 5
Alc./Vol.	15.0%
RRP	$24.00 Ⓢ ⓥ

Battle of Bosworth White Boar Shiraz

Quality	❚ ❚ ❚ ❙
Value	★ ★ ┤
Rating	88
Grapes	shiraz
Region	McLaren Vale, SA
Cellar	▮ 4
Alc./Vol.	15.0%
RRP	$45.00 Ⓢ Ⓥ

Produced using the unusual method of cordon cutting to allow the grapes to partially dry on the vine, this is an unusual red made in a formidably big, alcoholic style.
CURRENT RELEASE 2004   There's an oxidised thread to this shiraz on the nose, and the high-toned stewed-plum, berry and chocolatey-fruit character, and alcoholic power are hard to ignore. It's a big broad mouthful of wine with fumy heat to it, and almost an impression of sweetness. It finishes dry with ripe tannins. Serve it with firm cheese and dried fruits.

Beresford McLaren Vale Shiraz

Quality	❚ ❚ ❚ ❚ ❙
Value	★ ★ ★ ★
Rating	92
Grapes	shiraz
Region	McLaren Vale, SA
Cellar	▮ 5
Alc./Vol.	13.5%
RRP	$20.00 ⧳

Beresford's McLaren Vale Shiraz is made in a generous, full-flavoured style that is always a crowd-pleaser. The price has crept up a little over the years, but it's still good value. Maker: Rob Dundon.
CURRENT RELEASE 2003   This is the best Beresford shiraz for a while. It has deep colour and a lusciously ripe, seductive nose based on syrupy blackberry fruit, subtle spice, and a balanced measure of coconutty oak. The palate is velvety, ripe and long with just the right level of grainy tannins in support. A crowd-pleasing shiraz to serve with roast beef.

Berrys Bridge Shiraz

Quality	❚ ❚ ❚ ❚ ❙
Value	★ ★ ★
Rating	94
Grapes	shiraz
Region	Pyrenees, Vic.
Cellar	▮ 3
Alc./Vol.	15.0%
RRP	$42.00 Ⓢ

At their most formidable, Pyrenees shirazes are among the biggest, most concentrated red wines in Australia. Long age is desirable with some wines, with these it's essential.
CURRENT RELEASE 2002   A dense, deep shiraz with powerful aromas of boiled-down black plums, spices and cedar. And while it doesn't have the excessive eucalypt of some big Pyrenees reds, there's a whisper of the gum tree about it. Overall the nose is like a plush essence of super-ripe shiraz. The palate is full-bodied and strongly flavoured with warmth and generosity; a great wall of tannins supports the whole. Serve it with rib roast of beef.

Bress Heathcote & Bendigo Shiraz

Bendigo and surrounding districts like Heathcote were known to produce excellent wine in the nineteenth century, but phylloxera infestation caused their demise before the turn of the twentieth century. Now these regions have been reborn and quality is ever improving. CURRENT RELEASE 2005 A deeply coloured young red made in the smooth Bress style, this has clean mixed berry and spice aromas of good intensity. The palate is finely balanced with intense flavour, yet no heaviness, finishing with well-tuned, dry tannins. Works a treat with pumpkin and sage tagliatelle.

Quality	♟ ♟ ♟ ♟ ♟
Value	★ ★ ★ ★ ┥
Rating	93
Grapes	shiraz
Region	Heathcote & Bendigo, Vic.
Cellar	♦ 6
Alc./Vol.	14.0%
RRP	$19.00 ⬚

Bress Heathcote Shiraz

The Bress way with Heathcote shiraz is to make it into a smoother, easier red than some. It's still pretty muscular, especially in the warm 2004 vintage. Maker: Adam Marks. CURRENT RELEASE 2004 There are a number of wines around now showcasing just what makes Heathcote one of Australia's finest shiraz regions, and Bress is one of them. This shiraz has dark-berry, spice and foresty notes on the nose that offer a great feeling of harmony in the wine. The palate has velvety texture with lovely depth of flavour, and seamlessly integrated tannins lead through a dry, firm-ish finish. Good with roasted vegetables.

Quality	♟ ♟ ♟ ♟ ♟
Value	★ ★ ★ ★
Rating	95
Grapes	shiraz
Region	Heathcote, Vic.
Cellar	➠1–10+
Alc./Vol.	14.5%
RRP	$40.00 ⬚

Bridgewater Mill Shiraz Viognier

Brian Croser's first Bridgewater Mill shirazes of a decade or so ago could be formidable critters, with firm tannins and plenty of character. It's still a big wine, but its current flirtation with viognier makes it a little more genteel. CURRENT RELEASE 2003 There's good concentration of jammy-blueberry, spice, musk and peppery notes on the nose in this vintage, and the influence of viognier is thankfully toned down compared to some of the competition. In the mouth it has medium to full body with good flavour development and richness. It finishes with nicely grainy ripe tannins and an aromatic, long aftertaste. Serve it with lamb and kidney pie.

Quality	♟ ♟ ♟ ♟ ♟
Value	★ ★ ★ ★ ┥
Rating	93
Grapes	shiraz; viognier
Region	Adelaide Hills, SA
Cellar	♦ 8
Alc./Vol.	14.5%
RRP	$24.00 ⬚

Brokenwood Rayner Vineyard Shiraz

Quality	♥♥♥♥♥
Value	★★★
Rating	97
Grapes	shiraz
Region	McLaren Vale, SA
Cellar	▮ 10
Alc./Vol.	14.0%
RRP	$69.00 ⮺

The Rayner Vineyard was planted at McLaren Vale by David Rayner in 1950. Four generations of Rayners have been grapegrowers in the region. The quality of their fruit is exemplary.

CURRENT RELEASE 2003   A full-flavoured, rich shiraz that sums up the best McLaren Vale type. It's deep in colour, and it smells invitingly of dark chocolate, blackberries, spice and sweet oak. In the mouth it shows lovely ripe flavours of good concentration, but it retains a certain freshness that's sadly lacking in some of today's super-shirazes. It finishes with ripe tannins and a long, slightly minty aftertaste. A classically built wine to serve with kangaroo.
Previous outstanding vintages: 1996, 2001,'02

Brokenwood Wade Block 2 Shiraz

Quality	♥♥♥♥♥
Value	★★★
Rating	94
Grapes	shiraz
Region	McLaren Vale, SA
Cellar	➾1–8+
Alc./Vol.	14.5%
RRP	$39.00 ⮺

Wade Block 2 is a McLaren Vale vineyard situated a little away from the heart of things in the slightly cooler Blewitt Springs sub-region. Yields are kept low to enhance intensity in the wine.

CURRENT RELEASE 2003   Initially this has a rather old-fashioned feel to it with some earthy, leathery touches to plum and mocha aromas. Raspberry and blackberry flavours have real concentration and presence, and it has a smooth mouth-feel, finishing with a spicy aftertaste and soft tannins. Try it with a steak pie.

Brown Brothers Patricia Shiraz

Quality	♥♥♥♥♥
Value	★★★
Rating	92
Grapes	shiraz
Region	north-east Vic.
Cellar	▮ 8
Alc./Vol.	14.5%
RRP	$44.95

Brown Brothers were concentrating on developing their table wines long before many of their north-east Victorian comrades. Experimentation with varieties and techniques stood them in good stead as the wine boom accelerated through the 1970s. Patricia Shiraz is one of their current-day flagships.

CURRENT RELEASE 2002   Quite a lot of toasty, sweet American oak kicks things off with this shiraz, but syrupy-berry aromas aren't lost in the wood. The palate is long and smooth with concentrated rich flavours of dark fruits and sweet oak. It has a mouth-coating quality that will endear it to many, and it finishes dry with perfectly integrated ripe tannins. A ripe, full Australian shiraz to enjoy with a Turkish-inspired mixed grill.

Bullers Beverford Shiraz

The Beverford vineyard in the Murray Valley near Swan Hill is the source of Bullers' cheap-and-cheerful ranges of wines. The best of them fit simple quaffing specifications well, but we feel that the reasonably priced wines from a number of other Murray Valley vineyards have left them behind in the quality stakes.

CURRENT RELEASE 2003   There are hints of earthy, spicy, berry and licorice aromas here that are appealing, if fairly light. In the mouth it has straightforward flavour, light to middling body and very soft tannins. A drink-now sort of shiraz to serve with pizza.

Quality	♥ ♥ ♥ ♥
Value	★ ★ ★ ↓
Rating	88
Grapes	shiraz
Region	Murray Valley, Vic.
Cellar	🍷 2
Alc./Vol.	14.5%
RRP	$14.90

Bullers Caspia Shiraz

Caspia is a Greek word with connotations of flora and fauna. The name is used on this range of wines in recognition of Mrs Val Buller's dedication to her garden and native birds. At the Buller winery a fascinating bird park of aviaries is testament to her interests.

CURRENT RELEASE 2005   A young wine with a bit more freshness and substance than the Buller Beverford range. It smells of dark plums, berries and earth with a slightly porty overtone. In the mouth it has fruit-sweet berry flavour that's direct and easy, good depth and body, finishing with soft, easy tannins. Try it with a delicious meat pie.

Quality	♥ ♥ ♥ ♥
Value	★ ★ ★ ★
Rating	88
Grapes	shiraz
Region	not stated
Cellar	🍷 2
Alc./Vol.	15.5%
RRP	$11.60 🍷

Castagna Sauvage

Sauvage is the label Julian Castagna uses when he declassifies wine – in this case, wine that might otherwise appear under the top label, Genesis. The 2003 vintage was a notoriously difficult year at Beechworth and the King Valley, with heat, drought and bushfires. Diam-sealed.

CURRENT RELEASE 2003   This is a good drink, but clearly not in the class of recent releases of Genesis. The aromas are slightly forward-developed, leathery, chaffy and moderately complex. The palate is slightly lacking in fruit and freshness but is not without its charms. There's a little drying harshness at the back of the palate. It's good with food, especially rare grilled steak.

Quality	♥ ♥ ♥ ♥
Value	★ ★ ★
Rating	88
Grapes	shiraz; viognier
Region	Beechworth, Vic.
Cellar	🍷 5
Alc./Vol.	14.0%
RRP	$35.00 🍷
	(cellar door)

Centennial Vineyards Reserve Shiraz Viognier

Quality	🍷🍷🍷🍷
Value	★★★⧸
Rating	90
Grapes	shiraz; viognier 6%
Region	Hilltops, NSW
Cellar	🍾 8+
Alc./Vol.	14.8%
RRP	$27.00 (cellar door)

This winery is at Bowral in the New South Wales Southern Highlands, but many of their wines are made from grapes sourced in other regions, such as Orange and Hilltops. The latest crop of releases are all sealed with Procork, which seems like a good move. Winemaker is Tony Cosgriff.
CURRENT RELEASE 2004   A somewhat drying style of red, here, with bay-leaf and walnut aromas together with dried spices and a hint of jam. It's intense, lively, has length and elegance, but a touch of firmness and very drying tannins to close. It would suit braised lamb shanks.

Chateau Mildura Psyche Smuggler Shiraz

Quality	🍷🍷🍷
Value	★★★★
Rating	87
Grapes	shiraz
Region	Riverland, Vic.
Cellar	🍾 3
Alc./Vol.	14.5%
RRP	$12.50 ⑤ ≋

In Roman mythology, Psyche was a beautiful princess, the forbidden lover of Cupid, wasn't she? What this has to do with this wine is anyone's guess!
CURRENT RELEASE 2005   This is just a pup. It's as virginal as Psyche, before she met Cupid. Vivid purple–red colour, raw fruity aromas of violets and plums, simple and probably unwooded, it is all about the grapes. In the mouth, it's bold and direct, recalling plum juice or syrup. It has lots of fruit, and doesn't appear to be sugar-sweet, like so many reds released too young. Plenty of bang for your bucks. Food? It's not really a food wine, but you could try hard cheeses.

Cheviot Bridge Heathcote Shiraz

Quality	🍷🍷🍷
Value	★★★★
Rating	87
Grapes	shiraz
Region	Heathcote, Vic.
Cellar	🍾 4+
Alc./Vol.	14.0%
RRP	$13.50 ⑤ ≋

The Cheviot Bridge Wine Co. is a fast-growing public company that specialises in giving the average drinker what they want – a decent drink at a modest price. It's building a reputation for very reliable value for money.
CURRENT RELEASE 2004   This is a good introduction to Heathcote shiraz at an amazingly low price. It is a straightforward, fruit-driven style (they didn't waste any cash on expensive barrels) that allows the sweetly ripe cherry/plum shiraz fruit to shine. The palate is soft, fruit-sweet and low in tannin; persistence is moderate. It's good value, and would suit a lamb shank stew.

Cheviot Bridge Yea Valley Shiraz

While it is a 'virtual wine company', i.e. not owning infrastructure like vineyards and wineries, various Cheviot partners do own vineyards, especially in the Yea Valley – which is just a little way north of the Yarra Valley boundary.
CURRENT RELEASE 2003   The colour is good for a three-year-old and this light- to medium-bodied red has a slightly grippy tannin finish coupled with a modest depth of fruit. The nose is somewhat smoky – which may or may not be a symptom of the notorious bushfire year in northern Victoria. There are some attractive spicy/earthy shiraz characters, as well. Try it with lamb and barley casserole.

Quality	♟ ♟ ♟
Value	★ ★ ★
Rating	86
Grapes	shiraz
Region	Yea Valley, Vic.
Cellar	▮ 3
Alc./Vol.	14.0%
RRP	$19.00 Ⓢ ⮒

Cigale Shiraz

The producer's name is Domaine Jardin. And it's not French, it's Barossa. Yet another new brand doing good stuff in small doses. This runs out at just 200 cases.
CURRENT RELEASE 2004   Great colour: deep purple–red, and it doesn't disappoint from there on. It's a big Barossa style, with lots of alcohol warmth and fruit-sweet aniseed flavours, plus a slightly rustic broadness of structure. Plummy and super-ripe, it's bright and fruit-driven with very surreptitious oak. It would suit reggiano cheese.

Quality	♟ ♟ ♟ ♟ ♟
Value	★ ★ ★ ★ ⮒
Rating	92
Grapes	shiraz
Region	Barossa Valley, SA
Cellar	▮ 6+
Alc./Vol.	15.0%
RRP	$23.00

Cobaw Ridge Shiraz Viognier

Cobaw Ridge was one of the earliest vineyards to start fooling around with a little viognier mixed into shiraz. Now everybody's doing it – with mixed success.
CURRENT RELEASE 2004   A very fragrant young wine with complex aromas of plums, berries, spice and mint. Oak is seamlessly folded into it. The palate is silky and long with persistent, gently spicy cherry flavour, beautifully fine, soft tannins and a lingering aftertaste. A gentle wine to have with roast duck.

Quality	♟ ♟ ♟ ♟ ♟
Value	★ ★ ★ ⮒
Rating	93
Grapes	shiraz; viognier
Region	Macedon Ranges, Vic.
Cellar	▮ 5
Alc./Vol.	13.0%
RRP	$42.00

The Colonial Estate Explorateur Shiraz

Quality	??? ?
Value	★★★）
Rating	92
Grapes	shiraz
Region	Barossa Valley, SA
Cellar	8+
Alc./Vol.	14.5%
RRP	$36.00

Jonathan Maltus has a number of wine properties in Bordeaux, including Chateau Teyssier in St Emilion, as well as the Barossa. His Barossa wines are expensive and generally not to our taste. But we liked this one.
CURRENT RELEASE 2004 It's a big wine: earthy, walnutty, spicy and savoury – not fruity at all, indeed more the kind of wine someone with French experience might make. It has lots of flesh and tannin grip and the flavours are long barrel-matured as opposed to primary fruit. Quite well balanced, too. It goes with Heidi gruyère cheese.

Connor Park Shiraz

Quality	??? ?
Value	★★★
Rating	91
Grapes	shiraz
Region	Bendigo, Vic.
Cellar	4
Alc./Vol.	14.5%
RRP	$25.00

Connor Park is based on a small vineyard planted in the late 1960s by present proprietor Ross Lougoon's uncle, Tom. Ross and wife Robyn have since extended the plantings and built a winery. The wines are made in the flavoury Bendigo style.
CURRENT RELEASE 2002 This has the nose of a ripe, solidly built Bendigo-region red, but with less of the typical mint and eucalypt shown by some of the district's shiraz. The palate is ripe and intense, with good depth, medium body and well-integrated tannins. Easy to like with a thick steak.

Craiglee Shiraz

Quality	???? ?
Value	★★★）
Rating	94
Grapes	shiraz
Region	Sunbury, Vic.
Cellar	2–10
Alc./Vol.	14.5%
RRP	$42.00

Craiglee Shiraz is one of our favourite Australian shirazes made in the European style. Wines produced from this piece of ground can also age amazingly well, evidenced by the fact that some bottles of the 1872 vintage lived for 100 years.
CURRENT RELEASE 2004 At only two years of age, this wine is big and unevolved with raw raspberry and plum aromas, and an earthy, slightly reductive touch. It needs air, and after breathing it reveals smooth spice and savoury notes, good texture and length. It finishes long, dry and spicy, and should build complexity with the years, but right now there's a rather stewed character to it that puts it out of the Craiglee mainstream. Cellar it, then serve it with roast rib of beef.

d'Arenberg d'Arry's Original

A historic wine descended from the shiraz-grenache 'Burgundy' made by Francis d'Arry Osborn back in the 1960s. Perhaps we shouldn't say it, but these modern wines are much better than those pongy drops ever were. CURRENT RELEASE 2004   This has a subdued, complex aroma that reminds us of earth, leather, dry undergrowth and stewed raspberries. In the mouth it has a smooth, easy disposition, again with nicely restrained ripe fruit and complex, savoury overtones. Tannins are fine-grained and unassertive. All round a wine style we'd prefer to drink with a meal over many much ballyhooed modern shiraz-grenaches. Enjoy it with an old-fashioned mixed grill.

Quality	♟♟♟♟♟
Value	★★★★
Rating	92
Grapes	shiraz 50%; grenache 50%
Region	McLaren Vale, SA
Cellar	🍾 4
Alc./Vol.	14.5%
RRP	$19.95 ⬚

d'Arenberg The Dead Arm

Dead Arm is a disease of old vines that kills one part of the vine, while preserving the rest to produce intensely concentrated fruit. d'Arenberg's shiraz vines so afflicted are the basis of this flagship wine.
CURRENT RELEASE 2003   A powerful essay in McLaren Vale shiraz, but a wine of some elegance, not just brute power. The nose has deep blackberry, dark-chocolate, game and smoky/spicy oak aromas. That oak is a definite component, but we don't think it's overdone. In the mouth it has deliciously ripe, refined fruit that's sweet and intense. The palate has classy balance and great texture now, but we think its best days are ahead of it. Try it with racks of lamb.

Quality	♟♟♟♟♟
Value	★★★⟩
Rating	95
Grapes	shiraz
Region	McLaren Vale, SA
Cellar	➡2–12
Alc./Vol.	14.5%
RRP	$60.00

d'Arenberg The Laughing Magpie

The 'laughing magpies' of the d'Arenberg vineyard are two tame kookaburras that frequent the vineyard. They were so-named by winemaker Chester Osborn's two young daughters.
CURRENT RELEASE 2004   Some shiraz-viognier blends overdo the viognier component, giving red wines a disconcertingly strong aroma of apricots and musky perfume. The Laughing Magpie is at the other end of the spectrum; viognier makes a barely perceptible contribution, adding a whisper of spice and a floral note to a core of black-fruit, olive-like and earthy aromas. The middleweight palate is flavoursome and persistent with a solid backbone of ripe tannins. Good with a lamb tagine.

Quality	♟♟♟♟♟
Value	★★★★
Rating	94
Grapes	shiraz; viognier
Region	McLaren Vale, SA
Cellar	🍾 5+
Alc./Vol.	14.5%
RRP	$30.00

De Bortoli Reserve Release Syrah

Quality	♟ ♟ ♟ ♟ ♟
Value	★ ★ ★ ★
Rating	96
Grapes	shiraz
Region	Yarra Valley, Vic.
Cellar	▮ 5
Alc./Vol.	14.0%
RRP	$45.00

This is a very European-inspired take on Yarra Valley shiraz, which explains the use of the French term *syrah* on the label. It reflects winemaker Steve Webber's exploration of the French technique with shiraz and pinot noir.
CURRENT RELEASE 2004   This is well out of the mainstream of Australian shiraz, and as such it will be ignored by those who love the big porty styles – a good thing, as it means there'll be more for the rest of us! It's an earthy, musky, slightly wild expression of shiraz, with meaty and spicy notes woven through plummy fruit. The palate is silky and fine in texture, again with quite exotic smoky, musky flavours in excellent harmony with fine-grained tannins. Serve it with braised duck and prunes.

De Bortoli Sacred Hill Shiraz Cabernet

Quality	♟ ♟ ♟ ♟
Value	★ ★ ★ ★ ⸱
Rating	88
Grapes	shiraz; cabernet sauvignon
Region	Riverina, NSW
Cellar	▮ 1
Alc./Vol.	13.5%
RRP	$6.99

We've said it before elsewhere, but why buy anonymous, inexpensive cleanskin wines of unknown provenance, when a modest Riverina red like this offers so much. De Bortoli's Sacred Hills are perennial bargains for easy everyday supping.
CURRENT RELEASE 2005   The nose has earthy/berry aromas, touched lightly by hints of spice. In the mouth there's plenty of smooth flavour, and a balanced hint of fruit sweetness stops well short of cloying. It finishes soft and easy. A bargain. Drink it with meat pies in front of the TV.

De Bortoli Windy Peak Shiraz Viognier

Quality	♟ ♟ ♟ ♟
Value	★ ★ ★ ★
Rating	89
Grapes	shiraz; viognier
Region	various, Vic.
Cellar	▮ 3
Alc./Vol.	14.0%
RRP	$13.00 Ⓢ ⬗

The shiraz-viognier blends just keep on comin'. This is one of the lower-priced versions and it shows viognier's influence without being too showy. The Windy Peak range has a new label which is a lot classier looking than the old one.
CURRENT RELEASE 2003   This has a restrained nose of plummy fruit with subtle notes of exotic, earthy spice. Viognier is more apparent in the mouth, where a soft, stone-fruity touch adds another layer of interest to red-berry-like shiraz fruit. It's medium-bodied and there are no sharp edges to it at all. Try it with a rustic terrine and crusty bread.

Deakin Estate Shiraz

Standards have been constantly improving in the Murray Valley's vineyards over the past decade. Some wines punch well above their weight, and others remain in the cheap-and-cheerful category. Deakin Estate Shiraz sits in the latter camp.

CURRENT RELEASE 2004 The first thing you notice here is a typically earthy Riverland-type aroma but there's a bit more to it. There are touches of plummy fruit, seasoned with mixed spice and slightly raw oak, and it tastes smooth and satisfying with fruit flavour dominating the palate and light dry tannins in support. Try it with a Chilean-style meat pie (empanada).

Quality	
Value	★★★★
Rating	**88**
Grapes	shiraz
Region	Murray Valley, SA
Cellar	2
Alc./Vol.	14.0%
RRP	$10.75

Elderton Command Shiraz

'Your wish is my command' used to be the slogan behind the naming of this shiraz, which is the flagship of Elderton's range. It's an unapologetically full-on shiraz, which stretches the use of oak, and often alcohol, to the limits.

CURRENT RELEASE 2002 The colour is deep and starting to show some maturity; the bouquet is completely taken over by timber-like oak aromas, together with mocha/chocolate characters derived from oak maturation. It's a gutsy, big-boned wine with a lot of presence but not much grace or elegance. No doubt the oakiness of the bouquet would be subdued by prolonged aeration – or further bottle-age. It's very impressive in a perverse way. While not to our personal tastes, we acknowledge that thousands will love it. It would work with any aged hard cheeses.

Quality	
Value	★★½
Rating	**95**
Grapes	shiraz
Region	Barossa Valley, SA
Cellar	2–12+
Alc./Vol.	14.5%
RRP	$95.00

Elderton Friends Shiraz

Nice that the Ashmeads of Elderton consider all their growers as friends! The Friends group of wines are sourced from other people's vineyards, but still in the Barossa Valley.

CURRENT RELEASE 2003 This tastes as though it has residual sugar, although it could be just the ultra-ripe fruit and high alcohol. It's a good wine at an attractive price: spicy, charcuterie/meaty aromas, turning sweet and lush on the palate. It's soft and quite well balanced, although the finish falls away a bit soon. It would suit roast buffalo fillet.

Quality	
Value	★★★★
Rating	**89**
Grapes	shiraz
Region	Barossa Valley, SA
Cellar	4+
Alc./Vol.	14.5%
RRP	$20.00

elgo estate shiraz

Quality	▼▼▼▼
Value	★★★
Rating	88
Grapes	shiraz
Region	Strathbogie Ranges, Vic.
Cellar	▮ 7+
Alc./Vol.	14.5%
RRP	$26.00 ⬥

how far do you take this fashion of dropping the capital letter off everything? it seems just a wee bit affected to us. elgo estate is at longwood in the strathbogies and has substantial vineyard plantings on granitic soils in three locations.

CURRENT RELEASE 2004   The style of this wine is a touch lighter-bodied than most modern shiraz, and together with its high acidity this suggests the fruit was grown in a cool vineyard site. The colour is nice and deep; the nose is all about spicy, meaty and berry aromas that are most attractive, but then the palate is a trifle unbalanced. No doubt the acidity would taste more balanced when it's drunk with food: we suggest a hearty beef casserole.

Euroa Creeks Reserve Shiraz

Quality	▼▼▼▼▼
Value	★★★★
Rating	96
Grapes	shiraz
Region	central Vic.
Cellar	▮ 10+
Alc./Vol.	14.5%
RRP	$42.00

Made by David Lloyd at Eldridge Estate on the Mornington Peninsula. The 2002 was the first vintage; just 250 cases were made of the '04.

CURRENT RELEASE 2002   This is a delicious red. It still has a deep red–purple colour and the taste is soft, round and smooth with lovely balance and ample sweet fruit. It's plummy and is already showing some complexity. The palate is deep, layered and well structured, with plenty of backbone. An exciting new star in the Victorian shiraz firmament. Serve with scaloppine limone.

Quality	▼▼▼▼
Value	★★★
Rating	90
Grapes	shiraz
Region	central Vic.
Cellar	➤ 2–12+
Alc./Vol.	14.5%
RRP	$42.00 ⬥

CURRENT RELEASE 2004   The colour is dense and youthfully purple; the wine is leaner and spicier than previous vintages, with a nettley herbal overtone, together with aniseed and plum-cake aromas. There's no lack of ripeness in the fruit. It has sweet fruit as well as lively acidity on palate. The tannins turn a shade hard on the finish. It needs more time. A pretty stylish red to team with vitello tonnato.

Faber Vineyard Reserve Shiraz

After making some excellent cooler-climate Western Australian wines while at Houghton, John Griffiths is now carrying the standard for the unequivocally hot Swan Valley. He's a lover of big, soft, warm-climate reds, and believes he can reveal a new face of Swan Valley wine. CURRENT RELEASE 2003 A statuesque shiraz that is quite oaky in youth but surely has a long life ahead of it. Deep purple–red hue, toasty oak and ultra-ripe blackberry, prune and chocolate aromas, then a concentrated palate of great depth and gravity, held together by a good tannin backbone. A touch less oak would have been even better. Try steak and kidney pie.

Quality	♟♟♟♟
Value	★★★
Rating	91
Grapes	shiraz
Region	Swan Valley, WA
Cellar	➥1–10
Alc./Vol.	14.5%
RRP	$40.00 🍾

Faber Vineyard Riche Shiraz

Winemaker John Griffiths uses the word 'riche' to signify a red wine that has been subjected to the *saignée* method, which means a proportion of juice was bled off the tank before the fermentation began, concentrating what is left behind. This is supposed to give extra richness and tannin. And it works!
CURRENT RELEASE 2001 Quite a savoury, oak-driven red, this is medium- to full-bodied and grippingly tannic, with a pronounced drying aftertaste. The palate is thick, chewy and dense, and the tannins still need time to soften. Serve it with hard, aged cheeses.

Quality	♟♟♟◗
Value	★★★◗
Rating	88
Grapes	shiraz
Region	Swan Valley, WA
Cellar	🍾6+
Alc./Vol.	13.5%
RRP	$16.50 (cellar door)

CURRENT RELEASE 2004 The nose is very smoky from charred oak, which tends to dominate at this juncture. The palate is fleshy and quite high in tannin; it's a less grippingly full-on wine than the 2001 but still formidable. Vanilla, dark berries, toasty barrels – a surprising wine. We'd suggest a hearty meat casserole.

Quality	♟♟♟◗
Value	★★★◗
Rating	88
Grapes	shiraz
Region	Swan Valley, WA
Cellar	🍾5
Alc./Vol.	14.0%
RRP	$16.50 (cellar door)

Ferngrove Dragon Shiraz

Quality	♟♟♟♟
Value	★★★
Rating	93
Grapes	shiraz
Region	Frankland River, WA
Cellar	➡2–10
Alc./Vol.	14.5%
RRP	$25.00

This wine's name comes from the dragon orchid that grows in this part of south-west Western Australia. It's present in a tract of old-growth forest preserved from development at Ferngrove.
CURRENT RELEASE 2004   There's a distinctive smoky quality to this blackish-purple shiraz. The nose also shows peppery notes, dark-cherry fruit, dried herb and cedar aromas – very savoury rather than sweet in fruit. In the mouth it's densely packed with smoky-berry fruit and it has attractive succulence thanks to a well-measured fruit-tannin-acid equation. After some time in bottle it should suit shanks of lamb braised in full-flavoured red wine.

Four Emus Shiraz

Quality	♟♟♟♟
Value	★★★★★
Rating	90
Grapes	shiraz
Region	not stated
Cellar	▮2
Alc./Vol.	13.5%
RRP	$9.99 ⑤ ≋

Foreign markets seem to have an insatiable appetite for clichéd Aussie labels. Who knows what will come along next in the way of Aussie fauna gracing wine labels?
CURRENT RELEASE 2004   This is a very acceptable red on a budget with attractively deep colour and an appealing ripe, sweet-fruited nose. Plummy aromas and spice are the main elements, and the palate follows the formula of smooth, agreeable flavour and texture leading through to a very soft finish. It's an informal red that's not as reliant on sweetness as some in this price range. Serve it with emu – no, better make that chicken braised in red wine.

Fox Creek Reserve Shiraz

Quality	♟♟♟♟
Value	★★★
Rating	93
Grapes	shiraz
Region	McLaren Vale, SA
Cellar	➡3–10+
Alc./Vol.	14.5%
RRP	$70.00 ≋

Fox Creek is one of the new generation of McLaren Vale enterprises offering the sort of powerfully flavoured red wines that the world wants.
CURRENT RELEASE 2004   An impenetrable, purplish, glass-staining colour suggests great levels of fruit extract in this immature McLaren Vale shiraz, and the nose confirms it with spicy-blackberry, funky-earthy and vanillin-oak aromas of great concentration. In the mouth it's a big, generously constructed red that's a bit muscular and obvious now, but we reckon that it will develop into a velvet-textured, complex, rich mouthful with enough bottle-age. Firm tannins offer a very solid foundation to it all. A good match for braised oxtail.

Gemtree Uncut Shiraz

All of the Gemtree wines are named after a precious stone, e.g. Obsidian, Cinnabar and Bloodstone. This one is Uncut, which could mean the wine is a bit rough and ready, but we wouldn't agree with that interpretation at all. Maker: Mike Brown; viticulturalist: Melissa Brown.
CURRENT RELEASE 2004   This is a bread-and-butter shiraz that punches well above its weight. It won a gold medal at the 2005 Adelaide Wine Show. Dense colour, excellent concentration of plummy, meaty, earthy fruit coupled with toasty oak. There is a rather dominant barrel-ferment oaky meatiness that will become more integrated as it matures. Try it with chargrilled steak.

Quality	♥ ♥ ♥ ♥
Value	★ ★ ★ ★
Rating	90
Grapes	shiraz
Region	McLaren Vale, SA
Cellar	▮ 6
Alc./Vol.	14.5%
RRP	$20.00 ⑤ ⊗

Giaconda Warner Vineyard Shiraz

In the space of a few short years Giaconda's shiraz has staked a claim as one of Australia's best. A totally different creature to the big South Australian style, it combines subtlety and complexity with great presence.
CURRENT RELEASE 2004   A deeply coloured shiraz with a complex smoky/Frenchy nose of forest berries, plums, spices and savoury peppery notes. It's smooth and subtle in the mouth with great depth, but not great weight, ending long and fine with understated sandy tannins. It needs at least a couple of years' bottle-age, then it will be a perfect companion to Cantonese roast duck.

Quality	♥ ♥ ♥ ♥ ♥
Value	★ ★ ★
Rating	96
Grapes	shiraz
Region	Beechworth, Vic.
Cellar	▬ 2–8+
Alc./Vol.	13.5%
RRP	$87.00

Grampians Estate Streeton Reserve Shiraz

The Guthrie family's grazing property Thermopylae and small vineyard were almost completely burnt in the January 2006 Grampians bushfire. Happily, they are re-planting what has in a short space of time proven to be a great site. Maker: Simon Clayfield. Cellar door is at Garden Gully vineyard, Great Western.
CURRENT RELEASE 2003   This winner of three trophies and four gold medals is a stunning shiraz in a style that shouts Great Western. Very ripe yet spicy aromas – big but elegant at the same time – strikingly perfumed and flavoured, this is an amazing success from what were quite young vines. It has great structure: abundant tannins run the full length of the palate and provide backbone without heaviness or excess grip. Wholly delicious! Serve it with pink roast lamb leg.

Quality	♥ ♥ ♥ ♥ ♥
Value	★ ★ ★ ★
Rating	95
Grapes	shiraz
Region	Grampians, Vic.
Cellar	▮ 12+
Alc./Vol.	14.6%
RRP	$55.00 ▮
	(cellar door)

Grant Burge Miamba Shiraz

Quality	🍷🍷🍷🍷🍷
Value	★★★★★
Rating	92
Grapes	shiraz
Region	Barossa Valley, SA
Cellar	🍾 5
Alc./Vol.	14.0%
RRP	$20.00 ⑤

That man Burge just keeps on making better and better wine – and more and more of it! If you want an example of exactly what Barossa shiraz tastes like, without the layers of oak that usually accompany the better ones, you could do worse than to try Miamba.

CURRENT RELEASE 2004   This is a lovely, genuine, fruit-driven Barossa shiraz, scented with sweet, ripe plum and cherry and a saucing of melted dark chocolate. There's a hint of charcuterie, too. It has appealing depth and grip in the mouth, preceded by a sweet fruit mid-palate. Then a clean, firm tannin finish. Hard to imagine better value for money, really. A good match with Barossa mettwurst.

Groom Barossa Shiraz

Quality	🍷🍷🍷🍷
Value	★★⁺
Rating	89
Grapes	shiraz
Region	Barossa Valley, SA
Cellar	🍾 5
Alc./Vol.	13.8%
RRP	$48.00

This is a new label to us. The only information we have is that East End Cellars of Adelaide are retailing it.

CURRENT RELEASE 2004   If you like very sweetly fruited warm-climate shiraz, and don't mind a bit of oak, this could be for you. The aromas are dominated by new oak at this stage; we'd love to see it with less of that. The palate continues the same theme, except that far from being hardened by the oak it's incredibly soft, sweet and seductive. The texture is impressive. But whether it's the sort of wine you want to drink is a personal matter. We have our reservations. Food choice: grana padano.

Hanging Rock Cambrian Rise Shiraz

Quality	🍷🍷🍷🍷
Value	★★★
Rating	91
Grapes	shiraz
Region	Heathcote, Vic.
Cellar	🍾 4
Alc./Vol.	14.5%
RRP	$27.00

The Heathcote region is starting to realise its promise with shiraz, although we see too many porty, raisined, alcoholic wines that in our view do the region's reputation no good at all. Hanging Rock's Heathcote shirazes always have a much better sense of equilibrium.

CURRENT RELEASE 2003   Asian spice and slightly jammy loganberry fruit fill the nose with appetising, succulent aromas. In the mouth it shows satiny berry fruit that's perhaps a trifle hollow and a wee bit short, but the flavour is kept fresh and tangy by good acidity and fine, dry tannins. Try it with lamb loin chops.

Hanging Rock Heathcote Shiraz

Hanging Rock's base vineyard, beside the mystical geological formation of the same name, is decidedly cool climate – not good country for shiraz. These Hanging Rock reds are sourced further afield in the emerging high-quality red wine region of Heathcote.
CURRENT RELEASE 2003   A rich Heathcote shiraz with a nose of dark chocolate, coconut and sweet forest berries. It's full-bodied and very ripe in flavour with amazing depth and length of flavour. It has a slightly fumy edge of alcohol to it, but it fits the style. There's some oaky grip as well as grainy tannins at the end, and it has a warm afterglow of aromatic berry flavour to finish. Serve it with red-wine-braised oxtail.

Quality	♟ ♟ ♟ ♟ ♟
Value	★ ★ ★
Rating	92
Grapes	shiraz
Region	Heathcote, Vic.
Cellar	🍷 8
Alc./Vol.	15.0%
RRP	$60.00

Hanging Rock Rowbottoms Shiraz

This wine is from the Treehouse vineyard, an isolated plot on Rowbottoms Track in the ironbark forest west of Heathcote township. Its low-yielding vines give distinctive shiraz.
CURRENT RELEASE 2003   This has good depth of colour and a complex nose of dried spices, plum, red berries, vanilla and eucalypt forest. It has good concentration in the mouth, more dense and husky than Hanging Rock's Cambrian Rise of the same year, and there is a touch of ironstone to its ripe-berry flavours. Tannins are grippy and chunky, and it finishes with good length. Cellar it mid-term, then match it with daube of beef.

Quality	♟ ♟ ♟ ♟ ♟
Value	★ ★ ★ ★
Rating	92
Grapes	shiraz
Region	Heathcote, Vic.
Cellar	🍷 6
Alc./Vol.	14.0%
RRP	$33.00

Hardys Eileen Hardy Shiraz

Eileen Hardy has been a Hardys flagship since 1970. It began as a label for the red wine Hardys considered the best of the vintage, irrespective of the grape variety. Thus the first wine was a shiraz but it switched to cabernet sauvignon the following year. Now it's established as the best shiraz of the year.
CURRENT RELEASE 2002   A deep, dense wine with a peaty/oaky nose that suggests old highland malt whisky. The palate is rather unyielding with plum and oak-derived flavours that lack generosity, and woody tannins and a slightly metallic touch dominate the finish. It's very concentrated, but to us it lacks the flesh and generosity we expect in a McLaren Vale flagship wine. It will undoubtedly live for many years but will the fruit last? Cellar it, then serve it with roast leg of lamb.

Quality	♟ ♟ ♟ ♟
Value	★ ★ ⸱
Rating	91
Grapes	shiraz
Region	McLaren Vale, SA
Cellar	⬤—2–8+
Alc./Vol.	14.0%
RRP	$96.00

Hardys Nottage Hill Shiraz

Quality	♟ ♟ ♟ ៛
Value	★★★★
Rating	89
Grapes	shiraz
Region	not stated
Cellar	▮ 3
Alc./Vol.	13.5%
RRP	$10.60 ⑤

The lower-priced shirazes of the Hardys group of wineries take a lot of beating for value. Nottage Hill isn't just another inexpensive red; it has real depth and personality. A wine for Australians to be proud of.
CURRENT RELEASE 2004   Good depth of colour here, and the nose has clean, ripe loganberry-like varietal aroma. Oak is subliminal and the palate has more than adequate intensity and length of flavour. The finish is soft and easy. Drink it with moussaka.

Hardys Oomoo Shiraz

Quality	♟ ♟ ♟ ♟ ៛
Value	★★★★★
Rating	92
Grapes	shiraz
Region	McLaren Vale, SA
Cellar	▮ 3
Alc./Vol.	14.0%
RRP	$17.00 ⑤

Sometimes over the years, we've seen a reasonably priced and very high-quality red launched with great fanfare, only to see the quality fall away in subsequent vintages. With Oomoo, that hasn't happened; in fact, Oomoo seems to get better each year. Oomoo may be a resurrection of a Hardys label from the 1800s, but we reckon the modern wine would be much better than its predecessor.
CURRENT RELEASE 2004   This is right on form again in the quality stakes, and the price makes it an incredible bargain. Intense blackberry, spice and peppery aromas are seasoned lightly with sweet oak, and the ripely flavoured palate is smooth, clean, long, and in perfect balance. One of the best buys of the year. Enjoy it with barbecued lamb kebabs.

Haselgrove HRS Reserve Shiraz

Quality	♟ ♟ ♟ ♟ ៛
Value	★★★★
Rating	92
Grapes	shiraz
Region	McLaren Vale, SA
Cellar	▮ 6
Alc./Vol.	14.0%
RRP	$25.00 ⊗

Haselgrove is an old Australian wine name, but in its present incarnation it has a slightly confusing profile with many different wines across a range that runs from around $10 to $25. Wine quality is generally good.
CURRENT RELEASE 2003   This shiraz has a dense colour and a very good, mainstream nose of syrupy dark berries with a whisper of toasted coconut from oak input. The palate has deep fruity/meaty richness and very smooth texture with a juicy balance of acidity and tannins. It finishes with a light grip and good length. Try it with roasted winter vegetables and crusty bread.

Hazyblur Kangaroo Island Shiraz

The idyllic South Australian holiday spot of Kangaroo Island now has an assortment of vineyards vying for the tourist dollar. Wine quality is varied, but the best are intense and flavoursome.
CURRENT RELEASE 2004   This has a big blackberry-jam nose with some slightly porty overtones. Touches of spice and dark chocolate, and a balanced overlay of sweet American oak give it real impact. The mouth-filling rich fruit flavour is backed by drying tannins. A big obvious red but one with hearty appeal. We'd suggest pairing it with beef and winter vegetable casserole.

Quality	🍷🍷🍷🍷
Value	★★★⟩
Rating	90
Grapes	shiraz
Region	Kangaroo Island, SA
Cellar	🍾 10
Alc./Vol.	14.5%
RRP	$23.10

Hazyblur McLaren Vale Shiraz

'The vines so drenched with sunlight, appeared to be radiating rays themselves. A magical sight to experience: a hallowed blurry haze.' Hence the name. The wines show the definite influence of lots of sunshine.
CURRENT RELEASE 2004   This is a very ripe, almost fruit-sweet red wine that smells of black plums and berries with a touch of peppery spice and an overlay of dark chocolate. In the mouth it's velvety in texture with spicy, ripe flavour and plenty of sticky fruit character. The palate has good length and it finishes warm with briary dry tannins. Good with a suitably sticky beef dish, say braised oxtail.

Quality	🍷🍷🍷🍷🍷
Value	★★★★
Rating	92
Grapes	shiraz
Region	Wrattonbully, SA
Cellar	🍾 8
Alc./Vol.	14.5%
RRP	$25.60

Heathcote Estate Shiraz

In only a few short years this great Victorian shiraz has become one of those impressive wines that we can't wait to taste each year. Made without compromise, it's fast becoming a regional benchmark.
CURRENT RELEASE 2004   There were a few stewed, alcoholic and soupy '04 Heathcote shiraz reds, but this isn't one of them. It has a nose of blackberry, mocha, spice, vanilla, and charry oak. The palate is full-bodied but also smoothly textured and fine, with deep, layered flavour, excellent length and ripe, beautifully integrated tannins. Try it with beef fillet.

Quality	🍷🍷🍷🍷🍷
Value	★★★★
Rating	96
Grapes	shiraz
Region	Heathcote, Vic.
Cellar	🍾 10+
Alc./Vol.	14.0%
RRP	$45.00

Henschke Henry's Seven

Quality 🍷🍷🍷🍷½
Value ★★★½
Rating 93
Grapes shiraz 60%; grenache 30%; mourvèdre 5%; viognier 5%
Region Barossa Valley, SA
Cellar 4
Alc./Vol. 15.0%
RRP $32.00

Henry's Seven commemorates Keyneton's original seven-acre vineyard planted near where the Henschke winery now stands. Henry Evans planted it in 1853, but after his death in 1868 his wife, a committed teetotaller, closed the winery and pulled out all the vines.

CURRENT RELEASE 2004 There's only 5 per cent viognier in this red, but it shows. Floral, apricot- and plum-brandy aromas confirm its presence, and some raspberry-like fruit chimes in, adding attractive complexity. The palate is smooth and jammy with good length of flavour and a persistent finish. Tannins are ripe and relatively unassertive. Satisfying with a sticky veal shank dish.

Henschke Hill of Grace

Quality 🍷🍷🍷🍷🍷
Value ★★
Rating 97
Grapes shiraz
Region Eden Valley, SA
Cellar 10+
Alc./Vol. 14.5%
RRP $500.00

Hill of Grace occupies a space alongside Penfolds Grange as Australia's most collected red wine. Unlike Grange, which is a multi-regional blend, Hill of Grace is a single-estate wine sourced from an isolated vineyard full of doddering, wizened old vines in the hills near Eden Valley. Fruit quality is usually superb, translating into an Australian classic.

CURRENT RELEASE 2001 Those ancient Hill of Grace vines make an eloquent statement. The bouquet is lush, essency and still youthful, smelling of summer pudding, black fruits, spice, vanilla and sweet soy. Beautifully handled oak makes a balanced counterpoint. It tastes deliciously concentrated but very fine, finishing with poised tannins and a super-long aftertaste. Serve it with venison and wild mushrooms.

Previous outstanding vintages: 1980, '82, '84, '86, '88, '90,'91, '92, '94, '96, '98, '99

Henschke Keyneton Estate Euphonium

Quality 🍷🍷🍷🍷½
Value ★★★
Rating 94
Grapes shiraz
Region Barossa Valley, SA
Cellar 6
Alc./Vol. 14.5%
RRP $40.00

The euphonium in question is a musical instrument kept at the Henschke winery as a memorial to the Henschke Family Brass Band that entertained locals many years ago.

CURRENT RELEASE 2002 One of the best Keyneton Estates in years, this has succulent blackberry and raspberry-like fruit, with some sweet oak folded in seamlessly. Peppery/spicy notes season it well, and everything is in fine balance. The medium-weight palate is smooth and long with integrated, ripe tannins providing exactly the right balance. A good choice with lamb kebabs.

Previous outstanding vintages: 1988, '90, '91, '93, '94, '96, '98

Henschke Mount Edelstone

Mount Edelstone is one of Henschke's two most famous vineyards; the other is Hill of Grace. Mount Edelstone occupies a special place for many reasons including the age of its vines (nearly 95 years), and the fact that it was first produced as a single-vineyard wine in 1952 at a time when most Aussie red wines were blends.
CURRENT RELEASE 2003   Mount Edelstone has recovered from a quality hiccup a few years ago, and the '03 measures up well to the estate's lofty reputation. It has great purity of old-vine fruit character, with intense dark-berry and plum fruit, lovely sweet spice, and subtle oak. The palate is seamless and long with ripe tannins and a lingering aromatic finish. Serve it at a big-occasion dinner of roast beef.
Previous outstanding vintages: 1978, '80, '84, '86, '88, '90, '91, '92, '93, 94, '96, 2001, '02

Quality	♟♟♟♟♟
Value	★★★
Rating	97
Grapes	shiraz
Region	Eden Valley, SA
Cellar	➥1–10+
Alc./Vol.	14.5%
RRP	$86.00

Henschke Tappa Pass Shiraz

A number of new labels have appeared from the previously conservative Henschke winery in recent years, and more grapes are being sourced from the nearby Barossa Valley. Tappa Pass is a 'special' made from distinguished vineyard sites in the Tappa Pass and Ebenezer districts of the Barossa.
CURRENT RELEASE 2002   This deep-purplish shiraz smells superb: sumptuous blackberry, juicy black plum, subtle spice and restrained oak aromas. The palate is velvety and chocolatey rich, finishing deliciously long. It doesn't go into blockbuster territory, despite having relatively high alcohol. Instead it offers complex, ripe flavours while retaining balance and restraint. Great with fillet of beef.

Quality	♟♟♟♟♟
Value	★★★★
Rating	97
Grapes	shiraz
Region	Barossa Valley, SA
Cellar	8+
Alc./Vol.	15.0%
RRP	$55.00

Hewitson Ned & Henry's Shiraz

The Hewitson red wines are made to express old Barossa vineyards without too much messing around with oak and winemaking tricks. The results speak for themselves.
CURRENT RELEASE 2004   A mellow Barossa red that stays well away from the bigger-is-better malaise that grips many these days. The nose evokes spices like nutmeg and cloves, giving a savoury touch to focused cherry and black fruits, and a hint of dark chocolate. In the mouth it's a velvety, seamless statement of Barossa shiraz, medium- to full-bodied with great depth and presence. Beautifully integrated fine-grained tannins complete the picture. Try it with venison pie.

Quality	♟♟♟♟♟
Value	★★★★
Rating	94
Grapes	shiraz
Region	Barossa Valley, SA
Cellar	8
Alc./Vol.	14.5%
RRP	$25.00

Huntington Estate Special Reserve Shiraz Bin FB19

Quality	♥ ♥ ♥ ♥
Value	★ ★ ★
Rating	90
Grapes	shiraz
Region	Mudgee, NSW
Cellar	▮ 10
Alc./Vol.	13.5%
RRP	$31.50 Ⓢ ▮

The new owners of Huntington, Tim and Connie Stevens of Abercorn, have vowed to maintain the traditional style of Huntington wines, which have always been subtly different from those of next door Abercorn. Maker: Susie Roberts.
CURRENT RELEASE 2001   This is a good Huntington shiraz without being a top vintage: it's a bit drying on the palate and falls ever so slightly short. The bouquet offers chocolate, earth, plum and subtle spice. A big but somewhat bony warmer-year wine, it would go well with barbecued beef sausages.

Ingoldby Shiraz

Quality	♥ ♥ ♥ ♥
Value	★ ★ ★ ↓
Rating	89
Grapes	shiraz
Region	McLaren Vale, SA
Cellar	▮ 6+
Alc./Vol.	14.0%
RRP	$26.00 Ⓢ

McLaren Vale used to be referred to as the middle palate of Australian wine, and this is a pretty good example. Maker: Matt O'Leary.
CURRENT RELEASE 2004   A rich, fleshy, chocolatey palate is the hallmark of this maker's style. It's fully ripe tasting and oak has been used generously. Plum, herb and chocolate flavours abound in the plush palate. Ample soft tannins complete the picture with some acidity showing on the finish. We'd suggest matching it with porterhouse steak.

Innocent Bystander Shiraz Viognier

Quality	♥ ♥ ♥ ♥
Value	★ ★ ★ ★
Rating	88
Grapes	shiraz; viognier
Region	various, Vic.
Cellar	▮ 4
Alc./Vol.	13.5%
RRP	$21.00 ⧈

Phil Sexton (of Giant Steps) is known for thinking up intriguing names for his wines. He explains that this one reflects his feelings on a wine industry dominated by huge multi-national companies and a retailing environment dominated by massive store chains. There is more than an echo of Michael Leunig in it, too.
CURRENT RELEASE 2004   A clean, well-made, easygoing red without great depth or complexity but lots of free-flowing easy-drinking charm. The colour is excellent; the aromas are of plum and mixed spices. It's fruit-driven and just falls away a little at the finish. A very good commercial style to serve with tasty pork sausages.

Izway Bruce Shiraz

It's almost as though the Izway wines are private wines made for home consumption. They have little dedications on the back labels that may mean something to the makers, but not to the public at large; such as: 'Traditionally, Bruce is a man of very few words.' Que?

CURRENT RELEASE 2004   We're not sure who drinks all these humungous, treacley Barossa reds, but someone apparently does. This is like a boiled-down essence of wine: it's dense, thick and over-the-top concentrated. At least it's not over-oaked: the vivid blackberry, cassis, mulberry-like fruit is given free expression. For all its (over)ripeness, the tannins seem slightly harsh at the finish. A wine to cellar – and throw away the key! If you do drink this, you'll need a slab of aged reggiano.

Quality	♟♟♟♟
Value	★★★
Rating	90
Grapes	shiraz
Region	Barossa Valley, SA
Cellar	➥4–10+
Alc./Vol.	15.5%
RRP	$37.00 🍾

Jamiesons Run Country Selection Shiraz

The first Jamiesons Run wine was a 1985 vintage blend of cabernet sauvignon, shiraz, malbec, merlot and cabernet franc. Its success was such that it spawned a whole range of Jamiesons Run wines, both red and white.

CURRENT RELEASE 2003   A good middle-of-the-road shiraz in the easy-drinking house style. It smells of ripe plums and berries touched by spice and a layer of slightly raw oak which isn't quite integrated yet. The smooth, mainstream palate has satisfying intensity and soft tannins finish things off well. Try it with good sausages.

Quality	♟♟♟♟
Value	★★★
Rating	90
Grapes	shiraz
Region	Coonawarra, SA
Cellar	🍷4
Alc./Vol.	14.0%
RRP	$22.00 ⑤

Jasper Hill Georgia's Paddock Shiraz

Jasper Hill's rare Heathcote reds have enjoyed cult status for years. In style they've evolved into bigger and bigger wines, and the hot, dry 2004 vintage has provided true whoppers.

CURRENT RELEASE 2004   This was our pick of the '04 Jasper Hills. It showed less raisiny, stewed, hot-vintage characters than some of its siblings, and while still a truly formidable critter it also had real complexity and interest. It smells of black plums, smoked meats, mint, Vegemite and spices, leading to a big, warmly alcoholic palate supported by butch tannins. It's not a red for wimps by any means. Give it age, then enjoy it with rare rump steak.

Quality	♟♟♟♟♟
Value	★★⌐
Rating	93
Grapes	shiraz
Region	Heathcote, Vic.
Cellar	➥3–10+
Alc./Vol.	15.0%
RRP	$90.00

Jim Barry The Armagh

Quality	♛ ♛ ♛ ♛ ♛
Value	★ ★ ⸕
Rating	95
Grapes	shiraz
Region	Clare Valley, SA
Cellar	⭢ 2–15
Alc./Vol.	15.5%
RRP	$185.00 🍾

The Armagh is one of those bigger-than-Ben-Hur types of red, a huge wine of amazing power.

CURRENT RELEASE 2002 The concentrated appearance sets the stage for a powerful, potently alcoholic nose reminiscent of raisins and prunes, spices and mint, blackberries and mocha – complex and challenging. In the mouth it's ultra-dense with roasted fruit character, spice and sweet oak flavours of great depth, length and impact. A firm underpinning of ripe tannins holds it all together, and there's a lingering warm, slightly fumy aftertaste. This is one of the better examples of the body-slamming mod-Oz shiraz type that has many adherents both here and in the US. Good with beef ribs.

Previous outstanding vintages: 1990, '91, '92, '93, '95, '96, '98, '99

Jim Barry The McRae Wood Shiraz

Quality	♛ ♛ ♛ ♛
Value	★ ★ ★
Rating	90
Grapes	shiraz
Region	Clare Valley, SA
Cellar	⭢ 2–8+
Alc./Vol.	15.5%
RRP	$29.25 🍾

The McRae Wood vineyard produces wine of more tight, structured character and herby flavour than the Clare Valley norm. The '02 shows the style well.

CURRENT RELEASE 2002 The pronounced minty qualities that have always marked McRae Wood Shiraz are here in good measure, but there seems to be more dense ripe-berry fruit than usual in this edition. Aromas and flavours of blackberries, mint, eucalypt, spices and vanillin oak are very concentrated, and it has plenty of alcoholic warmth. There's good palate length, but its firm finish borders on being a tad too astringent for us. Try it with roast lamb.

John Duval Entity Shiraz

Quality	♛ ♛ ♛ ♛ ♛
Value	★ ★ ★ ★ ⸕
Rating	97
Grapes	shiraz
Region	Barossa Valley, SA
Cellar	⭢ 2–10
Alc./Vol.	14.5%
RRP	$36.00

PENGUIN BEST RED WINE and BEST SHIRAZ

John Duval needs little introduction. As Penfolds chief red winemaker he oversaw the production of Australia's most famous wine, Grange, for 28 years. His own label continues to showcase his considerable skill with high-quality, old-vine grapes.

CURRENT RELEASE 2004 A wonderfully concentrated, yet elegant statement of Barossa shiraz, this wine is all class. Aromas of stewed plums, berries, spice, polished new leather, cedar and wood smoke are deliciously complex. All is harmony in the mouth too, with velvety texture, persistent flavour, seamless structure and a super-long finish. Delicious with fillet of beef.

Jones L.J. Shiraz

This old vineyard took on a new lease of life when Mandy Jones, Leanne Schoen and Arthur Jones took it over from their uncle, Les Jones, in 1998. Mandy makes wine both here and in France each year, and her Rutherglen table wines are usually regional high-points.
CURRENT RELEASE 2003 A concentrated warm-area nose has deep plum and blackberry-jam aromas, with a rich chocolatey touch. There's none of the portiness that sometimes marks Rutherglen reds, and the palate is big and generously flavoured, finishing with firm, ripe tannins. A robust red with a real countrified charm. Enjoy it with roasted lamb shanks.

Quality	♟♟♟♟
Value	★★★
Rating	91
Grapes	shiraz
Region	Rutherglen, Vic.
Cellar	▬1–10
Alc./Vol.	14.8%
RRP	$42.00

Journeys End Arrival Shiraz

Journeys End has a very large range of wines, with nearly all of them based on various permutations of McLaren Vale shiraz. Their avowed aim of over-delivering in terms of value for money is no idle claim; most of the wines are excellent buys.
CURRENT RELEASE 2003 A 'serious' McLaren Vale shiraz of real pedigree, this has a deep, liqueurish, high-toned aroma of super-ripe black fruits, spices, musk and charry oak. The palate is velvet-smooth and lusciously proportioned with complex, spicy shiraz flavour of great depth. It finishes ripe and long with very finely grained dry tannins and some alcoholic heat. We'd sugggest matching it with slow-roasted leg of lamb.

Quality	♟♟♟♟♟
Value	★★★┩
Rating	95
Grapes	shiraz
Region	McLaren Vale, SA
Cellar	▬2–12
Alc./Vol.	15.0%
RRP	$45.00

CURRENT RELEASE 2004 A deliciously concentrated shiraz with aromas of crushed blackberries, dark chocolate and bakery spice. It tastes concentrated and full, but it isn't so big and powerful that it's difficult to drink. On the contrary, it gets better with each glass, and its velvety texture dovetails with ripe dry tannins in excellent balance. A long-liver, but you could serve it now with roast beef.

Quality	♟♟♟♟♟
Value	★★★┩
Rating	96
Grapes	shiraz
Region	McLaren Vale, SA
Cellar	▬2–10+
Alc./Vol.	14.5%
RRP	$45.00

Journeys End Ascent Shiraz

Quality	♟♟♟♟♟
Value	★★★★
Rating	96
Grapes	shiraz
Region	McLaren Vale, SA
Cellar	➴1–10
Alc./Vol.	14.5%
RRP	$35.00

The name of this wine refers to Australia's gradual ascent to winemaking heights, which began with Gregory Blaxland's first export of Australian wine in 1822. Journeys End winemaker Ben Riggs has a good sense of history, which is a great thing.

CURRENT RELEASE 2004   Deep and dense in appearance, this young shiraz is packed with ripe black-plum fruit, dressed in chocolatey notes. Very typically McLaren Vale but without the strong earthiness that marks some of the region's reds. It's pure and concentrated with lush texture and long spicy flavours, finishing dry and savoury with very dry, fine-grained tannins. Try it with a navarin of lamb.

Journeys End Beginning Shiraz

Quality	♟♟♟♟♟
Value	★★★¹
Rating	94
Grapes	shiraz
Region	McLaren Vale, SA
Cellar	➴2–10
Alc./Vol.	15.0%
RRP	$25.00

Clone Wars. There is an international obsession among some viticulturists and obsessive wine buffs with the clones of particular grape vines. So for those interested, this wine is made from shiraz clones: SA 1654, SA 2626, SA 1127, SA 712 and BVRC30. So now you know. By the way, it tastes pretty good.

CURRENT RELEASE 2003   This is a deep-coloured, syrupy, strong type of McLaren Vale shiraz. It smells of chocolate-coated liqueur fruits, assorted spices, berries and has a slightly gamey touch. It's a big mouthful with a ripe, boiled-down sort of concentration. The mellow palate is big-flavoured with a warm finish and attractive grainy tannins. Perfect with a tasty corned beef meal.

Quality	♟♟♟♟♟
Value	★★★¹
Rating	93
Grapes	shiraz
Region	McLaren Vale, SA
Cellar	▮8+
Alc./Vol.	14.5%
RRP	$25.00

CURRENT RELEASE 2004   The Journeys End red wines have impressed us very much in the five years since they arrived on the market. This is typically characterful: a deep-coloured shiraz with a big nose of blackberries, sweet spice and gravelly soil. It tastes ripe and profound with unctuous mouth-feel, spicy-berry flavour, fine-grained tannins and a long finish. A high-quality McLaren Vale shiraz to serve with crumbed veal cutlets.

Kangarilla Road Shiraz

What could be simpler or more logical than naming your winery after the road it's on? Not everyone is that lucky: you could find yourself on Flyblown Wombat Road or, as one memorable New Zealander did, Swamp Road. Makers: Kevin O'Brien and Mike Brown.

CURRENT RELEASE 2003   Lots of bang for your bucks here. Pepper/spice fruit and toasty oak combine to give an appealing bouquet, while the palate is rich and fleshy, laden with melted Club chocolate and sweet blackberry flavours. It has grip and density: a solid, robust red that could take some cellaring, or serve it now with barbecued kangaroo.

Quality	♥ ♥ ♥ ♥
Value	★★★★ꜝ
Rating	91
Grapes	shiraz
Region	McLaren Vale, SA
Cellar	▮ 8+
Alc./Vol.	14.5%
RRP	$21.50 ⑤

Katnook Estate Prodigy Shiraz

One of the several meanings of the word prodigy is: 'a child of precocious genius'. The implication is that the wine will develop into something special if you look after it properly – in your cellar. Maker: Wayne Stehbens.

CURRENT RELEASE 2002   This is a confusing wine. It is somewhat forward in development and seems to have spent a lot of time in barrel. There are some leafy/minty aromas – possibly because the '02 season was a very cool one – and yet there are some very ripe flavours as well, such as fruitcake and chocolate. Meaty, earthy and olive-oil characters also chime in. The palate is thick and chewy with lots of tannin. It's an acquired taste. Try it with hard cheeses like parmesan.

Quality	♥ ♥ ♥ ♥
Value	★★★ꜝ
Rating	90
Grapes	shiraz
Region	Coonawarra, SA
Cellar	▬1–8+
Alc./Vol.	14.0%
RRP	$100.00 ▮

Kingston Estate Shiraz

Kingston Estate takes its name from the town where it's located: Kingston-on-Murray. The family wine business was started by proprietor Bill Moularadellis's father, Sarantos. And they named a wine after him, too.

CURRENT RELEASE 2005   A very appealing red for the modest price, without the greenness or excessive sweetness you taste in many cheaper Aussie reds these days. The colour is deep and youthful, the aromas remind of licorice and blackberry jam, while the palate is lively, lean and perhaps lacks flesh, but is enjoyable to drink young. Take it to a barbecue.

Quality	♥ ♥ ♥
Value	★★★ꜝ
Rating	86
Grapes	shiraz
Region	Adelaide Plains & Clare Valley, SA
Cellar	▮ 3
Alc./Vol.	14.5%
RRP	$13.00 ⑤

Knappstein Shiraz

Quality	▼▼▼▼
Value	★★★★ᐟ
Rating	92
Grapes	shiraz
Region	Clare Valley, SA
Cellar	🍷 10+
Alc./Vol.	14.0%
RRP	$21.00 Ⓢ

Knappstein is part of the Lion Nathan group since Petaluma was taken over by that company. Former winemaker Andrew Hardy is now general manager of the Lion wine group, while Paul Smith has taken over as winemaker at Knappstein.

CURRENT RELEASE 2003 A generously flavoured red in typical Clare fashion. Nice deep colour; rich, properly ripe chocolate, aniseed, plum and vanilla aromas; excellent depth of palate flavour with a little fieriness that is typical of the area. It's a vigorous wine with plenty of tannin lending a final grip, and will age well. It also drinks well now with rare rump steak.

Langmeil Valley Floor Shiraz

Quality	▼▼▼▼▼
Value	★★★
Rating	93
Grapes	shiraz
Region	Barossa Valley, SA
Cellar	🍷 8
Alc./Vol.	14.5%
RRP	$27.50

The Barossa 'valley floor' was once considered by some to be slightly lesser wine country, with the higher vineyards in the Barossa and Eden valleys more prized. The bigger-is-better crowd, led by the American gurus, has turned that around and now the warm vineyards are the ones to go for. Langmeil's Valley Floor is more moderate in style than a lot.

CURRENT RELEASE 2004 A slightly jammy shiraz, but it has plenty of immediate appeal for its ripe-berry fruit character and earthy, spicy complexities. Vanillin oak is there too, but it's in the background. Its texture is syrupy and the palate is sustained and likeable. We'd suggest porterhouse roasted in the piece.

Lark Hill Shiraz Viognier

Quality	▼▼▼▼▼
Value	★★★ᐟ
Rating	92
Grapes	shiraz; viognier
Region	Canberra district, NSW
Cellar	⬤–1–6
Alc./Vol.	13.8%
RRP	$32.00

The Lark Hill vineyard is one of the older vineyards in the Canberra district. It's in cool, dry country above Lake George, once full of water but now more like a broad meadow of grass.

CURRENT RELEASE 2004 This has an intense purplish colour and a fragrant, aromatic nose, which reflect its cool-climate origins. It smells of spice, florals, loganberry and there's a whisper of liqueur apricot from the viognier component. The complex palate is silky smooth and rich in flavour with good depth and body, finishing long with soft tannins. Good with cotechino sausage.

Leasingham Bastion Shiraz Cabernet

Since its arrival a few years ago, Leasingham's Bastion range has won a lot of friends for capturing the authentic spirit of the region and variety so well. We prefer this shiraz-cabernet blend to its slightly pongy companion, the straight cabernet.
CURRENT RELEASE 2003   There's a hint of regional mintiness on the nose, and intense berry aromas show freshness and vitality. Oak is very subdued. The palate is middling in weight with moderate extract and good balance of fruit and dry tannins; there's some savoury grip to it that really works well with something like rump steak.

Quality	♥♥♥♥
Value	★★★★
Rating	90
Grapes	shiraz; cabernet sauvignon
Region	Clare Valley, SA
Cellar	5
Alc./Vol.	14.0%
RRP	$15.70 (S)

Leasingham Bin 61 Shiraz

The Clare Valley naturally makes shiraz of strength and personality. Leasingham's wines are more modern types than some, ripe and full, and usually influenced by sweet oak. It can sometimes be heavily discounted far below normal retail price – as with many commercial wines it's best to shop around.
CURRENT RELEASE 2003   Bin 61 has a deep glass-staining colour that suggests power and extract and it delivers in similar vein. The nose is powerful with ripe-blackberry, black-chocolate and vanilla aromas, and savoury, earthy, meaty notes add dimension. It's rich and ripe in the mouth and quite full-bodied, with a strong foundation of very firm, grippy tannins. Like some previous Bin 61s this should be a good cellaring proposition. We'd partner it with steak and kidney pie.

Quality	♥♥♥♥
Value	★★★
Rating	91
Grapes	shiraz
Region	Clare Valley, SA
Cellar	6
Alc./Vol.	14.0%
RRP	$24.50 (S)

Lindemans Bin 50 Shiraz

Lindemans Bin 50 was created as a partner for the successful Bin 65 Chardonnay. Soon, there was a whole family of bin-numbered varietals at the same cheap-and-cheerful price-point.
CURRENT RELEASE 2005   This has a simple nose of raspberries, blackberries and spicy aromas. The medium-bodied, uncomplicated palate is young and fresh with fruity berry flavour and unusual presence at the price. Drink it young with pizza.

Quality	♥♥♥♥
Value	★★★★
Rating	88
Grapes	shiraz
Region	not stated
Cellar	1
Alc./Vol.	14.0%
RRP	$10.50 (S)

Lindemans Reserve Padthaway Shiraz

Quality	♟ ♟ ♟ ♟
Value	★★★★⁺
Rating	90
Grapes	shiraz
Region	Padthaway, SA
Cellar	▮ 3
Alc./Vol.	14.0%
RRP	$16.00 Ⓢ

A lot of moderately priced table wines look . . . well . . . cheap, but Lindemans Reserve range are labelled like wines costing a lot more. The smart presentation reflects some smart winemaking, and these wines are often surprising value. They're frequently discounted well below standard retail, too.

CURRENT RELEASE 2004   This is a no-fuss sort of red that offers pleasantly intense berry and plum-like shiraz fruit. Hints of vanilla and spice add dimension, and the palate is medium-bodied with balanced ripe tannins in support. Great-value drinking with empinadas (Spanish meat pies).

Longview Yakka Shiraz Viognier

Quality	♟ ♟ ♟ ♟ ⁙
Value	★★★⁺
Rating	92
Grapes	shiraz; viognier
Region	Adelaide Hills, SA
Cellar	▮ 4
Alc./Vol.	14.5%
RRP	$26.00

It's hard yakka tasting wines all day, but Longview's Yakka reds are easier to cope with than the big blockbusters.

CURRENT RELEASE 2004   This has a penetrating nose of ripe cherries with lifted minty and spicy notes, and a dab of licorice strap. It smells savoury but nicely ripe, and the palate has a smooth, generous feel with long, spicy flavour and a fine finish of ripe tannins. It doesn't have great power, but it has intensity and finesse. Try it with paella made with mixed meats and vegetables.

Lost Valley Thousand Hills Shiraz

Quality	♟ ♟ ♟ ♟
Value	★★★
Rating	91
Grapes	shiraz
Region	Upper Goulburn, Vic.
Cellar	▮ 8
Alc./Vol.	14.0%
RRP	$34.00

Lost Valley is in a remote spot among the beautiful hills and mountains of Victoria's Great Dividing Range. It's cool-climate wine production, indeed, but recent warm years have helped shiraz obtain good ripeness levels.

CURRENT RELEASE 2003   Plum, pepper, earth and smoky-oak aromas are complex and appealing, and the palate is smooth and satisfying with good length and a succulent finish. Tannins are moderate, offering balanced firmness and a dry finish. It would go well with slow-roasted pork belly.

Maglieri Shiraz

Maglieri's reds have for many years been among the great bargains of Australian wine. We're not sure why. Could it be the oceans of lambrusco they make have held their image down? Maker: Charles 'Chilly' Hargrave.
CURRENT RELEASE 2004   Maglieri's style is typical of McLaren Vale: soft, rounded and chocolatey, with plenty of extract and smooth, supple tannin. The flavours are ripely plummy and length is medium. It's the kind of wine that will never strike a bad reaction with the guests. Just the red to serve with beef satays.

Quality	♟♟♟♟
Value	★★★★
Rating	90
Grapes	shiraz
Region	McLaren Vale, SA
Cellar	6+
Alc./Vol.	14.0%
RRP	$21.50 Ⓢ

Magpie Estate The Sack Shiraz

Magpie Estate is a brand started by Veritas winemaker Rolf Binder and his British importer. The names and labels of all the wines are mysterious, to say the least! You'll have fun trying to work them out. Maker: Rolf Binder.
CURRENT RELEASE 2003   It has a developing bouquet of toasty, smoky, earthy aromas, with some spices and aniseed. Peppercorns as well. In the mouth it has good flavour, style, balance and depth. There is plenty of oak which is well married in. It's a pretty stylish wine of excellent drinkability, but it has a future, too. We'd suggest pork spare ribs.

Quality	♟♟♟♟
Value	★★★
Rating	90
Grapes	shiraz
Region	Barossa Valley, SA
Cellar	6
Alc./Vol.	14.5%
RRP	$25.00

Margan Shiraz

Hunter Valley shiraz is seldom big and gutsy like those from warm South Australian regions such as the Barossa and McLaren Vale. It's often a welcome antidote to the high-alcohol blockbusters that seem everywhere these days. Maker Andrew Margan uses grapes only from the Broke Fordwich sub-region.
CURRENT RELEASE 2004   This lovely young shiraz has a deep-purple robe and a clean, vibrant nose of cherry, plum, pepper and other spices in a fruit-driven (i.e. non-oaky) style. There's a touch of leathery Hunter character. It's a bit young now, but is pleasingly smooth in its tannins, which are fine-grained and lend pleasing structure. It's only medium-bodied but the style is all about drinkability. Serve it with barbecued lamb loin chops.

Quality	♟♟♟♟
Value	★★★★
Rating	89
Grapes	shiraz
Region	Hunter Valley, NSW
Cellar	1–8+
Alc./Vol.	13.5%
RRP	$20.00

Marius Simpatico Shiraz

Quality	♟♟♟♟
Value	★★★★
Rating	90
Grapes	shiraz
Region	McLaren Vale, SA
Cellar	🍶 10
Alc./Vol.	14.5%
RRP	$25.00 ⊗

The people at Marius set great store by the fact that both their shirazes are single-vineyard wines. Their Home Block vineyard is just four acres, so don't expect to see the wines in cut-case floor displays at every Liquorland outlet! CURRENT RELEASE 2004 The colour is nice and deep, the nose is very ripe and rich, with plenty of oak and a hint of sweatiness. The taste is excellent: full-bodied, powerful and tightly packed with rich fruit, some eucalyptus touches, and a firm tannin/acid finish. It could be cellared, but right now it goes well with rare steak.

Marius Symphony Shiraz

Quality	♟♟♟♟♟
Value	★★★↓
Rating	92
Grapes	shiraz
Region	McLaren Vale, SA
Cellar	⊷2–12+
Alc./Vol.	14.5%
RRP	$35.00 🍶⊗

This is made from the fruit of a special section of the four-acre Home Block, and is therefore a tiny production wine. Hand-picked, open-fermented, basket-pressed, aged in new and second-use French oak – all done on the property at Willunga. It is truly a handmade wine. CURRENT RELEASE 2004 This is a shy young shiraz that took time to open up in the glass. It's a more elegant wine than the Simpatico, but also reveals more body and richness, more fullness and length when you get to know it. It is a beautifully balanced wine that should reward cellaring. Then serve with an aged, hard cheese such as cheddar.

McIvor Estate Shiraz

Quality	♟♟♟♟
Value	★★★
Rating	90
Grapes	shiraz
Region	Heathcote, Vic.
Cellar	⊷2–6
Alc./Vol.	14.5%
RRP	$30.00

McIvor Estate is at the southern end of the Heathcote region, a place that seems to produce a fairly angular type of shiraz. This vineyard was established in 1997. CURRENT RELEASE 2003 There are some typically central-Victorian shiraz qualities here: deep colour, traces of mint and eucalypt on the nose, Heathcote-style black cherry and spicy fruitcake, with a subtle thread of oak. The palate is medium-bodied, dry and tightly structured with some rather austere, astringent tannins behind it. It needs bottle-age to soften and harmonise, then try it with roast lamb.

Merum Pemberton Shiraz

At 13.3%, this is amongst the lowest-alcohol shiraz wines that we've seen in this country for years. Maker: Jan McIntosh.
CURRENT RELEASE 2004   This is a very elegant shiraz; spicy and smoky in bouquet, it's fine, light- to medium-bodied and turns peppery on the palate – but not green. It's fine-boned and elegant. The savoury complexity grows on you as you sip. A very good food wine: we'd suggest matching it with Chinese five-spice quail.

Quality	🍷🍷🍷🍷
Value	★★★★
Rating	92
Grapes	shiraz
Region	Pemberton, WA
Cellar	🍾 6
Alc./Vol.	13.3%
RRP	$28.00 🗳

Mistletoe Reserve Shiraz

The grapes were hand-picked from a single 35-year-old vineyard in the Pokolbin area of the Hunter, and the wine was aged in new French oak hogsheads.
CURRENT RELEASE 2004   The coconutty aromas are consistent with the new oak, and we find the oak a little too raw and edgy. It needs time to integrate better with the wine. There are pepper and mixed spice (cloves, nutmeg) aromas too, while the palate is oaky and disjointed. There is certainly big flavour and loads of fruit lurking in there; it just needs time to come together. Hard to judge now; it could gain a higher rating later. Put it away for a while before broaching with a hearty T-bone steak.

Quality	🍷🍷🍷🍷
Value	★★★
Rating	88
Grapes	shiraz
Region	Hunter Valley, NSW
Cellar	⬤–3–15+
Alc./Vol.	13.0%
RRP	$26.00 🍾 🗳
	(cellar door)

Mistletoe Shiraz

The grapes were hand-picked from three vineyards: Mistletoe's own, and two neighbours on Hermitage Road, Pokolbin. It was aged in French and American oak, and 300 cases were produced. Maker: Nick Paterson.
CURRENT RELEASE 2004   There are smoky, oak characters in this wine that suggest it will benefit from a little cellar time, but it has the body and youthful vigour to reward patience. The fruit has some chaffy/vegetal spice characters and the palate adds savoury walnut flavours and drying tannins, which are quite chewy and firm. Cellar it, then drink with roast nut of veal.

Quality	🍷🍷🍷
Value	★★★
Rating	87
Grapes	shiraz
Region	Hunter Valley, NSW
Cellar	⬤–2–6+
Alc./Vol.	13.0%
RRP	$20.00 🗳
	(cellar door)

Mitolo Jester Shiraz

Quality 🍷🍷🍷🍷
Value ★★★½
Rating **92**
Grapes shiraz
Region McLaren Vale, SA
Cellar 5+
Alc./Vol. 14.5%
RRP $28.00

The Jester label is the entry-level Mitolo wine, and is sourced from the sections of Mitolo's own McLaren Vale vineyard that don't make the cut for the Savitar or G.A.M. shirazes. Winemaker Ben Glaetzer does a sterling job with these wines: they invariably over-deliver.

CURRENT RELEASE 2005 The colour is promisingly dark and it has a slightly raw, youthful plum and chaff aroma with little oak to speak of, but bags of fruit. This is repeated in the mouth, where it has abundant richness and weight of well-ripened fruit. Licorice, mocha and chocolate are suggested, while the tannins are thick and coat the mouth. It's a chewy, though not very elegant, wine but the alcohol is nicely in balance. Try it with any hard, aged cheese, like Italian pecorino.

Moondah Brook Shiraz

Quality 🍷🍷🍷🍷
Value ★★★★★
Rating **90**
Grapes shiraz
Region various, WA
Cellar 5+
Alc./Vol. 14.0%
RRP $16.50 ($)

There is actually a place called Moondah Brook, and the Hardy group has a major vineyard there. But we suspect the brand has long ago outgrown that vineyard and now includes blend components from several regions of Western Australia.

CURRENT RELEASE 2002 As reliable as clockwork, this excellent red delivers lots of flavour and impeccable quality year after year. The colour is youthful and deep; the bouquet is all about ripe plum, vanilla and chocolate, while the taste is smooth and fleshy with good depth of fruit. The oak is controlled and tannins don't get in the way. It goes well with a steak sandwich.

Mornington Estate Shiraz Viognier

Quality 🍷🍷🍷½
Value ★★★½
Rating **88**
Grapes shiraz; viognier
Region Mornington Peninsula, Vic.
Cellar 4+
Alc./Vol. 14.0%
RRP $20.00

The Mornington Peninsula is not the first region one thinks of for great Aussie shiraz. While there are some great vineyard sites there, such as Paringa Estate's, much of the region, in all but the warmest seasons, is too cool for shiraz. Maker: Rollo Crittenden.

CURRENT RELEASE 2004 This has the hallmarks of a cool-grown shiraz: pronounced spicy aromas with some herbal, pea-pod, vegetal accents. The palate is light- to medium-bodied, lean, tangy/spicy and attractive in its way, with weight and presence and some oaky tannins on the back-palate. It's not complex, but it is attractively priced. Serve it with peppered steak.

Morris Rutherglen Shiraz

This wine's moment of glory was winning the trophy for the best wine under $25 in the Great Australian Shiraz Challenge. Well deserved, too, we'd say. A superb red at a modest price. Maker: David Morris.

CURRENT RELEASE 2001 This is a typically robust Rutherglen red, but much more balanced and measured in its ripeness and alcohol strength than some of its neighbours in the region. Earthy, herbal and minty aromas are starting to show some mellow bottle-age, and the taste is smooth and mellowing, with medium depth of fruit. It could use just a touch more primary fruit. It would go well with savoury meatballs.

Quality	🍷🍷🍷🍷
Value	★★★★½
Rating	**90**
Grapes	shiraz
Region	Rutherglen, Vic.
Cellar	6
Alc./Vol.	13.5%
RRP	$17.50

Mount Horrocks Watervale Shiraz

When the '04 vintage was fresh in the tanks, the word around the country was that the wines suffered from over-cropping. But as they've started to come onto the market, we find ourselves highly impressed with the quality and style of many '04 reds. Winemaker Stephanie Toole has excelled herself here.

CURRENT RELEASE 2004 This is a deeply coloured, big, gutsy shiraz that needs time and is a bit too young to open now. It's perfumed and very attractive with licorice/anise and floral/violet aromas, while the palate is somewhat aggressive and callow, with impressively deep flavour and some firm tannin astringency. It should be a superb red in a few years. Then drink it with aged Italian parmesan.

Quality	🍷🍷🍷🍷½
Value	★★★½
Rating	**93**
Grapes	shiraz
Region	Clare Valley, SA
Cellar	2–15+
Alc./Vol.	14.0%
RRP	$32.00

Mount Langi Ghiran Billi Billi Shiraz

The (blue label) Langi Shiraz '02 was deleted because of a miocrobiological problem, but the good news is that both the Billi Billi and Cliff Edge shirazes of that year are spectacular value. Makers: Trevor Mast and Dan Buckle.

CURRENT RELEASE 2002 Sweet plum/cherry and dusty/earthy shiraz aromas with a twist of spice. There's a suggestion of volatility which doesn't intrude. The wine has plenty of acid – a feature of all Langi reds – and good palate length, while the tannins are typically fine-grained. It's soft and ready to drink. This is the drink-now Langi but it won't disappoint if you keep it a few years. Food: pink roast lamb.

Quality	🍷🍷🍷½
Value	★★★★
Rating	**88**
Grapes	shiraz
Region	Grampians, Vic.
Cellar	4+
Alc./Vol.	13.5%
RRP	$16.60 ($)

Mount Langi Ghiran Langi Shiraz

Quality	♟ ♟ ♟ ♟ ♟
Value	★★★★⟩
Rating	95
Grapes	shiraz
Region	Grampians, Vic.
Cellar	▮ 15+
Alc./Vol.	15.0%
RRP	$55.00 ▮

After skipping a year in 2002 – scrapped because of microbial problems – Langi makes a welcome return with this crackerjack wine. The Grampians area has a long tradition of great shiraz and the granitic soil is increasingly mentioned. This tallies with the northern Rhône Valley in France, which also specialises in shiraz.

CURRENT RELEASE 2003 From a very hot, dry year, this is predictably a much less peppery Langi shiraz than usual. Despite the 15 per cent alcohol it's not a big wine: rather, it's smooth, gentle, elegant and intensely flavoured, with marvellous balance. Aromas are of sweet plum, earth and faint spices; it's a classic, elegant, medium- to full-bodied shiraz of warmth and generosity. Great with rare fillet steak. *Previous outstanding vintages: 1986, '90, '91, '92, '94, '95, '96, '98, 2000*

Mr Riggs The Gaffer Shiraz

Quality	♟ ♟ ♟ ♟
Value	★★★★
Rating	90
Grapes	shiraz
Region	McLaren Vale, SA
Cellar	▮ 6+
Alc./Vol.	15.0%
RRP	$22.00 Ⓢ ≋

Ben Riggs makes an awesome array of shiraz-based red wines under a number of labels. This junior label upstaged many more expensive wines, including some of Riggs's own, no doubt, at the McLaren Vale Wine Show, winning a trophy.

CURRENT RELEASE 2004 We like it, but we're not sure it's *that* good. Mulchy, chocolatey aromas are mixed up with meaty, spicy and aniseedy notes. The alcohol is a bit high, leading to some end-palate harshness and heat. It's a bit over the top for our tastes, but many will love it. Roast saddle of hare, with some chocolate in the sauce, would work well.

Murchison Shiraz

Quality	♟ ♟ ♟ ♟
Value	★★★⟩
Rating	90
Grapes	shiraz
Region	Goulburn Valley, Vic.
Cellar	▮ 4
Alc./Vol.	14.3%
RRP	$18.50 ≋

The ex-Longleat vineyard has a new lease of life under the stewardship of Guido and Sandra Vazzoler as Murchison Wines. It's a lovely little corner of Victoria, nestled among the river gums by the Goulburn River.

CURRENT RELEASE 2004 A complete, balanced young shiraz that drinks well right now. It has pleasant berry aromas and plenty of savoury interest in the mix as well. The palate is smooth and easy with attractive berry and mocha flavours, finishing soft and friendly. A good match for mushroom and cheese pasta.

Narkoojee Myrtle Point Shiraz

Although Narkoojee is situated near the Strzelecki Ranges and the picturesque old mining village of Walhalla in central Gippsland, the cool Myrtle Point vineyard is much further east, near Bairnsdale.
CURRENT RELEASE 2004 Typically cool-grown cues are here on the nose, but it still has attractive levels of ripeness. Spices, herbs and pepper-like aromas add savoury qualities to black-cherry fruit. The mid-weight palate is aromatically flavoured with a pleasantly drinkable, gentle feel to it, finishing soft, long and savoury. Serve it with mild pepper steak.

Quality	♀ ♀ ♀ ♀
Value	★ ★ ★
Rating	88
Grapes	shiraz
Region	Gippsland, Vic.
Cellar	4
Alc./Vol.	14.0%
RRP	$20.00

Neagles Rock Shiraz

For the first time, the 2004 Neagles Rock Shiraz has shiraz from the old Duncan Block vineyard in it, giving the wine more intensity and depth.
CURRENT RELEASE 2004 A big warm shiraz that verges on being a bit too soupy and alcoholic, not the thing for those who like more elegant reds. It truly reflects a hot vintage with its jammy-berry fruit nose and lightly earthy/funky notes. It's full-bodied and obvious in flavour, with a long, hot finish and balanced ripe tannins. Good with rich lamb biryani.

Quality	♀ ♀ ♀ ♀
Value	★ ★ ★ ﹥
Rating	90
Grapes	shiraz
Region	Clare Valley, SA
Cellar	6
Alc./Vol.	15.0%
RRP	$22.00

Norfolk Rise Shiraz

Norfolk Rise is the largest winemaking enterprise in South Australia's Mount Benson region. Its Belgian ownership gives it a strong export focus.
CURRENT RELEASE 2004 Spicy/peppery cool-climate notes are the first things we noticed on the nose of this wine, with black-cherry fruit and subtle background oak emerging on further acquaintance. The palate has smooth spicy flavour that's savoury and long, but a little ungiving at the moment. Give it a year or two, then enjoy it with some pork sausages and onions.

Quality	♀ ♀ ♀ ♀
Value	★ ★ ★ ﹥
Rating	91
Grapes	shiraz
Region	Mount Benson, SA
Cellar	1–5
Alc./Vol.	14.0%
RRP	$16.55

Oakridge 864 Shiraz

Quality	♥♥♥♥
Value	★★★
Rating	90
Grapes	shiraz
Region	Yarra Valley, Vic.
Cellar	🍷 8+
Alc./Vol.	13.5%
RRP	$50.00 ⊗
	(cellar door)

We do like what David Bicknell is doing at Oakridge. He has raised the standard to the best yet, and the new 864 range – a de facto reserve range, only available at cellar door and in restaurants – is truly superb.
CURRENT RELEASE 2003   This opened up a bit funky and sweaty, but after extended airing it revealed itself as a very tight, elegant, traditional-style shiraz of moderate alcohol and fine balance. Red cherry and raspberry aromas are expressed in the bouquet and it has the kind of understated elegance that will really grow and develop with time in the bottle. It's a world apart from the fat, chocolate and plum-jam style of the warmer climates. We'd suggest peppered steak.

Oakridge Shiraz

Quality	♥♥♥♥↑
Value	★★★★
Rating	93
Grapes	shiraz
Region	Yarra Valley, Vic.
Cellar	🍷 10+
Alc./Vol.	14.5%
RRP	$25.00 ⊗

Winemaker David Bicknell likes to source his white grapes from the highest and coolest sites on the edges of the Yarra Valley. With reds, the opposite is true: he wants grapes from the lower, warmer sites in the central valley, where the ripest fruit is found.
CURRENT RELEASE 2003   There's a slightly sweaty overtone that we often find in young screw-capped reds, but it's a minor issue and the wine is very good all the same. It has loads of appealing toasty barrel-ferment character, and the taste is medium-bodied, elegant and nicely balanced. It's smooth, gentle, up-front and drinks beautifully already. We liked it more and more as it 'came up' in the glass. It would go well with veal standing rib roast.

O'Leary Walker Clare Valley McLaren Vale Shiraz

Quality	♥♥♥♥
Value	★★★★★
Rating	92
Grapes	shiraz
Region	Clare Valley & McLaren Vale, SA
Cellar	➦1–12+
Alc./Vol.	14.5%
RRP	$21.50 ⊗

This company has its winery and base in Clare, but takes grapes from wherever it needs to in order to make the kind of wine it desires. Winemakers are David O'Leary and Nick Walker.
CURRENT RELEASE 2004   A generously flavoured red, and great value for money. The colour stains the glass impressively. It's big and concentrated with violet, licorice and blackberry perfumes, laced with fruitcake and mixed spices. There's quite a contribution from oak, and lashings of tannin to firm up the finish. Delicious wine with big cellaring potential. It needs a rare, bloody steak.

Orlando Lawson's Shiraz

A winner of three gold medals in wine shows, and Orlando have done us a favour by holding it back for six years' maturation before release. That's part of the story behind the price tag. Chief red winemaker: Sam Kurtz.
CURRENT RELEASE 2000 This is typical Padthaway and typical Lawson's style: intense peppermint aromas and terrific concentration. It's holding its age well and starting to enter its peak drinking window. The taste is smooth and full of mocha and chocolate flavours, with sweetness, flesh and succulence. But it's not especially complex: is that because of the domineering mintiness? We'd suggest aged cheddar and biscuits.

Quality	🍷🍷🍷🍷
Value	★★★
Rating	91
Grapes	shiraz
Region	Padthaway, SA
Cellar	🍷 5
Alc./Vol.	14.0%
RRP	$60.00 🍷

Paringa Estate Reserve Shiraz

Lindsay McCall of Paringa Estate usually makes this Special Barrel Selection Reserve wine in warm, dry years on the Mornington Peninsula. So far it's only appeared in 2000, 2003 and 2004. It's quite a rarity but worth seeking out.
CURRENT RELEASE 2004 Cool-climate shiraz at its best, this seductive wine shows more of itself with each sip, opening with aromas of fleshy black cherry, spices and cracked black pepper, then evolving savoury notes of wood smoke, wild game and earth. Cedary oak plays a definite role, yet it doesn't intrude. The mid-palate is silky and long, with fine flavour and subtle complexity. Tannins are in good harmony at the finish, although some oak tannin needs time to soften and integrate. It's just right with Cantonese roast duck and Chinese pickles.

Quality	🍷🍷🍷🍷🍷
Value	★★★
Rating	95
Grapes	shiraz
Region	Mornington Peninsula, Vic.
Cellar	➥ 1–6
Alc./Vol.	14.4%
RRP	$90.00 🍷

Peerick Reserve Shiraz

The Moonambel district is well known for substantial red wines that are often more aromatically regional than others in the Pyrenees region.
CURRENT RELEASE 2002 This has a very peppery nose with cherry and plum fruit mixed in. There's good meaty intensity to it and a measured dose of slightly resiny oak adds seasoning. Although it shows little of the typical regional eucalypt character on the nose, it's there on the palate adding savoury dimension and pungency. It's medium in body and long in flavour, with a backbone of rather sinewy tannins. Enjoy it with roast lamb.

Quality	🍷🍷🍷🍷
Value	★★★⯪
Rating	90
Grapes	shiraz
Region	Pyrenees, Vic.
Cellar	🍷 6
Alc./Vol.	14.0%
RRP	$28.00

Penfolds Bin 28 Kalimna Shiraz

Quality	♟♟♟♟
Value	★★★
Rating	91
Grapes	shiraz
Region	McLaren Vale, Langhorne Creek & Barossa Valley, SA
Cellar	🍶 7
Alc./Vol.	14.0%
RRP	$26.00 ⑤

Bin 28 has an illustrious history going back 40 years. These days the wine occupies a slightly lower niche, but it's still a distinguished member of Australia's premier red wine family. CURRENT RELEASE 2003 Bin 28 always offers a touch of Penfolds class, and the '03 is a typically generous member of the family. The nose has juicy fruits-of-the-forest aromas, with hints of spice and a balanced veneer of mocha-like sweet oak. The palate is medium in body with an attractive rounded mouth-feel and a backing of ripe integrated tannins. Good with veal chops.
Previous outstanding vintages: 1971, '81, '86, '90, '91, '92, '96, '98

Penfolds Grange

Quality	♟♟♟♟♟
Value	★★
Rating	98
Grapes	shiraz
Region	Barossa Valley & other regions, SA
Cellar	➡2–20
Alc./Vol.	14.5%
RRP	$450–$500

What's in a name? A few years ago one of the authors opened a bottle of Grange and it was corked. He put it aside. A dinner guest that night noticed it and, despite entreaties, proceeded to drink almost the whole bottle of musty, stale, dank wine. Grange. The name has such magic. CURRENT RELEASE 2001 After a disappointing 2000 vintage (we think it should have been declassified and blended into other Penfolds reds) the 2001 is a welcome return to form. A deeply coloured wine with intense spicy, blackberry fruit and powerful vanillin oak, which is more than matched by that perfectly ripe, super-concentrated fruit. The palate is profound, seamless and wonderfully textured with extraordinary length of flavour, and ripe, ultra-fine tannins in perfect integration. Grange at its best. Food: roast rib of beef and all the flash trimmings.
Previous outstanding vintages: 1953, '55, '62, '63, '66, '71, '72, '76, '80, '83, '86, '88, '90, '91,'92, '94,'96,'97, '98, '99

Penfolds Koonunga Hill Shiraz

Quality	♟♟♟♟
Value	★★★⟩
Rating	88
Grapes	shiraz
Region	various, SA
Cellar	🍶 4
Alc./Vol.	14.0%
RRP	$15.60 ⑤ ⧢

The Koonunga Hill reds continue to be some of Australia's best-value-for-money wines, and unlike many in their price-point, they can often improve with a fair bit of bottle-age. CURRENT RELEASE 2003 A straightforward Penfolds red wine, this has a fresh nose that's reminiscent of raspberries, blackberries, spice and there's a bit of chocolatey richness underneath. In the mouth it's a bit lighter than Penfolds' tradition would dictate, but it has the intensity and smooth texture to be a real crowd-pleaser. Try it with moussaka.

Penfolds Magill Estate Shiraz

Most of the famous Penfolds red wines are multi-regional blends, but Magill Estate is a true estate wine, grown on the same ground Dr Christopher Rawson Penfold first planted in 1844. The estate is a real showplace these days, with an excellent restaurant and other facilities.
CURRENT RELEASE 2003   A concentrated Magill Estate with a powerful nose of ripe dark berries, bread and Vegemite, bakery spices and vanilla that's very attractive. The palate shows plenty of stuffing with rich smoky flavour, great depth and velvety texture, leading to a solid foundation of ripe tannins. A bigger style than usual, that works well with roast beef.

Quality	♟♟♟♟♟
Value	★★★
Rating	93
Grapes	shiraz
Region	Adelaide, SA
Cellar	➥2–8+
Alc./Vol.	14.0%
RRP	$95.00

Penfolds RWT Shiraz

RWT, which stands for Red Wine Trial, is a sort of alter-ego to the famous Penfolds Grange. It's a single-region wine instead of a multi-regional wine; it's less concentrated, less tannic and approachable earlier, and it sees civilised French oak rather than brash American. In every way it's a worthy companion to its famous stablemate.
CURRENT RELEASE 2003   Typically deep in colour, '03 RWT is a less obvious wine at this stage in its life than previous vintages. Ripe loganberry, spice and dusty oak aromas are subtle and complete, and by comparison with most of Penfolds' super-dooper reds, it shows more restraint and finesse. The palate is still ripely concentrated, and very harmonious, with perfectly integrated tannins on a very long finish. A fine, silky RWT, and a good one. Serve it with pot-roasted lamb and lentils.

Quality	♟♟♟♟♟
Value	★★★
Rating	97
Grapes	shiraz
Region	Barossa Valley, SA
Cellar	➥1–10
Alc./Vol.	14.5%
RRP	$130.00

Pepperjack Shiraz

Pepperjack is one of the modern incarnations of the Saltram vineyard that once produced so many classic Australian red wines. Maker: Nigel Dolan.
CURRENT RELEASE 2004   This epitomises the mod-Oz type of Barossa shiraz that we think needs to be encouraged. It's alive with jammy black-fruit characters, touches of spice and nicely handled, definite sweet oak, and it tastes forward, seamless and well-muscled. It finishes with a mellow lick of ripe tannins that give structure and dry out the finish well. A friendly, well-put-together red to enjoy with steak and kidney pie.

Quality	♟♟♟♟
Value	★★★
Rating	90
Grapes	shiraz
Region	Barossa Valley, SA
Cellar	▮5
Alc./Vol.	14.0%
RRP	$23.00 Ⓢ

Peter Lehmann Barossa Shiraz Grenache

Quality	▼▼▼▼
Value	★★★★﹜
Rating	88
Grapes	shiraz; grenache
Region	Barossa Valley, SA
Cellar	▋2
Alc./Vol.	14.0%
RRP	$13.00 ⑤ 彡

This easy quaffer employs the two stalwart old Barossa red varieties, shiraz and grenache, to make an eminently chug-a-luggable red for early consumption.
CURRENT RELEASE 2005   A fresh red that sits at the less exuberant end of the Barossa spectrum. It's pleasantly fragrant, with bright cherry and berry aromas that are sweetly fruity, yet with a savoury, earthy, spicy grenache touch. The palate has warm flavours, but its lightish, medium body keeps it easy to quaff, and its appealing softness has a bit of the Côtes du Rhône to it. Try it with pissaladière (Provençale onion pizza).

Peter Lehmann The Futures Shiraz

Quality	▼▼▼▼▼
Value	★★★★﹜
Rating	96
Grapes	shiraz
Region	Barossa Valley, SA
Cellar	▬2–10
Alc./Vol.	14.5%
RRP	$29.00

Peter Lehmann is a larger-than-life figure in the Barossa Valley. Over many years he's helped maintain the region's impetus by supporting local growers and helping to define its wine styles, sometimes in difficult times for the industry.
CURRENT RELEASE 2003   A very complete Barossa shiraz that offers lovely intensity and texture while retaining a refined feel. At its heart is syrupy blackberry and spicy shiraz fruit, and a veneer of spicy oak; while still slightly raw, it is in excellent balance. The palate follows the theme through with great depth and length, finishing in ripe, fine-grained tannins. The building blocks are in place and all it needs is time to evolve further. It suits braised and roasted lamb shanks perfectly.

Pettavel Southern Émigré Shiraz Viognier

Quality	▼▼▼▼
Value	★★★
Rating	92
Grapes	shiraz
Region	Geelong, Vic.
Cellar	▋6
Alc./Vol.	14.5%
RRP	$42.00

Pettavel was one of the original Geelong vineyards of the nineteenth century. Now resurrected across the road from its original site, it's more than just a vineyard and winery, an excellent restaurant makes it a wonderful place to visit.
CURRENT RELEASE 2003   This Geelong shiraz is an unusually complex, quite exotic wine. The nose has pungent aromas of spice, herbs, smoked meats and truffles, with liqueur-ish berry fruit at the core. The palate is medium- to full-bodied, spicy-rich and deep in flavour with a very long, smoky finish. A fascinatingly different red to serve with a mixed mushroom risotto drizzled with truffle oil.

Pikes Eastside Shiraz

The grapes for this smooth shiraz were grown on the east side of the Clare Valley, which might have something to do with the name. Maker: Neil Pike.
CURRENT RELEASE 2003   A straightforward wine with some herby touches to dark berry fruit. It lacks a little of the richness of the usual Pikes shiraz style, with medium-intensity berry flavours backed by rather bony, astringent tannins. It's a style that lends itself to foods like pasta with a meaty sauce.

Quality	▼▼▼▼
Value	★★★
Rating	90
Grapes	shiraz
Region	Clare Valley, SA
Cellar	▮ 4
Alc./Vol.	14.5%
RRP	$26.50 ✇

Pirramimma Stock's Hill Shiraz

The Pirramimma red wines have a very traditional McLaren Vale personality, although screw-caps now add a modern touch. Stock's Hill is the winery's most elevated vineyard.
CURRENT RELEASE 2003   A notably earthy regionality marks the nose of this shiraz. It has blackberry and spice, and a slightly feral, meaty aroma that takes us back to the McLaren Vale reds of our youth. The medium-bodied palate continues the rustic themes with a slightly metallic thread to the finish. It's one for the traditionalists. Try it with a beef casserole.

Quality	▼▼▼▽
Value	★★★
Rating	88
Grapes	shiraz
Region	McLaren Vale, SA
Cellar	▮ 3
Alc./Vol.	14.0%
RRP	$17.50 ✇

Plunkett Strathbogie Ranges Reserve Shiraz

The Plunketts have been doing a lot of work on their shiraz in recent years and it shows. Although the wines are sourced from fairly cool vineyards, ripeness levels are good. A couple of hot years have helped out as well.
CURRENT RELEASE 2003   This latest release builds on the reputation of the '02 with a deep glass-staining colour, a dense-packed nose, and poised, intense palate. It smells of spicy fruitcake, black chocolate, a light herbal thread and there's a subtle interplay with spicy-sweet oak. The middleweight, spicy palate is mouth-wateringly vibrant, and fine-grained tannins lead through a long savoury signature. Great with crumbed veal cutlet.

Quality	▼▼▼▼▽
Value	★★★
Rating	94
Grapes	shiraz
Region	Strathbogie Ranges, Vic.
Cellar	▮ 8
Alc./Vol.	14.5%
RRP	$98.00

Pyren Vineyard Block E Shiraz

Quality	🍷🍷🍷🍷
Value	★★★
Rating	91
Grapes	shiraz
Region	Pyrenees, Vic.
Cellar	🍷 8
Alc./Vol.	14.2%
RRP	$26.00

The new labels just keep on coming. This smartly packaged wine hails from one of the newest in Victoria's Pyrenees region, and it encapsulates the regional personality very well.

CURRENT RELEASE 2004   This shows what the French would call *typicité* – the essential qualities of a region. It smells of after-dinner mints with a pinch of eucalypt, as well as all the other savoury Pyrenees hallmarks of mixed spice and dark berries. It has good depth in the mouth with a core of ripe shiraz fruit and a savoury/minty seasoning. Dry tannins give some grip and form at the end of the palate. Excellent with a beef and Vietnamese mint stirfry.

Pyrenees Ridge Reserve Shiraz

Quality	🍷🍷🍷🍷🍷
Value	★★★
Rating	97
Grapes	shiraz
Region	Pyrenees, Vic.
Cellar	➦ 2–10+
Alc./Vol.	14.5%
RRP	$45.00

Although Graeme and Sally Jukes only established Pyrenees Ridge less than 10 years ago, the wines have attracted quite a following already. They are robust drops of strong personality that don't stray too much into the super-minty/ eucalypty type so common in the area.

CURRENT RELEASE 2004   A powerfully concentrated nose leaps out of the glass here. It has aromas of pepper, spice, syrupy blackberries and chocolate sauce with a balanced overlay of toasty vanillin oak. The deliciously ripe palate is mellow and warm with finely tuned, ripe tannins and a long mellow aftertaste. It would work well with roast Scotch fillet of beef.

Ravensworth Shiraz Viognier

Quality	🍷🍷🍷🍷🍷
Value	★★★★⸼
Rating	96
Grapes	shiraz 95%;
	viognier 5%
Region	Canberra, ACT
Cellar	➦ 2–8
Alc./Vol.	14.0%
RRP	$25.00 🍷

Ravensworth's Bryan Martin is assistant winemaker to Tim Kirk at Clonakilla, the Canberra region's (and Australia's?) master of the shiraz-viognier blend. Bryan's wine seems more influenced by the white viognier than Clonakilla's version, but it's pretty good all the same.

CURRENT RELEASE 2005   A pungent, aromatic red wine that's impossible to ignore in a line-up of shirazes. It has floral pot-pourri, plum, pepper and spice on the nose, with a seasoning of lightly toasty oak. It smells intense and it tastes deliciously smooth with pepper and dark-cherry flavours of length and concentration, leading through dry and firm, but not harsh, tannins. It needs bottle-age, then serve it with roast duck.

Raydon Estate Tails South Shiraz

The fifth generation of the Borrett family own Raydon Estate. It was originally founded by John Borrett, who jumped ship in Adelaide in 1839 in search of adventure and fortune.
CURRENT RELEASE 2003   A big deep Langhorne Creek red, this has a slightly porty note to its ripe-berry fruit. A dab of coconutty American oak adds another facet, and the palate is full-bodied, rich and alcoholic with a dry underpinning of ripe tannins. It's not particularly complex, but it does have impact. Serve it with beef goulash.

Quality	♟♟♟♟
Value	★★★＋
Rating	91
Grapes	shiraz
Region	Langhorne Creek, SA
Cellar	▮ 5
Alc./Vol.	15.0%
RRP	$20.00

Red Edge Degree Shiraz

Peter Dredge's Red Edge reds (how's that for a tongue-twister?) from Victoria's outstanding Heathcote region are always rare, but this junior version is made in somewhat larger quantities. It's still not easy to find, but those who succeed will get a snapshot of why these wines are so exciting.
CURRENT RELEASE 2004   Heathcote shiraz always has real concentration, and this is no exception, but it is less formidable than the drought-influenced '04 flagship wines. The nose has blackberry, red-earth and minerally aromas, with threads of sweet/savoury spice and hints of raisin and prune. In the mouth it's full-flavoured with good body and depth, lasting long on the palate and finishing grippy and dry. A fine match for roast topside of beef.

Quality	♟♟♟♟
Value	★★★★
Rating	91
Grapes	shiraz; mourvèdre
Region	Heathcote, Vic.
Cellar	▬ 1–6
Alc./Vol.	14.0%
RRP	$25.00

Red Knot McLaren Vale Shiraz

Red Knot is one of a number of wines to emerge recently from the McLaren Vale region sealed with a 'Zork'. It sounds like the name of a visitor from the planet Zarquon, but it is another twist on the 'anything but cork' theme. It's like a plug of black plastic that goes 'pop' when you unpeel the seal and pull it out.
CURRENT RELEASE 2004   This is a very pleasant McLaren Vale shiraz to drink young. Its sweet blueberry, spice and vanillin aromas are immediately inviting, and some deeper chocolatey richness adds another layer. The palate has ripe dark-fruit flavours, smooth mouth-feel and just enough ripe tannin for balance. Drink it with kebabs.

Quality	♟♟♟♟
Value	★★★★
Rating	91
Grapes	shiraz
Region	McLaren Vale, SA
Cellar	▮ 4
Alc./Vol.	14.0%
RRP	$16.90

Redden Bridge Gully Shiraz

Quality	♟♟♟♟
Value	★★★
Rating	92
Grapes	shiraz
Region	Limestone Coast, SA
Cellar	▮ 5
Alc./Vol.	14.1%
RRP	$29.00 ⬙

Redden Bridge crosses the evocatively named Mosquito Creek Gully to enter this Wrattonbully vineyard. The name comes from Agnes Redden, who was a particularly dedicated local schoolteacher.

CURRENT RELEASE 2003   A fresh shiraz with a nose of mint, raspberry and black fruits, plus a touch of spicy vanillin oak. In the mouth it shows medium body and intensity with minty-berry flavours and some savoury barrel influence, finishing in ultra-fine ripe tannins. Try it with roast lamb.

Rees Miller Thousand Hills Shiraz

Quality	♟♟♟♟♟
Value	★★★⭑
Rating	92
Grapes	shiraz
Region	Yea Valley, Vic.
Cellar	▮ 4
Alc./Vol.	15.0%
RRP	$25.00

Rees Miller's label advertises that it's a 'vegan friendly' wine. We've said it before, but we think it's commendable to have someone brightening the vegan lifestyle with a drop of wine! These wines are also suitable for unreconstructed carnivores.

CURRENT RELEASE 2003   The deep, dense colour promises much, and the nose delivers with intense aromas of mint, dark fruits, earth, licorice straps and spice. It really does smell good. The palate follows with concentrated ripe, spicy flavours of good length and middling weight, leading to a ripe, fine finish of soft tannins. Serve it alongside wholemeal pasta with grilled eggplant, braised chickpeas and tomato, or serve a rare steak instead.

Richmond Grove Black Cat Shiraz

Quality	♟♟♟♟
Value	★★★★⭑
Rating	90
Grapes	shiraz
Region	not stated, SA
Cellar	▮ 3
Alc./Vol.	14.0%
RRP	$14.00 Ⓢ ⬙

Richmond Grove's silver series of budget-priced wines have been relaunched with a number of quirky names like the Black Cat. Most wineries seem to have a cat hanging around the place, so it's probably a more appropriate moniker than all those 'Swaggie's Armpit' and 'Wallaby's Nose' names that populate our wine shops' shelves.

CURRENT RELEASE 2004   Ripe plums and berries meet the nose, and attractive hints of spice add interest. The palate has good flavour development, depth and length, and although the flavour is ripe and juicy, thankfully it's not boosted with sugar-sweetness like many reds in this price range. Good value with lasagna.

Robert Johnson Vineyards Shiraz Viognier

This was one of our 'discovery' wines last year, when the '03 vintage gained a five-glass rating. The maker has a small 4.5-hectare vineyard in Eden Valley and also buys Adelaide Hills grapes for his second label, Alan & Veitch. CURRENT RELEASE 2004   The colour and nose suggest a very youthful, gently evolving wine. The aromas of pepper, cloves and nutmeg spice, roast meats and toasted oak are tantalising. The more it airs, the more apricotty-viognier aromas show out, which detracts a little. It's intense and lively without being tannic, although the alcohol warmth does tend to make it a little syrupy. The powerful flavours are focused and deliciously balanced. It should cellar well but it also drinks well now, perhaps with vitello tonnato. *Previous outstanding vintage: 2003*

Quality	♟ ♟ ♟ ♟ ♟
Value	★ ★ ★ ⋆
Rating	93
Grapes	shiraz; viognier
Region	Eden Valley, SA
Cellar	🍷 10+
Alc./Vol.	14.5%
RRP	$33.00

Robertson's Well Shiraz

John Robertson dug a well into the limestone of Coonawarra in the 1840s to support his vast sheep property. The land is now part of the famous Coonawarra wine region. CURRENT RELEASE 2004   Deliciously ripe aromas of blackberries, spice, earth and sweet oak meet the nose here, and the medium-bodied palate is a velvet-smooth progression of generous ripe fruit flavours. It finishes with a long blueberry-ish aftertaste and finely textured, drying tannins at the end. Try it with thick chargrilled veal chops with sage.

Quality	♟ ♟ ♟ ♟ ♟
Value	★ ★ ★ ★
Rating	92
Grapes	shiraz
Region	Coonawarra, SA
Cellar	🍷 7
Alc./Vol.	14.5%
RRP	$23.50

Rockbare Shiraz

The moody rock star-style pics on the back label look very cool indeed, and there's a certain self-conscious hipness about the whole Rockbare thing, but the authors of the *Guide* are pretty slick dudes, so we get it totally. Oh, and the wines are very good too. CURRENT RELEASE 2004   Tim Burvill's Rockbare Shiraz has impressed us mightily for value in the couple of vintages we've seen, and the '04 is true to form. It has deep colour and a ripe, generous nose that suggests Club chocolate, plums and spice. The smooth palate has deliciously ripe-berry flavour with some gentle oak input, a persistent feel and nicely integrated dry tannins underneath. Try it with mixed cheese lasagna.

Quality	♟ ♟ ♟ ♟ ♟
Value	★ ★ ★ ★ ⋆
Rating	93
Grapes	shiraz
Region	McLaren Vale, SA
Cellar	🍷 5
Alc./Vol.	14.5%
RRP	$20.00 ⊜

Rolling Shiraz

Quality	♟ ♟ ♟ ♟
Value	★ ★ ★ ★
Rating	91
Grapes	shiraz
Region	Central Ranges, NSW
Cellar	🍷 2
Alc./Vol.	13.5%
RRP	$15.00 ⑤ ⬥

The rolling hills of the New South Wales Central Ranges is a cool-climate wine region that shows a lot of promise. This wine from ex-Rosemount and Southcorp winemaker Philip Shaw sums up the region's well-balanced wines well.
CURRENT RELEASE 2004   Lifted red-berry and spice aromas are fresh and pleasing, with a summer-pudding-like succulence to them. In the mouth it has attractive equilibrium with soft, juicy-fruit flavours of length and finesse. The finish is soft and agreeable. A perfumed shiraz to drink young with hearty egg and bacon pie.

Rosabrook Shiraz

Quality	♟ ♟ ♟ ♟
Value	★ ★ ★
Rating	90
Grapes	shiraz
Region	Margaret River, WA
Cellar	🍷 4
Alc./Vol.	13.0%
RRP	$28.00 ⬥

Past vintages of Rosabrook's Shiraz have sometimes tended to be a little too extractive and hard on the palate, but the quality of fruit was always there. This latest incarnation is a more friendly drop.
CURRENT RELEASE 2003   A deep ruby-coloured shiraz with an intense nose of liqueur cherries, a hint of cassis, and a subtle veneer of savoury older French oak. The juicy palate is on the light side of medium-bodied but it has good flavour intensity nevertheless. It falls away slightly in the mouth, but overall it's a well-made, nicely balanced wine. Serve it with veal scaloppine.

Rosemount Estate Shiraz Cabernet

Quality	♟ ♟ ♟ ♟
Value	★ ★ ★ ⁂
Rating	88
Grapes	shiraz; cabernet sauvignon
Region	not stated
Cellar	➙2
Alc./Vol.	14.0%
RRP	$11.00 ⑤

Rosemount's Diamond Label wines are found just about everywhere and the red wine style has sometimes been committed to a measure of sweetness. Is it the secret of commercial success? It would appear so, especially in the US.
CURRENT RELEASE 2005   Bright-purplish colour looks good, and the nose shows typical sweet plummy fruit and earthy notes. The palate is plump and juicy with plenty of ripe flavour, and soft tannins add a grainy thread that's savoury and appealing. Try it with spaghetti bolognese.

S.C. Pannell McLaren Vale Shiraz

Stephen Pannell is a former Hardys' chief red winemaker, now working at Shaw & Smith and doing some consulting, as well as making small quantities of his own wines on the side. This was made from 90-year-old vines.
CURRENT RELEASE 2004   The first feature you notice is the great colour. Then it unfolds sweetly ripe plummy shiraz aromas, the fruit is perfectly ripe and there is no overt oak interfering with it. The palate is soft and smooth as expected from this region, yet it also has a backbone of finely measured tannin. It is very long and pure-tasting. Sheer class – and it will have a big future. Drink with any hard cheeses.

Quality	♥ ♥ ♥ ♥ ♥
Value	★ ★ ★ ★ ⁾
Rating	97
Grapes	shiraz
Region	McLaren Vale, SA
Cellar	▮ 12+
Alc./Vol.	14.0%
RRP	$45.00 (mail order) ▮

S.C. Pannell Shiraz Grenache

The quality of the packaging matches the wine in the bottle. It comes in a heavy glass burgundy-shaped bottle, and the cork is the best available. You can tell it's expensive: it's very long and springy, with few blemishes. Unfortunately, that doesn't guarantee it's taint-free!
CURRENT RELEASE 2004   This is a stunningly good red. It's concentrated in all respects – colour, nose and palate. There is little wood intruding but instead the bouquet is all about spices, especially clove and nutmeg. In the mouth it is big, rich and fleshy, with ample tannins but not over-built. There's lovely fruit-sweetness without any hint of jamminess. Some aniseed and ironstone characters chime in and the tannins provide excellent structure. A rip-snorter with a huge future. Rare rump steak is the go.

Quality	♥ ♥ ♥ ♥ ♥
Value	★ ★ ★ ★ ⁾
Rating	96
Grapes	shiraz; grenache
Region	McLaren Vale, SA
Cellar	▮ 12+
Alc./Vol.	14.5%
RRP	$45.00 (mail order)

Salomon Finniss River Shiraz

The Finniss River is a very new winegrowing region about half an hour south of McLaren Vale on the Fleurieu Peninsula. The vineyard is owned by Bert Salomon, who runs his family's white wine estate, Salomon Undhof, in Austria's Kremstal region, on the Danube River.
CURRENT RELEASE 2001   A bold, pungent, fruit-driven red smelling of mint and herbs, licorice, earth and pepper/spice. It's medium-bodied, with a moderate alcohol strength, and fairly assertive savoury drying tannins. A grippy red that needs to be drunk with red meats or cheeses.

Quality	♥ ♥ ♥ ⁾
Value	★ ★ ★
Rating	89
Grapes	shiraz
Region	Fleurieu Peninsula, SA
Cellar	⇒ 1–7+
Alc./Vol.	13.5%
RRP	$30.00 ▮

Sandhurst Ridge Reserve Shiraz

Quality	♟ ♟ ♟ ♟ ♟
Value	★★★
Rating	93
Grapes	shiraz
Region	Bendigo, Vic.
Cellar	➥ 2–10
Alc./Vol.	14.5%
RRP	$36.00

Sandhurst was the original name of Bendigo in the nineteenth century. It was a thriving source of wine then, and now former glories are being restored at estates like Sandhurst Ridge. Makers: Paul and George Greblo. CURRENT RELEASE 2003 A deep-coloured shiraz with a powerfully ripe, plummy nose of warm, sweet, spicy notes and a veneer of vanillin oak. The palate is full-bodied with real density of essency fruit and notable American oak flavour. It finishes long with a slight hint of raspberry on the aftertaste. Firm tannins stop short of taking over and it has a lingering dry aftertaste. Serve it with roast beef.

Schild Estate Shiraz

Quality	♟ ♟ ♟ ♟
Value	★★★★
Rating	91
Grapes	shiraz
Region	Barossa Valley, SA
Cellar	🍾 5
Alc./Vol.	14.5%
RRP	$24.00 (cellar door)

Ed Schild established his first vineyard in the Barossa in 1952. The winery and cellar door are located in Lyndoch, in the southern end of the valley. Schild has 157 hectares, and a minority of the grapes are kept for their own wines. CURRENT RELEASE 2004 Vanilla, dark-chocolate, sweet plum aromas are the order of the day. It's a very slippery, smooth red without much backbone. Those who are into texture will like this. But it seems to have a slight hollow in the middle, which is not totally covered up by the lashings of oak. A seductive but not really complex young shiraz. Further age may help. Food: gourmet bangers and mash.

Seppelt Chalambar Shiraz

Quality	♟ ♟ ♟ ♟ ♟
Value	★★★★
Rating	95
Grapes	shiraz
Region	Grampians & Bendigo, Vic.
Cellar	🍾 12+
Alc./Vol.	13.0%
RRP	$30.00 Ⓢ 🍾 ≋

Chalambar has been one of the best-value red wines in the entire country for the past few years. We are mightily impressed with what Southcorp/Foster's is doing at the Great Western winery, where this is made. Chief winemaker there is Arthur O'Connor. Bendigo fruit is increasingly being used in the Seppelt blends, with great results. CURRENT RELEASE 2004 This is a more tannic, less fleshy Chalambar than we were expecting, and we guess that's the beauty of vintage variation – there's light and shade from year to year. The wine is full of aniseed, plum and dark-berry aromas gently garnished with spices; the palate is medium- to full-bodied with balanced but firm-finishing tannins. It will surely cellar well, but if you open it young, give it plenty of air and serve protein-rich food, such as rare beef fillet and demiglaze.
Previous outstanding vintages: 1998, 2001, '02, '03

Seppelt Victoria Shiraz

When other companies put 'Victoria' on their labels, they usually mean somewhere along the vast Murray Valley. Not so Seppelt. The grapes for this lovely shiraz come from regions like Bendigo, the Pyrenees and the Grampians. Maker: Arthur O'Connor and team.

CURRENT RELEASE 2004 Again, this is one of the greatest red bargains of the year. It is a soft, fruity, spicy, gorgeous quaffing red, with distinctly cool-grown aromatics and the sort of fleshy, fruit-sweet palate that every drink-now red under $20 should have, but few do. Flavours of vanilla, plum, dark chocolate abound, and it has just enough grip to lend it real authority. If ever a wine punched above its weight, this does. Serve with shish kebabs.

Quality	🍷🍷🍷🍷
Value	★★★★★
Rating	**90**
Grapes	shiraz
Region	central and southern Vic.
Cellar	5
Alc./Vol.	13.5%
RRP	$18.50

Sevenhill Shiraz

Sevenhill was originally established as a monastery or school for Jesuit priests. The winery was added to make wine for the altar. Now it's pretty much all about the wine. Winemaker is Brother John May.

CURRENT RELEASE 2002 The trademark of Sevenhill reds is their eucalyptus/mint aroma, and this has it in spades. There are also tomato ketchup, blackberry and oaky aromas, while the palate is medium-bodied, with intensity, length and structure. It's a good drink-or-cellar style. Shepherd's pie would suit.

Quality	🍷🍷🍷½
Value	★★★½
Rating	**88**
Grapes	shiraz
Region	Clare Valley, SA
Cellar	10
Alc./Vol.	13.5%
RRP	$24.50

Shaw and Smith Shiraz

This is only the third vintage of this wine and already we regard it in the top echelon of Australian shiraz. It contains a tiny viognier component but there is no mention of it on the bottle. The '03 was our Best Shiraz and Best Red Wine in last year's *Guide*. Makers: Martin Shaw and Daryl Catlin.

CURRENT RELEASE 2004 A most impressive red, even better than the lovely '03. It's very clean, rich and ripe, while at the same time capturing cooler-grown elements of pepper and spices, together with sweeter berry and plum flavours. It's deep and well-structured on the palate, superbly balanced and full of beautifully ripe but spicy flavours, which are concentrated and long. Sheer magic! Delicious with duck sausages.

Previous outstanding vintages: 2002, '03

Quality	🍷🍷🍷🍷🍷
Value	★★★★
Rating	**96**
Grapes	shiraz; viognier
Region	Adelaide Hills, SA
Cellar	15+
Alc./Vol.	14.0%
RRP	$38.00

Shelmerdine Heathcote Shiraz

Quality	♟♟♟♟
Value	★★★★
Rating	90
Grapes	shiraz
Region	Heathcote, Vic.
Cellar	🍾 8+
Alc./Vol.	13.5%
RRP	$28.00 ⑤ 🥂

The Shelmerdine family owns vineyards at both ends of the Heathcote strip, the hottest part in the north and the coolest in the south – which Stephen Shelmerdine calls the Côte Rôtie of Heathcote, partly because of its granitic soils. This wine is more evocative of the south than the north. CURRENT RELEASE 2004 Shelmerdine deliberately makes a more elegant, lower-alcohol style of shiraz than most in Heathcote. If you want guts, look elsewhere. The '04 is a nicely balanced red with savoury earth, black-olive and dry-spice characters. The tannins are mild and measured. It has very good balance and drinkability. It suits drinking with veal escalopes and mushroom sauce.

St Hallett Faith Shiraz

Quality	♟♟♟♟
Value	★★★★⌐
Rating	90
Grapes	shiraz
Region	Barossa Valley, SA
Cellar	🍾 6
Alc./Vol.	14.0%
RRP	$21.50 ⑤

The name came from a vineyard near the Faith Lutheran church in the Barossa Valley, which originally supplied the grapes. Winemakers: Stuart Blackwell and Matt Gant. CURRENT RELEASE 2004 This is one of the most reliable labels in the Barossa for good drinking at a reasonable price. Classic regional meaty/charcuterie and plum/raspberry flavours, not oaky but more fruit-driven. It's medium-bodied but doesn't stint on flavour. Indeed, it's more digestible than most of the famous Barossa blockbusters and has some fruit sweetness and lovely balance. Enjoy it with gourmet meat pies.

St Leonards Shiraz Viognier

Quality	♟♟♟♟
Value	★★★
Rating	88
Grapes	shiraz; viognier
Region	Rutherglen, Vic.
Cellar	🍾 4
Alc./Vol.	14.0%
RRP	$25.00 🥂

The Browns of Wahgunyah are a very saintly family – they own All Saints as well as St Leonards. There was a time when people named wineries after saints – must be a sign of the times that these things are no longer considered so important. CURRENT RELEASE 2004 A fairly modest depth of colour is the first thing to note. It has a soft, mellow, semi-mature bouquet of earthy dark-berry and plum fruit, the 5 per cent viognier component is not too obvious, and oak has been used discreetly. The taste is soft, mellow, easy-drinking and smooth. Gentle, balanced and ready to go. Try it with savoury meatballs.

Stella Bella Shiraz

The Stella Bella labels are a marvellous example of design. We love 'em. They depict a mass of fruits and flowers being squeezed in a dirty great big G-clamp. The resultant ooze of red juice trickles down the label. Maker: Janice McDonald.

CURRENT RELEASE 2004   The Stella Bella style is bold, fruit-driven and vibrant, and this conforms precisely to that model. Aromas of dark berries and plums are supported by high-quality oak, and the wine is full-bodied, intense and lively on the palate. Well-concentrated fruit, polished tannins and youthful exuberance are the keys. It would cellar well, and drink nicely with a rare T-bone steak.

Quality	♀ ♀ ♀ ♀ ♀
Value	★ ★ ★ ★
Rating	92
Grapes	shiraz
Region	Margaret River, WA
Cellar	🍾 10
Alc./Vol.	14.5%
RRP	$24.00 ➓

Stringy Brae Shiraz

Stringy-bark is a type of eucalyptus tree, characterised by its tough, fibrous bark. It is reputed to thrive on the poorest soils – of which they have plenty in the Clare Valley's picturesque Sevenhill area, where this vineyard is found.

CURRENT RELEASE 2002   This is a boots-and-all style of big-boy shiraz. There are some gumleaf, wormwood and tomato ketchup aromas about it, mixed in with some sweaty/feral reductive notes. It's big, fruit-sweet and gutsy, a bit rough and grippy perhaps, and a touch overripe, but certainly you won't feel short-changed! It's got plenty of everything – except price: at well under $20, it's good value. Pair it with game pie.

Quality	♀ ♀ ♀ ♀
Value	★ ★ ★ ⁺
Rating	88
Grapes	shiraz
Region	Clare Valley, SA
Cellar	🍾 13+
Alc./Vol.	14.5%
RRP	$18.50 ➓ 🍶

Syrahmi SV2 Heathcote Shiraz Viognier

Adam Foster is a former chef (Melbourne's Adelphi and Pomme) who became a winemaker. This is his first effort, and there's just 95 cases! SV2 refers to shiraz viognier as well as 'single vineyard'.

CURRENT RELEASE 2004   This is an impressive first attempt. The lad knows how to make wine. Great depth of red–purple colour leads into a very ripe aroma which treads the fine line – there are hints of raisin and prune but it avoids portiness or 'dead-fruit'. The taste is big and chewy, voluptuous even. It's big and obvious, not a wine of subtlety, but generous, fleshy and rich, with some savoury characteristics and great balance. We'd suggest osso buco here.

Quality	♀ ♀ ♀ ♀ ♀
Value	★ ★ ★ ⁺
Rating	93
Grapes	shiraz; viognier 3.4%
Region	Heathcote, Vic.
Cellar	🍾 6+
Alc./Vol.	14.0%
RRP	$34.00 ➓

Tahbilk 1860 Vines Shiraz

Quality	♀♀♀♀
Value	★★
Rating	90
Grapes	shiraz
Region	Nagambie Lakes, Vic.
Cellar	▮ 6+
Alc./Vol.	13.5%
RRP	$121.60

Tahbilk 1860 Vines is a single-block wine made from the oldest shiraz vines planted at this wonderfully atmospheric, historic winery. Quality varies according to vintage, and in some recent years we've preferred its sibling, the less expensive old-vine Reserve Shiraz. At its best 1860 is a lovely expression of this unique *terroir*.
CURRENT RELEASE 2000 The nose is all old spice, leather and maturity, and as usual it's a bit of a time capsule of how Aussie shiraz used to be. It lacks the weight and depth of the best years, and there's a rather rustic thread, but aficionados of the style probably won't mind. It finishes with a long, mature aftertaste. Try it with slow-roasted leg of lamb.
Previous outstanding vintages: 1984, '86, '91, '92, '95, '98, '99

Taltarni Heathcote Shiraz

Quality	♀♀♀♀▯
Value	★★★↓
Rating	93
Grapes	shiraz
Region	Heathcote, Vic.
Cellar	⟵2–10
Alc./Vol.	14.5%
RRP	$44.00 ⬚

Taltarni's reds are traditionally hefty styles, so the hearty shiraz of Heathcote has a natural affinity with the house style. Taltarni has joined the growing band of wineries safeguarding their reds with a screw-cap instead of a cork.
CURRENT RELEASE 2004 Not as potent as some '04 Heathcote shiraz, this deeply coloured young red has a very seductive nose of dark fruits, spices, ferrous stones and subtle smoky oak. In the mouth it has structured, inky blackberry fruit of ripe intensity, which hasn't become soupy and fumy with alcohol due to the hot vintage. The texture is fine; it lingers on the palate, and the dry firm tannins are starting to integrate. It needs age to be at its best. A good mate for rare rib of beef.

Tatachilla Keystone Shiraz Viognier

Quality	♀♀♀♀
Value	★★★★
Rating	90
Grapes	shiraz 93%; viognier 7%
Region	McLaren Vale, SA
Cellar	▮ 3
Alc./Vol.	14.8%
RRP	$17.95 Ⓢ ⬚

Shiraz-viognier blends are the flavour of the month, so it was only a matter of time before they started popping up in budget brands. Tatachilla's Keystone does an excellent job of showing off the style at a moderate price.
CURRENT RELEASE 2004 The nose has earthy, cherry and spice aromas with a whisper of floral scent courtesy of the viognier component and subtle oak. The medium-weight palate continues with plummy flavour and velvety texture, ahead of fine tannins on the finish. Try it with mushroom risotto.

Taylors Shiraz

According to a December 1995 A.C.Nielsen survey, Taylors Shiraz dominates its varietal category in the $14–$20 price range. The formula of generous, ripe wine at a fair price always works well.
CURRENT RELEASE 2004   From an excellent Clare Valley vintage, this wine typifies the successful Taylors style. The nose has earth and blackberry aromas with a whisper of mint and a hint of vanilla. In the mouth it has a smooth rich flavour that's ripe and satisfying, finishing with just the right amount of tannic edge. We'd recommend spaghetti bolognese with parmesan.

Quality	♟♟♟♟
Value	★★★★
Rating	90
Grapes	shiraz
Region	Clare Valley, SA
Cellar	▮ 4
Alc./Vol.	14.5%
RRP	$17.95 ⑤ 🛇

Tenet Estate Shiraz

Tenet Estate is a new Barossa label, exclusive to Vintage Cellars and associated stores. Pricing is very reasonable.
CURRENT RELEASE 2004   This is a ripe commercial wine, bolstered by a touch of sweetness to make a plummy style with a hint of spice on the nose. The palate is clean and of middling body with intense plum and licorice flavours and a very soft finish. Try it with a steak.

Quality	♟♟♟♟
Value	★★★
Rating	88
Grapes	shiraz
Region	Barossa Valley, SA
Cellar	▮ 2
Alc./Vol.	14.0%
RRP	$18.00 🛇

Terra Felix Shiraz Viognier

'. . . and the exciting couples come together in a way that is both classic and surprising.' The Terra Felix wines each have a similar esoteric quote on the label. It's all very arty and well above our heads, but wine quality is excellent, especially given the moderate price tag.
CURRENT RELEASE 2005   An aromatic floral note betrays the viognier component in this well-priced red, and the peppery red-berry fruit is bright and breezy, yet there's plenty to interest us. It has a definite Rhône-ish accent, but more Mediterranean than the shiraz-viognier composition would suggest. It's flavoursome, dry and savoury with a moderate bite of tannin. A new-fashioned Australian red of high quality made in an easy food-friendly style. Enjoy it with a pork terrine.

Quality	♟♟♟♟
Value	★★★★
Rating	91
Grapes	shiraz; viognier
Region	Upper Goulburn, Vic.
Cellar	▮ 2
Alc./Vol.	14.3%
RRP	$15.00 🛇

PENGUIN WINE OF THE YEAR
and BEST-VALUE RED WINE

Tibooburra Shiraz

Quality	🍷🍷🍷🍷🍷
Value	★★★
Rating	93
Grapes	shiraz
Region	Yarra Valley, SA
Cellar	🍾 5
Alc./Vol.	13.0%
RRP	$30.00

The Tibooburra property in the picturesque southern hills of the Yarra Valley isn't just a producer of good wine. It was the first place in Victoria to produce black truffles, which have been exported to the truffle fanatics of the world.
CURRENT RELEASE 2004   This has a loose-knit nose of juicy loganberries, gentle spices and subtle smoky oak. It tastes smooth and satisfying with medium body, ripe-berry flavour and a long, gentle finish. It makes a great contrast to the potent, super-ripe, alcoholic shiraz type and slips down a lot easier over a meal. Serve it with tagliatelle with truffle oil and shaved parmigiano.

Tim Adams Shiraz

Quality	🍷🍷🍷🍷
Value	★★★
Rating	92
Grapes	shiraz
Region	Clare Valley, SA
Cellar	⬤–1–8
Alc./Vol.	14.0%
RRP	$26.00 🥂

We always see some traditional minerally qualities in Tim Adams Shiraz that are missing from most of the more 'modern' Clare wines, and it's something we like a lot. The wine isn't traditional in another significant way: Tim Adams has smoothly made the transition to screw-caps on his shiraz.
CURRENT RELEASE 2004   This has a very spicy and slightly meaty nose to start, then ripe-berry and redcurrant aromas enter the equation on further acquaintance. A thread of slightly raw oak doesn't intrude unduly, and the generous palate has good texture and real poise and balance. It should develop well in bottle and be a good match for a lamb casserole.

Tim Smith Wines Barossa Shiraz

Quality	🍷🍷🍷🍷🍷
Value	★★★
Rating	94
Grapes	shiraz
Region	Barossa Valley, SA
Cellar	⬤–2–10
Alc./Vol.	14.5%
RRP	$33.00 🥂

Where once we were inundated with new labels from emerging wine regions, now we seem to receive just as many from old established places like the Barossa. This is one of them.
CURRENT RELEASE 2004   This young Barossa shiraz has great visual impact: the colour is a glass-staining black–purple. On the nose it has deep, boiled-down, black-fruit aromas of great intensity. Touches of five-spice and ironstone add complexity and impact, oak is a background player. The palate has densely packed blackberry and blackcurrant flavours with a high-toned edge adding definition. It finishes long and fine, with attractively ripe tannins in support. Serve it with braised steak and winter vegetables.

Tinkers Hill Shiraz

Tinkers Hill is a new, small vineyard in the rugged
Woolshed Valley near Beechworth in north-eastern Victoria.
It's a region worth visiting for its impressive countryside
and the lovely old gold-rush town at its heart.
CURRENT RELEASE 2005   A fair effort for a young
vineyard, this has a medium-intensity nose of raspberries,
leather, spices and a slightly barnyardy touch. The palate
is better: light to middling in body with rustic cherry and
berry flavours, ahead of a very soft, agreeable finish. It falls
away a bit on the palate but its no-fuss personality has
some charm. Serve it with pasta and wild mushrooms.

Quality	▇ ▇ ▇ ▌
Value	★ ★ ★
Rating	90
Grapes	shiraz
Region	Beechworth, Vic.
Cellar	▌ 1
Alc./Vol.	14.0%
RRP	$26.50

Tollana TR16 Shiraz

Tollana's reds deliver generous fruit in spades, making
them excellent value. We're thankful to Tollana's
Southcorp/Foster's owners for reintroducing this
good-value brand.
CURRENT RELEASE 2004   Exactly what we expect from
Tollana. TR16 has aromas and flavours of vanilla, chocolate
and dense blackberry-ish fruit in velvety harmony with soft,
ripe tannins. It has succulent balance and good length.
A red of quality and value. Enjoy it with cassoulet.

Quality	▇ ▇ ▇ ▇ ▌
Value	★ ★ ★ ★
Rating	92
Grapes	shiraz
Region	Adelaide Hills & Clare Valley, SA
Cellar	▌ 5
Alc./Vol.	14.0%
RRP	$19.50 Ⓢ ⬗

Torbreck Descendant

Descendant is a sort of understudy to the more
stratospherically priced Torbreck flagship, RunRig; it is also
made from shiraz with some viognier influence. We often
enjoy it more than its big brother.
CURRENT RELEASE 2004   This is another for the Torbreck
aficionados – a very dark dense wine with a powerful plum-
jam nose, touched by notable spice and floral notes. Fruit-
sweet, ripe flavours have spicy and chocolatey trimmings,
and the palate has great depth and length of flavour, but it
seems to lack true complexity to us. It's still a pup though,
and age could well build new dimensions. It rests on firm,
grippy tannins that will mellow in bottle. We'd suggest
Chinese red-cooked beef.

Quality	▇ ▇ ▇ ▇
Value	★ ★
Rating	91
Grapes	shiraz; viognier
Region	Barossa Valley, SA
Cellar	▌ 10
Alc./Vol.	14.8%
RRP	$150.00

Torbreck RunRig

Quality	♉♉♉♉
Value	★→
Rating	90
Grapes	shiraz; viognier
Region	Barossa Valley, SA
Cellar	➦2–10+
Alc./Vol.	14.5%
RRP	$250.00

This is Torbreck's top red, a collectors' wine in the US and among some Australians who like wines of immense power and raisiny concentration. We usually think Torbreck's less-cultish reds are easier to drink.

CURRENT RELEASE 2003   Another rather stewed effort under the RunRig ticket, but it's a tad less porty and one-dimensional than the '02. It has profound plum and blackberry fruit with some floral fragrance, and the palate is thick in texture, mouth-filling and firm on the finish. It lacks real mid-palate interest and complexity, perhaps that will develop with bottle-age – it's still very youthful – but we'd like to see more dimension right now. Try it with mature cheddar.

Torbreck The Factor

Quality	♉♉♉♉♉
Value	★★
Rating	93
Grapes	shiraz
Region	Barossa Valley, SA
Cellar	▮8+
Alc./Vol.	14.5%
RRP	$140.00

We've been in a quandary over the Torbreck style in recent years. Perhaps it's a vintage thing, but the top wines have been getting bigger and more port-like, and we often prefer the lesser wines to the high-priced super-dooper versions.

CURRENT RELEASE 2003   The nose is slightly fumy and there are some wild meaty notes to it, too, but the main game is lush berry fruit, licorice and spice notes, a raisiny, almost muscaty touch and barely perceptible oak. It's a little like a dry vintage port in some ways, and the velvet-smooth palate has a very long finish with perfectly integrated tannins. It's one of the better of the super-ripe, demiglaze-like genre of Barossa red. Serve it with roast rump of beef. *Previous outstanding vintages: 1999, 2000, '02*

Torbreck The Struie

Quality	♉♉♉♉
Value	★★★
Rating	92
Grapes	shiraz
Region	Barossa & Eden valleys, SA
Cellar	▮10+
Alc./Vol.	14.5%
RRP	$46.00

Torbreck's wines have as their essence the ancient, dry-grown, bush vines of the Barossa Valley.

CURRENT RELEASE 2004   This Struie has a glass-staining purplish colour, and the nose has concentrated aromas of dark cherries, crushed red berries, spice, earth and a floral/minty touch. The palate is plump and deeply flavoured with warm plummy fruit in the middle, and a very long fine-grained finish. It's a powerful Barossa statement, and it stops short of being overwhelming, but to us it lacks the interesting facets that keep you pouring another glass. What sort of food do you serve with big, jammy wines like this? Hare or some other rich furred game is worth a try.

Train Trak Shiraz

The railway line that carried passengers through the verdant hills of the Yarra Valley still passes the Train Trak vineyard. Today its rusty rails carry an occasional trolley of tourists, but the days of 'real' trains are gone.
CURRENT RELEASE 2004   A smoothly proportioned cool-climate shiraz with mellow blackberry aromas, some restrained hints of spice, and understated oak. In the mouth it's rounded and juicy with moderate, dry tannins and a long succulent finish. Try it with veal kidneys.

Quality	♟♟♟♟♟
Value	★★★★
Rating	93
Grapes	shiraz
Region	Yarra Valley, Vic.
Cellar	▮ 5
Alc./Vol.	14.0%
RRP	$26.00 ≋

Trevor Jones Wild Witch Reserve Shiraz

Wild Witch is an old shiraz vineyard at the Lyndoch end of the Barossa Valley. Trevor Jones's motto 'my way, boots and all' is borne out in the big brash style of his wines.
WARNING: This wine has one of the heaviest bottles we've ever seen. Don't drop it on your toe!
CURRENT RELEASE 2002   This has a warm, powerful nose of spicy dark berries and boiled fruitcake all dressed up in lots of high-toned vanillin and coconutty oak. The opulent palate has plenty of ripe fruit and oak flavours in balance, and tannins of surprising finesse precede a very long, ripe aftertaste. A macho red and then some! It would work well with sticky braised oxtail.

Quality	♟♟♟♟♟
Value	★★★
Rating	92
Grapes	shiraz
Region	Barossa Valley, SA
Cellar	▮ 10
Alc./Vol.	14.8%
RRP	$58.80

Turkey Flat Shiraz

The nucleus of Turkey Flat Shiraz is a vineyard containing shiraz vines that are among the oldest in the world. Planted in 1847, they have quietly lived through the trials and traumas of the past 160 years, a living link with the early days of Australian wine.
CURRENT RELEASE 2004   Deep, glass-staining colour and rich, sweet, ultra-ripe aromas of blood plums and fruits of the forest introduce this very concentrated shiraz. It's fruit-driven with oak in the background, and the big, dense palate is powerfully flavoured and intense, if just a tad soupy. Grippy tannins hold it in a firm embrace. A generous, honest Barossa red that takes ripeness and alcohol to the limit, less would have been better perhaps, but it will please a lot of people. Serve it with a rich beef casserole.

Quality	♟♟♟♟♟
Value	★★★
Rating	93
Grapes	shiraz
Region	Barossa Valley, SA
Cellar	▬ 2–15
Alc./Vol.	15.0%
RRP	$45.00

Two Hands Max's Garden Shiraz

Quality	🍷🍷🍷🍷🍷
Value	★★★
Rating	92
Grapes	shiraz
Region	Heathcote, Vic.
Cellar	➙2–8+
Alc./Vol.	14.5%
RRP	$55.00

The arrival of a Heathcote shiraz under the Two Hands label is a surprise. In the past Two Hands has been strongly associated with hefty South Australian reds. The resulting wine is less formidable (and in our opinion more drinkable) than its '04 vintage South Oz siblings.
CURRENT RELEASE 2004   This has a deeply saturated purple colour and the aromatic nose is a departure from the usual Two Hands fashion. It has black-cherry, raisin, chocolate-nougat, mint and spice aromas that are seductively lush and ripe. In the mouth it shows great depth of flavour along with a freshness that keeps it lively. It finishes with dry, fine-grained tannins. We'd suggest braised veal and winter vegetables.

Tyrrell's Rufus Stone Heathcote Shiraz

Quality	🍷🍷🍷🍷🍷
Value	★★★★
Rating	94
Grapes	shiraz
Region	Heathcote, Vic.
Cellar	➙1–8
Alc./Vol.	14.0%
RRP	$25.00 ⬧

Sir Walter Tyrrell, an ancestor of the Hunter Valley Tyrrells, is supposed to have accidentally killed King William II (aka 'Rufus') in a hunting accident about 900 years ago. The site of the event is marked today by the Rufus Stone.
CURRENT RELEASE 2004   Tyrrells are super-impressed with Heathcote shiraz, and their wines so far have supported their enthusiasm. More mellow than some Heathcote reds, the '04 shiraz shows delicious, blackberry-like fruit character with sweet spice and chocolatey notes adding richness and complexity. Oak is deftly handled, and it has a rounded, smooth texture, very long flavour, and lovely ripe, integrated tannins. Great with beef fillet.

Ulithorne Frux Frugus Shiraz

Quality	🍷🍷🍷🍷
Value	★★★
Rating	90
Grapes	shiraz
Region	McLaren Vale, SA
Cellar	➙1–10+
Alc./Vol.	14.5%
RRP	$42.00 🍾

Full marks to Rose Kentish and Sam Harrison, the owners, for originality in naming the wine (it's Latin for 'fruit of the earth'). It comes from a 28-hectare shiraz vineyard in the Onkaparinga Hills, planted in 1971. Contract winemaker is the accomplished Brian Light.
CURRENT RELEASE 2004   The colour is impressively dark and youthful, while the bouquet has some raisined, overripe, slightly porty aspects. In the mouth, the wine is big and concentrated, thick and chewy – we wouldn't call it elegant! It's a huge, dense, chocolatey red with loads of tannin. Definitely one for those who love body-slammers. You could try it with aged Heidi gruyère cheese.

Vasarelli Family Reserve Shiraz

The Vasarellis arrived in Australia in the 1960s and found the McLaren Vale district had everything they needed to grow grapes and produce the sort of food they'd enjoyed in their European homeland. Now their own wines are made in an easy-drinking style that's perfect on the regional table.
CURRENT RELEASE 2003   The nose is driven by juicy red- and black-fruit aromas, with some attractive savoury earthiness underneath. Sweet oak seasons it lightly, and the palate follows suit with ripe, smooth flavour, good balance and a poised underpinning of ripe tannins. The rather high alcohol doesn't intrude too much. A harmonious red wine to enjoy with homemade pasta, tomatoes and cheese.

Quality	♥ ♥ ♥ ♥
Value	★ ★ ★ ⌐
Rating	92
Grapes	shiraz
Region	McLaren Vale, SA
Cellar	▮ 4
Alc./Vol.	15.0%
RRP	$23.50 ⋧

Wandin Valley Estate Shiraz

Wandin Valley Estate is a showpiece wine property with a picturesque location on Wilderness Road, Lovedale. Owners James and Philippa Davern created not just a winery, but a restaurant, accommodation, cricket oval and pavilion.
CURRENT RELEASE 2004   There's a very smoky/charry character about this wine that could polarise tasters. It's a common feature of Hunter reds and goes hand in hand with a drying, savoury earthiness that is the opposite of the bold fruity style of red that we see from other regions. This style tends to come into its own with food. We'd try a peppered steak.

Quality	♥ ♥ ♥
Value	★ ★ ★
Rating	86
Grapes	shiraz
Region	Hunter Valley, NSW
Cellar	▮ 5+
Alc./Vol.	13.5%
RRP	$18.00 ⋧

Water Wheel Shiraz

The Cumming family celebrated 30 vintages at Water Wheel in 2006. Winemaker Peter Cumming is on record as saying he'd like to see less alcohol in his reds, and we would agree: this admits to 15.5 per cent and tastes like it, too. Curiously, it didn't stop the (palate-fatigued?) judges at the 2005 Royal Melbourne Wine Show awarding it a gold medal.
CURRENT RELEASE 2004   We find this kind of wine wellnigh undrinkable. It is clumsy, shapeless and syrupy; sweet-fruited, rich and fat; but most of all it's hot and spirity from all that alcohol. To those who like this kind of wine, we say go for it. One thing that's beyond argument is that Water Wheel wines are always modestly priced, and often good value. It's a style thing. Hard cheese, such as parmesan, is about the only thing to pair this with.

Quality	♥ ♥ ♥
Value	★ ★ ★
Rating	86
Grapes	shiraz
Region	Bendigo, Vic.
Cellar	▮ 3
Alc./Vol.	15.5%
RRP	$18.00 Ⓢ ⋧

West Cape Howe Two Steps Shiraz Viognier

Quality	♟♟♟♟♟
Value	★★★★
Rating	93
Grapes	shiraz; viognier
Region	Great Southern, WA
Cellar	▮ 5+
Alc./Vol.	15.0%
RRP	$24.00

It's amazing how many wineries are suddenly finding some viognier and turning out a shiraz-viognier blend. It would be easy to be cynical and say it's all a marketing ploy, but the evidence of our tastebuds is that a lot of these wines are absolutely delish. So, why not? Maker: Gavin Berry.
CURRENT RELEASE 2004   The colour is deep and of excellent hue while the bouquet reveals a floral viognier influence at first sniff. There are apricot, pencil-shavings and earthy-spice notes. It's very rich and deep in the mouth and boasts lashings of vanilla, berry, plum and jam flavours, with admirable fleshy extract. There's a lot of bang for your 24 bucks – including alcohol and tannin to burn. Serve it with slow-braised Greek lamb with olives.

Westend Three Bridges Reserve Limited Release Shiraz

Quality	♟♟♟♟♟
Value	★★★★
Rating	95
Grapes	shiraz
Region	Riverina, NSW
Cellar	▮ 5+
Alc./Vol.	14.5%
RRP	$25.00 ▮

Westend Wines started life as Calabria, after the owners, the family of Bill Calabria – perhaps Australia's only non-drinking winemaker. Westend has a smart cellar-door facility in the main street of Griffith.
CURRENT RELEASE 2003   A big wine with a lot of stuffing, this shows what can be achieved with Riverina fruit. Correct fruit ripeness plus smart oak well handled has given a stylish, savoury wine with lots more than just simple grapey fruit. Leathery, savoury and spicy, it has a structured, tannic palate and could take some age, too. It drinks well now, with salami, cheese and crusty bread.

Westgate Endurance Shiraz

Quality	♟♟♟♟♟
Value	★★★⒈
Rating	92
Grapes	shiraz
Region	Grampians, Vic.
Cellar	▮ 15+
Alc./Vol.	13.5%
RRP	$53.00 ▮ ⌷

This flagship shiraz comes from 35-year-old vines on Bruce and Robyn Dalkin's Westgate property near Great Western. Bruce Dalkin is the sixth generation of his family to run the primarily wool-growing property. They've been selling grapes to other wineries for many years, but only recently begun to market wine of their own.
CURRENT RELEASE 2004   This is a delicious shiraz that grows on you as it opens up in the glass. It has typical Great Western shiraz spice, perhaps due to the 'original Great Western clone' as much as the site. There are dark-cherry, herbal and medicinal overtones as well; the palate has length and plenty of stuffing, finishing with abundant ripe tannins that dry the finish. It suits hard cheeses: try reggiano.
Previous outstanding vintages: 2002, '03

Wirra Wirra RSW Shiraz

RSW stands for the founder of Wirra Wirra – Robert Strangways Wigley – which seems an appropriately odd name for such a reputedly eccentric man. RSW, the wine, is becoming more powerfully concentrated, and expensive, as time passes. Maker: Samantha Connew.
CURRENT RELEASE 2003   Our sample seemed to be developing quite rapidly, but it's a big, rich, dense wine that will no doubt handle bottle-age well. There are dark-chocolate, earthy, dusty and savoury barrel-aged aromas, while in the mouth it's smooth, fleshy, velvety and profoundly flavoursome. There's a lot of oak here but it's been well handled. It already drinks well, pair it with aged cheddar.

Quality	♟♟♟♟
Value	★★★
Rating	91
Grapes	shiraz
Region	McLaren Vale, SA
Cellar	▮ 10+
Alc./Vol.	14.5%
RRP	$50.00 ▮

Wolf Blass Gold Label Shiraz

Herr Wolfgang Blass still has his signature on the labels of Wolf Blass wines, which is a puzzle, as he hasn't had much to do with them for years. Caroline Dunn is the chief red winemaker.
CURRENT RELEASE 2003   This has more focus and structural tightness than many warm-grown shirazes. It seems to have the kind of structure that will age well, as opposed to a big fat blob of sweet fruit that tastes flattering at a couple of years. Aromas of pepper and mixed spices are bound up with charry/toasty American oak notes. The palate is dry and lean-ish, with almost a touch of austerity. It's a good food wine: osso buco would work well.

Quality	♟♟♟♟
Value	★★★★
Rating	91
Grapes	shiraz
Region	Barossa Valley, SA
Cellar	▮ 10+
Alc./Vol.	14.0%
RRP	$23.00 ⑤ ≋

Wolf Blass Grey Label Shiraz

'No wood, no good', was the Wolf Blass/John Glaetzer motto for the first 35 years. Neither Glaetzer nor Blass works in the company today, but no reason to change now – we guess.
CURRENT RELEASE 2004   This is a big, thick, dense wine with chewy tannins and a lot of extraction, but it's a bit overdone for our likes. The bouquet is all about wood at this stage: it reeks of coconut, vanillin American oak. The tannins are assertive, mouth-coating and chewy, and it's too young to drink. At least, we couldn't enjoy drinking it now; you might be different. It's just a baby and certainly has the legs to age. We'd recommend cellaring, then serve with standing rib roast of beef.

Quality	♟♟♟♟
Value	★★ ⌐
Rating	89
Grapes	shiraz
Region	McLaren Vale, SA
Cellar	➥2–10+
Alc./Vol.	14.5%
RRP	$40.00 ▮ ≋

Wolf Blass Platinum Label Shiraz

Quality	❦❦❦❦
Value	★★
Rating	88
Grapes	shiraz
Region	Barossa Valley, SA
Cellar	➞2–7
Alc./Vol.	15.5%
RRP	$180.00

This is the top of the many-branched Wolf Blass red-wine tree. It is breathtakingly expensive and we wonder what the intention is with style: in the few vintages sold thus far the style has wandered a fair bit. This is possibly the least convincing release that we've seen.
CURRENT RELEASE 2003   This tastes like a desperate attempt to join the Barossa's Robert Parker club. It is a very dense, concentrated wine with a blackish colour and a thick, chewy, oaky, alcoholic style that completely lacks elegance and refinement. It's big and brutish, with borderline 'dead fruit' and essency, earthy, woody and slightly minty flavours. It's difficult to enjoy at this young stage; however, we have trouble imagining it any better with age. And we certainly can't see $180 worth in it.

Wood Park Kneebone's Gap Shiraz

Quality	❦❦❦❦
Value	★★★
Rating	88
Grapes	shiraz
Region	King Valley, Vic.
Cellar	5+
Alc./Vol.	14.0%
RRP	$23.00

Apparently Kneebone's Gap is a local landmark. The vineyard's address is Kneebone's Gap Road, Markwood. Many of the names on Wood Park's wines relate to a small vineyard that supplied the grapes, but this one is off John Stokes's own Wood Park vineyard.
CURRENT RELEASE 2005   Wood Park wasted no time getting its '05 reds on the market. The most surprising thing was how approachable they were from the outset. This has a vivid purple–red colour and a bright, berry/ cherry and plum-like fruit-led bouquet, with a faint touch of spice. It's balanced in the mouth, with good intensity, and although the tannins are fairly evident, they're smooth and fluffy. A good wine to serve with a beefy casserole.

Woodstock Shiraz

Quality	❦❦❦❦
Value	★★★★
Rating	92
Grapes	shiraz
Region	McLaren Vale, SA
Cellar	➞1–8+
Alc./Vol.	14.0%
RRP	$20.00
	(cellar door)

Woodstock's owner Scott Collett is part-owner of Barossa Vintners, Tanunda, where Qantas Medallist/Young Winemaker of the Year Ben Glaetzer practises his craft. Both men sign the Woodstock back labels these days, and we've seen a marked improvement in the wines of late.
CURRENT RELEASE 2004   The colour is deep and full of promise; the nose is very fragrant with peppermint, raspberry, blackberry and blueberry aromas. In the mouth, it's concentrated and essency, with lashings of fruit and youthful vim; it's very young and just oozes potential. We'd cellar it, then serve it with spaghetti bolognese.

Woodstock The Stocks Single Vineyard Shiraz

This single-vineyard shiraz is the big kahuna in the Woodstock portfolio. It is always made in a big, tannic, gutsy regional style that demands cellaring, hearty food, and a taste for whopper red wines. The '04 comes in a flash new, etched-glass bottle. Makers: Scott Collett and Ben Glaetzer.
CURRENT RELEASE 2004   Dark red–purple in colour, this is a big, rich, thickly textured, oaky shiraz. There's a lot of tannin but it's remarkably smooth, and it's a seductive style although we'd like to see less oak. It does have a core of rich, ripe fruit but it finishes with oak flavour, which is not ideal. It's a crowd-pleaser and would probably do justice to a piece of beef à la mode.

Quality	▼▼▼▼▼
Value	★★★
Rating	92
Grapes	shiraz
Region	McLaren Vale, SA
Cellar	➡ 2–8+
Alc./Vol.	14.5%
RRP	$50.00 (cellar door)

Wynns Coonawarra Estate Michael Shiraz

Things have changed at Wynns, since the last of the old-style Michaels rolled off the bottling line. The last was the '98; the new model is lighter and more elegant with less alcohol, less tannin, and above all less oak – and it's French instead of raucous American. Makers: Sue Hodder and Sarah Pidgeon.
CURRENT RELEASE 2003   The colour is more youthful than most '03s, and it has a bright, fresh, fruit-driven aroma of rose petal and raspberry, with low-key oak of a subtle kind and plenty of primary fruit showing through. The palate is lively and quite intense, with understated sweet fruit, mild fine-grained tannins and excellent length. This should be cellared further for maximum reward, then enjoy it with hard Swiss-style cheeses.
Previous outstanding vintages: 1990, '91, '94, '96, '98

Quality	▼▼▼▼▼
Value	★★★↓
Rating	92
Grapes	shiraz
Region	Coonawarra, SA
Cellar	➡ 2–15+
Alc./Vol.	13.5%
RRP	$75.00

Yalumba Y Series Shiraz Viognier

Shiraz-viognier blends are all the rage and some of them are quite expensive, too. This is the best introduction to the style we've yet found. It's great value for an entry-level wine of its quality.
CURRENT RELEASE 2003   This is tremendously good value for money. The colour is medium-dark red–purple and the nose carries spices and oak, red and black fruits, with a slight whiff of apricot from the viognier. The palate adds a smoky charcuterie (possibly from charred oak) character. The palate is nicely focused and has remarkable intensity for the price. Surprisingly elegant, it suits grilled lamb chops.

Quality	▼▼▼▼
Value	★★★★★
Rating	90
Grapes	shiraz; viognier
Region	not stated
Cellar	▮ 4
Alc./Vol.	14.0%
RRP	$13.75 ⑤

Yarra Ridge Shiraz

Quality	♟ ♟ ♟ ♟
Value	★ ★ ★ ★ ⫯
Rating	90
Grapes	shiraz
Region	Yarra Valley, Vic.
Cellar	🍷 8
Alc./Vol.	14.5%
RRP	$21.00 Ⓢ ≋

When it comes to kicking back and drinking a few glasses of red with dinner, we'd much prefer this kind of medium-bodied shiraz than any of the hordes of blockbusters that seem to be taking over the world.

CURRENT RELEASE 2004   This is a very 'drinkable' shiraz: in other words, it's no show-stopper but it goes well with a meal and is a very agreeable drink, without any shortcomings. The colour is nice and deep; the bouquet shows nicely integrated fruit and oak with spicy earthy aromas and plenty of interest. It's a lighter-bodied style, medium-weight at best, smooth and balanced, with fine-grained tannins. We'd recommend pink medallions of roast beef fillet.

YarraLoch The Collection Shiraz Viognier

Quality	♟ ♟ ♟ ♟ ⵗ
Value	★ ★ ★ ★
Rating	94
Grapes	shiraz; viognier
Region	Heathcote, Vic.
Cellar	➥ 1–10+
Alc./Vol.	14.0%
RRP	$40.00 🍷

The company spiel says: 'YarraLoch differs from the plethora of new producers who have emerged in recent years in its total and uncompromising commitment to quality.' Well, they all say that; difference is, YarraLoch's wines bear it out. The proof of the pudding is in the eating. The 2 per cent of viognier was co-fermented with the shiraz.

CURRENT RELEASE 2004   Hey, this is a delicious shiraz! Nice dark colour leads the way to a big, intense bouquet of minty, herbal, ripe-plummy fruit, with vanilla and chocolate grace notes. The palate is big flavoured and dense, concentrated and gutsy, brawny and tannic – it just needs a little more time to come together properly. Then serve it with gourmet sausages.

Yellow Tail Premium Shiraz

Quality	♟ ♟ ♟ ♟ ⵗ
Value	★ ★ ★ ⫯
Rating	93
Grapes	shiraz
Region	McLaren Vale, SA
Cellar	🍷 7
Alc./Vol.	13.5%
RRP	$50.00 🍷

Yellow Tail is known for cheap $10 wines, so imagine the eyebrow raising that went on when it released two $50 reds late in 2005. This one won the Stodart Trophy in Brisbane for the best one-year-old red wine of show (as a barrel sample).

CURRENT RELEASE 2003   This is a typical McLaren Vale blockbuster 'show style' with masses of toasty American oak showing, and a fleshy, rich, smooth, opulent palate. It's oaky but not excessively so. There's a lot of mocha, fruitcake, chocolate and vanilla in there, too. A real hedonistic bombshell. It might go with parmesan cheese.

Yering Station Shiraz Viognier

Yering Station has quickly become one of the wineries most famous for shiraz viognier. Their Reserve wines have won many trophies and gold medals. In 2004, they didn't bottle a Reserve. Hence all the best fruit went into this, their regular label. Maker: Tom Carson.

CURRENT RELEASE 2004   We could drink a bucket of this. It's so soft and fleshy and fruit-sweet. Rich, melted-chocolate aromas fill the glass. There are spices as well, and a hint of viognier apricot. The tannins are very gentle and the texture is a delight. But it also has length and substance, far from being just a fruit bomb. Serve with aged pecorino cheese.

Quality	♟♟♟♟♟
Value	★★★★★
Rating	95
Grapes	shiraz; viognier
Region	Yarra Valley, Vic.
Cellar	▮ 7+
Alc./Vol.	14.0%
RRP	$23.50 ⓢ

Zonte's Footstep Shiraz Viognier

This brand is a joint venture between marketer Zar Brooks, winemaker Ben Riggs and viticulturists John Pargeter and Geoff Hardy. The footprint on the label is that of the now-extinct giant wombat, which inhabited the area in days long gone.

CURRENT RELEASE 2004   Another crowd-pleaser in the generous, user-friendly style we've quickly come to associate with this marque. The colour is deep; the bouquet carries plum-jam, herb and dark-chocolate aromas with little oak influence, while the palate is very soft and fruity, almost sweet, with a hint of overripe grapes. Drink with any hard cheeses.

Quality	♟♟♟♟
Value	★★★★⁺
Rating	90
Grapes	shiraz; viognier
Region	Langhorne Creek, SA
Cellar	▮ 5
Alc./Vol.	14.5%
RRP	$18.50 Ⓢ ⓢ

Tempranillo

Tempranillo is a newcomer to Australia and it is exciting interest in many of our wine-growing areas. In its country of origin, Spain, it's the most famous indigenous grape variety, being made either as a straight varietal or blended into savoury, sunny reds of distinctive character. In style it can vary from fairly light to surprisingly full bodied, and its berry, spice and earthy characters lend themselves to modern Australian dining, particularly dishes of Mediterranean origin. No one region has emerged as the ideal Australian location; it shows promise in a range of places.

Centennial Vineyards Limited Release Reserve Tempranillo

Quality	🍷🍷🍷🍷
Value	★★★★
Rating	93
Grapes	tempranillo
Region	Hilltops, NSW
Cellar	🍶 8+
Alc./Vol.	14.0%
RRP	$30.00 (cellar door)

Centennial Vineyards is the biggest producer in the New South Wales Southern Highlands, which is just off the Hume Highway around Bowral and Mittagong. It has a restaurant, function centre, smart cellar door and very well-equipped modern winery. A wholly professional operation. CURRENT RELEASE 2004   This tempranillo is a gutsy, concentrated red that has a fruit-forward style, redolent of exotic spices, dried cherry and dark plum. Oak plays a minor role. It's clean and vibrant on nose and palate. The tannin profile is tight, firm and long. It has a real air of authority. Try it with tuna seared on the barbecue.

Pondalowie MT Tempranillo

Quality	🍷🍷🍷🍷
Value	★★★★
Rating	92
Grapes	tempranillo
Region	Bendigo, Vic.
Cellar	🍶 2
Alc./Vol.	14.0%
RRP	$24.00 🥂

PENGUIN BEST OTHER REDS AND BLENDS

MT stands for 'minya terra', an expression Portuguese vignerons use to describe their individual plots of vineyard, reflecting Dominic and Krystyna Morris's experience making wine in Portugal. The 'terra' in question here is their Pondalowie vineyard, near Bendigo.
CURRENT RELEASE 2005   A more-ish young wine, more successful than just about any Aussie tempranillos we've tasted. The colour is bright and youthful, and the nose has appetising aromas suggesting fleshy dark cherries and licorice. The makers see cola and sarsaparilla as well, and we won't argue – it certainly is different. The medium-weight palate is smooth with ripe flavours in a savoury 'euro' fashion. Drink it young with jamon and vegetable pastries.

Stella Bella Tempranillo

The Spanish workhorse red grape is becoming more and more popular in Australia, but there aren't too many emanating from Margaret River. This one is made by Janice McDonald. The Stella Bella stable also includes the Suckfizzle and Skuttlebutt wines.

CURRENT RELEASE 2004 The nose is a tad subdued but the action is all happening on the palate. It's well endowed with peppermint, red-berry and faintly herbal flavours which are fruit-dominant and fairly tight in the mouth – almost forbiddingly so. The finish dries off rapidly and the wine is improved by food, especially aged parmesan cheese.

Quality	🍷🍷🍷½
Value	★★★
Rating	**89**
Grapes	tempranillo
Region	Margaret River, WA
Cellar	5+
Alc./Vol.	14.5%
RRP	$27.00

Tokar Estate Tempranillo

Tokar Estate describes this as 'an essence of Spain in the Yarra Valley'. It does have authentic Spanish traits, not least of which is the liberal use of American oak – which can be a significant component in Spain as well.

CURRENT RELEASE 2003 A densely coloured wine with a concentrated nose of licorice, dark chocolate, dry leaves and blackcurrants; power-dressed in strong vanillin oak. In the mouth it's dense in texture and very flavoursome, with abundant deep fruit and sweet-oak flavours. It finishes dry with some slightly astringent tannins. It should develop well, but it will always be oaky. Pair it with chargrilled meats.

Quality	🍷🍷🍷🍷
Value	★★★
Rating	**91**
Grapes	tempranillo
Region	Yarra Valley, Vic.
Cellar	7
Alc./Vol.	14.5%
RRP	$45.00

Other reds and blends

In the earliest days of Australian wine, growers often planted an enormous variety of grapes in their vineyards. After a while most of them learnt what went well, produced the best crops and made the best-quality wine. Slowly but surely the wide range of grape varieties used in Australia dwindled as growers increasingly played it safe with the most versatile types, and so it continued for the first three-quarters of the twentieth century. Then the wine boom arrived and experimentation became the order of the day. Thus gamay, petit verdot, nebbiolo, tempranillo and a score of other red grapes appeared in vineyards alongside shiraz, plus new blends of different varieties both familiar and arcane arrived – and an exciting new era dawned for Aussie wine consumers.

Bremerton Malbec

Quality	♥♥♥♥
Value	★★★
Rating	91
Grapes	malbec
Region	Langhorne Creek, SA
Cellar	▮ 4
Alc./Vol.	13.5%
RRP	$27.00 ≋

Malbec has a long history at Langhorne Creek, and it provided the first dry-red table wine made in the district. Its star is on the wane these days but Bremerton's Rebecca Willson has done a good job with a special parcel of it in this limited-release wine.

CURRENT RELEASE 2004   This is pretty good malbec with spice, plum and floral aromas leading to an agreeable palate of concentrated plummy fruit that's long-flavoured and soft. Its friendly texture makes it very easy to drink, yet it has enough interest to keep you pouring another glass. Try it with moussaka.

Cape Mentelle Zinfandel

Quality	♥♥♥♥♥
Value	★★★
Rating	95
Grapes	zinfandel
Region	Margaret River, WA
Cellar	▮ 7+
Alc./Vol.	16.0%
RRP	$51.00 ▮ ≋

Cape Mentelle pioneered the zinfandel grape in Australia, first planting it in 1972. The inspiration was founder David Hohnen's time spent in California where he attended winemaking university at Fresno.

CURRENT RELEASE 2004   This wine can be top-heavy with alcohol some vintages, but even with the declared 16 per cent we really like the flavour and balance of the '04. It has a rich, dark colour and a noseful of morello cherries, anise, mint and flowers. There is substantial oak input, but it's well handled. The palate is amazingly powerful, concentrated and muscular. It's a whopper, in the high-alcohol, sweet-fruit genre. It'll impress those who are impressed by size. We were! Serve with hard cheeses.

Centennial Vineyards Limited Release Reserve Rondinella Corvina

Sealed, like all the latest Centennial reds, with a Procork (membrane coated cork), this is a style inspired by the great amarone wines of northern Italy's Veneto. To that end, it's been made from partially air-dried grapes, and the varieties are also those of amarone.
CURRENT RELEASE 2004   A most impressive interpretation of amarone. This is a superb red, deeply flavoured, tightly focused and powerful, with an excellent tannin grip that runs the full length of the palate and adds great authority and presence. There is no underripe or porty character, and the fruit flavours are of cherry and plum, both fresh and dried. Terrific length. A real triumph. Try it with aged reggiano cheese.

Quality	♛♛♛♛♛
Value	★★★★
Rating	95
Grapes	rondinella 57%; corvina 43%
Region	Hilltops, NSW
Cellar	🍷 10+
Alc./Vol.	15.2%
RRP	$30.00 (cellar door)

Cobaw Ridge Lagrein

Lagrein is a rather obscure grape variety native to north-eastern Italy. Alan and Nelly Cooper have made a speciality of it in their Macedon Ranges vineyard. We can only think of two other Australian examples. Good on 'em for showing such innovative spirit.
CURRENT RELEASE 2004   This is always a very distinctive wine. The '04 has deep colour and there was a wee tingle of gas on opening, but the initial aromas are very seductive. It reminds us of tar, cherries, spices and that peculiar mint/aniseed sort of perfume the Italians call *liquorizia.* The palate is on the light side of medium-bodied but it has fair intensity and persistence. The finish is light and soft. Pair it with prosciutto crudo and roasted vegetables.

Quality	♛♛♛♛
Value	★★★
Rating	91
Grapes	lagrein
Region	Macedon Ranges, Vic.
Cellar	🍷 2
Alc./Vol.	12.5%
RRP	$60.00

Coldstone Tarrango

Just when HH has burst into print wondering why no other winery has bothered to compete with Brown Brothers' highly successful tarrango, along comes this one. Coldstone is a new brand from the Vic Alps Winery, near Myrtleford.
CURRENT RELEASE 2005   It has a light purple–red hue, like a deeper-coloured rosé. The bouquet has distinct meaty overtones that remind us of carbonic maceration wines such as beaujolais. It's a grapey, simple, fruit-driven light red with a bit more sharpness than we'd have liked, in the form of acid and tannin. It needs the softening effect of food, such as herbed meatballs in tomato sauce.

Quality	♛♛♛
Value	★★★
Rating	84
Grapes	tarrango
Region	Victoria
Cellar	🍷 2
Alc./Vol.	12.5%
RRP	$13.00 🏷

Deen De Bortoli Vat 4 Petit Verdot

Quality	❦❦❦❦
Value	★★★★ⁱ
Rating	91
Grapes	petit verdot
Region	Riverina, NSW
Cellar	▮ 3
Alc./Vol.	13.5%
RRP	$10.85 ⊜

Petit verdot has found an unlikely home in the warm regions of the Riverina and the Murray Valley. It originates in the very different climate of Bordeaux, where it rarely achieves optimum ripeness; it's a different story in Oz. CURRENT RELEASE 2004 Another hot-climate petit verdot confirming how well-suited this Bordeaux variety is to certain parts of Australia. It's a dense young wine with a ripe nose of syrupy blackberries and dark plums, and a balanced spicing of oak. In the mouth it shows abundant rich, ripe flavour of good depth, trimmed in soft tannins. A good companion to meaty continental sausages.

Grant Burge Abednego Shiraz Grenache Mourvèdre

Quality	❦❦❦❦
Value	★★★
Rating	90
Grapes	shiraz; grenache; mourvèdre
Region	Barossa Valley, SA
Cellar	▮ 5+
Alc./Vol.	14.0%
RRP	$60.00 ▮

Abednego was the third of the three wise men who followed that famous star to Bethlehem. The others, Meshach and Shadrach, have already had wines named after them by Grant Burge. CURRENT RELEASE 2002 With a degree of bottle-age, this is starting to develop attractive savoury, mellow complexities. The nose has a lacing of garden mint and is chocolatey, mellowing into leather and fresh earth. The palate is smooth and mellow, with plenty of drying tannin and, again, chocolate, mint and honey flavours. This would suit shepherd's pie.

Hewitson Old Garden Mourvèdre

Quality	❦❦❦❦❦
Value	★★★
Rating	94
Grapes	mourvèdre
Region	Barossa Valley, SA
Cellar	⬤━1–8
Alc./Vol.	14.5%
RRP	$49.00

From an old Barossa vineyard planted in 1853, this wine shows what satisfying wine can come from mourvèdre. Known as mataro for most of its existence in Australia, mourvèdre is enjoying some well-deserved trendiness lately. CURRENT RELEASE 2004 The elements that make good Barossa mourvèdre so appealing are all here. It has an intense nose of blackberries, spices and rum 'n' raisin chocolate. There's a measure of smoky-sweet oak in the background. The full, round, velvety palate has just enough gravelly mourvèdre structure to give it some savouriness, and ripe tannins give it balanced support. We'd suggest pot-roasted topside.

Margan Barbera

Nicknamed Il Nove Barbera, this wine's front label proudly declares it to be 'Estate Grown & Made'. Andrew Margan planted the vines himself, behind his winery.
CURRENT RELEASE 2004   A remarkably good first attempt from young vines, this has more than a passing resemblance to an Italian red wine. The nose is coconutty and oxidative, without much vibrant berry-fruit aroma, and there's a charred-timber kind of savoury note that runs throughout the wine. The palate has good depth and structure, and, despite the savoury style, there is some fruit sweetness. Enjoy it with spit-roasted quails.

Quality	♟♟♟♟
Value	★★★✦
Rating	91
Grapes	barbera
Region	Hunter Valley, NSW
Cellar	🍾 5+
Alc./Vol.	14.0%
RRP	$25.00 🥂

Murray Darling Collection Aglianico

Aglianico is a rare bird in Australia; indeed, this could be the very first to hit the market. It is the grape variety that makes the famous central Italian red, taurasi. If you've ever had a top taurasi from, say, Feudi di San Gregorio, you'll know it can be a superb wine. Maker: Sandro Mosele; grapegrower: Bruce Chalmers. Diam-sealed.
CURRENT RELEASE 2004   This is a light-weight wine compared to the abovementioned taurasi. It has a medium-light colour, similar to a pinot noir, and a raspberry-cordial, tutti-frutti nose which is fruit-driven and simple, but clean and pleasantly aromatic. There's no oak to remark on. It's a plain but attractive, well-balanced, easy-drinking light red, and would suit game birds such as quail.

Quality	♟♟♟♟
Value	★★★
Rating	88
Grapes	aglianico
Region	Riverland, Vic.
Cellar	🍾 3
Alc./Vol.	12.5%
RRP	$33.00

Pepper Tree Grand Reserve Tannat

Tannat is, as the name might suggest, the ultra-tannic red grape used to make the strong wines of Madiran in south-west France. As Australian winemakers grow ever more adventurous we can expect more unusual grape varieties to appear on the shelves.
CURRENT RELEASE 2004   A deeply coloured wine with an extraordinary nose that's a bit like spearmint with some blackberry, cedar and vanillin notes underneath. The palate is a deeply flavoured, minty mouthful with medium body and a very grippy tannic backbone. An unusual wine that needs time to soften a little. It should be served with a hefty rump steak.

Quality	♟♟♟♟
Value	★★★
Rating	92
Grapes	tannat
Region	Wrattonbully, SA
Cellar	▬2–6+
Alc./Vol.	14.5%
RRP	$55.00

Roundstone Gamay

Quality	🍷🍷🍷
Value	★★★
Rating	88
Grapes	gamay
Region	Yarra Valley, Vic.
Cellar	🍷 1
Alc./Vol.	13.1%
RRP	$18.00 ⊜

There isn't much gamay grown in Australia, yet its light red wine style would seem to recommend itself to this country's sunny, outdoor lifestyle. It wasn't always so. In the 1970s and '80s fashionable Australians guzzled French beaujolais (made from gamay) in vast quantities.
CURRENT RELEASE 2005   A light red with a bright appearance and a light, high-toned varietal nose suggesting cherries and red fruits. It also has a slightly stemmy edge. The palate is light, dry and fruity with low tannin. Try it with a Lyonnaise sausage salad.

Terra Felix Mourvèdre

Quality	🍷🍷🍷
Value	★★★
Rating	89
Grapes	mourvèdre
Region	upper Goulburn Valley, Vic.
Cellar	🍷 2
Alc./Vol.	14.8%
RRP	$15.00 ⊜

Terra Felix has produced some of the most interesting wines in the $15-price range in Australia in the last couple of vintages. It's the second label of the Tallarook vineyard north of Melbourne.
CURRENT RELEASE 2005   Meaty mourvèdre scents kick things off in a savoury direction here, then peppery-spice, dark-plum and earthy complexities chime in. The palate is light- to medium-bodied, and attractively dry with good texture. It finishes with soft dry tannins. A European-accented red to enjoy with braised veal and red peppers.

Tscharke The Curse Zinfandel

Quality	🍷🍷🍷🍷
Value	★★★⁺
Rating	90
Grapes	primitivo (aka zinfandel)
Region	Barossa Valley, SA
Cellar	🍷 10
Alc./Vol.	16.1%
RRP	$30.00 ⊜

The Curse refers to the expletives that are thrown around the Tscharke vineyard because of the temperamental nature of these zinfandel vines. The vines respond to all this abuse by producing wines of dreadnought-like power. Beware.
CURRENT RELEASE 2004   All the over-the-top plum-pud, jammy, spicy, vanillin, come-on-and-give-us-a-kiss zinfandel characteristics are here, as well as a belt of alcohol that warms things up very quickly. It tastes voluptuous and powerful with a slightly spirity thing. You wonder with what and with whom you would drink a thing like this. We'd drink it with brontosaurus ribs in the company of WWF wrestlers. That said, it's well-made, clean and friendly, and a lot livelier and better to drink than some 15 to 16+ per cent alcohol juggernauts.

Tscharke The Monster Montepulciano

Damien Tscharke employs quite a few left-field grape
varieties in his range of potent red wines. The results are
always interesting, and good viticulture and winemaking
technique elevates them well above the sometimes awful
'experimentals' of other makers. Good work, Damien.
CURRENT RELEASE 2004   Dense and purplish, this is
another hard-to-ignore Tscharke red. It smells powerfully of
ripe cherries, marzipan, tar, earth and a whisper of coconut:
very ripe but also savoury. The palate is concentrated but
friendly in disposition with attractive ripe-berry flavours of
good depth and body, leading to fine tannins and warmth
at the end. A good match for sticky braised oxtail.

Quality	▼▼▼▼▼
Value	★★★★
Rating	93
Grapes	montepulciano
Region	Barossa Valley, SA
Cellar	8+
Alc./Vol.	15.0%
RRP	$30.00

Wood Park Zinfandel

There are only a handful of good zins in the entire
Australian continent, and this is one of them. The grapes
come from Prescott's vineyard, on the side of the high-
altitude Whitfield Plateau. Maker: John Stokes.
CURRENT RELEASE 2005   Zin has a high degree of difficulty
and this is a ripper of a wine, with lovely flavours of perfectly
ripened grapes and no detracting greenness. Rose petals,
cassis and herbs to sniff; the palate is smooth and medium-
to full-bodied, with more elegance than you might expect.
The profile is smooth, and plenty of raspberry, cassis and
cherry flavours in the mouth. It's fruit driven and well
balanced, with loads of class but without excessive alcohol.
Delicious with braised meats or hard cheeses.
Previous outstanding vintage: 2003

Quality	▼▼▼▼▼
Value	★★★★↑
Rating	95
Grapes	zinfandel
Region	King Valley, Vic.
Cellar	8+
Alc./Vol.	14.0%
RRP	$35.00

Zilzie Petit Verdot

The increasing number of petit verdot reds coming from
the Murray Valley has given us a new slant on this relatively
obscure French grape variety. In its Bordeaux home it's not
known for its ripe, plump fruit and depth, but it is here.
CURRENT RELEASE 2004   Zilzie's Petit Verdot is a deeply
coloured young wine with plenty of personality. The nose
has well-concentrated aromas of ripe loganberries, licorice,
spices and dark earth. In the mouth it follows the promise
of the nose with warm, intense ripe-berry and spice
flavours, medium-bodied and well balanced. Oak input is
pleasantly understated and it finishes with integrated dry
tannins. Try it beside pasta with braised beef ragu.

Quality	▼▼▼▼
Value	★★★★↑
Rating	91
Grapes	petit verdot
Region	Murray Valley, Vic.
Cellar	3
Alc./Vol.	14.0%
RRP	$15.00

Sweet Wines

Perhaps it's an obsession with diet, but we seem to be drinking less sweet wine (and maybe we're eating less of the sweet desserts or fatty cheeses they tend to be drunk with). Also there appear to be fewer 'stickies' around these days, the prolonged dry conditions in rural areas have probably not helped by keeping botrytis out of our vineyards. But the authors feel that there's still a place for a small glass of sweet wine at the dinner table. There's a variety of them: ranging from golden to syrupy Riverina botrytis semillons through to lighter, less domineering styles from cooler areas, often made from riesling, and non-botrytis late-picked whites such as frontignac.

Bimbadgen Myall Road Botrytis Semillon

Quality	▼▼▼▼
Value	★★★↓
Rating	89
Grapes	semillon
Region	Riverina, NSW
Cellar	▮ 3
Alc./Vol.	10.0%
RRP	$18.50 (375ml) (cellar door)

Myall Road is in Yenda, near Griffith in the Riverina – home of some of the most luscious sweet wines that Australia produces. Bimbadgen is a Hunter Valley winery but like many outside the Riverina, it makes a Riverina sticky.
CURRENT RELEASE 2004   Orange and grapefruit peel are evident here, as well as a hint of citron. It's a rich wine with a tight, intense palate which is at the same time slightly hard in its acidity. It could benefit from a little more bottle-age. Then serve with a fruit flan and cream.

Brown Brothers Moscato

Quality	▼▼▼▼
Value	★★★★↓
Rating	90
Grapes	muscat gordo blanco
Region	north-east Vic.
Cellar	▮ 1
Alc./Vol.	5.5%
RRP	$15.20

Brown Brothers Moscato follows the Italian formula accurately: a tingle of gas, sweet fruity aroma and flavour, succulence, a clean finish, and very low alcohol. It's like a crushed handful of ripe grapes.
CURRENT RELEASE 2005   Fragrant with floral, grapey aromas, this is a super mouthful of sherbetty, muscat fruit: light, sweet and tingly with gorgeously refreshing succulence. It finishes with a length of aromatic flavour that belies its very low alcohol, and it leaves the palate clean and crisp. Delightful. Delicious with a piece of cake.

Brown Brothers Spatlese Lexia

This sweetish white wine from Brown Brothers can be found in just about every corner of Australia. Its formula of juicy, grapey flavour, slightly reduced alcohol and easy drinkability is a winner.

CURRENT RELEASE 2005   Very scented floral aromas and muscaty notes are sweet and inviting, and the palate has penetrating, grapey varietal character that's sweet, but in a fruity rather than a sugary way. It finishes clean and juicy. Try it with chilled fresh fruits.

Quality	♀ ♀ ♀ ⸗
Value	★ ★ ★ ⸗
Rating	88
Grapes	muscat gordo blanco
Region	north-east Vic.
Cellar	🍾 1
Alc./Vol.	11.0%
RRP	$12.75

Capercaillie Dessert Style Gewürztraminer

The capercaillie is a kind of grouse found in Scotland. The Sutherlands of Capercaillie winery found that an export market for their wines opened up quite readily in Scotland thanks to the name, the bird, and no doubt the wine quality.

CURRENT RELEASE 2004   A pleasant medium-sweet wine, it has little if any botrytis character and not much lusciousness or complexity. Think of it as more a late-picked style rather than a full-on sticky. It has some spicy, muscaty-gewurz aromatics, and the palate has moderate depth and length, without a great deal of intensity. It suits fresh fruit.

Quality	♀ ♀ ♀
Value	★ ★ ★
Rating	86
Grapes	gewürztraminer
Region	Hunter Valley, NSW
Cellar	🍾 2
Alc./Vol.	9.0%
RRP	$18.00 (375ml)
	(cellar door)

Charles Melton Sotto di Ferro

The name means 'under the iron' – which refers to the barrel-ageing that took place directly under the warming corrugated iron roof of the winery. Before that, though, the grapes were strung up indoors and allowed to dry out a little, concentrating in them all the good things before fermentation. It's a technique borrowed from Tuscany's vin santo.

CURRENT RELEASE 2001   This is an astonishing, remarkable wine. It's tremendously sweet and luscious, wonderfully complex and multi-layered with flavours that come eerily close to the sweeter Tuscan vin santo styles. The colour is dark amber, almost tawny. Oak adds extra complexity but doesn't dominate. Dried wildflower, mixed citrus peels, toasty vanillin oak. An irresistible package! Serve it sparingly, in small glasses with sweet biscuits.

Quality	♀ ♀ ♀ ♀ ♀
Value	★ ★ ★ ★
Rating	96
Grapes	pedro ximenez;
	muscadelle
Region	Barossa Valley, SA
Cellar	🍾 3+
Alc./Vol.	10.5%
RRP	$55.00 (375ml)

Cookoothama Botrytis Semillon

Quality	♀ ♀ ♀ ♀
Value	★★★★
Rating	91
Grapes	semillon
Region	Riverina, NSW
Cellar	▮ 2
Alc./Vol.	11.5%
RRP	$23.00 (375ml) Ⓢ

The Nugan family, owners of Cookoothama, are one of the top-20 Australian wine exporters, and the eighteenth-largest wine producer in the country (measured in hectares of vines), according to the Australian & New Zealand Wine Industry Directory. Winemaker is Daren Owers.
CURRENT RELEASE 2004   The colour is already full amber and it's acquired a lot of caramel development, toast and vanilla, and a trace of cold tea-leaves – which is common in these wines. The palate is soft and mellow; oily and viscous. It's tempting to say it's a touch flat – although there is no shortage of acid. Maybe the problem is that it's not all natural acid. Still, a terrific sweet wine, to drink with crème caramel.

Craiglee Glacier

Quality	♀ ♀ ♀ ♀ ♀
Value	★★★
Rating	92
Grapes	sauvignon blanc
Region	Sunbury, Vic.
Cellar	▮ 3
Alc./Vol.	14.0%
RRP	$20.00 (375ml)

Pat Carmody at Craiglee produces some of Australia's leading shirazes, but we'd never seen a sweet white from him before this. Made from late-picked sauvignon blanc, it has a European accent.
CURRENT RELEASE 2005   The nose has scented aromas of stone fruits and guava, honey and slightly sulphury French traits, trimmed in subtle oak. There's a vague reminiscence of Bordeaux sweet white wine about it, and the palate continues the theme with lush sweet flavour of surprising complexity, finishing long and dry with a touch of phenolic hardness. An unusual sweet white to serve with apple cake.

Cullen Late Harvest Chenin Blanc Semillon

Quality	♀ ♀ ♀
Value	★★★
Rating	86
Grapes	chenin blanc; semillon
Region	Margaret River, WA
Cellar	▮ 1
Alc./Vol.	9.5%
RRP	$25.00 (375ml) 🍷

Chenin blanc is a great grape for sweet wines – in the right climatic regions. The best come from France's central Loire Valley, in such regions as Vouvray, Anjou, Quarts de Chaume, etc. It's much colder there than in Margaret River.
CURRENT RELEASE 2004   The colour is medium-deep gold, which fits the rather forward, early-drinking style of this sweetie. The aromas suggest raisined, vine-dried grapes rather than botrytis. There is a fig-jam, lightly spiced, raisined-grape aroma with some headiness, perhaps from alcohol. It's sweet and rather broad in the mouth and perhaps a touch low in acid. It could go well with washed-rind cheeses like Milawa Gold.

De Bortoli Noble One

The grand-daddy of all Australian botrytised sweeties just keeps getting better, with Darren De Bortoli tweaking the style all the time to improve it.
CURRENT RELEASE 2003   A simply gorgeous Noble One, the '03 sums the line up beautifully. The usual glace-apricot, candied-citrus, honey and spice characters are there on the nose, and a thread of spicy French oak is woven through it, adding its own savoury touch. The palate is lusciously sweet and persistent, and it has that extra dimension of finesse that's marked the recent vintages of Noble One. Tangy acidity sits in perfect counterpoint to the lush botrytised fruit, keeping it clean and vibrant. Delicious with old-fashioned bread and butter custard.

Quality	🍷🍷🍷🍷🍷
Value	★★★★★
Rating	98
Grapes	semillon
Region	Riverina, NSW
Cellar	🍾 10
Alc./Vol.	10.5%
RRP	$29.00 (375 ml)

Deen De Bortoli Vat 5 Botrytis Semillon

Vat 5 is the understudy to the excellent Noble One in De Bortoli's botrytis hierarchy. It's a perennial bargain, offering delicious botrytised characters on a budget.
CURRENT RELEASE 2004   A bright-gold wine with a juicy-sweet nose of glace peaches and apricots, orange peel, honey and a thread of spicy oak. It tastes sweet and luscious, but tangy acidity keeps it clean and balanced. A little dab of phenolic firmness at the end gives it structure. A sensationally good buy. Try it with peaches grilled with brown sugar and sweet white wine.

Quality	🍷🍷🍷🍷🍷
Value	★★★★★
Rating	94
Grapes	semillon
Region	Riverina, NSW
Cellar	🍾 3
Alc./Vol.	11.5%
RRP	$10.80 (375 ml)

The Gorge Mosto

This is an unusual wine, and the name is even more unusual. But why not? It suggests a sweet wine (*mosto* is Italian for must, or grape-juice), and why confuse the issue with the grape variety. It's a creative move by a boutique-sized maker, and deserves to succeed. Maker: David Hook.
CURRENT RELEASE 2005   This is a light, grapey, medium-sweet white wine that is fairly straightforward in character. It could use a little extra time in bottle before opening, on account of the 'free' sulphur dioxide evident when we opened our sample. There is a fairly high level of residual sugar, which makes this a very easy wine to enjoy. We'd pair it with cake, say, a passionfruit-iced sponge, for afternoon tea.

Quality	🍷🍷🍷
Value	★★★
Rating	86
Grapes	semillon
Region	Hunter Valley, NSW
Cellar	🍾 1
Alc./Vol.	10.5%
RRP	$20.00

Idlewild Succo del Sol

Quality	🍷🍷🍷🍷
Value	★★★
Rating	**90**
Grapes	semillon; sauvignon blanc
Region	Hunter Valley, NSW
Cellar	4+
Alc./Vol.	11.0%
RRP	$45.00 (375ml) (cellar door)

The name means 'juice of the sun', and the grapes were air-dried on racks to concentrate their sugars, before crushing and fermentation. The result is a wine very much in the style of Tuscany's vin santo. Producers are Tina and Matthew Ryan of Broke Estate.

CURRENT RELEASE *non-vintage* It's a remarkably good attempt at vin santo, down to the amber–orange colour and the curiously oxidative bouquet of tea-leaves, dried orange peel, dusty wood and old-cedar chests. It has a lot of viscosity and is very sweet and rich, almost like molasses. Indeed, in aroma and taste it has echoes of a rum distillery. The sugar level is high and it truly deserves the epithet 'sticky'. A fascinating drink, to serve with Italian biscotti.

Keith Tulloch Botrytis Semillon

Quality	🍷🍷🍷🍷
Value	★★★
Rating	**92**
Grapes	semillon
Region	Hunter Valley, NSW
Cellar	2+
Alc./Vol.	14.0%
RRP	$28.00 (375 ml)

Keith Tulloch is one of the most serious small makers in the Hunter, a Roseworthy graduate who has earned his stripes working for people like Len Evans at Rothbury and the Evans Wine Company.

CURRENT RELEASE 2004 With its deep-amber colour and developed bouquet and flavour, this is a forward style of sticky but an excellent drink right now. It's loaded with toffee, crème brûlée aromas that tend to slightly burnt sugar, and the palate is rich and full with lots of substance – possibly assisted by a little oak, and plenty of alcohol. It's a big, generous wine with impressive length and a complex array of flavours. Try it with milder blue cheeses.

Little Brother Late Harvest Riesling

Quality	🍷🍷🍷🍷
Value	★★★½
Rating	**91**
Grapes	riesling
Region	Porongurup, WA
Cellar	1
Alc./Vol.	11.0%
RRP	$16.00

Once upon a time, sweetish Australian rieslings like this had quite a following. Usually labelled 'late picked', 'late harvest', 'spatlese' or some such, most of these wines fell out of fashion by the 1990s.

CURRENT RELEASE 2005 A bright, fruity, sweetish white with a succulent aroma that reminds us of stewed apples, lime marmalade and spice. It's fairly sweet in the mouth, with a juicy feel, but tight acidity and dry finish keep it in balance. Sip it icy-cold on a hot afternoon.

Margan Botrytis Semillon

Andrew Margan consistently makes a surprising botrytised sticky from grapes grown in the Hunter sub-region of Broke Fordwich. It's surprising, because the Hunter is not an easy place to harvest grapes with a clean botrytis infection. If the season is wet enough for botrytis to come, the grapes often have other less-desirable moulds as well. A particularly suitable vineyard and scrupulous viticulture are the keys.

CURRENT RELEASE 2005   The colour is deep yellow–gold and the bouquet showcases fragrant honey, spice and citrus-peel aromas. There is a generous quota of sweetness and while the wine is not especially complex, it is delicious: very clean and technically well-made. There is a degree of richness and the balance is good, although at the sweeter end of the spectrum. It would be a treat with pavlova.

Quality	♀♀♀♀♀
Value	★★★★
Rating	94
Grapes	semillon
Region	Hunter Valley, NSW
Cellar	🍾 3
Alc./Vol.	10.5%
RRP	$30.00 (375 ml) 🥂

McWilliams Limited Release Botrytis Semillon

McWilliams wins a lot of gold medals with its stickies, and this one hasn't disappointed. It won the Hanaminno Trophy for the best sweet white wine at the 2006 Sydney Royal Wine Show.

CURRENT RELEASE 2004   McWilliams continues to refine this style. The subtle use of oak cleverly adds extra layers of complexity, making it uncannily sauternes-like in top vintages like '04. Honey, crème brûlée, vanilla and butterscotch come to mind on sniffing the bouquet, while the palate is very fine and harmonious but also rich, sweet and lush. It finishes cleanly so that you want another sip. Try it with mango millefeuille.

Quality	♀♀♀♀♀
Value	★★★★
Rating	95
Grapes	semillon
Region	Riverina, NSW
Cellar	🍾 4+
Alc./Vol.	12.5%
RRP	$30.00 (375 ml)

Mistletoe Petite Muscat

Quality	♀ ♀ ♀
Value	✱ ✱ ✱
Rating	86
Grapes	muscat blanc à petits grains
Region	Hunter Valley, NSW
Cellar	🍷 3+
Alc./Vol.	15.5%
RRP	$16.50 (375 ml) (cellar door)

Mistletoe's owner Ken Sloan believes his is the only vineyard with muscat blanc à petits grains in the Hunter Valley. He planted it especially to make this wine, which is modelled on Muscat de Beaumes de Venise. It is essentially unfermented, fortified grapejuice.
CURRENT RELEASE 2004   The colour is deep yellow–amber with rose–gold tinges. It smells like fortified grape-juice, with a heady spirit edge and straw/hay-like fruit character. It finishes with a lot of alcohol hotness, and the final impression is somewhat astringent. It needs food: try a stinky washed-rind cheese!

Quality	♀ ♀ ♀ ♀
Value	✱ ✱ ✱ ✛
Rating	90
Grapes	muscat blanc à petits grains
Region	Hunter Valley, NSW
Cellar	🍷 3+
Alc./Vol.	15.5%
RRP	$17.50 (375 ml) (cellar door) 🐚

CURRENT RELEASE 2005   We agree with its maker – the '05 is clearly the best of the line so far. It's a very stylish wine. The spirit is slightly hot and obvious to the sniff, but the taste is attractively spicy, fruity and well balanced. It's sweet but not over the top like some botrytis stickies – which is refreshing. It has length and balance – without spirit dominating the palate – and the finish is clean and drying. It doesn't overwhelm with size or sweetness. You could sip it with biscuits and soft cheeses.

Moorilla Estate Botrytis Sauvignon Blanc

Quality	♀ ♀ ♀ ♀ ♀
Value	✱ ✱ ✱ ✛
Rating	93
Grapes	sauvignon blanc
Region	Tasmania
Cellar	🍷 5
Alc./Vol.	12.0%
RRP	$26.50 (375 ml)

Some of the Moorilla wines are labelled Moorilla Estate and some just Moorilla. We assume they're respecting truth in labelling, as the word 'estate' usually denotes a wine made from grapes grown on the company's own vineyards.
CURRENT RELEASE 2004   It's not obvious what the grape variety is, but this is probably a good thing! It is a delightful sweet white, mid-yellow in hue with aromas of flowers and honey and hints of spices. There is some botrytis evident and the palate is luscious and high in sweetness. It has lovely palate balance: a wine of great elegance and subtlety. It would suit fresh fruit salad.

Mount Horrocks Cordon Cut Riesling

The cordon cut method is aimed at increasing the concentration of sugar and flavour in the must. It's achieved by partially cutting the branches of the vine to stop the sap flowing; the bunches partially dehydrate and then they're picked. No botrytis is involved.
CURRENT RELEASE 2005 A beautifully made sweetie that smells of honey and intensely focused riesling fruit, but lacks the complexity of the best botrytis wines. The taste is super-intense and lively with acid, but just lacks the richness and layering of botrytis wines. A thoroughly delicious sweetie all the same. Delicious with passionfruit pavlova.

Quality	🍷🍷🍷🍷🍷
Value	★★★★
Rating	95
Grapes	riesling
Region	Clare Valley, SA
Cellar	3+
Alc./Vol.	11.5%
RRP	$32.00 (375 ml)

Oakridge 864 Riesling

Enterprising winemaker David Bicknell used a refrigerated shipping container to make this pseudo icewine. He refrigerated the freshly picked riesling grapes till the water inside them froze, then quickly pressed them, resulting in a very sweet, concentrated juice, which was fermented to make this great 'sticky'.
CURRENT RELEASE 2005 This is a superb lighter style of late-picked riesling, not showing any botrytis of course but with a typical riesling nose of minerals and a hint of petrol (in the positive Alsace sense). The colour is still pale, the palate very fine and tautly structured, filled with green-apple and floral riesling flavours, with lots of sweetness matched by lively acid. It's a delicious style of wine and would go perfectly with a fresh, sweet peach.

Quality	🍷🍷🍷🍷🍷
Value	★★★
Rating	92
Grapes	riesling
Region	Yarra Valley, Vic.
Cellar	5+
Alc./Vol.	9.0%
RRP	$50.00 (375 ml)

Peter Lehmann Botrytis Semillon

Peter Lehmann's Botrytis Semillon comes from a small block on the Para River at Tanunda in the Barossa Valley. When in those parts, make sure you visit the Peter Lehmann cellar door, it's one of the best-kept and most picturesque in the whole valley.
CURRENT RELEASE 2005 A lighter, brighter botrytised semillon than some of the competition, this shows candied-peach, honey and mixed-citrus aromas of zippy freshness. The palate is sweet with a very fine feel to it. Sweet stone-fruit and citrus-peel flavours last long and lively on the palate, backed up by brisk acidity. Try it with a mild, creamy blue cheese.

Quality	🍷🍷🍷🍷🍷
Value	★★★★
Rating	93
Grapes	semillon
Region	Barossa Valley, SA
Cellar	3
Alc./Vol.	12.0%
RRP	$15.65 (375 ml)

Pettavel Evening Star Late Harvest Riesling

Quality	▼▼▼▼⬗
Value	★★★⬩
Rating	93
Grapes	riesling
Region	Geelong, Vic.
Cellar	▮ 4
Alc./Vol.	10.5%
RRP	$18.00 (375 ml)

A sweet Australian riesling without the complexing influence of botrytis has become a rarity. Once they were all the rage. Pettavel's is a modern interpretation of the genre.
CURRENT RELEASE 2005   A brilliant yellow–gold wine with a super-aromatic aroma of exotic spice, stone fruit and cumquat. The palate is lush and sweet with a delicious pineappley flavour that's soft and mellow. A slight nuttiness from fermentation in old oak adds dimension, and it has a long sweet finish that's kept zesty by succulent acid balance. Enjoy it with pineapple flambé with vanilla ice-cream.

Rymill June Traminer

Quality	▼▼▼▼⬗
Value	★★★★⬩
Rating	94
Grapes	gewürztraminer
Region	Coonawarra, SA
Cellar	▮ 2
Alc./Vol.	12.5%
RRP	$16.00 (375 ml) 🥂

When conditions are just right, Rymill winemaker John Innes leaves a small portion of gewürztraminer to become naturally infected with *botrytis cinerea*, the noble rot that helps produce the greatest sweet white wines of Europe. This 2005 vintage was the first in eight years that it was possible.
CURRENT RELEASE 2005   A curious sweet wine that shows how botrytis and ultra-late harvesting can create something very special from gewürztraminer. It's a bright golden thing with a lush-smelling nose of honey, candied peel, glace apricots and a dab of spicy oak. A wee bit of volatility is typical of the style but it's not out of balance. The palate is very sweet and luscious, yet with enough balancing acidity to keep it fresh and zesty. It finishes with an intriguing lychee-like aftertaste. Good with blue cheese.

Stella Bella Pink Muscat

Quality	▼▼▼⬗
Value	★★★
Rating	88
Grapes	red frontignac
Region	Margaret River, WA
Cellar	▮ 2
Alc./Vol.	8.0%
RRP	$17.00 (375 ml) 🥂

This is a perennial favourite of the authors. There should be more wines of this type as they are so popular with the drinkers – not necessarily the wine cognoscenti, but the regular wine-drinking public. The colourful label and cute packaging is also a winner.
CURRENT RELEASE 2005   It's a very pale shade of pink and has a slight spritz in the glass. The aroma is a lovely fresh, clean muscat-grape fragrance, which really invites you to take a sip. The alcohol is low and the body very light, so don't expect a lot of flavour. The fruit is lifted by some residual sugar and it's a lovely sipping wine – or you could accompany it with a piece of fresh fruit, especially a bunch of grapes.

Trentham Estate La Famiglia Moscato

Trentham Estate is in the sunny Murray Valley, an ideal place to sip grapey, low-alcohol moscato like this.

CURRENT RELEASE 2005 This has a light grapey/crushed muscatel aroma and a leafy/chlorophylly edge; traits that suggest freshness and gardens in summer. The palate is light and sweet with juicy, lively, grapey flavour. Drink it with chilled fresh fruit on a warm evening.

Quality	🍷🍷🍷½
Value	★★★★
Rating	**88**
Grapes	muscat
Region	Murray Valley, NSW
Cellar	1
Alc./Vol.	7.5%
RRP	$10.00

Turkey Flat The Last Straw Marsanne

This is an unusual wine made from part-dried marsanne grapes, somewhat along the lines of the sweet Italian *passito* wines. It's fermented in oak, adding another distinctive facet to it.

CURRENT RELEASE 2003 A complex, pale-golden wine with aromas of nutty and vanillin barrel-ferment, honeyed fruits, dried figs and peel. The palate is luscious, with very fine complex flavour that's long and ideally balanced. The oak input matches the lush fruit intensity perfectly, and it has taut acidity at the finish. It should build depth and complexity with further bottle-age. Delicious. Serve it with little almond biscuits.

Quality	🍷🍷🍷🍷🍷
Value	★★★
Rating	**95**
Grapes	marsanne
Region	Barossa Valley, SA
Cellar	5+
Alc./Vol.	14.0%
RRP	$40.00 (375 ml)

Two Hands Brilliant Disguise Moscato

Brilliant Disguise Moscato is based on an old Barossa white frontignac vineyard that was recently resurrected. Such vines, once highly prized, have made way for more fashionable grape varieties as Australians have turned away from sweet wines.

CURRENT RELEASE 2005 This pale moscato opens with that little frizzle of bubbles that marks the Italian prototype, adding a tiny tingle of gas to the experience. It smells quite lifted and less overtly grapey than Italian moscato, in some ways more like southern French muscats, at least in fruit character. In the mouth it's juicy and light with the sweetness moderated by very brisk acidity. Try it with fresh fruit.

Quality	🍷🍷🍷🍷
Value	★★★★
Rating	**91**
Grapes	white frontignac
Region	Barossa Valley, SA
Cellar	1
Alc./Vol.	6.5%
RRP	$13.50

Wellington Iced Riesling

Quality	�♦
Value	★★★
Rating	93
Grapes	riesling
Region	southern Tasmania
Cellar	🍷 3
Alc./Vol.	10.0%
RRP	$25.00 (375 ml) 🥂

Wellington Iced Riesling is made by Wellington's Andrew Hood using freeze-concentration of riesling juice to concentrate flavour elements and sweetness.

CURRENT RELEASE 2004   Intense aromas of lemon cordial, spice, honey and pineapple provide a sweet, inviting introduction. The sweet palate is taut with acidity, keeping it clean and tangy despite the high sugar level, and it finishes dry and lemony. It lacks the final complexity of botrytised wines, but its purity of juicy riesling fruit is very attractive. Pair it with little fresh fruit tarts.

Westend Three Bridges Golden Mist Botrytis Semillon

Quality	♟♟♟♟♟
Value	★★★★⁴
Rating	95
Grapes	semillon
Region	Riverina, NSW
Cellar	🍷 2+
Alc./Vol.	12.5%
RRP	$23.50 (375 ml) Ⓢ

That's a lot of names for one wine – but then, there is a helluva lot of wine in the bottle! Westend has been at the top of the Riverina sticky makers' list for some years now. Winemaker is Bryan Currie, with owner Bill Calabria looking over his shoulder.

CURRENT RELEASE 2003   The colour is dark amber, which suggests this wine is already fully mature. But experience shows these wines can hold on for many more years – although they reach their peaks within two or three. This has a toasty, developed, orange-peel and almost sherry-like aged bouquet. The taste is lovely: smooth and rich, unctuous, deep and soft. It's well rounded with some brandy-snap flavours and a hint of oak. A real mouthful: drink soon, with crème brûlée.

PENGUIN BEST SWEET WINE

Woodstock Recioto Style Barbera

Quality	♟♟⁵
Value	★★★
Rating	84
Grapes	barbera
Region	Langhorne Creek, SA
Cellar	🍷 4+
Alc./Vol.	16.0%
RRP	$20.00 (375 ml) 🍾🥂

This is a sweet-red wine that's been loosely modelled on the recioto amarone wines of the Veneto, in Italy. They are made with partially air-dried grapes. Maker Scott Collett recommends drinking it with sheep or goat cheese; we tried it with parmesan (cow's milk) and it went pretty well.

CURRENT RELEASE 2003   This is a most unusual wine that will mystify most tasters: it is mid-tawny–red in colour and smells stale, oxidised and earthy – a bit sweaty, a bit jammy. The taste is very tannic and drying, with some bitterness, some sugar and virtually no primary fruit flavour. It's more enjoyable sipped with cheese, but we're in two minds about its merits. We frankly prefer the Woodstock ports to drink at the end of a meal. But we support the idea and the braveness of the attempt. Any kind of hard, aged cheese will do.

Yalumba Late Harvest Viognier

Yalumba can lay serious claim to being the leader in viognier in Australia. Not only have they been growing it as long as anyone, they've made far more wines than anyone else, including sweet late-picked styles.

CURRENT RELEASE 2005   We're not sure this kind of wine is the future of Wrattonbully, but it is a decent drink. The nose is odd – it has some grassy/herbal characters together with more normal viognier spice and some floral notes, but the wine seems a little dank. The palate carries a fair whack of phenolics (tannins) that tend to toughen the finish. It does leave you with a clean, dry aftertaste. We'd suggest dried fruits and nuts.

Quality	♟ ♟ ♟
Value	★ ★ ★
Rating	86
Grapes	viognier
Region	Wrattonbully, SA
Cellar	▮ 3+
Alc./Vol.	12.0%
RRP	$25.00 (375 ml) Ⓢ

Fortified Wines

Some of Australia's greatest wines are fortifieds. Muscats and tokays from north-east Victoria, port styles from the Barossa and McLaren Vale, and a few dinosaur sherry styles. The market has shrunk so much that those players left in the game are the best, and the quality and value-for-money they offer are exceptional. What could be better than a glass of decadently rich port or muscat after a meal? All you need is a small glass, and the wine does you the unique favour of tasting just as good when you next access the bottle, days or even weeks later. We should all enjoy more of these great wines. As the boffins in the halls of economic rationalism say: use it or lose it!

All Saints Rutherglen Muscat

Quality	♟ ♟ ♟ ♦
Value	★★★
Rating	89
Grapes	red frontignac
Region	Rutherglen, Vic.
Cellar	♦
Alc./Vol.	18.0%
RRP	$19.00 (375 ml)

All Saints was inhabited by the Sutherland Smith family for most of its existence but was in the wilderness till bought by Brown Brothers in the 1990s. Peter Brown took it over on his own in 1999 and his family has run it ever since, with a greater than ever emphasis on quality. This is mainly three- to five-year-old material with some 15- to 20-year-old blending wines to give it depth of character.
CURRENT RELEASE *non-vintage* The colour is mid-amber and it has a lovely fresh, fruity young muscat nose; raisiny and distinctive with some tea-leafy overtones. There's a note of cured meadow-hay as well, and lots of sweetness. It's light and fruity on the tongue and lacks the concentration of a higher-grade wine. Good to sip after dinner or pour on ice-cream.

Baileys Founder Muscat

Quality	♟ ♟ ♟ ♟
Value	★★★★
Rating	92
Grapes	red frontignac
Region	Glenrowan, Vic.
Cellar	♦
Alc./Vol.	17.0%
RRP	$23.20

The Baileys winery is a historic place, rather like a living museum. The old winery machinery, stables, working-men's cottages and the original tiny nineteenth-century winery are still there. Although things have generally progressed a lot where winemaking is concerned, the Baileys fortifieds are still like a taste of yesterday.
CURRENT RELEASE *non-vintage* Still the best of the three Founder series fortified wines, this muscat has real depth and body with typically north-east Victorian toffee and raisiny qualities. It shows some attractive complexity and it strikes a great balance between lusciousness and drinkability. Serve it with good vanilla ice-cream.

Baileys Founder Tokay

Richard Bailey, who founded this historic winery in 1870, must have been in residence when Ned Kelly had his last stand with the troopers at nearby Glenrowan.
CURRENT RELEASE *non-vintage* This youngish tokay has heaps of varietal appeal with floral, tea-leaf, malt and honey aromas of succulent sweetness. It's very sweet in the mouth with a forward immediate appeal. Complexity is on hold, but the lush, fruity sweetness carries the day. Try it with an old-fashioned steamed pudding.

Quality	♟♟♟♟
Value	★★★★
Rating	90
Grapes	muscadelle
Region	Glenrowan, Vic.
Cellar	⬦
Alc./Vol.	17.5%
RRP	$23.20

Baileys Wine Maker Selection Old Tokay

The town of Glenrowan could be renamed Kellyville, such is its infatuation with the famous outlaw Ned Kelly. If you find all the tourist hype just too much, head for the hills. In the nearby Warby Ranges is the old Baileys winery where you can fortify yourself with some of Australia's best fortifieds.
CURRENT RELEASE *non-vintage* The colour of long wood ageing shows here. It's a viscous walnut-brown elixir with an almost olive tinge. The bouquet is powerfully luscious with concentrated aromas of butterscotch, plum pudding, and mum's toffee. The palate has gorgeous syrupy intensity, yet it's not over the top. It's smooth, luscious and profound with a delicious lingering aftertaste. Enjoy it with blue cheese.

Quality	♟♟♟♟♟
Value	★★★★★
Rating	96
Grapes	muscadelle
Region	Glenrowan, Vic.
Cellar	⬦
Alc./Vol.	17.0%
RRP	$33.00 (375 ml)

Brown Brothers Reserve Muscat

This north-east Victorian muscat has impressed us greatly over some years. Its relatively modest pricing in no way reflects its very high quality, making it a perennial bargain. Put it on your shopping list.
CURRENT RELEASE *non-vintage* The essency/raisiny fruit on the nose has lovely purity and hints of malty complexity and nutty-aged material add extra facets, but the dominant character is deliciously grapey, youthful flavour of great satiny depth and persistence. Excellent with a cheese selection.

Quality	♟♟♟♟♟
Value	★★★★★
Rating	94
Grapes	red frontignac
Region	north-east Vic.
Cellar	⬦
Alc./Vol.	18.0%
RRP	$14.75

Campbells Classic Rutherglen Muscat

Quality	🍷🍷🍷🍷
Value	★★★
Rating	91
Grapes	red frontignac
Region	Rutherglen, Vic.
Cellar	🍾
Alc./Vol.	17.5%
RRP	$42.00 (500 ml)

We confess to being slightly confused by the Campbells muscat and tokay packaging. The cheapest wine, the Rutherglen, is in a 375ml format; the next one up is in 500ml and then they revert to 375ml again. The price increments are fair, though: the Rutherglen works out at $40 a full bottle and this one, $60.

CURRENT RELEASE *non-vintage* The colour is slightly darker than the cheaper Campbells muscat, and the bouquet is nicely mellow and more developed, with vanilla, toffee, caramel and varietal muscat fruit. The mouth-feel is oily and viscous and high in sweetness with almost luscious toffee, raisin and Turkish-delight flavours. It has beguiling flavour of intensity and length. Drink with good espresso and chocolates.

Campbells Rutherglen Muscat

Quality	🍷🍷🍷🍷
Value	★★★⅃
Rating	90
Grapes	red frontignac
Region	Rutherglen, Vic.
Cellar	🍾
Alc./Vol.	17.5%
RRP	$19.50 (375 ml)

'Rutherglen Muscat' is the base level of the official Rutherglen liqueur muscat table of quality; from there it goes up to Classic, then Grand and finally Rare, which is the ultimate in aged character and complexity.

CURRENT RELEASE *non-vintage* With a light–medium tawny–red colour and a lovely fresh, fruity, muscat grape nose, this is a typical young muscat of the region and a fine after-dinner sipper. There are caramel and Turkish-delight notes as well, and the palate is very sweet and confectionery-like, with good intensity of muscat varietal character and excellent length. An alternative use is as an ice-cream topping.

d'Arenberg Vintage Fortified

Quality	🍷🍷🍷🍷
Value	★★★
Rating	91
Grapes	shiraz
Region	McLaren Vale, SA
Cellar	➌–15
Alc./Vol.	17.5%
RRP	$34.95 (750 ml); $19.95 (375 ml)

Once called 'vintage port', this wine now adheres to international conventions with the rather less evocative title 'vintage fortified'. This almost-forgotten Australian wine type deserves a wider audience.

CURRENT RELEASE 2004 The regional McLaren Vale indicators are here in an earthy overlay to ripe black-fruit and spicy spirit aromas. The palate is lush and sweet with syrupy dark-berry and cherry-fruit flavour, good depth and an initial velvety texture. Halfway down the palate some solid tannins intervene with a hard edge. Still a pup, this deserves many long years' age before maturity, then it should partner mature cheddar well.

De Bortoli Black Noble

This oddity from De Bortoli is a by-product of their botrytised sweet semillon program. Botrytis-affected grapes are made into sweet wine, then fortified and cask-aged for some years before bottling. The result is a delicious alternative to things like muscat, tokay and port.
CURRENT RELEASE *non-vintage* This has an average age of less than 10 years, but it seems older. The nose has burnt-sugar aromas, almost like very old tokay, along with nutty, raisiny and honeyed complexities. The palate has a slight candied-citrus character that betrays the botrytised wine, and the lush sweetness has an almost Madeira-like acid tang to it. It has less unctuously rich sweetness than, say, a liqueur muscat, but it has equal intensity. It would suit a creamy blue cheese.

Quality	♟♟♟♟♟
Value	★★★
Rating	93
Grapes	semillon; pedro ximenez
Region	Riverina, NSW
Cellar	🍾
Alc./Vol.	17.5%
RRP	$33.75 (375 ml)

Director's Special 10 Year Old Tawny

Yes, company directors and the like used to sip this wine after high-powered business lunches back in the days before .05, healthy lifestyles and fringe benefits tax. It remains a good standard Oz tawny with 10 years' wood-age imparting mellowness and interest.
CURRENT RELEASE *non-vintage* Attractive aged characters give the nose raisin, peel and nutty notes. The palate has the light freshness of a true tawny type, rather than the syrupy qualities of some others, but it has enough depth, richness and length of nutty sweet flavour to satisfy any directors you know. Drink it with coffee and Florentines.

Quality	♟♟♟♟
Value	★★★★
Rating	90
Grapes	mainly shiraz and grenache
Region	Barossa Valley, SA
Cellar	🍾
Alc./Vol.	17.5%
RRP	$12.60

PENGUIN BEST-VALUE
FORTIFIED WINE

Grant Burge Aged Tawny

The Barossa Valley could mount a strong case for being the outstanding tawny port region in Australia. If only that style of wine were fashionable once more, more people might care. The Burge family have been top port producers for a long time.
CURRENT RELEASE *non-vintage* The colour is light tawny–brown and it looks and smells as though it might have a fair whack of sweet sherry material in it. It doesn't seem to be all red grapes by a long shot. There's good rancio on the nose, which signifies age, but it's still very fruity. It's mellow, easy-drinking, moderately complex and has a clean, dry finish – which is unexpected in a wine so inexpensive. Serve with creamy blue cheese and crackers.

Quality	♟♟♟♟
Value	★★★★★
Rating	90
Grapes	grenache; shiraz; mataro
Region	Barossa Valley, SA
Cellar	🍾
Alc./Vol.	19.0%
RRP	$13.25 ⑤

Knappstein Single Vineyard Fortified Shiraz

Quality	▼▼▼▼
Value	★★★⟩
Rating	90
Grapes	shiraz
Region	Clare Valley, SA
Cellar	⬤→2–15+
Alc./Vol.	18.5%
RRP	$22.00 (375 ml) 🍾

A vintage port by another name, this wine was sourced from the company's Yertabulti vineyard, and fortified with eight-year-old brandy spirit. We like the half-bottle: it overcomes some of the resistance people feel to opening a VP, and not being able to finish it. Winemaker: Andrew Hardy.

CURRENT RELEASE 2001   The colour is deep and dense, the bouquet is nutty, toasty, rich-fruited and shows some oak, as well as fine, complexing spirit aromatics. The palate is quite sweet and packed with appealing blackberry and licorice flavours, while the tannins are less aggressive than a lot of young VPs. It would, however, benefit from further cellaring. The best accompaniment is a blue cheese such as stilton.

Lillypilly VP Fortified Shiraz

Quality	▼▼▼⟩
Value	★★★★⟩
Rating	88
Grapes	shiraz
Region	Riverina, NSW
Cellar	🍾 5
Alc./Vol.	18.5%
RRP	$13.50 (375 ml) 🍾🥂

Lillypilly's Robert Fiumara was among the first to get behind screw-caps in a big way, as evidenced by this 1995 vintage port. But the most extraordinary thing about this wine is the price: an 11-year-old mature VP selling for $13.50 a half is an act of great charity.

CURRENT RELEASE 1995   Now drinking at its peak, this lovely VP has a medium-deep red colour with brick-red edges, and a bouquet of aged dusty/earthy notes over plum-jam and blackberry aromas. It's mellowed off nicely on the plate, where the tannins are very soft and easy, and the style of the wine is quite elegant. It has a touch of acid on the finish and is not especially long, but these are minor points. It's a very good drink at a bargain price. Serve with mild blue cheese, such as Blue Castello.

Morris Premium Amontillado

Quality	▼▼▼▼▼
Value	★★★⟩
Rating	95
Grapes	palomino; pedro ximenez
Region	Rutherglen, Vic.
Cellar	🍾
Alc./Vol.	22.0%
RRP	$43.00 (500 ml)

This has won many accolades over the years, including our Penguin Award for Best Fortified Wine. In this day and age, table wines rule, which means few people avail themselves of the joys of this sort of wine. But there's nothing better with French onion soup on a cold winter's night.

CURRENT RELEASE non-vintage   This is quite full-bodied for an amontillado and fairly sweet. It has a full-amber colour and a bouquet of chocolate, vanilla, dried citrus peel and new leather, without much obvious flor-yeast character. It has a rich, soft taste with a significant amount of sweetness – again, within the style parameters but sweeter than some other labels. Delicious with onion soup.

Morris Premium Liqueur Tokay

The price continues to inch upwards, but this is still a great wine and good value. But the Orlando Wyndham Group, which owns Morris, still resists the Rutherglen winemakers' innovation of standardising names for the quality levels of muscat and tokay.

CURRENT RELEASE *non-vintage*   The deep, burnished-walnut colour prepares you for something special, and there's no disappointment. The bouquet is fantastic: concentrated, mellow, toffee-like rancio-aged complexities that go way beyond the cold-tea and malty aromas of younger tokays. It's a multi-dimensional wine with wonderful balance and softness on palate. It glides across the tongue. Try it with coffee and caramels.

Quality	♛♛♛♛♛
Value	★★★⟩
Rating	96
Grapes	muscadelle
Region	Rutherglen, Vic.
Cellar	▮
Alc./Vol.	18.0%
RRP	$57.00 (500 ml)

Noon VP

This vintage port style was made from the hand-picked fruit of grenache bush-vines (untrellised, that is) planted in the 1930s, and vinified by Drew Noon. It's common to see a tawny port style made from grenache; much less so a vintage port.

CURRENT RELEASE 2004   Another superb VP from the sure hand of Drew Noon. It has very concentrated cherry/blackberry jam fruit and fine brandy spirit lending floral and vanilla high-notes. Fully sweet, rich and round on the palate, it's a succulent, opulent, powerful wine with a terrifically long carry. It drinks well now, with Siena cake, and will continue to age well. The price is a gift!

Quality	♛♛♛♛♛
Value	★★★★★
Rating	95
Grapes	grenache
Region	McLaren Vale, SA
Cellar	▮6+
Alc./Vol.	19.3%
RRP	$18.00 (500 ml)
	(cellar door) ▮

Peel Estate Liqueur Shiraz 471

Blended from 1997, 1994 and 1991 vintage fortified shiraz, this is an unusual style that shows elements of both tawny and late-bottled vintage port types.

CURRENT RELEASE *non-vintage*   A deeply coloured wine with a very complex bouquet of raisined fruit, nutty rancio and vanilla. There's also a fair level of volatile acidity that might offend some people. We think it's a bit too high, but there's lovely tangy fruit in its midst, and the sweet, liqueurish palate is very long and rich. Serve it with chocolates and coffee.

Quality	♛♛♛♛
Value	★★★
Rating	91
Grapes	shiraz
Region	Baldivis, WA
Cellar	▮
Alc./Vol.	19.5%
RRP	$39.00 (500 ml)

Peel Estate Vintage Quattro

Quality	🍷🍷🍷🍷🍷
Value	★★★⭤
Rating	93
Grapes	touriga nacional; tinta cão; tinta amarella; souzão
Region	Baldivis, WA
Cellar	⭲2–10
Alc./Vol.	19.5%
RRP	$25.00 (500 ml)

The 'Quattro' refers to the four varieties blended into this vintage port style: touriga nacional, tinta cão, tinta amarella and souzão. They are all Portuguese port varieties which shows where the inspiration for this fortified wine came from. .

CURRENT RELEASE 2002   There's a definite Portuguese accent here; it has spice, licorice, black-cherry, bitter-chocolate, and peppery-lifted-spirit aromas of focused intensity. The palate is lighter and finer than the traditional Aussie VP type, with penetrating flavour, measured sweetness, fine tannins and a long finish. An oddball type that would work well with cheddar.

Penfolds Bluestone Tawny

Quality	🍷🍷🍷🍷
Value	★★★
Rating	91
Grapes	shiraz; mourvèdre; muscadelle
Region	Barossa Valley, SA
Cellar	🍷
Alc./Vol.	19.5%
RRP	$22.20

This aged tawny is named after the locally quarried bluestone that was used in constructing Penfolds Magill Cellars. Any self-respecting Australian wine fan must make the pilgrimage to Magill at least once, it's a wonderful place to tour and the restaurant with its panoramic Adelaide views is outstanding.

CURRENT RELEASE non-vintage   A very good liqueur tawny type with well-concentrated raisin, toffee and nutty characters, edged in clean spirit. In the mouth it has deep, sustained flavour that finishes with a lingering aromatic aftertaste. Serve it with nuts and dried fruits.

Penfolds Club Reserve Tawny

Quality	🍷🍷🍷🍷
Value	★★★★
Rating	89
Grapes	shiraz; grenache; mourvèdre
Region	Barossa Valley, SA
Cellar	🍷
Alc./Vol.	18.5%
RRP	$13.60

Penfolds Club has a long history and our great-grandfathers (if we had any still around) would probably be familiar with it from days of yore. Club Reserve is a more recent addition to the range and we think it's a better buy than the standard label.

CURRENT RELEASE non-vintage   Malty-raisin and nutty aromas are quite fine, and the palate has fair concentration for such a reasonably priced wine. It tastes rich, sweet and persistent with straightforward flavour and a long, clean finish. We'd suggest almond brittle and coffee.

Penfolds Grandfather

Many strange things happened in the 1970s. Where wine was concerned one of the strangest was the crazy cult/investment frenzy that surrounded the old vintages of Seppelt Para Liqueur Port. Swept up in it was Penfolds Grandfather, with vintage-dated wines like the 1945 commanding handsome prices. The bubble burst of course, and Grandfather, no longer vintage-dated, remains as always an excellent tawny.

CURRENT RELEASE *non-vintage* **Complexity is the thing here with an elaborate set of aromas and flavours that can keep you sipping for a long time. The colour is mahogany and it has a bouquet of raisins, vanilla, grilled nuts and aromatic spirit. In the mouth it's sweet yet not cloying with a lovely silky texture and a lingering, toasted toffee and almond-flavoured dry finish. Enjoy it by the fire on a winter night.**

Quality	♟♟♟♟♟
Value	★★★⟩
Rating	96
Grapes	shiraz; mataro
Region	Barossa Valley, SA
Cellar	▮
Alc./Vol.	19.0%
RRP	$92.00

PENGUIN BEST FORTIFIED WINE

Penfolds Great Grandfather

History in a bottle, this ancient blend has elements going back to the early twentieth century. Some wineries keep these liquid keepsakes of a bygone age as a curiosity, released occasionally and priced according to rarity and quality.
CURRENT RELEASE *non-vintage* This reveals its age in the olive-edged walnut-brown colour, and the ultra-concentrated bouquet has malt-toffee, vanilla, roasted-almond and sweet aged spirit in gorgeous harmony. In the mouth it's very rich and potent with lush, syrupy fruit, hints of mocha and toasted nuts with a very long, fascinating aftertaste. If you ever score a bottle of this, keep it away from your freeloading friends and relations, and sip it in quiet contemplation.

Quality	♟♟♟♟♟
Value	★★★
Rating	98
Grapes	not stated
Region	Barossa Valley, SA
Cellar	▮
Alc./Vol.	19.0%
RRP	$326.50

Pfeiffer Christopher's VP

These wines were made from shiraz, but some makers employ Portuguese port varieties with good results. The Pfeiffers from Rutherglen use touriga to make a wine of rare grace.
CURRENT RELEASE 2004 Complex and fragrant, this young port type shows elegance that's missing in its shiraz-based brethren. It smells of roses, black cherries, licorice and prunes, with an edge of clean spirit to lift the aromatics. In the mouth it's intense and fine in texture, without any heaviness or jamminess. The finish is very long, clean and perfumed. Try it with coffee and Florentines.

Quality	♟♟♟♟♟
Value	★★★★★
Rating	97
Grapes	touriga
Region	Rutherglen, Vic.
Cellar	➛2–12
Alc./Vol.	18.0%
RRP	$22.50 ⮞

Seppelt Barossa Valley Amontillado DP116

Quality	🍷🍷🍷🍷🍷
Value	★★★★★
Rating	96
Grapes	palomino; pedro ximenez
Region	Barossa Valley, SA
Cellar	🍾
Alc./Vol.	22.0%
RRP	$21.50

Do not adjust your set: that is the correct price – for a 750 ml bottle! Back in 2003, Southcorp made a price adjustment that meant the Seppelt fortifieds effectively halved in price, they were so eager to move some stock.
CURRENT RELEASE *non-vintage* Year after year we go into fits of ecstasy over this unfashionable but great wine. It is a thing of beauty. It's medium golden–amber in colour and exudes aromas of vanilla, caramel and mixed peel, with a veneer of leathery aged rancio. The palate is clean and relatively dry, with a pronounced tangy attack followed by piercing intensity on the mid-palate. A marvellous aperitif-style wine that also happens to be a wonderful accompaniment for a consommé.

Seppelt Barossa Valley Fino DP117

Quality	🍷🍷🍷🍷🍷
Value	★★★★⯀
Rating	92
Grapes	palomino
Region	Barossa Valley, SA
Cellar	🍾
Alc./Vol.	15.5%
RRP	$21.50

Seppelt is a specialist at this sort of wine, and if you tour the Seppeltsfield winery in the Barossa, you'll encounter entire warehouses with barrels that contain sherry of various types, gently sleeping away and maturing. Maker: James Godfrey.
CURRENT RELEASE *non-vintage* The colour is light mid-yellow and it smells invitingly of flor yeast, green apple, freshly shelled cashews, a hint of fresh cheese and an almost salty tang. In the mouth the seaside flavours pick up momentum, with a crisp texture that stimulates the tastebuds and sharpens the appetite. The finish is bone-dry. It calls out for anchovy-stuffed green olives.

Seppelt Barossa Valley Oloroso DP38

Quality	🍷🍷🍷🍷🍷
Value	★★★★★
Rating	95
Grapes	palomino; pedro ximenez
Region	Barossa Valley, SA
Cellar	🍾
Alc./Vol.	20.0%
RRP	$21.50

Unlike fino and amontillado, oloroso sherry is usually made without the help of the mysterious flor – a special type of yeast that floats on the ullaged wine's surface – adding its unique character. This wine spends its life in full barrels, and the flor is prevented from growing.
CURRENT RELEASE *non-vintage* The colour is dark amber–orange which suggests considerable age, and this is confirmed by a very complex bouquet of vanilla, caramel, chocolate, rancio and Violet Crumble. Some background oak is evident. The palate is sweet and rich, soft, gentle and rounded, with a lovely long, harmonious aftertaste. It's great to serve with clear soups.

Seppelt Rutherglen Tokay DP37

Seppelt has long ceased to have a winery in the Rutherglen area, its fortified wine base camp is in the Barossa. But it continues to source its muscats and tokays exclusively from Rutherglen because there is simply no better place to produce grapes for those styles of wine. Maker: James Godfrey.
CURRENT RELEASE *non-vintage*   The colour raises your expectations: a deep-amber hue with orange reflections. It has the classic tokay bouquet of cold tea-leaves and malt extract. It's lush in the mouth with lots of malty flavour and sweetness, very grapey and fruity with youthful vigour and a little spirit hotness towards the finish. It's a fine wine without great aged complexity, which would be well suited to creamy blue cheese, such as Blue Castello.

Quality	♟♟♟♟
Value	★★★★★
Rating	92
Grapes	muscadelle
Region	Rutherglen, Vic.
Cellar	🍶
Alc./Vol.	17.0%
RRP	$18.00

Skillogalee Liqueur Frontignac

Somewhat tragically, so the back label tells us, this is an unrepeatable wine – the white frontignac vines were replaced with some other variety after this was made. Maker/proprietor: Dave Palmer.
CURRENT RELEASE *non-vintage*   This is a pretty smart fortified – pity there will be no more. It reminds us of what used to be called Old Sweet White: not really a sweet sherry, madeira, tokay or white port but something else. It has a medium-light tawny colour with a yellow rim, and smells of vanilla, toasted nuts, toffee and butterscotch. The palate is sweet but not too syrupy; very pleasing, balanced and clean, with good but not great depth of aged character. It would go with nuts and dried fruits after a meal.

Quality	♟♟♟
Value	★★★
Rating	89
Grapes	white frontignac
Region	Clare Valley, SA
Cellar	🍶
Alc./Vol.	18.0%
RRP	$38.50 (500 ml)

Wolf Blass Red Label Reserve Tawny

So far, Australian winemakers are still permitted to use the name tawny although the word port has been consigned to the out-tray. Australia's bilateral wine treaty with the EU is behind these changes, and we believe the word tawny may eventually be banned, too.
CURRENT RELEASE *non-vintage*   A pleasant, if unremarkable, tawny port style that is very well priced. It has a youthful red to tawny–red colour and a spicy, honeyed, wood-aged character on the nose, with hints of molasses and cedar. It's soft and fairly sweet, medium-bodied and of modest intensity and length. A good sipper with dried fruit and nuts after dinner.

Quality	♟♟♟
Value	★★★┤
Rating	86
Grapes	not stated
Region	not stated
Cellar	🍶
Alc./Vol.	18.0%
RRP	$14.40 Ⓢ

Woodstock Vintage Fortified Shiraz

Quality 🍷🍷🍷½
Value ★★★
Rating 88
Grapes shiraz
Region McLaren Vale, SA
Cellar 5–12+
Alc./Vol. 18.0%
RRP $20.00 (375 ml) (cellar door)

It's a great pity wines like this have to be released so young; little more than 12 months after the harvest is way too soon to drink this kind of thing. Scott Collett, the maker, is relying on you to cellar it before drinking. On the back label, he encourages us to cellar it without saying for how long.

CURRENT RELEASE 2005 The colour is very deep, opaque purple and it smells raw, fresh and brazenly fruity: blackberry jam and attractive spirit are quite appealing even at this tender age. The palate is very sweet and jammy: a little clumsy, with the tannins and sugar quite separate and disjointed just now. It needs cellaring. In style it's more like a 'blackberry nip' than a classic Portuguese vintage port. Put it away and, a few years down the track, drink it with a sharp blue cheese like stilton.

Wine Terms

The following are commonly used winemaking terms.

Acid   There are many acids that occur naturally in grapes and it's in the winemaker's interest to retain the favourable ones because these promote freshness and longevity.

Agrafe   A metal clip used to secure champagne corks during secondary bottle fermentation.

Alcohol   Ethyl alcohol (C_2H_5OH) is a by-product of fermentation of sugars. It's the stuff that makes people happy and it adds warmth and texture to wine.

Alcohol by Volume (A/V)   The measurement of the amount of alcohol in a wine. It's expressed as a percentage, e.g. 13.0% A/V means there is 13.0% pure alcohol as a percentage of the total volume.

Aldehyde   An unwanted and unpleasant organic compound formed between acid and alcohol by oxidation. It's removed by sulphur dioxide.

Allier   A type of oak harvested in the French forest of the same name.

Aperitif   A wine that stimulates the appetite.

Aromatic   A family of grape varieties that have a high terpene content. Riesling and gewürztraminer are examples, and terpenes produce their floral qualities.

Autolysis   A Vegemite or freshly baked bread taste and smell imparted by spent yeast cells in sparkling wines.

Back Blend   To add unfermented grape juice to wine or to add young wine to old wine in fortifieds.

Barrel Fermentation   The process of fermenting a red or white wine in a small barrel, thereby adding a creamy texture and toasty or nutty characters, and better integrating the wood and fruit flavours.

Barrique   A 225-litre barrel.

Baumé   The measure of sugar in grape juice used to estimate potential alcohol content. It's usually expressed as a degree, e.g. 12 degrees Baumé juice will produce approximately 12.0% A/V if it's fermented to dryness. The alternative brix scale is approximately double Baumé and must be divided by 1.8 to estimate potential alcohol.

Bentonite   A fine clay (drillers mud) used as a clarifying (fining) agent.

Blend   A combination of two or more grape varieties and/or vintages. *See also* Cuvée.

Botrytis Cinerea   A mould that thrives on grapevines in humid conditions and sucks out the water of the grapes thereby concentrating the flavour. Good in white wine but not so good in red. (There is also a loss in quantity.)

Breathing   Uncorking a wine and allowing it to stand for a couple of hours before serving. This introduces oxygen and dissipates bottle odours. Decanting aids breathing.

Brix   *see* Baumé.

Brut   The second lowest level of sweetness in sparkling wine; it does not mean there is no added sugar.

Bush Vine   Although pruned the vine is self-supporting in a low-to-the-ground bush. (Still common in the Barossa Valley.)

Carbonic Maceration   Fermentation in whole (uncrushed) bunches. This is a popular technique in Beaujolais. It produces bright colour and soften tannins.

Charmat Process   A process for making sparkling wine where the wine is fermented in a tank rather than in a bottle.

Clone (Clonal)   A recognisable subspecies of vine within a varietal family, e.g. there are numerous clones of pinot noir and these all have subtle character differences.

Cold Fermentation   (Also Controlled Temperature Fermentation) Usually applied to white wines where the ferment is kept at a low temperature (10–12 degrees Centigrade).

Cordon   The arms of the trained grapevine that bear the fruit.

Cordon Cut   A technique of cutting the fruit-bearing arms and allowing the berries to dehydrate to concentrate the flavour.

Crush   Crushing the berries to liberate the free-run juice (*q.v.*). Also used as an expression of a wine company's output: 'This winery has a 1000-tonne crush'.

Cuvée   A Champagne term meaning a selected blend or batch.

Disgorge   The process of removing the yeast lees from a sparkling wine. It involves freezing the neck of the bottle and firing out a plug of ice and yeast. The bottle is then topped up and recorked.

Dosage   Sweetened wine added to a sparkling wine after disgorgement.

Downy Mildew   A disease that attacks vine leaves and fruit. It's associated with humidity and lack of air circulation.

Drip Irrigation   An accurate way of watering a vineyard. Each vine has its own dripper and a controlled amount of water is applied.

Dryland Vineyard   A vineyard that has no irrigation.

Esters   Volatile compounds that can occur during fermentation or maturation. They impart a distinctive chemical taste.

Fermentation   The process by which yeast converts sugar to alcohol with a by-product of carbon dioxide.

Fining   The process of removing solids from wine to make it clear. There are several methods used.

Fortify   The addition of spirit to increase the amount of alcohol in a wine.

Free-run Juice   The first juice to come out of the press or drainer (as opposed to pressings).

Generic   Wines labelled after their district of origin rather than their grape variety, e.g. Burgundy, Chablis, Champagne etc. These terms can no longer legally be used on Australian labels. *Cf.* Varietal.

Graft   Changing the nature/variety of a vine by grafting a different variety onto a root stock.

Imperial   A 6-litre bottle (contains eight 750-ml bottles).

Jeroboam   A 4.5-litre champagne bottle.

Laccase A milky condition on the surface of red wine caused by noble rot. The wine is usually pasteurised.

Lactic Acid One of the acids found in grape juice; as the name suggests, it's milky and soft.

Lactobacillus A micro-organism that ferments carbohydrates (glucose) or malic acid to produce lactic acid.

Lees The sediment left after fermentation. It consists mainly of dead yeast cells.

Malic Acid One of the acids found in grape juice. It has a hard/sharp taste like a Granny Smith apple.

Malolactic Fermentation A secondary process that converts malic acid into lactic acid. It's encouraged in red wines when they are in barrel. If it occurs after bottling, the wine will be fizzy and cloudy.

Mercaptan Ethyl mercaptan is a sulphur compound with a smell like garlic, burnt rubber or asparagus water.

Méthode Champenoise The French method for producing effervescence in the bottle; a secondary fermentation process where the carbon dioxide produced is dissolved into the wine.

Methoxypyrazines Substances that give sauvignon blanc and cabernet sauvignon that added herbaceousness when the grapes aren't fully ripe.

Mousse The froth or head on sparkling wines.

Must *see* Free-run juice.

Negociant A French word that describes a person or organisation that produces and sells wine from grapes and/or bulk wine bought-in from other people.

Noble Rot *see* Botrytis cinerea.

Non-vintage A wine that is a blend of two or more years.

Oak The least porous wood, genus *Quercus*, and used for wine storage containers.

Oenology The science of winemaking.

Organic Viticulture Growing grapes without the use of pesticides, fungicides or chemical fertilisers. Certain chemicals, e.g. copper sulphate, are permitted.

Organic Wines Wines made from organically grown fruit without the addition of chemicals.

Oxidation Browning and dullness of aroma and flavour caused by excessive exposure to air.

pH The measure of the strength of acidity. The higher the pH the higher the alkalinity and the lower the acidity. Wines with high pH values should not be cellared.

Phenolics A group of chemical compounds which includes the tannins and colour pigments of grapes. A white wine described as 'phenolic' has an excess of tannin, making it taste coarse.

Phylloxera A louse that attacks the roots of a vine, eventually killing the plant.

Pigeage To foot-press the grapes.

Pressings The juice extracted by applying pressure to the skins after the free-run juice has been drained.

Pricked A wine that is spoilt and smells of vinegar, due to excessive volatile acidity. *Cf*. Volatile.

Puncheon   A 500-litre barrel.

Racking   Draining off wine from the lees or other sediment to clarify it.

Saignée   French for bleeding: the winemaker has run off part of the juice of a red fermentation to concentrate what's left.

Skin Contact   Allowing the free-run juice to remain in contact with the skins; in the case of white wines, usually for a very short time.

Solero System   Usually a stack of barrels used for blending maturing wines. The oldest material is at the bottom and is topped up with younger material from the top barrels.

Solids   Minute particles suspended in a wine.

Sulphur Dioxide (SO₂)   (Code 220) A chemical added since Roman times to wine as a preservative and a bactericide.

Sur Lie   Wine that has been kept on lees and not racked or filtered before bottling.

Taché   A French term that means 'stained', usually by the addition of a small amount of red wine to sparkling wine to turn it pink.

Tannin   A complex substance derived from skins, pips and stalks of grapes as well as the oak casks. It has a preservative function and imparts dryness and grip to the finish.

Terroir   Arcane French expression that describes the complete growing environment of the vine, including climate, aspect, soil, etc., and the direct effect this has on the character of its wine.

Varietal   An industry-coined term used to refer to a wine by its grape variety, e.g. 'a shiraz'. *Cf.* Generic.

Véraison   The moment when the grapes change colour and gain sugar.

Vertical Tasting   A tasting of consecutive vintages of one wine.

Vigneron   A grapegrower or vineyard worker.

Vinegar   Acetic acid produced from fruit.

Vinify   The process of turning grapes into wine.

Vintage   The year of harvest, and the produce of a particular yeast.

Volatile   Excessive volatile acids in a wine.

Yeast   The micro-organism that converts sugar into alcohol.

Tasting Terms

The following terms refer to the sensory evaluation of wine.

Aftertaste   The taste (sensation) after the wine has been swallowed. It's usually called the finish.

Astringent (Astringency)   Applies to the finish of a wine. Astringency is caused by tannins that produce a mouth-puckering sensation and coat the teeth with dryness.

Balance   'The state of . . .'; the harmony between components of a wine.

Bilgy   An unfortunate aroma like the bilge of a ship. Usually caused by mouldy old oak.

Bitterness   A sensation detected at the back of the tongue. It's not correct in wine but is desirable in beer.

Bouquet   The aroma of a finished or mature wine.

Brettanomyces (Brett)   A spoilage yeast that produces chemical compounds that are present in most red wines but usually at small concentrations. In large doses, these cause aromas reminiscent of bandaids, sweaty horses and other unappetising things, as well as a metallic taste and bitter tannins on the palate. A recent scourge of the Australian wine industry.

Broad   A wine that lacks fruit definition; usually qualified as soft or coarse.

Burnt Match   A sulphide-related odour, often associated with wild or indigenous yeast fermentations in chardonnay. In small doses, can be a positive factor, adding complexity.

Cassis   A blackcurrant flavour common in cabernet sauvignon. It refers to a liqueur produced in France.

Chalky   An extremely dry sensation on the finish.

Cheesy   A dairy character sometimes found in wine, particularly sherries.

Cigar Box   A smell of tobacco and wood found in cabernet sauvignon.

Cloudiness   A fault in wine that is caused by suspended solids that make it look dull.

Cloying   Excessive sweetness that clogs the palate.

Corked   Spoiled wine that has reacted with a tainted cork, and smells like wet cardboard. (The taint is caused by trichloroanisole.)

Creamy   The feeling of cream in the mouth, a texture.

Crisp   Clean acid on the finish of a white wine.

Depth   The amount of fruit on the palate.

Dry   A wine that does not register sugar in the mouth.

Dull   Pertaining to colour; the wine is not bright or shining.

Dumb   Lacking nose or flavour on the palate.

Dusty   Applies to a very dry tannic finish; a sensation.

Earthy   Not as bad as it sounds, this is a loamy/mineral character that can add interest to the palate.

Finesse   The state of a wine. It refers to balance and style.

Finish   *see* Aftertaste.

Firm   Wine with strong, unyielding tannins.

Flabby   Wine with insufficient acid to balance ripe fruit flavours.

Fleshy   Wines of substance with plenty of fruit.

Flinty   A character on the finish that is akin to sucking dry creek pebbles.

Flor yeast   A yeast that grows on the surface of young sherry in partly filled barrels, producing aldehydes that are a key part of the flavour and aroma of fino and manzanilla sherries.

Garlic   *see* Mercaptan (in Wine Terms).

Grassy   A cut-grass odour, usually found in semillon and sauvignon blancs.

Grip   The effect on the mouth of tannin on the finish; a puckering sensation.

Hard   More tannin or acid than fruit flavour.

Herbaceous   Herbal smells or flavour in wine.

Hollow   A wine with a lack of flavour in the middle palate.

Hot   Wines high in alcohol that give a feeling of warmth and a slippery texture.

Hydrogen Sulphide   A rotten-egg-like character, usually created by yeasts during fermentation.

Implicit Sweetness   A just detectable sweetness from the presence of glycerin (rather than residual sugar).

Inky   Tannate of iron present in a wine which imparts a metallic taste.

Integrated (Well)   The component parts of a wine fit together without gaps or disorders.

Jammy   Ripe fruit that takes on the character of stewed jam.

Leathery   A smell like old leather, not necessarily bad if it's in balance.

Length (Long)   The measure of the registration of flavour in the mouth. (The longer the better.)

Lifted   The wine is given a lift by the presence of either volatile acid or wood tannins, e.g. vanillin oak lift.

Limpid   A colour term usually applied to star-bright white wine.

Madeirised   Wine that has aged to the point where it tastes like a madeira.

Mouldy   Smells like bathroom mould; dank.

Mouth-feel   The sensation the wine causes in the mouth; a textural term.

Musty   Stale, flat, out-of-condition wine.

Pepper   A component in either the nose or the palate that smells or tastes like cracked pepper.

Pungent   Wine with a strong nose.

Rancio   A nutty character found in aged fortifieds that is imparted by time on wood.

Reductive   *see* Hydrogen Sulphide.

Residual Sugar   The presence of unfermented grape sugar on the palate; common in sweet wines.

Rough Unpleasant, aggressive wines.

Round A full-bodied wine with plenty of mouth-feel (*q.v.*).

Sappy A herbaceous character that resembles sap.

Short A wine lacking in taste and structure. *See also* Length.

Sous-bois The French word for undergrowth. Used in describing some pinot noirs, especially those made with stalks included in the fermentation.

Spicy A wine with a high aromatic content; spicy character can also be imparted by wood.

Stalky Exposure to stalks, e.g. during fermentation. Leaves a bitter character in the wine.

Tart A lively wine with a lot of fresh acid.

Toasty A smell of cooked bread.

Vanillin The smell and taste of vanilla beans; usually imparted by oak ageing.

Varietal Refers to the distinguishing qualities of the grape variety used in the wine.

Principal Wine Regions

WESTERN AUSTRALIA
1 Swan Valley
2 Perth Hills
3 Geographe
4 Margaret River
5 Pemberton/Manjimup
6 Great Southern

SOUTH AUSTRALIA
7 Riverland
8 Clare Valley
9 Barossa Valley
10 Eden Valley
11 Adelaide Hills
12 McLaren Vale
13 Langhorne Creek
14 Coonawarra

TASMANIA
15 Tamar Valley
16 Derwent Valley
17 Coal River
18 East Coast
19 Piper's River

VICTORIA
20 Henty/Drumborg
21 Murray Valley
22 Sunraysia
23 Gippsland
24 Mornington Peninsula

25 Yarra Valley
26 Sunbury
27 Geelong/Bellarine
   Peninsula
28 Grampians/Great Western
29 Macedon Ranges
30 Heathcote
31 Bendigo
32 Pyrenees
33 Rutherglen
34 Beechworth
35 King Valley
36 Goulburn Valley

NEW SOUTH WALES
37 Murray Valley
38 Tumbarumba
39 Riverina
40 Canberra District
41 Hilltops/Young
42 Cowra
43 Shoalhaven
44 Southern Highlands
45 Orange
46 Mudgee
47 Hunter Valley
48 Hastings Valley

QUEENSLAND
49 Granite Belt
50 South Burnett

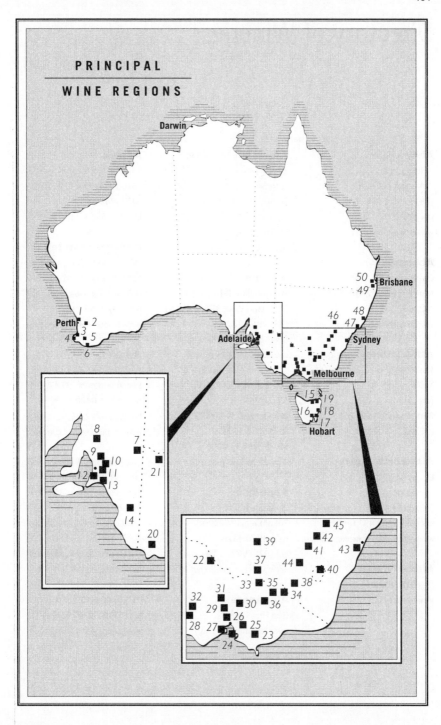

PRINCIPAL

WINE REGIONS

Darwin

Brisbane
50
49

Perth
1
2
3
5
4
6

Adelaide

46
48
47

Sydney

Melbourne

0

15
16
19
18
17

Hobart

8
9
7
10
12
11
13
21
14
20

45
42
39
41
43
22
37
44
40
33
35
38
32
31
34
29
30
36
28
26
27
25
24
23

Directory of Wineries

Abbey Vale
Wildwood Rd
Yallingup WA 6282
(08) 9755 2121
fax (08) 9755 2286
www.abbeyvale.com.au

Abercorn
Cassilis Rd
Mudgee NSW 2850
(02) 6373 3106
www.abercornwine.com.au

Affleck Vineyard
RMB 244
Millynn Rd
(off Gundaroo Rd)
Bungendore NSW 2651
(02) 6236 9276

Ainsworth Estate
Ducks Lane
Seville Vic. 3139
(03) 5964 4711
fax (03) 5964 4311
www.ainsworth-estate.com.au

Alan & Veitch
(see Robert Johnson
Vineyards)

Albert River Wines
1–117 Mundoolun
Connection Rd
Tamborine Qld 4270
(07) 5543 6622
fax (07) 5543 6627
www.albertriverwines.com.au

Alkoomi
Wingebellup Rd
Frankland WA 6396
(08) 9855 2229
fax (08) 9855 2284
www.alkoomiwines.com.au

All Saints Estate
All Saints Rd
Wahgunyah Vic. 3687
(02) 6035 2222
fax (02) 6035 2200
www.allsaintswine.com.au

Allandale
Lovedale Rd
Pokolbin NSW 2320
(02) 4990 4526
fax (02) 4990 1714
www.allandalewinery.com.au

Allanmere
(see First Creek)
www.allanmere.com.au

Allinda
119 Lorimer's Lane
Dixon's Creek Vic. 3775
(03) 5965 2450
fax (03) 5965 2467

Amberley Estate
Wildwood & Thornton Rds
Yallingup WA 6282
(08) 9755 2288
fax (08) 9755 2171
www.amberleyestate.com.au

Amulet
Wangaratta Rd
Beechworth Vic. 3747
(03) 5727 0420
fax (03) 5727 0421
www.amuletvineyard.com.au

Anderson Winery
Lot 13 Chiltern Rd
Rutherglen Vic. 3685
(03) 6032 8111
www.andersonwinery.com.au

Andraos Bros. Wines
150 Vineyard Rd
Sunbury Vic. 3429
(03) 9740 9703
fax (03) 9740 9795
www.andraosbros.com.au

Andrew Harris
Sydney Rd
Mudgee NSW 2850
(02) 6373 1213
fax (02) 6373 1296
www.andrewharris.com.au

Angove's
Bookmark Ave
Renmark SA 5341
(08) 8580 3100
fax (08) 8580 3155
www.angoves.com.au

Annie's Lane
Main North Rd
Watervale SA 5452
(08) 8843 0003
fax (08) 8843 0096
www.annieslane.com.au

Antcliffe's Chase
RMB 4510
Caveat
via Seymour Vic. 3660
(03) 5790 4333

Anvers
(no cellar door)
(08) 8374 1787
fax (08) 8374 2102
www.annvers.com.au

Apsley Gorge
'The Gulch'
Bicheno Tas. 7215
(03) 6375 1221
fax (03) 6375 1589

Arakoon
229 Main Rd
McLaren Vale SA 5171
(08) 8323 7339
fax (02) 6566 6288

Arlewood
Harmans South Rd
Wilyabrup WA 6284
Phone/fax (08) 9755 6267
www.arlewood.com.au

Armstrong Vineyards
(not open to public)
(08) 8277 6073
fax (08) 8277 6035

Arrowfield
Golden Hwy
Jerry's Plains NSW 2330
(02) 6576 4041
fax (02) 6576 4144
www.arrowfieldwines.com.au

Arthurs Creek Estate
(not open to public)
(03) 9714 8202

Ashton Hills
Tregarthen Rd
Ashton SA 5137
(08) 8390 1243
fax (08) 8390 1243

Ashwood Grove
(not open to public)
(03) 5030 5291

Auldstone
Booth's Rd
Taminick via Glenrowan
Vic. 3675
(03) 5766 2237
www.auldstone.com.au

Austins Barrabool
870 Steiglitz Rd
Sutherlands Creek Vic. 3331
(03) 5281 1799
fax (03) 5281 1673
www.abwines.com.au

Avalon
4480Wangaratta–WhitfieldRd
Whitfield Vic. 3733
(03) 5729 3629
www.avalonwines.com.au

Baileys
Taminick Gap Rd
Glenrowan Vic. 3675
(03) 5766 2392
fax (03) 5766 2596
www.baileysofglenrowan.com.au

Baldivis Estate
(see Palandri)

Balgownie
Hermitage Rd
Maiden Gully Vic. 3551
(03) 5449 6222
fax (03) 5449 6506
www.balgownieestate.com

Balnaves
Main Rd
Coonawarra SA 5263
(08) 8737 2946
fax (08) 8737 2945
www.balnaves.com.au

Bannockburn
(not open to public)
Midland Hwy
Bannockburn Vic. 3331
tel/fax (03) 5243 7094
www.bannockburnvineyards.com

Banrock Station
(see Hardys)

Barak's Bridge
(see Yering Station)

Barambah Ridge
79 Goschnicks Rd
Redgate via Murgon
Qld 4605
(07) 4168 4766
fax (07) 4168 4770
www.barambahridge.com.au

Barossa Settlers
Trial Hill Rd
Lyndoch SA 5351
(08) 8524 4017

Barossa Valley Estate
Seppeltsfield Rd
Marananga SA 5355
(08) 8562 3599
fax (08) 8562 4255
www.brlhardy.com.au

Barratt
(not open to public)
PO Box 204
Summertown SA 5141
tel/fax (08) 8390 1788
www.barrattwines.com.au

Barwang
(see McWilliams)

Bass Phillip
(by appointment)
Cnr Tosch's & Hunts Rds
Leongatha South Vic. 3953
(03) 5664 3341

Batista
Franklin Rd
Middlesex WA 6258
tel/fax (08) 9772 3530

Bay of Fires
(see Hardys)

Belgenny
Level 8, 261 George St
Sydney NSW 2000
(02) 9247 5577
fax (02) 9247 7273
www.belgenny.com.au

Beresford
26 Kangarilla Rd
McLaren Vale SA 5171
(08) 8323 8899
fax (08) 8323 7911
www.beresfordwines.com.au

Beringer Blass
77 Southbank Blvd
Southbank Vic. 3000
(03) 8626 3300
fax (03) 8626 3450
www.beringerblass.com.au

Berrys Bridge
633 Carapooee Rd
St Arnaud Vic. 3478
(03) 5496 3220
fax (03) 5496 3322
www.berrysbridge.com.au

Best's Great Western
Western Hwy
Great Western Vic. 3377
(03) 5356 2250
fax (03) 5356 2430

Bethany
Bethany Rd
Bethany
via Tanunda SA 5352
(08) 8563 2086
fax (08) 8563 2086
www.bethany.com.au

Bianchet
187 Victoria Rd
Lilydale Vic. 3140
(03) 9739 1779
fax (03) 9739 1277
www.bianchet.com

Bidgeebong
(no cellar door)
PO Box 5393
Wagga Wagga NSW 2650
(02) 6931 9955
www.bidgeebong.com

Bindi
(not open to public)
343 Melton Rd
Gisborne Vic. 3437
(03) 5428 2564
fax (03) 5428 2564

Bird in Hand
Pfeiffer & Bird In Hand Rds
Woodside SA 5244
(08) 8389 9488
fax (08) 8389 9511
www.olivesoilwine.com

Birdwood Estate
Mannum Rd
Birdwood SA 5234
(08) 8263 0986

Blackjack Vineyard

Calder Hwy
Harcourt Vic. 3452
tel/fax (03) 5474 2355
www.blackjackwines.com.au

Bleasdale

Wellington Rd
Langhorne Creek SA 5255
(08) 8537 3001
www.bleasdale.com.au

Blewitt Springs

Recreational Rd
McLaren Vale SA 5171
(08) 8323 8689
www.hillsview.com.au

Bloodwood Estate

4 Griffin Rd
via Orange NSW 2800
(02) 6362 5631
www.bloodwood.com.au

Blue Pyrenees Estate

Vinoca Rd
Avoca Vic. 3467
(03) 5465 3202
fax (03) 5465 3529
www.bluepyrenees.com.au

Bookpurnong Hill

Bookpurnong Rd
Bookpurnong Hill
Loxton SA 5333
(08) 8584 1333
fax (08) 8584 1388
www.salenaestate.com.au

Boston Bay

Lincoln Hwy
Port Lincoln SA 5605
(08) 8684 3600
www.bostonbaywines.com.au

Botobolar

Botobolar Lane
PO Box 212
Mudgee NSW 2850
(02) 6373 3840
fax (02) 6373 3789
www.botobolar.com

Bowen Estate

Riddoch Hwy
Coonawarra SA 5263
(08) 8737 2229
fax (08) 8737 2173

Boyntons of Bright

Great Alpine Rd
Porepunkah Vic. 3740
(03) 5756 2356

Brands of Coonawarra

Naracoorte Hwy
Coonawarra SA 5263
(08) 8736 3260
fax (08) 8736 3208
www.mcwilliams.com.au

Brangayne

49 Pinnacle Rd
Orange NSW 2800
(02) 6365 3229
www.brangaynewines.com

Bremerton

Strathalbyn Rd
Langhorne Creek SA 5255
(08) 8537 3093
fax (08) 8537 3109
www.bremerton.com.au

Briagolong Estate

Valencia-Briagalong Rd
Briagalong Vic. 3860
tel/fax (03) 5147 2322

Brian Barry

(not open to public)
(08) 8363 6211

Briar Ridge

593 Mount View Rd
Mt View NSW 2321
tel/fax (02) 4990 3670
www.briarridge.com.au

Bridgewater Mill

(see Petaluma)

Brindabella Hills

Woodgrove Cl.
via Hall ACT 2618
(02) 6230 2583

Broke Estate

(see Ryan Family Wines)

Brokenwood

McDonalds Rd
Pokolbin NSW 2321
(02) 4998 7559
fax (02) 4998 7893
www.brokenwood.com.au

Brookland Valley

Caves Rd
Wilyabrup WA 6280
(08) 9755 6042
fax (08) 9755 6038
www.brooklandvalley.com.au

Brown Brothers

Meadow Crk Rd
(off the Snow Rd)
Milawa Vic. 3678
(03) 5720 5500
fax (03) 5720 5511
www.brown-brothers.com.au

Browns of Padthaway
PMB 196
Naracoorte SA 5271
(08) 8765 6040
fax (08) 8765 6003
www.browns-of-padthaway.com

Buller & Sons, R.L.
Three Chain Rd
Rutherglen Vic. 3685
(02) 6032 9660
www.rlbullerandson.com.au

Burge Family Winemakers
Barossa Hwy
Lyndoch SA 5351
(08) 8524 4644
fax (08) 8524 4444
www.burgefamily.com.au

Burnbrae
Hargraves Rd
Erudgere
Mudgee NSW 2850
(02) 6373 3504
fax (02) 6373 3435

By Farr
(no cellar door)
101 Kelly Lane
Bannockburn Vic. 3331
(03) 5281 1733
tel/fax (03) 5281 1433

Calais Estate
Palmers Lane
Pokolbin NSW 2321
(02) 4998 7654
fax (02) 4998 7813

Caledonia Australis Estate
(not open to public)
PO Box 626
North Melbourne Vic. 3051
1800 225 287
fax (03) 9416 4157
www.caledoniaaustralis.com

Cambewarra Estate
520 Illaroo Rd
Cambewarra NSW 2541
(02) 4446 0170
fax (02) 4446 0170

Campbells
Murray Valley Hwy
Rutherglen Vic. 3685
(02) 6032 9458
fax (02) 6032 9870
www.campbellswines.com.au

Cannibal Creek
260 Tynong North Rd
Tynong North Vic. 3813
(03) 5942 8380
fax (03) 5942 8202

Canobolas-Smith
Boree Lane (off Cargo Rd)
Orange NSW 2800
tel/fax (02) 6365 6113

Canonbah Bridge
Merryanbone Station
Warren NSW 2824
(02) 6833 9966
www.canonbah.com.au

Cape Mentelle
Wallcliffe Rd
Margaret River WA 6285
(08) 9757 0888
fax (08) 9757 3233
www.capementelle.com.au

Capel Vale
Lot 5 Capel North West Rd
Capel WA 6271
(08) 9727 0111
fax (08) 9727 0136
www.capelvale.com

Capercaillie
Londons Rd
Lovedale NSW 2325
(02) 4990 2904
fax (02) 4991 1886
www.capercailliewine.com.au

Carlei Green Vineyards
1 Albers Rd
Upper Beaconsfield Vic. 3808
(03) 5944 4599
www.carlei.com.au

Carlyle
(see Pfeiffer)

Casa Freschi
Ridge Rd
Summertown SA 5141
tel/fax (08) 8536 4569
www.casafreschi.com.au

Cascabel
Rogers Rd
Willunga SA 5172
(08) 8557 4434
fax (08) 8557 4435

Casella Carramar Estate
Wakley Rd
Yenda NSW 2681
(02) 6961 3000
www.casellawines.com.au

Cassegrain
Fern Bank Crk Rd
Port Macquarie NSW 2444
(02) 6583 7777
fax (02) 6584 0353
www.cassegrainwines.com.au

Castagna
(by appointment)
88 Ressom Lane
Beechworth Vic. 3747
(03) 5728 2888
fax (03) 5728 2898
www.castagna.com.au

Castle Rock Estate
Porongurup Rd
Porongurup WA 6324
(08) 9853 1035
fax (08) 9853 1010
www.castlerockestate.com.au

Centennial Vineyards
Centennial Rd
Bowral NSW 2076
(02) 4861 8700
fax (02) 4861 8777
www.centennial.net.au

Chain of Ponds
Main Adelaide Rd
Gumeracha SA 5233
(08) 8389 1415
fax (08) 8389 1877
www.chainofpondswines.com.au

Chalkers Crossing
387 Grenfell Rd
Young NSW 2594
(02) 6382 6900
fax (02) 6382 5068
www.chalkerscrossing.com.au

Chambers Rosewood
Corowa–Rutherglen Rd
Rutherglen Vic. 3685
(02) 6032 8641
fax (02) 6032 8101

Chandon
Maroondah Hwy
Coldstream Vic. 3770
(03) 9739 1110
fax (03) 9739 1095
www.chandon.com.au

Chapel Hill
Chapel Hill Rd
McLaren Vale SA 5171
(08) 8323 8429
fax (08) 8323 9245
www.chapelhillwine.com.au

Charles Cimicky
Hermann Thumm Dve
Lyndoch SA 5351
(08) 8524 4025
fax (08) 8524 4772

Charles Melton
Krondorf Rd
Tanunda SA 5352
(08) 8563 3606
fax (08) 8563 3422
www.charlesmeltonwines.com.au

Charles Sturt University
Boorooma St
North Wagga Wagga
NSW 2678
(02) 6933 2435
fax (02) 6933 4072
www.csu.edu.au/winery

Chateau Leamon
5528 Calder Hwy
Bendigo Vic. 3550
(03) 5447 7995
www.chateauleamon.com.au

Chatsfield
O'Neill Rd
Mount Barker WA 6324
tel/fax (08) 9851 2660
www.chatsfield.com.au

Chatto
(see First Creek)

Chestnut Grove
Perup Rd
Manjimup WA 6258
(08) 9772 4255
fax (08) 9772 4543
www.chestnutgrove.com.au

Cheviot Bridge
(no cellar door)
(03) 9820 9080
fax (03) 9820 9070
www.cheviotbridge.com.au

Chrismont
Upper King Valley Rd
Cheshunt Vic. 3678
(03) 5729 8220
fax (03) 5729 8253
www.chrismontwines.com.au

Clairault Estate
via Caves Rd
or Bussell Hwy
CMB Carbunup River
WA 6280
(08) 9755 6225
fax (08) 9755 6229

Clarendon Hills
(not open to public)
(08) 8364 1484
www.clarendonhills.com.au

Classic McLaren
PO Box 245
McLaren Vale SA 5171
tel/fax (08) 8323 9551

Cleveland
Shannons Rd
Lancefield Vic. 3435
(03) 5429 9000
fax (03) 5429 2143
www.clevelandwinery.com.au

Clonakilla
Crisps Lane
Murrumbateman NSW 2582
(02) 6227 5877
www.clonakilla.com.au

Cloudy Bay
(see Cape Mentelle)

Clover Hill
(see Taltarni Vineyards)

Cobaw Ridge
Perc Boyer's Lane
East Pastoria
via Kyneton Vic. 3444
tel/fax (03) 5423 5227
www.cobawridge.com.au

Cockfighter's Ghost
(see Poole's Rock)

Cofield
Distillery Rd
Wahgunyah Vic. 3687
(03) 6033 3798
www.cofieldwines.com

Coldstream Hills
31 Maddens Lane
Coldstream Vic. 3770
(03) 5964 9410
fax (03) 5964 9389
www.coldstreamhills.com.au

Connor Park
59 Connor Road
Leichardt Vic. 3516
(03) 5437 5234
fax (03) 5437 5204
www.bendigowine.com.au

Constable Hershon
1 Gillards Rd
Pokolbin NSW 2320
(02) 4998 7887
fax (02) 4998 6555
www.constablehershon.com.au

Cookoothama
(see Nugan Estate)

Coolangatta Estate
1355 Bolong Rd
Shoalhaven Heads NSW 2535
(02) 4448 7131
fax (02) 4448 7997
www.coolangattaestate.com.au

Coombend
Swansea Tas. 7190
(03) 6257 8256
fax (03) 6257 8484

Cope-Williams
Glenfern Rd
Romsey Vic. 3434
(03) 5429 5428
fax (03) 5429 5655
www.cope-williams.com.au

Coriole
Chaffeys Rd
McLaren Vale SA 5171
(08) 8323 8305
fax (08) 8323 9136
www.coriole.com

Cowra Estate
Boorowa Rd
Cowra NSW 2794
(02) 6342 3650

Crabtree of Watervale
North Tce
Watervale SA 5452
(08) 8843 0069
fax (08) 8843 0144

Craig Avon
Craig Avon Lane
Merricks North Vic. 3926
(03) 5989 7465

Craigie Knowe
Cranbrook Tas. 7190
(03) 6223 5620

Craiglee
Sunbury Rd
Sunbury Vic. 3429
(03) 9744 4489
fax (03) 9744 4489

Craigmoor
Craigmoor Rd
Mudgee NSW 2850
(02) 6372 2208

Craigow
Richmond Rd
Cambridge Tas. 7170
(03) 6248 5482

Craneford
Moorundie St
Truro SA 5356
(08) 8564 0003
fax (08) 8564 0008
www.cranefordwines.com

Cranswick Estate
(see Evans & Tate)

Crawford River
Condah Vic. 3303
(03) 5578 2267

Crittenden at Dromana
25 Harrisons Rd
Dromana Vic. 3936
(03) 5981 8322
fax (03) 5981 8366

Crofters
(see Houghton)

Cullens
Caves Rd
Wilyabrup
via Cowaramup WA 6284
tel/fax (08) 9755 5277
www.cullenwines.com.au

Curly Flat Vineyard
263 Collivers Rd
Lancefield Vic. 3435
(03) 5429 1956
fax (03) 5429 2256
www.curlyflat.com

Currency Creek
Winery Rd
Currency Creek SA 5214
(08) 8555 4069
www.currencycreekwines.com.au

Dal Zotto
Edi Rd
Cheshunt Vic. 3678
(03) 5729 8321
fax (03) 5729 8490

Dalfarras
(see Tahbilk)

Dalrymple
Pipers Brook Rd
Pipers Brook Tas. 7254
(03) 6382 7222

Dalwhinnie
Taltarni Rd
Moonambel Vic. 3478
(03) 5467 2388
www.dalwhinnie.com.au

d'Arenberg
Osborn Rd
McLaren Vale SA 5171
(08) 8323 8206
www.darenberg.com.au

Darling Estate
(by appointment only)
Whitfield Rd
Cheshunt Vic. 3678
(03) 5729 8396
fax (03) 5729 8396

Darling Park
232 Red Hill Rd
Red Hill 3937
tel/fax (03) 5989 2324
www.darlingparkwinery.com

David Traeger
139 High St
Nagambie Vic. 3608
(03) 5794 2514

De Bortoli
De Bortoli Rd
Bibul NSW 2680
(02) 6966 0100
fax (02) 6966 0199
or
Pinnacle Lane
Dixons Creek Vic. 3775
(03) 5965 2423
Fax (03) 5965 2464
www.debortoli.com.au

De Iuliis
Lot 21 Broke Rd
Pokolbin NSW 2320
(02) 4993 8000
fax (02) 4998 7168

Deakin Estate
(see Katnook Estate)

Delamere
4238 Bridport Rd
Pipers Brook Tas. 7254
(03) 6382 7190

Delatite
Stoney's Rd
Mansfield Vic. 3722
(03) 5775 2922
fax (03) 5775 2911
www.delatitewinery.com.au

Dennis
Kangarilla Rd
McLaren Vale SA 5171
(08) 8323 8665
fax (08) 8323 9121
www.denniswines.com.au

Devil's Lair
(not open to public)
PO Box 212
Margaret River WA 6285
(08) 9757 7573
fax (08) 9757 7533
www.devilslair.com.au

Diamond Valley Vineyards
Kinglake Rd
St Andrews Vic. 3761
(03) 9722 0840
fax (03) 9722 2373
www.diamondvalley.com.au

Dominion Wines
Upton Rd, via Avenel
Strathbogie Ranges Vic. 3664
(03) 5796 2718
fax (03) 5796 2719
www.dominionwines.com

Doonkuna Estate
Barton Hwy
Murrumbateman NSW 2582
(02) 6227 5811
fax (02) 6227 5085
www.doonkuna.com.au

Dowie Doole
182 Main Rd
McLaren Vale SA 5171
(08) 8323 7314
fax (08) 8323 7305

Drayton's Bellevue
Oakey Creek Rd
Pokolbin NSW 2320
(02) 4998 7513
fax (02) 4998 7743
www.draytonswines.com.au

Dromana Estate
RMB 555 Old Moorooduc Rd
Tuerong Vic. 3933
office (03) 5974 3899
fax (03) 5974 1155
www.dromanaestate.com.au

Elderton
3 Tanunda Rd
Nuriootpa SA 5355
(08) 8568 7878
fax (08) 8568 7879
www.eldertonwines.com.au

Eldridge Estate
120 Arthurs Seat Rd
Red Hill Vic. 3937
(03) 5989 2644
fax (03) 5989 2089
www.eldridge-estate.com.au

Elgee Park
(no cellar door)
Junction Rd
Merricks Nth Vic. 3926
(03) 5989 7338
fax (03) 5989 7553
www.elgeeparkwines.com.au

elgo Estate
(by appointment only)
Upton Rd
Longwood Vic. 3665
(03) 5798 5563
fax (03) 5798 5524
www.elgoestate.com.au

Eppalock Ridge
Metcalfe Pool Rd
Redesdale Vic. 3444
(03) 5425 3135

Evans & Tate
Lionel's Vineyard
Payne Rd
Jindong WA 6280
(08) 9755 8855
fax (08) 9755 4362
www.evansandtate.com.au

Evans Family
Palmers Lane
Pokolbin NSW 2320
(02) 4998 7333

Fergusson's
84 Wills Rd
Yarra Glen Vic. 3775
(03) 5965 2237
www.fergussonwinery.com.au

Fermoy Estate
Metricup Rd
Wilyabrup WA 6284
(08) 9755 6285
fax (08) 9755 6251
www.fermoy.com.au

Fern Hill Estate
Ingoldby Rd
McLaren Flat SA 5171
(08) 8323 9666
fax (08) 8323 9280
www.fernhillestate.com.au

Ferngrove
Ferngrove Rd
Frankland WA 6396
(08) 9855 2378
fax (08) 9855 2368
www.ferngrove.com.au

Fettler's Rest
(see Jindalee)

Fire Gully
(see Pierro)

First Creek
Monarch Wines
McDonalds Rd
Pokolbin NSW 2320
(02) 4998 7293
fax (02) 4998 7294
www.firstcreekwines.com.au

Fleur De Lys
(see Seppelt)

Flinders Bay
(see Old Station)

Fontys Pool
(see Cape Mentelle)

Fox Creek
Malpas Rd
Willunga SA 5172
(08) 8556 2403
fax (08) 8556 2104
www.foxcreekwines.com.au

Fox River
(see Goundrey)

Frankland Estate
Frankland Rd
Frankland WA 6396
(08) 9855 1544
fax (08) 9855 1549
www.franklandestate.com.au

Freycinet Vineyard
Tasman Hwy
Bicheno Tas. 7215
(03) 6257 8574
fax (03) 6257 8454

Gabriel's Paddocks
Deasy's Rd
Pokolbin NSW 2321
(02) 4998 7650
fax (02) 4998 7603
www.gabrielspaddocks.com.au

Galafrey
Quangellup Rd
Mount Barker WA 6324
(08) 9851 2022
fax (08) 9851 2324

Galah Wines
Box 231
Ashton SA 5137
(08) 8390 1243

Gapsted Wines
Great Alpine Rd
Gapsted Vic. 3737
(03) 5751 1383
fax (03) 5751 1368
www.gapstedwines.com

Garden Gully
Western Hwy
Great Western Vic. 3377
(03) 5356 2400
www.gardengully.com.au

Gartelmann
Lovedale Rd
Lovedale NSW 2321
(02) 4930 7113
fax (02) 4930 7114
www.gartelmann.com.au

Gembrook Hill
(by appointment only)
Launching Place Rd
Gemrook Vic. 3783
(03) 5968 1622
fax (03) 5968 1699

Gemtree
Kangarilla Rd
McLaren Vale SA 5171
(08) 8323 8199
fax (08) 8323 7889
www.gemtreevineyards.com.au

Geoff Merrill
291 Pimpala Rd
Woodcroft SA 5162
(08) 8381 6877
fax (08) 8322 2244
www.geoffmerrillwines.com.au

Geoff Weaver
(not open to public)
2 Gilpin Lane
Mitcham SA 5062
(08) 8272 2105
fax (08) 8271 0177
www.geoffweaver.com.au

Giaconda
(not open to public)
Beechworth Vic.
(03) 5727 0246
www.giaconda.com.au

Gilbert Wines
Albany Hwy
Kendenup WA 6323
(08) 9851 4028
(08) 9851 4021

Glaetzer
34 Barossa Valley Way
Tanunda SA 5352
(08) 8563 0288
fax (08) 8563 0218
www.glaetzer.com

Glenara
126 Range Rd Nth
Upper Hermitage SA 5131
(08) 8380 5277
fax (08) 8380 5056
www.glenara.com.au

Glenguin
Boutique Wine Centre
Broke NSW 2330
tel/fax (02) 4998 7474

Golden Grove Estate
Sundown Rd
Ballandean Qld 4382
(07) 4684 1291
www.goldengrove.com.au

Goona Warra
790 Sunbury Rd
Sunbury Vic. 3429
(03) 9740 7766
fax (03) 9744 7648
www.goonawarra.com.au

The Gorge
(see Pothana Vineyard)

Goundrey
Muir Hwy
Mount Barker WA 6324
(08) 9892 1777
fax (08) 9851 1997
www.goundrey.com

Gramp's
(see Orlando)

Grand Cru Estate
Ross Dewell's Rd
Springton SA 5235
(08) 8568 2378

Granite Hills
Burke and Wills Track
Baynton
via Kyneton Vic. 3444
(03) 5423 7273
fax (03) 5423 7288
www.granitehills.com.au

Grant Burge
Jacobs Creek
Barossa Valley Hwy
Tanunda SA 5352
(08) 8563 3700
Fax (08) 8563 2807
www.grantburgewines.com.au

Green Point
(see Chandon)

Greenock Creek
Radford Rd
Seppeltsfield SA 5360
(08) 8562 8103
fax (08) 8562 8259

Grosset
King St
Auburn SA 5451
(08) 8849 2175
fax (08) 8849 2292
www.grosset.com.au

Grove Estate
Murringo Rd
Young NSW 2594
(02) 6382 6999
fax (02) 6382 4527
www.groveestate.com.au

Gulf Station
(see De Bortoli)

Hainault
255 Walnut Road
Bickley WA 6076
(08) 9293 8339
fax (08) 9293 8339
www.hainault.com.au

Half Mile Creek
(see Beringer Blass)

Hamilton
Willunga Vineyards
Main South Rd
Willunga SA 5172
(08) 8556 2288
fax (08) 8556 2868
www.hamiltonwinegroup.com.au

Hamilton's Ewell
Barossa Valley Way
Nuriootpa SA 5355
(08) 8562 4600
fax (08) 8562 4611
www.hamiltonewell.com.au

Hanging Rock
Jim Rd
Newham Vic. 3442
(03) 5427 0542
fax (03) 5427 0310
www.hangingrock.com.au

Hanson Wines
'Oolorong'
49 Cleveland Ave
Lower Plenty Vic. 3093
(03) 9439 7425

Happs
Commonage Rd
Dunsborough WA 6281
(08) 9755 3300
fax (08) 9755 3846
www.happs.com.au

Harcourt Valley
Calder Hwy
Harcourt Vic. 3453
(03) 5474 2223

Hardys
Reynella Rd
Reynella SA 5161
(08) 8392 2222
fax (08) 8392 2202
www.hardywines.com.au

Harewood Estate
Scotsdale Rd
Denmark WA 6333
(08) 9840 9078
fax (08) 9840 9053

Haselgrove Wines
Sand Rd
McLaren Vale SA 5171
(08) 8323 8706
fax (08) 8323 8049
www.haselgrove.com.au

Hay Shed Hill
Harmans Mill Rd
Wilyabrup WA 6285
(08) 9755 6046
fax (08) 9758 5988
www.hayshedhill.com.au

Heathcote Winery
183 High St
Heathcote Vic. 3523
(03) 5433 2595
fax (03) 5433 3081
www.heathcotewinery.com.au

Heathfield Ridge
Caves Rd
Naracoorte SA 5271
(08) 8363 5800
fax (08) 8363 1980
www.heathfieldridgewines.com.au

Heggies
(see Yalumba)

Helm's
Yass River Rd
Murrumbateman NSW 2582
(02) 6227 5953
fax (02) 6227 0207
www.helmwines.com.au

Henschke
Moculta Rd
Keyneton SA 5353
(08) 8564 8223
fax (08) 8564 8294
www.henschke.com.au

Heritage Wines
Seppeltsfield Rd
Marananga
via Tununda SA 5352
(08) 8562 2880

Hewitson
16 McGowan Ave
Unley SA 5061
(08) 8271 5755
fax (08) 8271 5570
www.hewitson.com.au

Hickinbotham
Nepean Hwy
Dromana Vic. 3936
(03) 5981 0355
fax (03) 5987 0692
www.hickinbotham.biz

Highbank
Riddoch Hwy
Coonawarra SA 5263
(08) 8736 3311
www.highbank.com.au

Highwood
(see Beresford)

Hill Smith Estate
(see Yalumba)

Hillstowe Wines
104 Main Rd
Hahndorf SA 5245
(08) 8388 1400
fax (08) 8388 1411
www.hillstowe.com.au

Hollick
Racecourse Rd
Coonawarra SA 5263
(08) 8737 2318
fax (08) 8737 2952
www.hollick.com

Holm Oak
11 West Bay Rd
Rowella, Tas. 7270
(03) 6394 7577
fax (03) 6394 7350
www.holm-oak.com

Home Hill
38 Nairn St
Ranelagh Tas. 7109
(03) 6264 1200
fax (03) 6264 1069
www.homehillwines.com.au

Homes
(see Massoni Home)

Honeytree
130 Gillards Rd
Pokolbin NSW 2321
tel/fax (02) 4998 7693
www.honeytree.wines.com

Hope Estate
Cobcroft Rd
Broke NSW 2330
(02) 6579 1161
fax (02) 6579 1373

Horseshoe Vineyard
Horseshoe Rd
Horseshoe Valley
Denman NSW 2328
(02) 6541 3512

Houghton
Dale Rd
Middle Swan WA 6056
(08) 9274 5100
fax (08) 9250 3872
www.houghton-wines.com.au

House of Certain Views
(see Margan)

Howard Park
Scotsdale Rd
Denmark WA 6333
(08) 9848 2345
fax (08) 9848 2064
www.howardparkwines.com.au

Hugh Hamilton Wines
McMurtrie Rd
McLaren Vale SA 5171
(08) 8323 8689
fax (08) 8323 9488
www.hamiltonwines.com.au

Hugo
Elliott Rd
McLaren Flat SA 5171
(08) 8383 0098
fax (08) 8383 0446

Hungerford Hill
(see Cassegrain)

Ingoldby
Kangarilla Rd
McLaren Vale SA 5171
(08) 8383 0005
www.beringerblass.com.au

Innisfail
(not open to public)
(03) 5276 1258

Ivanhoe
Marrowbone Rd
Pokolbin NSW 2320
(02) 4998 7325
www.ivanhoewines.com.au

James Irvine
Roeslers Rd
Eden Valley SA 5235
PO Box 308
Angaston SA 5353
(08) 8564 1046
fax (08) 8564 1314
www.irvinewines.com.au

Jamiesons Run
(see Beringer Blass)

Jane Brook
Toodyay Rd
Middle Swan WA 6056
(08) 9274 1432
fax (08) 9274 1211
www.janebrook.com.au

Jansz
(see Yalumba)

Jasper Hill
Drummonds Lane
Heathcote Vic. 3523
(03) 5433 2528
fax (03) 5433 3143

Jeanneret
Jeanneret Rd
Sevenhill SA 5453
(08) 8843 4308
fax (08) 8843 4251
www.ascl.com/j-wines

Jeir Creek Wines
Gooda Creek Rd
Murrumbateman NSW 2582
(02) 6227 5999

Jenke Vineyards
Jenke Rd
Rowland Flat SA 5352
(08) 8524 4154
fax (08) 8524 4154
www.jenkevineyards.com

Jim Barry
Main North Rd
Clare SA 5453
(08) 8842 2261
fax (08) 8842 3752

Jindalee
(not open to public)
(03) 5276 1280
fax 5276 1537
www.jindaleewines.com.au

Jingalla
Bolganup Dam Rd
Porongurup WA 6324
(08) 9853 1023
fax (08) 9853 1023
www.jingallawines.com.au

John Gehrig
80 Gehrig's Lane
Oxley Vic. 3678
(03) 5727 3395
www.johngehrigwines.com.au

Jones Winery
61 Jones Rd
Rutherglen Vic. 3685
www.joneswinery.com

Joseph
(see Primo Estate)

Juniper Estate
Harmans Rd Sth
Cowaramup WA 6284
(08) 9755 9000
fax (08) 9755 9100
www.juniperestate.com.au

Kangarilla Road Winery
Kangarilla Rd
McLaren Flat SA 5171
(08) 8383 0533
fax (08) 8383 0044
www.kangarillaroad.com.au

Kara Kara
Sunraysia Hwy
St Arnaud Vic. 3478
tel/fax (03) 5496 3294
www.pyrenees.org.au/karakara.htm

Karina Vineyards
35 Harrisons Rd
Dromana Vic. 3936
(03) 5981 0137

Karl Seppelt
(see Grand Cru Estate)

Karrivale
Woodlands Rd
Porongurup WA 6324
(08) 9853 1009
fax (08) 9853 1129

Karriview
RMB 913
Roberts Rd
Denmark WA 6333
(08) 9840 9381
www.karriviewwines.com.au

Katnook Estate
Riddoch Hwy
Coonawarra SA 5263
(08) 8737 2394
fax (08) 8737 2397
www.katnookestate.com.au

Kays Amery
Kay's Rd
McLaren Vale SA 5171
(08) 8323 8201
fax (08) 8323 9199
www.kaybrothersamerywines.com

Keith Tulloch
Hunter Ridge Winery
Hermitage Rd
Pokolbin NSW 2320
(02) 4998 7500
fax (02) 4998 7211
www.keithtullochwine.com.au

Kies Estate
Barossa Valley Way
Lyndoch SA 5351
(08) 8524 4110
www.kieswines.com.au

Kilikanoon
PO Box 205
Auburn SA 5451
tel/fax (08) 8843 4377
www.kilikanoon.com.au

Killawarra
(see Southcorp Wines)

Killerby
Minnimup Rd
Gelorup WA 6230
(08) 9795 7222
fax (08) 9795 7835
www.killerby.com.au

Kingston Estate
Sturt Hwy
Kingston-on-Murray SA 5331
(08) 8583 0500
fax (08) 8583 0304
www.kingstonestatewines.com

Kirrihill Estates
Farrell Flat Rd
Clare SA 5453
(08) 8842 1233
fax (08) 8842 1556
www.kirrihillestates.com.au

Knappstein Wines
2 Pioneer Ave
Clare SA 5453
(08) 8842 2600
fax (08) 8842 3831
www.knappsteinwines.com.au

Kooyong
110 Hunts Rd
Tuerong Vic. 3933
(03) 5989 7355
fax (03) 5989 7677
www.kooyong.com

Koppamurra
(no cellar door)
PO Box 110
Blackwood SA 5051
(08) 8271 4127
fax (08) 8271 0726
www.koppamurrawines.com.au

Kulkunbulla
Brokenback Estate
1595 Broke Rd
Pokolbin NSW 2320
(02) 4998 7140
fax (02) 4998 7142
www.kulkunbulla.com.au

Kyeema
(not open to public)
PO Box 282
Belconnen ACT 2616
(02) 6254 7557

Laanecoorie
(cellar door by arrangement)
RMB 1330
Dunolly Vic. 3472
(03) 5468 7260

Lake Breeze
Step Rd
Langhorne Creek SA 5255
(08) 8537 3017
fax (08) 8537 3267
www.lakebreeze.com.au

Lake's Folly
Broke Rd
Pokolbin NSW 2320
(02) 4998 7507
fax (02) 4998 7322
www.lakesfolly.com.au

Lamont's
Bisdee Rd
Millendon WA 6056
(08) 9296 4485
fax (08) 9296 1663
www.lamonts.com.au

Lancefield Winery
Woodend Rd
Lancefield Vic. 3435
(03) 5433 5292

The Lane
Ravenswood Lane
Hahndorf SA 5245
(08) 8388 1250
fax (08) 8388 7233
www.ravenswoodlane.com.au

Langmeil
Cnr Langmeil & Para Rds
Tanunda SA 5352
(08) 8563 2595
fax (08) 8563 3622
www.langmeilwinery.com.au

Lark Hill
521 Bungendore Rd
Bungendore NSW 2621
(02) 6238 1393
www.larkhillwine.com.au

Laurel Bank
(by appointment only)
130 Black Snake Lane
Granton Tas. 7030
(03) 6263 5977
fax (03) 6263 3117

Leasingham
7 Dominic St
Clare SA 5453
(08) 8842 2555
fax (08) 8842 3293
www.leasingham-wines.com.au

Leconfield
Riddoch Hwy
Coonawarra SA 5263
(08) 8737 2326
fax (08) 8737 2285
www.leconfield.com.au

Leeuwin Estate
Stevens Rd
Margaret River WA 6285
(08) 9757 0000
fax (08) 9757 0001
www.leeuwinestate.com.au

Leland Estate
PO Lenswood SA 5240
(08) 8389 6928
www.lelandestate.com.au

Lengs & Cooter
24 Lindsay Tce
Belair SA 5052
tel/fax (08) 8278 3998
www.lengscooter.com.au

Lenswood Vineyards
3 Cyril John Crt
Athelstone SA 5076
tel/fax (08) 8365 3766
www.knappsteinlenswood.com.au

Lenton Brae
Caves Rd
Wilyabrup WA 6280
(08) 9755 6255
fax (08) 9755 6268
www.lentonbrae.com

Leo Buring
(see Southcorp Wines)

Lillydale Vineyards
Davross Crt
Seville Vic. 3139
(03) 5964 2016
www.mcwilliams.com.au

Lillypilly Estate
Farm 16, Lilly Pilly Rd
Leeton NSW 2705
(02) 6953 4069
fax (02) 6953 4980
www.lillypilly.com

Lindemans
McDonalds Rd
Pokolbin NSW 2320
(02) 4998 7501
fax (02) 4998 7682
www.southcorp.com.au

**The Little Wine
Company**
824 Milbrodale Rd
Broke NSW 2330
(02) 6579 1111
fax (02) 6579 1440
www.thelittlewinecompany.
com.au

Logan
(not open to public)
(02) 9958 6844
www.loganwines.com.au

Long Gully
Long Gully Rd
Healesville Vic. 3777
tel/fax (03) 5962 3663
www.longgullyestate.com

Lovegrove
Heidelberg–Kinglake Road
Cottlesbridge Vic. 3099
(03) 9718 1569
fax (03) 9718 1028

Lowe Family
Ashbourne Vineyard
Tinja Lane
Mudgee NSW 2850
(02) 6372 0800
fax (02) 6372 0811
www.lowewine.com.au

Madew
Westering Vineyard
Federal Hwy
Lake George NSW 2581
(02) 4848 0026
fax (02) 4848 0026
www.madewwines.com.au

Madfish
(see Howard Park)

Maglieri
RSD 295 Douglas Gully Rd
McLaren Flat SA 5171
(08) 8383 2211
fax (08) 8383 0735
www.beringerblass.com.au

Main Ridge
Lot 48 Williams Rd
Red Hill Vic. 3937
(03) 5989 2686
www.mre.com.au

Majella
Lynn Rd
Coonawarra SA 5263
(08) 8736 3055
fax (08) 8736 3057
www.majellawines.com.au

Malcolm Creek
(open weekends and public
holidays)
Bonython Rd
Kersbrook SA 5231
tel/fax (08) 8389 3235

Margan Family
1238 Milbrodale Rd
Broke NSW 2330
tel/fax (02) 6579 1317
www.margan.com.au

Maritime Estate
Tuck's Rd
Red Hill Vic. 3937
(03) 5989 2735

Marius Wines
(not open to public)
PO Box 545
Willunga SA 5172
(08) 8556 2421
fax (08) 8556 4839
www.mariuswines.com.au

Massoni Home
(by appointment only)
Mornington–Flinders Rd
Red Hill Vic. 3937
(03) 5981 8008
fax (03) 5981 2014
www.massoniwines.com

Maxwell
Cnr Olivers & Chalkhill Rds
McLaren Vale SA 5171
(08) 8323 8200
www.maxwellwines.com.au

McAlister
(not open to public)
RMB 6810
Longford Vic. 3851
(03) 5149 7229

McGuigan
Cnr Broke & McDonalds Rds
Pokolbin NSW 2320
(02) 4998 7700
fax (02) 4998 7401
www.mcguiganwines.com.au

McWilliams
Hanwood NSW 2680
(02) 6963 0001
fax (02) 6963 0002
www.mcwilliams.com.au

Meadowbank
Denholms Rd
Cambridge Tas. 7170
(03) 6248 4484
fax (03) 6248 4485
www.meadowbankwines.com.au

Meerea Park
Lot 3 Palmers Lane
Pokolbin NSW 2320
(02) 4998 7006
fax (02) 4998 7005
www.meereapark.com.au

Merricks Creek
(by appointment only)
44 Merricks Rd
Merricks Vic. 3916
(03) 5989 8868
fax (03) 5989 9070
www.merrickscreek.com

Merricks Estate
Cnr Thompsons Lane &
Frankston–Flinders Rd
Merricks Vic. 3916
(03) 5989 8416
fax (03) 9613 4242

Miceli
60 Main Creek Rd
Arthur's Seat Vic. 3936
(03) 5989 2755

Middleton Estate
Flagstaff Hill Rd
Middleton SA 5213
(08) 8555 4136
fax (08) 8555 4108

The Mill
(see Windowrie Estate)

Mintaro Cellars
Leasingham Rd
Mintaro SA 5415
(08) 8843 9150
www.mintarowines.com.au

Miramar
Henry Lawson Dr.
Mudgee NSW 2850
(02) 6960 3000
www.miramarwines.com.au

Miranda Wines
57 Jordaryan Ave
Griffith NSW 2680
(02) 6960 3000
fax (02) 6962 6944
www.mirandawines.com.au

Mirrool Creek
(see Miranda Wines)

Mitchell
Hughes Park Rd
Sevenhill via Clare SA 5453
(08) 8843 4258
www.mitchellwines.com

Mitchelton Wines
Mitcheltstown
Nagambie 3608
(03) 5736 2222
fax (03) 5736 2266
www.mitchelton.com.au

Molly Morgan
Talga Rd
Lovedale NSW 2321
(02) 4930 7695
fax (02) 9816 2680
www.mollymorgan.com

Monichino
70 Berry's Rd
Katunga Vic. 3640
(03) 5864 6452
fax (03) 5864 6538

Montalto
33 Shoreham Rd
Red Hill South Vic. 3937
(03) 5989 8412
fax (03) 5989 8417
www.montalto.com.au

Montara
Chalambar Rd
Ararat Vic. 3377
(03) 5352 3868
fax (03) 5352 4968
www.montara.com.au

**Montrose/Poets
Corner**
Henry Lawson Dr.
Mudgee NSW 2850
(02) 6372 2208
www.poetscornerwines.com.au

Moondah Brook
(see Houghton)

Moorilla Estate
655 Main Rd
Berridale Tas. 7011
(03) 6277 9900
www.moorilla.com.au

Moorooduc Estate
Derril Rd
Moorooduc Vic. 3933
(03) 5971 8506
www.moorooducestate.com.au

**Mornington Vineyards
Estate**
(see Dromana Estate)

Morris
off Murray Valley Hwy
Mia Mia Vineyards
Rutherglen Vic. 3685
(02) 6026 7303
fax (02) 6026 7445
www.orlandowyndhamgroup.com

Moss Brothers
Caves Rd
Wilyabrup WA 6280
(08) 9755 6270
fax (08) 9755 6298
www.mossbrothers.com.au

Moss Wood
Metricup Rd
Wilyabrup WA 6284
(08) 9755 6266
fax (08) 9755 6303
www.mosswood.com.au

Mount Avoca
Moates Lane
Avoca Vic. 3467
(03) 5465 3282
www.mountavoca.com

Mount Horrocks
Curling St
Auburn SA 5451
(08) 8849 2202
fax (08) 8849 2265
www.mounthorrocks.com

Mount Hurtle
(see Geoff Merrill)

Mount Ida
(see Beringer Blass)

Mount Langi Ghiran
Warrak Rd
Buangor Vic. 3375
(03) 5354 3207
fax (03) 5354 3277
www.langi.com.au

Mount Mary
(not open to public)
(03) 9739 1761
fax (03) 9739 0137

Mount Pleasant
Marrowbone Rd
Pokolbin NSW 2321
(02) 4998 7505
fax (02) 4998 7761
www.mcwilliams.com.au

Mount Prior Vineyard
Cnr River Rd & Popes Lane
Rutherglen Vic. 3685
(02) 6026 5591
fax (02) 6026 5590

Mount William Winery
Mount William Rd
Tantaraboo Vic. 3764
(03) 5429 1595
fax (03) 5429 1998
www.mtwilliamwinery.com.au

Mountadam
High Eden Ridge
Eden Valley SA 5235
(08) 8564 1900
www.mountadam.com

Mulyan
North Logan Rd
Cowra NSW 2794
(02) 6342 1336
fax (02) 6341 1015
www.mulyan.com.au

Murchison Wines
Old Weir Rd
Murchison Vic. 3610
(03) 5826 2294
fax (03) 5826 2510
www.murchisonwines.com.au.

Murrindindi
(not open to public)
(03) 5797 8217

Narkoojee
170 Francis Rd
Glengarry Vic. 3854
(03) 5192 4257
fax (03) 5192 4238
www.narkoojee.com

Neagle's Rock
Main North Rd
Clare SA 5453
(08) 8843 4020
www.neaglesrock.com

Nepenthe Vineyards
(not open to public)
(08) 8389 8218
www.nepenthe.com.au

Nicholson River
Liddells Rd
Nicholson Vic. 3882
(03) 5156 8241
www.nicholsonriverwinery.com.au

Ninth Island
(see Pipers Brook)

Noon Winery
(cellar door seasonal)
Rifle Range Rd
McLaren Vale SA 5171
tel/fax (08) 8323 8290

Normans
(see Xanadu)

Notley Gorge
(see Rosevears Estate)

Nugan Estate
Darlington Point Rd
Wilbriggie NSW 2680
(02) 6968 5311
fax (02) 6962 5399

Oakridge Estate
864 Maroondah Hwy
Coldstream Vic. 3770
(03) 9739 1920
fax (03) 9739 1923
www.oakridgeestate.com.au

Oakvale Winery
1596 Broke Rd
Pokolbin NSW 2320
(02) 4998 7088
www.oakvalewines.com.au

Old Kent River
Turpin Rd
Rocky Gully WA 6397
(08) 9855 1589
fax (08) 9855 1589

Old Station
PO Box 40
Watervale SA 5452
(02) 9144 1925

O'Leary Walker
Main Rd
Leasingham SA 5452
(08) 8843 0022
fax 08 8843 0004
www.olearywalkerwines.com

Olivine
(see The Little Wine
Company)

Orlando
Barossa Valley Way
Rowland Flat SA 5352
(08) 8521 3111
fax (08) 8521 3102
www.orlandowyndhamgroup.com

Osborns
166 Foxeys Rd
Merricks North Vic. 3926
(03) 5989 7417
fax (03) 5989 7510

Padthaway Estate
Riddoch Hwy
Padthaway SA 5271
(08) 8765 5235
fax (08) 8765 5294
www.padthawayestate.com

Palandri
Cnr Boundary Rd & Bussell
Hwy
Margaret River WA 6285
(08) 9756 5100
fax (08) 9755 5722
www.palandri.com.au

Palmer Wines
Caves Rd
Wilyabrup WA 6280
(08) 9756 7388
fax (08) 9756 7399

Pankhurst Wines
Woodgrove Rd
Hall ACT 2618
(02) 6230 2592
www.pankhurstwines.com.au

Panorama
1848 Cygnet Coast Rd
Cradoc Tas. 7109
Tel/fax (03) 6266 3409
www.panoramavineyard.com.au

Paracombe
Paracombe Rd
Paracombe SA 5132
(08) 8380 5058
fax (08) 8380 5488
www.paracombewines.com

Paradise Enough
(open weekends & holidays)
Stewarts Rd
Kongwak Vic. 3951
(03) 5657 4241
www.paradiseenough.com.au

Paringa Estate
44 Paringa Rd
Red Hill South Vic. 3937
(03) 5989 2669
www.paringaestate.com.au

**Parker Coonawarra
Estate**
Riddoch Hwy
Coonawarra SA 5263
(08) 8737 3525
fax (08) 8737 3527
www.parkercoonawarraestate.
com.au

Passing Clouds
Powlett Rd
via Inglewood
Kingower Vic. 3517
(03) 5438 8257

Pattersons
St Werburghs Rd
Mount Barker WA 6324
tel/fax (08) 9851 2063

Paul Conti
529 Wanneroo Rd
Woodvale WA 6026
(08) 9409 9160
fax (08) 9309 1634
www.paulcontiwines.com.au

Paul Osicka
Majors Creek Vineyard
Graytown Vic. 3608
(03) 5794 9235
fax (03) 5794 9288

Paulett Wines
Polish Hill River Rd
Sevenhill SA 5453
(08) 8843 4328
fax (08) 8843 4202
www.paulettwines.com.au

Peel Estate
Fletcher Rd
Baldivis WA 6171
(08) 9524 1221
www.peelwine.com.au

Pendarves Estate
110 Old North Rd
Belford NSW 2335
(02) 6574 7222

Penfolds
(see Southcorp Wines)

Penley Estate
McLean's Rd
Coonawarra 5263
(08) 8736 3211
fax (08) 8736 3124
www.penley.com.au

Penny's Hill
Main Rd
McLaren Vale SA 5171
(08) 8556 4460
fax (08) 8556 4462
www.pennyshill.com.au

Pepper Tree Wines
Halls Rd
Pokolbin NSW 2320
(02) 4998 7539
fax (02) 4998 7746
www.peppertreewines.com.au

Pepperjack
(see Beringer Blass)

Peppers Creek
Cnr Ekerts & Broke Rds
Pokolbin NSW 2321
(02) 4998 7532

Petaluma
Spring Valley Rd
Piccadilly SA 5151
(08) 8339 9300
fax (08) 8339 9301
www.petaluma.com.au

Peter Lehmann
Para Rd
Tanunda SA 5352
(08) 8563 2500
fax (08) 8563 3402
www.peterlehmannwines.com.au

Petersons
Lot 21 Mount View Rd
Mount View NSW 2325
(02) 4990 1704
www.petersonswines.com.au

Pewsey Vale
(see Yalumba)

Pfeiffer
Distillery Rd
Wahgunyah Vic. 3687
(02) 6033 2805
www.pfeifferwines.com.au

Phillip Island Wines
Lot 1 Berrys Beach Rd
Phillip Island Vic. 3922
(03) 5956 8465
www.phillipislandwines.com.au

Pibbin Farm
Greenhill Rd
Balhannah SA 5242
(08) 8388 4794

Picardy
(not open to public)
tel/fax (08) 9776 0036
www.picardy.com.au

Pierro
Caves Rd
Wilyabrup WA 6280
(08) 9755 6220
fax (08) 9755 6308

Pikes
Polish Hill River Rd
Seven Hill SA 5453
(08) 8843 4370
fax (08) 8843 4353
www.pikeswines.com.au

Pipers Brook
3959 Bridport Hwy
Pipers Brook Tas. 7254
(03) 6332 4444
fax (03) 6334 9112
www.pbv.com.au

Pirramimma
Johnston Rd
McLaren Vale SA 5171
(08) 8323 8205
fax (08) 8323 9224
www.pirramimma.com.au

Pizzini
King Valley Rd
Whitfield Vic. 3678
(03) 5729 8278
fax (03) 5729 8495
www.pizzini.com.au

Plantagenet
Albany Hwy
Mount Barker WA 6324
(08) 9851 2150
fax (08) 9851 1839

Plunkett's
Cnr Lambing Gully Rd &
Hume Fwy
Avenel Vic. 3664
(03) 5796 2150
fax (03) 5796 2147
www.plunkett.com.au

Poole's Rock
McDonalds Rd
Pokolbin NSW 2320
(02) 4998 7501
fax (02) 4998 7682
www.poolesrock.com.au

Port Phillip Estate
261 Red Hill Rd
Red Hill Vic. 3937
(03) 5989 2708
fax (03) 5989 2891
www.portphillip.net

Portree Vineyard
72 Powell's Track
Lancefield Vic. 3435
(03) 5429 1422
fax (03) 5429 2205
www.portreevineyard.com.au

Pothana Vineyard
Pothana Lane
Belford NSW 2335
(02) 6574 7164
fax (02) 6574 7209

Preece
(see Mitchelton Wines)

Prentice
(see Tuck's Ridge)

Preston Peak
31 Preston Peak Lane
Preston Qld 4352
tel/fax (07) 4630 9499
www.prestonpeak.com

Primo Estate
Cnr Old Port Wakefield &
Angle Vale Rds
Virginia SA 5120
(08) 8380 9442
fax (08) 8380 9696
www.primoestate.com.au

Prince Albert
Lemins Rd
Waurn Ponds Vic. 3221
(03) 5243 5091
fax (03) 5241 8091

Provenance
(by appointment)
PO Box 74
Bannockburn Vic. 3331
(03) 5265 6055
fax (03) 5265 6077
www.provenancewines.com.au

Providence
236 Lalla Rd
Lalla Tas. 7267
(03) 6395 1290
fax (03) 6395 2088
www.providence-vineyards.com.au

Punt Road
St Huberts Rd
Coldstream Vic. 3770
(03) 9739 0666
fax (03) 9739 0633
www.puntroadwines.com.au

Punters Corner
Cnr Riddoch Hwy &
Racecourse Rd
Coonawarra SA 5263
(08) 8737 2007
www.punterscorner.com.au

Queen Adelaide
(see Southcorp)

Radenti
(see Freycinet Vineyard)

Ralph Fowler
Lot 101 Limestone Coast Rd
Mount Benson SA 5275
tel/fax (08) 8768 5008
www.ralphfowlerwines.com.au

Red Edge
(not open to public)
Heathcote Vic. 3523
(03) 9337 5695

Red Hill Estate
53 Shoreham Rd
Red Hill South Vic. 3937
(03) 5989 2838
www.redhillestate.com.au

Redbank Winery
1 Sally's Lane
Redbank Vic. 3478
(03) 5467 7255
www.sallyspaddock.com.au

Redgate
Cnr Caves & Boodjidup Rds
Margaret River WA 6285
(08) 9757 6488
fax (08) 9757 6308
www.redgatewines.com.au

Redman
Riddoch Hwy
Coonawarra SA 5263
(08) 8736 3331
fax (08) 8736 3013

Renmano
Renmark Ave
Renmark SA 5341
(08) 8586 6771
fax (08) 8586 5939
www.hardywines.com.au

Reynell
(see Hardys)

Ribbon Vale Estate
(see Moss Wood)

Richmond Grove
(see Orlando)

Riddoch
(see Katnook Estate)

Rimfire
via Bismarck St
Maclagan Qld 4352
(07) 4692 1129
www.rimfirewinery.com.au

Riverina Estate
700 Kidman Way
Griffith NSW 2680
(02) 6963 8300
fax (02) 6962 4628

Robinvale Wines
Sealake Rd
Robinvale Vic. 3549
(03) 5026 3955
fax (03) 5026 1123
www.organicwines.com

Rochford
Cnr Maroondah Hwy & Hill Rd
Coldstream Vic. 3770
(03) 5962 2119
www.rochfordwines.com.au

Rockford
Krondorf Rd
Tanunda SA 5352
(08) 8563 2720
info@rockfordwines.com.au

Rosabrook Estate
Rosa Brook Rd
Margaret River WA 6285
(08) 9758 2286
fax (08) 9758 8226
www.rosabrook.com

Rosemount
Rosemount Rd
Denman NSW 2328
(02) 6549 6450
fax (02) 6549 6588
www.rosemountestate.com.au

Rosevears Estate
1A Waldhorn Dve
Rosevears Tas. 7277
(03) 6330 1800
fax (03) 6330 1810
www.rosevearsestate.com.au

Rosily Vineyard
Yelverton Rd
Wilyabrup WA 6280
tel/fax (08) 9755 6336
www.rosily.com.au

Rothbury Estate
Broke Rd
Pokolbin NSW 2321
(02) 4998 7555
fax (02) 4998 7553
www.beringerblass.com.au

Rothvale
Deasy's Rd
Pokolbin NSW 2321
(02) 4998 7290
www.rothvale.com.au

Rufus Stone
(see Tyrrell's)

Rumball
(no cellar door)
(08) 8332 2761
fax (08) 8364 0188

Ryan Family Wines
Broke Estate
Broke Rd
Broke NSW 2330
tel/fax (02) 6579 1065
www.ryanwines.com.au

Ryecroft
Ingoldby Rd
McLaren Flat SA 5171
(08) 8383 0001
www.southcorp.com.au

Rymill
The Riddoch Run Vineyards
(off Main Rd)
Coonawarra SA 5263
(08) 8736 5001
fax (08) 8736 5040
www.rymill.com.au

Saddlers Creek
Marrowbone Rd
Pokolbin NSW 2321
(02) 4991 1770
fax (02) 4991 2482
www.saddlerscreekwines.com.au

Salisbury
(see Evans & Tate)

Salitage
Vasse Hwy
Pemberton WA 6260
(08) 9776 1771
fax (08) 9776 1772
www.salitage.com.au

Saltram
Nuriootpa Rd
Angaston SA 5353
(08) 8564 3355
www.saltramwines.com.au

Sandalford
West Swan Rd
Caversham WA 6055
(08) 9374 9374
fax (08) 9274 2154
www.sandalford.com

Sandhurst Ridge
156 Forest Dve
Marong Vic. 3515
(03) 5435 2534
fax (03) 5435 2548
www.sandhurstridge.com

Sandstone Vineyard
(cellar door by appointment)
Caves & Johnson Rds
Wilyabrup WA 6280
(08) 9755 6271
fax (08) 9755 6292

Savaterre
(not open to public)
PO Box 337
Beechworth Vic. 3747
tel/fax (03) 5727 0551
www.savaterre.com

Scarborough Wines
Gillards Rd
Pokolbin NSW 2321
(02) 4998 7563
www.scarboroughwine.com.au

Scarpantoni
Scarpantoni Dve
McLaren Flat SA 5171
(08) 8383 0186
fax (08) 8383 0490
www.scarpantoni-wines.com.au

Schinus
(see Crittenden at Dromana)

Scotchman's Hill
Scotchmans Rd
Drysdale Vic. 3222
(03) 5251 3176
fax (03) 5253 1743
www.scotchmanshill.com.au

Seaview
Chaffeys Rd
McLaren Vale SA 5171
(08) 8323 8250
www.southcorp.com.au

Seppelt
Seppeltsfield
via Tanunda SA 5352
(08) 8562 8028
fax (08) 8562 8333
www.southcorp.com.au

Sevenhill
College Rd
Sevenhill
via Clare SA 5453
(08) 8843 4222
fax (08) 8843 4382
www.sevenhillcellars.com.au

Seville Estate
Linwood Rd
Seville Vic. 3139
(03) 5964 2622
fax (03) 5964 2633
www.sevilleestate.com.au

Shadowfax
K Road
Werribee Vic. 3030
(03) 9731 4420
fax (03) 9731 4421
www.shadowfax.com.au

Shantell
Melba Hwy
Dixons Creek Vic. 3775
(03) 5965 2155
fax (03) 5965 2331
www.shantellvineyard.com.au

Sharefarmers
(see Petaluma)

Shaw and Smith
(weekends only)
Lot 4 Jones Rd
Balhannah SA 5242
(08) 8398 0500
fax (08) 8398 0600
www.shawandsmith.com.au

Shottesbrooke
1 Bagshaws Rd
McLaren Flat SA 5171
(08) 8383 0002
fax (08) 8383 0222
www.shottesbrooke.com.au

Simon Hackett
(not open to public)
(08) 8331 7348

Skillogalee
Skillogalee Rd
via Sevenhill SA 5453
(08) 8843 4311
fax (08) 8843 4343
www.skillogalee.com.au

Smithbrook
(not open to public)
(08) 9772 3557
fax (08) 9772 3579
www.smithbrook.com.au

Smiths Vineyard
(open weekends & public
holidays)
Croom Lane
Beechworth Vic. 3747
0412 475 328
www.smithsvineyard.com.au

Sorrenberg
Alma Rd
Beechworth Vic. 3747
(03) 5728 2278
www.sorrenberg.com

Southcorp Wines
Tanunda Rd
Nuriootpa SA 5355
(08) 8568 9389
fax (08) 8568 9489
www.southcorp.com.au

St Hallett
St Halletts Rd
Tanunda SA 5352
(08) 8563 7000
fax (08) 8563 7001
www.sthallett.com.au

St Huberts
Maroondah Hwy
Coldstream Vic. 3770
(03) 9739 1118
fax (03) 9739 1096
www.sthuberts.com.au

St Leonards
St Leonard Rd
Wahgunyah Vic. 3687
(02) 6033 1004
fax (02) 6033 3636
www.stleonardswine.com.au

St Mary's Vineyard
V and A Lane
via Coonawarra SA 5263
(08) 8736 6070
fax (08) 8736 6045
www.stmaryswines.com.au

St Matthias
(see Moorilla Estate)

Stanley Brothers
Barossa Valley Way
Tanunda SA 5352
(08) 8563 3375
fax (08) 8563 3758
www.stanleybrothers.com.au

Stanton & Killeen
Murray Valley Hwy
Rutherglen Vic. 3685
(02) 6032 9457
www.stantonandkilleenwines.
com.au

Starvedog Lane
(see Hardys)

Stein's Wines
Pipeclay Rd
Mudgee NSW 2850
(02) 6373 3991
fax (02) 6373 3709

Stella Bella/Suckfizzle
(no cellar door)
PO Box 536
Margaret River WA 6285
(08) 9757 6377
fax (08) 9757 6022
www.stellabella.com.au

Stephen John Wines
Government Rd
Watervale SA 5452
tel/fax (08) 8843 0105

Stonehaven
(see Hardys)

**Stoney Vineyard/
Domaine A**
Teatree Rd
Campania Tas. 7026
(03) 6260 4174
fax (03) 6260 4390

Stonier
362 Frankston–Flinders Rd
Merricks Vic. 3916
(03) 5989 8300
fax (03) 5989 8709
www.stoniers.com.au

Stumpy Gully
1247 Stumpy Gully Rd
Moorooduc Vic. 3933
(03) 5978 8429
fax (03) 5978 8419

Summerfield
Main Rd
Moonambel Vic. 3478
(03) 5467 2264
fax (03) 5467 2380
www.summerfieldwines.com.au

Tahbilk
Tahbilk Vic. 3607
via Nagambie
(03) 5794 2555
fax (03) 5794 2360
www.tahbilk.com.au

Talijancich
26 Hyem Rd
Herne Hill WA 6056
(08) 9296 4289
fax (08) 9296 1762

Tallarook
(not open to public)
(03) 9818 3455
www.tallarook.com

Taltarni Vineyards
Taltarni Rd
Moonambel Vic. 3478
(03) 5459 7900
fax (03) 5467 2306
www.taltarni.com.au

Talunga
Lot 101 Adelaide-Mannum Rd
Gumeracha SA 5233
(08) 8389 1222
fax (08) 8389 1233
www.talunga.com.au

Tamar Ridge
Auburn Rd
Kayena Tas. 7270
(03) 6394 7002
fax (03) 6394 7003

Tamburlaine Wines
McDonalds Rd
Pokolbin NSW 2321
(02) 4998 7570
fax (02) 4998 7763
www.tamburlaine.com.au

Tanglewood Downs
Bulldog Creek Rd
Merricks North
(03) 5974 3325
www.tanglewoodestate.com.au

Tapestry
Merrivale Wines
Olivers Rd
McLaren Vale SA 5171
(08) 8323 9196
fax (08) 8323 9746
www.merrivale.com.au

TarraWarra
Healesville Rd
Yarra Glen Vic. 3775
(03) 5962 3311
fax (03) 5962 3887
www.tarrawarra.com.au

Tatachilla Winery
151 Main Rd
McLaren Vale SA 5171
(08) 8323 8656
fax (08) 8323 9096
www.tatachillawinery.com.au

Taylors
Mintaro Rd
Auburn SA 5451
(08) 8849 2008
www.taylorswines.com.au

Temple Bruer
Angas River Delta
via Strathalbyn SA 5255
(08) 8537 0203
fax (08) 8537 0131
www.templebruer.net.au

Tempus Two
(see McGuigan)

T'Gallant
1385 Mornington–Flinders Rd
Main Ridge Vic. 3937
(03) 5989 6565
fax (03) 5989 6577

Thalgara Estate
De Beyers Rd
Pokolbin NSW 2321
(02) 4998 7717
www.thalgara.com.au

Thomas Wines
PO Box 606
Cessnock NSW 2325
tel/fax (02) 6574 7371
www.thomaswines.com.au

Thorn-Clarke
PO Box 402
Angaston SA 5353
(08) 8564 3373
fax (08) 8564 3255
www.thornclarkewines.com.au

Tim Adams
Warenda Rd
Clare SA 5453
(08) 8842 2429
fax (08) 8842 3550
www.timadamswines.com.au

Tim Gramp
Mintaro/Leasingham Rd
Watervale SA 5452
(08) 8843 0199
fax (08) 8843 0299
www.timgrampwines.com.au

Tin Cows
(see TarraWarra)

Tintilla
Hermitage Rd
Pokolbin NSW 2335
(02) 6574 7093
fax (02) 6574 7094
www.tintilla.com

Tisdall
Cornelia Creek Rd
Echuca Vic. 3564
(03) 5482 1911
fax (03) 5482 2516

Torbreck
Roennfeldt Rd
Marananga SA 5360
(08) 8562 4155
fax (08) 8562 3418
www.torbreck.com

Torresan Estate
Estate Dve
Flagstaff Hill SA 5159
(08) 8270 2500

Tower Estate
Cnr Broke & Halls Rds
Pokolbin NSW 2321
(02) 4998 7989
www.towerestatewines.com.au

Trentham Estate
Sturt Hwy
Trentham Cliffs
via Gol Gol NSW 2738
(03) 5024 8888
fax (03) 5024 8800
www.trenthamestate.com.au

Tuck's Ridge
37 Red Hill–Shoreham Rd
Red Hill South Vic. 3937
(03) 5989 8660
fax (03) 5989 8579
www.tucksridge.com.au

Turkey Flat
Bethany Rd
Tanunda SA 5352
(08) 8563 2851
fax (08) 8563 3610
www.turkeyflat.com.au

Turramurra Estate
295 Wallaces Rd
Dromana Vic. 3936
(03) 5987 1146
fax (03) 5987 1286
www.turramuraestate.com.au

Two Hands
Neldner Rd
Marananga SA 5355
(08) 8562 4566
fax (08) 8562 4744
www.twohandswines.com

Two Rivers
18 Craig Street
Artarmon NSW 2064
(02) 9436 3022
fax (02) 9439 7930

Tyrrell's
Broke Rd
Pokolbin NSW 2321
(02) 4993 7000
fax (02) 4998 7723
www.winefutures.com.au

Vasse Felix
Cnr Caves & Harmans Rds
Cowaramup WA 6284
(08) 9756 5000
fax (08) 9755 5425
www.vassefelix.com.au

Veritas
Cnr Seppeltsfield & Stelzer Rds
Dorrien SA 5355
(08) 8562 3300
www.veritaswinery.com

Virgin Hills
(not open to public)
(03) 5422 3032
www.virginhills.com.au

Voyager Estate
Stevens Rd
Margaret River WA 6285
(08) 9757 6354
fax (08) 9757 6494
www.voyagerestate.com.au

Wandin Valley Estate
Wilderness Rd
Lovedale NSW 2320
(02) 4930 7317
fax (02) 4930 7814
www.wandinvalley.com.au

Wantirna Estate
(not open to public)
(03) 9801 2367
www.wantirnaestate.com.au

Warburn Estate
(see Riverina Estate)

Wards Gateway Cellars
Barossa Valley Hwy
Lyndoch SA 5351
(08) 8524 4138

Warrabilla
Murray Valley Hwy
Rutherglen Vic. 3687
tel/fax (02) 6035 7242
www.warrabillawines.com.au

Warramate
27 Maddens Lane
Gruyere Vic. 3770
(03) 5964 9219

Warrenmang
Mountain Ck Rd
Moonambel Vic. 3478
(03) 5467 2233
fax (03) 5467 2309
www.bazzani.com.au/warrenmang

Waterwheel Vineyards
Raywood Rd
Bridgewater Vic. 3516
(03) 5437 3060
fax (03) 5437 3082
www.waterwheelwine.com

Wedgetail
(not open to public)
(03) 9714 8661
www.wedgetailestate.com.au

Wellington
(Hood Wines)
489 Richmond Rd
Cambridge Tas. 7170
(03) 6248 5844
fax (03) 6248 5855

Wendouree
Wendouree Rd
Clare SA 5453
(08) 8842 2896

Westend
1283 Brayne Rd
Griffith NSW 2680
(02) 6964 1506
fax (02) 6962 1673

Westfield
Memorial Ave
Baskerville WA 6056
(08) 9296 4356

Wetherall
Naracoorte Rd
Coonawarra SA 5263
(08) 8737 2104
fax (08) 8737 2105

Wignalls
Chester Pass Rd
Albany WA 6330
(08) 9841 2848
www.wignallswines.com.au

Wild Duck Creek
(by appointment only)
Springflat Rd
Heathcote Vic. 3523
(03) 5433 3133

Wildwood
St Johns Lane
via Wildwood Vic. 3428
(03) 9307 1118
www.wildwoodvineyards.com.au

Will Taylor
1 Simpson Pde
Goodwood SA 5034
(08) 8271 6122

Willespie
Harmans Mill Rd
Wilyabrup WA 6280
(08) 9755 6248
fax (08) 9755 6210
www.willespie.com.au

Willow Creek
166 Balnarring Rd
Merricks North Vic. 3926
(03) 5989 7448
fax (03) 5989 7584
www.willow-creek.com

The Willows Vineyard
Light Pass Rd
Barossa Valley SA 5355
(08) 8562 1080
www.thewillowsvineyard.com.au

The Wilson Vineyard
Polish Hill River
via Clare SA 5453
(08) 8843 4310
www.wilsonvineyard.com.au

Winchelsea Estate
C/- Nicks Wine Merchants
(03) 9639 0696

Windowrie Estate
Windowrie Rd
Canowindra NSW 2804
(02) 6344 3598
fax (02) 6344 3597
www.windowrie.com.au

Winstead
Winstead Rd
Bagdad Tas. 7030
(03) 6268 6417

Wirilda Creek
Lot 32 McMurtrie Rd
McLaren Vale SA 5171
(08) 8323 9688

Wirra Wirra
McMurtrie Rd
McLaren Vale SA 5171
(08) 8323 8414
fax (08) 8323 8596
www.wirra.com.au

Wolf Blass
Sturt Hwy
Nuriootpa SA 5355
(08) 8568 7300
fax (08) 8568 7380
www.wolfblass.com.au

Wood Park
Kneebones Gap Rd
Bobinawarrah Vic. 3678
(03) 5727 3367
fax (03) 5727 3682
www.woodpark.com.au

Woodstock
Douglas Gully Rd
McLaren Flat SA 5171
(08) 8383 0156
fax (08) 8383 0437
www.woodstockwine.com.au

Woody Nook
Metricup Rd
Metricup WA 6280
(08) 9755 7547
fax (08) 9755 7007
www.woodynook.com.au

Wyanga Park
Baades Rd
Lakes Entrance Vic. 3909
(03) 5155 1508
fax (03) 5155 1443

Wyndham Estate
Dalwood Rd
Dalwood NSW 2321
(02) 4938 3444
fax (02) 4938 3555
www.wyndhamestate.com.au

Wynns
Memorial Dve
Coonawarra SA 5263
(08) 8736 3266
fax (08) 8736 3202
www.wynns.com.au

Xanadu
Boodjidup Rd
Margaret River WA 6285
(08) 9757 2581
fax (08) 9757 3389
www.xanaduwines.com.au

Yabby Lake
(no cellar door)
(03) 9667 6644
fax (03) 9639 0540
www.yabbylake.com

Yaldara
Gomersal Rd
Lyndoch SA 5351
(08) 8524 0200
fax (08) 8524 0240
www.yaldara.com.au

Yalumba
Eden Valley Rd
Angaston SA 5353
(08) 8561 3200
fax (08) 8561 3393
www.yalumba.com

Yarra Burn
Settlement Rd
Yarra Junction Vic. 3797
(03) 5967 1428
fax (03) 5967 1146
www.hardywines.com.au

Yarra Ridge
Glenview Rd
Yarra Glen Vic. 3775
(03) 9730 1022
fax (03) 9730 1131
www.beringerblass.com.au

Yarra Valley Hills
(see Dromana Estate)

Yarra Yering
Briarty Rd
Gruyere Vic. 3770
(03) 5964 9267

YarraLoch
(not open to public)
11 Range Rd
Coldstream Vic. 3770
(03) 9525 4275
fax (03) 9534 7539
www.yarraloch.com.au

Yarraman Estate
700 Yarraman Rd
Wybong NSW 2333
(02) 6547 8118
fax (02) 6547 8039
www.yarramanestate.com.au

Yellow Tail
(see Casella)

Yellowglen
White's Rd
Smythesdale Vic. 3351
(03) 5342 8617
www.yellowglen.com.au

Yeringberg
(not open to public)
(03) 9739 1453
fax (03) 9739 0048

Yering Station
Melba Hwy
Yering Vic. 3775
(03) 9730 0100
fax (03) 9739 0135
www.yering.com

Zarephath
Moorialup Rd
East Porongurup WA 6324
tel/fax (08) 9853 1152
www.zarephathwines.com

Zema Estate
Riddoch Hwy
Coonawarra SA 5263
(08) 8736 3219
fax (08) 8736 3280
www.zema.com.au

Zilzie
Lot 66 Kulkyne Way
Karadoc Vic. 3496
(03) 5025 8100
fax (03) 5025 8116
www.zilziewines.com

Index

The Sydney Morning Herald Good Food Guide 2007

Simon Thomsen & Cath Keenan

For more than two decades, *The Sydney Morning Herald Good Food Guide* has provided expert advice on negotiating Sydney's restaurant scene, keeping residents and visitors in touch with the best, the most interesting, and the most innovative places to dine in the city and suburbs, and further afield in regional New South Wales.

In this expanded 2007 edition, food connoisseurs Simon Thomsen and Cath Keenan and their team review over 400 restaurants, and numerous bars, cafes and provedores, setting down their impressions with the flair, insight and razor-sharp wit for which the guide has become known. And, of course, the *Good Food Guide 2007* reveals this year's much anticipated award-winning restaurants.

The Age Good Food Guide 2007

John Lethlean & Necia Wilden

The Age Good Food Guide is Melbourne's most respected guide to eating out. Edited for the first time by well-known restaurant critic John Lethlean and deputy editor of *Epicure* Necia Wilden, this edition brings you an entertaining insider's guide to the best and newest stars of the Melbourne food scene.

With nearly 300 reviews of Melbourne restaurants and extensive coverage of establishments further afield, as well as the eagerly awaited winners of *The Age Good Food Guide* awards, it is an essential reference in helping you choose the right place for every occasion.